R. Gupta's®

POPULAR MASTER GUIDE

Madhya Pradesh

Middle School Teacher Eligibility Test

For

English Language Teacher

- **Part-A:** सामान्य हिन्दी; General English; General Knowledge & Current Affair, Reasoning and Numerical Ability; Pedagogy • **Part-B:** English Language

Conducted by

Madhya Pradesh Employees Selection Board, Bhopal

by

RPH Editorial Board

RAMESH PUBLISHING HOUSE, NEW DELHI

Published by

O.P. Gupta *for* Ramesh Publishing House

Admin. Office

12-H, New Daryaganj Road, Opp. Officers' Mess,
New Delhi-110002 ✆ 23275224, 23245124

E-mail: info@rameshpublishinghouse.com
For Online Shopping: www.rameshpublishinghouse.com

Showroom

- Balaji Market, Nai Sarak, Delhi-110006 ✆ 23282525 📱 9354373464
- 4457, Nai Sarak, Delhi-110006

Book Code: R-2002

ISBN: 978-93-87918-85-6

Price: ₹ 390

Printed at: Deepak Offset, Delhi

Contents

---

* For Part-A

** For Part-B

Scheme of Examination

1. All questions will be compulsory.
2. There will be one question paper of 150 marks for the eligibility test. The duration of the exam will be 2.30 hours.
3. All the questions in the Eligibility Test will be of Multiple Choice Type (MCQs) with four options and one option will be correct.
4. Each question will carry 1 mark. There will be negative marking. 1 mark will be deducted for every 4 questions wrongly answered.
5. There will be two parts in the question paper: Part-A and Part-B. Part-A will be compulsory for all. One has to choose any one subject from the subjects included under Part-B.
6. **Part-A** will have 4 sections with weightage of marks as follows:

Section	Contents	Number of Questions	Total Marks
1.	General Hindi	08	08
2.	General English	05	05
3.	General Knowledge and Current Affairs, Reasoning & Numerical Ability	07	07
4.	Pedagogy	10	10
	Total	**30**	**30**

7. **Part-B** will be of 120 marks and 120 multiple choice questions will be asked in this question paper.

Subject	No. of Questions	Total Marks
English Language	120	120

8. Level of content
   - The level of the content of General Knowledge and Current Affairs, Reasoning and Numerical Ability, Pedagogy in Part-A of the question paper will be equivalent to the mental level of a higher secondary school student. The level of Hindi and English subjects will be equivalent to the Higher Secondary School Examination.
   - The level of content in Part-B of the question paper will be equivalent to that of graduation. In this question paper, questions will be based on the prevailing syllabus of classes 9 and 10 in the M.P. state but their difficulty level and linkage (linkage) will be of graduate level. The question paper will be based on understanding of concepts, problem solving and pedagogy.

Previous Paper (Solved)

Madhya Pradesh Middle School Teacher Eligibility Test, 2019*

(For English Language Teacher)

Child Development & Pedagogy

1. Which of the following is not a child-centered learning practice?
   A. Make the student more active in acquiring knowledge and skills
   B. Make the student more aware of what they are doing and why they are doing it
   C. Working under teacher's direction and decisions
   D. Focus on interaction, such as the use of tutorials and other discussion groups
2. Which of the following is used in tests of attitude?
   A. Aptitude test B. Achievement test
   C. IQ test D. Likert scale
3. Multicultural awareness in the field of education includes the appreciation for and understanding of differences in students in terms of their ______.
   A. skills and abilities
   B. special needs and giftedness
   C. socioeconomic status and religious backgrounds
   D. behaviours and dispositions
4. The anti-anxiety drug is a drug whose primary behavioural effect is the reduction of anxiety but it functions as Central Nervous System (CNS) ______.
   A. Activator B. Depressant
   C. Stimulant D. Modifier
5. Which of the following mainly causes children to fail in examinations?
   A. Environment in the classroom
   B. Physical strength
   C. Fear of Examination
   D. Lack of patience during examination
6. "Learning by doing" is when learning is:
   A. Teacher centred
   B. Relevant and practical
   C. Passive and theoretical
   D. Rote or didactic
7. Which of the following compares the human cognition to the working of a computer?
   A. Neural Processing
   B. Network mapping
   C. Information Processing
   D. Mind mapping
8. Children who deviate considerably from the normal children are known as:
   A. Autistic children B. Abnormal children
   C. Intelligent children D. Exceptional children
9. Gender refers to the ______ constructed differences in persons.
   A. Educationally B. Emotionally
   C. Biologically D. Socially
10. The psychologist, who conducted experiments of trial and error learning, was ______.
    A. Thorndike B. Kohler
    C. Skinner D. Pavlov
11. The term *Abstract Thinking* refers to:
    A. Personality B. Attitude
    C. Intelligence D. Motivation
12. The learning that happens in the formal environment is studied by ______.
    A. Anthropologists
    B. Educational psychologists
    C. Clinical psychologists
    D. Social psychologists
13. Which profession uses the aptitude tests most?
    A. Guidance Counsellor B. Doctors
    C. Lawyers D. Engineers
14. Which of the following theories of motivation does not focus in any way on biological aspects and needs?
    A. Drive theory
    B. Hierarchy of needs theory
    C. Manifest needs theory
    D. Instinct theory
15. Which of the following is not considered a cognitive form of learning?
    A. Vicarious conditioning B. Latent learning
    C. Observational learning D. Classical conditioning
16. Which of the following principle can be used to make the students curious about the topic?
    A. Already know
    B. Willing to know
    C. Not willing to know
    D. Don't know

* Exam held on 18 February, 2019.

17. Which of the following statements is true regarding a Constructivist classroom?
A. The classroom environment is intellectually, emotionally and physically safe.
B. The learning process lacks structure.
C. Student-student interactions have no role to play in a constructivist classroom.
D. The method of instruction is purely didactic in a constructivist classroom.

18. In what type of memory is the skill of riding a cycle stored?
A. Procedural memory B. Iconic memory
C. Episodic memory D. Declarative memory

19. Self-improvement is given importance in ______ approaches to personality.
A. Cognitive B. Psychoanalytic
C. Humanistic D. Biological

20. What is described as the pattern of enduring characteristics that defines a person and produces consistency and individuality?
A. Personality B. Learning
C. Intelligence D. Motivation

21. What kind a learner is a child who seems to learn best when carrying out a physical activity related to the subject?
A. Aural B. Reading/writing
C. Visual D. Kinesthetic

22. Learning is defined as a process of bringing relatively permanent changes in the ______ of an organism.
A. Behaviour B. Thought
C. Personality D. Intelligence

23. In the *Fearless Peer* experiment by Bandura, who played the role of the model?
A. The experimenter B. The fearless child
C. The friendly dog D. The fearful child

24. Study of meaning in language is known as:
A. Morphology B. Linguistics
C. Syntax D. Semantics

25. In view of Piaget the stage of development from the age 7 to 12 years is called:
A. Concrete operational B. Formal operational
C. Pre operational D. Sensory motor stage

26. Four limbs of the body are affected in case of ______.
A. Triplegia B. Biplegia
C. Quadriplegia D. Hemiplegia

27. Developing one's personality helps in:
A. Quicken the process of maturation.
B. Increasing body stature.
C. Dealing with social situations.
D. Overcome congenital disorders.

28. According to Thorndike's theory, the frequency of stimulus-response pairings determine the formation of:
A. Reinforcements B. Habits
C. Punishments D. Conditioning

29. Which of the following is an example of creative thinking?
A. Arguing B. Managing time
C. Active listening D. Questioning

30. Language is which of the following types of content?
A. Auditory B. Pedantic
C. Visual D. Symbolic

भाषा-I हिन्दी

निर्देश (प्र.सं. 31 से 45): *गद्यांश को पढ़कर निम्नलिखित प्रश्नों में* **सबसे उचित** *विकल्प चुनिए।*

गद्यांश

एक था किसान। गोमा मोरी नाम था उसका। गुजर-बसर लायक खेती थी। एक गाय, एक जोड़ी बैल, बीस बकरियाँ थीं। छोटा-सा घर। घर के सामने पशु बाँधने का बाड़ा। तीन साल से वर्षा बहुत कम हुई थी। न फसलें हुईं थी न चारा। इस वर्ष भी आषाढ़ सूखा ही रह गया। वर्षा की कोई आशा नहीं बंधी थी। "खेत जोतकर क्या करूँगा?" गोमा ने एक लम्बी सांस छोड़ी और मन ही मन सोचा। वह बैलों को हाँकते हुए वापिस घर की ओर चल पड़ा। अगले दिन गोमा बड़े सवेरे सोकर उठा। गया, बैल व बकरियों को बाड़े से निकाला। उसकी पत्नी बकरियों को घेरकर उन्हें चराने चली गई। उसने फिर हिम्मत बटोरी और हल को बैलों के कंधे पर रखकर चल पड़ा खेतों की ओर। रास्ते में उसे कई किसानों ने टोककर कहा कि "गोमा! खेत जोतने से क्या होगा? वर्षा के तो कुछ भी आसार नहीं दिख रहे।" गोमा ने सब की बात सुनी। कई बार उसका मन डाँवाडोल भी हुआ फिर भी उसने हिम्मत रखी और कुछ सोचकर खेत पर पहुँच गया।

31. गोमा के पास कौन-सा जानवर नहीं था?
A. बकरी B. गाय
C. भेड़ D. बैल

32. 'आशा' शब्द का पर्यायवाची शब्द कौन-सा है?
A. उलाहना
B. वासना
C. सांत्वना
D. आकांक्षा

33. निम्न में से क्या गोमा की परेशानी नहीं थी?
A. जंगल B. वर्षा
C. फसलें D. चारा

34. गोमा कौन था?
A. एक किसान
B. एक बनिया
C. एक लोहार
D. एक सोनार

35. गोमा के मन में खेत न जोतने का विचार क्यों आ रहा था?
A. क्योंकि वह बहुत थक गया था।
B. क्योंकि उसकी पत्नी नहीं चाहती थी।
C. क्योंकि और लोग खेत नहीं जोत रहे थे।
D. क्योंकि वर्षा होने का कोई आसार नहीं था।

36. गोमा कैसा व्यक्ति था?
A. मूर्ख B. आशावादी
C. कामचोर D. पागल

37. बकरियों को कौन चरा रहा था?
A. गोमा B. गाँव वाले
C. गोमा की पत्नी D. उपरोक्त सभी

38. 'डाँवाडोल' शब्द का क्या अभिप्राय है?
A. स्थिर B. अस्थिर
C. असाधारण D. साधारण

39. 'आषाढ़' महीने के बाद कौन-सा महीना आता है?
A. बैशाख B. कार्तिक
C. सावन D. ज्येष्ठ

40. गुजर-बसर में कौन-सा समास है?
A. द्वंद्व समास B. बहुब्रीहि समास
C. अव्ययीभाव समास D. द्विगु समास

41. कितने वर्षों से वर्षा कम हुई है?
A. पाँच वर्षों से B. चार वर्षों से
C. तीन वर्षों से D. दो वर्षों से

42. बैलों का खेती में क्या योगदान है?
A. पीटे जाने का B. खेत जोतने का
C. चराए जाने का D. हांके जाने का

43. प्रस्तुत गद्य खण्ड में 'खेत जोत कर क्या करूंगा' प्रश्न गोमा किससे पूछता है?
A. स्वयं से B. किसानों से
C. जानवरों से D. पत्नी से

44. 'गोमा एक किसान था' में कौन-सा काल होगा?
A. इनमें से कोई नहीं B. वर्तमान
C. भूत D. भविष्य

45. 'बाड़ा' शब्द क्या है?
A. विदेशी B. देशज
C. तत्सम D. तद्भव

निर्देश (प्र.सं. 46 से 60): *निम्न पद्यांश को पढ़कर निम्नलिखित प्रश्नों में* ***सबसे उचित*** *विकल्प चुनिए।*

पद्यांश

जाति न पूछो साधु की, पूछ लीजिए ज्ञान।
मोल करो तरवार का, पड़ा रहन दो म्यान।।
माला तो कर में फिरै, जीभ फिरै मुख माँहि।
मनुवाँ तो दहुँ दिसि फिरै, यह तौ सुमिरन नाहिं।।

46. 'जीभ' शब्द निम्न में से क्या है?
A. स्त्रीलिंग B. इनमें से कोई नहीं
C. पुल्लिंग D. नपुंसकलिंग

47. ''जाति न पूछो साधु की, पूछ लीजिए ज्ञान'' के माध्यम से कवि ने किसके महत्व को प्राथमिकता दी है?
A. जाति B. साधु
C. ज्ञान D. तलवार

48. 'कर' का क्या अर्थ है?
A. कान B. नाक
C. मुंह D. हाथ

49. 'पड़ा रहन दो म्यान' से क्या तात्पर्य है?
A. आभूषण का सौन्दर्य B. म्यान का महत्वहीन होना
C. म्यान को रंग देना D. उपरोक्त सभी

50. 'दहुँ दिसि फिरै' का क्या तात्पर्य है?
A. मन का भटकाव B. चारों राज्य
C. चारों लोक D. चारों कुल

51. सुमिरन के अंतर्गत क्या आता है?
A. केवल चिंतन B. केवल स्मरण
C. केवल मनन D. उपरोक्त सभी

52. प्रस्तुत पंक्तियाँ किस छन्द में रचित हैं?
A. इनमें से कोई नहीं B. सबद
C. रमैनी D. साखी

53. प्रस्तुत पंक्ति में कवि क्या पूछने से मना करता है?
A. जाति B. ज्ञान
C. वैराग्य D. उपरोक्त सभी

54. प्रस्तुत पंक्ति में कबीर ने किसके महत्व को दर्शाया है?
A. म्यान B. तलवार
C. अज्ञान D. उपरोक्त सभी

55. तलवार शब्द का पर्यायवाची शब्द क्या नहीं है?
A. कृपाण B. खड्ग
C. असि D. तरकस

56. मन कहाँ फिरता रहता है?
A. ज्ञान में B. उपवन में
C. चारों दिशाओं में D. सुमिरन में

57. ''मनुवाँ तो दहुँ दिसि फिरै, यह तौ सुमिरन नाहिं'' पंक्ति में कवि ने किस बाट का विरोध किया है?
A. भक्ति का B. ज्ञान का
C. जाति का D. कर्मकाण्ड का

58. कबीर ने सुमिरन किसे नहीं माना है?
A. केवल जीभ डुलाने को
B. केवल मन को चारों दिशाओं में घुमाने को
C. केवल माला फेरने को
D. उपरोक्त सभी

59. 'साधु' शब्द का स्त्रीलिंग क्या है?
A. साधुओं
B. शाध्वी
C. साधुई
D. साध्वी

60. 'सुमिरन' का क्या अर्थ है?
A. भगवान के नाम का स्मरण
B. क्रोध करना
C. मृत्यु को प्राप्त करना
D. इनमें से कोई नहीं

Language-II English

61. Fill in the blank with the most appropriate preposition in the given sentence:
Most people like cricket, but ______ my opinion it is too chaotic.
A. of
B. from
C. with
D. in

62. Fill in the blank with the correct option in the given sentence:
The school conducted the annual sports day success--.
A. -ion
B. -ive
C. -fully
D. -ful

63. Fill in the blank with the correct option in the given sentence:
If ______ is low, they will cancel the class.
A. enrolling
B. enrolled
C. enrollee
D. enrollment

64. Fill in the blank with the correct option in the given sentence:
The students requested the school management to conduct a --exam mock test.
A. pro-
B. post-
C. multi-
D. pre-

65. Choose an appropriate modal for the given sentence:
______ you have orange juice?
A. Might
B. Shall
C. Will
D. Should

66. Choose the most suitable pronouns for the given sentence:
______ house is as big as ______.
A. My ... yours
B. Our ... your
C. Our ... ourselves
D. Their ... theirs

67. Choose the appropriate tenses to fill in the blanks in the given sentence :
______ the degree to his ward for personal reasons, the dean ______ to make it public.
A. Denied, was not wanting
B. Having denied, didn't want
C. Having denying, would want
D. Denying, didn't wanted

68. Choose the appropriate conjunction to fill in the blank in the given sentence:
Do your duty without ______ ado.
A. many
B. all
C. little
D. much

69. Choose the appropriate antonym for the highlighted word in the given sentence.
Incessant rains inundated low lying areas.
A. Occasional
B. Uninterrupted
C. Connual
D. Ceaseless

70. Choose the appropriate option that rewrites the given sentence in its passive voice.
Everybody loves Mr. Brown.
A. Mr. Brown was loved by everybody.
B. Mr. Brown is loving everybody.
C. Mr. Brown is loved by everybody.
D. Everybody is loved by Mr. Brown.

71. Choose the appropriate synonym for the highlighted word in the given sentence.
Western leaders are looking beyond traditional indices of economic and social well being and turning to ways of measuring national happiness.
A. Theories
B. Masterpieces
C. Indicators
D. Dices

72. Choose the appropriate prepositions for the given sentence:
Jawaharlal Nehru was the brain ______ the project and it gave a fillip ______ the relations ______ the two countries.
A. in, on, about
B. for, from, to
C. to, behind, between
D. behind, to, between

73. Choose the option that best combines the following two sentences.
There was a cyclonic storm. The schools were closed.
A. The schools were closed, but there was a cyclonic storm.
B. The schools were closed, so there was a cyclonic storm.
C. There was a cyclonic storm, so only the schools were closed.
D. There was a cyclonic storm, so the schools were closed.

74. Choose the option that best transforms the sentence into its Indirect form:
"You must not tell anyone," my mother said.
A. My mother warned me not to tell to anyone.

B. My mother warned me not to tell anyone.
C. My mother warned me that I must not to tell anyone.
D. My mother warns me that not to tell anyone.

75. Choose the option that best explains the highlighted expression:

Wild horses cannot drag me to the party tonight.

A. Nothing can pull me
B. Only wild horses can take me
C. Everything is undecided
D. Even the wild horses cannot go

76. Choose the option that best explains the highlighted expression:

1. The insurance advisor met the so-called prospect for the seventh time.
2. I heard that. Tell him not to flog a dead horse.

A. to waste one's efforts B. to spend one's money
C. to kill someone D. to revive things

77. Choose appropriate articles for the given sentence:

______ bird that cannot fly is ______ anomaly.

A. No article required, a B. A, no article required
C. The, no article required D. A, an

78. Read the sentence carefully and choose the option that has an error in it:

It is the dream of every mountaineers to climb the world's highest peak.

A. the world's highest peak B. of every mountaineers
C. to climb D. It is the dream

Directions (Qs. 79 to 82): *Read the passage carefully and answer the questions given below:*

Passage

Magnetic levitation trains also known as 'maglev trains' is a floating land transportation which works on the principles of electromagnetic attraction or repulsion. It has been in commercial use since 1984.

Maglev trains uses the basic concept of magnets 'like poles repel each other' to lift, propel and guide the train on its track. Thus, eliminating the force of friction. However, it needs to overcome air pressure. This enables the maglev train to reach higher speeds when compared with the conventional trains. It can travel in excess of 500 kmph.

The advantages of Maglev trains are not only that it travels faster, it has unlikely chances of derailing, less operating and maintenance costs, quieter when compared and also produces little or no air pollution.

Due to air pressure the maglev trains are only slightly more energy efficient than conventional trains. Maglev trains are little affected by snow, ice and wind.

79. Which of the following concepts is involved in the working of Maglev trains?

A. Electromagnetic induction
B. Electromagnetic distraction
C. Electromagnetic repulsion
D. Electromagnet radiation

80. The disadvantage of maglev train is:

A. Less friction to overcome
B. More air pressure to overcome
C. More speed and faster travel
D. Less operation cost

81. Maglev trains are affected by:

A. convention B. attraction
C. snow D. friction

82. In the passage, what does the sentence, 'Maglev trains have unlikely chances of derailing' mean?

It will not ______.

A. serve as a train B. move like a train
C. be considered a train D. get off its track

Directions (Qs. 83 to 86): *Read the poem carefully and answer the questions given below:*

Poem

Living a life full of lies
Invites a battle to rise
Anytime your world can break
Giving you a bitter taste.

So open your eyes
And smile all your life
The doors are open to a real world
Which is far more adventurous.

Every time sharpen your mind
Learn a lesson from time
You know you can do it
Say this as you lose it.

You will get a closer look
To your fortune trailer
Your dreams are not too far
If you know who you are.

83. Living a life full of lies invites a:

A. Battle to rise B. Place of peace
C. Place to hide D. Taste of pies

84. You will know your dreams when you know about ______.

A. yourself B. adventure
C. the world D. death

85. When the speaker describes the world as adventurous, she means that it is:

A. Sad B. Thrilling
C. Gloomy D. Happy

86. The speaker advises the reader that lies can make life ______.

A. adventurous B. fun
C. scary D. difficult

87. Choose the right tag:

You do a lot of experiments, ______?

A. do you B. don't you
C. won't you D. aren't you

88. Choose the option that substitutes the given phrase appropriately.

The science which studies human societies, cultures and their development

A. Anatomy B. Archaeology
C. Acupuncture D. Anthropology

89. Change the given statement from direct speech to indirect speech.
He said, "I will arrive at 7 pm today."

A. He said that I was arriving at 7 pm that day.
B. He said that he would arrive at 7 pm today.
C. He said that he would arrive at 7 pm that day.
D. He said that I would arrive at 7 pm today.

90. Choose the most appropriate determiner in the given sentence.

______ of the dogs was given a bone to play with.

A. All B. Every
C. Each D. Any

Main Language : English

91. Choose the synonym for the underlined word in the given sentence.

Their uncouth laughter sounded loud in the room.

A. gracious B. suave
C. civilized D. coarse

92. Choose the antonym for the underlined word in the given sentence.

The instructions look very complicated, but I will try to fix it.

A. tortuous
B. meandering
C. convoluted
D. straightforward

93. Choose the appropriate suffix to get the noun form of the underlined word in the given sentence.

The Taj Mahal is a magnificent building.

A. magnificence B. magnanimous
C. magnanimity D. magnificently

94. Choose the appropriate modal to fill in the blanks.

If it ______ rain, they will not come.

A. can B. may
C. might D. should

95. Choose the appropriate adverbial clause to fill in the blank.

The stolen goods were found ______.

A. outside the garage
B. where the dacoits usually hid things
C. in the dacoit's hiding place
D. and the police confiscated them all

96. Choose the appropriate tense to fill in the blanks.

Everyday, the shop ______ at 8 in the morning.

A. will opens B. would opened
C. opens D. open

97. Choose the appropriate phrase preposition to fill in the blank.

______ introduction, he made some pertinent remarks.

A. On way of B. On the way
C. By way of D. In the way

98. Choose the appropriate phrase to fill in the blank.
She ______ the people standing nearby.

A. yelled at B. yelled into
C. yelled out D. yelled off

99. Choose the appropriate articles to fill in the blanks.
______ hour at ______ house is enough to give you an impression about the family that lives there.

A. a, a B. a, an
C. an, a D. an, an

100. Choose the appropriate noun clause that could replace the underlined part of the given sentence.

______ hurts me.

A. Cheating
B. The statement
C. That you should cheat me
D. Even the thought of his suffering

101. Choose the appropriate idiom to fill in the blank.

There will be ______ in today's interview.

A. no holds barred
B. holding pattern
C. hold of
D. hold all

102. Choose the appropriate idiom to fill in the blank.
Despite the slump in crimes, the Superintendent has been ______.

A. at the wrong foot of the sergeant
B. running the sergeant off her feet
C. landing the sergeant in her feet
D. rushed the sergeant into her feet

103. Choose the appropriate determiner to fill in the blank.

The climate of Belgavi is like ______ of Pune.

A. these B. this
C. that D. those

104. Choose the option that correctly changes the voice in the given sentence.

The officer asked me my name and he jotted it down.

A. I asked my name by the officer and jotted it down by him.
B. I was asked my name by the officer and it was jotted down by him.

C. My name was being asked and had been jotted down by the officer.
D. My name was asked by the officer and he jotted it down.

105. Choose the option that correctly changes the voice in the given sentence.

The captive was bound to a tree.

A. The captive was bound to a tree by someone.
B. A tree was bound to the captive by someone.
C. Someone bound the captive to a tree.
D. Someone bound the tree to a captive.

106. Choose the option that best transforms the simple sentence into a compound sentence.

To his eternal disgrace, he betrayed his country.

A. His betrayal of the country brought him disgrace.
B. He was disgraced by the betrayal of his country.
C. Eternal disgrace is the result of the country being betrayed by him.
D. He betrayed his country, and this was to his eternal disgrace.

107. Choose the option that best transforms the given interrogative sentence into an assertive sentence.

Why waste time reading trash?

A. Is it wasting time when one reads trash all the time.
B. It is extremely foolish to waste time in reading trash.
C. Must you waste time reading trash foolishly.
D. Wasting time is foolish because one reads trash, isn't it?

108. Which of the following is not one of the characteristics of English Language?

A. It is evolving over the years
B. It is used for communication
C. It is inborn and need not be learnt
D. It is acquired through training

109. Which of the following is true in the context of using effective teaching learning materials in class?

A. Teaching without any materials helps in enhancing creativity
B. Use of materials fail to break the monotony of the teacher-centered classrooms
C. Use of relevant materials makes completion of the task very difficult
D. A task without any material seems quite boring and burdensome

110. Read the following letter and answer the given question.

To,
Whomsoever it May Concern

I have had the pleasure of employing Joy Jen for five years. Joy has handled many responsibilities in these five years. She has handled customer interaction, inventorying, and content writing for our website, Joy is an intelligent, responsible, energetic lady who never loses her cool in any crisis. I am sure that Joy will perform any responsibility given to her with care and maturity.

Yours sincerely
Susan Sanders
CEO
J.O. Enterprises

According to Susan, which of the following comments is true about Joy?

A. she will be composed in the face of a crisis
B. she will panic in the face of a crisis
C. she will handle all crisis with trepidation
D. she will handle all crisis with apprehension

111. Read the following report and answer the question given below:

Healthy Eating Mela

Students from the Ganapur High School organized a Healthy Eating Mela to spread the message of good food habits. The competition included events like Cooking without Fire, Conjuring Salads, and Watch the Calories. Our chief guest for the day was the famous nutritionist Ms. Kamala Madhav. She spoke to the students about what is healthy and what is unhealthy food. The day must certainly have found several converts from junk to healthy food.

Based on this given report, what does the author say must have been the consequence of the event?

A. Students would abandon healthy food habits and turn to junk food
B. Students would give up junk food and adopt healthy eating habits
C. Students would think that junk food is healthy and continue to eat it
D. Students would understand that junk food is not unhealthy

Directions (Qs. 112 to 119): *Read the passages carefully to answer the given questions:*

Passage-1

Make in India initiative was launched on September 25, 2014, with the primary goal of making India a global manufacturing hub, by encouraging both multinational as well as domestic companies to manufacture their products within the country. Led by the Department of Industrial Policy and Promotion, the initiative aims to raise the contribution of the manufacturing sector to 25% of the Gross Domestic Product (GDP) by the year 2025 from its current 16%. Make in India has introduced multiple new initiatives, promoting foreign direct investment, implementing intellectual property rights and developing the manufacturing sector. It targets 25 sectors of the economy which range from automobile to Information Technology (IT) & Business Process Management (BPM), the details of each can be viewed on the official site. It also seeks to facilitate job creation, foster innovation, enhance skill development and protect intellectual property. The logo of 'Make in India' – a lion made of gear wheels – itself reflects the integral role of manufacturing in government's vision and national development.

112. Apart from making India a global manufacturing hub, the Make in India initiative seeks to do a few more things. Which one of the following options in NOT one of them?
A. safeguard intellectual property
B. encumber skill development
C. nurture innovation
D. succor job creation

113. According to the passage, which of the following is not among the sectors of economy about which details could be obtained from the official website?
A. Information Technology B. GDP
C. BPM D. Automobile

114. Which of the following options best expounds the logo of Make in India as given in the passage?
A. the lion indicates the integral role of the foreign manufacturing sector and the gear wheels symbolize their nation
B. the lion indicates the integral role of the multinational companies and the gear wheels symbolize the domestic companies
C. the gear wheels indicate the integral role of the Indian manufacturing sector and the lion symbolizes the nation
D. the gear wheels indicates the integral role of the Information Technology and the lion symbolizes the Business Process Management (BPM)

115. According to the passage, which of the following is NOT one of the initiatives introduced as part of Make in India?
A. promote foreign direct investment
B. develop the manufacturing sector
C. protect multinational companies
D. implement intellectual property rights

Passage-2

Most of his wife's opinions were heirlooms, and he took a quaint pleasure in tracing their descent. She was proud of their age, and saw no reason for discarding them while they were still serviceable. Some, of course, were so fine that she kept them for state occasions, like her great-grandmother's Crown Derby; but from the lady known as Aunt Sophronia she had inherited a stout set of every-day prejudices that were practically as good as new; whereas her husband's, as she noticed, were always having to be replaced. In the early days she had fancied there might be a certain satisfaction in taxing him with the fact; but she had long since been silenced by the reply: "My dear, I'm not a rich man, but I never use an opinion twice if I can help it."

116. How did the husband's opinions differ from the wife's?
A. They were always as good as new
B. They were always serviceable with no reason to discard
C. They were always having to be replaced
D. They were practically never having to be replaced

117. What were practically 'as good as new' and inherited by the wife?
A. quaint pleasure opinions
B. everyday prejudices
C. serviceable heirlooms
D. stout set of practical ideas

118. What is the implication when the author calls the wife's opinions 'heirlooms'?
A. that they gave pleasure
B. that they were about her hair
C. that they were inherited
D. that she was proud of them

119. According to the passage, the wife's everyday prejudices were inherited from ______?
A. the Crown derby B. Aunt Sophronia
C. her husband D. her great grandmother

Directions (Qs. 120 to 123): *Read the poem carefully before answering question:*

Poem

Once upon a midnight dreary,
while I pondered, weak and weary,
Over many a quaint and curious
volume of forgotten lore—
While I nodded, nearly napping,
suddenly there came a tapping,
As of some one gently rapping,
rapping at my chamber door.
"Tis some visitor," I muttered,
"tapping at my chamber door—
Only this and nothing more."

Ah, distinctly I remember
it was in the bleak December;
And each separate dying ember
wrought its ghost upon the floor.
Eagerly I wished the morrow;—
vainly I had sought to borrow
From my books surcease of sorrow—
sorrow for the lost Lenore—
For the rare and radiant maiden
whom the angels name Lenore—
Nameless here for evermore.

And the silken, sad, uncertain
rustling of each purple curtain
Thrilled me—filled me with fantastic
terrors never felt before;
So that now, to still the beating of
my heart, I stood repeating
"Tis some visitor entreating entrance
at my chamber door—
Some late visitor entreating entrance
at my chamber door;—
This it is and nothing more."

120. Whose loss is the poet mourning?
A. maiden Lenore B. forgotten lore
C. a late visitor D. bleak December

121. What is the rhythmic structure evident in the first line?
A. iambic pentameter B. spondaic hexameter
C. anapestic monometer D. trochaic octameter

122. What does the poet eagerly wish for even in the midst of his sadness?
A. visitor B. books
C. books of sorrow D. tomorrow

123. Which of the following figures of speech best describes the use of the words 'tapping' and 'rapping' in lines three, four, and five?
A. Alliteration B. Litotes
C. Personification D. Onomatopoeia

124. Read the following notice and answer the given question.

Green National School, Mathura

NOTICE

28 January 2019

This is to inform all students that our school is organizing a 2 day field trip to the Wipro Industrial Estate. The details are as follows:

Classes: VIII to X

Dates: 23 February to 25 February

Those who are keen on registering for the trip must pay 1500 rupees to Ms. Ritu, Biology teacher before 31 January.

Principal

Where will the students be going during the field trip?
A. Mathura Industries
B. Wipro Industrial Estate
C. Biology lab in Mathura
D. Fields near the school

125. Read the following advertisement and answer the given question.

ADVERTISEMENT

KENDRIYA VIDYALAYA, AMEERPET

Walk-in Interview for part time SQUASH COACH on 3rd July, 2018 at 10 a.m at the Vidyalaya campus. For more details please visit kvameer@kv.in. Eligible candidates must attend the interview with original and attested copies of educational qualification and work experience. No TA/DA will be paid for attending the interview.

Sd/-

Principal

What are the documents that the interviewees ought to carry to the interview?
A. Both Notarized and photocopies of documents related to education and work experience
B. Both original and attested copies of documents related to education and work experience
C. Only attested copies of documents related to education and work experience
D. Only original documents related to education and work experience

126. Read the following poster and answer the given question

DJ SCHOOL CLUB

is

organising a Diwali Mela

to

bring light and happiness into everyone's life

Venue: TK Stadium, North Campus

Date: 7th to 9th November

Time: 6 p.m. to 9 p.m.

Entry fee: Adults 20/- Children 5/-

Let's make this Diwali cracker free

Sponsored by

Ronex

Which of the following statements is not true based on the information from the poster?
A. The Mela is sponsored by Ronex and organized by the DJ School Club
B. The club will charge an entry fee for those who wish to join the Mela
C. The organizers will distribute free crackers during the celebrations
D. There will be no pyro techniques displayed during the Mela

127. Read the following letter and answer the given question.

Dear Dev

How are you? I am sure that your studies must be keeping you busy. I am glad to tell you that I have now been selected to the theatre group. We have a play coming up next month at Rangashankara. It is a big deal. Remember, we had once met the who's who of theatre and cinema at Rangashankara. Maybe, my dream might come true and someone will notice me for a small role in the movies. Well, enough of day dreaming. How are things at your end? When is that big test of yours? Do write to me as soon as you could.

Yours truly

Jo

According to the letter, what does Jo hope might happen at Rangashankara?
A. he will be noticed by an influential person who might offer him a role in the movies
B. he will be introduced to the greatest personalities from theatre and cinema
C. he will fumble his part in the upcoming play and lose his face
D. he will win the best actor award at the upcoming play

128. Read the following letter and answer the given question.

To,
The Recruitment Officer,
Anganwadi, Bidar
Dear Sir,
I wish to apply for the post of Anganwadi worker at Bidar. I have completed my Matriculation with First class. The Principal of my school, Bidar High School, is willing to give you a reference for my conduct. Please consider my application. I will work hard and do my best.
Thank you.
Kishan Raj

Fill in the details based on the letter.
Name: ________
Post: ________
Education: ________
Referee: ________

A. Recruitment Officer, Anganwadi worker, 12th Grade, Principal of Bidar High School
B. Recruitment Officer, Anganwadi worker, First Class, Principal of Bidar High School
C. Kishan Raj, Recruitment Officer, Matriculation, Anganwadi worker at Bidar High School
D. Kishan Raj, Anganwadi worker, Matriculation, Principal of Bidar High School

129. Read the following letter and answer the given question.

To,
The Editor,
The Hindu,
Dear Sir,
In response to the news about the Municipal Corporation of Hibbalpur converting the public park into a bus stand, I would like to express my strong displeasure as a citizen. There are very few public parks in the Hibbalpur locality. Moreover, shifting the bus stand there will increase pollution in an otherwise clean residential area. The Corporation is sure to face more severe protest from the residents of Hibbalpur in the coming week.
Yours faithfully,
Krishna Swamy

What would be the dominant tone of this letter?

A. complaisant
B. congenial
C. irate
D. insolent

130. Read the following letter and answer the given question.

To,
Communications Skills Training
Munnar, Kerala
Dear Sir,
I write to enquire whether your company would offer a 5 day Communications skills workshop for our new recruits at HR Customer Services, Munnar. We have a group of 25 fresh graduates who need training in customer interaction, etiquettes, presentation and such other skills. If you could send us the details about your training program, the cost, and the trainer profile, we could fix an appointment accordingly.
Thank you
Manager
HR Customer Services

Which of the following are among the details that the Manager asked for from the Communications Skills Training company?

A. the details about the program offered by Communications Skills Training
B. the profile of the new recruits at HR Customer Services
C. the cost of several communication skills materials available in the market
D. the cost of their Time Management course

131. Read the following letter and answer the given question.

Dear Kaite
I hope you are well. I am waiting for the summer holidays. I'm writing to you because I want to invite you to visit me during the holiday season. We could visit the heritage centers and museums or spend the day at the movies or wander around the shopping malls. Let me know what you think. We could plan everything then.
Hoping to see you.
Jainne

Which of the following is not one of the things that Jainne suggests she and Kaite could do during the summer holidays?

A. spend the day at the movies
B. visit the heritage centers and museums
C. go swimming on the sunny beaches
D. wander around the shopping malls

132. Read the following instructions and answer the given question.

Follow these guidelines when there are children with disabilities in the class.

FOR MATERIALS

- Get audiobooks through services like Bookshare, a free online library for students with disabilities
- Provide pictures of directions and schedules
  Use large-print text for worksheets
- Simplify directions with key words for most important ideas
- Provide coloured strips or bookmarks to use when reading

According to the instructions given, which of the following options is not among the things that a teacher should do for the students with disabilities?
A. Use audiobooks whenever possible
B. Use simple, key words to give important directions
C. Provide notes in advance for all the chapters in the text
D. Provide coloured bookmarks to enable them to track their reading

133. What is one of the major drawbacks of the structural approach?
A. it taught language in meaningful contexts that learners could relate to
B. led to a fragmentation and trivialisation of thought by breaking up language into structures and skills
C. It gave learners language that could be used in real life situations instead of just the ability to use correct sentences in classrooms
D. it bridged the gap between "linguistic age" and "mental age"

134. What is one of the major problems faced in the implementation of the Continuous and Comprehensive Evaluation (CCE)?
A. teachers largely consider CCE as an integral part of the assessment process
B. the teachers integrate the assessment with the teaching-learning process
C. it is considered by teachers as an external activity that is to be followed after the completion of a topic/lesson
D. it is given significant attention by teachers to integrate into the teaching learning process

135. What is a major aim of remedial teaching?
A. to enable detention practices that would instill fear in a child
B. to dictate notes of every chapter so that a child could learn everything by heart
C. to put a child through grueling hours of drill so that he despises learning
D. to bring a child to minimal acceptable levels in each class

136. What is the role of grammar in teaching language?
A. sensitise the child to language-sound structures
B. develop the imagination
C. reconstruction of the meaning of the attempted expression through imperfect English
D. tool for increasing the language repertoire and for understanding the construction of text "rhetoric" and argumentation

137. What is the one of the methods adopted by the government to tackle the challenge of the multilingual nature of the Indian society?
A. the grammar-translation method
B. the information technology curriculum
C. the modern language policy
D. the three language formula

138. In mother tongue learning, speech progresses from ______ through ______ to ______.
A. one word, one sentence, several sentences
B. one sentence, two sentence stage, multi-sentences
C. one phoneme, a few morphemes, multi-vowel stage
D. one word, two word stage, multi-word sentences

139. According to Norbert Schmit (2000) "whereas the ______ of a language is largely in place by the time a child is 10 years old ... , ______ continues to be learned throughout one's lifetime."
A. grammar, vocabulary B. order, structure
C. structure, order D. vocabulary, grammar

140. Listening and Reading proficiency in language learners mainly develop ____ skills.
A. expression B. comprehension
C. articulation D. delivery

141. Which one of the following is NOT a correct statement?
A. Writing is an important Language Skill
B. Listening is an important Language Skill
C. Reading is an important Language Skill
D. Reckoning is an important Language Skill

142. Which of the following statements is true in the context of sentence construction in a language?
A. When compared to organizing words, there is no order of organizing sentences in any language
B. Like in the case of organizing sentences, there is no order of organizing sentences in any language
C. As compared to the level of sentences, language is more tightly organised at the level of words
D. As compared to the level of words, language is more tightly organised at the level of sentences

143. Which of the following is an important consideration when choosing teaching materials for a class?
A. need to be as confounding as possible in the extend of texts that will be used
B. need to be sensitive to perspectives of equity (gender and societal) and harmony
C. need to be rigid and inconsiderate to the cultural and local contexts of learning
D. need to be circuitous when deciding the concepts to be dealt with in class

144. Which of the following is one of the aims of teaching English Poetry?
A. enable students to solve puzzles
B. enable students to write an essay
C. enable learners to prepare reports and brochure
D. enable learners to appreciate rhythm and feeling

145. In the case of English words like 'fun', 'rain', and 'fish', how would you convert them into adjectives?
A. add 'ion' at the end
B. add 'in' at the beginning
C. add 'y' at the end
D. add 'a' at the beginning

146. Choose the closest meaning of the underlined phrase in the given sentence.

The act of burying a dead person sometimes becomes mundane for an undertaker.

A. Internment
B. Interstitial
C. Interment
D. Intermittent

147. Choose the closest meaning of the underlined phrase in the given sentence.

After the event he felt weak and tired.

A. encomiastic
B. energized
C. enervated
D. engineered

148. Satish was out of office when he got a call from the onsite supervisor asking him to immediately send the office assistant with the BMP approval form to the Head Office in Andheri. Govind, Satish's colleague, has to fill the following out of office form passing on the message.

____ (Name), send ____ with ____ to ____ in Andheri.

A. Office assistant, Govind, BMP approval form, onsite supervisor
B. Govind, Satish, Head Office, BMP approval form
C. Satish, office assistant, BMP approval form, Head Office
D. Satish, Govind, BMP approval form, Head Office

149. Change the given sentence into direct speech.

He urged them to be quiet and listen to his words.

A. He wished, "that they were quiet and listening to his words."
B. He enquired, "are you quiet to listen to my words?"
C. He exclaimed, "you are quiet and listening to my words!"
D. He said, "be quiet and listen to my words."

150. Change the given sentence into indirect speech.

He said to them, "will you listen to such a man?"

A. He asked them to listen to such a man
B. He asked them whether they would listen to such a man.
C. He said that they will listen to such a man.
D. He said to them that they will have to listen to such a man.

ANSWERS

1	2	3	4	5	6	7	8	9	10
C	D	C	B	C	B	C	D	D	A
11	**12**	**13**	**14**	**15**	**16**	**17**	**18**	**19**	**20**
C	B	A	C	D	D	A	A	C	A
21	**22**	**23**	**24**	**25**	**26**	**27**	**28**	**29**	**30**
D	A	B	D	A	C	C	B	D	D
31	**32**	**33**	**34**	**35**	**36**	**37**	**38**	**39**	**40**
C	D	A	A	D	B	C	B	C	A
41	**42**	**43**	**44**	**45**	**46**	**47**	**48**	**49**	**50**
C	B	A	C	B	A	C	D	B	A
51	**52**	**53**	**54**	**55**	**56**	**57**	**58**	**59**	**60**
D	D	A	B	D	C	D	D	D	A
61	**62**	**63**	**64**	**65**	**66**	**67**	**68**	**69**	**70**
D	C	D	D	C	A	B	D	A	C
71	**72**	**73**	**74**	**75**	**76**	**77**	**78**	**79**	**80**
C	D	C	B	A	A	D	B	C	B
81	**82**	**83**	**84**	**85**	**86**	**87**	**88**	**89**	**90**
C	D	A	A	B	D	B	D	C	C
91	**92**	**93**	**94**	**95**	**96**	**97**	**98**	**99**	**100**
D	D	A	D	B	C	C	A	C	C
101	**102**	**103**	**104**	**105**	**106**	**107**	**108**	**109**	**110**
A	B	C	B	C	D	B	C	D	A
111	**112**	**113**	**114**	**115**	**116**	**117**	**118**	**119**	**120**
B	B	B	C	C	C	B	C	B	A
121	**122**	**123**	**124**	**125**	**126**	**127**	**128**	**129**	**130**
D	D	D	B	B	C	A	D	C	A
131	**132**	**133**	**134**	**135**	**136**	**137**	**138**	**139**	**140**
C	C	B	C	D	D	D	D	A	B
141	**142**	**143**	**144**	**145**	**146**	**147**	**148**	**149**	**150**
D	D	B	D	C	C	C	C	D	B

Child Development & Pedagogy

CHILD DEVELOPMENT

CONCEPT OF DEVELOPMENT

Development refers to interaction of a person with his environmental surroundings whose after product is to increase:

- The strength
- The degree of differentiation
- The organization of personality

Development refers to those effects upon the person's cognitive and emotional systems which strengthen one or more abilities of the person in the desired manner. Thus, development is the qualitative changes in the organism. Environment has very important role to play in the process of development.

Three Concepts of Development

1. *Development is maturation :* According to **Arnold Gessell**, the role of physical changes is very important in development. The development from infancy to adolescence is governed by physical changes. When physical growth of the particular stage gets matured only then development in that stage is possible. For example, a growing nervous system changes systematically and automatically and this results in predictable changes in bones and muscles. Thus major changes in the organism are based on maturation.

   According to Gessell, there is internal programming toward physical and cognitive growth and each year is characterized by certain behavioural changes. Development is always guided and controlled by these changes.

2. *Development is learning :* According to **Baer**, "development is the behavioural changes which require programming and programming requires time but not enough of it to call it age."

   Programming here means the sequence of learning which may happen naturally or it may be arranged in the life of an individual with the help of the environment. Thus, according to this definition, development is genetic and environmental both. Whatever we learn in the process of our life is related to development of us.

3. *Development is the synthesis of abilities :* According to **Jean Piaget**, there are four basic elements that take part in the process of development and development is the result of synthesis of all these elements. They are given below:

I. Maturation	An automatic and innate process
II. Social transmission	Learning through language, schooling or training given by parents
III. Experiences	Obtained from the outer environment informally
IV. Equilibration	Whatever is learnt or gained internally or externally is equilibrated here.

STAGES OF DEVELOPMENT

From infancy to adulthood human being undergoes the following stages of development.

1	Infancy	-	0-2 years
2	Early childhood	-	3-6 years
3	Later childhood	-	7-12 years
4	Adolescence	-	13-17 years
5	Adulthood	-	18-25 years

At each stage of human development, certain physical, intellectual, language, emotional and social changes occur which may be similar or entirely different from the preceding age. We will describe all these stages one by one.

Dimensions (Areas) of Development

Before coming to the stages of development it is better to know what the physical, intellectual, emotional and social development are:

1. **Physical development :** Important characteristics of physical growth and development are given below:
   - Physical growth is curvilinear not steady or regular. Rapid growth is followed by slow growth and then again rapid growth may be there.
   - Different parts (organs) of the body have its own unique way of development. Whatever changes we see in hands and legs cannot be seen in heart or lung.
   - Physical growth and development is affected by climatic conditions. For example, cold countries have more favourable conditions of growth and development than hot or humid countries.
   - Heredity fixes a limit of physical growth and development. The descendents of five feeted man is not supposed to have a height of more than 6 feet or 5½ feet.
   - Physical growth is very rapid in the infancy and in the later childhood. It is again fast in the start of adolescence.

Dimensions of Physical Growth : Important dimensions of physical growth and development are as follows:

(i) Height : A new born baby is 19-20 inches in length at the time of birth. As soon as the baby grows, his height also increases.

(ii) Weight : Human baby has a weight of 2.5 kg. –3.5 kg. at the time of birth. Girl babies are generally lighter than male babies here. When a baby becomes an adult he acquires a weight of 55 kg. at the height 5.5 feet. The weight of boys are generally higher than girls due to increased height. If height is more, weight will also be high.

(iii) Body proportion : Some organs of the body are more developed at the time of birth than others. But as soon as the baby grows and reaches to the period of adulthood, proportionate change and growth are seen. For example, head is already somewhat developed at the time of birth but it grows less proportionately than other parts of body.

(iv) Internal organs : Internal organs of the body also develop with age. As the child grows, the heart beat which is 100-120 per minute in infancy, becomes regular and normal, *i.e.*, 72 times per minute. Respiration also becomes slower, deeper and regular, food takes longer time to pass the digestive tract, the body temperature becomes stable and so on and all this happens due to growth and development of the internal organs of the body. This increase in efficiency enables the older children and adults to adapt to the environmental changes.

It is pitutory gland which is responsible for growth in the early years of life. Sex gland is also activated under the influence of this gland, and influence the pitutory gland as well. If sex hormones did not restrain the function of pitutory gland the human being would become a giant.

2. **Motor development :** Motor development includes movement of hands, lags, mouth and other related muscles of the body. Important features of motor development are as follows:
   - Motor development occurs in those structures which lie nearest to the main axis especially near the vaist, thighs, legs etc. The child learns to control the muscles of his arms earlier than those of fingers.
   - Bilateral to unilateral trend in the coordination and control of muscles is seen. The child first uses both of his hands then he gradually learns to use only one hand in specialized manner.
   - From general to specific trend in motor development is seen.
   - An orderly sequence of motor development is also seen. **Hurlock** found that motor development in the head region takes place first, followed by the motor development of arms, hands, legs, etc. This trend is not reversed any how.
   - If motor development of the child is delayed by any reason, his emotional and social development will also be delayed or disturbed.

3. **Intellectual development :** Intellectual development includes attending, perceiving, observing, thinking, recalling, analyzing, evaluating, problem solving and the development of language and concepts. These aspects of mind grow and change with age. Generally these activities of mind are inter related. Important features of intellectual development are as follows:

- Mental development is a continuous but steady process and all activities of mind are inter-related also.
- As long as the experiences of the child increase, his mental horizon expands. He learns not only to differentiate but to integrate different elements of the physical as well as meta-physical world.
- Factors affecting mental development are maturation and learning.
- Mental activities are guided and controlled by nervous system. Brain which is an important part of nervous system plays the key role in the mental development of the child.
- Sensation and perception are the primary aspects of mental activities. In fact, mental activities start from these two aspects. Sensation is the first step to knowledge which is accompanied by perception.
- Perceptual experience leads to concept formation. Concept formation takes place on the basis of general and common qualities of an object, e.g., concept of "book" is developed after seeing so many things like books and then we say that books are for reading. Thus, concept is developed on the basis of common qualities of an object. It involves discrimination and generalization both.
- Concept of an object or idea changes with the change in experiences for example, cold season of December may have different meaning for the people of Kolkata and Srinagar due to difference of experiences.
- Child's concepts change with the increase in his age. For example, a small child may develop a unique concept of ghost. But when he becomes an adult, his concept of ghost changes.

4. **Language development :** Language development is actually the verbalization of concepts which is learnt by imitation (hearing). If child is deaf, his language development will be zero. Important features of language development are given below.
   - Language is a tool to be used for all types of communication. Without proper language development, no communication from one person to the other is possible.
   - Language is used as a tool in acquiring knowledge. When knowledge increases, vocabulary also increases.
   - Language development starts with mere names of objects or events and when it reaches at its peak it develops ideas into universal concepts.
   - Growth and maturity of speech is an important aspect of language development. Four needs of the child motivates him to learn speech.

Desire to secure information more and more (Interrogative sentences).

(a) Desire to give commands or to do requests (Imperative sentences).

(b) Desire to come into social relationship with others.

(c) Desire to express feelings and thoughts (Exclamatory and Assertive sentences)

- There are spurts or rest in the speech development. It is not constant throughout life. Sometimes it is very rapid and sometimes very slow.
- The development of thinking moves from simple to complex and from the concrete to the abstract.
- An individual stops growing intellectually upto the age of 20 years in general.

5. **Emotional development :** Emotion is a strong feeling that is so strong that it can be observed overtly. There are **four qualities of emotional experiences:**
   - Every emotional experience involves feeling
   - Every emotional experience is accompanied by marked physiological changes
   - An emotional experience includes an impulse towards some kind of action, ie, overt response is seen
   - Emotion involves awareness or perception of what it is or what it might be that causes these impulses and feelings

Important features of emotional development are as follows :

(a) Emotions start immediately after birth. For example, an infant shows fear, anger, love etc, though his emotions are not clear at this age, according to Sherman.

(b) Children's emotions are very intense as compared to adults. As they grow they begin to exercise restraint over their emotions. They learn to modify and hide their emotions also.

(c) Child's emotions last only for a few minutes and then it ends all of a sudden. The transitory nature of the child's emotions lies in a rapid shift from one emotion to another. When he shows anger, he at the next moment smiles.

(d) In the beginning, the emotional expression is diffused and generalized. It becomes stable, differentiated, selective, moderate and graded as the child grows older.

(e) Emotional development is also determined by the socio-economic background of the child. If a child belongs to a cultured family, he will show more emotional maturity.

(f) Emotional development is affected by the physical development of the child also. For example, if a child is physically weak due to malnutrition or diseases, his emotions will be less stable and less subtle.

6. **Social development :** Human baby is the only organism in the world that takes maximum and longer time to be socially and economically self dependent. He needs help from others more than any other creature. This dependence of the child on others helps him to learn how to interact with others in diverse situations. The more a person is healthy in his social interactions, the more he is said to be socially developed. Important features of social development are as follows:

- Social development starts with the process of socialization, a process which enables a child to acquire his social status according to his age. It is the process of socialization that helps the child to learn social traditions, customs and culture.
- The child increases his social circles gradually. These circles increase further when the child grows with age. It makes very difficult for the child to adjust with different types of people in the society. Thus, social development is actually an adjustment training.
- Social development means to share joy and sorrows with others, to work as a member of a group, to cooperate with others and to develop social perception for the purpose of developing belongingness with the rest of the society.
- The end points of social development is social maturity, ie, to adapt successfully to the social environment without frustration. A socially matured person is one who is fair in his dealing, courteous in his behaviour and honest in his character. His sense of responsibility, his self confidence, and his leadership quality make him distinct from others. He confirms what is acceptable to others and denies what is antagonistic to him.

Lifespan and Development

(A) Infancy and development : Various dimensions of development during the period of infancy are given below.

1. **Physical development :** This period is marked by following characteristics of physical development.

(i) Physical development is very rapid during this period. For example size increases ten inches upto second year. Weight also becomes almost double at the age 4½ months, i.e., from 3 kg at birth to almost 6 kg. At the age of 4½ month.

(ii) Though sex organs are totally undeveloped and inactive during this period, yet a tendency to sexual development is seen in the second year of life. Child actually passes through three stages of sexual development. First stage, the stage of self love belongs to infancy. Here the child derives pleasure from his body, by sucking his thumbs of hand or legs or by touching his sex organs. The other two stages- homosexual or hetero sexual belong to early childhood.

(iii) At the time of birth, boys are heavier than girls. 7% weight loss is seen in the first seven days then the baby start to gain weight.

(iv) Study shows that boys are on the average heavier than girls at all age levels except from 11-14 years of age in which girls are found heavier than boys.

(v) Head is more developed than other parts of the body at birth. It grows proportionately at lesser speed than other parts of the body. At 6 years, the child gains 90% of the adult size of head.

(vi) Facial skeleton is found larger in proportion to cranium from birth to seven years of age.

(vii) Nose is proportionately small and flat on the face in the first four years. It gains full size at the age of 13 or 14.

(viii) Trunk is found heavy during the period of infancy. It along with legs lengthens gradually.

(ix) At birth, the weight of the brain is one fourth of an adult brain. It is one half by the age of 9 months and three fourth by the age of two years.

(x) In the first year of the baby the heart beat is very irregular and its speed is very high. As the child grows, the heart beat becomes regular and slower. Other physical changes are given below.

- Food takes longer time to pass through the digestive tract and to reach the intestines.
- Urine bladder can retain urine for a longer period of time.
- Body temperature becomes more stable.
- Composition of blood does not change.

(xi) The weight becomes almost three times the birth weight at the end of first year. By the age of 2, it becomes 3½ times the birth weight.

2. Nervous system :

(i) Nerve cells attain maturity during this period

(ii) Brain also grows rapidly and its size and weight increases

(iii) Improvement in the functioning and structure of sensory organs is seen. Thus, by the end of this period the child is able to perform all the functions of seeing, hearing, smelling, tasting and touching properly.

3. Motor development :

(i) Co-ordination and control of bodily movements are seen.

(ii) The child starts grasping objects in the fourth month of his life.

(iii) He sits in the sixth month. He crawls in the seventh or eighth month. He stands with the help of support in the ninth month and in the 12th month he begins to walk slowly without support.

(iv) Running begins in the second year of his life

(v) Greater muscular involvement is seen during infancy

4. Language development :

(i) It starts with vocalization in the form of cries or explosive sounds. This vocalization may be described as pre speech form.

(ii) The child only cries at the time of birth to express his emotions or desires. This crying is used even in the second year of life to express desires and needs.

(iii) He begins to utter few words by the end of the first year like mama, dada etc. Some unintelligible words spoken by the child may be seen in the seventh or eighth month.

(iv) Language development properly begins in the beginning of the second year. The rate of language development becomes rapid at the age of 1.5 years and the child crames any new learnt word just in order to retain it in his mind.

(v) By the end of two years he begins to speak proper but short sentences, though grammatical mistakes may be there.

5. Intellectual development :

(i) No clear cut sign of intellectual development is seen during infancy. His capacity to grasp new words is totally based on rote memory, though his cramming is without reason or intellect.

(ii) He lacks abstract understanding. His understanding is exclusively restricted to concrete materials but he thinks that heavier is one which is bigger in size. Thus, a plastic ball of bigger size is heavier than a metal ball of smaller size for the child.

(iii) Sign of creativity is seen at the end of the 2nd year. The infant often engages himself in collecting many articles.

(iv) This is a period of make belief. When he attains the age of 2, he believes in what he is told by his elders.

(v) A baby perceives an unfamiliar object as a form or as a figure. He has an innate tendency to organize his sense field and to perceive the object as a whole but this perception lacks definiteness.

6. Social development :

(i) He learns social skills in the company of his mother and fathers. When he is responded by them he learns how to respond to others. Thus, he learns all his social experiences from his family members in the first year but in the second year his horizon expands to his neighbourhood.

(ii) By the end of two years he begins to take the notice of other infants and plays with them.

(iii) He totally depends upon his family members for the fulfillment of his social, psychological and physical needs.

(iv) He expects that every body around him should love him and care him. When this expectation is not fulfilled he becomes irritated and cries.

(v) The baby becomes aware of other persons around him at the age of one month. In the second month, he smiles in response to the attentions of adults and he is able to distinguish his mother and other women. In the third month he waves his hands and legs when he is talked to. In the fourth month, he makes anticipatory adjustment to being lifted by someone. In the fifth month, he attends to the human face and looks in the direction of the person who leaves him. He smiles in response to the person who speaks and plays with him. In the sixth month, he reacts differently to

smiling and scolding and shows negative responses to strangers. In the ninth month, he tries to imitate the speech of others. He copies simple acts and gestures of others after observation in the tenth month. In the 12th month, he can refrain from doing things when he is forbidden to do so.

In the second year of life he exhibits fear and dislike for strangers by crying or withdrawing. When the baby attains the age of 18 months, he shows negativism in the form of stubborn resistance to the demands of adults.

(vi) In the first two years, the child's play is self centred. He does not like to be interfered by other children or adults. He plays in his own way. He is generally non-cooperative and has to be handled with patience and tacts. In short, the baby is socially underdeveloped.

(vii) Hurlock has presented the social development taking place during first two years of infancy as under :

1. First month	Understand human and other voices
2. Second month	Recognizes human voices and greets with smile
3. Third month	Recognizes mother and distresses on her being away
4. Fourth month	Recognizes human faces
5. Fifth month	Understands the tone of voices i.e. love and hate
6. Sixth or Seventh month	Welcomes the known with smile
7. 8th or 9th month	Plays with his own shadow
8. 24th month	Participates in elder's work

7. Emotional development:

(i) He is completely egocentric and selfish. When he reaches the age of 2, he even does not want to share his toys.

(ii) He is irritated and cries when he is chided by his family members.

(iii) His emotions are intense, frequent and totally unstable though emotional reactions become distinct in the beginning of the second year. These emotions are spontaneous and he can not control them.

(iv) He cannot hide his feelings thus, his entire emotions are in the overt form.

(v) Emotions of anger, fear, disgust, elation, love and affections are seen. For example, when he is loved by his mother, he shows his affection by his activities. Similarly, when he is not attended by his family members, he feels disgusted. He also feels pleasure in the company of his mother or his father.

(vi) A number of psychologists are of the view that infants are able to undergo emotional experiences. Emotions of fear, anger, joy, hate etc. are seen in them even in the first year.

(vii) During the period of infancy only those conditions arouse emotional responses which affect the child's immediate needs and well being, but when the child grows, his spectrum increases and he becomes responsive to a number of stimuli.

(viii) It has been noticed that babies and children show their pronounced emotional disturbance just before eating, sleeping, or waking up. For example, when a baby wakes up after sleep, he cries whether he is hungry or not.

(ix) Intellectually dull children are less emotionally disturbed than the normal children.

(x) Infants show smiling response to any human face whether familiar or stranger between eight and twenty weeks of age. Negative responses to strangers starts after 20 weeks of age and continues upto 40 weeks.

(B) Early childhood and development : Various dimensions of development during the period of early childhood (3-6 years) are as follows:

1. Physical and motor development :

(i) He acquires many motor skills like catching, throwing, running, jumping, climbing, using simple tools, riding a tricycle etc.

(ii) Growth in outer parts of the body especially height, weight, formation of muscles etc. is not as fast as it was during infancy. The child, however begins to assume the body proportion of an adult.

(iii) The growth of legs is rapid and it acquires about half of an adult size. The growth of head is, however, very slow and that of trunk is medium.

(iv) The height of a three years old child is 38 inches on an average though Indian children may be slightly lower than this size. Similarly, the weight should also be 33 pounds at the age of three. By the age of five years, the average weight of children is 43 pounds and average height for boys is 43 inches.

Motor	2 years	3 years	4 and 5 years
Development	Walks without help, jumps, runs	Skips, hops	Free and active movement responds to music
Fine motor coordination	Copying	Can match shapes, sees similarities and differences	Can name colours
Perceptual	Identifies self, matches colours	Can fit nuts, boxes	Matches shapes and colours, distinguishes names
Vocalization	200 words, uses few words	900 words, follows commands	Can repeat 4 digits-2000 to 3000 words, can define familiar words
Adaptive behaviour	Bowel control	Builds blocks, can draw a man	4 digits, draws body with details

(v) Muscles develop at a very rapid speed due to excess involvement of the child in motor activities.

(vi) The rate of heart beat and pulse slow down and blood pressure goes up steadily.

(vii) By the age of 5-6 the child acquires 90% of the adult weight of brain. Nerve fibres in the brain areas also come to almost maturity by the end of the period of early childhood. It should be noted that the growth of brain and nerve fibres is very rapid from birth to four years.

(viii) Self feeding, self dressing, self bathing, combing the hair, brushing the teeth, playing with toys, using pencils for writing or sketching etc are also seen during this period.

2. Intellectual development :

(i) Perceptual development begins from mass movement to differentiation. Norms for perceptual development is given in the callout table.

(ii) The child perceives those things quickly and clearly which are concerned with his mental set and interest.

(iii) The child begins to explore his social environment and acquire new experiences at the age of three.

(iv) By the age of six, the child develops clear perception of size, shape, colour, time and distance. He does not consider all bigger objects as heavier too.

(v) The child begins to form concepts of physical and social reality. For example, he does not do any thing against the wishes of his family members. If he does so, he hides the same.

(vi) The child starts learning many materials by rote memorization. His capacity to retain learnt material increases.

(vii) Imagination begins to grow and creativity is seen. He manipulates or breaks his toys to understand its mechanism. But his thinking process is restricted to concrete objects only.

(viii) Span of attention increases from 7 minutes to 20 minutes.

(ix) His curiosity forces him to explore the environment. He asks so many questions from his elders for this purpose.

(x) The child is now able to use symbols in language and mathematics.

(xi) The child develops a lot of concepts during this period but many of his concepts cannot be verbalized by him due to limited vocabulary.

(xii) During this period, children's concepts of spatial relations, distance and depth are vague. This makes the children awkward in their behaviour. For example they calculate height and distance wrongly.

(xiii) By the age of five, they are able to distinguish between past, present and future, ie, between yesterday, tomorrow and day after tomorrow etc.

(xiv) The concepts of number and quantity also become clear to them. According to Piaget, children acquire concept of number even before they are able to count.

(xv) Children's social concepts are influenced by the nature of inter-personal relationship.

(xvi) This stage is also called the stage of fantasy. The child takes shelter into his imaginary world in order to escape the harsh realities of his world at home and neighbourhood. If he is given more chance to interact with people, his social concepts will be rich.

3. Language development

(i) The child has to master four major tasks in the process of learning to speak properly.

- Comprehension of the speech of others
- Building a vocabulary
- Using and combining words into sentences
- Pronouncing the words correctly

By the end of the period of early childhood, the child is able to master all these four tasks.

(ii) Language development of a child actually begins from birth cry. When he is responded by his mother after crying, he comes to understand the meaning and importance of crying.

(iii) A ten month old child is able to use one or two words only but by the end of the first year his vocabulary increases to four, as **Smith** has observed. By the end of 2nd year, he can use 272 words. In the third year, his vocabulary increase to 896. when he attains the age of four, he can use 1560 words and at the age of 6 he can use 2562 words as Smith has observed.

(iv) Language development of children is not uniform. It depends upon better socio-economic environment at home, better schooling and independent living of the child.

4. Social development:

(i) Feeling of autonomy develops in children. They try to explore and manipulate their environment independently.

(ii) The child learns how to behave, talk and interact with the family members and neighbourhood.

(iii) The child may be frustrated if social atmosphere of the neighbourhood is not similar to that of the atmosphere at home.

(iv) The child's play no longer remains a solitary play after the age of three. The child selects his playmates and develops casual friendship with them. He learns cooperation, competition, sympathy, jealousy, teasing, bullying, quarrelling, etc. in the company of his playmates.

(v) Imitation, timidity, shyness, desire for possession etc. are other forms of social behaviour that develop during this period.

(vi) The child who is resistive upto the age of three years becomes cooperative and friendly and seeks approval of adults upto the age of four years. That is why he does not object to exchange his toys with his best friends.

(vii) At the age of 5-6 he begins to pride about his parents and boast about other members of his family after six.

(viii) Most of the children want to dominate in their respective groups at the age of six. Thus group leader changes every time in the group. In this way, the child learns how to adjust in the society in varied situations.

(ix) Children of both sexes play together without any discrimination.

(x) They also take part in those games which involve physical energy and motor activity like hide and seek.

(xi) They take interest in fairy tales and animal stories in which they want that someone should win in the fighting. They are very much interested to know which animal is stronger and strongest out of so many at the age of 4-5.

(xii) Negativism increases during this period. It is believed that the more a child is frustrated by the interference of adults, the more negativistic his behaviour will be.

(xiii) Girls have been found more dominating than boys in social and group situations.

5. Emotional development : Contributions of emotions are very much recognized in the personal and social adjustment of the individuals. Important features of emotional development during this period are given below.

(i) Emotions of the child are exhibited only for a very short period. It means that child shifts from one emotion to another very rapidly. For example, if a three or four years old child who is weeping loudly is given a toffee, he will become pleased at once.

(ii) Emotions of children are intense irrespective of the intensity of the stimulus. A very simple stimulus can create a very intense emotional experience.

(iii) Children are helpless to hide their emotions and they express them by different activities like crying, throwing objects, nail biting, bullying, thumb sucking and speech difficulties. Emotions of hope, disappointment, fear, anxiety, shame, jealousy, hatred etc. are expressed during this period in different ways.

(iv) He is still guided by his innate tendencies and instincts.

(v) His moral behaviour is also guided by his emotions-pleasure and pain.

(vi) Emotions of submission and elation are alternately seen in the child.

(vii) At the age of five his emotions begin to organize into sentiment. The most primitive sentiment is his love for his own self and his love for his toys. Due to this reason, this stage is also called "Narcissism autoerotism" or self love. This word **narcissism** has been derived from Greek language which means falling in love with one self.

(viii) The child also develops a deep sentiment of affection for his parents. At the age of 6-7 it is very painful for the child to see his/her father or mother ailing. Here Freud is of the opinion that girl is very much attached to her father and boy feels more attachment to his mother. Former is called Elektra complex and later is called Oedipus complex.

(ix) The child begins to show "moodiness" expressed in sulking and bad emotions at the age of four. This emotion reaches to its peak during the period of adolescence.

(x) Most of the emotional responses are learned by children by imitating parents and other family members. Thus, emotions are innate but emotional responses are innate and learnt both.

Educational Implications of the Period of Early Childhood

Early childhood is basically a pre-school period. The formal education of the child begins when he attains the age of five so, sixth year of life of the child is very important from point of view of educating the child. Since success of education of this period will depend on the pre-school education, so, the whole period from 3-6 becomes very important. Following strategies must be adopted by the school to develop the child educationally.

(i) The teacher in the school should first see whether the child has proper physical and motor development. Regular medical and health check up programme should be organized in the school for this purpose.

(ii) Parents should also be consulted if teacher finds some problem in the physical or motor development of the child.

(iii) It is the teacher who will first notice the physical or motor problems of the child. Hence, he should know the norms of physical and social development of children. On the basis of his very report, the child will be sent to the doctor for further diagnosis and investigation.

(iv) Various types of games and play activities should be organized in the school according to the age of children and they should be motivated to participate in those activities.

(v) The child is very active physically during this period. He mostly takes part in those activities, which involve muscular movement. Seeing this, he should be given rich diet to eat. If child is not getting proper nutrition, he will not gain height or weight properly.

(vi) This is a period of taking shift from dependence to self help, so child should be given more and more freedom to do in whatever manner he likes and to manipulate his environment in his own way.

(vii) This is a period of rapid intellectual growth. Hence, he should be sent to pre-primary school for learning through plays.

(viii) He should also be taught religious and moral principles so that he may become an acceptable member of the society.

(ix) He should be given freedom to manipulate objects so that he may develop his creative potentials.

(x) The teacher should narrate the stories of animals before such children. It will develop their vocabulary and imaginative power.

(xi) The child can concentrate for a longer period. Hence, the teacher can teach him any thing systematically. Even mathematics can be taught to him because he can understand symbols.

(xii) Efforts should be made to increase the vocabulary of the child as much as possible so that he can verbalize all the concepts that he knows.

(xiii) In order to save the child from frustration, he should not be interfered by the adults or parents.

(xiv) The child can increase his vocabulary mostly by hearing, so, he should be talked more and more. Better environment created at home means better language development.

(xv) Group activities are most suitable for such children. They should be given chance to get involve in such activities. Through these activities they would learn competition, cooperation, sympathy and the like feeling.

(xvi) The child seeks approval of adults. Adults should not be miserly in giving such approvals. They should rather love him.

(xvii) Girls and boys can be educated in a co-setting. This arrangement will create no administrative problem.

(xviii) If the child disobeys the parents they should not mind it. It is a natural phenomenon and will come down in the later childhood.

(xix) Girls should be preferred to be given the role of group leaders.

(xx) A teacher can control intense emotions of the child by his loving behaviour.

(xxi) Since children of this age can not hide their emotions, it is very easier for the teacher to deal these children effectively.

(xxii) Early childhood is a period in which the child can be emotionally attached to any body who loves him. The emotional attachment with parents may be generalized and extended to teachers in the school. A teacher can exploit this tendency and get the students involved in so many types of tasks.

(C) Later childhood and development : This is the period between the age of 6-12 years. At the end of this period, puberty symptoms begin to grow and the period of adolescence starts. This period is marked by **pseudo maturity** and excellence in different fields. As far as sexual maturity is concerned, it remains completely dormant during this period, but this sex emerges with a great force at the end of this period. Because of the dormant nature of sex, this stage is also called **latency period**. Various dimensions of development during this period are given below.

1. Physical development :

(i) Steady and slow but uniform growth in the external as well as internal organs are seen.

(ii) Milk teeth are replaced by permanent set.

(iii) Auscification of bones takes place due to increase in height and weight.

(iv) Refinement in motor skills are seen.

(v) The child is physically restless during this period. He finds himself engaged in one activity or the other.

(vi) The brain acquires the size of an adult.

(vii) It is the period of best health of the individual during his whole life. During this period children never get tired. They burn their calories in physical activities and eat to the maximum level possible.

(viii) Girls are ahead of boys by two years in height and weight physiologically. Girls at the age of 11 are ahead of boys by at least one year.

(ix) Shedding of milk teeth and growth of permanent teeth change the shape of mouth, like flattening of forehead, sharpening nose and broadening of the chest.

(x) Important physical characteristics of this period are increased manual dexterity, high muscular strength, increased resistance to fatigue, increased endurance for play activities and so on.

2. Intellectual development :

(i) The child develops the powers of observation, reasoning and abstract thinking.

(ii) He can accumulate huge amount of knowledge in his mind. He can derive information and pleasure from books.

(iii) His perceptual ability, memory, and application of mental powers become keener.

(iv) The IQ of the child becomes stable and determines his IQ level in future. In short, it is a period of intellectual maturity.

(v) Boys love adventure and fairy tales and girls love mild form of romance and biographies.

(vi) The child begins to admire things and people around him and he begins to imitate the behaviour of those people who he likes.

(vii) The child begins to make clear distinction between himself and the outer world. He starts working on reality principles according to Freud.

(viii) The concept of natural laws becomes fully developed at the end of this period.

(ix) Capacity of logical thinking and power of reasoning increases.

(x) Interest in science fictions and stories reaches at its peak by the end of later childhood.

(xi) Courage and loyalty both increase simultaneously.

(xii) The child starts day dreaming and he defeats his rivals in his imaginative plays.

(xiii) The early imaginary fears are disappeared by the end of 12 years.

(xiv) When a child attains the age of ten, he shows high ability of generalization.

(xv) Children of this age are concerned with immediate cause and effect relationship and current happening. They live in the realm of present and don't care for future.

(xvi) The child begins to understand conceptual problem very well. He can analyse it and can give suggestions for its solutions.

(xvii) The physical growth is slow and steady during this period but intellectual growth and the functioning of mind are very rapid during this period.

(xviii) The child develops clear concepts of length, breath, time and distance.

3. Sexual development :

(i) From this angle this stage of the child is called latency period. Generally sexual energy at this age remains dormant but it becomes very active immediately after the age of 12 years.

(ii) Indifferent and antagonistic attitude towards the opposite sex are seen by the age of 10-11. As a result of this attitude, boys do not like to mix up with girls and girls are antagonistic to mix up with boys. Due to this reason upper primary education (from VIth –VIIIth) in co educational setting is not suited in school.

4. Emotional development :

(i) Rapid shift from one type of emotion to another is not seen and the child learns how to control his emotions in a variety of social situations. For example, he avoids weeping in the company of his friends.

(ii) Emotional responses of the child become less diffused and undifferentiated, ie, intensity of emotions is reduced.

(iii) Emotions are expressed even in the absence of concrete materials.

(iv) Fear of animals, ghosts, loneliness and high place that was found in the early childhood, no longer persists in the later childhood.

(v) Certain new fear appear during this stage like fear of failing in the attempt such as games examinations, etc, fear of supernatural objects, such as heaven or hell etc and fear of being ridiculed etc.

(vi) The child gets angry if he is thwarted, teased or prejudiced. If he is compared with other children wrongly, he is interfered in his activities or he is ridiculed by elders, all these things will make the child angry.

(vii) If child thinks that some other children are being favoured by elders, he again gets angry. He becomes jealous of those children who are favoured. Emotion of jealousy is found in girls more than in boys.

(viii) All emotions like joy, love, curiosity, grief and affection appear during this stage in a stable manner. The child can hide his emotions. He expresses only those emotions which are approved socially.

(ix) Emotions are structured into sentiments. Various types of sentiments like religious, moral, patriotic and aesthetic sentiments develop during this period.

(x) Complex of superiority develops during this period. Boys consider themselves superior to girls.

5. Social development :

(i) He loves to play in groups and shares his toys with other children. Team spirit and group loyalties are commonly seen in such children in a more matured form.

(ii) Social horizon of the child increases to neighbourhood and school and he looses the shackles of his family ties. He becomes independent of his parents and does many things against their wishes.

(iii) He wants to become hero or leader in the group in the same way as we see in the period of early childrenhood.

(iv) He cares himself more than others. His self centred behaviour sometimes gives rise to rivalries and aggression.

(v) He accepts social norms. He feels pride to be ruled by public opinions. He is so much attached with his group that he can defy even the orders of his parents if they do not match with the norms of the group to which the child belongs. This tendency in children continues upto the age of 17-18.

(vi) Social development of the child mostly takes place in the play ground. The child mostly takes interest in those games which require stiff competition like football, hockey, kabaddi and kho kho.

(vii) Girls mostly prefer indoor games but if they are exposed to outdoor games they enjoy more than boys. Badminton, tennis and skipping are their favorite games.

(viii) When something wrong happens, boys indulge into physical combat and girls into verbal fights or pulling each others hairs. The behaviour of the child is largely influenced by the group to which child belongs.

(ix) The age from 10-12 is referred to gang age when children take much interest in gang activities and adhere to gang loyalties. That is why we see that every child in the age group of 10-12 necessarily joins a group and follows its rules and regulations strictly.

(x) Sex differentiation becomes sharp,i.e., girls play with girls only. The child does not like to play with girls during this period.

He accepts only those girls in his group which are very energetic and courageous.

(xi) It is the period of peak unruliness in schools and homes especially when child is thwarted by his peers and relatives. Here, the child rejects many of the standards set by the adults or his family members and tries to live an independent life in his own circle.

(xii) Some delinquent acts like bullying, stealing, gang activities etc begin at the end of this period.

(xiii) Boys are more rebellion than girls and their groups or gangs are more organized than girls.

(xiv) Because of the excess involvement of boys and girls in their respective groups, this period is particularly known as gang age period.

6. Moral development:

(i) When the child attains the age of six, his capacity to understand relationship increases. He accepts lawful and unlawful social matters, though his concept of right and wrong may be different from his peers.

(ii) At the age of 8 he moves from specific response to generalized response and thus his concepts become more generalized. For example, he comes to realize that stealing of any thing is bad whether it be the matter of money or books.

(iii) During the period of later childhood morality is defined as performing good acts and maintaining the conventional social order. Children of this age are not deficient of this respect in any way.

(iv) At the age of 11-12, moral behaviour is oriented towards authority and maintaining the status quo which is considered to be a primary value. When the child changes his group loyalties, moral values may also change. It is because their conduct is mostly governed by the mores of his group.

(v) The development of right and wrong concepts begins at home in the period of early childhood, but it actually matures in the group. That is why we see that the child may float the authority of his parents but he may not go against the wishes of his gang. Such moral behaviour is dangerous only when the group is not following social and moral norms properly.

Educational Implications of the Period of Later Childhood

(i) Suitable freedom should be given to children to develop physically, emotionally and intellectually.

(ii) These children like games, sports and group activities very much. School should organize such activities and should make them an indispensable part of the curriculum.

(iii) A teacher should not try to compare boys with girls. It is because girls feel themselves superior to boys and vice versa. If a teacher does not follow this maxim, it will create hatred for girls in the minds of boys.

(iv) Most of the lessons should be taught to children of this age through group activities.

(v) A teacher must be democratic in dealing such children. If anything is imposed on them irrationally, they will not follow it.

(vi) It is also necessary for the teacher to express faith in such children. He should not suspect the integrity and honesty of these children without reason.

(vii) Many desirable behaviours come to light during this period. Such behaviours should be reinforced regularly.

(viii) Children should be allowed to go to neighbourhood to learn community experiences. Remember that only school experiences are not enough.

(ix) The parents should not take the gang activities of their sons and daughters with anger. The only thing that is needed is that the gang should be good in behaviour.

(x) Certain hobbies are developed during this period. They should be encouraged by teachers and parents.

(xi) Interest and liking of boys and girls differ. Hence, they should be assigned different types of works according to their liking.

(xii) Children should be motivated to take rich diet in order to develop their muscles and bones.

(xiii) Child is never at rest during this period. So, a teacher should always get them involve in certain activities—physical or mental. If child is free, he may be destructive and problematic for the family.

(xiv) If a teacher knows the norm of physical growth of these boys and girls, he can guide them accordingly in the class. If the child is not growing on a satisfactory line, the teacher can report to the parents of the child.

(xv) If a teacher is successful in developing reading habits as a part of their routine activity in students, they can accumulate huge amount of information and knowledge.

(xvi) The teacher should take the child to the laboratory for observation and experimentation. Lab work must start at the age of 12.

(xvii) Children of this age should be taught stories full of adventure and romance.

(xviii) The tendency of hero worshiping in such children should be exploited by the teacher.

(xix) Power of reasoning of the child should be utilized in understanding religion and mythology.

(xx) Parents should not forbid the child from doing a particular thing in a straight forward manner. They should give reason to the child why it should not be done.

(xxi) The child should be given chance to generalize laws and principles as mush as possible.

(xxii) Children of this age do not care much for their tomorrow. Hence, whatever good is done by them should be reinforced immediately.

(xxiii) At the age of ten, girls do not like to mix up with boys and vice versa. So, a teacher should guide them separately and co-education at the junior level is not recommended at all.

(xxiv) Children can hide any of their emotions at this age. So, a teacher should not study them in hurry and draw conclusion about the child.

(xxv) The behaviour of the teacher should be completely unbiased. He should not discriminate any child on any ground. Biased attitude and discrimination make the child angry.

(xxvi) The child should be given opportunity to lead at least one group in any curricular or co-curricular activities.

(xxvii) Religious and moral educations should properly begin at this stage.

(xxviii) Gang activities of children should not be discouraged by the teacher. Such activities are essential for self expression and exposure.

THEORIES OF CHILD DEVELOPMENT

Theories of child development can be classified into three broad categories. The first is psycho analytic theory propounded by Sigmund Freud and his associates. This theory gives much importance to unconscious motivation developed especially in the early period's of life and it determines the personality of the individual in the later parts of life also. The second is behaviouristic theory of child development which lays stress on the connection between stimulus and response. The major advantage of this category of theories is that it can be experimented and verified in clinical setting and thus these theories are more scientific in nature. The last category is cognitive theory of child development. It is a molar approach of explanation of human development and it takes the total situation facing the mind into account. It lays stress on perception and its organization responsible for learning and development.

Some of these theories are being described below:

1. **Psychoanalytic Theory (Freud) :** According to this theory, every child passes through five stages of psycho-sexual development. These stages are given below.

(a) *Oral stage:* At this stage focus of pleasure is mouth. When child sucks milk from the breast of her mother, he not only quenches his hunger but also gets pleasure by the excitement of mouth.

(b) *Anal stage :* When child attains the age of two the focus of pleasure shifts from mouth to anus. The child obtains pleasure from the activities related to anus during this period. That is why defecating is enjoying for the child.

(c) *Phallic stage :* This period starts at the age of three and lasts at the age of six. Here the focus of pleasure shifts from anus to sexual organs like pennis or vagina. That is why habit of masturbation is common in children. Two special complexes also develop during this period (1) Oedipus complex-here the male child wants his mother more but finds his father as a powerful rival. He wants to destroy this rival but he is unable to do so. (2) Elektra complex-Here female child comes closer to her father and hates her mother.

(d) *Latency stage :* During this period all earlier forms of sexual activities are stopped. The child takes interest in learning skills and in the development of social and religious values. This stage helps the child to develop his super ego on the basis of his ego.

(e) *Genital stage :* The focus of pleasure shifts to the member of the opposite sex by using genital organs here. This stage starts after 13 years.

2. Ericksons' Theory of Psychosocial Stages : Erickson has proposed another theory of stages of child development. He divides stages of development into eight phases marked by specific developmental characteristics. The stages are as follows :

S.No.	STAGE	PSYCHOSOCIAL CRISES
1	Birth to first year	Trust Vs mistrust
2	1 to 2 years	Autonomy Vs shame, doubt
3	3 to 5 years	Initiative Vs Guilt
4	6 to 12 years	Industry Vs inferiority
5	Adolescence	Identity Vs identity diffusion
6	Early adult period	Intimacy Vs Isolation
7	Young and middle adult	Generativity Vs self-absorption
8	Later adult period	Integrity Vs despair

A brief explanation of these stages are given below:

(i) The infant develops a sense of trust in himself as well as in the environment. This trust is developed when he finds others at the beck and call of his physiological needs. Contrary to this, if his needs are not fulfilled by the people around him, he aches and cries. As a result, he loses his faith in the people around him.

(ii) When the child attains the age of 1.5 years, he develops the sense of autonomy in him. He does not want help from others. If parents give them reasonable freedom, it will develop confidence in them. Children who are not given such freedom to explore the environment, develop suspicion and doubt about their abilities. When they perform a task they become shy and hesitant. They are afraid of their mistakes which can bring about shame for them.

(iii) At the age of three, rapid growth of children in all dimensions is seen. At this age, the child starts to take initiatives on various tasks. The social horizon of the child begins to spread from home to neighbourhood and then to school. At this age, children also begin to develop the sense of right or wrong. Feeling of guilt is developed when they do not follow moral principles and codes given by their parents and teachers.

(iv) Fourth stage of development in the life of a child starts at age of six and comes to an end just before adolescence. During this period child utilizes his energies for self improvement and for the conquest of the outer world. He shows his industry and hard labour in all directions with special emphasis to motor field. The child wants to understand different mechanisms of the world through his toys and other usable articles. If the above opportunities are not given to him and the child is still treated as a child of low mind, it develops inferiority complex in him.

(v) When the child attains the age of thirteen he begins to fight for his identity in his group. He wants to become a leader in various activities and through this he wants to gain popularity among girls. Contrary to this if he is completely disregarded in the group to which he belongs, his identity is diffused.

(vi) Adulthood period starts at the age of 17. In the early years of adulthood, the individual wants to increase his social circle as large as possible. If he is amiable by nature, he is liked by others and if he is selfish, self centred or intolerant or he is hated by others especially by the girls, he starts to live in isolation. Many tragic songs and dramas are written during this period.

(vii) In the middle years of adulthood, generativity is seen. The individual exposes himself through any outstanding efforts in any field. He wants to live for others. That is why he is very much interested to see a better and disciplined world around him. The condition of self absorption is seen when an individual does not receive any encouragement for his tasks from anywhere.

(viii) Last stage is known for the integrity of the person to his profession, group, organization and institution to which he belongs. When justice is not maintained or an individual is not paid and recognized according to his efforts, his integrity is turned into despair.

3. Robert Sears' Development Theory: This theory represents the behavioural approach to the study of child development. According to Robert Sears learning experiences of the child are the result of stimulus-response associations that may result either classical or operant conditioning procedures . Thus according to this theory, development is a process of observable social interaction. The more there is social interaction, the more there is learning which is enhanced by reinforcement also.

There are three broad phases of human development according to this theory which are given below-

(a) *Phase (I) Rudimentary behaviour :* Initial behavioural training starts during this period. The period of this stage is birth to sixteen months of age. During this period the infant is activated by his innate needs of hunger, thirst, motor movement, defecation etc. These needs create tension in him and in order to reduce this tension, the infant is motivated for action. When action of the infant is reinforced by positive response, his needs are satisfied. The infant is very much selfish in his behaviour in the beginning and does not care for any social world. But when social world (parents and relatives) fulfills his needs and infant is reinforced for his action of say crying learning takes place which makes the learner more learned and goal directed.

Since, the infant here depends on someone else for the gratification of needs, the development becomes a process of social interaction. It is a type of operant behaviour here. The social environment in which the child is born greatly influences the development of the child. If child is not reinforced by anybody, *i.e*, his needs are not fulfilled, no development will be there. Socio-economic condition of the family, birth order of the child, his sex, the education or profession of his parents etc., affect the development of the child.

In other words, we can say that the first phase of the child's development interlinks the biological endowments (innate abilities) of the child with his social environment. The more the social environment is conducive to the fulfillment of biological needs of the child, the more learning and development will be there.

(b) *Phase II (Secondary behaviour) :* When child is reinforced by his parents and other members of the family, and the child's biological needs are gratified, he comes to develop secondary behaviour system, *i.e.*, he has to respond to others. If his response is fine he will be motivated. If response of the child is not upto the mark, it will be corrected by others and thus the process of development of correct secondary behaviour goes on.

The secondary behaviour of children starts by imitation. If model to be imitated is good, behaviour of the child will also be fine. The secondary behaviour of children should also be reinforced by parents and others and use of punishment as a technique should be avoided as much as possible because it can create behaviour problems in the child.

During this phase when the child begins to fulfil his needs himself by learning some new behaviour, his dependency on others decreases with age till the child is grown up fully and becomes an independent member of the society.

(c) *Phase III (Behaviour motivated) :* After the age of 11-12 the social boundary of the child expands a lot. The child comes in contact with other parents and their sons and with many people in his school and thus his process of socialization is accelerated. His dependency on others is reduced further but some new dependency in the school increases also. If child is given approval by his parents and other persons of the society that his behaviour is fine, he motivated to repeat that behaviour again and thus the process of development expands.

As the number of environmental **reinforcers** increases, the child comes to identify those persons well who satisfy his needs and he accepts those people as his model.

4. **Bandura's Theory of Development :** He gives equal importance to reward and punishment in the development of behaviour. Thus Bandura is mainly concerned with the social development of the individual. He believed that responses which are reinforced are more likely to recur than those responses of children which are not reinforced. Behaviour is learned either through conditioning or observational learning. In early childhood many behaviours of children are not approved by parents. Children are rather punished for the execution of such behaviour. Due to this fear, children are conditioned not to repeat that behaviour even in the later periods of life. Thus reward and punishment both are necessary for the moral and social development of the child.

   Observation (imitation) is the second mechanism responsible for learning (or acquisition of behaviour. The child creates some models in his mind or he is impressed by the behaviour of some people and accepts them as his model. These models are imitated by the child. Imitation follows certain principles such as competency, social status, power and similarity of the model with the imitator.

5. **Jean Piaget's Theory of Development :** He has explained his theory in the context of cognitive (mental) development of the child. Before coming to various stages of

development according to this theory it is better to know various related concepts to understand the theory in detail. These concept are given below:

1. **The schema :** The concept of schema is applied to the sensory motor behaviour of the infant. The infant does various activities such as sucking milk from the mother's breast, looking at the objects of the environment and pointing at it and in the process he tries to comprehend and conceptualize the objects, animals or space. This process of conceptualization depends on the sequence of behaviour employed by the infant to adapt to his environment. This is called schema which is not the same in all the individuals. Basic structure, is however the same. Although a particular scheme derives its name from the sequence of behaviour which the schema denotes yet some internal organizational disposition is there to enable the sequence to adapt itself to a number of conditions. As the development of the individual takes place, each schema is enlarged, modified and co-ordinated with other schemas. In this way, more complex schemas are formed.

   The sensory motor scheme develops out of reflex behaviour of the infant. When this behaviour is repeated by the infant many times and is responded by others, it is internalized and is gradually converted into cognitive schema. For example, in northern India when a child says mum and is given water by the parents the child conceptualizes mum as water. Many such defects are corrected in the later stage of life.

   Piaget believes that schemed a (cognitive structure) exists in primitive form even at conception and develops progressively with age.

2. **Assimilation and accommodation :** The schemas which are acquired in infancy period are practiced and modified in the later stages of life. This process of practice and change is called assimilation and accommodation by the cognitive field theorists. These assimilation and accumulation processes go hand in hand. For example, during infancy when infant acquires grasping schema he pick up objects and grasps them. This grasping of objects is called assimilation. But if that particular object is too big or too small to grasp it., the child changes his schema in order to manage the new situation. It is called accommodation.

   The cognitive structure (schema) changes from one stage to another by the process of equilibration. Through this process the child tries to adapt to his changing environment every time to maintain equilibrium between him and the environment.

PRINCIPLES OF DEVELOPMENT

1. *Development is a product of interaction :* Development is a process which is the result of constant interchange of energy within the organism and his environment. Thus hereditary forces interact with environmental forces and the process of development goes further. These two forces are so closely interacted that it is very difficult to isolate the contribution of either of them. The contribution of gene may be 10% as compared to 90% contribution of environment in the process of development.

2. *Development follows an orderly sequence :* The rate of growth and development is different in different individuals depending upon a number of factors but it does follow an orderly sequence in all the individuals. The psychologists have reported three important directional trends in the process of development:

   (a) *Cephaulo caudal :* Development starts from head and proceed toward heel. We see that development of head of a child is well advanced as compared to other parts of the body.

   (b) *Proximodigital :* Development starts from the central part of the body. Then it spread to other outer or more distant parts of the body. We see that an infant uses his shoulders and elbows first to reach an object and then he uses his fingers and wrists.

   (c) *Locomotion :* Locomotion develops in a sequence in all the individuals belonging to different cultures of the world. The rate of development for different infants may be different but every infant will have to pass through these stages at all cost. For example, an infant first learns to crawl, then to sit, then to stand and finally to walk. No infant can walk directly in the first stage.

3. *Development is a continuous process :* Development is a continuous process which begins from the time of conception in the womb of the mother and continues till death. But this process is not always smooth or gradual. Ups and downs are most of the time seen in every stage of development. There are spurts in physical growth and psychological functioning. Sharp growth rate is seen at the time of spurts. For example, a sharp increase in height and weight in the early adolescent period, a fast rise in vocabulary during pre-school period, sudden improvement in problem solving abilities during adolescence and so on.

4. *Development goes from bilateral to unilateral trend :* Infants up to the age of 2.5 years use both of their hands with equal ease. Then they learn to use any of their hands preferably. Similarly, in the beginning of cycle learning we use both the hands to control it but when we become fully experts in cycle learning we can control the cycle single handedly. Thus, development is a process of specialization also.

5. *Inter-relationship of different aspects of development:* Different aspects of development are interdependent and inter related. For example child's social behaviour is interrelated with his physical development. If child is physically handicapped, his emotional development may also be slow with aggressive development in some emotions. Similarly, if social development of an individual is poor, his mental or physical development will also be slow.

6. *Development is individualized process :* All individuals develop in their own way depending on their genetic characteristics and the training received from the environment. Thus, each child has his own rate of physical, social, mental or emotional development. If we observe ten years old children in a society, we find that there are great differences in their height, weight, sociability, emotional expressions and learning readiness. Similarly, the rate of growth is very high during infancy or pre-adolescent period as compared to other periods of life. Thus, rate of growth also changes with the change in stages of life.

7. *Development is positive and negative both :* Up to a certain period of human's life all the faculties of the individual develop but after that retardation starts specially after the age of 70. Physical and emotional retardations are seen during this age with zero social development. Mental development still continues but it too ultimately starts diminishing with the increase in age. Death is nothing but the collapse of all these processes of development.

8. *Development is cumulative :* Development is a cumulative process. Certain changes impress the observer and it looks as these changes are sudden but actually they are not sudden. They are the cumulative effect of all the changes in the individual. The child climbs the steps of the development one by one and then he reaches the zenith. The child first of all learns the words, then he learns the phrases, then sentences and finally he comes to know how the stories or essays are written. Thus, each change in the child is the culmination of his prior growth and experiences.

9. *Development proceed from general to specific:* In all types of development we find the principle of mass differentiation and integration. At the time of birth, the world is like big blooming confusion for the child. Then by and by his behaviours are refined and become goal directed responses.

10. *Rate of development differs with sex :* There is slight difference in the process of development between boys and girls. Girls mature earlier than boys at least emotionally. Girls are taller and heavier than boys in pre adolescence period but by the end of this period boys surpass them.

Dimensions of Growth and Development

1. *Physical growth and development :* It refers to strengthening of body and muscles with better proficiency and coordination of motor organs, if a person is able to do heavy work with ease, if he is able to do the task in lesser time, if he is able to do the task with accuracy and if he is able to do the task with neatness and beauty, then it is said that physical growth and development of the person is satisfactory.

2. *Social growth and development :* It refers to improvement and refinement of behaviour of an individual in social situations. If a person is stable in his behaviour even in adverse situations, if the behaviour of the person is fully acceptable to the society and if he is able to influence the society by his behaviour, then it is said that the social growth and development of the person is satisfactory.

3. *Emotional growth and development :* It refers to the accuracy of responses that an individual will exhibit under the influence of his emotions. These exhibited responses will be real as well. For example, if anger is not exhibited at the abuse given by any other person, it means that emotional growth and development is not satisfactory. Expressing sorrow at losses but not so much sorrow as it is beyond control is emotional maturity. If a person gets angry at his insults but he fully controls his anger according to the situation, then it is said that his emotional growth and development is satisfactory. Same is the case with other emotions also.
4. *Intellectual growth and development :* It refers to the ability to draw out conclusion from jumbled informations and to apply the inferences to real life situations in order to make the life happy and meaningful. If a person normally does what he is expected to do, if he is able to mould the situation in his own favour, if he is able to manipulate the situation against the other and if he is not backward in any way in mental operations, then it is said that his mental growth and development is satisfactory.
5. *Language growth and development :* Language is means of expressing, thinking and action. Had we not been given this power, we would not have been able to interact with others and our social existence was not possible. Language may be verbal and non verbal both. Human being uses both types of languages at a time to inform others about his thinking and behaviour and to be informed about their thinking and behaviour. Thus, language development refers to the ability of a person to convince the people what he thinks right.

Factors Affecting Growth and Development

Many factors affect to these dimensions of growth and development. Some of them affect mental or social growth and development and some factors affect all of them. Important such factors are given below:

1. *Proper Diet :* There is direct relationship between nutrition and physical growth. If diet is not taken according to the physical activities, physical growth will be retarded which will in turn affect the social, mental and emotional growth and development also.
2. *Exercise :* Physical exercise on regular basis will also improve physical growth and development. If a person is slow in his physical activities, his health might be worsened. The more an organ of the body is used, the more it will become strong.
3. *Sanitation and hygiene :* A disease free body is likely to grow more freely. This is possible only when the person is following the norms of hygiene and live in a good sanitary condition. It will save the person from communicable diseases.
4. *Genetic factors :* Genes play very important role in the process of growth and development. Nobody can surpass his genetic characteristics. If a person belongs to a race which is genetically short in height he can not increase his height by taking nutritious food and doing exercises.
5. *Recognition in the society :* If the individuality of a person is recognized in the society and he is given full freedom to grow his potentialities, his physical as well as social growth and development will be maximum. Unnecessary restrictions imposed on a person hampers the process of growth and development.
6. *Sociability :* Social relations also affect growth and development of a person. If a person is discarded by the society and people are biased against him, he will get less chance of socialization. As a result, his social horizon will be limited which will reduce his social learning. This will deteriorate the social growth and development. In that case the person will get less chance of exposure in the society. It will reduce his physical development also. As far as language development is concerned, sociability is a must.
7. *Training :* Growth and development is science in itself. If proper training on scientific lines is given to the individual, he is likely to grow and develop by leaps and bounds. Physical and health education serves this purpose.
8. *Games and sports :* Games and sports are necessary for all types of growth and development. They release pent up feeling of the person on one hand and give more chance of physical activities on the other. They are an important source of recreation as well. All these things are very conducive to physical, social and emotional growth and development.
9. *Protection :* A person must feel secure in the society only then his growth and development will be natural and spontaneous. If an

individual is living in a surcharged atmosphere and his life and property is always in danger, he will develop negative thinking. Negative attitude towards life and society is an enemy of growth and development in general.

10. *Manipulation of the environment* : If a person is given full enhance to manipulate the environment, his thinking will expand. It will have a positive bearing on his mental and emotional development.

11. *Free exchange of ideas* : Language development takes place only when a person is exposed in the society. In such an environment free exchange of ideas takes place. It increase word power of a person.

12. *Self contentment* : Human desires have no ends. If first desire of the wants is satisfied, another desire replaces the first, thus man always becomes slave of desires. It creates a tension in the mind of man. On the other, if a man is fully contended with what he has, he becomes tension free. It can improve his process of growth and development to a great extent.

HEREDITY AND ITS INFLUENCE

All that which we inherit from our parents, grandparents, great grandparents and so on as a free gift is called heredity. It is of two types: (i) Biological heredity and (ii) *Social heredity*

Biological heredity is that which a person inherits from his forefathers in the forms of chromosomes and genes.

Social heredity means all that one generation receives from the preceding generation in the form of social traditions customs and skills.

Person belonging to Rajput race is generally found muscular with strong and wide bones. It is an example of biological heredity. And the son of a carpenter is also likely to be an expert carpenter. It is an example of social heredity.

We will talk in this part only about biological heredity which is determined by genes. These genes are located in chromosomes. A person inherits chromosomes from his forefathers. With the transfer of these chromosomes genes are also transferred which are actually the carrier of heredity. Sex of an individual is also determined by genes. In order to know how traits are fixed by genes, we must first of all know the principles of heredity.

Principles of Heredity

There are two principles in this regard :

(a) *Principle of resemblance* : This principle states that like begets like. A cat can only give birth to a kitten, a human can only give birth to a baby and so on. According to this principle children generally resemble their parents or relatives.

(b) *Principle of Variability* : Many children do not resemble their parents. There are many instances where intelligent parents have dull children or ugly parents have beautiful children. This variation is universal in nature. That is why we see every individual unique in certain respect. This is called principle of variability of inheritance.

Mechanism of Heredity

When human sperm and egg unite, they are fertilized into zygote. Each zygote has 23 pairs of chromosomes. Every egg in the body contains the same number of chromosomes. The number of chromosomes in a given species are same but different species have different number of chromosomes.

For example, all humans contain 46 chromosomes. Half of them come from mother and half of them come from father. Within the chromosomes there are thousands of minute particles called genes. They are actually the carriers of hereditary traits from one generation to another.

Chromosomes are made up of long organic molecules whose main substance is deoxyribo nucleic acid (DNA). It is found in the chromosomes as two long strands periodically connected by chemical bonds.

Our heredity information is not found in the two long strands of DNA but in their order of appearance between the two strands of DNA. One pair of chromosomes is related to sex (gender) also. Females have two x chromosomes and males have an x and a y chromosome. If sperm of x chromosomes unite with the egg of y chromosomes, then the child will be a girl. If on the other hand, the sperm of y unite with the egg of x chromosomes, then the offspring will be a male child.

The story of hereditary influence will not be complete without knowing the influence of genes on our traits. It is because traits are determined exclusively by genes.

Genes are of two types **(i) dominant and (ii) recessive**. We inherit the same qualities of our parents because of dominant genes. If same characteristics are not inherited it means that recessive gene is active there. If marriages between blood relations take place, the recessive genes are developed which can cause many deformities in the body, i.e., offspring may become physically or mentally handicapped.

Law of Inheritance

Gregor Mendel (1866) discovered the law of inheritance in hybrid peas growing in the garden of an Austrain monastery. His law was found applicable to animals also. His law can be summarized as under.

"If a man who is homozygous for blue eyes marries a woman who is homozygous for brown eyes, the children of the couple will have brown eyes only" (Homozygous condition is that condition in which information concerning a given characteristic differ in the paired gene position)

If a homozygous man marries to a heterozygous woman the distribution of children from the couple will be such that one fourth of them will be homozygous for brown eyes, one half of them, will he heterozygous and one fourth of them will be homozygous for blue eyes.

By this law, Mendel concluded that all genetic informations come to the individual in units rather than in graduated series. In other words, we receive from our ancestors genes controlling the development of specific unitary characteristics not a composite of traits called tendencies.

The second conclusion that can be drawn from this law is that characteristics of men do not remain constant. They tend to vary continuously along a dimension of genes.

Some Studies on Influence of Heredity

How great the role of inheritance is in shaping the personality of an individual by the process of growth and development can be understood by the following studies:

1. **Galton :** He was the first psychologist who conducted studies on the nature and extent of genetic influences in man. He studied 997 eminent British people and found that there were 322 people out of 997 who were also distinguished. He also studied 997 average people and found that only one of them was eminent. He thus concluded that eminent men were found in families which have already one eminent member at least. He also found that decreased instances of imminence were seen when eminent people decreased their relationship with eminent persons. Thus, according to him eminence is inherited from generation to generation.

   He also studied some people of U.S.A. who were given better educational facilities and compared them with the eminent people of U.K. who were given average educational facilities. He found that people of USA were not better performed than that of UK.

2. **Goddard (1914) :** He studied a Kalikak family of USA. Martia Kalikak who was a soldier in the American revolution, developed illegal sexual relation with a feeble-minded lady and an illegitimate child was born. 480 descendents were traced from the family tree of this illegitimate boy. Out of them 143 were feeble-minded, 291 were borderline normal and only 46 were found normal in intelligence.

   After the revolution when Mr. Kalikak married a normal lady a legitimate child was born. 496 descendents were traced from the family tree of this boy. All of them except two were found normal or above normal in intelligence and they became teachers, lawyers, businessmen etc. This study proves that intelligence is inherited from one generation to the next.

   These two studies show that heredity plays an important role in determining the traits. But the conclusions derived from these two studies can not be fully relied upon because of the following reasons.

   (i) They do not distinguish between biological and social inheritance. Their studies combine these two factors. So, it is very difficult to isolate the contribution of gene in shaping the personality.

   (ii) Testing material used in these studies was not perfect and the survey is also unsystematic and unreliable.

   (iii) The researchers were already biased in favour of hereditary factors. So, their conclusions can not be relied upon.

3. **Kellogg and Kellogg :** In order to study the relative influence of heredity and environment they conducted a systematic research by taking their own son and a chimpanzee. Their respective ages were 10 months and 7.5 months. Both of them were brought up in the same environment with similar type of facilities given to them. Their behaviours were systematically studied at regular intervals. It was found that in the beginning the chimpanzee surpassed the son in motor skills of jumping, running, climbing, etc. Chimpanzee also learned some social skills such as eating with spoon and drinking from a glass, but he could learn 93 words only. But later on, the son caught him up in all areas of development except physical strength.

   This study shows that heredity sets a limit for maximum development which can not be improved even by providing the best environment.

ENVIRONMENT AND ITS INFLUENCE

Environment here means social and cultural environment especially. Physical environment also becomes the part of social environment when it is used in the learning process. When an individual lives in a society, in a family, he learns many things from the social and cultural environment. These learnings bring about certain changes in his behaviour. Some of these changes may be of permanent nature. These permanent changes become the part and parcel of his habits. When these habits are converted into values after maturity, they become the representative traits of the individual. Individual is now recognized with these traits.

Influence of Environment in Shaping the Personality

The role or contribution of environment is no less than that of the heredity. In fact human being is a by product of heredity and environment both. The importance of environment in the process of growth and development can be understood by the following example.

A missionary in (Midnapur) Bihar found two children who were taken by wolves in early children hood. These children were reared in the company of wolves in beast environment. They learned to walk on four feet, ate raw flesh and verbalized like wolves. These children were brought back from the forest and kept in a hospital. One of them died next day and the other could hardly learn elementary things. This study shows that if suitable environment is not provided to a person, his genetic qualities will not flourish at all.

On the basis of studies on heredity and environment with regard to growth and development following conclusions can be drawn:

1. Heredity and environment both play combined role in the development of personality of an individual.
2. Heredity does not determine any trait of the personality in isolation. It only provides a base and then environment develops the trait.
3. Subjective traits of the individual like physique, colour of skin, resistance level of the body etc are determined by the hereditary factors. Certain diseases are also inherited because of low resistability of the body of the individual.
4. Bad environment can surpass good inheritance but good environment is not a substitute for poor heredity. It means heredity sets a limit for the maximum development. Even good training and experiences will not enable the person to cross this limit. On the other hand, even good man by genes can be made corrupt in a bad environment.
5. Training and experiences can improve the traits of an individual to a great extent. Even intelligence level can be improved to some extent.

Environmental Factors Affecting Growth and Development

Environmental influences begin since the time of conception of the child into the womb of his mother. Mental, physical and emotional conditions of mother also influence the development of foetus in the womb. When child opens his eyes in the physical world, he immediately comes in contact with the environment. Since he takes birth in a society, he is also influenced by a number of social and cultural factors. The impact of some of these factors on his growth and development is given below:

1. **Physical factors of the environment :** Physical and geographical conditions of the environment play an important role in shaping the personality of an individual. People living in deserts, hilly areas and plains have great difference in their body strength, height, structure, mode of living, habits etc. Climate of the region also affects the behaviour, body built and resistance to fight the environmental forces. For example, people living in Siberian region can tolerate lower degree of temperature than those who live in Indian sub continent. Personality traits are also determined by these environmental factors, for example, people living in African continent are more aggressive and get easily annoyed than those living in North America.
2. **Family of the individual :** Personality of an individual develops fully only when interaction between biological inheritance and environmental forces take place. Home is the first place of these interactions. Whatever early changes take place in the nature and pattern of personality formation in the initial life of an individual at home, they are generally upheld in the whole life. In the family, child comes in contact with his parents, grandparents, uncles, aunties and cousins. These people give full recognition to the child. They also respond him keeping his likes and dislikes. Several empirical evidences support that childhood experiences are decisive determinants of his personality in later life. For example, if a child is deprived of family love and other facilities, he may grow into

either an aggressive or totally submissive person in future. Margarets Ribble in 1944 started a series of investigations on the effects of some psychological deprivations in infancy. She studied 600 children in this regard and concluded that lack of adequate cuddling and other close physical contact with some friendly adults can impose serious handicaps on the growing infants.

Each and every characteristic of the family affects the personality of the child in future. We are taking here one more example of morale of the family. A low morale home does not present a good model before the child for imitation. Stort in 1939 on the basis of a questionnaire administered on 1800 adolescents concluded three things given below-

- Children coming from homes where good morale pattern dominated were better adjusted, more independent in thinking and action and more satisfactorily related to their parents than those who were average in this dimension.
- Adolescents who came from discarded and nagging families were poorly adjusted in the society.
- Economic factors also influence the development of personality. Poverty of parents and lack of money even to fulfil legitimate needs of their children led to certain kinds of frustrations in adolescents.

3. **School :** School is a miniature society in itself. Here individual stays for almost six hours daily in the early quarter period of his life. His personality is shaped by the school in the following ways.
   - School poses new problems before the child to be acquired and new models for imitation.
   - School provides new knowledge and expands the horizon of the child. These behavioural changes determine the pattern and direction of growth and development.
   - Social interaction with teachers, classmates and peers is possible in schools. These interaction also shape the personality of the individual.
4. **Teacher :** Teacher can play a very crucial role in shaping the personality of the individual. The way the teacher behaves and handles his students and the personality traits exhibited by him have an important effect on the future personality of students. He influences a child in the following ways.
   - The way the teacher carries out his role in the class will affect the emotional climate of the classroom. An authoritarian teacher will establish an autocratic climate and a democratic teacher will create a permissive climate in the classroom. Autocratic climate will tend to create aggression and bostility among students. If climate is democratic, it will develop constructive, thoughtful and cooperative behaviour among students. All good personality traits can be developed by democratic climate in the class. Because of this reason democratic dealing is preferred to autocratic dealing. The more a teacher is democratic in his attitude and behaviour, the more his students will be accommodative to others.
   - Studies have shown that children who repeatedly fail in the class are likely to be cruel, selfish, unfriendly, unhappy, impolite, boastful and quarrelsome. Thus, teacher tries to reduce the occurrence of failures in the class by his dedicated efforts.
   - Whatever model of character is presented by the teacher in the class, it is immediately copied down by the students. If teacher has ideal traits in him, students, are also likely to be idealistic.
5. **Language :** Language is the medium by which the society is structured and experiences of the race are transmitted from generation to generation. The child learns the languages of the society. He learns many experiences and knowledge by these languages. He also communicates the other members of the society by these languages. Thus, by these processes he becomes an integral part of the social environment.
6. **Social roles :** The word role has been derived from the theatre world. In theatres the actors play the role of different characters as the situation demands. Worlds is also a stage and human beings are just actors who play their respective roles. Man is a social animal. He comes in contact with different people in the society. As a result he has to play the role of a father, son, brother, friend, student etc. throughout his life at various stages of his development. Social roles are the process by which an individual interacts with other members of the society. Thus, social roles are the collection of behaviour and relevant attitudes towards others. These roles are learned by individuals through observation and imitation.

7. **Self concept :** Self concepts are the means by which we create our unique image and identity in the society. Self concept in the child is initiated by physical awareness. The other means of developing self concept are how we maintain our social status, how we dress ourselves and how we speak and respond to others. Self concept influences our personality development in two ways. The first is that if people hold us in high esteem, we feel exalted. And the second is that if others hold negative attitude towards us, it creates the feeling of worthlessness and it may lead to self defence or withdrawl from the social situation. If self concept is fully developed in an individual his rate of growth and development will be high.
8. **Identification :** Identification is the process by which we imitate the physical, social or mental characteristics of our model. When a boy identifies himself with his father by coping father's behaviour it means that he wants to be like him. If identifying models are solid physically, mentally or socially, the identification process will also be solid and healthy.
9. **Living standard :** Physical and mental health of a person is directly related to his living standard. If he is getting nutritious food and sufficient amount of time for sports and exercise, his rate of development will be high. People of developed countries are found very advanced because of this reason.
10. **Cultural heritage :** Every society is identified by its cultural heritage which is transmitted from one generation to the next. The transmission of cultural heritage may also be termed as social heredity. The personality of an individual is gradually shaped by the culture he is born in.

E.R. Tyler defined culture in the following words.

"It is that complex whole which includes knowledge, beliefs, morals law, customs and many other capabilities (skills) and habits acquired by man as a member of society."

Thus, culture refers to total life activities of a society. Whatever a person learns from the society by the process of interaction is called culture. In other words, what the people think, feel and do constitute the culture of a society. Biological inheritance is more or less the same all over the world but whatever differences are seen in the process of growth and development of personality among individuals it is because of the differences of social inheritance (culture). We can easily identify people reared in different cultures by the personality patterns they possess. English, Africans, Arabs and Indians can be identified by their cultural background more than by their biological heredity.

No single culture dominates in big countries. Sub cultures within the culture is also seen which brings about social conflicts. This conflict distorts the personality of individuals as well. Culture or sub cultures are silent educators and they mould the personality of individuals very silently.

The influence of cultural forces is so powerful that if three identical twins of a Hindu family are reared in three different cultures such as houses of Muslims, Christians and jews, the impact of their respective cultures will produce three distinct type of personality. These twins will not have any thing of their original Hindu culture.

The influence of culture can also be understood by the following words:

"Culture regulates our lives at every turn. From the moment we are born until we die, whether we are conscious of it or not, constant pressure on us forces us to follow certain types of behaviour that other men have created for us".

Culture influences the personality development of an individual in the following ways:

- Ideas, values, beliefs, customs and traditions are internationalized through the process of learning. A child who takes birth in a particular culture is reared in that very culture. He learns ideas, beliefs, values, customs etc. of his society and thus he acquires distinctive personality characteristics in the process.
- Various cultures are propagated by various institutions. When individual takes part in these activities actively or in a passive manner, he gets attached to these cultural institutions. Thus, his culture is institutionalized. This is the **second stage of culture formation**. When culture of a region reaches this stage it becomes very difficult to wipe it out by other cultures.

PIAGET'S STAGES OF COGNITIVE DEVELOPMENT

According to him, there is an orderly sequence of stages in cognitive development. Thus progression from one stage to another is always fixed. The child can not adopt the strategies of a later stage at an early stage of development. It is because he must have to acquire and exercise the strategies and schemas of earlier stages. For example, in order to understand words, the child must know letters first or we can not teach Electronic Physics to a child of primary class.

Ausbel commenting upon the development stages of Piaget writes "Piaget's stages are identifiable, sequential phases in an orderly progression of development that are qualitatively discriminable from adjacent phases and generally characteristic of most members of a broadly defined age range".

The stages of cognitive development are related in the sense that they represent forms of adaptation, but these forms are qualitatively different, that is the adaptive functions are transformed as the child moves from one stage to the next. This theory of development is quite different from the theory of associationists who emphasize the gradual accumulation of responses.

Important stages of Piaget's theory of mental development are given below.

I. Period of sensorimotor adaptation (from 0-2 years): The infant starts this stage by his reflex activities and then he reaches to the stage of sensorimotor schemes by practice and accommodation. The intellectual development at this stage is marked by the following characteristics.

(a) *Object concept formation :* Objects exist in the mind of an adult whether they are present before the person or not. But in the psychological world of a child, only those objects exist which have a psychological presence for the child, ie, he can look and touch it. As soon as they are removed from the eyes of the child, they cease to exist for the child. When the child experiences the same object repeatedly, he develops the concept of permanence of objects. This concept is developed in the first year of life. When this type of structure is formed in the mind, practice of concepts is started by the child.

(b) *Coordinated space :* Spatial world at first is totally uncoordinated for the child. Each sensory modality has its own space. By the end of two years, the child develops the concepts which are marked by the coordination among different objects and between objects and body of the child.

(c) *Objectified causalty :* The concept of cause and effect relationship is established when action of the child brings about an effect. Then this effect is taken as the cause of that event.

(d) *Objectification of time :* By the end of two years the child is also able to objectify time.

II. Period of symbolic and preconceptual thought (2-4 years): Ideas begin to develop in the mind of the child at the third year. By imitation and observation, he demonstrates that he is capable of extending his physical world to metaphysics. He begins to use symbols in the 4th year. Now he can represent the environment in the absence of perceptual cues only on the basis of ideas.

III. Period of intuitive thought (4-8 years): At this stage the child can use various concepts in different situations, *i.e.*, he is able to generalize his past and present experiences. His thoughts are not based on logical reasoning. It is rather governed by intution. The child can talk about this and that momentary static condition in a separate manner but he can not properly integrate various sets of conditions into an integrated whole due to lack of logical weakness, *i.e.*, logical coherence is not found here. For example, a child can write fine sentences representing various topics but he can not write a compact essay.

IV. The period of concrete operation (8-12 years): Here the child is able to direct his attention away from the static condition, ie, he can accommodate with all the successive changes taking place in the system. It means that he can reorganize his future on the basis of his past experience as well as trends at present. Reasoning power of the child is well developed during this period. Some examples of what a child can do are handling and manipulating the numbers in various ways by various operations, arrangement of objects and materials into various groups and sub groups, ordering of objects according to one or more attributes and so on. Piaget has described a term "grouping" for this stage of cognitive development.

This period also shows some logical inconsistency in the thinking of the child. Piaget has coined a term "syncretism" for this defect. Despite this, beginning of abstract operation is seen during this stage.

V. Period of formal (abstract) operation (12-18 years): During this period, the thought process of the child becomes systematic, consistent and reasonably well integrated. Reality guides the contemplation process of the child. The formal operation of thinking starts with the formulation of hypothesis, (deductive reasoning) and reaches at its peak when hypothesis is tested by experiments, ie, inductive reasoning. At this stage, the boy can manipulate any abstract idea in his own way and form new idea entirely different from the old one. His wisdom lies in the expertise administration of the unforeseen. Whenever an adolescent faces any problem with the help of formal operation of thought he identifies various relevant variables which may be helpful in the solution of that problem and then all these variables are manipulated by him.

Thus, development of formal operation capacity enables the adolescent to transfer understanding from one situation to another and to evaluate the results on the basis of its pros and cons. Physical (concrete) objects are never required for thinking (operation) during this period. The thought process is completely abstract here.

KOHLBERG'S THEORY OF DEVELOPMENT

According to him moral development of the child proceeds in sequential but distinctive stages. These stages are given below:

(a) **Stage-I :** In the early years of a child's life (from zero-four years) the physical consequences of an action determines its goodness or badness. If fire burns the child, he does not touch it. The child is ego-centric and standards of morality are external here.

(b) **Stage-II :** The child gives importance to his own point of view, (his self) and is able to take account of other's roles insofar as he can use them in his own way. This is a period of make belief. Right action is what which satisfies the needs of the child. The role of others is also important in the sense that a child does only what can bring approval of others. Thus, only that behaviour is moral which can satisfy not only self needs of the child but it must please others also.

(c) **Stage-III :** At this stage the child adopts the view pints of others on the basis of their consequences. He does not question the views of others. The child considers only that thing as right which are considered as right by others. Thus, the child is totally conformist to the standard of the society.

(d) **Stage-IV:** At this stage, the child is able to make any moral decision on his own without caring for the thinking of others. Though he considers laws and regulations set by the society as the essence of morality, yet he develops his own principles of morality on various occasions. Thus, he is a non-conformist to the norms of the society to a great extent.

(e) **Stage-V :** Standards and norms are more internalized here. The adolescents examine various view points prepared by different societies and recognize them. They think that the laws prepared by their own society are correct. Other societies may have good moral principles that must be adopted after careful appraisal.

(f) **Stage-VI :** This is the last stage of moral development according to Kohlberg. Here the universality of the view points of the individual is seen. He formulates his own universal moral principles which he thinks that all societies should adhere to it. True understanding of right and wrong is developed at this stage.

HAVIGHURST'S THEORY OF DEVELOPMENT

According to him at each stage of development, there are certain tasks, skills and understanding that must be completed before a person can proceed to a higher level of development.

Havighurst Says –

"At or about a certain period in the life of the individual, successful achievement leads to his happiness and to success with later tasks, while failure leads to unhappiness in the individual, disapproval by society and difficulty with later tasks".

LIST OF DEVELOPMENT TASKS GIVEN BY HAVIGHURST

S.No.	Birth to 6 years	6 to 12 years
1	Learning to walk	Learning physical skills, ordinary games.
2	Learning to take solid food	Building wholesome attitudes towards oneself as a growing organism
3	Learning to talk	Learning to get along with age mates
4	Learning to control the elimination of body wastes.	Learning an appropriate masculine or feminine role.
5	Learning sex differences	Developing fundamental skills in reading, writing and calculating.

6	Achieving physiological stability	Developing concepts necessary for everyday living
7	Forming simple concepts of social and physical reality	Developing the ability of manipulating the ideas and concepts.
8	Learning to relate oneself emotionally to parents, siblings and other people	Achieving personal independence
9	Learning to distinguish right and wrong and developing a conscience	Developing attitudes towards social groups and institutions

COMPARISON OF THREE CATEGORIES OF THEORIES

S. No.	Psycho analytic	Behaviouristic	Cognitive
1	Feeling is important here	Stimulus and behaviour of others are important here	Thinking is all responsible for development
2	In order to acquire moral principles, parental values are internalized	Moral values are adopted from either models or they are acquired by conditioning	Moral principles are acquired automatically with age, ie, mental development
3	Super ego, a moral conduct is formed at the age of five	Learning of morality is a life long process	Super ego is formed during the period of adolescence
4	Moral values are not free from culture	Same	Moral values are universal
5	Parents and relatives are agents of socialization	Adults and peers who give reinforcement are the main agents of socialization	People of the matured age are the agents of socialization

VYGOTSKY'S SOCIOCULTURAL THEORY

Both Jean Piaget and Lev Vygotsky believed that children build knowledge through experiences. Piaget believed this happened through exploration with hands-on activities. Vygotsky, on the other hand, believed that children learn through social and cultural experiences. Interactions with peers and adults help children in this process. While interacting with others, children learn the customs, values, beliefs, and language of their culture. For this reason, families and teachers should provide plently of social interaction for young children.

Vygotsky believed language is an important tool for thought and plays a key role in cognitive development. He introduced the term ***private speech***, or self-talk. This refers to when children ''think out loud''. After learning language, children engage in this self-talk to help guide their activity and develop their thinking. Generally, self-talk continues until children reach school age.

One of Vygotsky's most important contributions was the *zone of **proximal development*** (ZPD). This concept presents learning as a scale. One end of the scale or ''zone'' includes the tasks that are within the child's current development level. The other end of the scale includes tasks too difficult for children to accomplish, even with help. In the middle are the tasks children cannot accomplish alone. These are achieved with help from another knowledgeable peer or adult. The term used for this assistance is ***scaffolding***. Just as a painter needs a structure on which to stand and point a building, scaffolding provides the structure for learning to occur. For example, a teacher could scaffold a child's learning while constructing a puzzle. The teacher might demonstrate how a piece fits or provide clues regarding colour, shape or size. The ''zone'' is constantly changing. In contrast to Piaget, Vygotsky believed that learning was not limited by stage or maturation. Children move forward in their cognitive development with the right social interaction and guided learning.

CONCEPTS OF CHILD-CENTERED AND PROGRESSIVE EDUCATION

Child-Centered Education

Child-centered education is the idea that the needs and desires of the child should take precedence in structuring the learning day. The whole idea is that learning should be fun and engaging for the child, and is most likely to be that way if the child is incharge of the learning experience, rather than the adult parent or teacher.

Child-centered education is most characterised by learning 'centers' in a classroom that promote hands-on, active participation by the child. There may be magnifying glasses and bug slides in the science center, books and puppets that could be used to re-tell the stories in the language arts center, and wood blocks and shapes in the math center. The children are free to manipulate the objects in these centers. It is the process, the activity, the experience, that is valuable, not the facts, ideas, concepts or skills.

It is a relatively new approach to education. For centuries past, adults defined what education should be and children were the ones who did the adjusting. Education was considered work, not play.

Then came the softening influences of child psychologist Jean-Jacques Rousseau, as well as Dr. Marria Montessori, John Dewey, Jean Piaget and Lev Vygotsky, who all contended that a child's self-esteem and self-concept should be built up in order to create a better learner. Soon, the colleges of education were promoting child-centered education instead of instructionally centered education.

Role of Learner in Child-Centered Education

Learners are active as opposed to passive recipients of knowledge. Learners may assume a decision-making role in the classroom. Learners often decide what is to be learned, through which activities and at what pace. Learners can also produce materials and provide activities for the classroom.

Role of Teacher in Child-Centered Education

To put this approach into practice, teachers need to help students set achievable goals; they encourage students to assess themselves and their peers; help them to work co-operatively in groups and ensure that they know how to make use of all the available resources for learning.

Progressive Education

During most of the twentieth century, the term 'progressive education' has been used to describe ideas and practices that aim to make schools more effective agencies of a democratic society. Although there are numerous differences of style and emphasis among progressive educators, they share the conviction that democracy means active participation by all citizens in social, political and economic decisions that will affect their lives. The education of engaged citizens, according to this perspective, involves two essential elements: (1) respect for diversity, meaning that each individual should be recognised for his or her own abilities, interests, ideas, needs, and cultural identity, and (2) the development of critical, socially engaged intelligence, which enables individuals to understand and participate effectively in the affairs of their community in a collaborative effort to achieve a common good. These elements of progressive education have been termed 'child-centered' and 'social reconstruction' approaches, and while in extreme forms they have sometimes been separated, in the thought of John Dewey and other major theorists they are seen as being necessarily related to each other.

The term 'progressive' arose from a period (roughly 1890–1920) during which many Americans took a more careful look at the political and social effects of vast concentrations of corporate power and private wealth. Dewey, in particular, saw that with the decline of local community life and small scale enterprise, young people were losing valuable opportunities to learn the arts of democratic participation, and he concluded that education would need to make up for this loss. In his Laboratory School at the University of Chicago, where he worked between 1896 and 1904, Dewey tested ideas he shared with leading school reformers such as Francis W. Parker and Ella Flagg Young. Between 1899 and 1916 he circulated his ideas in works such as The School and Society, The Child and the Curriculum, Schools of Tomorrow, and Democracy and Education, and through numerous lectures and articles. During these years other experimental schools were established around the country, and in 1919 the Progressive Education Association was founded, aiming at "reforming the entire school system of America".

Therefore, progressive education is a reaction against the traditional style of teaching which teaches facts largely at the expense of understanding what is being taught. According to **John French,** "The progressive school teaches the child to think for himself instead of passively accepting stereotyped ideas. It keeps always in mind that each child is different from every other, and that what makes an educated person useful in his particular walk of life, what makes him interesting, what makes him an individual, is not his resemblance to other people, but his differences".

Philosophies and Practices of Progressive Education

1. Curriculum is strongly influenced by what the children are interested in, and is child-centered rather than adult driven.
2. Learning is 'hands-on', experiential and the emphasis is on process rather than product children are 'learning to learn'.
3. Children learn through integrated, theme-based units or inquiry projects and the 'theme' often emerges from the children.
4. Assessment is authentic and holistic. Children are well known by their teachers and peers. There are no tests or letter grades. Instead, narrative reports are written about children

that cover all aspects of their development: social, emotional, personal, physical and intellectual level.

5. Classes are usually of mixed ages and no ability grouping is used. Children are able to work at their own pace and cross-age friendships are encouraged.
6. Progressive education practices a developmental approach which holds that each child is a unique being unfolding and developing at their own pace according to a specific pattern. At each stage of development there are things that can be learned and things that should not be learned. Respecting a child's development is central to progressive education.

Types of Progressive Education

1. **Humanistic :** The humanistic form of progressive education focuses on the humanities, arts and social sciences. Its emphasis is on the individual child and not the curriculum. This type of progressivism aims to build a well-rounded individual with highly developed critical thinking and reasoning skills. The children learn think for themselves instead of accepting everything teachers tell them. Social development and interaction among the students are seen as valuable learning techniques.
2. **Constructivism :** Constructivism is a type of child-centered progressivism. It focuses on the child's creativity and learning abilities. Teachers should build the curriculum around the requirements and interests of the child. It maintains that education should consider children's developmental stages. Swiss psychologist **Jean Piaget** influenced the theories of constructivist education. Experiential learning, or learning by doing, allows students to construct their own knowledge.
3. **Montessori :** Italian doctor Marria Montessori started the Montessori progressive educational system. She developed her teaching theories by clinical observation and analysis of how children learn. Her method of education focused on how children naturally learn, all by themselves, without the help of adults. Maria Montessori concluded that children teach themselves, and it's the job of teachers to facilitate this process, not dominate it. Montessori teachers provide a sensory-rich environment and hands-on activities.

CRITICAL PERSPECTIVE OF THE CONSTRUCT OF INTELLIGENCE

Introduction

The most important variable that affects schooling or performance on a job is intelligence. Psychologists have interpreted the term intelligence in different ways and there is no consensus among them on the term even so far. In psychology this term is treated as a construct whose structure is different in different individuals.

The vagueness of the term arises due to the fact that intelligence is not a concrete material. It is rather abstraction from the behaviour of the individual which is indirectly inferred and elaborated as an adjective.

The dictionary meaning of term "intelligence" is the capacity to acquire and apply knowledge. **Boring** defines intelligence as intelligence is what an intelligence test measures.

Definitions of Intelligence

Several psychologists have classified and defined intelligence in several ways. Some of them are given below:

1. Vernon's Classification of Intelligence

(a) *Biological Approach:* Man is an organism among millions living on earth. Environment works as a foe for him. Intelligence is the capacity to adapt to the environment or new situations of life at every moment.

This definition of intelligence can be criticized on the ground that there have been many intelligent and renowned persons who were ill adapted to their social and physical environment. Besides, if we want to study individual differences in a society, this definition serves no practical purpose.

(b) *Psychological Approach :* According to psychologists intelligence is the relative effects of heredity and environment both. An English psychologist, **C. Burt** defined intelligence as the innate general cognitive ability.

In support of psychological definitions of intelligence **Hebb** and **R.B. Catell** distinguished two kinds of intelligence. The first is intelligence "A" which is Fluid intelligence and which is related to genetic potentialities or innate qualities of the individual's nervous system. Second is intelligence "B" which is crystalised "intelligence" and which is related to experiences, learning and environmental factors. These two types of intelligence in normal circumstances so much overlap on each other that they are practically indistinguishable.

(c) *Operational Approach :* These definitions help us to understand the concept of intelligence in clear and definite terms. In this approach scientific terms are first of all defined operationally and then observations are conducted with reference to these terms. For example, in order to determine a child's IQ, we first administer a test of a specific kind. Then we observe his performance on the test and finally draw certain conclusions in the context of the pre-determined objectives.

2. Freeman's Classification

(a) *Ability of adjustment :* An individual is intelligent to the extent to which he is able to adjust to new situations and problems of life. The more a person is intelligent, the more he is able to adapt to his environment in antagonistic conditions. The person who is low in intelligence has less capacity to adjust to the new situations of life.

(b) *Ability of learning :* Learning ability is also an index of intelligence. The more a person is intelligent, the more he will be able to learn new things.

(c) *Ability to carry on abstract thinking :* This category of definitions of intelligence is related to the effective use of concepts and symbols in dealing with situations and solving the problems through the use of verbal and numerical symbols. According to **Terman**, an individual is intelligent to the extent he is able to carry on abstract thinking.

3. E.L. Thorndike's Classification

(a) *Concrete intelligence :* The intellectual ability in relation to concrete materials is called concrete intelligence. It is the ability of a person to comprehend the actual situations and react to them adequately. This kind of intelligence is measured by using performance tests or picture tests in which the subject manipulates the concrete materials.

(b) *Abstract intelligence :* It is the ability to respond to words, letters, numbers or symbols. This type of intelligence is required in all academic activities in schools or outside the schools. The highest level of abstract intelligence is manifested in the thoughts of philosophers or in the inventions of scientists and mathematicians.

(c) *Social intelligence :* It is the ability of an individual to react to social situations of life. It is the ability to understand others and to react to them in such a manner that they may not feel unjust attitude regarding them.

4. Intelligence as a Global Capacity

A comprehensive definitions of intelligence : **Stoddard** (1943) and **Wechsler** (1944) have defined intelligence in the following words :

"Intelligence is the aggregate or the global capacity of the individual to act purposefully, to think rationally and to deal with the environment effectively".

Stoddard further elaborated that intelligence is the capacity of a person to undertake such activities which are: (*i*) difficult (*ii*) complex (*iii*) abstract (*iv*) economical (*v*) goal directed (*vi*) valuable from social view points (*vii*) original. These activities demand concentration of energy and a resistance to emotional forces.

Characteristics of Intelligence

From the above definitions of intelligence, we can draw the following characteristics of intelligence:

(*i*) Intelligence is the composite of several intellectual skills, such as thinking, doing, reasoning, dealing, learning etc.

(*ii*) Intelligence is displayed by the behaviour of the individual as a whole and intelligent behaviour is always goal directed.

(*iii*) Intelligence is the ability to adjust to abnormal and challenging situations of life.

(*iv*) Intelligence is not related to ordinary tasks of life. It is always related to extra ordinary manipulation.

(*v*) Wechsler has included the concepts of drive and incentive which are implied in his statement. "To act purposefully" and "to deal effectively". But many psychologists are of the view that drive and incentive are non-intellectual traits of personality and if they are included in a test of mental ability, more confusions will be created thereof.

(*vi*) There are seven fundamental elements of intelligence according to **Stoddard.** Intelligent person can undertake difficult and abstract tasks with ease. He can manipulate and deal the abstract ideas and concepts efficiently. Similarly, economy refers to the rate at which a mental task is done or a problem is solved. If "A" solves a problem sooner than 'B' then 'A' will be considered more intelligent than 'B'. The term social value indicates whether a mental task performed by a person is in accordance with the socially desirable and acceptable norms or not. The last term original refers to a person's, ability to discover something new and different, *i.e.*, this term is directly related to creative potential of a person. Discovery of some new facts and principles and inventions of new concrete materials by the scientists are few examples of originality.

Stoddard's definition of intelligence has been criticized on two grounds :

(a) It includes social values in intelligence, *i.e.*, intelligent task must be socially desirable. Psychologists criticize this point by saying that social value is a subjective phenomenon, *i.e.*, what is desirable for me, may not be necessarily desirable for others. So, there is no scope of subjectivity in an objective intelligence test.

(b) He has included two conditions of intelligent behaviour in his definition. First is concentration of energy and second is resistance to emotional forces. Psychologists say that these elements are non-intellectual traits and hence they should not be included in mental abilities at any cost.

Theories of Intelligence

1. Faculty theory of intelligence:

This is the oldest theory of intelligence given during the period of pre-experimental psychology. According to this theory mind is made up of different faculties like reasoning, logic, memory, imagination and discrimination. These faculties are independent of each other and can be developed by rigorous mental exercises of the difficult subject-matter.

This theory does not take the hereditary factors of intelligence into account and thus this theory was discarded by the later psychologists who believed that we can never improve the intellectual capacity of a person if he is mentally slow by birth.

2. Unifactor theory:

According to Alfred Binet (1916) intelligence is a general intellectual ability which is made up of several discrete abilities. These abilities include

(i) to reason well with abstract material

(ii) to comprehend well

(iii) to have a clear direction of thoughts

(iv) to relate thinking with the attainment of a desirable end and

(v) to be self-critical.

All these abilities combined together is called general mental ability. Thus, intelligence is a single but complex mental process which can be measured by different kinds of materials designed for the purpose.

3. Two factors theory:

This theory was developed by an English psychologist, **Charles Spearman** in 1904. According to him, intellectual abilities consist of two factors, general ability known as 'G' factors and specific abilities known as 'S' factors.

Characteristics of G factors

(i) It is universal inborn ability.

(ii) It is general mental energy.

(iii) It is constant, *i.e.*, it remains the same in all the individuals and does not change with time.

(iv) The amount of G differs from person to person depending on his genes.

(v) It is used in every life activity.

(vi) Greater the amount of G in an individual, larger is the chance of his success in life.

Characteristics of 'S' factors

(i) It is learnt and hence acquired in the environment.

(ii) It varies from activity to activity in the same individual.

(iii) The amount of S also differs from person to person due to his accessibility to learning situations.

(iv) 'S' factors are related to the specific activity. A low correlation between two or more functions or activities indicates the presence of 'S' factor involved in the activity. A person can be expert only in one or few activities because of the specific factors involved in the activity.

According to Spearman, out of these two factors 'G' factor is more important and thus it is an important measure of intelligence. So, any intelligence test should measure only 'G' factor because it provides most important basis of predicting a person's behaviour in different situations. Raven's Progressive Matrices and Catell's Culture Fair Test both measure 'G' factor.

Spearman has explained his theory with the help of a tetrad equation which is given below :

$$rap \times rbq - raq \times rbp = 0$$

Here,

a = opposites
b = discrimination
p = completion
q = cancellation

Thus, rap means correlation between opposites and completions, rbq means correlation between cancellation and discrimination, raq means correlation between opposite and cancellation and rbp means correlation between discrimination and completion. This theory can also be explained with the help of a diagram given below :

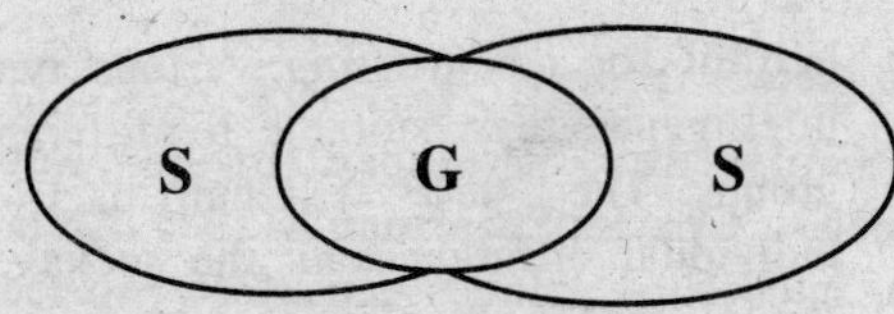

4. Multi-factors theory :

This theory was developed by an American psychologist, **E.L. Thorndike.** He opposed the theory of general intelligence by saying that there are specific stimuli and specific mental responses. Intelligence is nothing more than a potential specific connections between these stimuli and responses. Differences of intelligence among people are due to the different number of such connections in the neurological system. This theory is also called **atomistic theory** of intelligence. There are **four attributes of intelligence** according to him:

(a) *Level :* It refers to the difficulty of a task that can be removed by using intelligence. If different tasks are arranged in increasing difficulty order, then the height that a person can attain determines his level of intelligence. It is a kind of power test.

(b) *Range :* It refers to the number of tasks of the same difficulty value that a person can do in a certain period of time. Theoretically, an individual possessing a certain level of intelligence should be able to solve the whole range of tasks at a given level. It is a kind of speed test.

Range and level can not be completely isolated from each other. We can not measure range without altitude (level) and vice versa.

(c) *Area :* It refers to the total numbers of situations at each level to which the individual is able to respond. Area is the summation of all ranges at each level of intelligence. Area = Level × Range.

(d) *Speed :* It refers to the rapidity with which an individual can respond to a test items. Speed and level are positively correlated. It is different from range in the sense that no specific time is given here to complete a task.

Every intelligence test should consist of these four attributes.

5. Group factor structure of intelligence (PMA Test) :

This theory was developed by **L.L. Thurstone.** According to him, intelligence is not an expression of general factor but a combination of group of traits. They are intermediate factors, *i.e.*, they are not so universal as 'G' factor and they are not so specific as 'S' factor. This primary group of factors give the common mental abilities, a functional cohesiveness and then constitute a group. Another group of common mental abilities is said to have another primary factor and so on. In this way, there are a number of groups of mental abilities each of which has its own primary factors. On the basis of factor analysis of these groups, Thurstone identified the following seven group factors which are termed as primary mental abilities (PMA).

1. Number factor (N) : It is the ability to do numerical calculations rapidly and accurately.
2. Verbal factor (V) : They are related to the operations involving verbal comprehension.
3. Space factor (S) : It is related to the tasks in which subject manipulates an object imaginary in space.
4. Word fluency factor (W) : It is involved to the situation when the subject is asked to think of isolated words at a fast rate.
5. Reasoning factors (R) : It is used in those tasks that require the subject to discover a rule or principles involved in series or groups of letters.
6. Rote memory (M) : It is the ability to memorize a fact quickly.
7. Perceptual speed (P) : It is the ability to note perceptual (visual) details rapidly.

The point to be noted here is that these seven abilities are significantly correlated with each other.

6. Structure of intelligence (SI) model :

This model was given by **J.P. Guilford** in 1966 in the University of California on the basis of factor analysis of many tests. According to him human mind is composed of at least three dimensions—operations, contents and products, and each dimension of intellect is sufficiently distinct which can be detected by factor analysis. These three dimensions of mind are given below:

(A) Operations : Operations can be divided into five major groups of intellectual abilities.

- **Cognition :** It includes discovery, recognition of informations and new understanding of the facts.
- **Memory :** It is the ability to recognize or recall previously learnt material.
- **Divergent thinking :** This operation is closely associated with creative potential. It refers to the ability to search out and think in a novel out of track way.
- **Convergent thinking :** It refers to the generation of information from given information and drawing conclusion from the given facts.

- **Evaluation :** It is the ability to make judgement on the basis of merits and demerits of a phenomenon. Here, value judgement on knowledge and thoughts is placed after critically examining them.

(B) Contents : Five kinds of contents are involved here. Operations are performed on these contents.

- **Figural content :** It is the concrete material perceived through the senses. Visual materials have three properties, size, form and colour.
- **Auditory content :** It includes nature and characteristics of sound perceived.
- **Symbolic content :** It includes letters, digits and other conventional signs usually organised in general pattern.
- **Semantic content :** It refers to those verbal meanings, ideas and concepts for which no examples are necessary.
- **Behavioural content :** It includes knowledge regarding other persons.

(C) Products : When five operations are applied to five types of contents, six kinds of products are made.

- **Units :** It refers to the production of a single word, definition or isolated bits of informations.
- **Classes :** It refers to the production of a concept.
- **Relations :** It refers to the production of any form of relationship, such as, analogy, opposite or similar ones.
- **System :** It refers to the production of internally consistent set of classification of various forms.
- **Transformation :** It refers to the production of changes in meaning, organisation or some other arrangement.
- **Implication :** It refers to the production of such information which is beyond the data given.

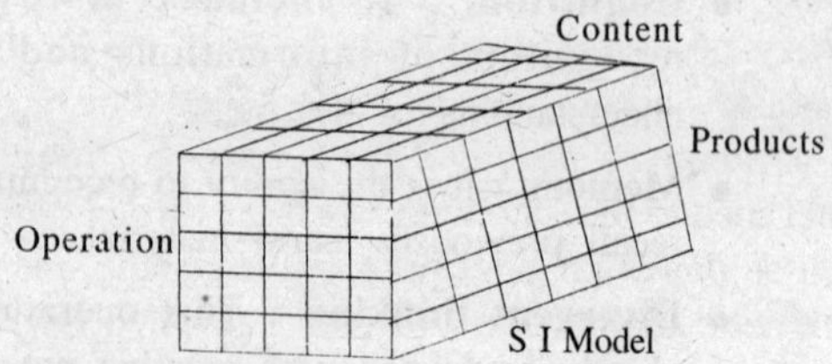

S I Model

On the basis of the model given above it can be stated that there are 5 × 5 × 6 = 150 factors involved in intelligent acts.

Educational Implication of the Model

(a) In psychology : This model is very much helpful for constructing various types of intelligence tests suitable to different age groups. These tests will help us to study individual differences in the society. This model is taxonomic in nature and has discovered many abilities which were not known before. If test maker has included items representing contents and operations, he can see whether products are same or different. Conversely, if products are shown by the subject through the test, the test maker can find out the content and operation and match them with the items given in the test.

(b) In vocational testing : This model shows that there are 150 intellectual abilities. This model predicts five kinds of mental abilities classified as content. This means that different kinds of test items are needed in vocational testing. Six types of products are also tested on the basis of items representing the products. For example, if a person is able to deal with items of figural contents, he can deal with machines, operators, engineers etc. and any or all of the six types of products can be made by him, such as, he can define a machine or any operator. He can give clear concept about how a machine is operated and so on.

(c) In the field of education : Conventionally, learner was considered to be a kind of stimulus response device. Once the stimulus is given to him, he will respond but the new conception of the learner in the light of SI model is that of electronic computer which not only stores information but uses that information to generate new information either by divergent or convergent thinking.

Thus, this model gives the idea that learning is not merely the association of informations but it is the discovery of information as well. Model suggests that in order to understand human learning and higher mental processes of thinking, some drastic modifications are to be made in our theory of curriculum construction and pedagogy of instruction. Similarly, education is no longer considered to be the training of mind. Now, main emphasis on education is given to the learning of specific skills and modification of behaviour and all these materials are not taught merely for the purpose of training the mind of humans.

7. Two Level Process Theory of Intelligence : This theory was developed by **Jensen** in 1968. According to him intelligence is a combination of two levels of processes. One is associative intelligence and the other is abstract intelligence. Associative intelligence includes those kinds of tests that depend upon memory and simple verbal association. Abstract intelligence includes those factors as concept learning, thinking, problem solving skills, multiple discrimination, principle learning etc.

8. Burt and Vernon's Hierarchy Theory :

Burt (1940) separated four factors of intelligence by using statistical techniques :

- General factors (common to all traits)
- Group factors (common to some of the traits)
- Specific factors (limited to few traits)
- Error factors (limited to a particular trait when it is measured)

When human mind is put at the top, there will be 5 level hierarchical model of intelligence where general factors will come next to intelligence and error factors will come in the last.

Vernon, on the other hand, suggested that intelligence tests measure an overall factor G as well as two other mental abilities. First are related to verbal, numerical and educational. Second are related to practical, mechanical, spatial and physical. These two major factors can be divided into minor group factors. These minor factors can further be divided into various specific factors and so on.

MEASUREMENT OF INTELLIGENCE

Historical development of mental testing can be divided into three periods for the purpose of convenience.

(A) Pre-Binet Period :

In the 19th century, there was a good deal of interest in the field of psychophysics in which attempts were made to develop general rule of sensory judgement. The functioning of sensory reactions of the typical individuals is actually studied in psycho-physics. Method of limits procedure was used here to measure the extent to which people were able to differentiate between stimuli. But the limitation of these experiments was that accurate generalization of the result was not possible.

Francis Galton was the first psychologist who took interest in studying whether individual characteristics are acquired or inherited. For this purpose, he studied the lives of prominent English men and in his book "Hereditary Genius" he demonstrated that personal characteristics, (mental and physical) of men are inherited. He developed a series of tests to measure these characteristics. It was the starting point of mental measurement.

The first laboratory of experimental psychology was established by **Wundt** in 1879 in Leiping. He employed two methods to test vision, hearing, reaction time and psychosomatic problems— *(i)* psycho-physical method *(ii)* Introspection method. He also developed mental tests which could measure the keenness of vision and hearing, muscular strength, reaction time and other sensory motor functions of body.

Many of **Galton's** ideas were brought to USA by an American psychologist **J.M. Catell.** Like **Galton** he also believed that intellectual functions can best be measured by the reaction time and sensory discrimination tests.

In the last quarter of the 19th century, many psychological laboratories came into existence and studies of individual differences in mental abilities started.

The word "**Mental Test**" was first used by Catell in 1890 but his tests were actually tests of sensory discrimination, speed of motor responses and the like.

Thus, upto this period mental ability was identified as sensory acuity of an individual. The correlation between mental abilities and academic achievements was not known at the time.

Drawbacks of this period:

- Psychologists were unable to identify and define the nature of intelligence. Keenness of sensory motor reactions were related to intelligence.
- They were unable to measure the complex functions of the body.
- Intelligence tests developed during this period were measuring other than intelligence.

(B) Binet Period :

An important incident led the people to think about mental measurement during this period. In the beginning of the 20th century in France, a large number of students failed in the examination. For this teachers and students blamed each other. Seeing this, superintendent of public instruction appointed a committee to device some techniques to screen out slow learners in the schools. Binet and Simon were among members of the committee. They developed a variety of paper pencil tests in their psychological laboratory established in 1889, to administer them on children of different ages. Through these tests Binet tried to measure more complex mental functions such as power of judgement and reasoning, memory, arithmetic ability, etc.

An important contribution of Binet and Simon is that they categorised their tests in terms of age levels by administering their test items to children of different ages. In this way, an age scale of intelligence was also developed. For example, if an item was correctly answered by majority of seven years old children but only few six years old children could respond it correctly, then this item was reserved for seven years old children. In this way, Binet and Simon developed separate tests for different ages.

Similarly, if an item suited to eight years old child was correctly answered by a child of 6 years and if the same trend was shown by the six years old child in most of the cases of a test, then the mental age of the child was considered to be eight years not six years, though his chronological age is six years only. Thus, the concept of mental age was also introduced by Binet and Simon for the first time in the history of mental testing and with the help of this concept we could assess the intellectual ability of a person. Some of the tests developed during this period are given below:

Binet-Simon Scale

The first scale of Binet-Simon was published in 1905. This scale consisted of 30 items arranged in increasing order of difficulty. This scale was a crude measure of intelligence of school going children.

In order to remove some of its defects they revised their scale in 1908. It was the first age based scale and it created a lot of interest among the psychologists across the world. The items in the tests were grouped according to the appropriate age levels from 3 to 13 years.

Some items for three years age

- Point to your nose, eyes and mouth.
- Repeat two digits 3, 5.
- Repeat sentences of six syllables.
- Enumerate objects in a picture.
- Give family names.

Some items of eight years age

- Read a passage and remember two lines.
- Add up the value of five coins.
- Name four colours.
- Count reverse from 20 to zero.
- Give differences between two objects.

1908 revision of Binet-Simon Scale was adopted by many psychologists of America, Switzerland and Germany and many suggestions were given by them for the improvement of the scale. Binet-Simon accepted their suggestions and revised their scale again in 1911.

Some sample items of 1911 scale are given below:

(A) Age = 8 years

- Gives difference between two objects.
- Counts reverse from 20 to zero.
- Points out omissions from unfinished pictures.
- Tells the dates correctly.
- Repeats the digits.

(B) Age = 10 years

- Arranges five blocks in order of increasing weights.
- Reproduces two geometric designs by using memory.
- Criticizes absurd statements.
- Comprehends and answers difficult questions.
- Uses three given words in two sentences.

Main Features of Binet-Simon Scale

(i) They are really scales, *i.e.*, items of the tests are arranged in the increasing difficulty order. Easiest items are put in the beginning and the most difficult item is put in the last. Thus, these scales measure the level or aptitude of an examinee and not their speed.

(ii) These tests measure the general abilities of intelligence instead of specific abilities.

(iii) They can also measure the mental growth of the subject because they are arranged according to different ages from 3 to 14 years.

(iv) They are administered on subjects individually.

(v) Their system of scoring is tied to age norms. A child's performance on the scale will be compared to that of children of his own age.

L.M. Terman's revision of Binet–Simon Scale: L.M. Terman of **Stanford** University revised this scale in 1916 to adapt to American situations. He introduced one new concept which was intelligence Quotient (IQ) in his revision. His scale consisted of 90 items ranging from 3 to 14 years of age. Some items of this scale are given below:

Age = 7 years

- Knows number of fingers on both hands.
- Describes pictures.
- Repeats five digits.
- Gives differences between paired objects.
- Ties a bowknot.

1937 Revision of Binet-Simon Scale : Terman along with his associate Merill revised 1916 scale again in 1937. This revision had two equivalent forms L and M. The number of items in the test was raised to 129 in each L M. forms. A new change was also introduced in the test which was the calculation of chronological age. Upto 13 years CA was taken to be as original but after 13 years CA was computed in the following manner.

At 14 years = 13 yrs+2/3 of 14th year = 13 2/3 years.

At 15 years = 13+2/3 of 2 years = 14 1/3 years.

At 16 years = 13+2/3 of 3 years = 15 years.

Besides, 16 years was taken to be the last age for calculation of IQ. After that, CA was taken to be constant.

LM form revision of 1960 : Binet-Simon scale was last revised in 1960 in which items of both L and M forms were included in the scale. This revision has a range of 2 years of mental age scores to 22 years and 11 months of mental age score. This form of the test measures abilities from 7 categories namely, language, memory, reasoning, social intelligence, conceptual phenomenon, numerical, reasoning and visual motor. Test items are in the form of words, objects and pictures and the responses given by the examinees are in the form of drawing, calculating, writing and speaking. Administration of the test requires one full hour. In this revision intelligence is expressed in terms of standard scores of the deviation IQ.

Wechsler Scale : This scale may be considered an improvement over Binet-Simon scale as it can measure the intelligence of adults very effectively. David Wechsler developed this scale in 1939. This scale was developed in two equivalent forms, each form consisted of ten subtests of which five tests were verbal and five were non-verbal or performance type. This scale was revised in 1955 and was renamed as Wechsler Adult Intelligence Scale (WAIS). It comprised of 11 sub tests of which six were verbal and five were non-verbal. This scale is used on persons above 16 years of age upto 64 and administration time of the scale is one hour. The detail of these 11 subtests are given below:

(a) Verbal subtests :

1. *Information* : 29 questions are given here to test the recall of knowledge concerning wide varieties of information.
2. *Comprehension* : 14 questions are given here to test understanding of knowledge concerning a particular subject or event.
3. *Arithmetic* : 14 questions are given here to test numerical ability. These questions are solved orally without using paper and pencil at all.
4. *Similarity* : 13 questions are given here to measure abstract verbal reasoning. Examinees are required here to compare two objects and find out the relationship between them.
5. *Digit span* : Memory for digits are measured here. In the first half, the examinee is asked to repeat in the same order, three to nine digits presented in the forward directions and in the second half, the digits are repeated in a backward direction.
6. *Vocabulary* : 40 words of increasing difficulty value are presented before the examinees here and they are asked to tell the meaning of these words.

(b) Non-verbal or performance subtests:

1. *Digit symbol* : Nine digits each with different digit symbols are given to the examinees here and they are asked to give the right code for each digits or symbols.
2. *Picture completion* : This subtest measures the ability of the examinees to analyse the parts from the whole. Examinees are given 21 cards containing incomplete pictures and they are asked to fill the missing part of each picture.
3. *Block design* : Its purpose is to measure the ability to analyse the complex whole. There are only 7 designs in these blocks which have red, white and red-white sides. Examinees are asked to produce a given design with the help of these blocks.
4. *Picture arrangement* : Its purpose is to measure the ability to identify the whole from the parts. Here six set of pictures are given to the examinees and they are asked to arrange them in an order which tells a meaningful story.
5. *Object assembly* : Its purpose is to measure the ability to synthesise the whole with the help of parts. Here examinees are given some puzzle pictures each representing some parts of the human body and they are asked to assemble them in the form of a complete man.

Speed and accuracy factors are also scored in Arithmetic, digit symbol, block design, picture arrangement and object assembly. Raw scores of each subject are converted into normalized standard scores with a mean of 10 and SD of 3. This makes the scores of each sub tests comparable. Separate IQ for verbal and non-verbal subtest forms is calculated by adding up the respective subtests of the two forms and if we add up scores on all the 11 subtests, we obtain total scale score. These standard scores are expressed in the form of deviation IQ with a mean of 100 and SD of 15.

Wechsler developed another scale known as Wechsler intelligence Scale for Children in 1949 to test the intelligence of children from 5 to 15 years of age. It also takes one hour to administer, though there are 12 subtests in this scale. Maze test is the only test which is extra in WISC. Maze subtest has eight mazes to be traced by the examinee with a pencil. These mazes are given in increasing order of difficulty.

The scoring system of both the tests WAIS and WISC are the same. Here also the total scores are converted into deviation IQ with a mean of 100 and SD of 15.

Advantages of Wechsler Scales

(i) Though Binet's scale and Wechsler's scale both are individual scales, yet the later can be

administered on small groups of children and adults.

(ii) Wechsler's scale is easier to administer than Binet's Scale and its scoring is also less complex than the former.

(iii) Wechsler has prepared separate scales for children and adults Binet's scale does not possess this advantage.

Other differences of Wechsler Scales and Stanford Binet Scale

(i) In Wechsler scale, items are not grouped in terms of mental age as is the case of Stanford-Binet scale. Points are given here for all correct responses. Thus, WAIS or WISC is a point scale.

(ii) In Stanford-Binet scale items are interpreted in terms of different age levels of the examinees but in WAIS or WISC similar types of items are grouped together to form subtests.

(iii) WAIS has separate age norms for adults but in SB Scale all the individuals above 18 are treated in a similar manner as far as computation of IQ is concerned. Thus, people of all age levels are treated as 18 years of age after 18.

(iv) In SB tests items are varied, unrelated and upgraded but in WAIS and WISC tests, items are graded according to various range of ages.

(v) SB scale is internally standardized and rigid but WAIS is externally standardized and flexible.

(vi) SB scale refers to qualitative evaluation while WAIS refers to quantitative evaluation.

(vii) Slight chance of statistical treatment is possible in SB scale but WAIS is fully subject to all statistical analysis.

(c) Post Binet period :

This period is particularly known for testing intelligence in groups and thus group test of intelligence became popular during this periods.

A group test is one that can be given to a number of subjects at a time by a single examiner. This type of test came into being during first World War for the purpose of classifying soldiers for various jobs in accordance with their mental abilities. Army Alpha and Army Beta, two tests were developed during this period. Army Alpha is a verbal group test of intelligence meant for literate people. Army beta is a non-verbal group test of intelligence meant for illiterate persons.

We will discuss here some more group test of intelligence :

1. **Catell's Culture Fair Test :** This test was developed by RB Catell and was published by IPAT (Institute for Personality and Ability Testing) in 1961. The test has three scales and can be administered on children and adults both.

   Scale I meant for 4-8 years

   Scale II meant for 8-15 years

   Scale III meant for 15 years and above

   This test measures the general intelligence factor and takes 30-60 minutes to administer. The test has been prepared in such a manner that previously learnt skill or knowledge does not help the examinee to score more on this test. That is why, it is said to be independent of school achievement, social advantages and environmental influences.

2. **Large Thorndike's Intelligence Test :** This test is meant for primary and secondary school children graded into five different levels. The purpose of the test is to measure verbal comprehension, numerical skill and reasoning abilities. Test has verbal as well as non-verbal items. Only non-verbals items are, however, included at the lower levels. The administration of the test takes 30 minutes in all.

3. **Raven Progressive Matrices Test :** This test was developed in England. It consists of geometric figures and designs. The subjects find out the relationship between figures and select appropriate parts for completion of each pattern of relations.

Classification of Intelligence Test

(A) Classification from the point of view of administration

1. **Individual intelligence test :** An individual intelligence test is one which is administered to only one person at a time. Binet-Simon is an example.

2. **Group intelligence test :** A group intelligence test is one which can be administered to more than one persons at a time. Army Alpha and Army Beta are two examples of such tests.

Some general characteristics of group intelligence tests are as follows :

(i) They have been developed on the assumption that intelligence is a general capacity and can be measured by sampling a variety of mental activities.

(ii) In group tests the similar types of items are pooled together in different subtests.

(iii) Every group test is standardized for a special range of ages or school grades.

(iv) Construction of individual test is also very difficult and costly as compared to group tests.

Their scoring and standardization is also time consuming process.

(v) It is very difficult to establish rapport between the examiner and the examinees and hence examinees can not be motivated properly in group tests of intelligence. These two limitations are not seen in individual tests.

(vi) Group tests are superior to individual tests in the sense that norms established here are more dependable than that of individual tests. It is because these norms are calculated on the basis of a very large sample.

(vii) Individual test provides qualitative performance of the individual while group tests are mostly point scale and express the performance in quantities.

(B) Classification from the point of view of nature of items of the test

1. **Verbal test :** Verbal test of intelligence is one in which instructions and items are produced before the examinees through the written language. So, examinees must be literate to take these tests. Mohsin's General intelligence Test, Joshi's General Mental Ability test and Jalota's Group General Mental Ability Test are some examples of verbal tests of intelligence of Indian origin.

2. **Non-verbal test :** A non-verbal test is one which requires the use of language only to impart instructions. The examinees are asked to manipulate the test materials in their own way. Since language is not needed to respond to items here, it can be administered to illiterate persons as well. They are also culturally free and hence they can be applied to any situation representing any culture. Test items are usually of figured relation type. Army Beta is a good example of non-language test.

3. **Performance test :** A performance test is one in which a subject has to perform some thing or to manipulate some concrete materials without much use of the language ability. Non-verbal and performance tests are useful for the following groups of people:

   (a) *Deaf and Dumb :* Those children who cannot hear or speak can be tested with the help of performance test.

   (b) *Illiterates :* Verbal test of intelligence is useless for those who cannot read or write. Performance test is useful for them.

   (c) *Shy children :* Many withdrawn children are hesitant to express before others. Performance and non-verbal test of intelligence will suit them very much.

   (d) *Educationally deficient children :* Verbal test of intelligence generally measure learning along with intelligence. If children are educationally poor, they will perform poorly on intelligence test too and thus they will be wrongly declared as children of below average intelligence. Such a problem can be overcome by using performance test or non-verbal intelligence test.

   (e) *Useful for children of other culture :* A particular culture dominates in every verbal intelligence test and thus the test can not be adopted by other cultures. Due to free from culture, performance test is suitable for these foreign students.

Some performance tests of intelligence are given below :

(a) Pintner Paterson Scale : This is the first systematic performance test. This scale was standardized in 1917. It consists of 15 subtests.

(b) Goodenough Drawing Test : This scale was developed by Florence Goodenough in 1926. Here child is asked to draw the picture of a man as best as possible without any time limit. This is especially useful for those children who are suspected to be mentally retarted.

Weaknesses of performance test :

- Here the subject can score high due to practice effect and chance success is more frequent than verbal tests. Because of this reason, reliability coefficient is very low.
- They fail to distinguish between gifted and average children due to limited scope of these tests.
- These scales fail to test fine mental abilities such as, ability to make abstraction or concept formation or evaluation abilities of mind.

Interpretation of Intelligence Test Scores : Intelligence test scores can be interpreted in the following three ways:

1. **Mental age :** This concept was first introduced by **Afred Binet** of France in 1908. It refers to a score that is determined by comparing a child's score with the scores obtained by younger or older children in the norming group. Here a child's score is compared with the average score of his own age. For example, if a 9-year-old child scores 60 on an intelligence test and suppose mental age norms for that scale are as follows:

   Mental age of 8 years = 60

   Mental age of 9 years = 70

   Mental age of 10 years = 80

Then, in that case, mental age of the child will be considered as 8 years instead of 9 though his chronological age is 9 years.

Similarly, if another child of 8 years obtains a score of 80, then his mental age will be 10 years, though his chronological age is 8 years only.

Thus, we can say that the mean performance of each age level becomes the mental age for that age level.

2. **Intelligent Quotient (IQ) :** IQ is also based on the concept of mental age. It is the ratio of mental age to the chronological age multiplied by 100.

$$IQ = \frac{MA}{CA} \times 100.$$

Suppose, the mental age of a 10-year-old child is 12 years on the basis of his scores on an intelligence test, his IQ will be

$$\frac{12}{10} \times 100 = 120.$$

Similarly, if mental age of a person is nine years two months and his age is 12 years 6 months, then his IQ will be

$$\frac{110}{150} \times 100 = 73.3.$$

General classification of persons in terms of IQ

IQ	Classification
140 and above	Genius
130-140	Very superior
120-130	Superior
110-120	Bright
90-110	Average
80-90	Dull
70-80	Borderline
Below 70	Mentally retarded.

Shortcomings of IQ: Some of the main short comings of IQ are as follows:

(i) It is a well-known fact that after 18 years, the mental age of a person tends to stabilize. Thus, if IQ is calculated after this age, the result will be misleading, *i.e.*, a person will be less intelligent if he grows in age.

(ii) Variability of IQ scores from one test to another is not the same. As a result IQ scores for different tests would not be directly comparable.

(iii) It has also been found that variability in IQ scores for the different age levels on the same test is not the same. In that case IQ scores would be a misleading index because it would indicate that a person's IQ may increase or decrease as he grows in age. An example will illustrate this point.

Age	IQ	SD
9 years old child	120	12
7 years old child	120	9

Here IQ of 120 of both the children is not the same due to difference in SD.

3. **Deviation IQ :** Now-a-days IQ ratio is converted into a normalized standard score with a fixed mean of 100 and SD of 15. This is known as DIQ. This fixed mean and SD remain constant through all the age levels. It means that if a child's score is 1 SD above the mean his DIQ will be 100 + 15 = 115. Similarly, if his score is 1 SD below the mean his DIQ will be 100 – 15 = 85 and so on. Thus, with the help of these **DIQ** scores inter age comparison is also possible.

Uses of Intelligence Test

Intelligence tests can be applied in the following situations.

1. **Measurement of general learning abilities:** Intelligence and achievement in schools are highly correlated. If a person is high on an intelligence test, he is expected to score high on school achievements also. Conversely if a person scores high on an intelligence test and still his school achievement is very poor, we can find out other reasons for his educational backwardness.
2. **Assessment of individual differences and categorization :** With the help of intelligence tests we can categories a particular class into several convenient groups and plan our instructional strategies accordingly. Thus, intelligence testing is very useful for educational guidance.
3. **Exact definition of mental retardation is possible :** It is said that those who are below 70 in IQ are retarded but to what extent they are mentally retarded can further be studied with the help of higher screening. We may define the three groups of mentally retarted in the following ways.

Category	IQ level
Morons	45-69
Imbeciles	25-45
Idiots	Below 25

4. **Identification of gifted children :** Gifted children are the treasure of the society. They must be identified in the earlier stages of their

lives so that they can be fully guided and helped for their better advancement which is directly related to the advancement of the society as well. Intelligence testing will help the concerned organisations to chalk out plans in the desired manner.

5. **Vocational guidance :** Some children are very forward in verbal abilities and some are superior in non-verbal abilities. This identification is possible only with the help of intelligence tests. Since academic subjects need verbal intelligence and technical subjects need non-verbal or performing abilities, hence children may be guided accordingly.
6. **Screening :** In today's age of competition and rush, screening has become a necessity. Every school has limited seats of admission and it has to select only those students who can raise the academic level of the school high and get name for it. Same is the case with appointments in jobs. For all these purposes, intelligence testing is a must.
7. **Study of mental growth :** Mental abilities develop in a sequential order onward. We can use intelligence tests for studying the trends of mental development of individuals. Intelligence tests have made it clear that mental development of children is a steady consistent process from year-to-year till the age of 25. Intelligence tests show that mind does not develop rapidly in the period of adolescence like the physical and emotional development, but in childhood, it develops rapidly.

Limitations of Intelligence Tests

1. Generally intelligence test shows what a person can do at a certain point of time. These abilities are tested on the basis of certain items included in the test. In order to make the results dependable, a proper size of the sample must be selected for standardization of the test.
2. Some people may be fatigued earlier than others when take a test. This extent of fatigue may reduce their scores and hence intelligence testing will not be accurate. So scores should be taken with caution.
3. No intelligence test is fully free from cultural influences. So, home or school background may affect the intelligence test scores of subjects.
4. Administration of the test also affects the scores of subjects. If proper rapport is there between the examiner and the examinee. IQ scores may be high. On the other hand, if children are frightened with the testing situation as is case of slow learners they will perform poorly on the test.
5. Taking intelligence scores in absolute form is misleading. Intelligence tests do not reveal all the mental abilities in most of the cases. So, intelligence test must be supplemented with clinical setting and case history method to collect detailed information about a subject as is done in clinics by physician who does not entirely believe in physical investigations. He rather takes the help of clinical diagnosis before giving remedial treatment to the patients.

THOUGHT AND LANGUAGE

In this section we examines the relationship between language and thought: that language determines thought, that thought determines language, and that thought and language have different origins. Let us examine these three viewpoints in some detail.

Language as Determinant of Thought

In Hindi and other Indian languages we use a number of different words for various kinship relationships. We have different terms for mother's brother, father's elder brother, father's younger brother, mother's sister's husband, father's sister's husband and so on. An English person uses just one word *uncle* to describe all these kinship relationships. In the English language there are dozens of words for colours whereas some tribal languages have only two to four colour terms. Do such differences matter for how we think? Does an Indian child find it easier to think about and differentiate between various kinship relationships compared to her English-speaking counterpart? Does our thinking process depend on how we describe it in our language?

Benjamin Lee Whorf was of the view that language determines the contents of thought. This view is known as **linguistic relativity hypothesis.** In its strong version, this hypothesis holds what and how individuals can possibly think is determined by the language and linguistic categories they use **(linguistic determinism).** Experimental evidence, however, maintains that it is possible to have the same level or quality of thoughts in all languages depending upon the availability of linguistic categories and structures. Some thoughts may be easier in one language compared to another.

Thought as Determinant of Language

The noted Swiss psychologist, Jean Piaget believed that thought not only determines language, but also precedes it. Piaget argued that children form an internal representation of the world through thinking. For example, when children see something and later copy it (a process called imitation), thinking does take place, which does not involve language. A child's observation of other's behaviour and imitation of the same behaviour, no doubt involves thinking but not language. Language is just one of the vehicles of thinking. As actions become internalised, language may affect children's range of symbolic thinking but is not necessary for the origins of thought. Piaget believed that though language can be taught to children, understanding of the words require knowledge of the underlying concepts (*i.e.* thinking). Thus, thought is basic, and necessary if language is to be understood.

Different Origins of Language and Thought

The Russian psychologist, Lev Vyogotsky, argued that thoughts and language develop in a child separately until about two years of age, when they merge. Before two years thought is preverbal and is experienced more in action (Piaget's sensory motor stage). The child's utterances are more automotic reflexes—crying when uncomfortable—than thought-based. Around two years of age, the child expresses thought verbally and her/his speech reflects rationality. Now children are able to manipulate thoughts using soundless speech. He believed that during this period the development of language and thinking become interdependent; the development of conceptual thinking depends upon the quality of inner speech and vice versa. Thought is used without language when the vehicle of thinking is non-verbal such as visual or movement-related. Language is used without thought when expressing feelings or exchanging pleasantries, for example ''Good morning! How are you?'' ''Very well, I am fine''. When the two functions overlap, they can be used together to produce verbal thought and rational speech.

Development of Language

Language is a complex system and unique to human beings. Psychologists have tried to teach sign language, use of symbols to chimpanzees, dolphins, parrots, etc. But it is observed that, human language is more complex, creative, and spontaneous than the system of communication other animals can learn. There is also a great deal of **regularity** with which children all over the world seem to be learning the language or languages to which they are exposed. When we compare individual children, we find that they differ a great deal in the rate of their language development as well as in how they go about it. But when we take a general view of children's acquisition of language all over the world we find some *predictable pattern* in which children proceed from almost no use of language to the point of becoming competent language users. Language develops through some of the stages discussed below.

Newborn babies and young infants make a variety of sounds, which gradually get modified to resemble words. The first sound produced by babies is crying. Initial crying is undifferentiated and similar across various situations. Gradually, the pattern of crying varies in its pitch and intensity to signify different states such as hunger, pain, and sleepiness, etc. These differentiated crying sounds gradually become more meaningful *cooing sounds* (like 'aaa', 'uuu', etc). usually to express happiness.

At around six months of age children enter the *babbling* stage. Babbling involves prolonged repetition of a variety of consonants and vowel sounds (for example, da—, aa—, ba—). By about nine months of age these sounds get elaborated to strings of some sound combinations, such as 'dadadadadada' into repetitive patterns called *echolalia.* While the early babblings are random or accidental in nature, the later babblings seem to be imitative of adult voices. Children show some understanding of a few words by the time they are six months old. Around the first birthday (the exact age varies from child-to-child) most children enter the *one-word-stage.* Their first word usually contains one syllable—*ma or da*, for instance. Gradually they move to one or more words which are combined to form whole sentences or phrases. So they are called *holophrases*. When they are 18 to 20 months of age, children enter a *two-word stage* and begin to use two words together. The two-word stage exemplifies *telegraphic speech.* Like telegrams (got admission, send money) it contains mostly nouns and verbs. Close to their third birthday, *i.e.* beyond two-and-a-half years, children's language development gets focused on rules of the language they hear.

How is language acquired? You must be wondering: ''How do we learn to speak?'' As with many other topics in psychology, the questions of whether a behaviour develops as a result of inherited characteristics (nature) or from the effects of learning (nurture) has been raised with regard to language. Most psychologists accept that both nature and nurture are important in language acquisition.

Behaviourist B.F. Skinner believed we learn language the same way as animals learn to pick keys or press bars. Language development, for the behaviourists follow the learning principles, such as association (the sight of bottle with the word 'bottle'), imitation (adults use of word ''bottle''), and reinforcement (smiles and hugs when the child says something right). There is also evidence that children produce sounds that are appropriate to a language of the parent or care-giver and are reinforced for having done so. The principle of shaping leads to successive approximation of the desired responses so that the child eventually speaks as well as the adult. Regional differences in pronunciation and phrasing illustrate how different patterns are reinforced in different areas.

Linguist Noam Chomsky put forth the innate proposition of development of language. For him the *rate at which children acquire words and grammar* without being taught can not be explained only by learning principles. Children also *create all sorts of sentences* they have never heard and, therefore, could not be imitating. Children throughout the world seem to have a *critical period*—a period when learning must occur if it is to occur successfully—for learning language. Children across the world also go through the same stages of language development. Chomsky believes language development is just like physical maturation given adequate care, it ''just happens to the child''. Children are born with ''universal grammar''. They readily learn the grammar of whatever language they hear.

Skinner's emphasis on learning explains why infants acquire the language they hear and how they add new words to their vocabularies. Chomsky's emphasis on our built-in readiness to learn grammar helps explain why children acquire language so readily without direct teaching.

GENDER AS A SOCIAL CONSTRUCT; GENDER ROLES, GENDER-BIAS AND EDUCATIONAL PRACTICE

Gender refers to the social distinctions between boys and girls and men and women that are socially constructed rather than biologically determined. These distinctions are reflected in the roles that boys and girls play in society and the status that they occupy within it. Gender roles tend to be dynamic. They vary from one culture and time period to another and are characterized by unequal power relationships.

Ending gender bias and discrimination is crucial to the empowerment of women and girls and to the achievement of gender equality in education. Applying a gender perspective helps to make differences in power relations visible. It also helps us to see more clearly the needs and rights of girls and boys in particular geographical, cultural and economic contexts.

The ultimate goal is to eliminate gender biases and discriminatory practices and policies, both overt and covert. This is at the heart of gender analysis. Gender analysis should therefore be a prerequisite for identifying and understanding problems as they relate to education, and especially to the continued exclusion of girls from quality schooling. Gender analysis guides the process of finding viable and sustainable solutions to the problems of access, quality and learning achievement.

Gender analysis of what learners bring to education (including early childhood socialization, feeding and health access, cultural heritage and language), the content of education, teaching and learning processes, learning environments and learning outcomes help to highlight bad (and good) educational practices and policies. This analysis, in turn, should form the basis for educational interventions that are sensitive to both gender and human rights.

Gender Bias in Teaching

A common response from teachers when asked about gender inequity in classrooms is that they treat all their students the same. There are two problems with this statement. First, students are diverse and have different learning issues, thus treating all students in the same way means that some students will have a better learning experience than their peers. Second, teachers may be ignoring their unconscious gender biases towards their students, their schools and themselves. If ignored, these gender biases, which may have developed from cultural norms, may lead to bias in the classroom.

Gender bias occurs when people make assumptions regarding behaviours, abilities or preferences of others based upon their gender. Because there are strong gender role stereotypes for masculinity and femininity, students who do not match them can encounter problems with teachers and with their peers. For example, the expectation is that boys naturally exhibit boisterous, unruly behaviour, are academically able, rational, and socially uncommunicative, whereas girls are quiet, polite, and studious. Girls are also expected to possess better social skills than boys and to excel at reading and the language arts. So girls who present discipline problems for teachers, or quiet, studious boys, may encounter a lack of understanding from peers and teachers. Within the classroom, these biases unfold in students' practices and teachers' acceptance of certain behaviours from one student or another based upon the students' gender. Also, bias due to a person's gender is not mutually exclusive of other social categories such as race, ethnicity, class, religion, and language. For example, some teachers may perceive African American or other Black girls as loud and uncontrollable because the girls do not exhibit the feminine behaviours associated with White women, such as quiet, self-effacing and malleable.

Gender bias can occur within subject areas and school activities. For example, in subjects such as mathematics and the sciences, there are different participation patterns for girls and boys. Gender bias promulgates a myth that boys are naturally better at mathematics and science than girls. The implications are that if girls succeed in these subjects it is due to their hard work, not their intelligence, whereas boys' success is credited to their natural talent. There are some signs that gender bias in schools may be decreasing in some areas. The percentage of girls participating in science has increased and achieved parity with boys in biology, chemistry and algebra. However, subjects that are prerequisites for college majors such as engineering or physics remain dominated by men. Only 25% of high school students enrolled in physics are female. Moreover, there has been little increase in the percentage of women in engineering programs.

Males are also more likely than females to be in remedial programs and students' race also impacts these patterns. For example, African American males are more likely than White or female peers to enroll in remedial reading and mathematics courses. And non-White students have a higher representation in vocational and noncollege preparatory courses than their White peers. Teachers are critical components in challenging gender bias in schooling, but they also can be major contributors to it as well, through their pedagogical practices, curriculum choices, and assessment strategies.

Gender Bias in Teachers

Teachers' unconscious gender biases can produce stereo-typic expectations for students' success and participation in the classroom. Teachers view male students' domination of the classroom and their time as typical masculine behaviour. However, these biases have consequences for the students and the classroom climate. More than two decades ago, researchers identified and named groups of students who dominated the teacher's time and the classroom resources as "target students" (Tobin & Gallagher, 1987). Target students were typically white and male. They answered most of the teacher's questions and also asked most of the questions. This behaviour pattern was particularly insidious in mathematics and science classrooms because teachers did not expect girls to have competent knowledge in these subject areas. Classroom observations documented that target students typically called out answers to the teacher's questions, thus denying other students the opportunity to engage in dialogue with the teacher or get to grips with the subject matter. Furthermore, because boys are perceived as having natural talent in science, teachers asked boys harder and more complicated questions than girls. If girls attempted to answer more difficult questions than boys and faltered, teachers often repeated the question and asked that another student, typically a boy, provide the answer. However, if a boy failed to answer correctly, teachers reframed the question or broke it into a series of simpler questions that could help the student find the answer. Teachers' unconscious stereotyped gender bias that boys are smarter than girls, especially in mathematics and the sciences, meant they were willing to work with boys to reach the answer because they perceived boys were capable of achieving that goal but girls were not. Conversely, teachers of subjects perceived as feminine will spend more time engaged with girls.

Teachers' gendered perceptions of students' ability is also reflected in the type of praise and expectations they have of their students. Teachers often give girls less meaningful and less critical praise than boys. Boys' work is described as unique or brilliant, while girls' work is often undervalued, critically ignored and praised for its appearance. This aspect of teachers' behaviour is particularly detrimental to girls because it means they do not receive feedback on their work that could help them develop deeper understandings of concepts (Liu, 2006).

Teachers also use target students to maintain the tempo and pace of classroom instruction. For example, in a lecture or whole class discussion when a teacher is posing questions to the class, he or she may encourage target students to call out answers in order to keep the lesson moving, rather than wait for the other students to process the question and provide an answer. This short "wait time" may be detrimental to learning. More than three decades ago, researchers found that if teachers waited three to five seconds before accepting a student's answer, more students became engaged in the classroom and also improved their understanding of the content. Moreover, the longer wait time meant that teachers began to ask more cognitively challenging questions. However, the existence of target students in classes who often call out answers without direction from teachers meant that fewer students, especially girls, engaged in the lessons. In the absence of proactive teacher intervention, these patterns in which males dominate classroom interactions also occur in mixed-gender, small groups.

Target students dominate classroom interactions and exchanges at all education levels. In the early 2000s, researchers identified these same patterns of engagement in a professional development program for science teachers. When alerted to the invasive behaviours of the male teachers in the cohort, faculty began using overt breaching strategies to stop the target students calling out answers, dominating the human and materials resources of the classroom, and showing disrespect to their peers (Martin Milne & Scantlebury, 2006).

Teachers' gender bias towards students can also extend to their response to students who challenge their authority. Such risk-taking behaviour in boys is expected and at times praised, but assertiveness in girls is viewed negatively and labelled unfeminine. Similarly, boys who do not exhibit stereotypic masculine behaviours may be ridiculed (Renold, 2006).

Teachers use gender expectations as a means of maintaining classroom control. For example, teachers will seat undisciplined boys next to girls as a classroom management strategy. Further, teachers use the gendered expectation that girls' nurturing characteristics will lead them to place others' needs before their own. In other words, teachers often ask girls to assume mothering roles towards students who have fallen behind with learning because of inattentiveness, absenteeism through truancy, or in-school disciplinary procedures, and often those students are male.

Effects of Gender Bias

Gender bias can impact students' attitudes towards learning and their engagement with the subject. If affected by gender bias, girls will tend to believe that any success they have is due to hard work rather than any innate talent or intelligence. Boys may be encouraged to believe that success in science and mathematics should come easily to them because of their gender. Some males report dropping out of college science and mathematics programs because they no longer perceive these subjects as easy. Overall, teachers have lower expectations for girls' academic success compared to boys, and their attitudes are shown through the type and quality of the student-teacher interaction. The type and quality of critique teachers give their students can also have an impact. Teachers' comments on girls' work focuses on its appearance but with boys' work teachers focus on the content. Girls often do not receive substantive comments or criticism from teachers from which they could improve their ability to learn. During the many hours spent in classrooms, girls receive less time and attention from teachers than their male peers. Teachers usually ask girls easier questions than they ask boys. Typically, girls receive fewer opportunities to engage in classroom discourse, use equipment and assert their knowledge in classrooms.

Reducing Gender Bias

Gender bias in education is a series of microinequities whose impact is cumulative and often ignored. Girls are rewarded and praised for compliant behaviour. Teachers do not challenge girls with questions and rarely offer criticisms of their works. Teachers can reduce and challenge gender bias through an examination of their pedagogical practices and by posing simple questions about their practices. For example, which students do they frequently interact with? Are target students evident in their classroom? If so, how does the teacher deal with those students? What questioning techniques does the teacher use to engage students? Does the teacher ask complicated questions to girls as well as boys? Does the teacher use a variety of pedagogical and assessment practices? Which students are engaged with the curriculum?

Another way of reducing gender bias would be for teachers to videotape their classes and review their interactions with the students. Or they could invite a colleague to watch their teaching and record which students are being asked questions and what type of questions. However, teachers must also prepare for the consequences of changing their practices. Girls are conditioned to receiving less of the teacher's attention, and they do not usually cause discipline problems if they are not receiving their fair share, but boys can react negatively to losing the teacher's attention, causing disruption to lessons and becoming discipline problems. Moreover, research has also shown that boys avoid written work and often have poor communication skills when asked to work in singlesex groups.

However, the gains in reducing gender bias in education may disappear with the requirements of high-stakes testing required by No Child Left Behind (NCLB). NCLB requires that states report academic achievement data in most social categories, except gender (Kahle, 2004). This may result in less attention being placed on gender bias and less data that might reveal it. Continued monitoring of gender bias is necessary to minimize its impact on students' opportunities for learning and achievement.

INDIVIDUAL DIFFERENCES AMONG LEARNERS

It is not unusual to find a wide range of differences among students in a class or a group. These differences are invariably identified in terms of student's characteristics such as physical (appearance, height, size, sex, colour, etc.), demographic (age, caste, socio-economic status, etc.) and cognitive behaviour (thinking, remembering, problem solving, creating idea, etc.). The differences that exist among students due to physical, demographic, affective behaviour and cognitive behaviour characteristics are referred to as individual differences.

Differences due to physical and demographic characteristics are conspicuous and easy to identify. However, the differences that exist in the way they solve problem in Mathematics or in their ability to interpret and explain ideas are not easily visible but are identified through their performance. Let us examine, for instance, the answers given by Bitto and

Neha, two students of the same class to the following proverb.

Interpret the saying, ''Pen is mighter than the sword''.

Bitto's Interpretation

It means that writing had always been able to influence mankind more than any amount of sheer physical strength; writing undoubtedly makes a more lasting impact in the minds of the people than any form of physical demonstration. In the case of the latter the impact might be forceful though less lasting. Great thinkers, writers and philosophers have from time immemovial been able to hold sway over the minds of the people by means of their profound knowledge through their writings. For example, Socrates won the wrath of a powerful state, because of his great ability to hold spellbound the young through his discourses. Similarly, the writing of Voltaire and Rousseau inspired the French to rise up in revolt.

Neha's Interpretation

It is a common proverb which simply means that through writing it is possible to win more victories than by using physical force and weapons. When any good book is read it is possible to retain in our memory the message it contains. On the other hand, success achieved through physical might is not for mankind.

The above illustration reflects the differences between Bitto and Neha in their interpretation of the proverb. While Bitto delves deep in her interpretation, Neha states only the meaning.

According to Skinner, individual differences in learner behaviours are the result of the organism's genetic endowment and reinforcement. Thus, Skinner believed that defective genetic endowment and/or defective reinforcement contingencies in an individual's experience result in a failure to acquire a variety of learned behaviours.

The process of an individual's mental activities such as remembering, analysing, interpreting, reasoning, problem solving and thinking are cognitive domain behaviours and are essential for learning and achievement. How we think, what and how we remember, how we solve problem and how we create ideas are cognitive domain behaviours and individuals differ by these behaviours. Such differences are often identified by psychologists in terms of intelligence, aptitude, creating and academic achievement.

Individual differences are crucial for teachers who are responsible for guiding all forms of learning. In fact, many educators would suggest that the primary role of teachers is to provide education to meet the individual differences and to develop student cognitive process.

Do Individuals Differ in Intelligence?

Well, they do differ. But how? Differences are due to the differences in the level of general intellectual ability and the underlying cognitive process among individuals.

How do we identify differences in intelligence?

Using suitable intelligence tests we can measure and identify the difference. An intelligence test may contain sub-tests (sub-sections) and each sub-test represents a different set of ability. The scores obtained in all sub-tests are added up to obtain a single score to represent the general ability of the student. Thus, the single score obtained for each individual in a test is expressed in terms of **intelligence quotient** (IQ). IQ is a measure of intelligence and is defined as the ratio of mental age (average age of children who give correct responses/ answers in an intelligence test) to the chronological age (actual age) multiplied by 100 (to avoid fraction). Thus mental age is:

$$IQ = \frac{\text{Mental age}}{\text{Chronological age}} \times 100$$

IQ scores help us estimate individual differences by categorising individuals on the basis of their IQs. These differences have important consequences for learning and performance. Let us examine the different categories of students based on their intelligence level.

Gifted : Those students who possess IQs of 130 or above are called gifted students. They are superior in intelligence and have high ability to reason. As compared to other children, they can perform academic activities grasping concepts, memorising, perceiving, seeing relationships, generalising, dealing with abstract ideas, critical thinking and solving problems more effectively and quickly. They have a broad attention span that permits concentration and the ability for a high level of academic performance. They take initiative in intellectual work and follow complex directions. Such individuals are small in number as compared to normal or average children. Normal groups have those children whose IQs range from 90 to 110 and they are able to profit from regular school programmes with varying degrees of effort.

Disabled : There are children with **disability** due to low level to intellectual functioning or specific learning deficits. Children with low level or below-average intellectual functioning are called mentally retarded. The children with inadequate level of intelligence are impaired in their ability to learn and to adapt to the demands of society. Mentally retarded children are of different categories. They can be:

- **Border line** (IQ ranges 90-70) and **educable mentally retarded** (IQ ranges 70-50) children can perform academic activities but are slow in their learning. Special instructional strategies can help them to profit from learning activities. They can take care of themselves and live independently as adults.
- **Trainable mentally retarded** (IQ ranges 50-35) are capable of learning only certain rudimentary literacy materials and simple occupational skills. They possess some ability to take care of their personal needs and can be trained in daily living skills. Such children require special classes or schools to study in.
- **Severely retarded** (IQ below 35) have quite limited adaptive behaviour and are never found in school. They are dependent on their families for their personal needs.

Children with specific learning defects are called learning disabled group. They are normal to above-average on intelligence but have difficulties in one or more psychological processes involved in understanding or in using language or numbers (written or spoken). The difficulties manifest in their ability to listen, think, speak, read, write, spell or do mathematical calculations. These difficulties are identified as **aphasia** (difficulty in grasping spoken language), **dylesia** (difficulty in reading), **hyperlexia** (little or no comprehension), **dyscalculia** (difficulty in doing arithmetic) and **dysgraphia** (difficulty in writing). Some are hyperactive in the sense that they are excessively active inattentive and behave impulsively. They follow instructions poorly and do not often complete the assigned tasks.

Instructional Strategies for Handling Individual Differences

- Organise instruction for the development of cognitive process.
- Use existing cognitive level as base.
- Strengthen memory.
- Formulate level specific instructional strategy.
- Use individual meeting.
- Provide instructions to overcome learning disability.

Do Individuals Differ in Aptitude?

Yes, they do differ. An individual may have a mechanical aptitude, another may have an aptitude for mathematics or yet another may have an aptitude for language, music or athletics. Such differences are due to the differences in the combination of abilities related to the cognitive processes, and the sensory and psychomotor components. For instance, when we talk of mechanical aptitude, we may deal with ability for spatial relations, ability to acquire information on mechanical matters and ability to comprehend mechanical relations, besides sensory and psychomotor abilities. Similarly, when we discuss aptitude in music, we may identify ability for musical memory, pitch discrimination, loudness discrimination, time discrimination and judgement of rhythm. Likewise, abilities required for science or mathematics are different and each requires a separate set of abilities.

The differences in aptitude can be identified using aptitude tests. Aptitude tests for areas such as mechanical skills, mathematics, science, language, music and graphic art can be used to identify the aptitude of students in each area of performance. You might have heard of the use of aptitude tests in medicine, engineering, business management, law or teacher training for selection of students for studies in the respective fields. The aptitude test, in fact, provides a measure of the candidates promise or teachability in a field of study, say, medicine. In other words, the test would tell whether the candidate possesses the required aptitude or readiness to profit from studies in the concerned field of study.

Instructional Strategy for Handling Individual Differences

The suggested approach for handling individual differences is **adaptive instructional system**. In this approach at least two alternative instructional treatments are needed to ensure academic success. Which is the most appropriate instructional treatment for the student depends upon his or her existing level of aptitude (learning readiness). Students with high aptitude may choose unstructured instructional strategy. With minimum guidance from teacher, they may be encouraged to learn through the discovery oriented approach. You may use the inductive process but instructional treatment is essentially learner-centered.

In contrast, highly structured instructional treatment for low aptitude learners is designed in small units through sequential steps and feedback. Frequent summary and review with simplified illustration, analogy and precise explanation of concepts and principles to be learned will facilitate progressive learning. Periodic achievement and aptitude assessments and comparison of these scores with the aptitude scores obtained at the start of instruction would tell the degree to which each learner in the specific treatment group has achieved.

However, for those who are unable to profit from either of the alternative treatments presented above, **compensatory aptitude training** is suggested. This consists of directed reading skill, study habits, self-learning skills, note taking and related activities. The main aim of compensatory aptitude training is to develop readiness for entry into structured treatment. Periodic monitoring should be formulated to identify the students who reach the required level for entry into alternative treatment.

Do Learners Differ in their Academic Achievements?

They do differ, but how? We have seen that those who possess appropriate pre-requisite knowledge learn more effectively than those who lack such knowledge. Differences in pre-requisite knowledge possessed by students create differences in the attainment of knowledge. Further, knowledge is attained progressively. Progressive differences in knowledge attainment leads to cumulative differences in knowledge attainment and this form of differences is often called **Mathew Effect.** It means that academically rich get richer and those who are poor continue to be poor. Thus, differences in pre-requisites and cumulative knowledge lead to differences in the knowledge possessed by the students likewise, they also differ in their capabilities to manipulate the knowledge in a given situation and the differences are identified in terms of the abilities to apply, analyse, synthesise and evaluate knowledge. In fact, ability is an essential condition for learning and the abilities related to intelligence, aptitude and creativity are important for academic achievement. We have seen the instructional strategies for meeting the differences in intelligence, aptitude and creativity through classroom situations. It means that differences in intelligence, aptitude and creativity do create differences in academic achievement.

The differences in academic achievement can be identified using an achievement test in the concerned subject. However, if the achievement test contains only knowledge level items (questions), it tells only knowledge level differences. On the other hand, if it contains items (questions) on knowledge and capabilities—comprehension, application, analysis, synthesis and evaluation—the various levels of differences can be identified. Besides, the total marks, each level-wise total is needed to identify the strengths and weaknesses of every student as well as the differences among students. As a teacher, if you know the strengths and weaknesses of your students in a subject, you may be able to adopt appropriate instructional strategies to suit their strenghts and weaknesses in that subject.

Apart from these achievement differences are quite often identified in terms of categories of achievers by classifying students as high, average and low achievers. Though there is no strict cut-off points, these categories can be created using marks. High achievers are those who possess higher level of knowledge and capabilities (say, with marks 66% and above) than the rest and those who possess average level of knowledge and capabilities (say, with marks 36% to 65%) are called average achievers. On the other extreme, you may find learners with low level knowledge and capabilities (with 35% and below marks). They are called low achievers. If you are interested in identifying the high, average and low achievers in a subject, say Science or language, the categories are created using the marks obtained in the concerned subject. However, categories can also be created based on the overall achievement in a class.

As a teacher, you may be curious to know the strategies for meeting the achievement differences in your classroom or the challenges posed by the strengths and weaknesses of the students in teaching-learning situations. Let us discuss important instructional strategies.

What are Instructional Strategies?

Let us discuss the major strategies to cope up with the differences in academic achievement.

- Provide appropriate pre-requisites to organise and learn new information.
- Use visual aids.
- Use analogy, example and illustration.
- Ensure learner's active involvement in learning.
- Periodic assessment.

EVALUATION AND ASSESSMENT

Evaluation

Evaluation, particularly educational evaluation is a series of activities designed to measure the effectiveness of the teaching-learning systems as a whole. According to Mary Thorpe (1980), "Evaluation is the collection, analysis and interpretation of information about any aspect of a programme of education." Teaching-learning process is a continuous activity. It needs to be evaluated from beginning to end. Evaluation during the learning process (continuous assessment), often termed as "formative evaluation", is important for learners and teachers alike.

The bases of evaluation are learning objectives, performance standards and achievement tests on the one hand, and learners' and experts' opinions on the other. Evaluation helps to build an educational programme, assess its achievement and improve upon its effectiveness. It also provides valuable feedback on the design, development and implementation of the programme. It is, of course, an important component of the teaching-learning process. It helps in making the value judgement, determining educational status, or measuring achievement of learners.

The scope of evaluation in schools extents to almost all the areas of learner's personality development. It includes both scholastic and non-scholastic areas. It reveals the strengths and weaknesses of the learners, so that the learners have better opportunity to understand and improve themselves.

Evaluation is helpful to teachers also. It provides feedback to them to reshape their teaching strategies according to the needs of the learners. Evaluation in education in general and in distance education in particular becomes imperative to know as to what extent the goals of education have been achieved.

Thus, evaluation is not merely assigning grades to learners. It is a continuous process of acquiring and processing information in order to improve one's learning and to assess decisions made in designing an instructional system. If we analyse the above statement we easily notice that it has three important implications for the entire teaching-learning system. They are as follows:

1. Evaluation is a continuous process and not a one time performance measurement, effected at the end of a course/programme. It starts at the stage of curriculum development and continues until the instruction ends.
2. Evaluation process is goal-directed. It is aimed at finding ways and means to improve learning and thereby to achieve learning objectives more effectively and more efficiently.
3. Evaluation requires the use of accurate and appropriate measuring instructions to collect information for taking decisions about the quality and operation of education.

It is clear that in designing an effective learning system, one of the earliest steps we need to take is to prepare a comprehensive evaluation plan, which should be developed soon after the learning objectives have been formulated. This practice will help us to:

- determine whether the objectives are attainable or need revisions before we start designing the instructional system;
- collect data/information in a form that suits our purposes adequately and at a time when it is available, otherwise the opportunity to collect specific information may be lost; and
- have sufficient time to test the effectiveness of a design.

Continuous and Comprehensive Evaluation (CCE)

Continuous and Comprehensive Evaluation (CCE) refers to a system of school based evaluation of a student that covers all aspects of a student development. It is a developmental process of student which emphasizes on two fold objectives. These objectives are continuity in evaluation and assessment of broad based learning and behaviourial outcomes on the other.

The term **'continuous'** is meant to emphasise that evaluation of identified aspects of students **'growth and development'** is a continuous process rather than an event, built into the total teaching-learning process and spread over the entire span of academic session. It means regularity of assessment, frequency of unit testing, diagnosis of learning gaps, use of corrective measures, retesting and feedback of evidence to teachers and students for their self evaluation.

The second term **'comprehensive'** means that the scheme attempts to cover both the scholastic and the co-scholastic aspects of the students' growth and development. Since abilities, attitudes and aptitudes can manifest themselves in forms other than the written word, the term refers to application of variety of tools and techniques (both testing and non-testing) and aims at assessing a learner's development in areas of learning, like:

- Knowledge
- Understanding
- Applying
- Analyzing
- Evaluating
- Creating

Objectives of CCE

- To help develop cognitive, psychomotor and affective skills.
- To lay emphasis on thought process and de-emphasise memorization.
- To make evaluation an integral part of teaching-learning process.
- To use evaluation for improvement of students achievement and teaching-learning strategies on the basis of regular diagnosis followed by remedial instructions.
- To use evaluation as a quality control device to maintain desired standard of performance.
- To determine social utility, desirability or effectiveness of a programme and take appropriate decisions about the learner, the process of learning and the learning environment.
- To make the process of teaching and learning a learner-centered activity.

Features of CCE

- The **'continuous'** aspect of CCE takes care of **'continual'** and **'periodicity'** aspect of evaluation.

- Continual means assessment of students in the beginning of instructions (placement evaluation) and assessment during the instructional process (**formative evaluation**) done informally using multiple techniques of evaluation.
- Periodicity means assessment of performance done frequently at the end of unit/term (**summative evaluation**).
- The **'comprehensive'** component of CCE takes care of assessment of all round development of the child's personality. It includes assessment in **Scholastic as well as Co-Scholastic** aspects of the pupil's growth.
- Scholastic aspects include curricular areas or subject specific areas, whereas Co-Scholastic aspects include Life Skills, Co-Curricular Activities, Attitudes and Values.
- Assessment in Scholastic areas is done informally and formally using multiple techniques of evaluation continually and periodically. The diagnostic evaluation takes place at the end of unit/term test. The causes of poor performance in some units are diagnosed using diagnostic tests. These are followed with appropriate interventions followed by retesting.
- Assessment in Co-Scholastic areas is done using multiple techniques on the basis of identified criteria, while assessment in Life Skills is done on the basis of Indicators of Assessment and Checklists.

Functions of CCE

- It helps the teacher to organize effective teaching strategies.
- Continuous evaluation helps in regular assessment to the extent and degree of Learner's progress (ability and achievement with reference to specific Scholastic and Co-Scholastic areas).
- Continuous evaluation serves to diagnose weaknesses and permits the teacher to ascertain an individual learner's strengths and weaknesses and her needs. It provides immediate feedback to the teacher, who can then decide whether a particular unit or concept needs a discussion again in the whole class or whether a few individuals are in need of remedial instruction.
- By continuous evaluation, children can know their strengths and weaknesses. It provides the child a realistic self assessment of how he/she studies. It can motivate children to develop good study habits, to correct errors, and to direct their activities towards the achievement of desired goals. It helps a learner to determine the areas of instruction in where more emphasis is required.
- Continuous and comprehensive evaluation identifies areas of aptitude and interest. It helps in identifying changes in attitudes and value systems.
- It helps in making decisions for the future, regarding choice of subjects, courses and careers.
- It provides information/reports on the progress of students in Scholastic and Co-Scholastic areas and thus helps in predicting the future success of the learner.

Continuous evaluation helps in bringing awareness of the achievement to the child, teachers and parents from time-to-time. They can look into the probable cause of the fall in performance if any, and may take remedial measures of instruction in which more emphasis is required. Many times, because of some personal reasons, family problems or adjustment problems, the children start neglecting their studies, resulting in sudden drop in their performance. If the teacher, child and parents do not notice the sudden drop in the performance of the child in academics, it could result in a permanent deficiency in the childs' learning.

The major emphasis of CCE is on the continuous growth of students ensuring their intellectual, emotional, physical, cultural and social development and therefore, it will not be merely limited to assessment of learner's scholastic attainments. CCE uses assessment as a means of motivating learners to provide feedback and follow up work to improve upon the learning in the classroom and to present a comprehensive picture of a learner's profile. It is this that has led to the emergence of the concept of **School Based Continuous and Comprehensive Evaluation.**

Scholastic and Co-Scholastic Assessment

In order to have Continuous and Comprehensive Evaluation, both Scholastic and Co-Scholastic aspects need to be given due recognition. Such a holistic assessment requires maintaining an ongoing and comprehensive profile for each learner that is honest, encouraging and discreet. While teachers frequently reflect, plan and implement remedial strategies, the child's ability to retain and articulate what has been learned over a period of time also requires periodic assessment. These assessments can take many forms but all of them should be as comprehensive and discreet as possible. **Weekly**, **fortnightly**, or **quarterly** reviews (depending on the learning area), that do not openly compare one learner with another are generally recommended. The objective is to promote and enhance not just learning and retention among children, but their soft skills as well.

Scholastic Assessment

The objectives of the Scholastic domain are:-

- Desirable behaviour related to the learner's knowledge, understanding, application, evaluation, analysis and the ability to apply it in an unfamiliar situation.
- To improve the teaching learning process.
- Assessment should be both **Formative** and **Summative**.

Summative and Formative Assessment

Assessment is often divided into formative and summative categories for the purpose of considering different objectives for assessment practices.

Summative Assessment

Summative assessment is intended to measure learning outcomes and report those outcomes to students, parents and administrators. In an educational setting, it generally occurs at the conclusion of a class, course, semester or academic year. In the context of a course summative assessments are typically used to assign students a course grade. It is also referred to in a learning context as **"assessment of learning"**. **Performance-based assessment** is similar to summative assessment, as it focuses on achievement. A well-defined task is identified and students are asked to create, produce, or do something, often in settings that involve real-world application of knowledge and skills. Proficiency is demonstrated by providing an extended response. Performance formats are further differentiated into products and performances. The performance may result in a product, such as a painting, portfolio, paper, or exhibition, or it may consist of a performance, such as a speech, athletic skill, musical recital, or reading.

Definitions of Summative Assessment

- "Good summative assessments—tests and other graded evaluations—must be demonstrably reliable, valid, and free of bias" (Angelo and Cross, 1993).
- '...assessment (that) has increasingly been used to sum up learning' (Black and William, 1999).
- '...looks at past achievements ... adds procedures or tests to existing work ... involves only marking and feedback grades to student ... is separated from teaching ... is carried out at intervals when achievement has to be summarized and reported.' (Harlen, 1998).

Features of Summative Assessment

- Assessment of learning.
- Generally taken by students at the end of a unit or semester to demonstrate the **"sum"** of what they have or have not learned.
- Summative assessment methods are the most traditional way of evaluating student work.

Formative Assessment

Formative assessment is generally carried out throughout a course or project. In an educational setting, formative assessment is used by teachers to consider approaches to teaching and next steps for individual learners and the class, and would not necessarily be used for grading purposes. Formative assessment, also referred to as **"educative assessment"** or **"assessment for learning"**, is used to aid learning. Assessment for learning is defined as "all those activities undertaken by teachers and/or students, which provide information to be used as feedback to modify the teaching and learning activities in which they are engaged" (Black and William 2004).

Definitions of Formative Assessment

- '... often means no more than that the assessment is carried out frequently and is planned at the same time as teaching'. (Black and William, 1999)
- '... provides feedback which leads to students recognizing the (learning) gap and closing it ... it is forward looking ...' (Harlen, 1998).
- '... includes both feedback and self-monitoring'. (Sadler, 1989)
- '... is used essentially to get a feedback into the teaching and learning process.' (Tunstall and Gipps, 1996)

Features of Formative Assessment

- Is diagnostic and remedial.
- Makes provision for effective feedback.
- Provides a platform for the active involvement of students in their own learning.
- Enables teachers to adjust teaching to take account of the results of assessment.
- Recognizes the profound influence assessment has on the motivation and self-esteem of students, both of which are crucial influences on learning.
- Recognizes the need for students to be able to assess themselves and understand how to improve.
- Builds on students' prior knowledge and experience in designing what is taught.
- Incorporates varied learning styles to decide how and what to teach.
- Encourages students to understand the criteria that will be used to judge their work.

- Offers an opportunity to students to improve their work after they get the feedback.
- Helps student to support their peer group and vice-versa.

A common form of formative assessment is **"diagnostic assessment"**. Diagnostic assessment measures a student's current knowledge and skills for the purpose of identifying a suitable program of learning. **"Self-assessment"** is a form of diagnostic assessment which involves students assessing themselves. **"Forward-looking assessment"** asks those being assessed to consider themselves in hypothetical future situations.

Co-Scholastic Assessment

The desirable behaviour related to learner's life skills, attitudes, interests, values, co-curricular activities and physical health are described as skills to be acquired in co-scholastic domain.

The process of assessing the students' progress in achieving objectives related to scholastic and co-scholastic domain is called comprehensive evaluation. It has been observed that usually under the scholastic domain such as knowledge and understanding of the facts, concepts, principles etc. of a subject are assessed. The Co-Scholastic elements are either altogether excluded from the evaluation process or they are not given adequate attention. For making the evaluation comprehensive, both Scholastic and Co-Scholastic aspects should be given importance. Simple and manageable means of assessment of Co-Scholastic aspects of growth must be included in the comprehensive evaluation scheme.

Comprehensive evaluation would necessitate the use of a variety of tools and techniques. This will be so because both different and specific areas of learner's growth can be evaluated through certain special techniques.

School Based CCE

School based Evaluation is held at school level unlike external examination conducted by the Boards of School Education. This is done by the teachers according to the schedule developed by the school and guidelines given by the Board. Though this evaluation has been done at school level all along, certain shortcomings have crept into this system. These shortcomings can be attributed to various factors. The basic factor is the misconception of teachers regarding the place of evaluation and its importance in the educational process. The other factor has been the imitation of the practice of external examination which is generally held at the end of the session.

In the School Based System of evaluation, the focus on the purpose of assessment has changed. Now, it includes readiness testing, screening of development, evaluation of performance in cognitive, affective and psychomotor domains more frequently, systematically and effectively.

In other words, School Based Evaluation is child-centred, school-centred and multidimensional evaluation. Hence, in its true spirit, it triggers an all round development of the learner. It encourages all kinds of learning in life both inside the school as well as outside it. It is child-centered as it attempts to consider the learner as a unique entity for its individual pattern of development. It builds on individual child's abilities, progress and development in achieving already set goals and objectives of education as an individual and not just his/her position in relation to other learners.

Further, this evaluation helps a learner to use his/her potential in a better manner and also provides insight to the teachers to discover the methods which may be helpful to the individual learner in resolving his/her problems and difficulties.

Besides being ***child-centred***, this evaluation is ***school-centred*** as well. It means that no outside agency interferes in this evaluation process. It is entirely school based and done by the teacher. The teacher is trusted and given full responsibility of evaluating students with the brief that the teacher knows best about his/her students.

School Based Evaluation is ***multidimensional***. Its multidimensional nature is reflected in recognizing and taking care of learners' social, emotional, physical, intellectual and other areas of development which are interrelated and cannot be considered in isolation. It also calls for the use of multiple techniques and tools of evaluation.

Aim of School Based CCE

- Elimination of chance element and subjectivity (as far as possible), de-emphasis on memorization, encouraging comprehensive evaluation incorporating both Scholastic and Co-Scholastic aspects of learners development.
- Continuous evaluation spread over the total span of the instructional time as an integral built-in aspect of the total teaching-learning process.
- Functional and meaningful declaration of results for effective use by teachers, students, parents and the society.
- Wider uses of test results for purposes not merely of the assessment of levels of pupils' achievements and proficiencies, but mainly for their improvement, thorough diagnosis and remedial/enrichment programmes.

- Improvement in the mechanics of conducting examinations for realizing a number of other allied purposes.
- Introduction of concomitant changes in instructional materials and methodology.
- Introduction of the semester system.
- The use of grades in place of marks in determining and declaring the level of pupil performance and proficiency.

Its Characteristics

School Based Evaluation has the following characteristics:

- Is broader, more comprehensive and continuous than traditional system.
- Aims primarily to help learners for systematic learning and development.
- Takes care of the needs of the learner as responsible citizens of the future.
- Is more transparent, futuristic and provides more scope for association among learners, teachers and parents.

School based evaluation provides opportunities to teachers to **know the following about their learners:**

- What they learn?
- How they learn?
- What type of difficulties/limitations they face in working in tandem?
- What do the children think?
- What do the children feel?
- What are their interests and dispositions?

The focus has shifted to developing a deep learning environment. There is a paradigm shift in the pedagogy and competencies from 'controlling' to 'enriching' to 'empowering' schools.

Traditional Schooling	Enriching Schooling	Empowering Schooling
• Teacher centred	• Student centred	• Experience centred
• Subjects and classes-teacher directed	• Self directed	• Virtual authenticity
• Sorting and ranking individuals	• Continuous assessment	• Multi literacies
Competency:	**Competency:**	**Competency:**
• Memory	• Critical thinking	• Risk taking
• Competitive	• Collaborative	• Ethical
	• Creative	• Interactive

Implementing School Based Assessment would mean:

- Elimination of chance element and subjectivity (as far as possible), de-emphasis of memorization, encouraging Comprehensive evaluation incorporating both scholastic and co-scholastic aspects of learners development.
- Continuous evaluation spread over the total span of the instructional time as an integral built-in aspect of the total teaching-learning process.
- Functional and meaningful declaration of results for effective use by teachers, students, parents and the society.
- Wider uses of test results for purposes not merely of the assessment of levels of pupils' achievements and proficiencies, but mainly for its improvement, through diagnosis and remedial/enrichment programmes.
- Improvements in the mechanics of conducting examinations for realizing a number of other allied purposes.
- Introduction of concomitant changes in instructional materials and methodology.
- Introduction of the semester system from the secondary stage onwards.
- The use of grades in place of marks in determining and declaring the level of pupil performance and proficiency.

The above goals are relevant for both external examination and evaluation in schools.

Shortcoming of Traditional External Examination

- It is a one shot examination at the end of a year at the terminal stage of schooling.
- It mainly evaluates only the scholastic aspects of learning of the students.
- It does not evaluate all the abilities of the children. On the basis of marks obtained in written examination the students are declared pass or fail and further classified into predetermined divisions.

- Pass and fail system causes frustration and is inhumane because the failed candidates come to feel that they are good for nothing.
- Co-scholastic areas are almost totally ignored and have no place in the currently prevalent scheme of education and evaluation.
- The practice of testing of untaught content also reflects poor learning achievement.
- Only limited techniques of evaluation without potential for judging a student are being used.
- The aim of evaluation is to improve learner's quality which is not served by external examination.
- The current practice of awarding marks suffers from many discrepancies due to variety of errors.
- The varied ranges of obtained scores of students in different subjects create the problem in declaring reliable results.
- Analysis and interpretation of test results is not done in a scientific way.

School Based Continuous and Comprehensive Evaluation System should be Established to:

- reduce stress on children.
- make evaluation comprehensive and regular.
- provide space for the teacher for creative teaching.
- provide a tool of diagnosis and remediation.
- produce learners with greater skills.

Four Assessment Paradigms

Assessment *of* Learning

The 'assessment **of** learning' is defined as a process whereby someone attempts to describe and quantify the knowledge, attitudes or skills possessed by another. Teacher direction is paramount and the student has little involvement in the design or implementation of the assessment process in these circumstances.

- Teacher designs learning
- Teacher collects evidence
- Teacher judges what has been learnt (and what has not been learnt)

Assessment *for* Learning

The 'assessment **for** learning' involves increased level of student autonomy, but not without teacher guidance and collaboration. The assessment **for** learning is sometimes seen as being akin to 'formative assessment'. There is more emphasis towards giving useful advice to the student and less emphasis on the giving of marks and the grading function.

- Teacher designs learning
- Teacher designs assessment with feedback to student
- Teacher judges what has been learnt (student develops insight into what has not)

Assessment *as* Learning

The 'assessment **as** learning' is perhaps more connected with diagnostic assessment and can be constructed with more of an emphasis on peer learning. Assessment **as** learning generates opportunities for self assessment and peer assessment. Students take on increased responsibility to generate quality information about their learning and that of others.

- Teacher and student co-construct learning
- Teacher and student co-construct assessment
- Teacher and student co-construct learning progress map

Assessment **for** learning and assessment **as** learning activities should be deeply embedded in teaching and learning and be the source of interactive feedback, allowing students to adjust, re-think and re-learn.

Assessment *in* Learning

The 'assessment **in** learning' places the question at the centre of teaching and learning. It deflects the teaching from its focus on a 'correct answer' to a focus on 'a fertile question'. Through enquiry students engage in processes that generates feedback about their learning, which come from multiple sources and activities. It contributes to the construction of other learning activities, line of enquiry and the generation of other questions.

- Student as the centre of learning
- Student monitors, assesses and reflects on learning
- Student initiates demonstration of learning (to self and others)
- Teacher as coach and mentor.

Teachers and students need to understand the purpose of each assessment strategy. The overall assessment 'package' being used by learners and teachers should accurately capture, generate and use meaningful learning information to generate deep learning and understanding.

ASSESSING LEARNERS

Any meaningful report on the quality and extent of a child's learning needs to be comprehensive. We need a curriculum whose creativity, innovativeness, and development of the whole being, the hallmark of a good education makes uniform tests that assess memorised facts and textbook-based learning obsolete. We need to redefine and seek new parameters for and ways of evaluation and feedback. In addition to the learner's achievements in specific subject areas that lend themselves to testing easily, assessment would need to encompass attitudes to learning, interest, and the ability to learn independently.

ASSESSMENT IN THE COURSE OF TEACHING

Preparing report cards is a way for the teacher to think about each individual child and review what she/he has learnt during the term, and what she/he needs to work on and improve. To be able to write such report cards, teachers would need to think about each individual child, and hence pay attention to them during their everyday teaching and interaction. One does not need special tests for this; learning activities themselves provide the basis for such ongoing observational and qualitative assessments of children. Maintaining a daily diary based on observation helps in continuous and comprehensive evaluation. An extract from the diary of a teacher for a week notes the following: ''Kiran enjoyed his work. He took an instant liking to the books that were informative and brief. He says that he likes simple and clear language. In noting down facts, he goes for short answers. He says that it helps him understand things easily. He favours a practical approach.'' Similarly, keeping samples and notes of the child's work at different stages provides both the teacher and the learner herself or himself with a systematic record of his/her learning progress.

The belief that assessment must lead to finding learning difficulties to then be remediated is often very impractical and not founded on a sound understanding of pedagogic practice. Problems regarding conceptual development cannot and do not wait for formal tests in order to be detected. A teacher can, in the course of teaching itself, come to know of such problems by asking questions that make children think or by giving them small assignments. She can then attend to them in the process of teaching—by ensuring that her planning is flexible and responsive to the learners and their learning.

CURRICULAR AREAS THAT CANNOT BE 'TESTED FOR MARKS'

Each area of the curriculum may not lend itself to being 'tested'; it may even be antithetical to the nature of learning in the curricular area. This includes areas such as work, health, yoga, physical education, music and art. While the skill-based component of physical education and yoga could be tested, the health aspect needs continuous and qualitative assessments. Currently, this has the effect of making these subjects and activities 'less important' in the curriculum; these areas are inadequately provided for in terms of material resources and curricular planning, and marked by a lack of seriousness. Further, the time allocated for them is also frequently sacrificed to accommodate special classes. This is a serious compromise with parts of the curriculum that have deep educational significance and potential.

Even if 'marks' cannot be given, children can be assessed for their development in these areas. Participation, interest, and level of involvement, and the extent to which abilities and skills have been honed, are some markers that can help teachers to gauge the benefits of what children learn and gain through such activities. Asking children to self-report on their learning can also provide teachers with insight into children's educational progress and give them feedback on improving curriculum or pedagogy.

DESIGN AND CONDUCT OF ASSESSMENT

Assessments and examinations must be credible, and based on valid ways of gauging learning.

As long as examinations and tests assess children's ability to remember and recall textbook knowledge, all attempts to redirect the curriculum towards learning will be thwarted. First, tests in knowledge-based subject areas must be able to gauge what children have learnt, and their ability to use this knowledge for problem solving and application in the real world. In addition, they must also be able to test the processes of thinking to gauge if the learner has also learnt where to find information, how to use new information, and to analyse and evaluate the same.

The types of questions that are set for assessment need to go beyond what is given in the book. Often children's learning is restricted as teachers do not accept their answers if they are different from what is presented in the guidebooks.

Questions that are open-ended and challenging could also be used. Designing good test items and questions is an art, and teachers should spend time thinking about and devising such questions. The interest and ability of teachers to design good questions can be promoted through district—or state-level competitions. All question papers must be designed graded for difficulty in order to permit all children to experience a level of success, and to gain confidence in their ability to answer and solve problems.

Trying to devise a good and effective open-book examination can be a challenge that we must try to take up in our curricular efforts at all levels of school. This would require teachers and examination setters to emphasise the interpretation and application of learning over the arguments and facts that can be located in the book. There have been successful demonstrations that such examinations can be carried out on a large scale, and that teachers can themselves be trusted with moderating the results of such examinations. In this way, the assessment of projects and lab work can also be made credible and sound.

It is important that after receiving their corrected papers, children rewrite the answers and that these are again reviewed by teachers to ensure that children have learnt and gained something out of the ordeal.

Competition is motivating, but it is an extrinsic rather than intrinsic form of motivation. It is, of course, much easier to establish and to manipulate, and therefore frequently resorted to by teachers and school systems as a way creating and nurturing the drive for excellence. Schools begin 'ranking' children as early as their pre-primary years as a way of inculcating in them a competitive spirit. Such a competitive drive has several negative side effects on learning, often superficial learning is sufficient to create and maintain impressions, and over time students lose their ability to take initiative or do things for the fulfilment of one's own interest; hence, areas that cannot be 'marked' are neglected. This has unhealthy consequences for classroom culture, making children individualistic and unsuited to team work. There is an absurd and unnecessary importance given to term examinations, often accompanied by extreme arrangements of invigilation and secrecy. While the physical and psychological effects of this may not be readily visible until middle school, they frequently lead to high levels of stress in children, and cause early burnout. Schools and teachers need to ask themselves whether there is really much to be gained out of such practices and to what extent learning requires such systems of marking and ranking.

SELF-ASSESSMENT AND FEEDBACK

The role of assessment is to gauge the progress that both learner and teacher have made towards achieving the aims that have been set and appraising how this could be done better. Opportunity for feedback, leading to revision and improvement of performance, should constantly be available, without exams and evaluations being used as a threat to study.

Grading and correction carried out in the presence of students and providing feedback on the answers they get right and wrong, and why. Asking children about why they answered what they did assists teachers in going beyond the written answer to engage with children's thinking. Such processes also take away the frightening judgemental quality of marks obtained in a test, and enable children to understand and focus on their mistakes and learn through these mistakes. Sometimes head teachers object, claiming that correction in the presence of the child reduces 'objectivity'. This is a misplaced concern for 'objectivity', stemming from a competitive system that believes in judging children. Such a concern for 'objectivity' is misplaced in evaluation, which is consistent with educational goals.

Not only learning outcomes but also learning experiences themselves must be evaluated. Learners happily comment on the totality of their experience. Exercises, both individual and collective, can be designed to enable them to reflect on and assess their learning experiences. Such experiences also provide them with self-regulatory capabilities essential for 'learning to learn'. Such information is also valuable feedback to the teacher, and can be used to modify the learning system as a whole.

Every classroom interaction with children requires their evaluation of their own work, and a discussion with them about what should be tested and the ways of finding out whether the competencies are being developed or not. Even very young children are able to give correct assessments of what they can or cannot do well. The role of teaching is to provide an opportunity to each child to learn to the best of his or her ability and provide learning experiences that develop cognitive qualities, physical well-being and athletic qualities, as also affective and aesthetic qualities.

Report cards need to present to children and parents a comprehensive and holistic view of the child's development in many fields. Teachers must be able to say things about each child/student, that conveys to them a sense of individualised attention, reaffirms a positive self-image, and communicates personal goals for them to work towards. Whether it is marks or grades that are reported, a qualitative statement by the teacher is necessary to support the assessment. Only through such a relationship with each child can any teacher succeed in influencing him/her, and contributing to his/her learning. Along with the teacher assessing each child, each student could also assess himself or herself and include this self-assessment in the report card.

Currently, many report cards carry information on subject areas and have nothing to say about other aspects of the child's development, including health, physical fitness and abilities in games, social skills, and abilities in art and craft. Qualitative statements about these aspects of children's education and development would provide a more holistic assessment of educational concerns.

AREAS THAT REQUIRE FRESH THINKING

There are many areas of the curriculum that can be assessed but for which we still do not have reliable and efficient instruments. This includes assessing learning that is carried out in groups, and learning in areas such as theatre, work and craft where skills and competencies develop over longer time scales and require careful observation.

Continuous and comprehensive evaluation has frequently been cited as the only meaningful kind of evaluation. This also requires much more careful thinking through about when it is to be employed in a system effectively. Such evaluation places a lot of demand on teachers' time and ability to maintain meticulous records if it is to be meaningfully executed and if it is to have any reliability as an assessment. If this simply increases stress on children by reducing all their activities into items for assessment, or making them experience the teacher's 'power', then it defeats the purpose of education. Unless a system is adequately geared for such assessment, it is better for teachers to engage in more limited forms of evaluation, but incorporating into them more features that will make the assessment a meaningful record of learning.

Finally, there is a need to evolve and maintain credibility in assessment so that they perform their function of providing feedback in a meaningful way.

ASSESSMENT AT DIFFERENT STAGES

ECCE and Classes I and II of the Elementary Stage: At this stage, assessment must be purely qualitative judgements of children's activities in various domains and an assessment of the status of their health and physical development, based on observations through everyday interactions. On no account should they be made to take any form of test, oral or written.

Class III to Class VIII of the Elementary Stage: A variety of methods may be used, including oral and written tests and observations. Children should be aware that they are being assessed, but this must be seen by them as a part of the teaching process and not as a fearful constant threat. Grades or marks along with qualitative judgements of achievement and areas requiring attention are essential at this stage. Children's own self-evaluation can also be a part of the report card from Class V onwards. Rather than examinations, there could be short tests from time-to-time, which are criterion based. Term-wise examinations could be commenced from Class VII onwards when children are more psychologically ready to study large chunks of material and, to spend a few hours in an examination room, working at answering questions. Again, the progress card must indicate general observations on health and nutrition, specific observations on the overall progress of the learner, and information and advice for the parents.

Class IX to Class XII of the Secondary and Higher Secondary Stages: Assessment may be based more on tests, examinations and project reports for the knowledge-based areas of the curriculum, along with self-assessment. Other areas would be assessed through observation and also through self-evaluation.

Reports could include much more analysis about the students, various skill/knowledge areas and percentiles, etc. This would assist them by pointing out the areas of study that they need to focus on, and also help them by providing a basis for further choices that they make regarding what to study thereafter.

CONCEPT OF INCLUSIVE EDUCATION & UNDERSTANDING CHILDREN WITH SPECIAL NEEDS

CONCEPT OF INCLUSIVE EDUCATION

Every child is special for his/her parent and, every child has a special need for love, acceptance and a feeling of belongingness. Here, we call **children with special needs** to those who are "different" from their cohorts. They are born equal with some limitations and with the help of inclusion be able to actively participate as equal citizens in all aspects of society and community life. Thus, children with special needs refer to "all those children who require adaptations to the normal process of education due to problems of vision, hearing, movement, learning and intellect." In other words, these children have some kind of **disability**.

Inclusive Education denotes that all children irrespective of their strengths and weaknesses will be part of the mainstream education. Thus, inclusive education means, "the act of ensuring that all children despite their differences, receive the opportunity of being part of the same classroom as other children of their age, and in the process get the opportunity to being exposed to the curriculum to their optimal potential."

EDUCATIONAL PROVISIONS FOR CHILDREN WITH SPECIAL NEEDS

The last two decades of the 19th century has witnessed the knowledge and processes of educating the disabled children through Christian Missionaries. The first school for the deaf was established in Mumbai in 1883 and the first school for the blind in Amritsar in 1887. At that time, it was believed that children with disabilities could not be educated alongwith normal children. Therefore, education to disabled children was offered through special school. This trend continued early sixties of the last century with the help of some international agencies who developed programme of integrated education. Here, children disabilities were placed in regular school so that they could study alongwith their non-disabled 'peers". The integrated education adopts various models for service deliver. Presently the emphasis is on the need to provide education for all in appropriate environment with inclusive philosophy through inclusive education.

INTEGRATED EDUCATION FOR THE DISABLED CHILDREN (IEDC)

With the development of science and technology and improvement in Medical Services and Aggressive neo-natal intervention has ensured that a large number of babies who would earlier have not survived but often with different abilities. The number of differently abled children is on the increasing trend but it is not possible to create the required number of special schools throughout the country to meet this challenge due to the high cost and also due to the fact that the population is so scattered. The best alternative under these situations is to make use of the infrastructural facilities already present in terms of regular schools and integrate children into the mainstream of education.

Consequent on the success of international institutions in introducing differently abled children in regular schools, the planning commission, Govt. of India, in 1971 includes in its plan a programme for integrated education. In 1974, the Union Government introduced a scheme called "Integrated Schools" to do just this. This scheme was later revised and a plan of action formulated. The important aims of IEDC includes:

- Provide educational opportunity to differently abled children in regular schools.
- Facilitate retention of differently abled in the school system.

- Integrate children from special school to common schools.

The scope of the scheme of IEDC includes pre-school training, counselling for the parents, and special training in skills for all kinds of differently abled children. It provides facilities in the form of books, stationary, uniforms and allowances for transport, reader and escort etc.

Project Integrated Education for the Disabled (PIED)

This scheme was launched by MHRD Govt. of India in collaboration with UNICEF in 1987 to strengthen the integration of differently abled into regular schools. Under this scheme, a cluster instead of individual school is given importance. This scheme is an improvement over the special schools in one or many ways and provides a way towards universalisation of elementary education and Education for All including for differently abled children.

Assumption About Integrated Education

Integrated education assumes a process of bringing disabled children into mainstream schools, where the system remains the same. As per the system, the child is the problem. So, it is essential to change the child where the resources are focused on the individual child. The failure is due to the child's problem; he is not able, not ready, not good enough to cope up with the system.

In integrated education; it is the children with disabilities who are seen as the problem, who must be "fixed", "changed" & "adapted" to suit the existing regular, mainstream school. It is the disabled child who is seen as a square peg in a round table. The system remains the same. The onus for successful integration therefore, is on the disabled child.

Assumption About Inclusive Education

Assumptions of inclusive education is opposite to integrated education. Inclusive education assumes that changes the system to fit the child. It is essential to addresses all types of individual needs, not just disability. Teachers and schools are held responsible for children's learning. It focuses on flexibility of curriculum, teacher training and change in environmental. Failure is the problem with the system not with the child. It is quite essential to assumes that all children can learn and that all children need their learning to be supported in diverse ways.

In this model of inclusive education, it is not the child, but the education system, which is seen as a problem. Therefore, it is the system (with all its components) with should be changed, modified & made flexible enough to accommodate the diverse needs of all learners, including children with disabilities. The onus for success is therefore on the flexibility of the system. It focuses on the environment, as the "disabling" cause because it fails to provide appropriate access to equal opportunities for all persons to participate fully in social life.

Though integrated education of differently abled children has gained momentum all over the country since 1974, there are some other possibilities too for these children to get education. For example, the NIOS (National Institute of Open Schooling) offers education which have the advantage of being specially adopted to the needs of every child as well as aimed at giving the child every opportunity to progress at his/her pace. Another example is alternative schooling and community-based rehabilitation programmes.

EDUCATION FOR A COHESIVE SOCIETY

Despite more than half a century of independence, India is struggling for freedom from various kinds of biases and imbalances such as rural/urban, rich/poor, and differences on the basis of caste, religion, ideology, gender etc. Education can play a very significant role in minimising and finally eliminating these differences by providing equality of access to quality education and opportunity.

Equality of opportunity means ensuring that every individual receives suitable education at a pace and through methods suited to his/her being. Children of the disadvantaged, and socially discriminated groups and also those suffering from specific challenges must be paid special attention.

Provision for equal opportunity to all not only in access, but also in the conditions for success is a precondition for the promotion of equality. The curriculum must create an awareness of the inherent equality of all with a view to removing prejudices and complexes transmitted through the social environment and the factor of birth.

EDUCATION OF GIRLS

Equality among sexes is a fundamental right under the constitution of India. The state, however, also has the right to exercise positive protective discrimination in favour of the disadvantaged population groups including women. Emphasis in education has moved from 'Equality of Educational Opportunity' (NPE, 1968) to 'Education for Women's Equality and Empowerment' (1986). As a result, the curricular and training strategies for the education of girls now demand more attention. Besides, making education accessible to more and more girls, especially rural girls, removing all gender discrimination and gender bias in school curriculum, textbooks and the process of transaction is absolutely necessary. There is a need to develop and implement gender inclusive and gender sensitive curricular strategies to nurture a generation of girls and boys who are equally competent and are sensitive to one another, and grow up in a caring and sharing mode as equals, and not as adversaries.

EDUCATION OF LEARNERS FROM DISADVANTAGED GROUPS

For achieving a cohesive society it would be essential to respond to specific educational needs of learners from different sections of the society with special emphasis on the Scheduled Castes, the Scheduled Tribes and the other socially and economically disadvantaged groups. In order to do so, there is a need for integrating the socio-cultural perspectives partly by showing concern for their linguistic specificities and pedagogic requirements. Implications of the multilingual and multicultural environment shall have to be taken care of through specifically devised methodology. Contextualisation of curriculum shall have to be effected through curricular materials. The fundamental rights of the disadvantaged groups have to be consciously incorporated in the curriculum. Even the problem of educating the migrating population shall have to be handled through specific condensed educational programmes based on the main ingredients of the national curriculum.

EDUCATION OF THE GIFTED AND TALENTED

An educational system has the dual role of promoting equality as well as excellence. Education is increasingly called upon to liberate all the creative potentialities of human consciousness. Man essentially fulfils himself in and through creation. It is in the context of this, that education of gifted and talented children assumes great importance. A curricular programme while on the one hand should identify such children, on the other it should also nurture their diverse creative abilities by paying them special attention. It is also important that the identification and nurturance begins right from the earliest stage of education. Moreover, the task of identifying the gifted and talented must be accomplished on the basis of a broad conceptualisation of the process from multiple perspectives rather than as a search for a unitary human attribute. Not only their IQ (Intelligence Quotient) but also their EQ (Emotional Quotient) and SQ (Spiritual Quotient) ought to be assessed.

NATIONAL LEVEL POLICY AND LEGISLATION

Kothari Commission (1964-66)

The Kothari Commission first suggested that the education of handicapped children has to be organised not merely on humanitarian grounds, but also an aspects of utility. The commission emphasised that the education of children with disability should be "an inseparable part of the general education system. The commission also specifically emphasised that the education of children with disability should be "an inseparable part of the general education system. The commission also specifically emphasised. the importance of integrated education in meeting this target as it is cost effective and useful in developing mutual understanding between children with and without disabilities.

National Policy on Education (1986)

The National Policy on Education was adopted by Indian Parliament in 1986. The policy emphasized the removal of disparities, and ensuring equalisation of educational opportunity under its para education of the disabled.

National Policies for Persons with Disabilities (2006)

This recognises that persons with disabilities are valuable human resources for the country and seek to create an environment that provides them equal opportunities, protection of their rights and full participation in society.

Persons with Disabilities (Equal Opportunities, Protection of Rights & Full Participation) Act, 1995

Landmark legislation in the history of special education in India is the persons with Disabilities Act, 1995. This comprehensive Act covers seven disabilities, namely blindness, low vision, hearing impaired, loco-motor impaired, mental retardation, leprosy cured and mental illness.

The Rehabilitation Council of India (RCI) Act, 1992

This Act was passed in 1992 for the purpose of constituting the Rehabilitation Professionals and for maintenance of a Central Rehabilitation Register. It was amended by Rehabilitation Council of India (Amendment) Act, 2000 to provide for monitoring the training of rehabilitation professionals and personal, promoting research in rehabilitation and special education as additional objectives of the council.

LEARNING AND PEDAGOGY

LEARNING

A considerable change in the behaviour of the organism is called learning. When organism comes in contact with his environment certain necessary adjustment in the behaviour is needed. This adjustment in behaviour is the result of acquision of various habits, skills, attitudes and knowledge which is actually learning in simple term

Thus, learning means change in response or behaviour (modification, elimination or acquisition of responses involving some degree of performance) caused partly or wholly by conscious or unconscious experiences. This learning does not include physiological changes such as fatigue, temporary sensory resistance or non functioning even after continued stimulation.

Definition of Learning

It is very difficult to give a universally acceptable definition of learning because psychologists have defined the concept from different angles on the basis of their experiments. The common feature among these definitions is that learning in psychology has the status of a construct which means an idea or image that can not be directly observed like electrons or genes but they are inferred from the behaviour of the organism.

Melvin H Marx has defined learning in the following words;

"Learning is a relatively enduring change in behaviour which is a function of prior behaviour (usually called practice)

Explanation : According to the definition given above learning has three attributes:

1. Learning is a some what permanent change in behaviour. Changes occurred due to illness, fatigue, maturation or the consumption of intoxicants is not learning.
2. Learning is not directly observable. It is inferred from the behaviour of the organism in the form of construct.
3. Learning is a function of practice and experience. Experiences adds learning and practice gives it an enduring nature.

Some other **definitions** of learning are given below;

"Learning is modification of behaviour through experiences." **— Gates**

"Learning involves the acquisition of habit knowledge and attitudes". **—Crow and Crow**

"Learning is any change in behaviour resulting from behaviour." **—Guilford**

"Learning includes both acquisition and retention." **—Skinner**

"Any activity can be called learning so far as it develops the individual (in any respect good or bad) and makes him after behaviour and experiences different from what that would otherwise have been."

—Woodworth

"The term learning covers every modification in behaviour to meet environmental requirement".

—Gardner Murply

"Learning is the process by which behaviour (in the broader sense) is originated or changed through practice or training." **—Kingsley and Garry**

"Learning is the acquisition of new behaviour or the strengthening or weakening of old behaviour as a result of experience." **—Henry P. Smith**

"Learning is an episode in which a motivated individual attempts to adapt his behaviour so as to succeed in a situation which he perceives as requiring action to attain a goal."

— Presey, Robinson & Horrocks

"Learning is the process by which an activity originates or is changed through reacting to an encountered situation, provided that the characteristics of the changes in activity can not be explained on the basis of native response tendencies maturation or temporary state of the organism (e.g. fatigue or drugs etc.)

—Milgard

Characteristics of Learning

On the basis of the meaning and definitions given above following characteristics of learning can be derived:

1. **Learning is a relatively permanent change in behaviour :** Temporary changes in behaviour brought about due to some accidents or consuming any drugs is not learning at all. Learning is a relatively permanent change in behaviour. It is in this context we can say that reading some selected material to pass an examination is not learning. It is because learnt material is forgotten immediately after the exam.
2. **Learning is a progress or growth of the organism :** Learning is a fundamental need of life. Without it, no progress or growth is possible. This process of growth is unending also. One achievement of the organism motivates him to go for further achievement and thus excellence in many cases is achieved.
3. **Learning is a life long process :** An organism needs learning (behavioural change) at every moment of life to adjust to new situations at every moment. He can not sit idle at any time. Situations all the time force him for the acquisition of new learning.
4. **Learning is not directly observable :** How much learning has taken place in an organism can not be directly observed. It is inferred from his behaviour which is manifested by some activities, mental or physical.
5. **Learning is the result of experiences :** Experiences are gained at every moment of life. Learning is the other name of these experiences.
6. **Learning is a goal directed process :** Learning is a purposeful activity. It is a goal directed process. Learning which is the result of unconscious efforts of the individual is not learning in actual sense.
7. **Learning is retained through practice :** Practice or exercise is a must to retain learning. If practice is not made, learning will be forgotten and the nature of learning will no longer remain permanent. Thus, learning is acquisition and retention both.
8. **Learning reinforces further learning :** Learning definitely gives satisfaction to the individual which further motivates him for higher level of learning. Similarly, learning which is accompanied by reinforcement is more likely to become permanent and motivating for further learning.
9. **Learning is motivated by adjustment :** Man has to adjust himself according to the new environment. In this way learning is an adjustment.
10. **Learning is aroused by individual and social needs :** Learning depends upon our social needs, problems, desires, and ideals. There are certain persons who learn very fast whereas others are slow in learning. It should be noticed that social environment affects learning. It is impossible to learn in the absence of environment.
11. **Learning is transferable :** It means that learning may change place but the quantum of change in the place may be different. Change in the place is caused by techniques, ideals and the process. Change of place takes place from one field of education to the other field and from one class to other class.
12. **Learning is a process not a product :** Learning is a product for public at large but a psychologist considers it a process which has got the following four shapes-Need, Goal, adjustment and change.
13. **Improvement in the behaviour through learning :** When man reacts to the environment there is progressive modification of behaviour through learning. That is why, learning is known as improvement.
14. **Learning is active and creative :** Learning is active and creative i.e. learning depends upon the active involvement of the learner. It is said that if the learner is not self active, he cannot learn.

    It is, therefore, said that learning is the result of active involvement and experience from the sender and the receiver both.
15. **Learning is universal :** Humans are not the only organism that learn ie, react to the environment for adjustment. Animals also go through the process of learning though their speed of learning may be slower than humans.

Learning differentiated from Some Concepts

1. **Learning and instinct :** Some behaviour of every organism is reflexive or inborn, eg, breathing, breast feeding etc. All such activities take place without the process of learning. As we move to lower animals reflexes or instincts are seen more and more in their behaviour. The least example of instincts are found in humans. These instincts are not the result of any learning or experiences. They are relatively invariant in form and are reliably elicited or released by a particular and usually very simple stimulus (R Habber 1966) Thus learning is not needed for instincts or reflexive behaviour.

2. **Learning and maturation :** Maturation means physiological development of the individual according to the norms of a particular age. Learning and maturation are very closely related in the sense that for a successful learning, a definite level of maturation is a must. Thus learning is induced by maturation. For example, we can not teach quantum mechanics to a six year old child due to lack of maturation.

   Maturation on the other hand, is qualitative changes in the organism which are not induced by learning. Maturation is an increase in competency and adaptability according to Baldwin.

   Thus, we see that maturation is purely an internal process in the organism and learning is an external process more than an internal change in the behaviour of the organism. Learning and training should start only when a child must have reached an appropriate level of maturation. Maturation is actually the readiness for an activity due to physiological preparation.

3. **Leaning and cramming :** Cramming does not bring about any change in the behaviour of a student. So, cramming can never be called as learning. Despite this fact, in order to make a durable or permanent change in the behaviour of an organism, cramming will be very much helpful.

4. **Learning and acquisition of knowledge :** Acquisition of knowledge and skills is generally termed as learning but if that change of behaviour in the organism is not applied in any situation in any manner, mere accumulation of facts and information is not learning in real sense.

5. **Learning and education :** As the meaning of education suggested by the Good's dictionary of education, education is the aggregate of all the processes, by means of which a persons develops his abilities, attitudes and other forms of behaviour of positive value in the society in which the organism lives. Learning is also a process of change in the behaviour of the organism but this change may be of positive and negative value both.

Mental Process Involved in Learning

Learning may be the result of conditioning of behaviour but following mental processes are also involved in learning:

1. **Direction :** The person must be directed to the process of learning. It means that he must be full attentive to the process. He must have a clear cut goal for learning and he must take full interest to achieve that goal.
2. **Interpretation :** Learning needs perception, reaction to the stimuli and then concepts formation. The organism must realize all these relations in his mind.
3. **Selection :** So many stimuli or experiences may be there before the organism at the time of learning. He selects and recalls only those stimuli and experiences which are relevant to the situation.
4. **Insight :** When organism comes across a number of stimuli and experiences, he tries to find out various types of relationship among them. An insight helps him to reach the correct relationship.
5. **Creation :** When learning takes place, certain new mental pattern is formed which forces the organism to think and act in a new way.
6. **Criticism :** When an organism learns something (his behaviour is changed) he does not accept it so easily. he evaluates all workable solutions in his mind before putting it into application or practice.

TYPES OF LEARNING

Different criteria of classification of learning are given below:

(A) Learning according to the development of body organs

Such type of learning can broadly be classified into two categories:

1. **Motor learning :** It involves motor and muscular parts of the body. Motor learning is

also of two types sensory motor and perceptual motor. Sensory motor learning is related to the acquisition of simple habits through sense organs. Learning of skills in nursery school play ground is a good example of sensory motor learning.

Perceptual motor learning is related to the acquisition of social habits and complex motor skills. Dancing, cycling, handwriting, typing, swimming, driving, playing a musical instrument, etc, are some examples of perceptual motor learning. It is very much objective in nature.

2. **Ideational learning :** In this type of learning, muscular or motor activity is not needed. It is related to the acquisition of concepts, ideas and mental associations. This type of learning is mostly subjective in nature.

Ideational learning can also be classified into the following categories.

(i) Perceptual learning which mostly comes through senses (direct experiences with the objects). Learning through concrete materials, learning through written or spoken symbols,, drawing a picture, nature study and sight seeing are some examples of perceptual learning

(ii) Conceptual learning is the other name of abstract learning. It is related to the acquisition of concepts and abstract ideas.

(iii) Associative learning is learned incidentally or by connecting two different types of learning. Prescribed sequence is followed while linking one information with the other.

(iv) Imaginative learning is the process by which things of the past, present and future are given a definite form. It involves the acquisition of images and understanding of things beyond the normal range of sensory experiences.

(B) Learning according to the domains of behaviour involved

Domains of human behaviour are three, cognitive, affective, and psychomotor so, learning can also be classified into these three categories.

1. **Cognitive learning :** It is related to the acquisition of knowledge, understanding of concepts, inter-relationship of various concepts and ideas etc. This type of learning is 90% emphasized in the classroom. Here only mind is brought into action. When this type of learning is well developed, a learner is able to generalize and evaluate concepts as well as personal experiences.

2. **Attitudinal learning :** Attitudes, values and social systems are also learnt by the individual. This type of learning begins with the feeling of belongingness of a person to his group. How a person should react to others in various types of emotional situations is the result of this type of learning.

3. **Skill learning and habit formation :** Motor behaviour of the individual along with feeling is involved here. Practice is an important aspect of this type of learning. Reading, writing, playing a certain game or doing some physical job with perfection is the result of this type of learning.

(C) Gagne's classification of learning

Gagne has classified learning into eight categories in a hierarchical order as given below.

1. **Signal learning :** This is called classical conditioning learning developed by Russian psychologist Pavlov. In this learning unconditioning stimulus (food) and conditioned stimulus, (sound of the bell are paired together and presented to a dog a number of times. Due to this paring sound of the bell (conditioned) stimulus also forces the dog to elicit the response (to salivate) This secretion of saliva by the sound of the bell is called conditioning. Sound of the bell works as signal here.

2. **Stimulus-response learning (operant conditioning) :** This study of operant conditioning started with the work of E.L. Thorndike He placed a hungry cat in a box and dish of food was kept outside. When cat manipulated the lever of the box correctly, it opened and cat could get food. Here manipulation of lever as a response is instrumental in producing the reward (food) here hence, this learning is also called instrumental conditioning. Instrumental conditioning is more flexible than classical one in the sense that responses are conditioned here to a variety of efforts. Such experiments were conducted and improved further by Skinner to explain operant nature of behaviour in a set form with the help of reinforcement.

3. **Chain learning :** Chaining means connection between S-R is formed in sequence Chaining is of two types, motor and verbal. Using remote controller to switch on or off a T V is an example of motor sequence and greeting a guest at home is an example of verbal sequence.

In verbal chaining, two or more previously learned verbal sequences in stimulus response form are chained. If first member or the second member word of the sequence comes, the other member will automatically come, such as mummy daddy, chhola bhatora, old, young etc. Opposite words are also used in the sequence to form a chain.

In motor chaining, a number of related activities are tied in such a sequence that one activity will necessarily be followed by the other. Driving a car or weaving cloth on a handloom are best examples of motor chain. The driver of a car comes to the next activity taking the gear into neutral position immediately after applying the brakes. This second activity is chained in a sequence.

It must be noted here that a chain can not be established unless the organism is capable of linking various acts in a sequence.

4. **Verbal associate learning :** In this type of learning verbal language is also used along with showing an object, ie, seeing is associated with a word. For example, we show an object to a child and say that it is monkey. Next time when the child will see an object exactly or almost similar to the object previously seen by him, he will name it as monkey.

Two types of chaining are involved here:

(i) Observing S-R connection that connects the appearance of the object and distinguishes it from other objects, i.e., the child distinguishes the object before him from the other objects not similar to it.

(ii) When object is clearly distinguished from the other objects it becomes next stimulus for the child and when the child say it is monkey, it is the second response. Thus, a connection between S-R is formed

In order to make this type of learning a success, the following points must be kept in mind:

(i) Verbal units must be presented in a proper sequence, *i.e.*, one chain must come after the other and the whole chain at a time.

(ii) Learner must be active enough to make responses required by every chain.

(iii) Cues may be used to facilitate verbal association.

(iv) Span of retention power of the individual determines the length of the chain. There is however, a limit of these verbal chains. Unlimited number of chains can not be retained at all.

(v) There must be provision for the confirmation of correct responses in the learning situation.

5. **Learning by discrimination :** When specific behaviour is shown to only one given stimulus and other stimuli are totally excluded it is called discrimination. This type of learning is seen from the beginning of life of the organism. An infant does not consider all women having breast or feeding him by their breast as mothers. Only one out of so many is her mother and that is well discriminated. The child discriminates a feeding bottle and other bottles, the child of the home and the child outside the home etc. thus, a relatively higher mental operation is involved in discrimination.

The concept opposite to discrimination is generalization. When after conditioning to a particular stimulus, other similar stimuli also cause to elicit same response, the process is called stimulus generalization. The point to be noted here is that without perfection in stimulus generalization, nobody will be able to learn by discrimination.

Fine discrimination takes place only out of the process of stimulus generalization. Initially the infant accepts every woman as mummy but when he does not get required response from every one, he narrows down the spirit of generalization and recognizes his real mummy on the basis of her responses.

Discrimination is also not similar to the word of differentiation. In discrimination, emphasis is placed on stimulus side, but in differentiation, emphasis is placed on the response side. In discrimination, we eliminate the unwanted responses to the other stimuli through selective reinforcement but in differenciation, we develop a very specific type of response on the basis of the stimuli presented through selective reinforcement after examining a number of related responses too.

6. **Concept learning :** Concept is developed on the basis of common characteristics of an object. When we identify an object or an idea on the basis of its common properties, which a class of objects share in common not specific to other objects or ideas, it is called concept learning. The properties of shape, size, colour, form, nature etc are used to discriminate an object from other objects of the same class. For example, trees are many but the concept of a mango tree is applied to a tree which has some very specific property.

Concept learning is the pre-requisite for learning a law or principle. Learning of abstract concept is more difficult than concrete concepts ;because discrimination is done here on the basis of ideation only.

7. **Learning of principles :** Learning of principles or laws takes place only after concept learning. It is because regular and constant relationship between two or more concepts is established in a principle. Knowledge of so many principles and laws are necessary to function properly in the environment and to save our time in repeated experimentations. Most of the learning obtained in schools is concentrated to laws, principles, systems etc.
8. **Problem solving :** It is the highest stage of learning in the hierarchy. When an individual has learned all laws and principles, he evaluates them from the point of view of utility or facticity. This evaluation helps him to solve various problems of life.

IMPORTANCE OF LEANING FOR TEACHERS

Learning is important for a teacher in the following ways:

1. A teacher can adopt learning centred approach of teaching such as, activity programme, project method, problem solving method etc., and avoid teaching centred approach. Former is autonomous process and later is a burden on students.
2. A teacher can use the whole and part learning methods alternately to benefit the poor and talented students equally in the class.
3. Verbalization on the part of the teacher along with other motor activity can explain and clarify the concepts and remove the difficulties of students. Cue is also used by the teacher in the class.
4. A teacher will not bank upon memorization from the very beginning of teaching. Desired change of behaviour is not related to memorization,
5. A teacher can keep the maturity level and inborn capacity of students in mind for effective learning.
6. A teacher can provide varied experiences to students in such a way that they can identify similarities and differences in objects, situations and concepts. This approach of learning will facilitate learning in the class.
7. The primary objective of schooling is to bring about desirable changes in the behaviour of learners through the process of learning. A teacher must know all these approaches and operations of learning and their relative significance. A teacher can adopt a better teaching strategy in the class only after knowing different approaches and operations of teaching.
8. A teacher can accommodate his teaching according to the individual differences of students only after knowing the process and theories of learning.
9. An important contribution of leaning psychology is that it has propounded and popularized the concept of motivation and its uses on scientific lines. We are now in a better position to use different techniques to motivate the students for verbal, mental or motor activity. The teacher can motivate the students in the class according to their age levels.
10. A teacher can know various procedures of remembering and forgetting and he can utilize various techniques of learning to minimize the share of forgetting in the class. He can help the students to transfer skills and informations acquired in the classroom to daily life situations outside the school and vice versa.
11. Modern psychology of learning lays much stree on social psychology of leaning and group dynamics. A teacher can improve social learning environment of the class by putting various theories and procedures of learning into practice.

THEORIES OF LEARNING

We may categories all these theories of learning into two groups.

1. Laboratory psychologists' theories of association or connection (S-R theories)
2. Cognitive field theories or gestalt psychology of learning. S-R theories of learning can further be classified into two categories as under

(A) **S-R theories without Reinforcement**	(B) **S-R theories with reinforcement**
1. Pavlov's conditioning theory	Thorndike's theory
2. Watson's learning theory	Hull's theory
3. Guthrie's learning theory	Skinner's theory

As far as field theories are concerned there are three important theories which are given below:

1. Gestalt theory of learning
2. Lewin's theory of leaning
3. Tolman's sign gestalt theory of learning

HOW CHILDREN THINK AND LEARN

Children learn from anything and everything they see and act upon. They have learnt a lot before they join school, and they continue to learn outside the school hours. If we believe that children learn only in school, it is because of what we wrongly regard as learning. When a child spends hours on trying to solve a Jigsaw puzzle (say), he/she is often reprimanded by adults for wasting study time. Little do the grown-ups realise that it is through such interesting games that this child may be increasing his/her understanding of shapes and size. And, this learning is taking place outside the school hours, without formal instruction. A curriculum built upon assumptions about children's learning, that ignore this aspect, is also responsible for children losing interest in mathematics or in any formal learning.

From the time a child is born, his/her interaction with the world around his/her starts. He/she perceives things around his/her, and gradually makes sense of them. He/she slowly begins to recognise people and objects, relate more and more to the environment, and observe things through the senses of touch, sight, taste, smell and sound. There are **four different stages** of learning or development that each child goes through.

Sensorimotor

This is from the ages of birth to about two years old. During this time the child's primary mode of learning occurs through the five senses. He/she learns to experience environment. The child touches things, holds, looks, listens, tastes, feels, bangs, and shakes everything in sight. When the child adds motor skills such as creeping, crawling and walking, his/her environment expands by leaps and bounds. The child is now exploring their environment with both senses and the ability to get around.

Preoperational

This is the stages between ages two and seven. During this stage the child is busy gathering information or learning, and then trying to figure out ways that they can used what they have learned to begin solving problems.

During this stage of his/her life child will be thinking in specifics and will find it very difficult to get generalise anything. This is the time when a child learns by asking questions. The child generally will not want a real answer to his question at this point. When he asks why do we have grass .... He simply wants to know that it is for him to play in. No technical answers for know. The child in this age group judges everything on the 'me' basis—How does it affect me? Do I like it?

Concrete Operations Period

This is the period of time when child is between the ages of seven to ten. This is a wonderful age as this is when children begin to manipulate data mentally. They take the information at hand and begin to define, compare and contrast it. They, however, still think concretely.

The concrete operational child is capable of logical thought. This child still learns through their senses, but no longer relies on only them to teach him. He now thinks as well. A good teacher for this age group would start each lesson at a concrete level and then more toward a generalised level. The child, during this period, is very literal in their thinking.

Formal Operations Period

The period begins at about age eleven. At this time the child will break through the barrier of literalism and more on to thinking in more abstract terms. He no longer restricts thinking to time and space. This child now starts to reflect, hypothesize and theorize. In the formal operation period, children need to develop cognitive abilities. The following is a list of six simple categories of cognitive abilities. The following is a list of six simple categories of cognitive abilities:

1. **Knowledge of facts and principals:** This is the direct recall of facts and principals. **Examples:** memorisation of dates, name, definition, vocabulary words.
2. **Comprehension:** Understanding of facts and ideas.
3. **Application:** Needs to know, rules, principles, and procedures and how to use them.
4. **Analysis:** Breaking down concepts into parts.
5. **Synthesis:** Putting together information or ideas.
6. **Evaluation:** Judging the value of information.

BASIC PROCESSES OF TEACHING AND LEARNING

Teaching-learning process is the heart of education. On it depends the fulfilment of the aims & objectives of education. It is the most powerful instrument of education to bring about desired changes in the students. Teaching learning are related terms. In teaching-learning process, the teacher, the learner, the curriculum & other variables are organised in a systematic way to attain some pre-determined goal.

Essential Aspects of the Teaching-learning Process

According to Diana Laurillard, there are four aspects of the teaching-learning process:

1. **Discussion**—between the teacher and learner.
2. **Interaction**—between the learner and some aspect of the world defined by the teacher.
3. **Adaptation**—of the world by the teacher and action by the learner.
4. **Reflection**—on the learner's performance by both teacher and learner.

According to **Burton** in the figure above

1. Teaching can become effective only by relating it to process of learning.
2. Teaching objective cannot be realised without being related to learning situation.
3. We may create and use teaching aids to create some appropriate learning situation.
4. The strategies and devices of teaching may be selected in such a manner that the optimal objectives of learning area achieved.
5. To understand principles, goals, objectives of education in right perspective.
6. Appropriate learning situation condition may be created for congenial and effective teaching.

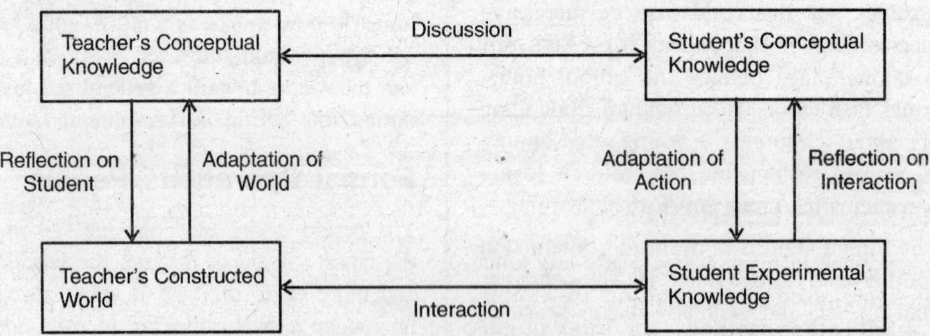

Fig. 1: *Essential aspects of the ideal teaching-learning process*

Approaches to Learning Theories

Aspect	Behaviourist	Cognitivist	Humanist
Learning theorists	Thorndike, Pavlov, Watson, Guthrie, Hull, Tolman, Skinner	Koffka, Kohler, Lewin, Piaget, Ausubel, Bruner, Gagne	Maslow, Rogers
View of the learning process	Change in behaviour	Internal mental process (including insight, information processing, memory, perception)	A personal act to fulfil potential
Locus of learning	Stimuli in external environment	Internal cognitive structuring	Affective and cognitive needs
Purpose in education	Produce behavioural change in desired direction	Develop capacity and skills to learn better	Become self-actualized autonomous
Educator's role	Arranges environment to elicit desired response	Structures content of learning activity	Facilitates development of the whole person
Manifestations in adult learning	Behavioural objectives	Cognitive development	Andragogy
	Competency-based education	Intelligence, learning and memory as function of age	Self-directed learning
	Skill development and training	Learning how to learn	

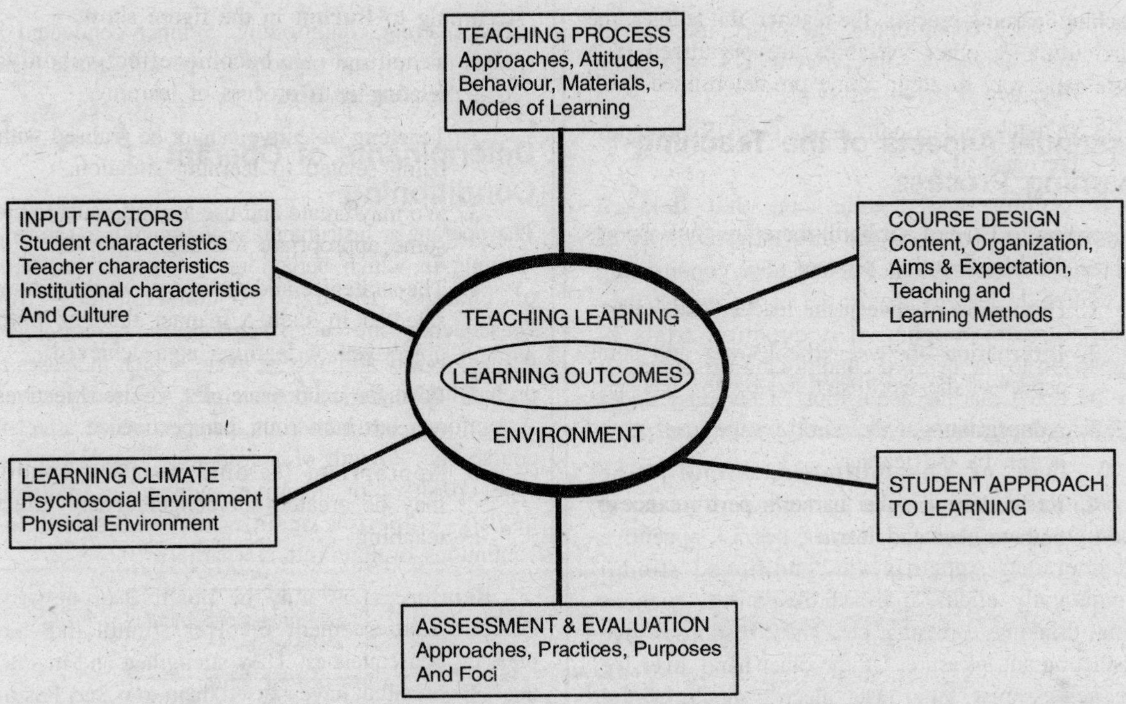

Fig. 2: *Teaching-Learning Environment*

PARADIGMS OF LEARNING

Learning takes place in many ways. There are some methods that are used in acquisition of simple responses while other methods are used in the acquisition of complex responses. The simplest kind of learning is called conditioning. Two types of conditioning have been identified. The first one is called classical conditioning and the second instrumental/operant conditioning. In addition, we have observational learning, cognitive learning, verbal learning, concept learning and skill learning.

Classical Conditioning

This type of learning was first investigated by Ivan P. Pavlov. Like many great scientific advances, classical conditioning was discovered accidentally. The nineteenth-century Russian physiologist Ivan Pavlov was looking at salivation in dogs in response to being fed, when he noticed that his dogs would begin to salivate whenever he entered the room, even when he was not bringing them food. However, when Pavlov discovered that any object or event which the dogs learnt to associate with food (such as the food bowl) would trigger the same response, he realised that he had made an important scientific discovery, and he devoted the rest of his career to studying this type of learning.

Classical conditioning is 'classical' in that it is the first systematic study of basic laws of learning. Classical conditioning involves learning to associate an unconditioned stimulus that already brings about a particular response (*i.e.* a reflex) with a new (conditioned) stimulus, so that the new stimulus brings about the same response. The unconditioned stimulus (or UCS) is the object or event that originally produces the reflexive/natural response.

Once the neutral stimulus has become associated with the unconditioned stimulus, it becomes a conditioned stimulus (CS). The conditioned response (CR) is the response to the conditioned stimulus. Thus, learning situation in classical conditioning is one of S-S learning in which one stimulus becomes a signal of another stimulus.

Determinants of Classical Conditioning

How quickly and strongly acquisition of a response occurs in classical conditioning depends on several factors. Some of the major factors influencing learning a CR are described below:

1. Time Relations between Stimuli: The classical conditioning procedures, discussed below, are basically of four types based on the time relations between the onset of conditioned stimulus (CS) and unconditioned stimulus (US). The first three are called forward conditioning procedures, and the fourth one is called backward conditioning procedure. The basic experimental arrangements of these procedures are as follows:

(*a*) When the CS and US are presented together, it is called simultaneous conditioning.

(*b*) In delayed conditioning, the onset of CS precedes the onset of US. The CS ends before the end of the US.

(*c*) In trace conditioning, the onset and end of the CS precedes the onset of US with some time gap between the two.

(*d*) In backward conditioning, the US precedes the onset of CS.

It is now well established that delayed conditioning procedure is the most effective way of acquiring a CR. Simultaneous and trace conditioning procedures do lead to acquisition of a CR, but they require greater number of acquisition trials in comparison to the delayed conditioning procedure. It may be noted that the acquisition of response under backward conditioning procedure is very rare.

2. Type of Unconditioned Stimuli: The unconditioned stimuli used in studies of classical conditioning are basically of two types, *i.e.* appetitive and aversive. Appetitive unconditioned stimuli automatically elicits approach responses, such as eating, drinking, caressing, etc. These responses give satisfaction and pleasure. On the other hand, aversive US, such as noise, bitter taste, electric shock, painful injections, etc. are painful, harmful, and elicit avoidance and escape responses. It has been found that appetitive classical conditioning is slower and requires greater number of acquisition trials, but aversive classical conditioning is established in one, two or three trials depending on the intensity of the aversive US.

3. Intensity of Conditioned Stimuli: This influences the course of both appetitive and aversive classical conditioning. More intense conditioned stimuli are more effective in accelerating the acquisition of conditioned responses. It means that the more intense the conditioned stimulus, the fewer are the number of acquisition trials needed for conditioning.

Operant/Instrumental Conditioning

B.F. Skinner is regarded as the father of operant conditioning, but his work was based on **Thorndike's law of effect.** In the late nineteenth century, psychologist Edward Thorndike proposed the law of effect. The law of effect states that any behaviour that has good consequences will tend to be repeated, and any behaviour that has bad consequences will tend to be avoided. In the 1930s, B.F. Skinner, extended this idea and began to study operant conditioning. Operant conditioning is a type of learning in which responses come to be controlled by their consequences.

Operants are those behaviours or responses, which are emitted by animals and human beings voluntarily and are under their control. The term operant is used because the organism operates on the environment. Conditioning of operant behaviour is called operant conditioning. Skinner conducted his studies on rats and pigeons in specially made boxes, called the Skinner Box.

Determinants of Operant Conditioning

The operant or instrumental conditioning is a form of learning in which behaviour is learned, maintained or changed through its consequences. Such consequences are called **reinforcers**. A reinforcer is defined as any stimulus or event, which increases the probability of the occurrence of a (desired) response. A reinforcer has numerous features, which affect the course and strength of a response. They include its type—positive or negative, number or frequency, quality—superior or inferior, and schedule—continuous or intermittent (partial).

Reinforcement may be positive or negative. Positive reinforcement involves stimuli that have pleasant consequences. They strengthen and maintain the responses that have caused them to occur. Positive reinforcers satisfy needs, which include food, water, medals, praise, money, status, information, etc. Negative reinforcers involve unpleasant and painful stimuli. Responses that lead organisms to get rid of painful stimuli or avoid and escape from them provide negative reinforcement. Thus, negative reinforcement leads to learning of avoidance and escape responses. For instance, one learns to put on woollen clothes, burn firewood or use electric heaters to avoid the unpleasant cold weather. One learns to move away from dangerous stimuli because they provide negative reinforcement. It may be noted that negative reinforcement is not punishment. Use of punishment reduces or suppresses the response while a negative reinforcer increases the probability of avoidance or escape response. For instance, drivers and co-drivers wear their seat belts to avoid getting injured in case of an accident or to avoid being fined by the traffic police.

Classical and Operant Conditioning : Differences

1. In classical conditioning, the responses are under the control of some stimulus because they are reflexes, automatically elicited by the appropriate stimuli. Such stimuli are selected as US and responses elicited by them as UR. Thus Pavlovian conditioning, in which US elicits responses, is often called respondent conditioning.

   In instrumental conditioning, responses are under the control of the organism and are voluntary responses or 'operants'. Thus, in the two forms of conditioning different types of responses are conditioned.

2. In classical conditioning, the CS and US are well-defined, but in operant conditioning CS is not defined. It can be inferred but is not directly known.
3. In classical conditioning, the experimenter controls the occurrence of US, while in operant conditioning the occurrence of the reinforcer is under the control of the organism that is learning. Thus, for US in classical conditioning the organism remains passive, while in operant conditioning the subject has to be active in order to be reinforced.
4. In the two forms of conditioning, the technical terms used to characterise the experimental proceedings are different. Moreover what is called reinforcer in operant conditioning is called US in classical conditioning. An US has two functions. In the beginning, it elicits the response and also reinforces the response to be associated and elicited later on by the CS.

OBSERVATIONAL LEARNING

The other form of learning takes place by observing others. Earlier this form of learning was called **imitation.** Bandura and his colleagues in a series of experimental studies investigated observational learning in detail. In this kind of learning, human beings learn social behaviours, therefore, it is sometimes called **social learning**. In many situations individuals do not know how to behave. They observe others and emulate their behaviour. This form of learning is called **modelling**.

Examples of observational learning abound in our social life. Fashion designers employ tall, pretty, and gracious young girls and tall, smart, and well-built young boys for popularising clothes of different designs and fabrics. People observe them on televised fashion shows and advertisements in magazines and newspapers. They imitate these models. Observing superiors and likeable persons and then emulating their behaviour in a novel social situation is a common experience.

The children observe adults' behaviours, at home and during social ceremonies and functions. They enact adults in their plays and games. For instance, young children play games of marriage ceremonies, birthday parties, thief and policeman, house keeping, etc. Actually they enact in their games what they observe in society, on television, and read in books.

Children learn most of the social behaviours by observing and emulating adults. The way to put on clothes, dress one's hair, and conduct oneself in society are learned through observing others. It has also been shown that children learn and develop various personality characteristics through observational learning. Aggressiveness, prosocial behaviour, courtesy, politeness, diligence, and indolence are acquired by this method of learning.

COGNITIVE LEARNING

Some psychologists view learning in terms of cognitive processes that underlie it. They have developed approaches that focus on such processes that occur during learning rather than concentrating solely on S-R and S-S connections. Thus, in cognitive learning, there is a change in what the learner knows rather than what he/she does. This form of learning shows up in insight learning and latent learning.

Insight Learning

Kohler demonstrated a model of learning which could not be readily explained by conditioning. He performed a series of experiments with chimpanzees that involved solving complex problems. Kohler placed chimpanzees in an enclosed play area where food was kept out of their reach. Tools such as poles and boxes were placed in the enclosure. The chimpanzees rapidly learned how to use a box to stand on or a pole to move the food in their direction. In this experiment, learning did not occur as a result of trial and error and reinforcement, but came about in sudden flashes of insight. The chimpanzees would roam about the enclosure for some time and then suddenly would stand on a box, grab a pole and strike a banana, which was out of normal reach above the enclosure. The chimpanzee exhibited what Kohler called insight learning—the process by which the solution to a problem suddenly becomes clear.

In a normal experiment on insight learning, a problem is presented, followed by a period of time when no apparent progress is made and finally a solution suddenly emerges. In insight learning, sudden solution is the rule. Once the solution has appeared, it can be repeated immediately the next time the problem is confronted. Thus, it is clear that what is learned is not a specific set of conditioned associations between stimuli and responses but a cognitive relationship between a means and an end. As a result, insight learning can be generalised to other similar problem situations.

Latent Learning

Another type of cognitive learning is known as latent learning. In latent learning, a new behaviour is learned but not demonstrated until reinforcement is provided for displaying it. Tolman made an early contribution to the concept of latent learning. To have an idea of latent learning, we may briefly understand his experiment. Tolman put two groups of rats in a maze and gave them an opportunity to explore. In one group, rats found food at the end of the maze and soon learned to make their way rapidly through the maze. On the other hand, rats in the second group were not rewarded and showed no apparent signs of learning. But later, when these rats were reinforced, they ran through the maze as efficiently as the rewarded group.

Tolman contended that the unrewarded rats had learned the layout of the maze early in their explorations. They just never displayed their latent learning until the reinforcement was provided. Instead, the rats developed a cognitive map of the maze, *i.e.* a mental representation of the spatial locations and directions, which they needed to reach their goal.

LEARNING AS A SOCIAL ACTIVITY

Learning is a social activity. Our learning is intimately associated with our connection with other human beings, our teachers, our peers, our family as well as casual acquaintances, including the people before us or next to us. We are more likely to be successful in our efforts to educate, if we recognise this principle rather than try to avoid it. Much of traditional education, as Dewey pointed out, is directed towards isolating the learner from all social interaction, and towards seeing education as a one-on-one relationship between the learner and the objective material to be learned. In contrast, progressive education (to continue to use Dewey's formulation) recognizes the social aspect of learning and uses conversations interaction with others, and the application of knowledge as an integral aspect of learning.

SOCIAL CONTEXT OF LEARNING

Social Learning theory

Social learning theory focuses on the learning that occurs within a social context. It considers that people learn from one another, including such concepts as observational learning, imitation, and modelling. Among others **Albert Bandura** is considered the leading proponent of this theory.

General Principles of Social Learning Theory Follows:

1. People can learn by observing the behaviour is of others and the outcomes of those behaviours.
2. Learning can occur without a change in behaviour. Behaviourists say that learning has to be represented by a permanent change in behaviour, in contrast social learning theorists say that because people can learn through observation alone, their learning may not necessarily be shown in their performance. Learning may or may not result in a behaviour change.
3. Cognition plays a role in learning. Over the last 40 years social learning theory has become increasingly cognitive in its interpretation of human learning. Awareness and expectations of future reinforcements or punishments can have a major effect on the behaviours that people exhibit.
4. Social learning theory can be considered a bridge or a transition between behaviourist learning theories and cognitive learning theories.

How the Environment Reinforces and Punishes Modelling:

People are often reinforced for modelling the behaviour of others. Bandura suggested that the environment also reinforces modelling. This is in several possible ways:

1. The observer is reinforced by the model. For example, a student who changes dress to fit in with a certain group of students has a strong likelihood of being accepted and thus reinforced by that group.
2. The observer is reinforced by a third person. The observer might be modelling the actions of someone else, for example, an outstanding class leader or student. The teacher notices this and compliments and praises the observer for modelling such behaviour thus reinforcing that behaviour.
3. The imitated behaviour itself leads to reinforcing consequences. Many behaviours that we learn from others produce satisfying or reinforcing results. For example, a student in my multimedia class could observe how the extra work a classmate does is fun. This student in turn would do the same extra work and also receive enjoyment.
4. Consequences of the model's behaviour affect the observers behaviour vicariously. This is known as vicarious reinforcement. This is where in the model is reinforced for a response and then the observer shows an increase in that same response. Bandura illustrated this by having students watch a film of a model hitting a inflated clown doll. One group of children saw the model being praised for such action. Without being reinforced, the group of children began to also hit the doll.

Contemporary Social Learning Perspective of Reinforcement and Punishment

1. Contemporary theory proposes that both reinforcement and punishment have indirect effects on learning. They are not the sole or main cause.
2. Reinforcement and punishment influence the extent to which an individual exhibits a behaviour that has been learned.
3. The expectation of reinforcement influences cognitive processes that promote learning. Therefore, attention pays a critical role in learning. And attention is influenced by the expectation of reinforcement. An example would be, where the teacher tells a group of students that what they will study next is not on the test. Students will not pay attention, because they do not expect to know the information for a test.

Cognitive Factors in Social Learning

Social learning theory has cognitive factors as well as behaviourist factors (actually operant factors).

1. **Learning without performance:** Bandura makes a distinction between learning through observation and the actual imitation of what has been learned.
2. **Cognitive processing during learning:** Social learning theorists contend that attention is a critical factor in learning.
3. **Expectations:** As a result of being reinforced, people form expectations about the consequences that future behaviours are likely to bring. They expect certain behaviours to bring reinforcements and others to bring punishment. The learner needs to be aware however, of the response reinforcements and response punishment. Reinforcement increases a response only when the learner is aware of that connection.
4. **Reciprocal causation:** Bandura proposed that behaviour can influence both the environment and the person. In fact each of these three variables, the person, the behaviour, and the environment can have an influence on each other.
5. **Modelling:** There are different types of models. There is the live model, and actual person demonstrating the behaviour. There can also be a symbolic model, which can be a person or action portrayed in some other medium, such as television, videotape, computer programs.

Behaviours that can be learned through modelling:

Many behaviours can be learned, at least partly, through modelling. Examples that can be cited are, students can watch parents read, students can watch the demonstrations of mathematics problems, or seen someone acting bravely and a fearful situation. Aggression can be learned through models. Much research indicate that children become more aggressive when they observed aggressive or violent models. Moral thinking and moral behaviour are influenced by observation and modelling. This includes moral judgments regarding right and wrong which can in part, develop through modelling.

Conditions Necessary for Effective Modelling to Occur:

Bandura mentions four conditions that are necessary before an individual can successfully model the behaviour of someone else:

1. **Attention:** the person must first pay attention to the model.
2. **Retention:** the observer must be able to remember the behaviour that has been observed. One way of increasing this is using the technique of rehearsal.
3. **Motor reproduction:** the third condition is the ability to replicate the behaviour that the model has just demonstrated. This means that the observer has to be able to replicate the action, which could be a problem with a learner who is not ready developmentally to replicate the action. For example, little children have difficulty doing complex physical motion.
4. **Motivation:** the final necessary ingredient for modelling to occur is motivation, learners must want to demonstrate what they have learned. Remember that since these four conditions vary among individuals, different people will reproduce the same behaviour differently.

Effects of Modelling on Behaviour:

Modelling teaches new behaviours.

Modelling influences the frequency of previously learned behaviours.

Modelling may encourage previously forbidden behaviours.

Modelling increases the frequency of similar behaviours. For example, a student might see a friend excel in basketball and he tries to excel in football because he is not tall enough for basketball.

Educational implications of social learning theory:

Social learning theory has numerous implications for classroom use.

1. Students often learn a great deal simply by observing other people.
2. Describing the consequences of behaviour is can effectively increase the appropriate behaviours and decrease inappropriate ones. This can involve discussing with learners about the rewards and consequences of various behaviours.
3. Modelling provides an alternative to shaping for teaching new behaviours. Instead of using shaping, which is operant conditioning, modelling can provide a faster, more efficient means for teaching new behaviour. To promote effective modelling a teacher must make sure that the four essential conditions exist; attention, retention, motor reproduction, and motivation.
4. Teachers and parents must model appropriate behaviours and take care that they do not model inappropriate behaviours.
5. Teachers should expose students to a variety of other models. This technique is especially important to break down traditional stereotypes.
6. Students must believe that they are capable of accomplishing school tasks. Thus, it is very important to develop a sense of self-efficacy for students. Teachers can promote such self-efficacy by having students receive confidence-building messages, watch others be successful, and experience success on their own.
7. Teachers should help students set realistic expectations for their academic accomplishments. In general in my class that means making sure that expectations are not set too low. I want to realistically challenge my students. However, sometimes the task is beyond a student's ability, example would be the cancer group.
8. Self-regulation techniques provide an effective method for improving student behaviour.

PLANNING FOR PROBLEM SOLVING

A curriculum that accommodates a variety of developmental levels as well as individual differences in young children sets the stage for problem solving. Choices, decision-making, and a curriculum framework that integrates learning, such as Katz and Chard's project method, are especially appropriate for young learners. The project approach facilitates cooperative learning and promotes diverse ideas. Donna Ogle's K-W-L (what you KNOW, what you WANT to know, and what you have LEARNED) is another method of organizing work that promotes problem solving. Themes, units, webbing, and the KWL method are all ways of organizing curriculum that can support problem solving. Beginning with the needs and interests of the children, problem solving develops from meaningful experiences important to the children. The teacher-designed curriculum provides the classroom basis for these experiences.

For example, a second grade investigation of waste materials from a classroom led one group of young children to explore the topic in an integrated way. Reading, writing, counting, measuring, interviews of community people, and science experiments were planned, initiated and reported. Solutions to many problems posed during the investigation were tried out and some were found to be successful. Through group work, individuals were able to participate and communicate as cognitive and social needs were met. Each child, at individual levels and in individual ways, was successful within the group experience. Problem solving empowers children.

Providing for Problem Solving

Problem solving is a skill that can be learned and must be practiced. It is facilitated by a classroom schedule that provides for integrated learning in large blocks of time, space for ongoing group projects, and many open-ended materials. The teacher provides the time, space, and materials necessary for in-depth learning.

1. Time: Teachers can provide for problem solving by enlarging blocks of learning time during the school day. Because making choices, discussing decisions, and evaluating mistakes takes time, large time blocks best suit the problem-solving process. It is important that children know they have time to identify and solve problems.

2. Space: Projects and group meetings may require an assessment of classroom space. Moving desks and tables together facilitates communication and cooperation in the classroom. Once the teacher has observed the patterns of traffic in the classroom, equipment can be moved or eliminated to promote problem solving.

3. Materials: The open-ended materials that are needed for the construction and concrete solving of problems should be safe, durable, and varied. Well-marked storage units should be easily accessible to children, and materials should be available for ongoing exploration and manipulation. Access to a variety of materials encourages children to use materials in new and diverse ways. This freedom promotes problem solving.

The Problem-Solving Model

Individuals or groups can solve problems. Group problem solving is important to young children because many diverse ideas are generated. Both individual and group processes should be included in the early childhood classroom. Becoming skillful at problem solving is based on the understanding and use of sequenced steps. These steps are:

1. Identifying the problem,
2. Brainstorming a variety of solutions,
3. Choosing one solution and trying it out, and
4. Evaluating what has happened.

Choosing Good Problems

Goffin provides teachers with guiding questions that will help them identify appropriate problems for young children. Some of these are:

1. Is the problem meaningful and interesting?
2. Can tne problem be solved at a variety of levels?
3. Must a new decision be made?
4. Can the actions be evaluated?

Problem solving is a way to make sense of the environment and, in fact, control it. The process allows children in an increasingly diverse world to be active participants and to implement changes. By including problem solving in the early childhood classroom, we equip children with a life-long skill that is useful in all areas of learning.

Obstacles to Solving Problems

Two major obstacles to solving a problem are mental set and lack of motivation.

Mental Set

Mental set is a tendency of a person to solve problems by following already tried mental operations or steps. Prior success with a particular strategy would sometimes help in solving a new problem. However, this tendency also creates a mental rigidity that obstructs the problem solver to think of any new rules or strategies. Thus, while in some situations mental set can enhance the quality and speed of problem solving, in other situations it hinders problem solving. You might have experienced this while solving mathematical problems. After completing a couple of questions, you form an idea of the steps that are required to solve these questions and subsequently you go on following the same steps, until a point where you fail. At this point you may experience difficulty in avoiding the already used steps. Those steps would interfere in your thought for new strategies. However, in day-to-day activities we often rely on past experiences with similar or related problems.

Like mental set, **functional fixedness** in problem solving occurs when people fail to solve a problem because they are fixed on a thing's usual function. If you have ever used a hardbound book to hammer a nail, then you have overcome functional fixedness.

Lack of Motivation

People might be great at solving problems, but all their skills and talents are of no use if they are not motivated. Sometimes people give up easily when they encounter a problem or failure in implementing the first step. Therefore, there is a need to persist in their effort to find a solution.

ALTERNATIVE CONCEPTIONS OF LEARNING

When teachers provide instruction on concepts in various subjects, they are teaching students who already have some pre-instructional knowledge about the topic. Student knowledge, however, can be erroneous, illogical or misinformed. These erroneous understandings are termed alternative conceptions or misconceptions (or intuitive theories). Alternative conceptions (misconceptions) are not unusual. In fact, they are a normal part of the learning process. We quite naturally form ideas from our everyday experience, but obviously not all the ideas we develop are correct with respect to the most current evidence and scholarship in a given discipline. Moreover, some concepts in different content areas are simply very difficult to grasp. They may be very abstract, counterintuitive or quite complex. Hence, our understanding of them is flawed. In addition, things we have already learned are sometimes unhelpful in learning new concepts/theories. This occurs when the new concept or theory is inconsistent with previously learned material. Accordingly, as noted, it is very typical for students (and adults) to have misconceptions in different domains (content knowledge areas). Indeed, researchers have found that there is a common set of alternative conceptions (misconceptions) that most students typically exhibit. There is one class of alternative theories (or misconceptions) that is very deeply entrenched. These are "ontological misconceptions," which relate to ontological beliefs (*i.e.*, beliefs about the fundamental categories and properties of the world).

Alternative conceptions (misconceptions) can impede learning for several reasons. First, students generally are unaware that the knowledge they have is wrong. Moreover, misconceptions can be very entrenched in student thinking. In addition, new experiences are interpreted through these erroneous understandings, thereby interfering with being able to correctly grasp new information. Also, alternative conceptions (misconceptions) tend to be very resistant to instruction because learning entails replacing or radically reorganizing student knowledge. Hence, conceptual change has to occur for learning to happen. This puts teachers in the very challenging position of needing to bring about significant conceptual change in student knowledge. Generally, ordinary forms of instruction, such as lectures, labs, discovery learning, or simply reading texts, are not very successful at overcoming student misconceptions. For all these reasons, misconceptions can be hard nuts for teachers to crack. However, several instructional strategies have been found to be effective in achieving conceptual change and helping students leave their alternative conceptions behind and learn correct concepts or theories.

Instructional strategies that can lead to change in students' alternative conceptions (misconceptions) and to learning of new concepts and theories

1. Present new concepts or theories that you are teaching in such a way that students see as plausible, high-quality, intelligible and generative.
2. Use students' correct conceptions and build on those by creating a bridge of examples to the new concept or theory that students are having trouble learning due to misconceptions they hold.
3. Use model-ased reasoning, which helps students construct new representations that vary from their intuitive theories.
4. Use diverse instruction, wherein you present a few examples that challenge multiple assumptions, rather than a larger number of examples that challenge just one assumption.
5. Help students become aware of (raise student metacognition about) their own alternative conceptions (misconceptions).
6. Present students with experiences that cause cognitive conflict in students' minds. Experiences (as in strategy 3 above) that can cause cognitive conflict are ones that get students to consider their erroneous (misconception) knowledge side-by-side with, or at the same time as, the correct concept or theory.
7. Engage in Interactive Conceptual Instruction (ICI).
8. Develop students' epistemological thinking, which incorporates beliefs and theories about the nature of knowledge and the nature of learning, in ways that will facilitate conceptual change. The more naive students' beliefs are about knowledge and learning, the less likely they are to revise their misconceptions.
9. Help students "self-repair" their misconceptions.
10. Once students have overcome their alternative conceptions (misconceptions).

Presenting new concepts or theories

In presenting new concepts or theories, teachers should be sure to show these theories or concepts as:

1. Plausible: The new information should be shown to be consistent with other knowledge and able to explain the available data. Learners must see how the new conception (theory) is consistent with other knowledge and a good explanation of the data.

2. High quality: Of course, the theory/concept to be taught is of high quality from a scientific point of view, since it is a correct theory. However, the presented theory should take a better account of the data than what students currently have available to them. For example, the instructor should deal with the problem from the perspective of the students (*e.g.*, students for whom a "flat earth" theory provides a better account of the data available than does a "spherical earth" theory). Hence, the quality of the new theory must be considered along with the kind of data that students know about.

3. Intelligible: Teachers should do what they can to increase the intelligibility of the new theory. Learners must be able to grasp how the new conception works. To increase intelligibility, teachers can use methods such as use of:

(*a*) analogies,

(*b*) models, and

(*c*) direct exposition.

4. Generative/fruitful: Teachers should show that the new concept/theory can be extended to open up new areas of inquiry. Learners must be able to extend the new conception to new areas of inquiry. Teachers might accomplish this by illustrating the application of the new concept/theory to a range of problems. These problems can include familiar ones and new ones.

UNDERSTANDING CHILDREN'S 'ERRORS' AS SIGNIFICANT STEPS IN THE LEARNING PROCESS

The legacy of Jean Piaget to the world of early childhood education is that he fundamentally altered the view of how a child learns. And a teacher, he believed, was more than a transmitter of knowledge she was also an essential observer and guide to helping children build their own knowledge.

As a university graduate, Swiss-born Piaget got a routine job in Paris standardizing Binet-Simon IQ tests, where the emphasis was on children getting the right answers. Piaget observed that many children of the same ages gave the same kinds of incorrect answers. What could be learned from this?

Piaget interviewed many hundreds of children and concluded that children who are allowed to make mistakes often go on to discover their errors and correct them, or find new solutions. In this process, children build their own way of learning. From children's errors, teachers can obtain insights into the child's view of the world and can tell where guidance is needed. They can provide appropriate materials, ask encouraging questions, and allow the child to construct his own knowledge.

Piaget's continued interactions with young children became part of his life-long research. After reading about a child who thought that the sun and moon followed him wherever he went, Piaget wanted to find out if all young children had a similar belief. He found that many did indeed believe this. Piaget went on to explore children's countless "why" questions, such as, "Why is the sun round?" or "Why is grass green?" He concluded that children do not think like adults. Their thought processes have their own distinct order and special logic. Children are not "empty vessels to be filled with knowledge" (as traditional pedagogical theory had it). They are "active builders of knowledge-little scientists who construct their own theories of the world."

COGNITION & EMOTIONS

What is Cognition?

Cognition is the ability to preceive, memorise, reason and understand. These abilities change with age. As the child grows, her thinking becomes more mature and efficient. Therefore, cognition can simply be defined as the process of acquiring, processing, organising and using knowledge. The development of cognition means development of all these abilities. A child's thinking changes as result of both age (maturation) and increased experiences.

Major Cognitive Characteristics of Children

Infancy

It is interesting to see the number of changes that take place in the first two years. Children at this stage are very active learners. Even when it seems the child is only lying and looking at nothing (e.g. 2 month old) she is actually looking at and trying to understand the things around her.

The first two years children begin by exploring their own bodies and move to the outside objects. Children at 2/3 months discover their thumb or hand or occasionally their own foot. These fascinate them they try to play with them. For a two month old a toy is not as satisfying as her/his own thumb in her/his mouth. Gradually, by about six months, children begin to play with objects outside the body. This could be the toy, the sheet, the bottle, etc. Later, by two years they can even indulge in pretend play [example doctor-doctor, house-house, etc.].

What children also achieve by two years is the understanding of object permanance. **Object permanance is the understanding that things exist even if you can not see them.** Let us take an example. If you show a five month old a toy she gets excited. If you hide the toy the child soon forgets that any toy even existed. This is because she thinks out of sight is out of mind. Do the same thing with a 1½ year old and you will find the child is either looking for it or asks you to find it. This is because she knows the toy exists even if she can not see it. This understanding, that things exist even if you can not see them, is called object permanance.

The other major development that happens by two years is that children begin to learn the symbols. What are symbols? A two year old can convey her thoughts and desires through language. All these are essential processes of cognition.

Early Childhood

This is a period when the childs mastery in use of symbols increases. We can observe this in the everyday behaviour and activities of the child, *i.e.* in what she plays, her language etc. Gradually her representations of objects become more flexible and less self centred. A one year old while playing does not need a toy phone to pretend speaking on the phone. She can use any object. This is indicative of flexibility in thinking. Gradually, children also start directing play between dolls, *e.g.,* one doll is the mother and the other doll the child. This is indicative of the child moving away from self to becoming less self centred.

Children at this stage also believe that all objects have feelings like human beings. That is why you will often see the child feeding her teddy bear.

Children at this stage can also focus on only one aspect of a situation and can not go back. Let us now take an example. You offer cola to a 4 yr old in a tall glass. You then change your mind and pour the coke from the tall glass to a short glass and give it to the child. You will find the child will say I want the big glass. This is because she can only focus on one aspect (height) at a time. Also, she is not able to go back mentally and realise that in the process of pouring from big to small glass, no cola was taken away.

Similarly, take two plates and put in one 6 pieces of chocolate spreadout and in the other make a tower of 6 pieces of chocolate. You will find the child thinking the spread out chocolate is more. This is because the child can only focus on one aspect at a time. This limitation seriously restricts the problem solving and logical thinking abilities of the child.

It also indicates the child's inability to understand that another point of view different from her own can exist, *e.g.,* you often find children responding to your question by nodding their heads, even if they are not in the same room as you. This is because they do not see another's point of view.

Middle Childhood

During this period, children begin to understand that another view point can exist. They are also able to focus on more than one aspect of a situation and go back and forth on their thinking. This makes their thinking more logical and efficient. However, children are only comfortable with concrete ideas/objects. It means, something that is real for them, *i.e.,* either something they have seen, *e.g.,* a house or something is in front of them, a plant or something linked to what they know, *e.g.,* blue like the sky. They are not able to think about abstract ideas, *e.g.,* what would happen if everyone could fly?

Emotion

Emotions, put simply, are feelings. In infants we can see these very clearly in the form of joy, anger and fear. These are similar to the emotions that adults have.

1. **The variety of emotions increases with age:** The basic emotions of joy, fear, anger are visible in infants. Gradually, as a sense of self develops; children begin to relate with people around them and value their opinions. Then we can see the emotion like pride, shame, sympathy, guilt also developing in them.
2. **The expression of emotion also changes with age:** Emotions are both innate and learnt. The instinctive response to a stimulus is innate but how to express that feeling is learnt, *e.g.* taking away of a toy makes the child angry (innate) but instead crying she is encouraged to ask for it back (learnt). Frustration tolerance increases with age. As children grow older, their responses change in both as well as instinctive method of expression, *e.g.,* when 2 year old falls downs she cries loudly and later forgets quickly. A 6 year old on the other hand, may not cry but forgets far less easily.
3. **The triggers or cause of emotions change with age:** The stimuli that elicit emotion also change with age, *e.g.,* an infant may cry on hearing the loud explosion of a cracker but a middle childhood child may laugh. Sucking a thumb may give great joy to an infant but provides no pleasure to a child is middle childhood.
4. **The coping techniques change with age:** Methods of coping with frustration and stress change with age. While a younger child may cry, or cling to the adult, an older child is likely to suppress the emotion.

Factors Affecting Emotional Development

If we look round in our environment, we will find that people differ in the emotions they experience and express. Some are happy, some are angry, some moody, some helpful. What then affects our emotional development?

1. **Parenting style:** Democratic parenting where induction is used as a method of disciplining allows for more mature emotional development and also for development of personal behaviour.
2. **Role model:** There are two factors which influence what a child ultimately learns:
   (i) How adults and others in the child's environment handle their emotions.
   (ii) How successful is the emotional expression in achieving their needs.
3. **Violence in the child's environment:** The kind of behaviour the child see in the community (*e.g.* during riots) or on TV will affect her expressions of emotions.
4. **Cultural norms:** Emotional expressions are learnt from the environment. It is the environment that tells us how to react in a situation (*e.g.* some people feel the emotion of fear when a black cat crosses their path). It is also the environment that tells us the acceptable way of expressing ones emotions (*e.g.* in many families it is unacceptable for boys to express their distress by crying). Therefore, our cultural beliefs and values also influence our emotional development.

MOTIVATION AND LEARNING

Definition of Motivation

1. **J.P. Guilford :** Motivation is any internal factor or conditions that needs to initiate or sustain an activity.
2. **B.F. Skinner :** Motivation in school learning involves arousing, persisting, sustaining and directing desirable behaviour .

3. **Lowell :** Motivation is psycho-physiological and internal process initiated by some needs which led to activity and which will satisfy those needs.

4. **Thompson :** Motivation is the act of stimulating interest in the pupils (individuals) where there is no such interest.

5. **Woodworth :** Motivation is the state of the individual which disposes him of certain behaviour for seeking goals.

Nature and Characteristics of Motivation

On the basis of above definitions following nature and characteristics of motivation are established:

1. Motivation is such a psychological factor which is controlled by physical conditions. This is an internal process. When this process becomes active in the body of an organism, he starts activity. This very process furthers the activity and directs the activity as well. As soon as the process stops activity also stops immediately.
2. In school environment motivation arouses the behaviour of pupils, directs it and helps the pupils to persist on it. A teacher can make any thing do by the students in the class by it.
3. A person is motivated to do an activity only when he is driven by any internal need for that job. When study becomes the need of the pupil, he is motivated to study. If this need is not there in him, it is created by the teacher from outside. This need gets satisfied at the fulfillment of the activity. The same job is performed by all sports and games coach in fields and playgrounds.
4. Need of life depends upon the objectives of life. If the student has fixed the objective of scoring 80% marks in the examination, this objective works as a need for him. Thus, teacher, by making the aimless students sensitive to objectives of life, motivates them to do better and better.
5. Motivation is an art of increasing the interest of students. Students can not be motivated to teaching learning process just by arousing their interest without creating the needs.

In conclusion we can say that need is the main factor behind motivation. Other factors are interest, objectives of life, curiosity, intelligence etc.

Needs : The feeling of want of something is called need. Condition of restlessness continues until the need is fulfilled. Man manifests any specific type of behaviour because of this very tension.

Maslow's Hierarchy of Human Needs

Abraham Maslow explained the theories of motivation in 1954 in the perspective of needs. He classified human needs in five levels in a continuum of pyramid. He termed the physiological, safety and belongingness needs as lower level needs and esteem and self-actualization needs as higher level needs.

1. **Physiological needs:** These primary needs are created in an individual by nature. Needs of air, water, food, defecation etc. are such needs. Unless these needs of the individual are satisfied, he can not even think of higher level needs. Meaning thereby, we can not motivate a hungry or thirsty pupil for learning in the class. If a child does not have even resources to fulfil these needs, he can defer these needs by his will power but only for a short duration, but ultimately these needs will have any how to be fulfilled.
2. **Safety needs:** After fulfilling the physiological needs an organism wants to be protected in the environment from his enemies whether they are his fellow being or the fury of the environment in the form of heat, cold, rain etc. In the school situation a child wants that he should not be teased by any body. If the school is unable to protect the child, the child can never be motivated for learning.
3. **Needs of belongingness:** Having the above two needs been fulfilled an individual wants to be associated with others. He wants love, affection and friendship from his fellow beings. In order to satisfy these very needs child participates in different types of programmes in the school. In order to draw the attention and love of his teachers, he fulfills the home works given to him. Those teachers who fail to satisfy these needs of their pupils, they cannot motivate them for learning as well.
4. **Esteem needs :** After the lower level of needs being fulfilled, an organism wants respects and recognition in the society. For this purpose he exhibits some extra ordinary performance on certain affairs. The organism wants some powers in his hand to use it in the society. For example, he wants to become monitor of the class or captain of football or cricket team. In order to motivate such students for learning, it is necessary that such needs of these students must be fulfilled to the maximum level possible.
5. **Needs of self actualization :** An individual comes to recognise his strengths and weakness fully before coming to this last level of needs.

On the basis of potentialities he wants to do such an extra-ordinary work so that he may acquire the top place in the eyes of the people. For example, talented students after a period of time come to know that they can top the class. In order to achieve this target they try their best. If a teacher fails to recognise the abilities of these students and does not respond properly at their achievement, these students lag behind their actual level of performance.

It is clear from the above classification that there are five groups of people found in every society. The first group gets satisfied only at the fulfillment of its first level needs and does not care for the next. Second group can be satisfied only at fulfilling the two levels of needs. The next two groups are smaller than these. They can be motivated only when their higher levels of needs are fulfilled. The last group is actually never contended. It always tries its best to excel more and more.

Types of Motivation

1. **Extrinsic Motivation :** In such type of motivation efforts are made to create such environment from outside that individual starts taking interest in the task. For example, if a student does not take interest in teaching learning process because of his hunger, thirst or lack of safety, first of all, these needs of the students are satisfied. Important other extrinsic motivations are reward and punishment, praise and blame, success and failure, competition and cooperation, and so on.
2. **Intrinsic Motivation :** These motivations are related to subject matter or activities of the students. This motivation stresses to fulfil the higher level of needs such as esteem or self actualization needs. Such type of individuals can hardly be motivated by extrinsic motivation. Here efforts are made to create such an environment from within the individual that higher performance becomes his needs and objective of life. Unless and until these needs are fulfilled, he never sits idle. Knowledge of progress, novelty in the procedure, and higher aspiration level, goals, etc, are important intrinsic motivating factors.
3. **External Internal Motivation :** This is the joint technique of motivation and is applied simultaneously on the individual.

Techniques of Motivation

Important extrinsic and intrinsic techniques of motivation are as follows:

1. Reward and Punishment

Student endeavours to do the best in order to get reward. He becomes pleased when he is given reward and greater enthusiasm on the part of the student is shown. Following things must be kept in mind while giving reward to an individual.

(a) The nature or amount of reward should be according to the level of performance. Additional reward is always fatal for the future progress of an individual.

(b) Individual must know the importance of reward. If reward is given to so many individuals at a time, the reward loses its validity.

(c) Reward should not be traditional or a routine activity. Different types of rewards should be given at different occasions.

(d) Reward should have some monetary or social value.

As far as punishment is concerned its fear leads an individual not to do unwanted jobs. The child comes to the class with full preparation in order to avoid punishment. Following things must be kept in mind before assigning any punishment:

(a) Punishment should not be regular. Such punishment can make the children habitual to punishment.

(b) Punishment should not be so severe. Such punishment can create hatred in the minds of children towards the whole system.

(c) Punishment should be given keeping in view the mental and physical resistance of children.

(d) Punishment should be judiciously distributed to all guilty persons.

Researches have made it clear that reward is better technique of motivation than punishment. Punishment is fatal to the psychological development of the organism also. So, punishment should be avoided as much as possible.

2. Praise and Blame

When a child is praised at his successes, he is overjoyed. As a result he works better than before. Following points must be kept in view while using praise as a technique of motivation:

(a) If an organism is praised at every big or small successes randomly, he will be addicted to listening the words of praise.

As a result no new behaviour is created due to praise.

(b) Weaker children should be praised even at their small bits of successes while talented children should be praised only when they have really done something very unique.

(c) Praise technique should be applied according to changing ratio schedule, i.e., sometimes, it should be used and sometimes not and the subject must not know at what time this is to be given.

As far as blame is concerned, students are directly blamed for their failures and they are made ashamed. But excess use of blame as a technique of motivation may frustrate the child. Following points must be kept in mind before blaming the students on their failures:

(a) Positive efforts of a child must be praised first before blaming him on his failure.

(b) Students should not be solely made responsible for their failure. Other related factors and conditions must also be included in the list of factors causing failures in life.

(c) The language of the blame should not be insulting for students. The self respect of every individual must be recognised.

3. Success and Failure

Success creates self confidence among individuals and possibility of more successes increases. Teacher creates such an environment in the class in which all the barriers in the way of success are removed.

Failure can also work as a source of motivation. Especially the talented students accepts the failure as a challenge for them. In order to use this technique in the classroom situation, the teacher presents such problems in the class which students are unable to solve. The bright students accept this challenge for future and thus they are motivated for work.

4. Competition and Cooperation

The feeling of competition is universal in humans. In the classroom situations weak students compare themselves with their own group and bright students compare their achievements with that of bright group of students. In this way the whole class is motivated. In games and sports too, competitions works as the best motivator. Every sports person does harder and harder efforts to raise his performance level. Such type of competition is called individual competition. Team competition also works as a good motivating force. These two types of competitive feelings are aroused by the teacher in the class in order to motivate the pupils.

The utility of cooperation as a technique of motivation is very limited. Here. Students are asked to work with mutual cooperation so that every one in the group may get opportunity to develop. Project method of teaching is a good example of this technique.

5. Knowledge of Progress

It is a traditional method of motivating the students that they are regularly told about their progress on the basis of formative evaluations. When they come to know about their achievements, they work harder to raise this level due to the feedback obtained from the knowledge of their progress. Teacher and sports teacher should regularly evaluate the achievement of students and students should be informed immediately about this. If any delay is made in evaluation or its reporting, the teachers will not be able to give any feedback to his students. For this purpose, regular tests should be conducted in the class and they should be evaluated with no delay. If evaluation and its reporting takes much time, students forget their mistakes or actual activities and as a result, they do not get any feedback from these.

6. Novelty

Researches have proved that monotony makes a man bored. In order to motivate such persons in their task novelty and change in the approach is essential. In the class room situation a teacher brings about novelty in his method of teaching at regular intervals. This makes the students come across to new experiences at every movement. Level of students must be kept in view while introducing novelty in the situation so that this novelty may not work as a bouncer.

7. Aspiration Level

Level of aspiration has a direct relationship with the objectives of life. An individual can achieve the objectives of his life when his aspiration level is high. A teacher tries to raise this level as much high as possible but it is always matched with the mental or physical potentialities of the pupils. If this level of aspiration is higher than physical or mental level, student will get frustrated at their successive failures. Contrary to this if this level is lower than the physical or mental level, it will reduce the activities of students and they will develop inferiority complex.

THEORIES OF MOTIVATION

1. Instinct Theory

This theory of motivation was propounded by an English psychologist **Mc Dougall**. He pleaded that every human being has some innate powers or instincts. These instincts work as motives also and influence our behaviour. Under the influence of these instincts relationship between the object and the individual is established. Sentiments are aroused as a result of this. These sentiments organise an individual's emotional life and bring about stability in his behaviour. Thus, sentiments are an important factor behind the force of motivation. He explained the importance of self respect regarding sentiments. An individual's character is evaluated in terms of the stability of his self respect. If organisation of moral sentiments is more stable than the sentiments regarding the self respect, the character of the person will be strong.

2. Psychoanalytic Theory : (By Freud, Young and Adler)

According to them conscious plays main role in controlling an individuals' behaviour. As against unconscious mind there is the role of repression. Repression is the elimination of painful and unhealthy experiences from the conscious mind. Thus, repression is a defense mechanism with the help of which an individual tries to adjust partially. This repression is necessary because as child grows, many of his needs and feelings are disliked by the people which were earlier liked. When these needs are eliminated from the conscious mind, they are collected into unconscious mind and affect human behaviour indirectly. Sometimes these repressed needs come to the conscious level also when they receive any stimulus from outside. Thus, according to these psychologists, human behaviour is influenced by such motives also about which he is totally unaware.

3. Maslow's Need Theory

This theory has already been explained under the head of Maslow's Hierarchy of needs.

4. Social Theory

This theory is of two type :

(a) **Cultural Pattern Theory** (by **Mead & Benedict**) **:** According to this theory, behaviour of a person is influenced by the respective culture in which he lives. For example, individuals of those castes which have strict controlling system on their members become foolish, dry and short tempered when they grow. On the contrary, the castes in which children are behaved affectionately, they manifest considerate behaviour when they grow. Thus, behaviour is very much influenced by the pattern of rearing of a person. In the classroom situation, a teacher can motivate his students by his own behaviour.

(b) **Field Theory** (by **Kurt Levin**) **:** According to this theory, the behaviour of an individual is not determined by his qualities or personality traits but all those forces which act between an individual and his environment. Thus, there is a close relationship between an individual and his environment. In the class room situation a child can be motivated by creating an environment suitable to the child.

5. Drive Theory

This theory is somewhat similar to need theory of Maslow. According to this theory an individual is driven to act when certain biological needs create some inner tension which is called drive. Thus drive is the primary cause of motivation.

The drawback of this theory is that it is helpless to explain why an individual, in the absence of inner drive behaves in a particular situation due to the effect of his environment as is explained by the social theory of motivation.

6. Incentive Theory

According to this theory, external incentives such as rewards, monetary benefits, promotion in the social status etc. can also motivate an individual to act in a certain direction.

7. Expectancy Theory

According to this theory an individual is not actually getting any reward or monetary benefits but the expectation of getting such a reward or benefits can motivate him to do the job in the best manner possible. In the field of games, a sportsman can be motivated to perform his best by giving him some incentive not at present but in the future.

8. Learning of behaviour Theory (Clark Hall)

According to this theory an individual's behaviour depends on the satisfaction or dissatisfaction of his needs. When his needs are satisfied, his psychological tensions are reduced and he retains the reaction of his learnt behaviour. When his organic needs are satisfied, he learns to link the social conditions with his primary needs and retains that particular behaviour.

9. Motivation Hygiene Theory (Fredrick Herzberg)

This theory was indoctrinated in the field of industry and commerce first. Herzberg interviewed farmers, account officers, nurses and house wives in Pistbarg University in 1966 and propounded this theory.

According to this theory motives enhance the efficiency by providing comforts and satisfactions to the pupils. Motives keep them delighted by increasing their achievement on one hand and pupils get satisfied by their motives on the other. This in turn enriches learning. Since the effect of motives are positive and persists for a longer period of time, as a result motives develop the following feelings in the pupils:

(*a*) Achievement

(*b*) Recognition

(*c*) Responsibility

(*d*) Advancement

(*e*) Personal growth

The above feeling are directly affected by hygiene factors. They are given below :

(*a*) Methods of supervision

(*b*) Condition of work

(*c*) Inter-personal relations

(*d*) Social policy and administration

(*e*) Status

(*f*) Security

If level of these factors is low, the individual becomes unhappy, and as a result, learning outcome will fall. It can also develop negative attitude among the learner. The learner can be motivated by raising the level of these six hygiene factors.

This theory has direct application in the field of education and sports along with other field of life. Performance of students of government schools is low only because of low level of some of hygiene factors. If organizational climate of the school is made good, it will automatically increase the achievement of pupils.

10. Operant Conditioning Model of Motivation

This model was presented by Skinner. It suggests that behaviour would change by the consequence of that very behaviour. If the result of a particular behaviour is satisfactory, it will be automatically reinforced and repeated in future. Reinforcement is given from outside also for the recurrence of desired behaviour.

Thus, this model does not give importance to the inner motivation of the individual. It ignores drives and needs of learners as well. Level of aspiration is also ignored by this model. This model is rather based on the observable and measurable overt behavioural responses which are modified slowly by giving proper reinforcement.

According to this model the desirable behaviours are first identified. Then conditions are created for the occurrence of these behaviours. And finally, once they occur, reinforcement is given for the recurrence of these behaviours.

Techniques of motivation and students' needs, teaching objectives and learning structures

Need (lower needs)	Teaching structure	Teaching objectives	Techniques of motivation (Extrinsic)
1. Physiological	1. Signal learning	1. Knowledge	1. Reward
2. Safety	2. Chain learning	2. Comprehension or understanding	2. Praise and reward
3. Belongingness (higher needs)	3. Multiple discrimination learning	3.Above + Analysis	3. Success and failure (extrinsic and intrinsic)
4. Esteem	4. Cocept learning	4.Application	4. Competition and cooperation
5. Self actualization	5. Principle learning	5.Creativity	5. Knowledge of result 6. Novelty 7. Level of aspiration 8. Self-motivation

Techniques of motivation and students' needs : The teacher should first of all find out the needs of his student's *i.e.*, at what level of needs the students are. Only then the teacher can give intrinsic or extrinsic motivation to his students. It is also likely that students do not have the capacity to think beyond the third level of Maslow's needs. In that case the teacher should create the other two needs in his students by telling the students about the goals of life and its related difficulties.

These very needs will motivate the students for effort and desired behaviour will be seen in future.

Motivation techniques and learning objectives

While selecting suitable techniques of motivation the teacher keeps this fact into account what learning objectives he had formulated in the beginning. Thus, a teacher takes 6 × 3 = 18 objectives into account while selecting motivation techniques. We will discuss these three domains of objectives in relation to motivation techniques below :

(a) *Cognitive Domain Objectives :* If teacher has restricted his objectives to the level of application only, then for realising these three levels of objectives, a composite techniques of motivation may be proved to be successful. But if the objectives are extended to analysis, synthesis or evaluation, motivation techniques will not work much. The teacher will rather have to take the help of teaching strategies and tactics such as self study, problem solving group discussion, symposium and seminars etc.

(b) *Affective objectives :* Lower level of affective objectives like receiving, responding and valuing etc, can be achieved by using techniques of motivation. But techniques of motivation are not very much helpful for achieving higher level of objectives and in that case, the teacher should use strategies of teaching like self study, brain storming , CAI etc. more than motivation techniques.

(c) *Psychomotor objectives :* Techniques of motivation are most helpful for realising objectives of psychomotor domain and extrinsic techniques are more powerful than intrinsic techniques here.

Motivation and Learning Structure

Various techniques of motivation should also he selected according to different structures of learning. These five structures are given here:

(a) **Signal learning** : Stimulus and responses are directly connected here. Extrinsic techniques of motivation are most suitable here.

(b) **Chain learning** : Chain is formed between stimuli and responses here. Environment is especially significant here so, extrinsic techniques are most suitable in chain learning.

(c) **Multiple discrimination learning** : So many stimuli are presented before the students simultaneously here and they respond to these stimuli on the basis of similarities and differences. Environment and content both are important here. In this type of learning structure, both types of motivation techniques are useful.

(d) **Concept learning** : In such type of learning content and its presentation are given preference here. Therefore, only intrinsic techniques of motivation are useful here.

(e) **Principle learning** : In this structure, various concepts are presented in the form of chain here. When this is done, they take the form of laws or principles. It means that only content is important here. So, only intrinsic techniques of motivation is useful here.

FACTORS CONTRIBUTING TO LEARNING

Introduction

Learning, can be considered as the process by which skills, attitudes, knowledge and concepts are acquired, understood, applied and extended. All human beings, whether grown ups or children engage in the process of learning, either consciously, sub-consciously or subliminally. It is through learning that their competence and ability to function in their environment get enhanced. It is important to understand that while we learn some ideas and concepts through instruction or teaching, we also learn through our feelings and experiences. Feelings and experiences are a tangible part of our lives and these greatly influence what we learn, how we learn and why we learn.

Learning has been considered partly a cognitive process and partly a social and affective one. It qualifies as a cognitive process because it involves the functions of attention, perception, reasoning, analysis, drawing of conclusions, making interpretations and giving meaning to the observed phenomena. All of these are mental processes which relate to the intellectual functions of the individual. Learning is a social and affective process, as the societal and cultural context in which we function and the feelings and experiences which we have, greatly influence our ideas, concepts, images and understanding of the world. These constitute inner subjective interpretations and represent our own unique, personalized constructions of the specific universe of functioning. Our knowledge, ideas, concepts, attitudes, beliefs and the skills which we acquire are a consequence of these combined processes.

CLASSIFICATION OF FACTORS: PERSONAL & ENVIRONMENT

To understand how we categorise the factors affecting learning, let us begin by considering the following examples:

- Ravi is sixteen year old and wants to please his mother by getting good results in his board examinations. He is so eager to please her, that he spends long hours of concentrated time and energy on his studies. He consciously tries to control other sources of distraction in his life and reduces the time spent on watching television, playing games and chatting with his friends.

- Rita Williams wants to be a famous tennis player. To achieve her goal, she practices tennis whenever she can, even though she gets no encouragement from her family. She makes it a point to watch tennis matches and maintain a good rapport with her sports teacher.
- Yuvraj is a good student, but lately he has been scoring very low marks at school. He is not able to concentrate or pay attention and his class work and home assignments reflect a very poor quality. Sources revealed that his parents fight a lot with each other and are about to get divorced.
- Arti and Kavita are two sisters. Arti is very good at art and craft and can sketch just about anything she sees. Kavita has a ear for music. She knows most songs and can sing them even if she has heard them only once. Both of them spend hours together pursuing their respective interest areas.
- Sayeeda is tall, attractive and has a very good figure. She wants to be a model or an air-hostess and nurtures this secretly as her dream. She is too scared to share her wishes with her family, since she belongs to an orthodox family, where girls at best can pursue teaching as a career. When she tries telling her mother what she wants, she is firmly told that she can only do her B.Ed and can go to the coaching classes for these.

The above cited examples illustrate that learning is a universal phenomenon mediated by a number of factors, both personal and environmental in nature. The dictum "everybody learns" is as true as its corollary, *i.e.*, everybody learns in accordance with his/her unique, individualized blend of personal and environmental factors. For example, in case of Ravi, the desire to please his mother, striving to do well in his board exams and managing his life situations appropriately constitute the key factors which influence him. For Rita Williams, it is her intrinsic desire to be a good tennis player which is paramount. She is not deterred by the lack of family support and continues to make efforts to promote her love for tennis on her own and fulfil her desire to be successful.

In case of Yuvraj, in spite of his innate capacity to study and perform well, his lack of achievement can be attributed to the emotional insecurity stemming from his parents' divorce. As far as Arti and Kavita are concerned, their special interests and talent in art and music respectively, seem to guide their activities.

For Sayeeda, the home environment and family culture and values determine her professional choice. Her own inner interests, desires and wishes are not to be taken into cognizance.

In all the examples cited, we can find evidence of both personal and environmental factors influencing the process of learning. Learning can thus be defined as a function of the interaction of personal and environmental factors.

$$L = f\,(EF \times PF)$$

L = learning; f = function; EF = environmental factors; PF = personal factors.

Personal factors are the intra individual factors like motivation, interests, abilities etc which predispose an individual towards learning as in the case of Rita Williams, Arti and Kavita. Environmental factors on the other hand, are those contextual factors which highlight the role of the environment in learning, such as the socio-emotional, societal and cultural factors as seen in the case of Yuvraj and Sayeeda. Although the two factors represent different categories, they operate in a common system. The environmental factors provide the context within which the personal factors, operate. The learner and the learning process can only be completely understood with reference to the interaction of both environmental and personal factors. This may be diagrammatically represented as follows:

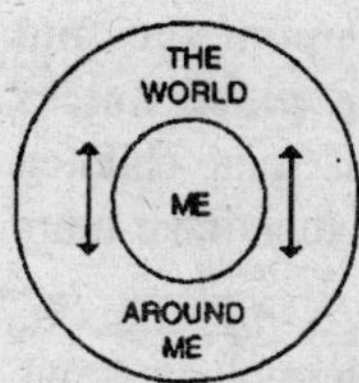

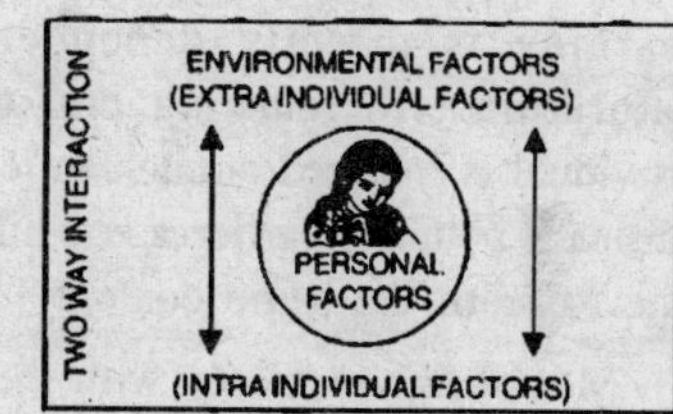

Fig: *Factors affecting learning*

Personal Factors Influencing Learning

The process of learning is influenced by a variety of personal factors. A thorough knowledge of these factors will prove very helpful for teachers and parents in understanding and guiding their children's learning. Some of the personal factors that influence the learning process may be classified as under : sensation and perception, fatigue and boredom, maturation, emotional condition, needs, interests, motivation, attention, intelligence, aptitude, attitude, etc. Let us discuss the important personal factors in the following sub-sections.

Sensation and Perception

Apart from the general health of the students, sensation and perception are the psychological factors which help in learning. Sensation is at the core of perception. There are five sense organs *i.e.*, skin, ears, tongue, eyes and nose. These sense organs are the gateways of knowledge and help in perception of various stimuli in the environment. Any defect in any of the sense organs will affect learning and hence acquisition of knowledge. For example, defects of vision such as myopia, hypermetropia, astigmatism, etc., cause headaches, nausia and general disinclination to study. A blind person depends upon the sense of touch or skin for learning and thus acquires knowledge and skills, as he can not visualise the objects. The stimuli are preceived and assimilated, and hence learnt through various sense organs. In this way we can say that sensation and perception is the bases of knowledge and learning.

Fatigue and Boredom

It is virtually boredom or lassitude rather than fatigue which bothers the students. The difference between the two is that fatigue is mental or physical tiredness which decreases in efficiency and competency to work. Boredom, on the other hand, is a lack of desire on an aversion to work. Such an aversion makes one feel fatigued without being actually fatigued. Studying seldom causes fatigue. It is mainly boredom which, besides causing the impression of fatigue, decreases student efficiency in learning.

Age and Maturation

Learning is directly dependent upon age and maturation. No learning can take place unless individual is matured enough to learn. Some children can learn better at earlier age while others take more time to learn the same content.

Mental age increases with the chronological age and ceases at about the age of sixteen years. Increase in age means intellectual maturation which helps in solving difficult problems. The principle of maturation warns us against enforcing learning on a child when he is not mature enough to learn the specific skills. Teachers should explain this principle to parents who are over ambitious or over enthusiastic in sending their children to school at the very early age.

Emotional Conditions

Desirable emotional conditions enhance the quality and speed of learning. Happiness, joy and satisfaction are always favourable for any type of learning. Adverse emotional conditons, on the other hand, hinder learning. Many studies have established the fact that emotional strain, stress, tensions, disturbances, etc., are extremely inimical to scholastic pursuits.

Needs

A need is the lack of something which, if provided, would facilitate child's usual behaviour. The lack of something is experienced by the child. The child then tries to perform that activity which culminates in the satisfaction of the need. Thus, the needs are associated with goals. Among human beings, the needs are realtively permanent tendencies which seek satisfaction in achieving certain specific goals. When these goals are achieved, the particular need is satisfied or met for the time being, but it recurs sooner or later and energises further activity. The needs in human beings can be physiological such as need for oxygen, food, water, etc. They may be social such as the need for affection, recognition, self-regard, etc. Social needs are however, quite different from physiological needs. Social needs might originate after physiological needs are satisfied. These needs have a complex structure and dominate the individual's behaviour.

There is not equal urgency in the satisfaction of all needs. Some have to be satisfied before others can manifest themselves.

In schools, children are not expected to do any intellectual thinking unless their physiological needs are satisfied. Poor, starved children may concentrate less on attainment of knowledge than on food. Similarly, very cold or hot classrooms or over-crowded seats will not be conducive to good learning. Likewise the need for safety, love and esteem, all act as powerful motives in the learning situations. If the child is afraid of the teacher or feels unsafe while in the school on account of too much beating or some other form of punishment, no learning can take place. Similarly, his needs for warmth and affection are very stimulating and hence results in effective learning.

Interests

Various types of interests of the students can be exploited to facilitate their learning. The interests during early infancy are mostly limited and short lived. As the child grows older his interests diversify and stabilize. You, a school teacher, should have thorough knowledge of children's interests. You can eliminate much drudgery, monotony and boredom from the school work if you make your instruction lively and stimulating and arouse student interest in it.

Once the students' interest is aroused in an activity you should expend more effort on it. No learning can be achieved without proper expenditure of effort on it. Students can even overcome distraction, fatigue and boredom if they feel interested in your instruction and class activities. It has often been found that, in most cases, fatigue in reality is loss of interest in the learning activity. Interest, should be exploited to yield results of greater quantity and quality learning in school.

Life is so exciting that many interesting things and activities often clamor to attract our attention.

Children frequently face the dilemma of mutually conflicting interests. Immediate interests often seem to be clashing with the remoter ones. A student might be in a quandary at least for the time being when his interest in sports impels him towards the play-field and his interest in studies force him to concentrate on books.

In such cases of conflicting interests a lot of hesitancy, wastage, frustration and unhappiness is bound to follow. What is needed is education at home and school which helps/trains children to achieve a healthy balance in their interests. They should be trained to budget their time in such a manner as to pay a reasonable attention to various interests, scholastic, athletic, social etc., within the time at their disposal.

Motivation

Motivation is the heart of the learning process. It generates the will in an individual to do something. Adequate motivation not only engages the student in an activity which results in learning, but also sustains and directs learning. Two types of motivation are commonly recognised. These are: intrinsic and extrinsic motivation.

Intelligence

Intelligence as expressed by an I.Q. score on an intelligence test is positively related to learning. Generally, students with higher I.Q. learn rapidly. However, higher I.Q. in itself is no guarantee for rapid learning, since other factors such as needs, interest, motivation, etc., of the students and the methods used for learning are also important.

Aptitude

A student who possesses appropriate aptitude for a particular subject of study or skill, will learn better and retain it for a longer time. On the other hand, he will require relatively longer time to study a subject for which he lacks natural aptitude. He is liable to forget it soon besides feeling bored and unhappy all the time while learning it. Hence, it is extremely desirable to analyse the aptitude of students before prescribing courses of study for them.

Attitude

The learning process is also influenced considerably by the attitude of the student. If he is alert, attentive and interested in the material to be learnt, he is bound to have a favourable attitude towards it. Such an attitude will enable him to tackle the learning situation economically, pleasantly and effectively. Conversely, if he is inattentive and is uninterested in the material his attitude is bound to be unfavourable. This will hinder the smooth learning of the material in hand besides involving undue strain and tension in the learner.

Environmental Factors

Environmental influences begin since the time of the conception of the child in the womb of the mother. Mother's mental, physical and emotional conditions influence the development of foetus in the womb. The external environment starts from the time of birth of the child. It (external environment) refers to the surroundings which prevail in home, school and locality. At these places, the child interacts with members of the family, teachers, classmates or peers and neighbours and establishes relationship with them. The relationship with the members of the society, and the surroundings may affect the development of the child and also the way he learns. Some of the environmental factors are discussed as follows:

Surrounding : Natural, Social and Cultural

As the title of the sub-section indicates, we shall discuss here natural, social and cultural environment the child interacts with and get influenced.

Natural surrounding covers the climatic and atmospheric condition. These conditions affect learning directly. It has been found that high temperature and humidity reduces mental efficiency. For a limited time, humidity and high temperature can be tolerated but prolonged humidity and high temperature become unbearable and decrease mental efficiency. The intellectual productivity and creativeness of people living in hot regions are much low. Likewise, the morning time is always better for mastering difficult tasks. Mental efficiency decreases due to increased humidity and temperature. Studies on the academic progress of evening school students shows losses of efficiency varying from one to six per cent.

Social surrounding includes especially the environment of home, school and locality. Physical conditions at home such as large family, small family, (specific place of the study), insufficient ventilation, improper lighting, uncomfortable temperature, noisy home environment due to use of radio, TV, etc., noisy neighbourhood, constant visits by friends or relatives, etc., influence the intellectual learning of the student. The socio-emotional factors such as child rearing practices, reward and punishment, scope for freedom and independence in activities and decision making, play and study facilities, ambitions and aspirations of the parents, disorganisation and discord among birth positions such as eldest, youngest or single child have their definite influence on learning. For example, a student who comes from a very poor family and never had any intellectual stimulation at home remains dull and unresponsive in the class. In some societies there is a strong sex bias. Girls are directly or indirectly told that education is not meant for them. In the middle class families, on the other hand, parents are rather over-ambitious. They wish their children to make quick academic progress, grow-up and find a respectable vocation preferably a white collar job. Such children, therefore get sufficient incentive from their families. This, of course, is most favourable to scholastic learning, although an overdose of family emphasis on acquiring academic excellence might affect the child's mental and physical health adversely. Similarly, school activities, study facilities and teaching methods and behaviour of teachers, principals and non-teaching staff have an impact upon learning. If the school atmosphere is unconducive, it adversely affects the learning process. Locality also has an influence on a child. If the locality is bad, the learning will be ineffective to some extent.

Cultural demands and social expectations also influence learning. The spirit of culture is reflected in its social and educational institutions. Children's learning, therefore, is greatly determined by the demands and expectations of their culture. Thus, for instance, in an industrialized culture the emphasis mostly centres mechanical sciences and preparing children for highly mechanised vocations. In an agriculture based community, on the other hand, the educational process focusses on preparing its members for those skills which are suited to the needs of an agrarian community.

The philosophical elements of culture also influence the spirit of children's learning. Children in a democratic culture tend to acquire democrative and values and attitudes. A feudal, aristocratic or dictatorial culture, on the other hand, promotes autocratic modes of thought and behaviour.

Relationship with Teacher, Parents and Peers

The teacher is an important constituent in the instructional process. She/he plays an important role in shaping the behaviour of students. The way he teaches and manages the students has an affect on their learning. An authoritarian teacher will create an aggression and hostility among students while a democratic teacher will create a participatory climate for learning. The democratic environment leads students to constructive, thoughtful and cooperative behaviour. Generally, students learn better in a democratic set up because they like democratic procedures. The teacher is no more an instructor or the director of learning in a democratic set up. She/he helps his/her students in their learning. The teachers no more dominate the scene, they can get better results by decentralizing authority, increasing independence of students. They can attend to the comments and questions of the students. They can encourage students to participate in learning activities in and outside the class. There should be more emphasis on activity-centred classroom where student's active participation in the teaching-learning process is encouraged and the teacher acts as a guide to promote learning.

Relationship with parents plays a vital role in the learning process of the student. If the child-parents relationship is based on mutual respect and faith, it can provide the child a congenial atmosphere which in turn can facilitate his/her learning. A distorted and unhealthy environment, on the other hand, adversely affects the learning of the student. The upward mobility brings resistance on the part of the student to learn. Students in such families find themselves unable to cope up. A subtle but powerful influence on the growing child arises from his/her position among the children in the family. The parents of the first born expect the child to act like miniature adults and hence the first-born are found to encounter a variety of expectations and stresses. Whereas parents tend to be more relaxed in their do's and dont's with the last-born. Factors like traumatic events at home, separation or death can also precipitate learning problems in the normal child.

A healthy peer group relationship also plays an important role in learning. Student-student relationship in the classroom, school, society, etc., create a particular type of emotional climate. The climate solely depends upon their relationships. A sound relationships provides a tension free environment to the student to learn more and to compete in the class. If the relationship among peers is not good, it adversely affects their learning. Therefore, to improve the classroom learning climate, free discussion should be there. You should help your students understand each other in formal or informal meetings. They should be encouraged to meet each other and their teachers freely. If any mis-understanding is created or developed, it should be immediately clarified so as to maintain the healthy climate and cordial relationship among peers.

Mass Media Influence on Learning

Today, mass media is all pervaive and omnipresent. Our day-to-day life is inundated with the presence of mass media. We can access mass media through television, radio and print. If, some years ago, radio and print were the main tools of mass communication, television seems to have taken over the place now.

Mass media is informative and influence the thinking of people. It creates a learning environment. Mass media is not controlled by a single agency and what it represents is neither organized learning (as in schools) nor the immediate reality surrounding you (as in home and community). Mass media offers a wide range of information and reality far removed from immediate reality. The informal learning environment created by mass media is intense and far reaching in impact than any other informal learning environment.

Learning through print medium presupposes the ability to read alike. Hence, its reach as an informal learning agency is limited. Radio is more effective than print as the listener requires only comprehension skill. The advent of twenty four hours television channels have redefined the role of mass media as an agency of informal learning. Television is more powerful and effective than radio and print as it exercises greater influence on the viewers through visual images.

Both radio and television appeal to literates and illiterates alike. The mass media-is not an agency of organized learning. However, the mass media is sometimes used by state agencies to effect purposeful and specific learning at a mass level. For example, the family planning, pulse polio, and HIV/AIDS programmes on mass media sponsored by the state are intended to bring about behaviour modification among the masses.

For children who have access to the mass media, especially the television, it becomes an additional and supportive source of learning in the context of organized learning. Children who are exposed to the mass media are well informsd and that often facilitate their reddiness for new learning in the organized learning context. However, learning through the mass media, especially the television is not always positive or constnictive learning. Through television viewing, children often pick up values that are not in conformity with the values of the family, school, or community. Thus, television or any other mass media teaches academic and cognitive skills and social behaviours but it can have both positive and negative influences on children.

These days television and radio are used as supportive agencies in imparting organized learning. For example, the Indira Gandhl National Open University utilizes the electronic media (television and radio) for teaching-learning purposes. We can say that the electronic media is used for creating a virtual learning environment. Through interactive radio counselling students sitting across the country are able to tune in to listen to their teachers and interact with them. Teleconferencing creates interactive virtual classroom. The virtual learning environment created on television or computer is found effective due to the presence of visual images and the use of multimedia. Then, there are noninteractive virtual learning environments, like the telecast of UGC's country-wideclassrooms. Decades ago when television was a rarity, the government of India used All India Radio to educate the Indian fanners about the technological advances in farming to bring in India's Green Revolution. Thus, mass media can play a significant role in formal and non-formal learning.

MULTIPLE CHOICE QUESTIONS

1. According to Piaget, during the first stage of development (birth to about 2 years age), a child learns best
   (a) by thinking in an abstract fashion
   (b) by applying newly acquired knowledge of language
   (c) by using the senses
   (d) by comprehending neutral words
2. The most intense and crucial socialization takes place
   (a) during early childhood
   (b) during adulthood
   (c) throughout the life of a person
   (d) during adolescence
3. Heredity is considered as a .... social structure.
   (a) dynamic (b) static
   (c) primary (d) secondary
4. Theory of learning which totally and only depends on '*observable behaviour*' is associated with .... theory of learning.
   (a) Behaviourist (b) Constructivist
   (c) Cognitivist (d) Developmental
5. Which of the following does ***not*** reflect 'teaching for understanding'?
   (a) Help students see similarities and differences and generate analogies
   (b) Enable students to memorize isolated facts and procedures
   (c) Ask students to explain a phenomenon or a concept in their own words
   (d) Teach students to provide examples to illustrate how a law works
6. Which of the following is ***not*** a characteristic feature of intrinsically motivated children?
   (a) They display a high level of energy while working
   (b) They like challenging tasks
   (c) They always succeed
   (d) They enjoy doing their work
7. A teacher wants the gifted children of her class to achieve their potential. Which of the following should she ***not*** do to achieve her objective?
   (a) Segregate them from their peers for special attention
   (b) Challenge them to enhance their creativity
   (c) Teach them to enjoy non-academic activities
   (d) Teach them to manage stress
8. Which of the following is ***not*** a sign of reading difficulty among young learners? Difficulty in
   (a) understanding words and ideas
   (b) spelling consistency
   (c) letter and word recognition
   (d) reading speed and fluency
9. 'Self-regulation' of learners refers to
   (a) rules and regulations made by the student body
   (b) self-discipline and control
   (c) their ability to monitor their own learning
   (d) creating regulations for student behaviour
10. Which of the following statements ***cannot*** be considered as a feature of 'learning'?
    (a) Study of behaviour is learning
    (b) Unlearning is also a part of learning
    (c) Learning is a process that mediates behaviour
    (d) Learning is something that occurs as a result of certain experiences
11. Constructivism as a theory
    (a) emphasises on memorising information and testing through recall
    (b) emphasises on the dominant role of the teacher
    (c) focuses on the role of imitation
    (d) emphasises the role of the learner in constructing his own view of the world
12. A creative learner refers to one who is
    (a) capable of scoring consistently good marks in tests
    (b) good at lateral thinking and problem solving
    (c) very talented in drawing and painting
    (d) highly intelligent
13. Development of concepts is primarily a part of
    (a) physical development
    (b) social development
    (c) emotional development
    (d) intellectual development

14. Individual learners differ from each other in
(*a*) sequence of development
(*b*) general capacity for development
(*c*) principles of growth and development
(*d*) rate of development

15. The statement : 'An important precondition for the proper development of a child is ensuring her/his healthy physical development'
(*a*) is true because physical development occupies the topmost place in the sequence of development
(*b*) is true because physical development is interrelated with other domains of development
(*c*) is untrue as physical development does not affect other domains of development in any way
(*d*) may be incorrect as development varies from individual to individual

16. Irfan breaks toys and dismantles them to explore their components. What would you do?
(*a*) Encourage his inquisitive nature and channelise his energy
(*b*) Make him understand that toys should not be broken
(*c*) Never let Irfan play with toys
(*d*) Always keep a close watch

17. Understanding the principles of development of a child helps a teacher in
(*a*) rationalizing why the learner ought to be taught
(*b*) effectively catering to the different learning styles of learners
(*c*) identifying the social status of the learner
(*d*) identifying the economic background of the learner

18. Every learner is unique means that
(*a*) A common curriculum for all learners is not possible
(*b*) It is impossible to develop the potential of learners in a heterogeneous class
(*c*) No two learners are alike in their abilities, interests and talents
(*d*) Learners do not have any common qualities, nor do they share common goals

19. The statement 'Men are generally more intelligent than women'
(*a*) shows gender bias
(*b*) is true for different domains of intelligence
(*c*) is ture
(*d*) may be true

20. Christina took her class for a field trip and after coming back, she discussed the trip with her students. It may be connotated as
(*a*) Learning for Assessment
(*b*) Learning of Assessment
(*c*) Assessment of Learning
(*d*) Assessment for Learning

21. Human development is based on certain principles. Which of the following is ***not*** a principle of human development?
(*a*) General to Specific
(*b*) Reversible
(*c*) Continuity
(*d*) Sequentiality

22. Centrally sponsored scheme of Integrated Education for disabled children aims at providing educational opportunities to children with disabilities in
(*a*) Open schools
(*b*) Blind Relief Association schools
(*c*) Regular schools
(*d*) Special schools

23. Which of the following statements is true about 'learning'?
(*a*) Learning is not affected by emotional factors at any stage of learning.
(*b*) Learning is fundamentally a mental activity.
(*c*) Errors made by children indicate that no learning has taken place.
(*d*) Learning is effective in an environment that is emotionally positive and satisfying for the learners.

24. The main purpose of assessment should be
(*a*) to decide if a student should be promoted to the next class
(*b*) to diagnose and remedy gaps in learning
(*c*) to point out the errors of the learners
(*d*) to measure the achievement of learners

25. Helping learners recapitulate or recall what they have already learnt is important because
(*a*) it is an effective way of revising old lessons
(*b*) it enhances the memory of learners thereby strengthening learning
(*c*) it is a convenient beginning for any classroom instruction
(*d*) relating new information to prior knowledge enhances learning

26. Creative answers require
(*a*) open-ended questions
(*b*) a highly disciplined classroom
(*c*) direct teaching and direct questions
(*d*) content-based questions

27. Learners should ***not*** be encouraged to
(*a*) participate in as many co-curricular activities as possible
(*b*) memorize all the answers to questions which the teacher may ask
(*c*) ask as many questions as possible both inside and outside the class

(*d*) actively interact with other learners in group work

28. Which of the following is ***not*** an appropriate tool for Formative Assessment?
(*a*) Term test (*b*) Quiz and games
(*c*) Assignment (*d*) Oral questions

29. Diagnosis of the gaps in the learning of students should be followed by
(*a*) systematic revision of all lessons
(*b*) reporting the findings to learners and parents
(*c*) appropriate remedial measures
(*d*) intensive drill and practice

30. Multilingual character of Indian society should be seen as
(*a*) a challenge to teacher's capacity to motivate students to learn
(*b*) a factor that makes school life a complex experience for the learners
(*c*) a hindrance in teaching-learning process
(*d*) a resource for enrichment of school life

31. Which of the following statements regarding personality traits is correct?
(*a*) Traits of personality can not be developed in isolation without taking the help of environment
(*b*) Subjective traits of the individual are determined by genetic factors
(*c*) Bad environment can surpass good inheritance but good environment is not a substitute for poor heredity
(*d*) All of these

32. Which of the following characteristics denote infancy period?
(*a*) Physical growth is curvilinear
(*b*) Physical growth is rapid
(*c*) Head grows at relatively slower rate as compared to other parts of the body
(*d*) All of these

33. Which of the following is not the characteristic of infancy period?
(*a*) From bilateral to unilateral trend in motor organs
(*b*) From general to specific trend in motor organs
(*c*) Emotional/social development is not associated with motor development
(*d*) Steady mental development

34. Which of the following illustrates conceptual development?
(*a*) Perception is the beginning of concept formation
(*b*) Concept changes with changes in experiences
(*c*) Concept changes with age
(*d*) All of these

35. There is one thing common in language and physical development what is that?
(*a*) Spurts of development at different ages
(*b*) Dependence on experience
(*c*) Dependence on training
(*d*) None of these

36. Which of the following characteristics is not associated with emotional development?
(*a*) Emotion is accompanied by physiological changes
(*b*) Emotions start immediately after birth
(*c*) Intense form of emotions are seen during early childhood period
(*d*) Emotions are unrelated to physical development

37. The child acquires about three fourth of the brain weight by the age of
(*a*) 2½ years (*b*) 2 years
(*c*) 6 years (*d*) 8 years

38. Social development of an infant depends on
(*a*) his chance of interaction with others
(*b*) love and affection shown to the child
(*c*) the extent to which he is able to attract the attention of others
(*d*) all of the above

39. In which of the following stages the child looks self centred?
(*a*) Infancy (*b*) Early childhood
(*c*) Adolescence (*d*) Adulthood

40. In the period of infancy, emotions are
(*a*) intense, frequent and unstable
(*b*) like an open book(overt)
(*c*) need based
(*d*) all of these

41. Which of the following organs of the body shows rapid growth in infancy?
(*a*) growth of hands (*b*) growth of head
(*c*) growth of legs (*d*) growth of fingers

42. In normal learning environment, forgetting is caused
(*a*) due to back of practice for a long time
(*b*) due to the interference of other learnt material
(*c*) due to lack of consolidation of memory traces
(*d*) all of these

43. Clear conception of size, weight, colour, time etc., is seen at the age of
(*a*) six (*b*) four
(*c*) four and half (*d*) five

44. Which of the following is not the characteristics of intellectual development of early childhood?
(*a*) increased span of attention
(*b*) exploration of the environment
(*c*) ability to verbalize all known concepts
(*d*) ability to distinguish past, present and future

45. Social development by the end of early childhood is marked by
(a) the feeling of autonomy
(b) the end of solitary plays
(c) the temperament of co-operation and friendliness
(d) all of these

46. Fictional world of the child starts at the age of
(a) 5-6 (b) 6-8
(c) 3-4 (d) 4-5

47. Girls are more dominating than boys in social situations in which of the following periods?
(a) pre-adolescent period
(b) early childhood period
(c) both of these
(d) none of these

48. In the period of early childhood, child is
(a) helpless to hide his emotions
(b) seen shifting his emotions very rapidly and frequently
(c) guided by his innate tendencies and instincts
(d) all of these

49. A nursery teacher should organize
(a) group games in the school
(b) those games which involve motor organs of the body
(c) those games which help the child to manipulate the environment
(d) all of these

50. Later childhood is called latency period because
(a) creative potentials are dormant
(b) sex remains dormant
(c) it is a period of inactivity
(d) all of these

51. Physical development of later childhood is marked by
(a) Auscification of bones
(b) Permanent teeth
(c) Excessive motor activity
(d) All of these

52. Girls surpass boys physically in
(a) infancy
(b) later childhood
(c) early childhood
(d) adolescence

53. The period of later childhood is marked by
(a) intellectual maturity
(b) high muscular energy
(c) hero worship
(d) all of these

54. Which of the following is not the characteristics of intellectual development of later childhood?
(a) High interest in science fiction
(b) Increased logical power
(c) Careful for future
(d) End of imaginary fears

55. Children are very much hateful or indifferent to opposite sex at the age of
(a) 11-12 (b) 13-14
(c) 10-11 (d) 15-16

56. Period of later childhood is marked by
(a) slow and steady physical growth
(b) stability in emotions
(c) anger against injustice
(d) all of these

57. At the end of later childhood period, the child
(a) feels himself superior to girls
(b) becomes independent of his family
(c) wants to become hero
(d) all of these

58. The best place of social development for a 12 years old child is
(a) neighbourhood
(b) family
(c) playground
(d) school

59. Group activities and group loyalties are at its peak at the age of
(a) 10-12 (b) 13-15
(c) 8-10 (d) 18-20

60. A teacher should not let a 12 years old child any time free because
(a) child is always interested to get involve in physical or mental activities
(b) spurts of creativity are seen at this age
(c) child is frustrated
(d) all of these

61. Elektra complex refers to
(a) daughter comes closer to the father
(b) son comes closer to the mother
(c) inferiority complex in the presence of girls
(d) none of these

62. According to Freud, super ego is properly developed during
(a) latency period (b) anal period
(c) phallic period (d) none of these

63. Development is a process of observable social interaction. This is the opinion of
(a) Erikson (b) Skinner
(c) Robert Sears (d) None of these

64. The secondary behaviour of the child according to Robert Sears starts with
(a) reinforcement (b) imitation
(c) modelling (d) none of these

65. The period of sensory motor adoptation of Piaget is
(a) 0-2 years (b) 1-3 years
(c) 3-5 years (d) 4-6 years

66. The child adopts the view points of others on the basis of consequences of these views in the
(*a*) third stage of Kohlberg's theory
(*b*) second stage of Kohlberg's theory
(*c*) fourth stage of Kohlberg's theory
(*d*) fifth stage of Kohlberg's theory

67. Which of the following is not the view point of cognitive theories of development?
(*a*) moral principles are acquired automatically with age
(*b*) super ego is formed during the period of adolescence
(*c*) Moral values are determined by culture
(*d*) Mural principles are universal

68. Organization of sensory experiences about a particular object is called
(*a*) percepts (*b*) reasoning
(*c*) concept (*d*) none of these

69. The concept building in a person depends on
(*a*) the age and maturity of the person
(*b*) past experiences of the learner
(*c*) intelligence of the learner
(*d*) all of these

70. Agreement on a concept is possible because
(*a*) concepts are subjective
(*b*) concepts are objective
(*c*) concepts are hierarchical
(*d*) b and c both

71. Which of the following statements about concepts is correct?
(*a*) Some concepts are more powerful than others
(*b*) All concepts are universal
(*c*) Concepts are differentiated on the basis of their attributes
(*d*) None of these

72. Which is the highest level of concept formation?
(*a*) formal level (*b*) sensory level
(*c*) concrete level (*d*) none of these

73. How many steps of problem solving has been given by Gates?
(*a*) Six (*b*) Seven
(*c*) Five (*d*) Ten

74. Freeman considers intelligence as an ability
(*a*) to adjust in an adverse situation
(*b*) to learn better and faster
(*c*) to manipulate abstract materials
(*d*) all of these

75. Single factor theory of intelligence was given by
(*a*) Alfred Binet (*b*) Thorndike
(*c*) Freeman (*d*) None of them

76. Which of the following is not the characteristics of 'S' factor according to Spearman ?
(*a*) It is the acquired capacity of the individual
(*b*) Specialization in only one trade is possible
(*c*) It varies from activity to activity in the same individual
(*d*) Individuals differ only in 'S' factor of intelligence

77. In multifactor theory, range is related to
(*a*) Number of tasks that a person can do in a limited period of time
(*b*) Difficulty level of items
(*c*) General intelligence of learners
(*d*) None of these

78. SI model of intelligence was given by I P Guilford in
(*a*) 1911 (*b*) 1904
(*c*) 1966 (*d*) 1975

79. Hierarchy theory of intelligence was given by
(*a*) Jenson
(*b*) Thorndike
(*c*) Burt and Vernon
(*d*) None of them

80. In the pre-Binet period, intelligence was considered as
(*a*) Sensory acuity of the individual
(*b*) Verbal ability of the individual
(*c*) Associative ability of the individual
(*d*) All of these

81. An age scale of intelligence was first developed by
(*a*) Spearman (*b*) Terman
(*c*) Binet-Simon (*d*) None of them

82. Binet-Simon scale of intelligence measures
(*a*) General mental abilities not specific ones.
(*b*) Mental growth of the individual over a period of time
(*c*) The aptitude or level of an examinee not their speed
(*d*) All of these

83. WAIS came into being in
(*a*) 1939 (*b*) 1955
(*c*) 1960 (*d*) 1964

84. Wechsler developed an intelligence test for children in
(*a*) 1939 (*b*) 1949
(*c*) 1955 (*d*) 1956

85. Catell's culture fair test of intelligence was developed in
(*a*) 1960 (*b*) 1961
(*c*) 1965 (*d*) 1955

86. Non-verbal test of intelligence is suitable for
(*a*) deaf and dumb
(*b*) illiterates
(*c*) backward children
(*d*) all of these

87. Intelligence testing is useful for knowing
(*a*) individual difference
(*b*) mental retardation

(*c*) educational backwardness
(*d*) all of these

88. Scores on intelligence tests can not be fully relied on because
(*a*) fatigue level can influence the performance
(*b*) cultural factors can influence the score
(*c*) they generally do not reveal all the mental abilities of a person
(*d*) all of these

89. Who among the following psychologists is of the view that a learner can be motivated by satisfying his needs?
(*a*) Henry Murray (*b*) Abraham Maslow
(*c*) Both of these (*d*) None of these

90. Permanent change in behaviour brought about by experience or training is called.
(*a*) Learning (*b*) Motivation
(*c*) Assimilation (*d*) None of these

91. The book "**Theory of Motivation**" has been written by
(*a*) K B Madson (*b*) Maslow
(*c*) Murray (*d*) None of them

92. Motivated behaviour of a person is
(*a*) Well directed and well guided towards the goal
(*b*) Agitated until the goal is achieved
(*c*) Both of these
(*d*) None of these

93. Factors affecting motivations are
(*a*) Physiological factors only
(*b*) Psychological factors only
(*c*) Psycho-social factors
(*d*) All of these

94. Process of motivation is affected by all except
(*a*) Habits
(*b*) Mental sets and values
(*c*) Physical factors
(*d*) None of these

95. Which of the following does not come under the category of social motives?
(*a*) Prestige and Status
(*b*) Social approval
(*c*) Personal goal
(*d*) Money hoarding

96. Our action and behaviour is motivated by the desire for getting pleasure and avoiding pain. This is the opinion of
(*a*) Thomas Hobbes (*b*) Descartes
(*c*) Kant (*d*) John Locke

97. Fundamental instincts of humans are inherited rather than acquired. These instincts are the spring of human behaviour. The above opinion was held by
(*a*) Charles Darwin (*b*) Mc Dougall
(*c*) Both of these (*d*) None of these

98. Instinct theory of behaviour was rejected by psychologists on which of the following grounds?
(*a*) Adult behaviour is guided by experience and learning also. It is not always guided by instinct
(*b*) Human behaviour is affected by the cultural factors also
(*c*) Human being is a rational animal. He is not supposed to be directed by instincts only
(*d*) All of these

99. Central motive state was explained by
(*a*) Morgan
(*b*) Mc Dougall
(*c*) Murray
(*d*) None of them

100. Abraham Maslow was basically a
(*a*) Pragmatist (*b*) Humanist
(*c*) Realist (*d*) All of them

101. A self actualized person is one who
(*a*) Does not accept restrictions imposed by the society
(*b*) Always seeks perfection
(*c*) Is very good in inter personal relationship with others
(*d*) All of these

102. The theory of achievement motivation was developed by Mc Clelland of Harward University in
(*a*) 1949 (*b*) 1951
(*c*) 1965 (*d*) 1944

103. Achievement motive in a child can be developed by
(*a*) Proper guidance and high expectation from the child
(*b*) Telling the stories of great men to the child
(*c*) Setting a realistic goal for the child
(*d*) All of these

104. Which of the following is not a characteristic of learning?
(*a*) Learning is a relatively permanent change in behaviour
(*b*) Learning is a growth of the organism
(*c*) Learning is directly observed
(*d*) Learning is a goal directed process

105. In the beginning of life, the baby is guided by
(*a*) maturation
(*b*) instincts
(*c*) learning
(*d*) none of these

106. Accumulation of knowledge or facts becomes learning when
(*a*) It is applied in real life situation
(*b*) It is done by the learner himself
(*c*) It is provided by the teacher
(*d*) None of these

107. Dancing, driving, writing etc are the examples of
(*a*) Mechanical learning
(*b*) Perceptual motor learning
(*c*) Psychomotor learning
(*d*) both (*b*) and (*c*)

108. In Gagne's hierarchy, learning has been divided into
(*a*) eight parts (*b*) nine parts
(*c*) seven parts (*d*) none of the above

109. Match the following:

(A)	(B)
(*i*) Classical conditioning	1. Kohler
(*ii*) Drive reduction	2. Hull
(*iii*) Sign gestalt	3. Pavlov
(*iv*) Learning by insight	4. Tolman

	(*i*)	(*ii*)	(*iii*)	(*iv*)
(*a*)	1	2	3	4
(*b*)	3	2	4	1
(*c*)	2	1	3	4
(*d*)	4	3	2	1

110. Reflexes are of two types according to Pavlov. They are physiological and
(*a*) Psychic (*b*) Neural
(*c*) Mental (*d*) None of these

111. In classical conditioning, extinction will take place when
(*a*) Organism is poor in generalization
(*b*) CS is given without UCS for a long time
(*c*) CS > UCS
(*d*) None of these

112. Backward conditioning will take place when
(*a*) UCS is presented prior to CS
(*b*) CS is presented prior to UCS
(*c*) Reward is not given to the organism
(*d*) None of these

113. When connection is not established between a CS and CR, due to any factor, that is called
(*a*) Spontaneous recovery
(*b*) Extinction
(*c*) Inhibition
(*d*) None of these

114. When a child responds to all women who wear black suit because of the black suit of her mother, it is the example of
(*a*) internal inhibition
(*b*) generalization
(*c*) assimilation
(*d*) all of these

115. Which of the following is not a behaviourist?
(*a*) Watson
(*b*) Skinner
(*c*) Pavlov
(*d*) Lewin

116. Learning according to Watson is
(*a*) the shifting of old responses to the new stimuli
(*b*) the result of connection between S-R formed in the brain
(*c*) both of these
(*d*) none of these

117. Which of the following points differentiates the theories of Watson and Guthrie?
(*a*) law of contiguity
(*b*) law of recency
(*c*) generalization
(*d*) law of frequency

118. In operant conditioning reward works as motives but in Guthrie's theory motives are
(*a*) Stimuli given to the learner
(*b*) Actions done by the learner
(*c*) Both of these
(*d*) None of these

119. We forget something not by disuse but by other learning. This is the theory of
(*a*) contiguity
(*b*) trial and error
(*c*) learning by insight
(*d*) perception

120. Which of the following is not an essential requirement for trial and error learning?
(*a*) Drive
(*b*) Barrier
(*c*) Chance success
(*d*) Selective movement of the organism

121. According to the law of trial and error, learning occurs when
(*a*) it is satisfying for the learner
(*b*) bond between S-R is strengthened by the repeated use
(*c*) drive is there in the learner to act
(*d*) all of these

122. Which of the following facilitates learning according to Thorndike?
(*a*) Transfer of training
(*b*) Mental set of the learner
(*c*) Law of contiguity
(*d*) All of these

123. In Hull's theory, for learning to occur, the S-R connection must be associated with the
(*a*) cognitive field of the learner
(*b*) diminution of the need
(*c*) both of these
(*d*) none of these

124. Reinforcement in Skinner's theory is similar to drive reduction in which theory
(*a*) Hull's theory
(*b*) Guthrie's theory
(*c*) Lewin's theory
(*d*) None of these

125. Which of the following theories is most quantitatively measurable?
(*a*) Pavlov's
(*b*) Skinner's
(*c*) Hull's
(*d*) None of these

126. In drive reduction theory, the effective stimulus in learning is the trace. It is formed
(*a*) in the brain
(*b*) by the bond of S-R
(*c*) in the nervous system
(*d*) none of these

127. In drive reduction theory, habit formation is a function of
(*a*) stimulus potential
(*b*) stimulus generalization
(*c*) reaction potential
(*d*) all of these

128. Hull may be considered superior to other S-R Theorists in the sense that he was able to measure
(*a*) latency of response
(*b*) reinforcement potential
(*c*) both of these
(*d*) none of these

129. Which of the following points differentiates Skinner from other S-R theorists?
(*a*) His operant conditioning (type R learning)
(*b*) His schedule of reinforcement
(*c*) His way of shaping behaviour
(*d*) All of these

130. Skinner's theory is more objective in nature than the others because
(*a*) operant behaviour is external
(*b*) reflexes never have zero strength
(*c*) reinforcement is followed by responses
(*d*) all of these

131. Aversive stimuli in operant conditioning means
(*a*) individual will not do a particular act because of fear of such stimuli
(*b*) individual will not do a particular act because of the disapproval from others
(*c*) both of these
(*d*) none of these

132. In Skinner's theory, reinforcement is given to the learner when
(*a*) his response is 100% correct
(*b*) his response is closer to the correct behaviour
(*c*) both of these
(*d*) none of these

133. Which of the following statements regarding S-R theories is not correct?
(*a*) Man behaves like a machine
(*b*) Behaviour is overt and can be objectively measured
(*c*) Learning proceeds from simple to complex
(*d*) Things are perceived in the context of figure ground *i.e.*, in relation to other things

134. Which of the following statements regarding field theories are correct?
(*a*) Learning is not additive
(*b*) Molar approach of behaviour is followed here
(*c*) Interaction between organism and the environment is essential for learning
(*d*) All of these

135. Operant conditioning is different from respondent conditioning in which of the following points
(*a*) In OC reinforcement is given after the response is made
(*b*) In operant conditioning, behaviour is controlled by central nervous system
(*c*) A chain of responses is needed for shaping the behaviour (learning)
(*d*) All of these

136. Thorndike and Skinner do not differ at all in
(*a*) the law of effect
(*b*) law of readiness
(*c*) law of contiguity
(*d*) all of these

137. According to gestalt psychologists, behaviour can not be quantified because
(*a*) it is always changeable
(*b*) it is governed by the configuration produced in the mind
(*c*) it is rarely overt
(*d*) all of these

138. Law of pragnanz is the other name of the law of
(*a*) continuity
(*b*) closure
(*c*) contiguity
(*d*) none of these

139. How does the law of similarity work according to field theorists?
(*a*) Similar ideas and experiences get associated to form a whole
(*b*) Similar objects or experiences are easily learnt
(*c*) Both of these
(*d*) None of these

140. Learning by insight looks similar to some extent to which of the following theories?
(*a*) Need reduction theory
(*b*) R type of learning
(*c*) Trial and error theory
(*d*) None of the above

141. The other name of conditioned reflexes is
(*a*) psychic reflexes
(*b*) motor reflexes

(*c*) physiological reflexes
(*d*) none of the above

142. According to Renzuli, a gifted child is one
(*a*) Who possesses above average ability in almost every field
(*b*) Who is committed to task and highly motivated
(*c*) Who is definitely creative
(*d*) All of these

143. Gifted and talented children must be identified as early as possible because
(*a*) If their potentials are not developed by proper guidance of the teacher, it is a loss of the society
(*b*) They are likely to create problems for others, if they are not given work according to their ability
(*c*) Ordinary level of curriculum will not suit to these children
(*d*) All of these

144. Achievement test can be a good indicator of intellectual power if
(*a*) It is conducted immediately after the teaching is over
(*b*) A student shows good performance consistently on different achievement test
(*c*) Both of these
(*d*) None of these

145. Which of the following skills does not require high intellectual ability?
(*a*) Technical skills
(*b*) Mechanical skills
(*c*) Teaching skills
(*d*) Management skills

146. Cognitive abilities related to giftedness are all except
(*a*) High comprehensive and analytical abilities
(*b*) High level of verbal intelligence
(*c*) High retention power
(*d*) None of these

147. A superior child is advanced to a normal child by at least
(*a*) 2½ years
(*b*) Four years
(*c*) 1 years
(*d*) 1½ years

148. A gifted child is
(*a*) realistic in his approach
(*b*) highly interested in solving social problems
(*c*) more frequently chosen by his age mates and peers
(*d*) all of these

149. Which of the following enrichment programmes is suitable for gifted children in the school?
(*a*) Mathematics or Science Olympiad
(*b*) Challenging home assignments
(*c*) Map work during studies
(*d*) All of these

150. Which of the following does not come under the category of acceleration for gifted children?
(*a*) Skipping of classes
(*b*) Early admission
(*c*) Extra laboratory work
(*d*) Organizing summer camps

151. Under achievers are those who
(*a*) Score low on intelligence tests
(*b*) Achieve low in the class consistently despite their superior intelligence
(*c*) Are unable to correspond their achievement to the level of their innate abilities
(*d*) Both (*b*) and (*c*)

152. Which of the following conditions must be satisfied in order to designate a person mentally retarded?
(*a*) Sub-normal intellectual functioning
(*b*) Very poor adaptive ability
(*c*) Dependability on others
(*d*) All of these

153. The best measure of identifying mildly mentally retarded is
(*a*) Administration of standardized intelligence test
(*b*) Administration of behaviour test
(*c*) Administration of adjustment test
(*d*) A combination of all

154. Physical trauma during pregnancy may cause
(*a*) Mental retardation
(*b*) Blindness
(*c*) Deafness
(*d*) All of these

155. All of the following may cause mental retardation except
(*a*) Blood incompatibility
(*b*) Action of toxic agent
(*c*) Radio-activity
(*d*) None of these

156. Which of the following is an important postnatal cause of mental retardation?
(*a*) Brain injury
(*b*) Infection
(*c*) Severe malnutrition
(*d*) All of these

157. Dullers do not differ from normal children in
(*a*) Physical characteristics
(*b*) Level of social expectancy
(*c*) Both of these
(*d*) None of these

158. Which of the following things is not required for educating mildly mentally retarded children?
(*a*) Regular counseling
(*b*) Remedial teaching

(c) Modification in the curriculum
(d) Regular evaluation

159. Teaching of which of the following skills is not suitable to borderline cases?
(a) Electric fitting
(b) Repairing of electric or electronic equipments
(c) Oratory skills
(d) Activity based skills

160. IQ range of morons are in the range of
(a) 60-90 (b) 50-75
(c) 60-80 (d) 30-50

161. Morons are slow in
(a) Physical growth
(b) Thinking and planning
(c) Taking initiative
(d) All of these

162. Unsatisfactory relation of a mentally retarded child with the environment is technically called
(a) Autism
(b) Maladjustment
(c) Pseudo-dullness
(d) None of these

163. All of the following are characteristics of morons except
(a) They are restricted to unskilled or semi skilled occupations
(b) They are likely to be delinquent more easily
(c) They have stronger sex drives than the normals
(d) They are educable upto normal level but at a slower rate

164. Which of the following modifications in the curriculum is needed for morons?
(a) Activity based curriculum
(b) Skill dominated curriculum
(c) Emphasis on social training
(d) All of these

165. Which of the following things can not be taught to Imbeciles?
(a) Self help skills
(b) Unskilled job to be performed under supervision
(c) Writing skills
(d) Social skills

166. In which of the following cases divergent thinking is required?
(a) Attempting a multiple choice items
(b) Writing an essay
(c) Doing a research activity
(d) Both (a) and (c)

167. Which of the following tests is similar to Guilford's test of cognitive abilities?
(a) Word association test
(b) Things test
(c) Hidden shapes test
(d) None of these

168. In Hidden shapes test of creativity, which of the following things is used?
(a) Pictures
(b) Words
(c) Things
(d) None of them

169. A creative child in the class can not be satisfied unless
(a) He is given freedom to manipulate ideas or things
(b) He is allowed to ask questions in his own way
(c) Both of these
(d) None of these

170. A creative child is one who
(a) Is ideationally productive and unconventional
(b) Does not stick to social and religious norms in a hard manner
(c) Is all the time restless to do something uncommon and unique
(d) All of these

171. For the development of creative potential of a child, the teacher should
(a) Allow him to be critical to ideas and people
(b) Give them chance of problem solving
(c) Both of these
(d) None of these

172. New ideas (Eureka) suddenly comes in the minds of the creative children in the stage of
(a) Preparation
(b) Illumination
(c) Revision
(d) Incubation

173. The technique to foster creativity in children is
(a) Brain storming
(b) Problem solving
(c) Both of these
(d) None of these

174. A teacher can foster creativity in children by
(a) Developing confidence in them
(b) Giving them opportunity to express
(c) Both of these
(d) None of these

175. Learning disabled children are
(a) Deficient in using potentials
(b) Low in intelligence
(c) Slow in activity
(d) None of these

176. Learning disabled children perform very poorly in
(a) academic areas
(b) technical areas

(*c*) both of these
(*d*) none of these

177. Problem of learning disability is more complex than that of other disabilities because
(*a*) Its causes can not be easily ascertained by applying usual tests
(*b*) It is associated to behaviour problems
(*c*) Both of these
(*d*) None of these

178. Educationally, learning disabled look similar to
(*a*) dullers
(*b*) backward children
(*c*) both of these
(*d*) none of these

179. In which of the following physical characteristics learning disabled children differ from the normal ones?
(*a*) They are all the time clumsy and awkward
(*b*) Poor coordination of motor abilities
(*c*) Height, weight and health
(*d*) All of these

180. Which of the following methods is most suitable for learning disabled children?
(*a*) Behaviour guidance method
(*b*) Remedial teaching
(*c*) Brain storming
(*d*) None of them

181. In order to improve work habits of learning disabled what should be done?
(*a*) Unattending behaviour should be penalized
(*b*) Close monitoring of the behaviour is needed
(*c*) Cues and prompt should be given
(*d*) All of these

182. Those who are normal in intelligence but slow in academic achievement due to psycho-social reasons are called
(*a*) Backward children
(*b*) Gifted under achievers
(*c*) Both of these
(*d*) None of these

183. Consistent low achievement leads to low intelligence because
(*a*) 50% intellectual ability is expressed in verbal form
(*b*) Learning develops thinking and reasoning power
(*c*) Both of these
(*d*) None of these

184. Which of the following situations may lead to educational backwardness?
(*a*) Sensory impairment
(*b*) Motor disability
(*c*) Long diseases and health problems.
(*d*) All of these

185. Emotional disturbances may lead to educational backwardness because
(*a*) Proper emotional development is necessary for social interactions
(*b*) Emotions will develop intellectual power, *i.e.*, emotional intelligence
(*c*) Both of these
(*d*) None of these

186. Which of the following factors will not lead to educational backwardness?
(*a*) Poor socio economic status of the family
(*b*) Poor educational environment of the school
(*c*) Occupation of the family
(*d*) Poor emotional climate of the family

187. Which of the following is an important cause of educational backwardness at primary level of education in India?
(*a*) Poor school organisation
(*b*) Lack of accountability
(*c*) Attitude of the masses towards education
(*d*) All of these

188. Which of the following measures should be adopted by the teacher to check educational backwardness?
(*a*) Continuous evaluation and regular feedback
(*b*) Remedial teaching
(*c*) Adjustment and behaviour training
(*d*) All of these

189. Teaching by small steps and frequent short assignment techniques are useful for
(*a*) Slow learners
(*b*) Learning disabled
(*c*) Educationally backward children
(*d*) Children of all types of disabilities

190. Special schools are required for backward children when
(*a*) Backwardness is due to any serious physical handicap
(*b*) The size of population of backward children in the society is very large as is the case of Gujarat where the achievement of students in mathematics is always seen very low
(*c*) Both of these
(*d*) None of these

191. Which of the following should be considered the most important quality of a teacher at primary level?
(*a*) Patience and perseverance
(*b*) Competence in methods of teaching and knowledge of subjects
(*c*) Competence to teach in highly standardised language
(*d*) Eagerness to teach

192. A teacher, because of his/her democratic nature, allows students to sit all over the class. Some sit together and discuss or do group reading. Some sit quietly and read themselves. A parent does not like it. Which of the following may be the best way to handle the situation?

(*a*) Parents should request the principal to change the section of their ward
(*b*) Parents should show trust in the teacher and discuss the problem with the teacher
(*c*) Parents should take away the child from that school
(*d*) Parents should complain against the teacher to the principal

193. The stage in which a child begins to think logically about objects and events is known as
(*a*) Formal operational stage
(*b*) Pre-operational stage
(*c*) Concrete operational stage
(*d*) Sensori-motor stage

194. 'Mind mapping' refers to
(*a*) a plan of action for an adventure
(*b*) drawing the picture of a mind
(*c*) researching the functioning of the mind
(*d*) a technique to enhance comprehension

195. The best way, specially at primary level, to address the learning difficulties of students is to use
(*a*) expensive and glossy support material
(*b*) easy and interesting textbooks
(*c*) story-telling method
(*d*) a variety of teaching methods suited to the disability

196. Which of the following will foster creativity among learners?
(*a*) Providing opportunities to question and to nurture the innate talents of every learner
(*b*) Emphasizing achievement goals from the beginning of school life
(*c*) Coaching students for good marks in examination
(*d*) Teaching the students the practical value of good education

197. According to Piaget, at which of the following stages does a child begin to think logically about abstract propositions?
(*a*) Formal operational stage (11 years and up)
(*b*) Sensori-motor stage (Birth–02 years)
(*c*) Pre-operational stage (02–07 years)
(*d*) Concrete operational stage (07–11 years)

198. Learning can be enriched if
(*a*) more and more teaching aids are used in the class
(*b*) teachers use different types of lectures and explanation
(*c*) due attention is paid to periodic tests in the class
(*d*) situations from the real world are brought into the class in which students interact with each other and the teahcer facilitates

199. Which of the following statements ***cannot*** be considered as a feature of the process of learning?
(*a*) Learning is a comprehensive process
(*b*) Learning is goal-oriented
(*c*) Unlearning is also a learning process
(*d*) Educational institutions are the only place where learning takes place

200. A student of V-grade with 'visual deficiency' should be
(*a*) helped with his/her routine-work by parents and friends
(*b*) treated normally in the classroom and provided support through Audio CDs
(*c*) given special treatment in the classroom
(*d*) excused to do a lower level of work

201. Which of the following is ***not*** related to the socio-psychological needs of the child?
(*a*) Need for emotional security
(*b*) Regular elimination of waste products from the body
(*c*) Need for company
(*d*) Need for appreciation or social approval

202. Which is the place where the child's 'cognitive' development is defined in the best way?
(*a*) School and classroom environment
(*b*) Auditorium
(*c*) Home
(*d*) Playground

203. .... is considered a sign of motivated teaching.
(*a*) Remedial work given by the teacher
(*b*) Questioning by students
(*c*) Pin drop silence in the class
(*d*) Maximum attendance in the class

204. Which of the following is ***not*** a sign of an intelligent young child?
(*a*) One who has the ability to communicate fluently and appropriately
(*b*) One who carries on thinking in an abstract manner
(*c*) One who can adjust oneself in a new environment
(*d*) One who has the ability to cram long essays very quickly

205. "Children actively construct their understanding of the world" is a statement attributed to
(*a*) Pavlov (*b*) Kohlberg
(*c*) Skinner (*d*) Piaget

206. Kritika who does ***not*** talk much at home, talks a lot at school. It shows that
(*a*) teachers demand that children should talk a lot at school
(*b*) she does not like her home at all
(*c*) her thoughts get ackrowledged at school
(*d*) the school provides opportunities to children to talk a lot

207. A teacher should make an attempt to understand the potentialities of her/his students. Which of the following fields is related to this objective?
(*a*) Social Philosophy
(*b*) Media – Psychology
(*c*) Educational Psychology
(*d*) Educational Sociology

208. Motivation, in the process of learning,
(*a*) differentiates new learning from old learning
(*b*) makes learners think unidirectionally
(*c*) creates interest for learning among young learners
(*d*) sharpens the memory of learners

209. The term 'curriculum' in the field of education refers to
(*a*) overall programme of the school which students experience on a day-to-day basis
(*b*) evaluation process
(*c*) text-material to be used in the class
(*d*) methods of teaching and the content to be taught

210. At lower classes, play-way method of teaching is based on
(*a*) principles of methods of teaching
(*b*) psychological principles of development and growth
(*c*) sociological principles of teaching
(*d*) theory of physical education programmes

211. "A young child responds to a new situation on the basis of the response made by him/her in a similar situation as in the past." This is related to
(*a*) 'Law of Effect' of learning
(*b*) 'Law of Attitude' of learning process
(*c*) 'Law of Readiness' of learning
(*d*) 'Law of Analogy' of learning

212. .... is ***not*** considered a sign of 'being gifted'.
(*a*) Fighting with others
(*b*) Novelty in expression
(*c*) Curiosity
(*d*) Creative ideas

213. Education of children with special needs should be provided
(*a*) by methods developed for special children in special schools
(*b*) in special schools
(*c*) by special teachers in special schools
(*d*) along with other normal children

214. To make assessment a 'useful and interesting' process, one should be careful about
(*a*) labelling students as intelligent or average learners
(*b*) using a variety of ways to collect information about the student's learning across the scholastic and co-scholastic boundaries
(*c*) using technical language to give feedback
(*d*) making comparisons between different students

215. 'Dyslexia' is associated with
(*a*) Mathematical disorder
(*b*) Reading disorder
(*c*) Behavioural disorder
(*d*) Mental disorder

216. Parents should play a .... role in the learning process of young children.
(*a*) proactive
(*b*) sympathetic
(*c*) neutral
(*d*) negative

217. "Development is a never ending process." This idea is associated with
(*a*) Principle of continuity
(*b*) Principle of integration
(*c*) Principle of interaction
(*d*) Principle of interrelation

218. The 'insight theory of learning' is promoted by
(*a*) Pavlov
(*b*) Jean Piaget
(*c*) Vygotsky
(*d*) 'Gestalt' theorists

219. In which of the following stages do children become active members of their peer group?
(*a*) Adulthood
(*b*) Early childhood
(*c*) Childhood
(*d*) Adolescence

220. Four distinct stages of children's intellectual development are identified by
(*a*) Erikson (*b*) Skinner
(*c*) Piaget (*d*) Kohlberg

221. Mass media, cinema and library are passive agencies of education because
(*a*) learner can not react to the feedback system of these agencies directly
(*b*) they provide informal education
(*c*) they can not come closer to the educant
(*d*) all of these

222. Education of a child really begins
(*a*) Once he takes birth
(*b*) Once he attains the age of three
(*c*) Once he is admitted to post nursery schools
(*d*) Once he learns to speak

223. Family is the original social institution from which all other institutions emerged, who said this
(*a*) Brown (*b*) Ballard
(*c*) Machiver (*d*) None of them

224. Which of the following is not the primary function of schools
(*a*) reorganization and reconstruction of Human experiences

(*b*) all-round development of the child
(*c*) to make the children self reliant
(*d*) advancement of culture

225. In a democratic country, school should reflect
(*a*) National aspirations
(*b*) Community related local aspirations
(*c*) Both of these
(*d*) None of these

226. The best teacher in a village school is he who
(*a*) carries community experiences to the class room
(*b*) prepares instructional programmes in the interest of the community
(*c*) carries classroom experiences to the community
(*d*) all of these

227. Universalisation of education is the concept adopted by
(*a*) modern state (*b*) democratic state
(*c*) totalitarian state (*d*) religious state

228. Secular education in India means
(*a*) an education opposed to religion
(*b*) an education indifferent to religion
(*c*) an education emphasizing equality of religions
(*d*) none of these

229. School works as a social sub system for
(*a*) transmission of culture
(*b*) preservation of culture
(*c*) advancement of culture
(*d*) all of these

230. "Society is nothing but a process of interaction among people." Who said this?
(*a*) Lapier (*b*) Cuber
(*c*) Reuter (*d*) Payne

231. The best model of schooling is
(*a*) Close interaction between education of society
(*b*) Self reliant society by education
(*c*) Reflection of openness by schools
(*d*) All of these

232. Special provisions have been made for socially and educationally backward classes of the nation under article
(*a*) 29 (*b*) 31
(*c*) 15 (*d*) 19

233. Religious education is prohibited in government schools and colleges under Article
(*a*) 29 (*b*) 28 (1).
(*c*) 39 (2) (*d*) 15 (a)

234. Religious and linguistic minorities shall have the right to establish and administer their own educational institutions under Article
(*a*) 30(1) (*b*) 31(2)
(*c*) 40 (*d*) 41

235. Article 351 is about
(*a*) education of tribals
(*b*) promotion of Hindi
(*c*) promotion of secularism
(*d*) English as official language

236. Status of central university is given to any educational institution under union list of
(*a*) Entry 65 (*b*) Entry 63
(*c*) Entry 66 (*d*) None of these

237. Entry 25 of concurrent list states about
(*a*) vocational and technical training of labour
(*b*) the education of working class
(*c*) the education of disabled
(*d*) none of the above

238. Education in the mother tongue at primary stage to children belonging to linguistic minorities has been mentioned in Article
(*a*) 250 (*b*) 350
(*c*) 349 (*d*) 351

239. Educational and economic interests of SCs and STs have been safeguarded under Article
(*a*) 46 (*b*) 45(a)
(*c*) 351 (*d*) 52

240. Education of union territories is administered by the central government under Article
(*a*) 350 (*b*) 229
(*c*) 239 (*d*) 50

241. Education was transferred from state list of subjects to concurrent list in
(*a*) 1976 (*b*) 1972
(*c*) 1980 (*d*) 1950

242. Which of the following statements about growth and development is not correct?
(*a*) Growth generally refers to quantitative changes while development refers to qualitative changes
(*b*) Growth is a function of the environment
(*c*) Growth is not possible without development and vice versa
(*d*) Growth is determined by intrinsic and genetic factors of the organism

243. The limit of growth is fixed by
(*a*) internal factors of the organism
(*b*) nutrition and exercise
(*c*) both of these
(*d*) none of these

244. Development is
(*a*) Maturation
(*b*) Learning
(*c*) Synthesis of abilities
(*d*) All of these

245. Development takes place when
(*a*) environmental forces work on the organism
(*b*) environmental forces interact with the hereditary forces in an organism

(*c*) both of these
(*d*) none of these

246. Which of the following statements about development is correct?
(*a*) Process of development can be improved by exercise and nutrition
(*b*) Development may be positive and negative both
(*c*) Development proceeds from general to specific
(*d*) All of these

247. The son of a goldsmith becomes an expert goldsmith. It is an example of a
(*a*) biological heredity
(*b*) social heredity
(*c*) transfer of instinct
(*d*) none of these

248. All humans contain .... chromosomes.
(*a*) 26 (*b*) 36
(*c*) 46 (*d*) 42

249. DNA test helps us to know
(*a*) the genetic traits of a person
(*b*) nature of personality and its composition
(*c*) both of these
(*d*) none of these

250. The law of inheritance was discovered by Gregor Mendel in
(*a*) 1866 (*b*) 1911
(*c*) 1888 (*d*) 1920

251. Everything which influences child's development is categorised under the 'Environment' other than 'Heredity.' This statement is given by
(*a*) Boring (*b*) Woodworth
(*c*) Douglas (*d*) Holland

252. During infancy which of the following aspect of development is not completed?
(*a*) Moral Development
(*b*) Emotional Development
(*c*) Social Development
(*d*) Language Development

253. A teacher who has given the responsibility of 'Infant education,' he must pay attention on
(*a*) The education must be child-centred
(*b*) The education must be mother-centred
(*c*) The education must be sport-centred
(*d*) The education must be school-centred

254. Which one of the following stage of child's development is popularly nicknamed as Mysterious period of the life?
(*a*) Infancy (*b*) Childhood
(*c*) Adolescence (*d*) Adulthood

255. Which one of the following is the defect of language development in children?
(*a*) Stammering (*b*) Talktiveness
(*c*) Scribbled writing (*d*) Reserve nature

256. The major change occurs in adolescent period is
(*a*) In voice
(*b*) In Bodily shape and organs
(*c*) In gestures and manners
(*d*) In all the above

257. In adolescent girls the following abilities are much better in comparison than the adolescent boys
(*a*) Language Abilities
(*b*) Functional Abilities
(*c*) Thinking Abilities
(*d*) Scientific Abilities

258. The psychologist who has given much importance to individual difference in children is
(*a*) Galton (*b*) Young
(*c*) Freud (*d*) Robert

259. In which age-group a child can differentiate between the anger and affection?
(*a*) In infancy (*b*) In childhood
(*c*) In adolescence (*d*) In adulthood

260. The chief social behaviour of infancy is
(*a*) Birth of group-feelings
(*b*) Exchange of toys
(*c*) Imitation of approved nouns
(*d*) All the above

261. The nearest emotion of distress which is developed after three months of the age in children
(*a*) Anger (*b*) Hate
(*c*) Fear (*d*) All the above

262. The best controlling powers of emotionally are displayed by
(*a*) Gifted children
(*b*) Mentally retarded
(*c*) Physically powerful children
(*d*) The children having escaping tendencies from work

263. Which one of the following does not having maximum development during adolescent stage?
(*a*) Intellectual abilities
(*b*) Mental abilities
(*c*) Interest-related abilities
(*d*) All of the above

264. In order to develop group-feelings among children, the provision in education required as
(*a*) The co-operative games and sports in school
(*b*) The group activities like dance, music and drama
(*c*) The mass drills and physical exercises on the games field
(*d*) All the above

265. It is said that in childhood, the children should be exposed to adventurous stories of great historical journeys which may develop the quality of
(a) Elimination of fear syndrome
(b) Discipline and obedience
(c) Delightfulness
(d) Enthusiasm and motivation

266. In early childhood, the children should be given education through
(a) Toys and games (b) Paper-Pencil
(c) Models (d) Plants

267. Which one of the following is not associated with the social development in childhood?
(a) Gang formation
(b) Formation of sex-groups
(c) Desire for social acceptance in children
(d) Attraction towards girls in boys

268. According to Piagent, infants in the sensorimotor thought stage cannot
(a) use sensory (b) use motor actions
(c) form symbolic (d) display reflexes

269. According to Piaget, the imaginary audience and the personal fable are both parts of
(a) intuitive (b) object
(c) conservation (d) adolescent

270. What is the term that Erikson coined?
(a) Oedipus Complex
(b) Self-fulfilling Prophecy
(c) Identity Crisis
(d) Positive Reinforcement

271. The two main personality differences identified by Eysenck are
(a) extroversion/introversion and neuroticism/stability
(b) pessimism/optimism and sufficiency/insecurity
(c) extroversion/introversion and shrewdness/insecurity
(d) neuroticism/stability and optimism/pessimism

272. Erik Erikson's theory is a good example of the .... approach.
(a) proactive (b) idiographic
(c) nomothetic (d) psychoanalytic

273. Attitudes are .... throughout life and are embodied our socialization process.
(a) constant (b) seen
(c) rigid (d) learned

274. Who is called as father of Conditioning?
(a) Pavlov (b) Koffka
(c) Wertheimer (d) Skinner

275. Which of the following concept in the basic element of conditioned Response?
(a) Associative Reflex
(b) Association Response
(c) Stimulus effect
(d) Latercy Response

276. When a child is asked that chocolate is not given to you, if you are telling-a-lie. This conditioning is an example of
(a) Non-reinforced training
(b) Discriminatory punishment training
(c) Escape training
(d) Discriminatory training

277. The meaning of the word conditioning is
(a) Relationship between the stimuli
(b) Substitution of organism behaviour with another behaviour
(c) Accommodation with new stimuli
(d) Learning through exercise

278. Which one of the following is not associated with Classical conditioning?
(a) Contemporary conditioning
(b) Delayed conditioning
(c) Trace conditioning
(d) Non-reinforced conditioning

279. Instrumental conditioning is also called as
(a) S-type conditioning
(b) Q-type conditioning
(c) C-type conditioning
(d) R-type conditioning

280. In which type of conditioning the reward is depend on the response?
(a) Classical conditioning
(b) Instrumental conditioning
(c) Respondents behaviour
(d) Operant behaviour

281. The ability of the learner to utilize or apply the acquired knowledge or skills in school to solve problems in similar or related situations at some future date is known as
(a) Knowledge acquisition
(b) Reinforcement
(c) Motivation
(d) Transfer of learning

282. In the learning of sciences and math's, scientifically their is no difference in performance as a result of gender. Which of the following influence gender based performance?
(a) Culture (b) Attitude
(c) Stereotyping (d) Race

283. Learning is best defined as a process that involves:
(a) Two stimuli being paired that produce a conditioned response over time
(b) An organism interacting with its environment, becoming changed by

experience, and thereby modifying subsequent behaviours

(*c*) An organism interacting with its environment through autoshaping and conditioning

(*d*) An organism responding to its environment based on reinforcement or punishment for behaviours

284. The basic understanding of the relationship between unconditoned response (UR) and conditioned response (CR) included which of the following ideas?

(*a*) The UR and Cr are not always the same response

(*b*) Organisms come to generally behave toward conditioned stimulus as they do unconditioned stimulus

(*c*) Stimulus substitution

(*d*) The UR and Cr are always the same response

285. Which of the following is accurate in relation to the law of effect?

(*a*) The law of effect relates to Pavlov's proposal that reward will strengthen the connection between the response that proceeded it and any stimuli present when it is delivere(d)

(*b*) In modern terminology, Thorndike's 'satisfiers' and 'annoyers' are called enforcers and punishers

(*c*) In the law of effect, a stimulus-response (S-R) association is learne(d)

(*d*) It is generally thought that the likelihood of an animal responding in a particular way cannot be controlled by the consequence of that response.

286. Which of the following statements applies to instrumental learning?

(*a*) Instrumental learning is the process by which an animal learns about the relationship between its behaviour and the consequence of that behaviour.

(*b*) Instrumentally trained responses are not entirely elicited by identifiable stimuli.

(*c*) Instrumental learning allows the animal to control the occurrence of environmental events.

(*d*) All of the above

287. Generally the construct of Personality can be defined in terms of

(*a*) Biological Approaches

(*b*) Psycho-sexual Approaches

(*c*) Psycho-physical Approaches

(*d*) Bio-chemical Approaches

288. The consistent and distinct style of behavioural tendencies are called as

(*a*) Habit (*b*) Trait

(*c*) Learning (*d*) Instinct

289. The personal changes that occur among the students through socialization can be judged through

(*a*) Inter-personal relationship among the specialised groups of the students

(*b*) The activities of the student

(*c*) Collecting the information from the parents

(*d*) Asking to the students

290. Co-operation is the fundamental basis of inter-personal relations which means

(*a*) It is self-centred in the early development of the children

(*b*) It is society-centred which is expressed in interpersonal relationship

(*c*) It can be learned through imitation and suggestibility

(*d*) It is voluntary in nature and can not be imposed

291. Personality is the sum total of all reactions which a person exhibits

(*a*) In context of environment

(*b*) In context of a person

(*c*) In context of society

(*d*) In context of himself

292. According to Sri Aurobindo, the basic elements of personality can be sequentially arranged as under

(*a*) Physical-Emotional-Intellectual-Spiritual-Super Mental

(*b*) Physical-Intellectual-Super Mental

(*c*) Physical-Intelecutual-Spiritual

(*d*) Physical-Emotional-Spiritual

293. Which of the following statements is correct in relation to values?

(*a*) Value is the dimension of arriving at an aim

(*b*) Value is a process which activated by a stimulus

(*c*) Value is a feeling which form through acts

(*d*) All the above

294. The need of the development of interest is felt in children

(*a*) They are playful in nature which leads them towards the development of constructive tendencies

(*b*) The interests make children's feelings more mature

(*c*) The interests enrich children's instincts

(*d*) All the above

295. The propounder of the Single factor theory of intelligence was

(*a*) Alfred Binet (*b*) Charles Spearman

(*c*) Burt (*d*) Guilford

296. Which of intelligence is accepted (recognised) by Trorndike?

(*a*) Simple-factor theory

(*b*) Bi-factor theory
(*c*) Multi-factor theory
(*d*) Three-dimensional theory

297. The two-factor theory of intelligence has been put forth by
(*a*) Burt and Vernon (*b*) Terman
(*c*) Spearman (*d*) Skinner

298. The factor which is most important in influencing the intellectual development of the individual is
(*a*) Family environment
(*b*) School environment
(*c*) Neighbourhood
(*d*) Cultural environment

299. The most important school related factor influencing child's intelligence is
(*a*) Curriculum
(*b*) Discipline
(*c*) Curriculum Activities
(*d*) All the above

300. Verbal intelligence tests are the better option for
(*a*) Literate persons (*b*) Illiterate persons
(*c*) Small children (*d*) Special children

ANSWERS

1	**2**	**3**	**4**	**5**	**6**	**7**	**8**	**9**	**10**
(*c*)	(*d*)	(*b*)	(*a*)	(*b*)	(*c*)	(*a*)	(*a*)	(*c*)	(*a*)
11	**12**	**13**	**14**	**15**	**16**	**17**	**18**	**19**	**20**
(*d*)	(*b*)	(*d*)	(*d*)	(*b*)	(*a*)	(*b*)	(*c*)	(*a*)	(*c*)
21	**22**	**23**	**24**	**25**	**26**	**27**	**28**	**29**	**30**
(*b*)	(*c*)	(*d*)	(*d*)	(*d*)	(*a*)	(*b*)	(*a*)	(*c*)	(*d*)
31	**32**	**33**	**34**	**35**	**36**	**37**	**38**	**39**	**40**
(*d*)	(*d*)	(*c*)	(*d*)	(*a*)	(*d*)	(*b*)	(*d*)	(*a*)	(*d*)
41	**42**	**43**	**44**	**45**	**46**	**47**	**48**	**49**	**50**
(*c*)	(*d*)	(*a*)	(*c*)	(*d*)	(*a*)	(*c*)	(*d*)	(*d*)	(*b*)
51	**52**	**53**	**54**	**55**	**56**	**57**	**58**	**59**	**60**
(*d*)	(*b*)	(*d*)	(*c*)	(*a*)	(*d*)	(*d*)	(*c*)	(*a*)	(*a*)
61	**62**	**63**	**64**	**65**	**66**	**67**	**68**	**69**	**70**
(*a*)	(*a*)	(*c*)	(*b*)	(*a*)	(*a*)	(*c*)	(*a*)	(*d*)	(*d*)
71	**72**	**73**	**74**	**75**	**76**	**77**	**78**	**79**	**80**
(*b*)	(*a*)	(*c*)	(*d*)	(*a*)	(*d*)	(*a*)	(*c*)	(*c*)	(*a*)
81	**82**	**83**	**84**	**85**	**86**	**87**	**88**	**89**	**90**
(*c*)	(*d*)	(*b*)	(*b*)	(*b*)	(*d*)	(*d*)	(*d*)	(*c*)	(*a*)
91	**92**	**93**	**94**	**95**	**96**	**97**	**98**	**99**	**100**
(*a*)	(*c*)	(*d*)	(*d*)	(*c*)	(*a*)	(*c*)	(*d*)	(*a*)	(*b*)
101	**102**	**103**	**104**	**105**	**106**	**107**	**108**	**109**	**110**
(*d*)	(*b*)	(*d*)	(*c*)	(*b*)	(*a*)	(*d*)	(*a*)	(*b*)	(*a*)
111	**112**	**113**	**114**	**115**	**116**	**117**	**118**	**119**	**120**
(*b*)	(*a*)	(*c*)	(*b*)	(*d*)	(*c*)	(*d*)	(*a*)	(*a*)	(*d*)
121	**122**	**123**	**124**	**125**	**126**	**127**	**128**	**129**	**130**
(*d*)	(*d*)	(*b*)	(*a*)	(*c*)	(*c*)	(*a*)	(*a*)	(*d*)	(*a*)
131	**132**	**133**	**134**	**135**	**136**	**137**	**138**	**139**	**140**
(*a*)	(*c*)	(*d*)	(*d*)	(*d*)	(*a*)	(*b*)	(*b*)	(*a*)	(*c*)
141	**142**	**143**	**144**	**145**	**146**	**147**	**148**	**149**	**150**
(*a*)	(*d*)	(*d*)	(*c*)	(*a*)	(*d*)	(*a*)	(*d*)	(*d*)	(*c*)
151	**152**	**153**	**154**	**155**	**156**	**157**	**158**	**159**	**160**
(*d*)	(*d*)	(*d*)	(*d*)	(*d*)	(*d*)	(*c*)	(*c*)	(*c*)	(*b*)
161	**162**	**163**	**164**	**165**	**166**	**167**	**168**	**169**	**170**
(*d*)	(*a*)	(*d*)	(*d*)	(*d*)	(*d*)	(*b*)	(*a*)	(*c*)	(*a*)

171	**172**	**173**	**174**	**175**	**176**	**177**	**178**	**179**	**180**
(*c*)	(*b*)	(*c*)	(*c*)	(*d*)	(*a*)	(*a*)	(*b*)	(*b*)	(*a*)
181	**182**	**183**	**184**	**185**	**186**	**187**	**188**	**189**	**190**
(*d*)	(*a*)	(*c*)	(*d*)	(*c*)	(*c*)	(*d*)	(*d*)	(*d*)	(*c*)
191	**192**	**193**	**194**	**195**	**196**	**197**	**198**	**199**	**200**
(*a*)	(*b*)	(*c*)	(*c*)	(*d*)	(*a*)	(*d*)	(*d*)	(*d*)	(*b*)
201	**202**	**203**	**204**	**205**	**206**	**207**	**208**	**209**	**210**
(*b*)	(*a*)	(*b*)	(*d*)	(*d*)	(*c*)	(*c*)	(*c*)	(*a*)	(*b*)
211	**212**	**213**	**214**	**215**	**216**	**217**	**218**	**219**	**220**
(*a*)	(*a*)	(*d*)	(*b*)	(*b*)	(*a*)	(*a*)	(*d*)	(*d*)	(*c*)
221	**222**	**223**	**224**	**225**	**226**	**227**	**228**	**229**	**230**
(*a*)	(*a*)	(*b*)	(*d*)	(*c*)	(*d*)	(*a*)	(*c*)	(*d*)	(*c*)
231	**232**	**233**	**234**	**235**	**236**	**237**	**238**	**239**	**240**
(*a*)	(*c*)	(*b*)	(*a*)	(*b*)	(*b*)	(*a*)	(*b*)	(*a*)	(*c*)
241	**242**	**243**	**244**	**245**	**246**	**247**	**248**	**249**	**250**
(*a*)	(*b*)	(*a*)	(*d*)	(*c*)	(*d*)	(*b*)	(*c*)	(*c*)	(*a*)
251	**252**	**253**	**254**	**255**	**256**	**257**	**258**	**259**	**260**
(*a*)	(*a*)	(*c*)	(*b*)	(*a*)	(*d*)	(*a*)	(*a*)	(*a*)	(*d*)
261	**262**	**263**	**264**	**265**	**266**	**267**	**268**	**269**	**270**
(*d*)	(*a*)	(*d*)	(*d*)	(*d*)	(*a*)	(*d*)	(*c*)	(*d*)	(*c*)
271	**272**	**273**	**274**	**275**	**276**	**277**	**278**	**279**	**280**
(*a*)	(*b*)	(*d*)	(*a*)	(*a*)	(*a*)	(*a*)	(*d*)	(*a*)	(*d*)
281	**282**	**283**	**284**	**285**	**286**	**287**	**288**	**289**	**290**
(*d*)	(*b*)	(*b*)	(*b*)	(*a*)	(*b*)	(*d*)	(*c*)	(*a*)	(*b*)
291	**292**	**293**	**294**	**295**	**296**	**297**	**298**	**299**	**300**
(*a*)	(*a*)	(*d*)	(*d*)	(*a*)	(*c*)	(*c*)	(*a*)	(*d*)	(*a*)

हिन्दी

SECTION a भाषा बोध : गद्यांश

परिचय

भाषा बोध के द्वारा व्यक्ति की समग्र अवबोधन क्षमता का मूल्यांकन किया जाता है। इससे अभ्यर्थी की समझ क्षमता एवं दिए गए अवतरण में छुपे गूढ़ विचारों को ग्रहण करने की क्षमता आंकी जाती है। इसके द्वारा अभ्यर्थी के निर्णय लेने की क्षमता की भी जांच की जाती है। ऐसा दिए गए प्रतिपाद्य के हृदयंगम द्वारा ही संभव है। इस प्रकार भाषा बोध व्यक्तित्व के बहुआयामी पहलुओं के परीक्षण की पद्धति है। इसके द्वारा भाषा-ज्ञान, निहितार्थ की समझ एवं अवबोधन क्षमता, निर्णय क्षमता एवं सही निष्कर्ष तक पहुंचने की क्षमता की जांच एक साथ की जाती है। जाहिर है, इतने सारे परीक्षणों के द्वारा व्यक्तित्व का समग्र उभार एवं निखार प्रकट हो जाता है। ऐसे में भाषा बोध के प्रश्नों को हल करने में अतिरिक्त सावधानी एवं सचेतता आवश्यक है। इस प्रकार के प्रश्नों के सही उत्तर देने के लिए निरंतर अभ्यास की आवश्यकता होती है।

उद्धरण को पढ़कर उसके मूलभाव या निहितार्थ को समझने की कोशिश करनी चाहिए। एक बार पढ़कर मूलभाव को समझने में कठिनाई हो तो उसे एक से अधिक बार पढ़ें। जबतक निहितार्थ समझ में न आए उसे दुबारा एवं तिबारा पढ़ें। निहितार्थ समझ लेने पर प्रश्नों का उत्तर देना आसान हो जाता है।

उद्धरण को पढ़ते समय महत्वपूर्ण बिंदुओं को रेखांकित करते चलें। ऐसे में मूल बिंदुओं को शीघ्रता से दुहरा सकते हैं। हो सकता है समयाभाव के कारण मूल अवतरण को बार-बार पढ़ना संभव न हो।

प्रश्नों के उत्तर दिए गए अवतरण पर ही आधारित हों। अपनी पूर्व की जानकारी के आधार पर निष्कर्ष न निकालें। यह संभव है कि अवतरण में दी गई जानकारी आपकी पूर्व की जानकारी या राय से भिन्न हो। ऐसे में अपनी जानकारी को अवतरण में दी गई सूचना के साथ घालमेल न करें। ऐसा करना आत्मघाती कदम हो सकता है।

कभी-कभी अवतरण में किसी शब्द के समानार्थक या विपरीतार्थक शब्द पूछे जाते हैं। ऐसे प्रश्नों के उत्तर देने में जल्दबाजी न करें। जाहिर है किसी एक शब्द के कई समानार्थक एवं विपरीतार्थक शब्द हो सकते हैं। ऐसे में उपयुक्त शब्द का चुनाव आवश्यक है। इसके लिए लेखक के मूल कथ्य और विचार को समझना आवश्यक है।

दिए गए अवतरण के लिए उपयुक्त शीर्षक लिखना एक चुनौतीपूर्ण कार्य होता है। यह प्रश्न काफी आसान भी है और कठिन भी। आसान इसलिए कि इनका उत्तर दिए अवतरण के आधार पर ही देना होता है और कठिन इसलिए कि अवतरण के मूल भाव को समझे बिना विषयांतर हो जाने की संभावना अक्सर बनी रहती है।

और, सबसे जरूरी चीज है-अभ्यास! अभ्यास के बिना आसान प्रश्न भी कठिन लगने लगते हैं। भाषा-बोध के प्रश्नों को हल करने के लिए भाषा में अभिरुचि एवं समझ विकसित करनी चाहिए।

गद्यांश-1

समकालीन भारत की अर्थव्यवस्था एक बड़ा विरोधाभास है। वह उत्कृष्ट उपलब्धियों और गंभीर विफलताओं का विचित्र संयोग है। स्वतंत्रता के बाद से भारत ने अपने आर्थिक पिछड़ेपन से ऊपर उठने में उल्लेखनीय प्रगति की है। वह जो 1950 के दशक में एक अत्यंत निर्धन देश था और 1960 के दशक के मध्य में सहायतार्थी देश था, वही आज विश्व की चौथी सबसे बड़ी अर्थव्यवस्था (क्रय-शक्ति क्षमता के आधार पर) के रूप में उभरा है। हमारी अर्थव्यवस्था विश्व की सबसे तेजी से संवर्द्धित होने वाली अर्थव्यवस्थाओं में आ गई है। अब यह देश विश्व ज्ञान अर्थव्यवस्था में एक अग्रणी खिलाड़ी बन गया है, जिसके पास अपार बौद्धिक पूंजी और तेजी से बढ़ने वाली सॉफ्टवेयर और सूचना प्रौद्योगिकी सेवाएं हैं। यद्यपि हमारा देश

विश्व के पांच सबसे अधिक तेजी से संवर्धित होने वाली अर्थव्यवस्थाओं के समूह में शामिल हो गया है फिर भी हम मानव विकास सूचकांक (ह्युमन डेवलपमेंट इंडेक्स) की दृष्टि से सबसे निचले 20 देशों में हैं। यद्यपि देश अपनी संवृद्धि दर और प्रौद्योगिकीय करामातों का जश्न मना रहा है, फिर भी वह सामाजिक विरोधाभासों तथा विकास के विरोधाभास और विडंबनाओं से गुजर रहा है। इस प्रकार समकालीन भारत में 'दो भारत' हैं।

1. भारतीय अर्थव्यवस्था को 'एक बड़ा विरोधाभास' क्यों माना जाता है?
   A. वह साक्षरता का निम्न स्तर होने के बावजूद सूचना प्रौद्योगिकी सेवाओं में एक अग्रणी खिलाड़ी है।
   B. कृषि जन्य उत्पादन की विपुलता के बीच गरीबी है।
   C. यह निम्न मानव विकास वाली एक सबसे बड़ी अर्थव्यवस्था है।
   D. सामाजिक विरोधाभासों के साथ ही उसकी वैज्ञानिक उपलब्धियाँ हैं।

2. भारत को विश्व ज्ञान अर्थव्यवस्था में एक अग्रणी खिलाड़ी क्यों कहा जा रहा है?
   A. विज्ञान और प्रौद्योगिकी में भारत के ज्ञान का आधार विश्व के सर्वोत्तम में से है।
   B. भारत के पास मानव बौद्धिक पूंजियों और सूचना प्रौद्योगिकी सेवाओं के विशाल भंडार हैं।
   C. भारत विश्व की पांच सबसे तेजी से संवर्द्धित होने वाली अर्थव्यवस्थाओं तथा प्रौद्योगिक भंडारों में से एक है।
   D. भारत के पास मानव पूँजी और वैज्ञानिक ज्ञान निर्यात संभाव्यता का विशाल भंडार है।

3. लेखक का 'दो भारत' से क्या तात्पर्य है?
   A. एक भारत है जिसके पास अपार बौद्धिक पूंजी है जबकि एक दूसरा है जो मुख्यतया निरक्षर है।
   B. एक भारत है जहाँ संवृद्धि में उछाल है तो वहीं व्यापक अभाव और विपन्नता वाला भारत भी है।
   C. एक प्रगतिशील मानसिकता वाला भारत है तो वहीं वह भारत भी है जो सामाजिक तौर पर दकियानूसी है।
   D. एक ऐसा भारत है जिसमें विशिष्ट उपलब्धियों के साथ ही विशाल विफलताएं हैं।

गद्यांश-2

भारतीय गणतंत्र में कानून एवं व्यवस्था राज्यों का विषय है इसीलिए मुख्यमंत्रियों को केंद्रीय दृष्टिकोण से लैस करने के क्लास को जरूरी समझा जाता है। विकास की दिशा में असमानता को दूर करने की कोई कारगर योजना भले ही नहीं दिखती हो लेकिन नक्सलियों से निपटने के लिए विशेष पुलिस फोर्स का गठन जरूरी बताया गया है। अब तक नक्सल प्रभावित क्षेत्रों के बारे में सरकारी कार्रवाईयों का अनुभव भी यही रहा है कि यहां पुलिस एक्शन तो बड़े पैमाने पर शुरू हो जाते हैं लेकिन नक्सली गतिविधियों की जड़ों में जो आर्थिक, राजनैतिक, सामाजिक असमानता के कारण को सत्ता जिम्मेदार मानती है, उसे दूर नहीं कर पाती है। भारत में यह खास तौर से देखा जाना चाहिए कि नक्सलियों की गतिविधियां उन्हीं राज्यों में हैं जहां दूसरी हथियारबंद शक्तियां नहीं हैं और जहां क्षेत्र विशेष की चरित्र वाली संसदीय शक्तियां अपनी पहचान खो चुकी हैं। इस तरह देश में किसी न किसी रूप में हथियारबंद समूहों की मौजूदगी की स्थितियां लगातार न केवल बनी हुई हैं बल्कि अंग्रेजों के जाने के बाद से विकसित हुई हैं। इस समय आंतरिक सुरक्षा और आदिवासी को खासतौर से जोड़कर देखा जा रहा है।

1. भारत में नक्सलवाद
   A. कानून एवं व्यवस्था की समस्या है।
   B. राज्यों की समस्या है।
   C. आर्थिक पिछड़ेपन एवं सामाजिक असमानता से उपजी समस्या है।
   D. हथियारबंद समूहों की समस्या है।

2. उपर्युक्त उद्धरण के आधार पर सही कथन का चयन कीजिए।
   A. नक्सलवाद से निपटने के लिए राज्य सरकारों के पास कोई स्वतंत्र कार्य योजना नहीं है।
   B. आर्थिक विकास की तुलना में विशेष पुलिस फोर्स पर अधिक निर्भरता की सरकारी नीति।
   C. नक्सलवाद की समस्या अंग्रेजों की फूट डालो और राज करो की नीति का ही परिणाम है।
   D. A एवं B दोनों।

3. निम्न में से कौन नक्सलवाद के उदय का कारण है?
   A. आर्थिक पिछड़ापन
   B. सामाजिक असमानता
   C. क्षेत्र विशेष की चरित्र वाली संसदीय शक्तियों का पहचान खोना
   D. उपरोक्त सभी।

गद्यांश-3

भारत के पूर्वी एशिया से गहरे ऐतिहासिक और सांस्कृतिक संबंध रहे हैं। प्राचीन काल में कई भारतीय सम्राटों ने दक्षिण पूर्व एशियाई देशों में भारत की संस्कृति का प्रचार किया। बौद्ध धर्म भी सम्पर्क का एक माध्यम बना। ये संबंध अठारहवीं शताब्दी तक रहे, लेकिन ब्रिटेन के आधिपत्य में आने के बाद अंतर्राष्ट्रीय जगत् में भारत एक स्वतंत्र खिलाड़ी नहीं रहा।

आजादी के बाद भारत ने फिर से पूरब की ओर देखने का प्रयास किया और नई दिल्ली में अप्रैल 1947 में 'एशियाई

बंधुत्व' कायम करने की इन आरम्भिक कोशिशों की परिणति 'हिन्दी चीनी भाई-भाई' जैसे नारों और बांडुंग सम्मेलन व गुटनिरपेक्ष आंदोलन के रूप में सामने आई, लेकिन चीन के साथ 1962 के युद्ध और शीतयुद्ध कालीन घटनाओं ने भारत को एक बार फिर पूरब से दूर कर दिया। पिछली शताब्दी में कई भारतीय इतिहासकारों ने नये साक्ष्यों के आधार पर दक्षिण-पूर्वी एशियाई देशों को भारत के 'सांस्कृतिक उपनिवेश' के रूप में पेश करके उन देशों में गलत संदेश दिया, क्योंकि कुछ ही समय पहले औपनिवेशिक गुलामी से आजाद हुए इन देशों में राष्ट्रवादी भावनाएं उफान पर थीं। भारत की पूर्वोन्मुखी नीति का वर्तमान स्वरूप 1992 में सामने आया जब शीतयुद्ध की समाप्ति हो चुकी थी और भारत आर्थिक उदारीकरण का मार्ग अपना चुका था। इस बार व्यापार और वाणिज्य संबंध का मुख्य आधार बने।

1. प्राचीन काल में भारत के पूर्व एशियाई देशों के साथ संबंध का मुख्य आधार क्या था?
A. व्यापार
B. राजनीतिक संबंध
C. धर्म
D. A एवं C दोनों

2. उपरोक्त उद्धरण के आधार पर निम्न में से कौन-सा कथन सही है?
A. प्राचीन काल में भारत के पूर्वी एशियाई देशों के साथ घनिष्ठ व्यापारिक संबंध थे।
B. मुसलमानों के आगमन के बाद भारत अंतर्राष्ट्रीय जगत में अलग-थलग पड़ गया।
C. गुट निरपेक्ष आंदोलन द्वारा एशियाई बंधुत्व को बढ़ावा दिया गया।
D. भारत की पूर्वोन्मुखी नीति का वर्तमान स्वरूप 1980 के दशक में सामने आया।

3. सांस्कृतिक उपनिवेश से लेखक का क्या अभिप्राय है?
A. सांस्कृतिक तौर पर समान होना
B. दूसरे की संस्कृति से प्रभावित होना
C. सांस्कृतिक विसंक्रमण
D. सांस्कृतिक आच्छादन

4. एशियाई देशों के साथ भारत के संबंध में सबसे बड़ी बाधा रही है--
A. राजनीतिक प्रतिस्पर्धा
B. सीमित व्यापार
C. इतिहास की गलत व्याख्या
D. उपरोक्त सभी

गद्यांश-4

अंतर्राष्ट्रीय मुद्राकोष के एक अध्ययन के मुताबिक भारत में रेमिटेंस इसलिए बढ़ा है, क्योंकि भारत से ऑस्ट्रेलिया, कनाडा और अमेरिका जाने वाले भारतीय प्रवासियों की संख्या तेजी से बढ़ी है। इन प्रवासियों में कुशल पेशेवरों की संख्या काफी है, जिन्हें वहां ऊंचा वेतन हासिल होता है। इससे भारतीय प्रवासियों की औसत आय बढ़ी है, लिहाजा भारत में रेमिटेंस ज्यादा आने लगा है। इन दिनों दुनिया के विकसित देशों के आर्थिक विकास की जो रिपोर्टें प्रकाशित हो रही है, उनमें बताया जा रहा है कि प्रवासी भारतीय विकसित देशों के सबसे महत्त्वपूर्ण विकास सहभागी बन गये हैं। कारण यह है कि दुनिया के विकसित देश प्रवासी भारतीयों को अधिक सम्मान देते हुए उन्हें अपने देश में रोकने के लिए हरसंभव प्रयास कर रहे हैं। आर्थिक सहयोग और विकास संगठन (ओईसीडी) के द्वारा जारी की गयी प्रवासी रिपोर्ट में भारतीयों को दुनिया का सबसे योग्य प्रवासी बताया गया है। रिपोर्ट में कहा गया है कि विकसित देशों में जाने वाले विभिन्न देशों के प्रवासियों में सेवा भावना, परिश्रम और ईमानदारी के परिप्रेक्ष्य में सबसे ज्यादा योग्य समुदाय भारतीय समुदाय ही है। उच्च कौशल सम्पन्न लोगों में सबसे ज्यादा (40 प्रतिशत से भी ज्यादा) संख्या भारतीयों की है।

1. विकसित देशों में भारतीय प्रवासियों को सम्मान की दृष्टि से देखा जाता है, क्यों?
A. प्रवासी भारतीय इन देशों की विकास प्रक्रिया में सहभागी हैं।
B. प्रवासी भारतीय इन देशों में भारतीय संस्कृति एवं मूल्यों का प्रसार कर रहे हैं।
C. A एवं B दोनों
D. दोनों में से कोई भी नहीं।

2. उपरोक्त उद्धरण के आधार पर निम्न में से कौन-सा कथन सही है?
A. विकसित देश प्रवासी भारतीयों को अपने यहां रोकने का हर संभव प्रयास करते हैं।
B. अन्य देशों की तुलना में भारतीय प्रवासी उच्च कौशल से संपन्न हैं।
C. विदेशों में भारतीयों के साथ भेदभाव किया जाता है।
D. A एवं B सही हैं।

3. लेखक के अनुसार भारत में रेमिटेंस बढ़ने का मुख्य कारण है–
A. भारत में सेवा क्षेत्र का विकास
B. प्रवासी भारतीयों द्वारा देश में भेजा जाने वाला धन
C. भारत में विदेशी निवेश में वृद्धि
D. उपरोक्त सभी

4. भारतीयों को दुनिया का सबसे योग्य प्रवासी माना जाता है, क्यों?
A. ये उच्च कौशल संपन्न हैं।
B. ये परिश्रमी एवं ईमानदार हैं।
C. इनमें सेवा भावना अधिक दिखती है।
D. उपरोक्त सभी

गद्यांश-5

आतंकवाद और तोड़फोड़ की तमाम घटनाएं, जिन्हें देश की संप्रभुता और स्थायित्व के दुश्मनों द्वारा अंजाम दिया जाता है, आंतरिक सुरक्षा की समस्या पैदा करती हैं। व्यापक पैमाने पर

हिंसा, जैसे मजहबी या जातीय दंगे, लोक व्यवस्था की परिधि में एक व्यक्ति या व्यक्तियों के एक समूह द्वारा किये जा रहे अपराध आते हैं। इन दोनों वर्गों के अपराधों की जांच-पड़ताल अलग-अलग तरीके से की जाती है। सबसे पहले कानून एवं व्यवस्था के मुद्दे को लेते हैं। यह निराशाजनक है कि आपराधिक मामलों की संख्या और उनके घटित होने की आशंका बढ़ती जा रही है, लेकिन न तो जांच-पड़ताल और कानूनी कार्रवाई के तौर-तरीके में बदलाव आ पा रहा है और न ही पुलिस बल का आचार-व्यवहार बेहतर हुआ है।

देश में बहुत बड़ी संख्या में मामले दर्ज नहीं कराए जाते या फिर पुलिस दर्ज नहीं करती। भारत में हर मिनट भारतीय दंड संहिता से संबद्ध औसतन तीन अपराध और विशेष व स्थानीय कानूनों से संबंधित छह अपराध होते हैं। महिलाओं के साथ होने वाले अपराधों की स्थिति तो विचलित कर देने वाली है। हर 15 मिनट में एक महिला के साथ छेड़छाड़, हर 29 मिनट में एक दुष्कर्म की घटना और हर 77 मिनट में दहेज हत्या होती है। इनमें भी केवल 30 फीसदी दर्ज मामलों पर ही अदालती कार्रवाई होती है।

1. निम्न में से कौन-सी समस्या आंतरिक सुरक्षा के लिए खतरा है?

A. आतंकवादी घटनाएं B. मजहबी हिंसा
C. जातीय दंगे D. उपरोक्त सभी

2. उपरोक्त उद्धरण के आधार पर निम्न में से कौन-सा कथन सही नहीं है?

A. देश में आपराधिक मामलों की संख्या में वृद्धि हुई है।
B. पिछले कुछ वर्षों में कानूनी कार्रवाई के तौर तरीकों में बदलाव हुआ है।
C. पुलिस का नजरिया भी इन वर्षों में बदला है।
D. B एवं C दोनों

3. महिलाओं के साथ होने वाले अपराध मुख्य रूप से किस श्रेणी में आते हैं?

A. राजनीतिक अपराध B. कानूनी अपराध
C. सामाजिक अपराध D. B एवं C दोनों

4. देश में बढ़ते अपराध का मुख्य कारण है–

A. कानून एवं व्यवस्था की खामियां
B. अपराधियों का राजनीतिक संरक्षण
C. सामाजिक जागरूकता का अभाव
D. उपरोक्त सभी

गद्यांश-6

एडम स्मिथ को मुक्त बाजार की अवधारणा का प्रतिपादक माना जाता है। उनकी मान्यता थी कि यदि आर्थिक प्रक्रिया में राज्य कोई हस्तक्षेप न करे तो उत्पादन में विकास होता जायेगा और एक 'अदृश्य हाथ' उसके लाभों को निम्नतम स्तर तक पहुंचा देगा। आजकल जिस उदारीकरण की नीति का बोलबाला है, उसका अर्थशास्त्रीय तात्विक आधार एडम स्मिथ ने अपने प्रसिद्ध ग्रंथ 'वेल्थ ऑफ नेशंस' में 1776 में प्रस्तुत किया था। भूमंडलीकरण इस उदारीकरण का ही स्वाभाविक अनुज, बल्कि उदारीकरण का अंतर्राष्ट्रीय अवतार है। इसका सीधा तात्पर्य यह है कि आर्थिक प्रक्रिया एक स्वायत्त प्रक्रिया है और उसमें हस्तक्षेप विकास को बाधित करता है।

अर्थशास्त्रीय दृष्टि से भी मुक्त बाजार की प्रतिस्पर्धा कीमतों को कम रखने और आर्थिक सेवाओं को अधिक कुशल बनाने में सहायक होंगी, जिसका स्वाभाविक परिणाम होगा उपभोक्ता अर्थात् समाज को कम कीमत में अधिक कुशल उत्पाद या सेवा मिलना। बाजार में प्रतिस्पर्धा की कमी एकाधिकारवादी आर्थिक प्रक्रिया का रास्ता सुगम करती है और इसके चलते वह उपभोक्ता के बजाय उत्पादक के लिए अधिक लाभकारी हो जाती है। आदर्श बाजार वह है जिसमें ग्राहक और उत्पादक दोनों पक्षों को मोलतोल करने की पूरी स्वतंत्रता और शक्ति हो और ऐसा केवल मुक्त बाजार की अर्थव्यवस्था में ही संभव है।

1. मुक्त बाजार की अवधारणा का क्या अभिप्राय है?

A. बाजार की गतिविधियों में सरकार का हस्तक्षेप न होना
B. बाजार की अंतःक्रिया में मांग एवं पूर्ति का हस्तक्षेप न होना
C. बाजार का बाह्य आर्थिक प्रभावों से मुक्त होना
D. A एवं C दोनों

2. उपरोक्त उद्धरण के आधार पर सही कथन का चयन कीजिए।

A. मुक्त बाजार की अवधारणा का प्रतिपादक एडम स्मिथ था।
B. वेल्थ ऑफ नेशंस का प्रकाशन 1876 में हुआ।
C. भूमंडलीकरण बाजार की गतिविधियों से स्वतंत्र आर्थिक क्रिया का समर्थक है।
D. A एवं C दोनों

3. आधुनिक आर्थिक तंत्र के बारे में निम्न में से कौन-सा कथन सही है?

A. बाजार प्रतिस्पर्धा के कारण कीमतों में कमी आती है।
B. भूमंडलीकरण के कारण बाजार की प्रतिस्पर्धा में कमी आई है, क्योंकि बड़ी कंपनियों ने बाजार पर अपना आधिपत्य कायम कर लिया है।
C. भूमंडलीकरण के कारण आर्थिक सेवाओं में अधिक कुशलता आई है।
D. A एवं C दोनों

4. एकाधिकारवादी आर्थिक क्रिया के लिए उत्तरदायी कारण है–

A. बाजार में प्रतिस्पर्धा की कमी
B. राज्य का आर्थिक क्रियाओं में हस्तक्षेप
C. बाह्य बाजार का हस्तक्षेप
D. A एवं C दोनों

गद्यांश-7

तिब्बत पर पूरी तरह शिकंजा कसने के लिए चीन सभी हथकंडे अपना चुका है। चीन ने बड़ी संख्या में हान वंशी चीनियों को तिब्बत में बसाया है। इससे वहां की जनांकिकी चीन के पक्ष में जाने का खतरा है। चीन जानबूझकर तिब्बत में हान वंशियों की वास्तविक संख्या नहीं बताता। यही सिलसिला चलता रहा तो वह दिन दूर नहीं जब तिब्बती बौद्ध अपने ही देश में अल्पसंख्यक बन कर रह जाएंगे। चीन ने 2006 में तिब्बत को चीन से जोड़ने वाले रेलमार्ग की शुरूआत की जिसका स्थानीय बौद्ध लोग काफी विरोध कर रहे हैं। उनका आरोप है कि नए रेलमार्ग से चीन को तिब्बत पर शिकंजा कसने में न केवल आसानी होगी, बल्कि तिब्बतवासी सांस्कृतिक और आर्थिक रूप से और अधिक हाशिये पर आ जाएंगे।

तिब्बतियों पर जिस तरह के कहर ढाये जा रहे हैं- उससे बहुत ज्यादा आश्चर्य नहीं करना चाहिए, क्योंकि साम्यवादी चीन को दमन के अलावा कोई दूसरा तरीका नहीं आता। चीन किसी भी लोकतांत्रिक आंदोलन को सख्ती से निपटाने में विश्वास करता है। दूसरी ओर भारत, बहुभाषी, बहुधर्मी और बहुसांस्कृतिक देश होने के कारण यह जानता है कि लोकतांत्रिक ढांचे के बिना स्थायी शांति संभव नहीं है। किसी आंदोलन को सैन्य शक्ति के सहारे दबाया तो जा सकता है, लेकिन उसे पूरी तरह खत्म नहीं किया जा सकता। चीन द्वारा तिब्बत पर अर्द्धशताब्दी से ज्यादा तक जबरन कब्जा करने के बावजूद तिब्बतियों के दिल में आजादी की ज्वाला अभी तक जल रही है और दलाई लामा के जीवित रहते हुए तो चीन अपनी साम्राज्यवादी मंशाओं को पूरा नहीं कर सकता।

1. तिब्बत पर अपना प्रभाव बढ़ाने के लिए चीन ने कौन-सा कदम उठाया है?
- A. तिब्बत में बड़ी संख्या में हानवंशी चीनियों को बसाया जा रहा है।
- B. तिब्बत के चीन में विलय का प्रस्ताव पारित कर दिया है।
- C. तिब्बत को चीन का स्वायत प्रदेश घोषित कर दिया है।
- D. उपरोक्त सभी

2. तिब्बत में चीन द्वारा निर्मित रेलमार्ग का विरोध किया जा रहा है, क्यों?
- A. इससे तिब्बत पर चीन के प्रभाव में वृद्धि होगी।
- B. तिब्बतवासी सांस्कृतिक एवं आर्थिक रूप से अधिक हाशिये पर चले जाएंगे।
- C. भारत के साथ तिब्बतियों का संबंध टूट जाएगा।
- D. A एवं B दोनों

3. तिब्बत में स्थायी शांति कैसे कायम हो सकती है?
- A. चीन के प्रभाव में कमी लाकर
- B. उसे चीनी प्रभाव से मुक्त स्वायत प्रदेश का दर्जा देकर
- C. लोकतांत्रिक ढांचे की स्थापना द्वारा
- D. B एवं C दोनों द्वारा

4. उपरोक्त उद्धरण के आधार पर सही कथन का चयन कीजिए।
- A. चीन तिब्बत में अपने सांस्कृतिक प्रभाव का विस्तार करना चाहता है।
- B. चीन ने तिब्बत में बड़ी संख्या में चीनियों को बसाना शुरू किया है।
- C. चीन अपने प्रभाव क्षेत्र में किसी भी प्रकार के लोकतांत्रिक आंदोलन का विरोधी है।
- D. उपरोक्त सभी

गद्यांश-8

आज की सियासत की सबसे बड़ी सच्चाई यह है कि हम गठबंधन यानी अलायंस के जमाने में चल रहे हैं। कोई नहीं जानता कि यह दौर कब खत्म होगा। ऐसे समय में गठबंधन धर्म को सबसे बड़े मंत्र की तरह दोहराया जाता है। गठबंधन बनाने और चलाने के चैलेंज का अहसास सबको है, लेकिन क्या वजह है कि इसके बावजूद हमारे देश में पॉलिटिकल अलायंस का कल्चर उस तरह से मजबूत नहीं हो पा रहा जैसा यूरोप के कई देशों में है। हमारे यहां अलायंस हमेशा कमजोर रहते हैं। उनका वजूद अक्सर खतरे में पड़ता दिखता है, जैसा हाल में दिखा। साझेदारी को लेकर तनाव पैदा होते रहते हैं और समर्थन के नाम पर सियासी ब्लैकमेलिंग का बोलबाला है। हमारे अलायंस रजामंदी का खेल नहीं मजबूरी का सौदा लगते हैं।

हमें यह नहीं भूलना चाहिए कि केंद्र में गठबंधन सरकारें कई कारकों का मिलाजुला नतीजा होती हैं। अगर कांग्रेस का कमजोर होना एक कारक है, तो बीजेपी को भी कुछ क्षेत्रों के अलावा पूरे देश में स्वीकार नहीं किया जाना गठबंधन सरकार को एक प्रभावी तंत्र के रूप में स्थापित करने वाला कारक है। इन दोनों विषयकों के अलावा अपने-अपने राज्यों में मजबूत जनाधार वाले क्षेत्रीय दलों का उभरना भी इन्हीं कारकों में शामिल है। यूपी में समाजवादी पार्टी, बहुजन समाज पार्टी, बिहार में जनता दल (एकीकृत), उड़ीसा में बीजू जनता दल, पंजाब में अकाली दल, आंध्र प्रदेश में तेलुगू देशम पार्टी, तमिलनाडु में एआईएडीएमके और डीएमके कुछ ऐसे क्षेत्रीय दलों के उदाहरण हैं जो क्षेत्रीय के साथ-साथ राष्ट्रीय राजनीति में भी अपनी महत्त्वपूर्ण भूमिका निभाते हैं। 2009 के लोकसभा चुनावों में क्षेत्रीय दलों का महत्व कुछ कम हुआ है और कांग्रेस पार्टी का विस्तार हुआ है। यह देश के लिए बहुत शुभ लक्षण है।

1. भारत में राजनीतिक गठबंधन की सबसे बड़ी कमी क्या है?
- A. इनमें बड़े और छोटे दल एक साथ शामिल होते हैं।
- B. हमारे यहाँ राजनीतिक गठबंधन वैचारिक समानता के आधार पर नहीं बनते बल्कि मजबूरी का सौदा होते हैं।

C. A एवं B दोनों।

D. दोनों में से कोई भी नहीं।

2. हाल ही में भारत में कई गठबंधन सरकारें बनी हैं। इसके लिए कौन-सा कारण उत्तरदायी है?

A. कांग्रेस का सिमटता जनाधार

B. कांग्रेस के प्रभावी विकल्प के रूप में किसी अन्य पार्टी का न उभर पाना

C. क्षेत्रीय पार्टियों का उभरना

D. उपरोक्त सभी

3. यूरोपीय देशों की तुलना में भारत में गठबंधन की संस्कृति कमजोर रही है, क्यों?

A. भारत में राजनीतिक दलों की बहुलता।

B. राजनीतिक दलों के बीच वैचारिक मतभेद।

C. संकीर्ण राजनीतिक हित एवं मानसिकता।

D. उपरोक्त सभी।

4. उपरोक्त उद्धरण के आधार पर सही कथन का चयन कीजिए।

A. 2009 के लोकसभा चुनाव में क्षेत्रीय दलों का महत्व कुछ कम हुआ है।

B. इस चुनाव में बिहार एवं बंगाल में कांग्रेस जनाधार का विस्तार हुआ है।

C. क्षेत्रीय पार्टियों को करारी हार का सामना करना पड़ा।

D. उपरोक्त सभी।

गद्यांश-9

कर्त्तव्य एक नैतिक बंधन है। यह एक तरह से ऋणी होने के समान है, जिस सामाजिक प्राणी के साथ हम रह रहे होते हैं। हमें अपने साथ रहने वालों के लिए इसकी अनुमति मिलनी चाहिए। हमारे जीवनवृत्ति का अधिकार संकेत देता है कि यह हमारा कर्त्तव्य है कि हम उन साथ रहने वाले प्राणियों को भी अपने समान ही जीवन की परिस्थितियां उपलब्ध कराएं। वास्तव में अधिकार और कर्त्तव्य परस्पर संबद्ध हैं। किसी एक के संबंध में अधिकार दूसरे का कर्त्तव्य हो सकता है। अधिकार और कर्त्तव्य एक सिक्के के दो पहलू हैं। हमें दूसरे के ओहदों का हमेशा ख्याल रखना चाहिए। नैतिक कर्त्तव्य, वैद्यानिक अधिकार की अपेक्षा ज्यादा प्रभावी होते हैं। नैतिक कर्त्तव्य वह कर्त्तव्य है जो लोगों को नैतिक स्तर पर बांध कर रखती है। यह हमारा नैतिक कर्त्तव्य है कि हम गरीबों की मदद करें क्योंकि वह एक प्राणी और समाज का अंग है।

हमें उन परिस्थितियों के निर्माण के लिए हमेशा प्रयास करना चाहिए जिनसे मानवता का कल्याण हो सके। यह हमारा अनुकरणीय कर्त्तव्य है कि हम अपने माता-पिता की आज्ञा मानें और उन्हें सम्मान दें। यह कर्त्तव्य जिम्मेवारी की चेतना से पैदा होता है जो कि प्रत्यक्षतः हमारे अंतःकरण से संबंधित है। इस प्रकार से यह एक नैतिक कर्त्तव्य है जिसमें कोई व्यक्ति बिना वैधानिक बंधन के ही ऋणी है।

कर्त्तव्य की चेतना, सही तरीके से सभ्यता के विकास की सर्वश्रेष्ठता है। पाखंड कर्त्तव्य की चेतना के एकदम विपरीत है। पाखंड में जहां दुरात्मा का समावेश है, वहीं कर्त्तव्य में यथार्थता और विश्वस्तता का समावेश है।

1. गद्यांश के अनुसार वैधानिक कर्त्तव्य है:

A. नैतिक कर्त्तव्य की अपेक्षा अधिक महत्त्वपूर्ण

B. नैतिक कर्त्तव्य की अपेक्षा कम महत्त्वपूर्ण

C. नैतिक कर्त्तव्य की अपेक्षा अधिक प्रभावी

D. नैतिक कर्त्तव्य की अपेक्षा कम प्रभावी

2. निम्न में से कौन-सा वाक्य गद्यांश के अनुसार सही नहीं है?

A. पाखंड में दुष्टता का समावेश

B. पाखंड का कर्त्तव्य के विपरीत होना

C. कर्त्तव्य में यथार्थता का समावेश

D. कर्त्तव्य की चेतना का सभ्यता के विकास के लिए महत्त्वपूर्ण न होना

3. निम्न में से किन नैतिक कर्त्तव्यों का उल्लेख गद्यांश में नहीं किया गया है?

A. नैतिक कर्त्तव्य हमारी मातृभूमि से बढ़कर है

B. नैतिक कर्त्तव्य हमारे माता-पिता से बढ़कर है

C. नैतिक कर्त्तव्य गरीब से बढ़कर है

D. नैतिक कर्त्तव्य मानव-कल्याण में योगदान है

4. निम्न में से कौन नैतिक कर्त्तव्य से संबंधित नहीं है?

A. जिम्मेवारी की चेतना

B. सद्विचार

C. पाखंड

D. यथार्थता

5. हमें माता-पिता के प्रति आज्ञाकारी और सम्मानपूर्ण होना चाहिए, क्योंकि:

A. यह जिम्मेवारी की चेतना है

B. यह वैधानिक बाध्यता है

C. यह सभ्यता है

D. यह पाखंड है

गद्यांश-10

ऐसे महान् चिन्तकों को जिनकी शिक्षाएँ वैश्विक हैं, अपने समय के संदर्भ से ही समझा जा सकता है। बुद्ध को व्यापक रुप में गलत समझा गया है। व्यवहारवादियों, अज्ञेयवादियों, निरीश्वरवादियों तथा नैतिक मानवतावादियों ने उन्हें अपने दर्शन का प्रचार करने वाला माना है। बुद्ध की शिक्षाओं को भारत की ईसा-पूर्व छठी शताब्दी को समझकर ही ठीक प्रकार से समझा जा सकता है क्योंकि उनका आविर्भाव उसी शताब्दी में हुआ था किन्तु ऐसा करना अपेक्षाकृत कठिन कार्य है।

ईसा-पूर्व छठी शताब्दी के भारत में बहुत प्रकार की विचारधाराएँ और सम्प्रदाय थे तथापि सभी सम्प्रदाय आत्मा के पुनर्जन्म, कर्म के दर्शन एवं मानव के चरम लक्ष्य निर्वाण के

विषय में सहमत थे। बुद्ध ने इन सिद्धान्तों को स्वीकार किया है, यद्यपि उन्होंने धार्मिक सिद्धान्तवाद को अस्वीकार किया है, किन्तु उनका योगदान नैतिकता तथा सदाचार की उत्कृष्टता को महत्वपूर्ण मानने में था। उन्होंने हृदय को शान्ति प्रदान करने की आवश्यकता तथा नैतिकता के नियमों के अनुसरण पर विशेष बल दिया। दुःखों का अन्त शरीर की भूख को शान्त करने तथा हमारे संवेगों पर दृढ़ता से नियंत्रण करने से हो सकता है।

बुद्ध की रुचि ईश्वर में नहीं थी बल्कि मनुष्य और मानव-प्रयासों में थी। अपनी साधना और अपने प्रयत्नों से मानव अपने आपको देवत्व की ऊँचाई तक उठा सकता है, यद्यपि भक्ति-सम्बन्धी तत्त्वों के बिना भी बुद्ध की शिक्षाएँ मुख्य रूप से धार्मिक हैं। बुद्ध के अन्दर आध्यात्मिक गहराई, नैतिक दृढ़ता तथा बौद्धिक स्पष्टता का भण्डार समाहित है। समय के व्यतीत होने के साथ-साथ उनके द्वारा की गई मानवता की सेवा का विश्वव्यापी समादर हो रहा है। उनका संदेश सभी काल के लिए सार्थक है।

1. बुद्ध ने अधिक महत्व प्रदान किया
- A. ईश्वर को न कि मनुष्य को
- B. मनुष्य तथा ईश्वर दोनों को
- C. न ईश्वर को और न मनुष्य को
- D. मनुष्य-मात्र को न कि ईश्वर को

2. महान विचारकों को ठीक से किसके द्वारा समझा जा सकता है?
- A. ई॰ पू॰ छठी शताब्दी के भारत को समझने से
- B. जिस काल में वे रहे हैं उस काल की सापेक्षता में उन्हें समझने से
- C. बुद्ध की शिक्षाओं का ठीक-ठीक समादर करने से
- D. उनके विचारों और दर्शन का अध्ययन करने तथा समझने से

3. बुद्ध ने किस पर जोर दिया?
- A. ईश्वर की भक्ति पर
- B. कर्मकाण्ड पर
- C. प्रार्थना पर
- D. आचारशास्त्र तथा नैतिक नियमों पर

4. परिच्छेद के अनुसार बुद्ध की शिक्षाएँ मुख्य रूप से धर्मसम्बन्धी हैं,
- A. आध्यात्मिक गहराई के कारण
- B. नैतिक दृढ़ता के कारण
- C. क्योंकि विशुद्ध रूप से बौद्धिक नहीं हैं
- D. उपर्युक्त सभी के कारण

गद्यांश-11

मनुष्य का सुखी जीवन संतुलित प्राकृतिक पर्यावरण पर निर्भर करता है। मानव की बढ़तीं जनसंख्या और तज्जन्य आवश्यकताएँ प्रकृति के संतुलन को बिगाड़ रही हैं। पर्यावरण में दूषित तत्त्वों की मात्रा आवश्यकता से अधिक बढ़ जाती है तो पर्यावरण का यह असन्तुलन प्रदूषण का रूप ले लेता है। मानव की आवासीय, औद्योगिक नगरीकरण, कृषि उत्पादन में वृद्धि करने की समस्याओं ने प्रकृति के संतुलन को बिगाड़कर प्रदूषण को बढ़ाया है। यातायात-साधनों की वृद्धि, वृक्षों की अंधाधुंध कटाई से वातावरण में ऑक्सीजन की कमी और कार्बन डाइ-आक्साइड की वृद्धि हो गई है। पॉप संगीत और रॉक संगीत तथा हॉर्न बजाने से ध्वनि प्रदूषण बढ़ रहा है। वातावरण को प्रदूषित कर हम अपनी मृत्यु को स्वयं ही निमंत्रण दे रहे हैं। प्रदूषण की वृद्धि के लिए मानव ही उत्तरदायी है। अतः इसके निवारण के लिए सर्वप्रथम अपने मानसिक प्रदूषण को दूर करना होगा। वृक्षारोपण, पेयजल-शुद्धीकरण, रासायनिक विस्फोटों पर नियंत्रण, कर्णभेदी ध्वनि विस्तारक यंत्रों, वाहनों और संगीत को रोकने के उपायों से मानव जीवन को प्रदूषण मुक्त बनाना होगा, तभी मानव जीवन सुखमय हो सकता है।

1. 'अपनी मृत्यु को स्वयं निमंत्रण देने' का अभिप्राय क्या है?
- A. आत्महत्या करना
- B. जीने की इच्छा छोड़ देना
- C. हताश हो जाना
- D. वातावरण को प्रदूषित करना

2. मानव जीवन को सुखी कैसे बनाया जा सकता है?
- A. औद्योगीकरण से
- B. जनसंख्या नियंत्रण से
- C. संतुलित पर्यावरण से
- D. यातायात साधनों की वृद्धि से

3. कर्णभेदी संगीत से किस प्रकार का प्रदूषण होता है?
- A. वायु प्रदूषण
- B. ध्वनि प्रदूषण
- C. पर्यावरण प्रदूषण
- D. मानसिक प्रदूषण

4. 'वृक्षारोपण' से प्रमुख लाभ क्या है?
- A. मृदा संरक्षण
- B. जड़ी-बूटियों, औषधियों की पूर्ति
- C. वातावरण में वायुशुद्धि
- D. रेगिस्तान वृद्धि की रोकथाम

5. पर्यावरण असन्तुलन के लिए कौन उत्तरदायी है?
- A. मानसिक प्रदूषण
- B. ध्वनि प्रदूषण
- C. वृक्षों की अंधाधुंध कटाई
- D. प्राकृतिक प्रकोप

गद्यांश-12

विकसित देशों के लोगों की अपेक्षा अविकसित देशों के लोगों की सोच ग्राम्यता के उत्प्रेरकों के सम्बन्ध में एकदम भिन्न है। वहाँ यह एक प्रकार से मानव के जीवित रहने की क्रिया के लिए केवल भौतिक आवश्कता है। तीसरी दुनिया के देशों में, जो मुख्य रूप से ग्रामीण हैं, उनका एकमात्र आधार ग्रामीण

विकास ही है, जिसके द्वारा मानव जीवन को इसके वर्तमान अवमानव स्तर से ऊपर उठाया जा सकता है। उन देशों में शताब्दियों से ग्रामीण जीवन जहाँ का तहाँ खड़ा अवरोधित है। उस ग्रामीण जनसंख्या की दशाओं को सुधारने के लिए कुछ नहीं किया गया जो अन्य चार पैर वाले प्रतिरूपों की तुलना में मामूली ढंग से भिन्न है। अविकसित एवं अर्द्धविकसित देशों में अज्ञान, कुस्वास्थ्य तथा गरीबी ग्रामीण जीवन के पर्याय बन गये हैं। लेकिन सबसे दुःखद स्थिति यह है कि इस प्रकार की मानव जनसंख्या ने ऐसा स्वीकार कर लिया है कि यह दुरवस्था अपरिवर्तनीय है। यह एक ऐसी स्थिति है जिसकी कोई दवा नहीं है। उनके जीवन से आशा की सभी किरणें दूर हो गयी हैं। इस प्रकार के देशों में, ग्रामीण विकास किसी प्रकार की भौतिक अथवा अभौतिक विकास के लिए अपरिहार्य शर्त है। इसलिए इन सभी देशों का प्रबुद्ध वर्ग ग्रामीण विकास के प्रश्न पर निरन्तर बढ़-चढ़कर रुचि ले रहा है।

उनके स्वतंत्रता संघर्ष की विरासत का यह एक अंग भी था। भारत जैसे देश में, इस बात को सभी जानते हैं कि स्वतंत्रता आन्दोलन में ग्रामीण विकास की कोशिश एक अविभाज्य अंग था। गाँधीजी जैसे नेताओं को भली-भाँति यह एहसास था कि वास्तविक भारत अवरोधग्रस्त ग्रामों में निवास करता है। शहर जो ज्यादातर पश्चिमी उपनिवेशवाद की उपज हैं, केवल दिखावटी दर्शनीय वस्तुएँ हैं। तब भी दो प्रकार की दुनिया थी – वह जहाँ तड़क-भड़क के जीवन वाले जो शाही रुचियों के सुविधासम्पन्न कुछ गिने-चुने सम्भ्रान्त क्षेत्रवासी रहते थे। वे क्षेत्र छोटे-छोटे टापू जैसे थे जिनको धूल-मिट्टी और गंदगी के विशाल समुद्र ने घेर रखा है और बहुसंख्यक लोग उन स्थानों का प्रतिनिधित्व करते थे।

भारत नगरों से किसी भी तरह अपरिचित नहीं रहा। प्राचीन भारत में, नगर देश के अंगभूत भाग थे जो मूलरूप से शेष सारे देश और समग्र समाज से सम्बन्धित थे। वे संस्कृति के सुमन की भाँति तथा राष्ट्र की कलात्मक उत्कृष्टता के परिचायक थे। आधुनिक नगर केवल दूसरों के शिकार करने वाले परजीवीमात्र हैं जो देश को कमजोर बना रहे हैं।

इसीलिए गाँधीजी ने 'गाँवों की ओर लौट चलो' यह ग्राम आन्दोलन प्रारम्भ किया था। उनके मतानुसार यह आन्दोलन ही भारत को स्वतंत्रता दिलवा सकता था और स्वतंत्रता को सुरक्षित रख सकता था। राष्ट्र की स्वतंत्रता के लिए अपनायी गयी उनकी रणनीति में ग्रामीण विकास गर्व का स्थान रखता था। इस प्रकार ग्रामीण विकास का उद्‌गम स्वतंत्रता संग्राम के मूल में सन्निहित है।

1. इस परिच्छेद के सन्दर्भ में निम्नलिखित में से कौन-सा कथन सत्य नहीं है?
   A. तीसरी दुनिया के देशों की ग्रामीण जनता की यह सोच है कि उनकी अवमानवीय स्थिति सुधर नहीं सकती।
   B. तीसरी दुनिया के देशों के लोगों का जीवन-स्तर केवल ग्रामीण विकास द्वारा उठाया जा सकता है।
   C. आधुनिक नगरों में रहने वाले अधिकांश धनाढ्य लोग वास्तव में ग्रामीण विकास के सम्बन्ध में चिन्तित हैं।
   D. किसी भी प्रकार की अन्य उन्नति और विकास के लिए ग्रामीण विकास सर्वप्रथम आवश्यक है।

2. लोग ग्रामीण विकास में अत्यधिक रुचि ले रहे हैं क्योंकि–
   A. उन्हें इसकी अपरिहार्यता का अनुभव हो चुका है
   B. वे घोर स्वास्थ्य-समस्याओं से दुःखी हैं
   C. निकट भविष्य में कुछ भी सार्थक करना सम्भव नहीं है
   D. अब वे इसके सम्बन्ध में आशावादी हो गए हैं

3. ग्रामीण विकास को भारत के स्वातंत्र्य आन्दोलन का एक अंग समझा गया था, क्योंकि–
   A. केवल ग्रामों में ही शाही रुचि निवास करती थी
   B. देश मुख्य रूप से ग्रामों से बना था
   C. गाँधीजी पश्चिमी उपनिवेशवाद के विरुद्ध थे
   D. उस समय वास्तविक भारत ब्रिटिश हुकूमत के मातहत था

4. परिच्छेद के सन्दर्भ में निम्नलिखित में से कौन-सा कथन सत्य है?
   A. तीसरी दुनिया के अधिकांश देशों का त्वरित गति से नगरीकरण हो रहा है।
   B. भारत का स्वतंत्रता आन्दोलन ग्रामीण विकास का अंगभूत समझा जाता है।
   C. ग्रामीण जनता अपनी दशा सुधारने के बारे में बहुत आशावादी है।
   D. वर्तमान सन्दर्भ में अज्ञान, निर्धनता तथा रुग्ण-स्वास्थ्य ग्रामीण जीवन के अविभाज्य अंग हैं।

5. निम्नलिखित में कौन-सा कथन आधुनिक नगरों वाली दो विपरीत दुनिया का सबसे उपयुक्त वर्णन करता है?
   A. कुछ धनी लोग और अधिक गरीब लोग
   B. चमक-दमक का क्षेत्र और धनाढ्य लोग
   C. वाणिज्यिक तथा औद्योगिक शोषण
   D. पश्चिमी उत्पादों के संरक्षक तथा शाही रुचियों के पोषक

गद्यांश-13

शिष्टजनों द्वारा अनुष्ठित आचरण मात्र कल्पना-उद्‌भूत सामाजिक शिष्टाचार नहीं है अपितु गंभीर वैज्ञानिक रहस्यों से ओत-प्रोत ऐसा संस्कार है जो मानव जीवन में गुणाधान प्रक्रिया को प्रशस्त करता है। भारतीय संस्कृति में शिष्टाचार का श्रीगणेश सामाजिक व्यवहार के सिंहद्वार – अभिवादन से होता है। ईश्वराभिवादन, पूज्यजनों को प्रणाम, नमस्कार, प्राञ्जलि, अञ्जलिपुट, प्रणिपात, नामोच्चारणपूर्वक नमन, प्रदक्षिणापूर्वक सम्मान तथा साष्टांग प्रणाम पर्यायभेद से अभिवादन के ही विविध रूप हैं। प्रतिदिन

या विशिष्ट अवसरों पर कर्म में सफलता और दीर्घायुष्य-प्राप्ति हेतु माता-पिता तथा गुरुजनों को अभिवादन करना केवल भारतीय संस्कृति में ही विद्यमान है। अध्यात्म-विज्ञान की मान्यता है कि किसी वरेण्य व्यक्ति के आगमन पर प्राणस्पन्दन की गति ऊर्ध्वमुखी होकर ऊर्जस्वित हो जाती है। उनका आशीर्वाद प्राप्त कर प्राण ऊर्जावान् बन जाते हैं। आज अन्य क्षेत्रों की भाँति शिष्टाचार के विधि-विधान में प्रदूषण और अवमूल्यन निर्बाध गति से हो रहा है। 'हाय', 'ही', 'हेलो' करने वालों को भला हाथ जोड़कर मस्तक झुकाना कैसे रास आ सकता है? त्याग-वैराग्यसम्पन्न अल्पवयस्क या वयोवृद्धों को अभिवादन करना हमारी पुरातन आचार-पद्धति है।

1. शिष्टाचार का प्रथम सोपान क्या है?

A. कुशलक्षेम पूछना B. मुस्कराते हुए बात करना
C. अभिवादन करना D. भेंट देना

2. गुरुजनों को अभिवादन करने का कौनसा कृत्य विधिसम्मत नहीं है?

A. चरण स्पर्श करना
B. हाथ जोड़कर सिर झुकाना
C. साष्टांग प्रणाम करना
D. हाथ मिलाना

3. आशीर्वाद ग्रहण करने का वैज्ञानिक रहस्य क्या है?

A. मन प्रसन्न हो जाता है
B. प्राण ऊर्जस्वित हो जाते हैं
C. असम्भव कार्य सम्भव हो जाता है।
D. हमारा आत्मविश्वास बढ़ता है

4. सामाजिक कुशलता प्राप्त करने का सिंहद्वार क्या है?

A. श्रीगणेश का पूजन
B. सहभोज का आयोजन
C. प्रत्येक व्यक्ति को अपना गुरु मानना
D. विधिपूर्वक यथायोग्य अभिवादन

5. 'सबहिं मानप्रद आप अमानी' का अभिप्राय है–

A. स्वयं सम्मान की चाह न कर सबको सम्मान देना
B. सबके मान की परवाह करने से पहले अपनी चिन्ता करना
C. मान पाकर आपा न खोना
D. अपने सम्मान के समान दूसरों का भी सम्मान करना

गद्यांश-14

शैक्षिक योजना का उद्देश्य सभी उम्र के वर्ग समूहों की कुल जनसंख्या की शैक्षिक आवश्यकताओं की पूर्ति करना होना चाहिए। निस्संदेह प्राथमिक स्तर से विश्वविद्यालयी स्तर तक शिक्षा का तीन स्तरीय पदानुक्रम परम्परागत शिक्षा की संरचना का सार भाग है तथापित हमें परिधीय शिक्षा जो उतनी ही महत्त्वपूर्ण है, की अवहेलना नहीं करनी चाहिए। आधुनिक अवस्थाओं के अंतर्गत, कार्यकर्त्ताओं को अपने उत्साह को तरोताजा करने की आवश्यकता है अथवा उन्हें एक नई दिशा में बढ़ने या अपने कौशलों को विश्वविद्यालयी प्रोफेसर के स्तर तक बढ़ाने की आवश्यकता है। सेवानिवृत और वृद्धों की भी अपनी आवश्यकताएँ होती हैं। शैक्षिक योजना ऐसी होनी चाहिए जिसमें प्रत्येक की आवश्यकताओं को ध्यान में रखा जाए। शिक्षा की हमारी संरचना इस मान्यता पर आधारित है कि शिक्षा का एक सीमावर्ती बिन्दु होता है। आजकल यह मूलभूत त्रुटि और अधिक हानिकारक बन गई है। एडगर फौरे तथा अन्य सदस्यों द्वारा रचित युनेस्को का 'लर्निंग टू बी' नामक प्रतिवेदन, जो 1973 में प्रकाशित हुआ, यह दावा करता है कि बच्चों की शिक्षा द्वारा स्व-अधिगम के विभिन्न रूपों के लिए भावी प्रौढ़ तैयार होने चाहिएँ। एक व्यवहार्य भावी शिक्षा पद्धति में ऐसे मोड्यूल होने चाहिए जिसमें विभिन्न प्रकार के प्रकार्य सम्मिलित हों और वह विविध सामाजिक अवयवों के लिए उपयोगी हों। और प्रमाण-पत्रों का आधार अध्ययन अवधि न होकर निष्पादन होना चाहिए। इसकी इबारत पहले से ही दीवार पर लिखी हुई है।

इस बात या तथ्य को ध्यान में रखते हुए कि जीवन-पर्यन्त अधिगम या आजन्म शिक्षा के प्रति प्रतिबद्धता के महत्त्व को आजकल शैक्षिक रूप से विकसित देशों में भी विवेचित किया जा रहा है, परंतु इस बात की सम्भाव्यता कि यह विचार शैक्षिक चिंतन का अभिन्न अंग बन जाए बहुत दूर की बात है। क्योंकि इस दिशा में आगे बढ़ने का अर्थ है वर्तमान शैक्षिक संगठनों की पुनर्व्यवस्था से कुछ अधिक करना। कम-से-कम विभिन्न वर्गों के वयस्क अध्येताओं के लिए मुक्त विश्वविद्यालयी प्रोग्राम विकसित करके और परम्परागत महाविद्यालयों और विद्यालयों में प्रसार-सेवाएँ आरंभ करके इसका शुभारंभ किया जा सकता है। साथ ही इन संस्थाओं को चाहिए कि असंख्य सामुदायिक संगठनों, जैसे पुस्तकालय, संग्रहालय, म्युनिसिपल मनोरंजन कार्यक्रम, स्वास्थ्य सेवाएँ आदि, के साथ सहयोग करते रहें।

1. परिच्छेद के अनुसार, वर्तमान शैक्षिक संरचनाएँ निम्नलिखित में से किसको मान्यता देती हैं?

A. सभी व्यक्तियों को उनकी आवश्यकताओं के अनुसार शिक्षित किया जा सकता है
B. वर्तमान में शैक्षिक योजना बहुत अधिक व्यवहार्य है
C. शिक्षा एक निश्चित समय में पूर्ण होने वाली प्रक्रिया है
D. जीवन-पर्यन्त शिक्षा (अधिगम) पर चर्चाएँ चलती रहनी चाहिए

2. दिए गए परिच्छेद के संदर्भ में निम्नलिखित में से कौन-सा सही नहीं है?

A. जीवन-पर्यन्त शिक्षा एक आधुनिक अवधारणा है
B. कर्मियों का ज्ञान तथा उनके कौशलों का निरंतर रूप से अद्यतन होते रहना चाहिए
C. 'लर्निंग टू बी' नामक ग्रंथ इस बात का समर्थन करता है कि शिक्षा का एक सीमांत बिन्दु होता है
D. विद्यालयों तथा महाविद्यालयों में भी विस्तार सेवाएँ आरंभ की जानी चाहिए

3. जीवन-पर्यन्त शिक्षा को शैक्षिक संरचना के साथ समेकित करने का अभिप्रेत होगा–
   A. परम्परागत विद्यालयों और महाविद्यालयों को बंद कर देना
   B. सभी औपचारिक पाठ्यक्रमों के लिए अधिक समयावधि
   C. वर्तमान शैक्षिक संगठनों का सामान्य पुनर्व्यवस्थापन
   D. इनमें से कोई नहीं
4. लेखक का मुख्य बल किस बात पर है?
   A. परम्परागत पद्धतियों को सुदृढ़ किया जाना चाहिए।
   B. औपचारिक शिक्षा, गैर-औपचारिक शिक्षा से अधिक महत्त्वपूर्ण है
   C. व्यक्ति को सीखना कभी बंद नहीं करना चाहिए
   D. मुक्त शिक्षा प्रणाली का कोई विकल्प नहीं है
5. लेखक के अनुसार, 'जीवन-पर्यन्त शिक्षा' की अवधारणा है
   A. इतनी पुरानी जितनी परम्परागत शिक्षा होती है
   B. जो अभी भी निर्माण अवस्था में हो
   C. जो विकसित देशों में प्रचलित है
   D. जो व्यवहार्य अथवा वांछनीय न हो

गद्यांश-15

मानव-जीवन के सौ वर्षों को चार भागों में बाँटा गया है। वास्तव में सम्पूर्ण जीवन सतत प्रयत्न करते हुए व्यक्तित्व का विकास करने के लिए है। व्यक्तित्व के विकास की दिशा अवस्था के अनुसार बदलती है। विशेष प्रकार की योग्यताओं को विकसित करने के लिए अनुकूल वातावरण की आवश्यकता पड़ती है। आश्रम-व्यवस्था के अनुसार जीवन-भार श्रम करते हुए मानव अधिकाधिक सफलता प्राप्त कर सकता है। जीवन का प्रथम आश्रम ब्रह्मचर्य अधिक से अधिक ज्ञान करने के लिए था। ब्रह्मचर्याश्रम में जो ज्ञान प्राप्त किया जाता है उसी की मात्रा के अनुरूप जीवन की सफलता होती है। इसी के बल पर गृहस्थाश्रम में वह अधिक से अधिक धन कमा कर लोक-कल्याण कर सकता है। मनुष्य की आध्यात्मिक प्रवृत्तियाँ स्वान्तः सुखाय होती हैं। इनके द्वारा वह वानप्रस्थ और संन्यास में शान्ति प्राप्त करता है।

1. वास्तव में सम्पूर्ण जीवन किसलिए है?
   A. सतत प्रयत्न करते हुए व्यक्तित्व के विकास के लिए
   B. श्रम करते हुए सफलता प्राप्त करने के लिए
   C. अधिक से अधिक धन कमाने के लिए
   D. अधिक से अधिक ज्ञान प्राप्त करने के लिए
2. व्यक्तित्व के विकास की दिशा कैसे बदलती है?
   A. योग्यताओं के विकास के अनुसार
   B. अनुकूल वातावरण के अनुसार
   C. अवस्था के अनुसार
   D. सतत प्रयत्नों के अनुसार
3. प्राप्त ज्ञान की मात्रा के अनुरूप क्या होता है?
   A. जीवन की सफलता B. सुख की प्राप्ति
   C. धन की प्राप्ति D. शान्ति की प्राप्ति
4. लोक-कल्याण कब अधिक किया जा सकता है?
   A. ब्रह्मचर्याश्रम में B. वानप्रस्थ में
   C. गृहस्थाश्रम में D. संन्यास में
5. मनुष्य शान्ति किसके द्वारा प्राप्त करता है?
   A. ज्ञान के द्वारा
   B. धन के द्वारा
   C. लोक-कल्याण के द्वारा
   D. आध्यात्मिक प्रवृत्तियों के द्वारा

गद्यांश-16

इन्द्र यह सुनकर स्वयं महर्षि दधीचि के आश्रम में गए और उन्हें मजबूरी कह सुनायी। ऋषि जग-कल्याण के लिए सहर्ष अपना शरीर त्यागने के लिए तैयार हो गए। उनकी हड्डियों से त्वष्ठा ने वज्र बनाया। इस वज्र को हाथ में लेकर इन्द्र दुगुने उत्साह से वृत्रासुर के सम्मुख गए। उनके मेघरूपी रथ के गर्जन से एक बार वृत्रासुर का कलेजा काँप गया। उनके साथ चलते हुए मरुत जोर-जोर से उनकी जयजयकार कर रहे थे। इन्द्र ने सबसे पहले अपने वज्र से वृत्रासुर की माया को काट दिया। फिर भी वह दैत्य बड़ा शक्तिशाली था। अपनी माया से विछिन्न होकर भी वह बहुत देर तक इन्द्र से जूझता रहा। लेकिन अन्त में इन्द्र ने वज्र के प्रहार से वृत्रासुर का सिर काट दिया। वृत्रासुर के मरते ही रुका हुआ जल बह निकला, नदी-नाले फिर से भर उठे और देखते-ही-देखते खेत लहलहा उठे।

1. महर्षि दधीचि एक ऐसे ऋषि थे जिन्होंने :
   A. देवताओं की रक्षा के लिए अपने शरीर का त्याग किया था
   B. योग बल से अपने शरीर को त्याग कर वृत्रासुर के वध हेतु वज्र बनाने के लिए इन्द्र को अपनी अस्थियाँ सुलभ करा दी थीं
   C. वृत्रासुर के वध में इन्द्र की सहायता की थी
   D. वृत्रासुर का वध किया था
2. हमें इस अवतरण से यह प्रेरणा मिलती है कि परोपकार के लिए आवश्यकता पड़ने पर :
   A. अपने शरीर भी दे देना चाहिए
   B. अपना सर्वस्व दे देना चाहिए
   C. अपनी अस्थियाँ दे देनी चाहिए
   D. अपनी सम्पत्ति दे देनी चाहिए
3. इस गद्यांश का उपयुक्त शीर्षक हो सकता है :
   A. दधीचि का आत्मदान
   B. दधीचि का सर्वस्व दान
   C. वृत्रासुर वध
   D. इन्द्र का कोप
4. निम्नलिखित में से सही कथन पर निशान लगाइए :
   A. वृत्रासुर इन्द्र का प्रतिद्वन्द्वी था
   B. वृत्रासुर एक आततायी राक्षस था

C. वृत्रासुर एक महाप्रतापी राक्षस था, जिसने जलावरोध कर रखा था
D. वृत्रासुर उपर्युक्त में से कोई नहीं था

इस उद्धरण में प्रयुक्त निम्नलिखित शब्दों के सही अर्थों पर निशान लगाइए :

5. महर्षि
A. मुनि
B. ऋषि जो ब्राह्मण न हो
C. ऋषि जो ब्राह्मण हो
D. ऋषियों का एक पद विशेष

6. जगकल्याण :
A. संसार का हित
B. संसार की भलाई
C. संसार को सुख देना
D. संसार के लिए आनन्द की व्यवस्था करना

7. वज्र :
A. एक प्रकार का बाजा
B. एक प्रकार का शस्त्र
C. एक प्रकार का आघात
D. पत्थर गिरना या बिजली गिरना

गद्यांश-17

आचार्य शुक्ल जी के गंभीर निबंध 'चिंतामणि' में संग्रहीत हैं। उनमें दो प्रकार के निबंध हैं, एक तो भावों के विश्लेषण से सम्बन्ध रखने वाले निबंध जो भाव-विषयक होते हुए भी आवश्यक नहीं हैं वरन् उच्चकोटि के विचारात्मक हैं, दूसरे साहित्यिक जिनमें कुछ सैद्धांतिक आलोचना से संबंध रखते हैं, जैसे—'साधारणीकरण और व्यक्ति वैचित्र्यवाद' और कुछ व्यावहारिक आलोचनाओं के हैं, जैसे 'भारतेन्दु हरिश्चन्द्र'। आचार्य शुक्ल जी के मनोवैज्ञानिक निबंधों की भी अन्विति उनकी आलोचनाओं से की जा सकती है, वे भारतीय रस सिद्धान्त पर अवलम्बित हैं और उनका सम्बन्ध जीवन सागर के निजी अवगाहन से है। इन निबंधों के भावों का विश्लेषण पर्याप्त मात्रा में हुआ है किन्तु जीवन से चुने हुए उपयुक्त उदाहरणों के कारण यह विश्लेषण दुरूह नहीं होने पाया है। 'लज्जा और ग्लानि' का आधार भारत की आत्मग्लानि है, 'लोभ और प्रीति' का अन्तर समझ लेने पर जायसी के 'रत्नसेन' के प्रेम की आलोचना भली प्रकार समझी जा सकती है।

—काव्य के रूप, डॉ. गुलाब राय

1. उक्त गद्यांश का सम्यक् अनुशीलन करने से पता चलता है कि लेखक ने :
A. शुक्ल जी को समझने में काफी प्रयास किया था
B. शुक्ल जी के साहित्य का सम्यक् अध्ययन किया था
C. शुक्ल जी से दिशाबोध ग्रहण किया था
D. शुक्ल जी को समीप से देखा था

2. डॉ. गुलाब राय की शैली थी :
A. कथा शैली
B. भावना प्रवण शैली
C. विवेचना प्रधान शैली
D. विश्लेषणात्मक शैली

3. डॉ. गुलाब राय ने आचार्य शुक्ल की शैलियों का जो वर्गीकरण किया है वह :
A. अत्यन्त वैज्ञानिक है   B. शोधपूर्ण है
C. सर्वांगीण है   D. यथातथ्य है

4. उक्त गद्यांश के लिए उचित शीर्षक होगा :
A. आचार्य शुक्ल की निबंध-शैली
B. शुक्ल जी की निबंध-कला
C. निबंध कला और शुक्ल जी
D. हिन्दी के श्रेष्ठ निबंधकार शुक्ल जी

5. अन्विति का अर्थ है :
A. अनुरक्ति   B. तालमेल
C. आलोचना   D. अर्चना

गद्यांश-18

चीन में न तो वर्ण व्यवस्था थी न जाति-पाँति का भेदभाव। परम्परा के अनुसार सम्मान के मुख्य पात्र क्रमशः विद्वान्, राज्य पदाधिकारी, योद्धा और अध्यापक थे। साधारण लोगों में नौ श्रेणियाँ थीं। अन्न उत्पन्न करने वाले, माली, लकड़हारे, पशु-पक्षी पालने वाले, बुनकर, नौकर-चाकर, कारीगर, व्यापारी और फुटकर काम करने वाले। कुलीनों तथा साधारण लोगों में अथवा श्रेणियों और व्यवसायों में ऊँच-नीच का भेद कायम था। पर यह विभेद नगण्य-सा था। अपनी योग्यता के अनुसार मनुष्य का स्थान घटता-बढ़ता था। लोग आपस में विवाह आदि बिना किसी बाधा के करते थे। चीनियों में विद्वान् और सेनापति विशेष आदर के पात्र समझे जाते थे। हिजड़े, भाँड, गुलाम, हरकारे, वेश्याएँ नीचे के स्तर के लोग थे। चीन में गुलामों की दशा उतनी खराब नहीं थी जितनी रोम तथा यूरोप के देशों के मध्य युग में थी। गुलामों से घरेलू काम कराये जाते थे। उनकी विशेष जाति नहीं थी। उन्हें यद्यपि खरीदा-बेचा जा सकता था तथापि उनसे न तो नीच काम कराए जाते थे और न उन्हें सताया जाता था।

—विश्व इतिहास, डॉ. रामप्रसाद त्रिपाठी

1. उक्त उद्धरण के अध्ययन से पता चलता है कि मध्यकालीन चीन में :
A. जाति प्रथा प्रचलित थी
B. सामाजिक जीवन काफी समुन्नत था
C. सामाजिक जीवन वैभवपूर्ण था
D. वर्ण-व्यवस्था से रहित था

2. उक्त उद्धरण का उपयुक्त शीर्षक हो सकता है :
A. मध्यकालीन चीन का सामाजिक जीवन
B. मध्यकालीन चीन में सामाजिक व्यवस्था
C. चीनी समाज में विविधता
D. चीनी समाज में गिरावट

3. उक्त गद्य खण्ड का सारांश एक पंक्ति में इस प्रकार व्यक्त किया जा सकता है :
A. अन्य तत्कालीन समाजों की तुलना में मध्यकाल में चीन का सामाजिक जीवन समुन्नत था

B. चीन का मध्यकालीन समाज विकास के शिखर पर था
C. चीन मध्यकालीन राज्यों में अग्रणी था
D. मध्यकालीन चीन का सामाजिक जीवन विकासोन्मुख था

4. चीन के सामाजिक इतिहास का अनुशीलन करने से पता चलता है कि चीन में :
A. सामाजिक भेदभाव अवश्य था भले ही वहाँ वर्ण-व्यवस्था नहीं थी
B. समाज के सभी सदस्य एक-सा जीवन नहीं जीते थे
C. चीनी समाज गुलामों को उत्पीड़ित करता था
D. मध्यकालीन चीन में नागरिक सुविधाओं का अभाव था

5. चीन में विशेष आदर के पात्र समझे जाते थे :
A. हिजड़े और भाँड B. विद्वान् और वेश्याएँ
C. विद्वान् और सेनापति D. कारीगर और व्यापारी

गद्यांश-19

आज से सप्तदशक पूर्व सम्पादकाचार्य पराड़करजी ने कहा था—हम सब सम्पादक पत्रों की उन्नति चाहते हैं। पर हमें स्मरण रखना चाहिए कि इस उन्नति के साथ-साथ हमारी स्वातंत्र्य-हानि अवश्यम्भावी है। उन्नति व्यापारी ढंग से ही हो सकती है; इसके लिए पूँजीपति और संचालक व्यवसाय की आवश्यकता है। इनके कथनानुसार और भी पत्र का सम्पादन करना असम्भव हो जाता है। इंग्लैण्ड और अमेरिका के पत्रों में स्पष्ट देखा जाता है कि इनके समाचार स्तम्भ, मनोरंजन स्तम्भ जितने ही अच्छे हो रहे हैं, उनके सम्पादकीय स्तम्भ उतने ही निकम्मे बनते जा रहे हैं। लन्दन के 'टाइम्स' जैसे दो-तीन पत्र इसके अपवाद हैं। पर साधारण नियम वही है जो बताया जा चुका है। एडिटर की अपेक्षा मैनेजिंग एडिटर का प्रभाव और गौरव अधिक बढ़ गया है। भावी हिन्दी समाचार-पत्रों में ऐसा ही होगा। पत्र निकालकर सफलतापूर्वक चलाना बड़े-बड़े धनियों अथवा सुसंघटित कम्पनियों के लिए संभव होगा। पत्र सर्वांगसुन्दर होंगे। आकार बड़े होंगे, छपाई अच्छी होगी, मनोहर, मनोरंजक और ज्ञानवर्द्धक चित्रों से सुसज्जित होंगे, लेखों में विविधता होगी, कल्पकता होगी, गम्भीर गवेषणा की झलक होगी और मनोहारिणी शक्ति भी होगी, ग्राहकों की संख्या लाखों में गिनी जाएगी। यह सब कुछ होगा पर पत्र प्राणहीन होंगे। पत्रों की नीति देशभक्त, धर्मभक्त अथवा मानवता के उपासक महाप्राण सम्पादकों की नीति न होगी—इन गुणों से सम्पन्न लेखक विकृत मस्तिष्क समझे जाएँगे, सम्पादक की कुर्सी तक उनकी पहुँच भी न होगी। वेतनभोगी सम्पादक मालिक का काम करेंगे और बड़ी खूबी के साथ करेंगे। वे हम लोगों से अच्छे होंगे। पर आज भी हमें जो स्वतन्त्रता प्राप्त है वह उन्हें न होगी। वस्तुत: पत्रों के जीवन में यही समय बहुमूल्य है। इंग्लैण्ड और अमेरिका के पत्रों ने उन्हीं दिनों सच्चा काम किया था जब उनके आकार छोटे थे, समाचार कम होते थे, ग्राहक थोड़े होते थे पर सम्पादक की लेखनी में ओज था और प्राण था। उन देशों की इस उन्नति के बहुत कुछ कारण वे ही सम्पादक थे जिनसे धनी घृणा करते थे, शासक क्रुद्ध रहा करते थे और जो हमारे ही जैसे, एक पैर जेल में रखकर धर्मबुद्धि से पत्र सम्पादन किया करते थे। उनके परिश्रम से और कष्ट से पत्रों की उन्नति हुई पर उनके वंश का लोप हो गया। अब संचालक और व्यवस्थापक सर्वेसर्वा हैं, सम्पादक कुछ नहीं है।

(ध्रुवतारा, अप्रैल-जून, 1996 के सौजन्य से)

1. नीचे लिखे विकल्पों में से कौन-सा उपर्युक्त गद्यांश की विषयवस्तु का सही प्रतिपादन करता है?
A. समाचार-पत्र B. समाचार-पत्र के स्वामी
C. सम्पादक का महत्त्व D. लेखक

2. इंग्लैण्ड और अमेरिका के समाचार-पत्रों की क्या विशेषता है?
A. मनोरंजन स्तम्भ अच्छे हैं
B. सम्पादक स्तम्भ अच्छे हैं
C. रंग-बिरंगे हैं
D. सस्ते हैं

3. 'सर्वांगसुन्दर' का क्या तात्पर्य है?
A. सभी गुणों का होना
B. समाचार-पत्र हर प्रकार से अच्छा हो
C. सबसे श्रेष्ठ
D. सबको लुभाने वाला

4. समाचार-पत्रों की उन्नति कैसे हो सकती है?
A. अच्छी मशीन लगाने से
B. व्यापारी ढंग से
C. सम्पादक के कारण
D. पूँजी लगाने से

5. स्वातन्त्र्य-हानि का क्या अर्थ है?
A. स्वतन्त्रता का नाश
B. पराधीनता
C. मनमानी करने पर रोक
D. कृपा

गद्यांश-20

हम विज्ञान युग में जी रहे हैं। हमसे ये आशा नहीं की जाती कि हम अविश्वसनीय मतों अथवा एकांतिक दैवी-संदेशों को सोचे-समझे बगैर आसानी से स्वीकार कर लेंगे। आज के युग में विज्ञान और प्रौद्योगिकी के नित-नूतन आविष्कार हो रहे हैं। प्रकृति के रहस्यों पर से आवरण क्रमशः हटता जा रहा है। यह युग मानववाद का भी है, जिसमें वे धर्म जो मानवीय बुराइयों तथा सामाजिक अपराधों के प्रति संवेदनशील नहीं हैं, आधुनिक व्यक्ति के गले नहीं उतरते। वे धर्म जो विभेद, वैमनस्य और अनैतिकता को बढ़ावा देते हैं तथा एकता, सद्भावना और सामंजस्य को प्रोत्साहित नहीं करते, वे मनुष्य को मनुष्य से लड़ाकर धर्मद्रोहियों के हाथ में अस्त्र बन जाते हैं। विज्ञान की प्रकृति कभी धर्म-विरोधी नहीं

रही है। धार्मिक मतों के पक्ष में मुख्य तर्क प्रायः ब्रह्मांड संबंधी वस्तुपरक विचारों पर आधारित होते हैं। प्राकृतिक धर्म कभी भी किन्हीं आप्त स्रोतों, इल्हामों या परंपराओं पर निर्भर नहीं करता, वह तो अनुभूत अनुभव सिद्ध प्रत्यक्ष तथ्यों के अध्ययन और व्यावहारिकता पर अवलंबित होता है। वैज्ञानिक विधि का अनुसरण करते हुए, प्राकृतिक तथ्यों का सर्वेक्षण करके, युक्तियुक्त तर्क देकर परमसत्ता-विषयक सिद्धान्त का प्रतिपादन किया जाता है। वैज्ञानिक धर्म में ब्रह्मांड को समझने की जिज्ञासा पर बल दिया जाता है। प्राकृतिक ऊर्जा व पदार्थों के जन्म तथा विनाश को समझ सकने की इच्छा होती है। विकास का क्रम ऊर्ध्वमुखी रहा है : यह अप्राण से सप्राण तक; सप्राण से संवेदनशील तक; संवेदनशील से सज्ञान जीवन तक विकसित होता है। सज्ञान प्राणी को आध्यात्मिक प्राणी के रूप में आत्मविकास करना पड़ता है। आध्यात्मिक प्राणी--विशुद्ध ज्ञानी या विचारवान् प्राणी से उतना ऊँचा होता है जितना ज्ञानवान प्राणी संवेदनशील प्राणी से उन्नत होता है। विज्ञान की चेतना में कहीं यह संकेत नहीं मिलता कि पदार्थ से ही सृष्टि का आरंभ हुआ था। परमाणु को विखंडित करने वाले मनुष्य का मन निश्चय ही परमाणु से कहीं अधिक श्रेष्ठ है। प्रकृत की व्यवस्था और प्रगति के अवलोकन से स्पष्ट हो जाता है कि अगणित क्रमबद्ध प्रणालियों का संचालन, किसी सर्वद्रष्टा परम-आत्मा द्वारा किया जा रहा है।

—(ध्रुवतारा—जनवरी, मार्च, 1996 के सौजन्य से)

1. वर्तमान युग का मनुष्य कैसे धर्म को सही समझ सकता है?

A. जो भय पैदा करे

B. वैज्ञानिक व सद्भावना पैदा करने वाला हो

C. जो वैमनस्य और अनैतिक को बढ़ावा दे

D. जो परंपरा पर आधारित हो

2. 'संवेदनशील' का सही अर्थ चुन कर बताएँ।

A. दूसरे को दुःख देने वाला

B. दूसरे का कष्ट महसूस करने वाला

C. दूसरे का संदेश देने वाला

D. दूसरों की भलाई सोचने वाला

3. 'आशा', 'अविश्वसनीय', 'प्रोत्साहित' तथा 'यह' शब्दों को क्रिया, विशेषण, सर्वनाम तथा संज्ञा के क्रम में व्यवस्थित करिए।

A. आशा, अविश्वसनीय, प्रोत्साहित, यह

B. यह, आशा, अविश्वसनीय, प्रोत्साहित

C. अविश्वसनीय, प्रोत्साहित, यह, आशा

D. प्रोत्साहित, अविश्वसनीय, यह, आशा

4. 'सामंजस्य' शब्द का सही अर्थ चयन करें :

A. सामना करना

B. आलस्य दूर करना

C. भेद-भाव हटाकर एक करना

D. अपना पक्ष प्रबल करना

5. उपर्युक्त गद्यांश में से 'प्राचीन' शब्द का विलोम चुनिए।

A. आधुनिक B. नित-नूतन

C. पारंपरिक D. ऊर्ध्वमुखी

गद्यांश-21

शान्ति और विश्वकल्याण की इसी उदात भावना के कारण युगों-युगों से विश्व हमारी संस्कृति हमारे साहित्य और हमारे विश्वबंधुत्व की ओर आकर्षित रहा है। इसी से प्रेरित होकर लोग भारत से सम्पर्क बढ़ाने के लिए हमारी राष्ट्रभाषा को सीखते-पढ़ते रहे हैं। उसी का सुफल है कि सोवियत संघ से लेकर अमेरिका तक, दक्षिण अफ्रीका से लेकर एशिया तक, यूरोप से लेकर कनाडा तक लाखों-लाखों विदेशी भारत प्रेमी लोग आज हिन्दी पढ़-लिख रहे हैं। इसलिए नहीं कि हिन्दी विश्व की तीसरी सबसे बड़ी भाषा है, इसलिए भी नहीं कि भारत विश्व का सबसे बड़ा लोकतंत्रीय देश है, इसलिए भी अधिक नहीं वह निर्गुट राष्ट्रों का एक मुखिया देश है, बल्कि सबसे अधिक इसलिए कि भारत के प्रति समीपता से उन्हें आत्मिक शान्ति प्राप्त होती है। वे भौतिकता से आध्यात्मिकता की ओर उन्मुख होते हैं। वे मनोविकारों से ऊपर उठकर स्वस्थ चिंतन में प्रवृत्त होते हैं और सबसे अधिक इसलिए कि भौतिकवाद की जिस कुन्ठा ने उन्हें ग्रसित कर रखा है उससे त्राण पाने का मार्ग उन्हें भारतीय संस्कृति और भारत की वाणी से सहज में ही सुलभ हो जाता है। क्योंकि हिन्दी आक्रान्ताओं की नहीं, आक्रमणों से मुक्ति पाने का सन्देश है। वह विश्व के साम्राज्यवादियों की भाषा नहीं, उनके द्वारा शोषित, सताए, लूटे और दलित बनाए जाने वाले लोगों की आत्मा की अदमनीय अनुगूंज है। वह समता का सन्देश देती है। वह सहअस्तित्व का पाठ पढ़ाती है। विश्व को युद्धों की विभीषिका से बचाकर उन्हें शांति का कर्त्तव्य बोध कराती है।

विश्व के लोगों के लिए हिन्दी वह भाषा है जो उन्हें वही देती है जिसकी वे तलाश में हैं। इसीलिए हम हिन्दी को भाषा नहीं विचार कहते हैं, संस्कृति कहते हैं और हम उसे मानवता का शांतिपाठ मानते हैं क्योंकि हिन्दी तलवार के बल पर नहीं, संतों के वचनामृत से फैली है। उसने द्वेष और छल से राष्ट्रों और व्यक्तियों का शोषण नहीं किया है। उसके साहित्य की पंक्ति-पंक्ति में प्रेम का सन्देश बिखरा हुआ है। वह प्रेम जो मनुष्य को मनुष्य से जोड़ता है और आत्मा को परमात्मा से जोड़ता है। इसलिए हिन्दी को हम जोड़ने वाली कड़ी कहते हैं, तोड़ने वाली हथौड़ी या छैनी नहीं। पढ़िए सूर को, तुलसी को, गाइए मीरा को और गुनगुनाइए कबीरा को, सुनिए मैथिलीशरण गुप्त को, प्रसाद को, महादेवी या निराला को। इन सभी महात्मा कवियों में आपको मानवीय संवेदना और प्रेम का एक ऐसा मधुर संगीत सुनाई देगा जो आपकी आत्मा को रसविभोर कर देगा। हिन्दी के उदात्त साहित्य में रस है, कामुकता नहीं, बौद्धिकता है, परन्तु जड़ शुष्कता नहीं, आनन्द की अनुभूति है, विरह के आँसू हैं, लेकिन जीवन की दुखान्त परिणति और कलुषित आक्रोश नहीं।

हिन्दी अपने इन्हीं गुणों के कारण विश्वमंच पर आज आदर से प्रतिष्ठित है। स्वार्थ और स्वामित्व की कुटिल विश्वनीति कितनी ही उसके मार्ग में बाधाएं उपस्थित करे, उनका कुहासा हिन्दी के दिव्य प्रकाश को फैलने से नहीं रोक सकता। क्योंकि हिन्दी के पीछे अन्य साम्राज्यवादी भाषाओं की तरह परपीड़न और शोषण का इतिहास नहीं है। उसने उपनिवेशों का शोषण करके अपने देश

और अपनी भाषा को ज्ञान-विज्ञान के मारक अस्त्र प्रदान नहीं किए। साम्राज्यवादी भाषाओं ने औपनिवेशिक देशों को जनता को ही नहीं वहां की संस्कृति, कला और साहित्य को भी दबाया है तथा उनके उत्कर्ष और विकास की खिल्ली उड़ाई है। उनके बुद्धिजीवियों और रचनाधर्मियों को सदैव अपने से हीन समझा है। जहां-जहां ये साम्राज्यवादी गए वहां-वहां अपनी संस्कृति और भाषा को थोपते रहे। जब वहां से हटे तो ऐसा कुचक्र रच गए कि वहां के शासक, श्रीमंत और बुद्धिजीवी इस तरह मानसिक दासता के चक्र में फंस गए कि उन्हें अपनी भाषा, कला, साहित्य-संस्कृति सब दीन-हीन लगने लगे। लेकिन भारत और अन्य देशों के साम्राज्यशाही चुंगल से छूटने के बाद शनैः-शनैः यह व्यामोह छूटने लगा है। राष्ट्रों में स्वाभिमान और स्वावलम्बन की प्रवृत्तियां उभर रही हैं। यह प्रक्रिया भाषा के क्षेत्र में भी प्रारंभ हुई है। राष्ट्रों में अपनी-अपनी भाषाएं अपना स्थान बना रही हैं और सम्पर्क सूत्र के रूप में अब अंग्रेजी ही नहीं अनेक देशों में विशेषकर तीसरी दुनिया के देशों में हिन्दी की भी छवि निखर कर ऊपर आने लगी है।

1. विदेशी आज हिन्दी सीख-पढ़ रहे हैं, क्योंकि :
A. हिन्दी विश्व की तीसरी सबसे बड़ी भाषा है
B. विदेशी हमसे सम्पर्क बढ़ाना चाहते हैं
C. भारत विश्व का सबसे बड़ा लोकतंत्रीय देश है
D. भारत निर्गुट राष्ट्रों का एक मुखिया देश है

2. विश्व हमारी संस्कृति की ओर आकर्षित हुआ :
A. शान्ति और विश्वकल्याण की उदात्त भावना के कारण
B. हमारी परमाणु शक्ति के विकास के कारण
C. अन्तर्राष्ट्रीय व्यापार मेलों के आयोजन के कारण
D. अनेक धार्मिक स्थलों के संरक्षण के कारण

3. हिन्दी मनुष्य को वही देती है :
A. जिसे वह नहीं चाहता है
B. जिसकी उसे चाह नहीं है
C. जिसकी उसे तलाश है
D. जिसे वह चाहती है

4. हिन्दी भाषा नहीं विचार है क्योंकि :
A. वह विश्व को सह-अस्तित्व का पाठ पढ़ाती है
B. वह विश्व को संत बनने का उपदेश देती है
C. वह विश्व को असंत बनाती है
D. वह विश्व को शान्ति का कर्तव्य-बोध कराती है

5. हिन्दी का मुख्य सन्देश है :
A. आक्रान्ताओं से मुक्ति पाने का सन्देश
B. कुन्ठा से ग्रसित होने का सन्देश
C. आक्रमणों से मुक्ति पाने का सन्देश
D. अकर्मण्यता का सन्देश

गद्यांश-22

अभिप्रेरण की संकल्पना अत्यंत जटिल है। इसका संबंध अनेक अभिलाषाओं, इच्छाओं, आवश्यकताओं एवं अनुभूतियों से है। वस्तुतः अभिप्रेरण की पूरी संकल्पना इन्हीं बलों पर आधारित है। यदि अभिप्रेरणा के विविध पक्षों का गंभीर अध्ययन करें तो यह सहज ही स्पष्ट हो जाता है कि यह वस्तुतः एक प्रकार की वैयक्तिक एवं आंतरिक भावना है या व्यक्ति विशेष के अंतःकरण में उत्पन्न होने वाला एक तरह का मनोवैज्ञानिक क्रम है। यह एक व्यावहारिक संकल्पना है जिससे मनुष्य का व्यवहार किसी निश्चित लक्ष्य की ओर निर्देशित और अग्रसर होगा। यह एक निरंतर चलती रहने वाली प्रक्रिया है। पर यदि एक ओर यह सकारात्मक हो सकती है तो दूसरी ओर नकारात्मक भी हो सकती है। प्रेरणा से व्यक्ति का व्यवहार प्रभावित होता है। प्रेरणा अभिप्रेरण के मूल में है। दूसरे शब्दों में यह अभिप्रेरण का मूलतत्व है। प्रेरणा के कारण व्यक्ति को कार्य करने की दिशा मिलती है। अतः किसी लक्ष्य या पुरस्कार की प्राप्ति के लिए ऊर्जा बढ़ाने की चाहत ही अभिप्रेरण है। यह एक ऐसी शक्ति है जिससे सुप्त ऊर्जा सक्रिय हो जाती है और व्यक्ति कार्य के प्रति उत्साहित एवं उन्मुख हो उठता है। मस्तिष्क किस प्रकार कार्य करता है इसे पूरी तरह समझ पाना अब संभव नहीं हो पाया है।

किंतु यह अवश्य ही सत्य है कि किसी भी व्यवस्था/तंत्र में मानवीय अंतःक्रिया की गुणवत्ता से ही संतोषजनक परिणाम मिल पाना संभव होता है। यह किसी ऐसे प्रतिफल की मांग द्वारा निर्धारित नहीं होती जिसे समाज में अनिवार्यतः हमेशा महत्व दिया जाता है बल्कि इसके मूल में एक ऐसे प्रतिफल की मांग होती है जो किसी खास संदर्भ में आवश्यक होता है। अतः यह समझना अपरिहार्य है कि अभिप्रेरण की वास्तविक दिशा क्या है? इसके लिए विभिन्न प्रकार की पद्धतियां अपनाई जाती हैं जिन्हें सामूहिक रूप से अभिप्रेरण-निर्देश की संज्ञा दी जाती है। इनमें से सबसे महत्वपूर्ण निर्देश वह है जिसके द्वारा यह ज्ञात करने की चेष्टा की जाती है कि अभिप्रेरित व्यक्ति या व्यक्ति समूह दायित्व से दूर भाग रहा है अथवा दायित्व के प्रति अभिमुखन दर्शा रहा है।

इस प्रकार के निर्देशों की दूसरी कोटि वह है जिनके जरिए यह निर्धारित करने का प्रयास किया जाता है कि अभिप्रेरण का मूलभाव स्वःअंतर्मुखी है अथवा अन्य-बहिर्मुखी है। तात्पर्य यह है कि अभिप्रेरित व्यक्ति स्वकेन्द्रित, आत्मसंतुष्टि पर आधारित प्रयोजनों के लिए अभिप्रेरित होता है या दूसरे व्यक्ति अथवा व्यक्तियों के लिए अभिप्रेरित होता है। तीसरे अभिप्रेरण निर्देश का आधार समानता और अंतर तथा चौथे निर्देश का आधार समग्र विवरण है।

1. अभिप्रेरण एक व्यावहारिक संकल्पना है जिससे मनुष्य का व्यवहार किसी निश्चित लक्ष्य की ओर निर्देशित और :
A. आधारित होता है B. अग्रसर होता है
C. निर्धारित होता है D. रूपायित होता है

2. अभिप्रेरण का संबंध अनेक अभिलाषाओं, इच्छाओं, आवश्यकताओं एवं :
A. अनुभूतियों से है B. भावनाओं से है
C. प्रकृति से है D. उत्थान से है

3. प्रेरणा के कारण व्यक्ति को कार्य करने :
A. का आधार मिलता है B. की शक्ति मिलती है
C. की दिशा मिलती है D. की दृष्टि मिलती है

4. दूसरे अभिप्रेरण-निर्देश के मूल में है :
A. व्यक्ति का अभिमुखन
B. व्यक्ति का दृष्टिकोण
C. व्यक्ति का लक्ष्य
D. व्यक्ति की लक्ष्य चेतना

5. अभिप्रेरण निर्धारित होता है :
A. प्रतिकार की मांग से
B. प्रतिकृति की मांग से
C. आवश्यक प्रतिफल की मांग से
D. प्रतिवाद से

गद्यांश-23

शस्त्र की परंपरा आगे बढ़ती जाती है। मानव की मूल प्रकृति में असुरक्षा का भय समाया रहता है। इसी भय से शस्त्र और सेना का जन्म होता है। प्रत्येक मानव किसी देश का निवासी है। देश रक्षा उसका प्रमुख कर्त्तव्य है। वह जन-जीवन, आत्म सम्मान और अपने धर्म की रक्षा करना, सर्वोपरि मानता है। युद्ध एक आवेश और मजबूरी है। युद्ध दीर्घकालीन जीवन शैली नहीं होता। युद्ध द्वारा आवेश की उत्तेजना का विरेचन हो जाता है। युद्ध केवल राष्ट्र के लिए खतरे में ही प्रासंगिक होता है, युद्ध की हिंसा में विनाश है शांति की अहिंसा में ही विकास है। युद्ध के बिना सारे विश्व जीवन का कार्य संभव है पर शांति के बिना असंभव। जब तक शस्त्रों का अस्तित्व है तो उसकी परंपरा अनिवार्यत: बढ़ती जाएगी। पूर्व प्रस्तर एवं प्रस्तर युगों में पत्थर के चाकू, कुल्हाड़ी और गदा जैसे शस्त्र थे। कालांतर में तीरकमान, भाले, तलवार, बंदूक, तोप, बारूद व विस्फोटक बम एवं परमाणु बम की परंपरा चलती गई। सभी देश एक-दूसरे से भयभीत होकर, शस्त्र निर्माण पर, देश की संपत्ति लुटाते जा रहे हैं। हिंसा से भय और भय से हिंसा का अन्तहीन, गतिमान अधोगामी चक्र चलता रहता है। मौलिक शस्त्र तो हमारा मन है, जो वाणी और कर्म द्वारा शस्त्रों की परंपरा को चलाता है, क्रिया-प्रतिक्रिया की मानसिक चेतना ही शस्त्र और अशस्त्र होती है। डार्विन के विकासवाद की आधारशिला संघर्ष और आक्रामकता है। डार्विन 'अस्तित्व के लिए संघर्ष और श्रेष्ठ का कायम रहना' विकास की प्रक्रिया मानते हैं। इस विचारधारा को खंडित सत्य ही मानना होगा। संसार के अनेक धर्म, आत्मा, को जड़-द्रव्य की कारा से विमुक्ति के लिए, सतत संघर्षरत मानते हैं। जड़-द्रव्य के आवरणों का निरंतर विरल होते जाना ही चेतना का अंत: प्रकाशन है। यही मानव का सच्चा विकास है। सामाजिक चेतना की मूल प्रेरणा का स्त्रोत प्रेम और सहयोग में निहित है। शस्त्र द्वारा तो हम भयजनित तनावयुक्त संतुलन को अस्थायी आधार पर कायम रखने का प्रयास करते हैं। तनाव अपनी सीमा पार करके स्वयं अशांति व मरणेच्छा में बदल जाता है। यह मन का बांध टूटते ही विनाश जन्म ले लेता है। मन से भय भगाकर ही हम सचमुच नि:शस्त्र हो सकते हैं। मन के अभय होने पर सच्ची शांति प्राप्त होती है।

1. नीचे दिए विकल्पों में से कौन-सा उपयुक्त गद्यांश की विषय वस्तु का प्रतिपादन करता है?
A. शस्त्र परम्परा | B. वास्तविक विकास
C. नि:शस्त्रीकरण | D. शस्त्र और शांति

2. 'प्रासंगिक शब्द का सही अर्थ चुनकर बताएं।
A. तराजू की डंडी से संबंधित
B. दरबान
C. मामले से जुडा हुआ
D. साथ निभाने वाला

3. शस्त्र व सेना के जन्म का मूल कारण है :
A. असुरक्षा
B. शक्ति प्रदर्शन
C. वैभव एवं समपन्नता
D. साम्राज्यवादी महत्वाकांक्षाएं

4. शस्त्रों की परंपरा चलाने वाला वास्तविक शस्त्र क्या है?
A. ज्ञान | B. बल
C. उत्साह | D. मन

5. उपर्युक्त गद्यांश में से 'चेतन' का विलोम चुनिए।
A. विरेचन | B. गतिमान
C. जड़ | D. जन्म

गद्यांश-24

भारत की सांस्कृतिक शक्ति लोगों को आकर्षित करती है। सिकन्दर पूरब की ओर आया, तो उसने राज कायम कर लौटने का रास्ता पकड़ा। बाबर आया, तो वह भी लौटने की तैयारी में था। फिर भी उसे भारत ने आकर्षित किया। भारत में पश्चिम के लौग अपने लिए बेहद शांतिप्रिय बसेरा पाते हैं। निकोलोई-श्वेतास्लाव रोरिख, नारा रिचर्ड, एल्फ्रेड बुर्फल ऐसे अनेक नामी गिरामी लोगों ने, जो बीसवीं शताब्दी में ऊँचाइयों पर पहुँचे, बिना किसी संकोच के भारत को अपना घर बनाया। सरला बहन और मीरा बहन गांधी जी की दो शिष्याएं थीं। मीरा बहन ने पक्षी कुंज में अपना निवास बनाया था, जहां से वह हर समय हिमालय की बर्फ से लदी चोटियां देखती थी। मुंबई शहर को एक जर्मन विद्वान लाइफर ने आवास चुना।

भारतीय संस्कृति अपनी शक्ति उस वैविध्य से पाती है, जिसे मोटे तौर पर हम बहुलतावाद के रूप में देखते हैं। तथापि वैविध्य में गुणसूत्रों में जो लोकव्यापी होने का सामर्थ्य रहता है, वही तत्व संस्कृति का जीवनदायी तत्व निर्धारित हो जाता है। यानी भारतीय संस्कृति को सजीव और सक्रिय रखने की प्रक्रिया के भीतर गुणों को आत्मसात कर अपना बनाने की जो प्रवृत्ति है, यही वह मूल बिंदु है, जिसका बोध कर हम आसानी से कह सकते हैं कि भारतीय संस्कृति वैश्वीकरण, विश्व बाजार या नयी प्रौद्योगिकी से जन्मे कल-पुर्जो के अति उपयोगकर्ता सभ्यता के हमले भी झेल लेगी।

1. पश्चिमी दुनिया के लोगों के भारत की ओर आकर्षित होने का मुख्य कारण क्या है?
A. भारत की संपदा
B. भारत की आकर्षक जलवायु
C. भारत की बहुलतावादी संस्कृति
D. उपरोक्त सभी

2. निम्न में से किसने मुम्बई को अपना आवास स्थल बनाया?
   A. लाइफर B. सरला बहन
   C. एल्फ्रेड बुर्फल D. उपरोक्त सभी
3. भारतीय संस्कृति को जीवनदायी तत्त्व मिलते हैं–
   A. लोक जीवन से
   B. सांस्कृतिक आदान-प्रदान से
   C. सांस्कृतिक विक्षेप से
   D. B एवं C दोनों से
4. उपरोक्त उद्धरण के आधार पर निम्न में से कौन-सा कथन सही है?
   A. भारत की संस्कृति ने सर्वदा ही विदेशियों को अपनी ओर आकर्षित किया है।
   B. भारत की संस्कृति अन्य संस्कृतियों से श्रेष्ठ है।
   C. भारत की संस्कृति एक बंद संस्कृति रही है।
   D. A एवं B दोनों

गद्यांश-25

अफ्रीका में चीन के बढ़ते हुए प्रभाव से अमेरिका को एक और चिंता ने घेर लिया है। इराक, ईरान और उत्तरी कोरिया के बारे में तो अमेरिकी शासक खुलकर बात करते आये हैं, किंतु चीन से मुचैटा लेने के मामले में वे भारी सावधानी बरतते हैं। आखिर वे चीन के भारी कर्जदार तो हैं ही और शायद ये भुलाना भी आसान नहीं है कि किस प्रकार दशकों तक चीन से शत्रुता रखने के बाद उन्हें शीतयुद्ध जीतने के लिए ,पाकिस्तान की मध्यस्थता के माध्यम से, चीन की ओर मित्रता का हाथ बढ़ाना पड़ा था। चीन जैसी बड़ी ताकत से अपने रिश्तों में विश्व की सोल-सुपरपावर भी वो रुख नहीं अपना सकती, जो वह इराक जैसे बरसों से पिटे-पिटाए देश के साथ अपना सका था, यह बात समझना कठिन नहीं है।

लेकिन फिर भी अगर खतरा बढ़ने लगे, प्रतिस्पर्धा से कतराना संभव न रहे और वामपंथियों का दबाव बढ़ता चला जाये तो आखिर कब तक उनका राष्ट्रपति हाथों पर हाथ रखकर बैठा रह सकता है? इसीलिए तमाम उलझनों के बावजूद पूर्व राष्ट्रपति बुश को चीन की चुनौती की ओर ध्यान देने के लिए विवश होना पड़ा।

1. अमेरिका के लिए सबसे बड़ी चुनौती क्या है?
   A. चीन का बढ़ता आर्थिक प्रभाव
   B. शीत युद्ध के बाद सुपर पावर बने रहने की चिंता
   C. दक्षिण पंथ का विस्तार
   D. उपरोक्त सभी
2. चीन से मुचैटा लेने में अमेरिका अक्सर सावधानी बरतता है, क्यों?
   A. चीन की बड़ी पूँजी अमेरिका के बाजार में लगी हुई है।
   B. अमेरिका चीन के साथ बेहतर संबंध बनाना चाहता है।
   C. चीन शीत युद्ध के दौरान तटस्थ रहा था।
   D. A एवं C दोनों
3. निम्न में कौन-सा कथन सही है?
   A. चीन एशिया एवं अफ्रीका में अपने प्रभाव क्षेत्र का विस्तार कर रहा है।
   B. अमेरिका चीन के साथ संबंध खराब न हो जाए, इसलिए उत्तरी कोरिया के खिलाफ खुलकर कुछ नहीं कहता।
   C. शीत युद्ध के दौरान अमेरिका ने चीन की ओर मित्रता का हाथ बढ़ाया था।
   D. अमेरिका को वास्तविक खतरा विश्व आतंकवाद से है।
4. अमेरिकी राष्ट्रपति बुश को चीन की चुनौती की ओर क्यों ध्यान देना पड़ा?
   A. चीन के बढ़ते आर्थिक प्रभाव के कारण
   B. चीन द्वारा पाकिस्तान को मिलने वाले समर्थन के कारण
   C. उत्तरी कोरिया का चीन द्वारा समर्थन के कारण
   D. वामपंथ के बढ़ते दबाव के कारण

गद्यांश-26

समकालीन विश्व राजनीति में पश्चिम एशिया एक ऐसे क्षेत्र के तौर पर कुख्यात हो चुका है जहां केवल आतंक, अशांति और अराजकता का बोलबाला है। दूसरे विश्व युद्ध के बाद से ही मिडिल ईस्ट या पश्चिम एशिया कई छोटे-बड़े युद्ध और अनगिनत हिंसक झगड़े झेल चुका है। हाल ही में फतह और हमास द्वारा फिलिस्तीन के अलग-अलग इलाकों पर कब्जा करने के बाद तो पश्चिम एशिया का सामरिक वातावरण और उलझ गया है। अगर आतंक के खिलाफ विश्वव्यापी जंग की बात करें तो वर्तमान हालात यही इशारा कर रहे हैं कि अगर अमेरिका यह जंग हार नहीं रहा तो जीत भी उससे कोसों दूर है। पूरा पश्चिम एशिया समस्याग्रस्त है और अमेरिकी विदेश नीति के पास इन समस्याओं से जूझने के लिए कोई ठोस रणनीति नहीं है।

फिलहाल सबसे विकट समस्या इराक को लेकर है। इराक पर हुए अमेरिकी हमलों के कई साल गुजर चुके हैं। लेकिन वहाँ अभी तक शांति कायम नहीं की जा सकी है। रोजमर्रा के शिया-सुन्नी झगड़ों और अमेरिकी आधिपत्य के खिलाफ जिहादी हिंसा ने इराक को जर्जर बना दिया है। दोनों प्रमुख सम्प्रदायों को समान रूप से स्वीकार्य एक राजनीतिक व्यवस्था अभी नहीं पनप पाई है। दरअसल इराक को शिया, सुन्नी और कुर्द इलाकों में बाँटने की केवल औपचारिक घोषणा होना ही शेष है। अमेरिका के लिए गले की फांस बन चुका इराक दुनिया भर में जिहादियों के लिए प्रशिक्षण केंद्र में तब्दील हो चुका है। सितम्बर 2010 में अमेरिकी राष्ट्रपति बराक ओबामा ने ऑपरेशन 'इराकी फ्रीडम' खत्म होने की घोषणा की है। अब वहाँ स्थिति और बिगड़ सकती है। आत्मघाती हमलों में बेगुनाह

इराकियों का मरना जारी है। अलकायदा दिन-प्रतिदिन अपनी ताकत में इजाफा कर रहा है। कट्टरपंथियों की फौज खड़ी हो रही है।

1. इराक में अमेरिका के लिए सबसे बड़ी चुनौती क्या है?
A. इराक में एक प्रतिनिधि सरकार स्थापित करना
B. इराक में शांति कायम करना
C. इराक में गठबंधन सेना के बीच समन्वय स्थापित करना
D. उपरोक्त सभी

2. उपरोक्त उद्धरण के आधार पर सही कथन का चयन कीजिए।
A. फतह एवं हमास गुट की सक्रियता के कारण पश्चिम एशिया की समस्या और भी उलझ गई है।
B. इराक में अमेरिका विरोधी जिहादी गुट लगातार सक्रिय हैं।
C. इराक पर अमेरिकी हमले के बाद वैश्विक आतंकवाद में कमी आई है।
D. A एवं B दोनों

3. इराक में शांति स्थापना में सबसे बड़ी बाधा क्या है?
A. अल कायदा की इस क्षेत्र में बढ़ती गतिविधियाँ
B. शिया-सुन्नी झगड़े
C. जिहादी हिंसा
D. A एवं C दोनों

4. पश्चिमी एशिया की पहचान निम्न में से किसके कारण है?
A. अरब-इजराइल युद्ध के कारण
B. इराक युद्ध के कारण
C. सीरिया में होने वाली शांति प्रक्रिया के कारण
D. उपरोक्त सभी के कारण

गद्यांश-27

किसी भी लोकतांत्रिक समाज का भविष्य, उसकी प्रगतिशीलता, वैज्ञानिकता और संवेदनशीलता पर निर्भर करता है। लोकतंत्र में मताधिकार योग्य व्यक्ति के चयन की कारगर व्यवस्था नहीं है। मतदाता की बौद्धिकता, वैज्ञानिकता और संवेदनशीलता ही सही निर्णय लेने में सहायक हो सकती है वरना चुनाव में तमाम हत्यारे अपराधी और गुंडे चुने जा सकते हैं। हमारे देश के ज्यादातर मतदाताओं में इन गुणों का अभाव है। वह मोबाइल युग में परम अवैज्ञानिक है। हम मतदाताओं की बौद्धिकता का अंदाज ऐसे लोगों को देखकर आसानी से लगा सकते हैं जो ओझा-तांत्रिक और नीम-हकीमों के चक्कर में फंसकर तिल-तिल मरने को मजबूर हैं। वह यह समझ पाने की स्थिति में नहीं है कि ओझा-तांत्रिक, नीम- हकीम वगैरह उनकी अज्ञानता का लाभ उठाकर, शोषण कर रहे हैं।

हम वर्तमान शिक्षा व्यवस्था में पनपे उस गरीब समाज को देखकर बौद्धिकता की असलियत जान सकते हैं, जो अपनी औलादों की बलि देकर कल्याण ढूंढ़ता है। जो पढ़ने-पढ़ाने का हक मांगने के बजाय, उन्हें 'मिड-डे-मिल' खाना खिलाकर धन्य हो रहा है। बौद्धिकता की असलियत समाज के उन वयस्क मतदाताओं से जानी जा सकती है, जो असामाजिक तत्वों, अपराधियों के गले में माला डालकर उनकी जय-जयकार करते हैं। ये मतदाता वैज्ञानिकों या समाजशास्त्रियों को चुनने के बजाय फूलनदेवी, मलखान सिंह, मुख्तार अंसारी या शहाबुद्दीन जैसे लोगों को चुनते हैं।

1. उपरोक्त उद्धरण के आधार पर सही कथन का चयन कीजिए।
A. भारतीय मतदाता पिछड़ी सोच वाला और अवैज्ञानिक है।
B. भारतीय लोकतंत्र में मताधिकार, योग्य व्यक्ति के चयन की कारगर व्यवस्था नहीं है।
C. भारतीय मतदाता अशिक्षित है।
D. उपरोक्त सभी।

2. लोकतंत्र का भविष्य किस पर निर्भर करता है?
A. समाज की प्रगतिशीलता पर
B. सामाजिक संवेदनशीलता पर
C. A एवं B दोनों पर
D. सामाजिक सुव्यवस्था पर

3. भारतीय लोकतांत्रिक व्यवस्था का सबसे बड़ा अंतर्विरोध क्या है?
A. भारत में गरीबी एवं असमानता व्याप्त है।
B. समाज में भूखमरी एवं अज्ञानता है।
C. बौद्धिकता के युग में ज्यादातर मतदाता घोर अवैज्ञानिक हैं।
D. उपरोक्त सभी।

4. चुनाव में अपराधी किस्म के लोगों का चुना जाना किस बात का संकेत है?
A. जनता की तटस्थता का
B. जनता की अबौद्धिक निर्णय क्षमता का
C. जनता की सक्रिय भागीदारी का
D. प्रशासनिक विफलता का

गद्यांश-28

देह-प्रदर्शन स्वेच्छा से किया जाए या सामाजिक दबाव के कारण, लेकिन उसके दुष्प्रभावों को नजरअंदाज नहीं किया जा सकता है। नारियों से छेड़छाड़, अश्लील हरकतें, बलात्कार, यौन अपराध, देह व्यापार आदि बुराइयों की जड़ देह प्रदर्शन है। यदि पुरुषों से यह पूछा जाए कि क्या नारी के देह-प्रदर्शन से तुम को लज्जा महसूस नहीं होती है तो उनका तर्क होता है कि जब नारी को देह-प्रदर्शन करने में लज्जा नहीं आती है तो हमको देखने में लज्जा क्यों आएगी? देह-प्रदर्शन करने वाली नारी को समाज में हेय दृष्टि से देखा जाता है। ऐसी नारी को सिर्फ देह मानकर उसे इस्तेमाल किया जा रहा है।

आजकल माता-पिता के लिए लड़की की परवरिश करना चुनौतीपूर्ण होता जा रहा है क्योंकि यौन अपराधों की संख्या में वृद्धि होती जा रही है। माता-पिता सोचते हैं कि यदि हम

बेटी की इज्जत की रक्षा न कर पाए तो बेटी को जन्म देने का क्या फायदा होगा? माता-पिता की यह सोच कन्या भ्रूण-हत्या का महत्त्वपूर्ण कारण है। जो नारी आर्थिक लाभ के लिए अंग प्रदर्शन करती है उसका यौवन व आकर्षण समाप्त हो जाने पर वह कुंठित हो जाती है। विषादग्रस्त होकर वह आत्महत्या भी कर सकती है। नारी देह के प्रति पुरुषों का आकर्षण यौवनावस्था में होता है, इसमें स्थायित्व नहीं होता है। ऐसी नारियाँ आकर्षणहीन हो जाने पर स्वयं को एकाकी महसूस करती हैं तथा कई प्रकार के मानसिक रोगों से ग्रस्त हो जाती हैं।

1. नारी देह-प्रदर्शन का स्वाभाविक परिणाम है–
A. उनके साथ छेड़छाड़
B. अश्लील हरकतें
C. यौन अपराध
D. उपरोक्त सभी

2. नारी देह-प्रदर्शन की बढ़ती प्रवृत्ति का मुख्य कारण है–
A. नारी की स्व इच्छा
B. सामाजिक दबाव एवं लोलुपता
C. शिक्षा का माहौल
D. A एवं B दोनों

3. लेखक के अनुसार कन्या भ्रूण-हत्या का महत्वपूर्ण कारण क्या है?
A. महिलाओं के साथ होनेवाला यौन शोषण
B. बच्चियों का उचित परवरिश न हो पाना
C. सामाजिक असुरक्षा की भावना
D. उपरोक्त सभी

4. उपरोक्त उद्धरण के आधार पर सही कथन का चयन कीजिए।
A. आर्थिक लाभ के कारण नारी में शरीर-प्रदर्शन की प्रवृत्ति बढ़ती जा रही है।
B. नारी के देह-प्रदर्शन के पीछे सामाजिक दबाव एक मुख्य कारण है।
C. अंग-प्रदर्शन करनेवाली नारियों को यौवन का आकर्षण समाप्त हो जाने पर कुंठा का सामना करना पड़ता है।
D. उपरोक्त सभी।

गद्यांश-29

'वर्तमान इतिहास में दो प्रवृत्तियां दिखाई देती हैं। एक प्रवृत्ति की दिशा वर्चस्व (हेजीमनी) की ओर है जो मानव-अस्तित्व (सरवाइवल) के लिए खतरा बन कर पागलपन के सैद्धांतिक चौखटे में तर्कपूर्ण ढंग से काम कर रही है। दूसरी प्रवृत्ति इस विश्वास को समर्पित है कि 'एक नयी दुनिया संभव है', जिन शब्दों से विश्व सामाजिक मंच प्रेरित है, जो शासक विचारात्मक प्रणालियों को चुनौती दे रहा है और जो विचार, कर्म और संस्थाओं का नया सृजनात्मक विकल्प बनाना चाहता है। इनमें कौन-सी प्रवृत्ति जीतेगी, कोई इसकी भविष्यवाणी नहीं कर सकता है। यह प्रक्रिया समूचे इतिहास में दिखाई देती है।'

चोमस्की का कहना है कि अस्सी के दशक में मुख्यधारा के अमेरिका, खासकर मध्य अमेरिका से संबंधित जो मानव एकता आंदोलन चले उन्होंने साम्राज्यवाद के इतिहास में नयी जमीन जोड़ी। इससे पहले कभी भी शासक समाज के लोग बड़ी संख्या में दुष्टतापूर्ण हमले के शिकार लोगों के साथ रहने और उन्हें कुछ मात्रा में सुरक्षा प्रदान करने नहीं गये थे। वैसे आम जनता में मानव अधिकारों की यह जागरूकता 1960 के दशक में तेज हुई थी और कई क्षेत्रों में जन-सक्रियता ने अपना सभ्यताकारी प्रभाव डाला। इससे अल्पसंख्यक समूहों, स्त्रियों, भावी पीढ़ियों के अधिकारों के आंदोलन और फिर पर्यावरण सुरक्षा के आंदोलन विकसित हुए थे।

1. वर्तमान इतिहास की दो महत्वपूर्ण प्रवृत्तियाँ कौन-सी हैं?
A. आशा एवं निराशा की।
B. हिंसा एवं सभ्यता की।
C. विश्व वर्चस्व की एवं एक नई दुनिया बसाने की।
D. साम्राज्यवाद एवं उदारवाद की।

2. आज मानव अस्तित्व के लिए सबसे बड़ा खतरा क्या है?
A. वर्चस्व की प्रवृत्ति
B. हिंसा की प्रवृत्ति
C. अधीनस्थता की प्रवृत्ति
D. उपरोक्त सभी

3. मानव एकता आंदोलन ने किस रूप में सकारात्मक भूमिका निभाई?
A. इसने शासक वर्ग की मानसिकता में बदलाव लाया।
B. इसने साम्राज्यवाद के इतिहास में एक नई जमीन जोड़ी।
C. इसने मानव अधिकारों को और भी सशक्त बनाया।
D. उपरोक्त सभी।

4. उपरोक्त उद्धरण के आधार पर सही कथन का चयन कीजिए।
A. हेजीमनी मानव अस्तित्व को बनाए रखने में सहायक है।
B. 'एक नई दुनिया संभव है' का विचार शासक विचारात्मक प्रणाली के लिए खतरा है।
C. मानव एकता आंदोलन का आरंभ दक्षिण अमेरिका से हुआ।
D. उपरोक्त सभी।

गद्यांश-30

इंडिया के लिए कॉमनवेल्थ गेम्स की सफलता ने एक साथ कई काम किए हैं। गेम्स शुरू होने से पहले दुनिया भर में बनी देश की नेगेटिव छवि धुलकर पॉजिटिव हो गई। इंडिया में निवेश करने वाले इन्वेस्टर्स अब शायद बेधड़क यहां पैसा लगाएंगे। ऑस्ट्रेलियाई और अंग्रेज अब शायद एक हिंदुस्तानी को नीचे नजर से न देख पाएं। इस सफलता ने भविष्य में ओलंपिक गेम्स जैसे बड़े आयोजन को लेकर भारत की दावेदारी को भी पुख्ता किया है। भारतीय खिलाड़ियों ने 71 देशों में

दूसरा स्थान हासिल कर देश के युवाओं को दिखाया है कि कैसे खेल भी उसके लिए नाम और रुतबे का जरिया बन सकते हैं। खेलों के आयोजन में हजारों करोड़ रुपये खर्च जरूर हुए मगर इससे देश की दो पीढ़ियों के करोड़ों लोगों में खेलों के प्रति नया जज्बा भी पैदा हुआ है। इन खेलों ने हमारे कई खिलाड़ियों को गुमनामी से निकाल कर रोशनी के घेरे में खड़ा कर दिया। दीपिका कुमारी, कृष्णा पूनिया, सुरंजय, ओंकार सिंह, जिन्हें मुट्ठी भर लोग ही जानते थे, अब नेशनल हीरो बन गए हैं। इनमें कई खिलाड़ी ऐसे हैं जिन्होंने अपने माता-पिता की सुरक्षित और बेहतर करियर अपनाने की नसीहतों के खिलाफ जाकर खेलों को अपनाया। गेम्स ने देश को उनकी कामयाबी दिखाई, उन्हें अपने देशवासियों के सामने अपनी मेहनत और अपनी जिद का उत्सव मनाने का मौका दिया।

देश की गरीब जनता की जरूरतों को भुलाकर एक सर्कस शो पर करोड़ों रुपये फूंकने की दलील देने वाले गेम्स के आलोचक आगे की बजाय पीछे देखते हुए ऐसा कह रहे हैं। वे यह नहीं समझ रहे कि भारत का एक बड़ी ताकत बनने का दावा सिर्फ आंकड़ों में कैद नहीं रहना चाहिए, तमाम क्षेत्रों में दिखना चाहिए। गेम्स की कामयाबी ने यही किया है। उसने इंडिया के फ्यूचर की तस्वीर पेश की है–आत्मविश्वास से भरा, बुनियादी सुविधाओं से लैस, सफलता का जश्न मनाता हुआ इंडिया।

1. कॉमन वेल्थ गेम्स की सफलता का सबसे बड़ा लाभ क्या हुआ है?

A. भारतीय खिलाड़ियों ने अंतर्राष्ट्रीय स्तर की खेल प्रतिभा का प्रदर्शन किया।

B. खेल के आयोजन में करोड़ों रुपये का घोटाला हुआ।

C. गेम्स के दौरान खिलाड़ियों को स्तरहीन सुविधाएँ उपलब्ध कराई गई।

D. भविष्य में ओलंपिक खेल जैसे बड़े आयोजन को लेकर भारत की दावेदारी पुख्ता हुई है।

2. आलोचकों की नजर में कॉमनवेल्थ गेम्स एक सर्कस शो क्यों था?

A. क्योंकि इसमें सर्कस की तरह तमाशे हुए।

B. आयोजन की तैयारी पूरी न हो पाने के कारण गेम्स एक तमाशा बनकर रह गया।

C. इसमें देश की गरीब जनता की जरूरतों को भुलाकर अनावश्यक खर्च किए गए।

D. उपरोक्त सभी

3. 'गुमनामी से निकालकर रोशनी के घेरे में खड़ा कर दिया' पदबंध का अर्थ बताइए–

A. अचानक प्रसिद्धि मिलना

B. अचानक बड़ी धनराशि मिलना

C. रोशनी से चकाचौंध होना

D. ऊँचा पद प्राप्त होना

4. उपरोक्त उद्धरण के आधार पर सही कथन का चयन कीजिए।

A. कॉमनवेल्थ गेम्स से दुनिया भर में देश की अच्छी छवि बनी है।

B. इससे दुनिया भर के निवेशक भारत में निवेश के लिए प्रोत्साहित होंगे।

C. इससे युवाओं में एक नई स्फूर्ति पैदा हुई है।

D. उपरोक्त सभी।

गद्यांश-31

देश में खाद्यान्न भंडारण की समस्या ने विकराल रूप धारण कर लिया है। इसकी भयावहता का अंदाजा इसी बात से लगाया जा सकता है कि एफसीआई के गोदामों में 67,542 टन अनाज नष्ट हो गया। इसकी कीमत 60 हजार करोड़ रुपए बताई गई है। सुप्रीम कोर्ट ने इसमें दखल देते हुए कहा है कि गोदामों में अनाज सड़ाने की जगह इसे गरीबों में बाँट देना चाहिए। सुप्रीम कोर्ट ने 12 अगस्त, 2010 को केन्द्र सरकार को आदेश देते हुए कहा कि वह फूड कॉरपोशन ऑफ इंडिया के गोदामों में अनाज सड़ाने की जगह गरीबों को मुफ्त बाँट दें।

जस्टिस दलवीर भंडारी और जस्टिस दीपक वर्मा की बेंच ने कहा कि और अनाज न सड़ने पाए, इसके लिए सरकार तुरंत कदम उठाए। वह उतने ही अनाज की खरीदारी करे, जितने को संभाल सकती है। साथ ही कोर्ट ने केन्द्र से प्रत्येक राज्य में एक बड़ा गोदाम और अलग-अलग जिलों व संभागों में विभिन्न गोदाम बनाने की व्यवस्था करने को कहा। इसके अलावा सरकार से यह सुनिश्चित करने को भी कहा कि उचित मूल्य की दुकानें पूरे महीने खुली रहें। कोर्ट ने सरकार को निर्देश दिया है कि वह 2010 के आंकड़ों के आधार पर बीपीएल (गरीबी रेखा से नीचे), एबीपीएल (गरीबी रेखा से ऊपर), एएवाई (अंत्योदय अन्न योजना) परिवारों का नए सिरे से सर्वे कराए। अधिकारी फायदे बांटने के लिए एक दशक पुराने आंकड़े पर भरोसा नहीं कर सकते।

बेंच ने अपना पहले का आदेश दोहराया कि एबीपीएल परिवार सब्सिडी वाला अनाज न हासिल करने पाएं। अगर सरकार उन्हें लाभ देना ही चाहती है तो उन परिवारों को दे, जिनकी सालाना आय 3 लाख रुपये से कम हो।

सुप्रसिद्ध अर्थशास्त्री डॉ. अमर्त्य सेन द्वारा 1981 में लिखी गई 'पावर्टी एंड फैमीन एंड एस्से ऑन इनटाइटिलमेंट एंड डिप्राइवेशन' (गरीबी और अकाल और पात्रता और वंचना पर निबंध) कृति में तर्क दिया गया कि अधिकांश मामलों में भूख और अकाल अनाज की उपलब्धता की कमी के कारण नहीं पड़ते, बल्कि उनका कारण असमानता और वितरण व्यवस्था की कमी होती है। उन्होंने जो बात 1981 में कही थी, संभवतः वह 2010 में भी सही है। हालांकि स्वतंत्रता प्राप्ति के बाद विगत तिरसठ वर्षों में भूख और वंचना से लड़ने के क्रम में हमने काफी अनुभव प्राप्त किया है।

1. अनाजों के भंडारण को लेकर सर्वोच्च न्यायालय ने कौन-से आदेश दिए हैं?

A. सरकार भंडारण के बराबर क्षमता के अनाज का ही क्रय करे।

B. सरकार अलग-अलग जिलों एवं संभागों में गोदाम बनाने की व्यवस्था करे।
C. उचित मूल्य की दुकानें महीने भर खुली रहें।
D. उपरोक्त सभी

2. देश में खाद्यान्न भंडारण की समस्या का मुख्य कारण क्या है?
A. खाद्यान्न भंडारण की सीमित क्षमता
B. अत्यधिक खाद्यान्नों की खरीद
C. समय पर खाद्यान्नों का वितरण न हो पाना
D. उपरोक्त सभी

3. प्रसिद्ध अर्थशास्त्री अमर्त्य सेन के अनुसार भूख एवं अकाल का कारण है–
A. राष्ट्रीय कृषि उपज में कमी
B. कृषि निर्यात की असमानता
C. अनाजों के उपयुक्त वितरण की समस्याएं
D. A एवं C

4. कोर्ट ने किस आधार पर बीपीएल, एबीपीएल एवं एएवाई परिवारों का सर्वे कराने को कहा है?
A. 2011 की जनगणना के आधार पर
B. 2005 के आंकड़ों के आधार पर
C. 2007 के योजना आयोग के आंकड़ों के आधार पर
D. 2010 के आंकड़ों के आधार पर

गद्यांश-32

वैश्वीकरण की दौड़ में क्षेत्रीय संगठनों का महत्व बढ़ा है। आज विश्व की स्थिति यह है कि राष्ट्र अपने आपसी मतभेदों को भुलाकर व्यापार एवं आर्थिक क्षेत्रों में एक-दूसरे को सहयोग कर रहे हैं। राष्ट्रों की पारस्परिक निर्भरता पहले की अपेक्षा काफी बढ़ी है। सार्क विश्व की 22 प्रतिशत आबादी को अपने दामन में रखने वाला विश्व का सबसे बड़ा क्षेत्रीय संगठन है। भारत विश्व की उभरती हुई आर्थिक शक्ति है। सार्क के सदस्य देश आपस में एक-दूसरे का आर्थिक सहयोग करें तो इस क्षेत्र से गरीबी, भुखमरी, अशिक्षा को सदा के लिए समाप्त किया जा सकता है। आज यूरोपियन संघ एवं आसियान जैसे क्षेत्रीय संगठनों ने जो आर्थिक सफलता पायी है। उससे सार्क के नेताओं को प्रेरणा लेनी चाहिए। इन क्षेत्रीय संगठनों ने आर्थिक एकजुटता के बल पर काफी उपलब्धियाँ हासिल की हैं। अब यह स्थिति स्पष्ट हो चुकी है कि आर्थिक विकास में क्षेत्रीय वैश्वीकरण की भूमिका अतिमहत्वपूर्ण है।

जनवरी 2009 में इस्लामाबाद में हुए सम्मेलन में इस तरह की स्पष्ट अभिव्यक्ति सामने आई। इस सम्मेलन में सार्क देशों ने 2012 तक दक्षिण एशियाई स्वतंत्र व्यापार क्षेत्र (साफ्टा) बनाने की इच्छा व्यक्त की है, लेकिन इस दिशा में अभी तक कोई ठोस कार्य नहीं हुआ है। साफ्टा के बारे में छोटे-छोटे देशों को यह भ्रम पैदा हो गया कि इससे भारत को ही अधिक लाभ होगा, जबकि सच्चाई यह नहीं है। उदाहरणस्वरूप अभी हम भारत, श्रीलंका के मुक्त व्यापार को देखें। दोनों देशों के बीच मुक्त व्यापार पिछले तीन वर्ष से चल रहा है। श्रीलंका का भारत को निर्यात 135 प्रतिशत सालाना की दर से बढ़ा है। इस तुलना में भारत का श्रीलंका को निर्यात 32 प्रतिशत की दर से बढ़ा है। अपितु मुक्त व्यापार के होने से श्रीलंका भारत की अपेक्षा अधिक लाभ की स्थिति में है। यही बात नेपाल एवं भूटान के साथ हैं। पाकिस्तान एवं बांग्लादेश के साथ भारत का व्यापार उतना नहीं बढ़ा है जितना बढ़ना चाहिए। इन देशों के असहयोग के कारण भी साफ्टा को लागू करने में कठिनाई है।

1. वैश्वीकरण के कारण क्षेत्रीय संगठनों का महत्व बढ़ा है–
A. क्योंकि वैश्वीकरण के दौरान विभिन्न देशों के बीच व्यापार बढ़ा है।
B. राष्ट्र अपने आपसी मतभेद को भूलाकर आर्थिक क्षेत्र में एक-दूसरे को सहयोग कर रहें हैं।
C. सभी राष्ट्रों ने व्यापार को सीमाकर मुक्त कर दिया है।
D. अंतर्राष्ट्रीय बाज़ार में डॉलर का मूल्य घटा है।

2. उपरोक्त उद्धरण के आधार पर सही कथन का चयन कीजिए।
A. हाल के वर्षों में राष्ट्रों के बीच पारस्परिक निर्भरता बढ़ी है।
B. सार्क दुनिया का सबसे बड़ा क्षेत्रीय संगठन है।
C. सार्क देशों में दुनिया की लगभग 1/4 आबादी रहती है।
D. उपरोक्त सभी।

3. सार्क देशों के बीच आपसी व्यापार में पर्याप्त वृद्धि नहीं हुई है, इसका क्या कारण है?
A. सार्क देशों के बीच व्यापार प्रतिबंध
B. आपसी सहयोग का अभाव
C. पश्चिमी देशों पर अत्यधिक निर्भरता
D. व्यापारिक निवेश का अभाव

4. साफ्टा को लेकर सार्क देशों में कौन-सा भ्रम फैला हुआ है?
A. इससे भारत को अधिक लाभ होगा।
B. भारत एक आर्थिक महाशक्ति बन जाएगा।
C. भारत का प्रभाव दुनिया के अन्य देशों में बढ़ जाएगा।
D. भारतीय रुपया और भी मजबूत होगा।

गद्यांश-33

महामशीन के महाप्रयोग का उद्देश्य परमाणु कणों की आपसी टक्कर को देखना है, जिनसे नए कण बन सकते हैं। उनका वेग और ऊर्जा मापकर मालूम हो सकता है कि आखिर शुरू में ब्रह्माण्ड कैसे बना और बाद में कैसे उसकी उत्पत्ति हुई। एलएचसी के इस प्रयोग में परमाणु कणों की बहुत अधिक वेग से अब तक की सबसे अधिक ऊर्जा से टक्कर हुई। आशा की जा रही है कि अब वैज्ञानिक भौतिकी की अनेक गुत्थियों को सुलझा लेंगे।

50,000 करोड़ रुपए की लागत से बना लार्ज हैड्रॉन कोलाइडर (LHC) 2008 में असफल हो गया था। उस समय इस सबसे बड़े एटम स्मैशर में दो शक्तिशाली चुम्बकों के बीच विद्युत कनेक्शन फ्यूज हो गया था। इन चुम्बक प्रोटॉनों को स्टीआर कहते हैं। इस खराबी से सुरंग में बड़े जोर का विस्फोट हुआ था, लेकिन इस बार का प्रयोग सफल रहा। एलएचसी प्रसिद्ध ईश्वरीय कण 'हिग्स बोसोन' के चिह्न की भी पहचान करेगा। बताया जाता है कि इसी कण के कारण ब्रह्माण्ड की सभी चीजों को पिण्ड भार मिलता है। इसके अलावा रहस्यमयी 'ब्लैक होल' की भी पहचान की जाएगी, जिससे काफी हद तक ब्रह्माण्ड बना है, लेकिन इसमें अंधेरा होने के कारण अब तक इसके दर्शन नहीं हुए हैं। वैज्ञानिकों का कहना है कि एलएचसी में जब कणों की टक्कर हुई, तब अनेक ऐसे मिनी बिग बैंग बने, जैसे आज से 13 अरब, 70 करोड़ वर्ष पहले बने थे।

इन असाधारण खोजों के अतिरिक्त मशीन बिग बैंग के पहले और बाद के कणों की नकल करेगी। गुरुत्वाकर्षण के रहस्य भी जानने के प्रयत्न किए जाएंगे। इस अनुसंधान में लगे वैज्ञानिकों का कहना है कि जब कणों की बीमों की टक्कर हुई तब सभी डिटेक्टरों ने अपने परमाणु कणों के बहुरंगी मार्गों की पहचान की। ये कण प्रत्येक दिशा में कार्यशील थे। भौतिकविद् का कहना है कि जब उप परमाणु कण बड़े वेग से आपस में टकराते हैं तो वे टूटकर नए तत्व बनाते हैं। आशा की जा रही है कि इसमें से एक तत्व हिग्स बोसोन होगा जिससे हमारे ब्रह्माण्ड बनने की गुत्थी सुलझेगी। वैज्ञानिकों का कहना है कि प्रयोग में उत्सर्जित ऊर्जा फील्ड को यदि ऊष्मा में बदल दिया जाए तो यह सूर्य की सतह से भी ज्यादा गर्म होगा।

1. महामशीन ब्रह्माण्ड की उत्पत्ति की जाँच किस आधार पर करेगा?
   A. परमाणु कणों की आपसी टक्कर से उत्पन्न वेग के आधार पर
   B. परमाणु कणों के बीच आपसी आकर्षण के आधार पर
   C. परमाणु कणों की आपसी टक्कर से उत्पन्न वेग एवं ऊर्जा के आधार पर
   D. परमाणु कणों के गुरुत्वाकर्षण के आधार पर

2. लार्ज हैड्रॉन कोलाइडर की पिछली असफलता का क्या कारण था?
   A. चुम्बकीय विद्युत कनेक्शन का फ्यूज होना
   B. हिग्स बोसोन कण का रिसाव
   C. परमाणु कणों के बीच तीव्र विकर्षण
   D. परमाणु कणों का विस्फोट

3. ब्रह्मांड के पिंडों का पिंड भार किस पर निर्भर करता है?
   A. पिंड के द्रव्यमान पर
   B. पिंड के घनत्व पर
   C. हिग्स बोसोन कण पर
   D. A एवं B दोनों पर

4. हिग्स बोसोन कण का निर्माण होता है–
   A. जब उप परमाणु कण तीव्र वेग से आपस में टकराते हैं।
   B. परमाणु कणों के बीच तीव्र आकर्षण बल के कारण।
   C. परमाणु कणों के बीमों के साथ टक्कर से।
   D. A एवं B दोनों

गद्यांश-34

विज्ञान शब्द की परिभाषा तथा इसके विस्तार, और प्रौद्योगिकी से इसके भेद को भी स्पष्ट रूप से समझ लेना जरूरी है। मानव जाति के भविष्य की कुंजी जिन कुछ शक्तिशाली ताकतों के हाथ में है, उनमें से विज्ञान संभवतः एकमात्र ऐसी ताकत है, जिसे एक अनूठा स्थान प्राप्त है क्योंकि वस्तुतः निरपवाद रूप से इसे सभी स्वीकार करते हैं। उन गिने-चुने व्यक्तियों के मामले में भी, जो विज्ञान के प्रति नफरत रखने वाले दिखाई देते हैं, उनके साथ भी एक बार बातचीत करने पर यह तथ्य उभरकर सामने आएगा कि वे वास्तव में विज्ञान के विरुद्ध नहीं हैं, बल्कि प्रौद्योगिकी के विरुद्ध हैं, जिसका सम्बन्ध मानव की विविध जरूरतों को पूरा करने के लिए विज्ञान के निष्कर्षों के अनुप्रयोगों से है।

वर्तमान समय में विज्ञान से हमारा अभिप्राय है हमारे विश्व तथा इसके परिवेश का मौलिक ज्ञान, उस ज्ञान का इसके सभी पहलुओं में, नियंत्रित तथा निरन्तर अनुसरण करना, इसके लिये जरूरी नहीं कि उसका प्रयोग सार्वजनिक प्रयोजनों के लिए किया जाए। प्रौद्योगिकी से हमारा आशय विज्ञान को मानव सेवा में लगाने के विभिन्न तरीकों से है, उन तरीकों का संकेन्द्रित अध्ययन जिनमें चीजों को मानव-प्रयोजन के लिए रचा या बदला जा सकता है। दोनों में स्पष्ट अन्तर करने के लिए इस समय आण्विक विज्ञान तथा टेक्नोलॉजी के सर्वाधिक लोकप्रिय क्षेत्रों से उदाहरण दिए जा सकते हैं। जब भारी धात्विक तत्व यूरेनियम के केन्द्रक का विखंडन या विस्फोटन होता है तब उससे निःसृत होने वाले कणों की संख्या तथा प्रकृति का मापन विज्ञान द्वारा ही किया जाता है। लेकिन, जब इस वैज्ञानिक ज्ञान का प्रयोग विद्युत उत्पादन के लिये परमाणु बिजली घर डिजाइन करने तथा बनाने अथवा एक परमाणु बम डिजाइन करने और बनाने के लिए किया जाता है तो यह प्रौद्योगिकी होती है। इस प्रकार, यह प्रौद्योगिकी ही होती है जो नैतिक रंग ले लेती है और इसे नैतिक या अनैतिक कहा जा सकता है। विज्ञान तटस्थ या नैतिकता से परे होता है और वह नैतिक-आचार या मानव कल्याण के विरुद्ध नहीं होता, हालांकि एक वैज्ञानिक एक मनुष्य तथा टेक्नोलाजिस्ट होने के नाते इसके विरुद्ध हो सकता है।

1. लेखक
   A. विज्ञान के प्रति बेहतर रवैया अपनाये जाने के लिए वकालत करने की कोशिश कर रहा है
   B. यह सुझाव देने की कोशिश कर रहा है कि हम विज्ञान का सार्वजनिक हित के लिए प्रयोग करें
   C. भौतिक विज्ञान के बजाय नैतिक विज्ञान का अध्ययन करने की कोशिश कर रहा है

D. विज्ञान तथा प्रौद्योगिकी (टेक्नोलाजी) के बीच भेद करने की कोशिश कर रहा है

2. लेखक के अनुसार, विज्ञान

A. एकमात्र ऐसी ताकत है, जो मानवजाति के भविष्य का निर्धारण करती है

B. मानव की नियति को निर्धारित करने वाली चन्द एक ताकतों में से एक है

C. भविष्य में मानवजाति की एकमात्र चिन्ता होगी

D. उन अनेक बाधाओं में से एक है जो मनुष्य की प्रगति में रुकावट डालती है

3. यह अवतरण

A. आलंकारिक है

B. वर्णनात्मक है

C. वृत्तात्मक है

D. व्याख्यात्मक है

4. यूरेनियम केन्द्रक के विस्फोट के अध्ययन को

A. आधुनिक प्रौद्योगिकी (टेक्नोलाजी) का एक उदाहरण कहा जा सकता है

B. विद्युत-सिद्धांतों का एक अनुप्रयोग कहा जा सकता है

C. ऐसा अध्ययन कहा जा सकता है जिसके कोई भौतिक निहितार्थ नहीं हैं

D. समूची मानवजाति के कल्याण के लिए महत्त्वपूर्ण कहा जा सकता है

गद्यांश-35

बच्चे किसी देश के सामाजिक तथा राजनीतिक दर्शन का अंग होते हैं। उनके प्रति जो रवैये अपनाये जाते हैं वे इस बात का निर्धारण करने में महत्त्वपूर्ण कारक होते हैं कि क्या उनकी जरूरतें पूरी होंगी तथा उनके अधिकार उन्हें मिलेंगे। भविष्योन्मुख कोई भी समाज इस बात का ध्यान रखेगा कि विपदा के समय बच्चों का ख्याल रखा जाये। इस समय विश्व के अनेक भागों में बच्चों को शांति तथा भाई-चारे की भावना के साथ पाले-पोसे जाने का कोई अवसर प्राप्त नहीं है। युद्ध तथा आतंकवाद के जो अत्यधिक भयावह रिकार्ड मिलते हैं वे हमेशा अपने घरों के खण्डहरों तथा अपने परिवारों के शवों के पास रोने के लिए बचे हुए शिशुओं या छोटे बच्चों की (या इतने सहमे हुए बच्चों की जो रो भी नहीं पाते) तस्वीरें होती हैं। ऐसे देशों में जहां लड़ाई-झगड़ा चल रहा हो या ऐसे समाजों में जहां ऐसी कार्यवाहियों को मनमोहक ढंग से पेश किया जाता हो, वहां बच्चों का निर्बाध रूप से खेलना जीवन की घटनाओं तथा/या ऐसी घटनाओं की सामाजिक स्वीकृति को परिलक्षित करेगा, जो हम सभी को यह सोचने पर मजबूर कर देगा कि क्या इस प्रकार के राष्ट्रीय दर्शनों से प्रभावित करोड़ों बच्चों को शांति की भावना के साथ बड़े होने के उनके अधिकार मिलने की कोई संभावना है। और निश्चय ही, "जाति, रंग, लिंग, राष्ट्रीय या सामाजिक मूल के धर्म" पर अकेले या कुछेक के मेल पर आधारित भेदभाव करोड़ों बच्चों को, जरूरतों की सार्वत्रिकता के बावजूद, जिन पर अधिकार आधारित होते हैं, इन अधिकारों से वंचित रखता है।

1. निम्नलिखित में से कौन-सा कथन बच्चों में शांति तथा भाई-चारे की भावना के विकास के लिए सहायक नहीं है?

A. जब वयोवृद्ध बच्चों को युद्ध के संत्रासों का अनुभव करने के लिए छोड़ देते हैं

B. जब प्रौढ़ लोग जातीय भेद-भाव का व्यवहार करते हैं

C. जब किसी देश का राजनीतिक दर्शन विश्वव्यापी भाई-चारे की वकालत करता है

D. जब समाज युद्ध के कार्यकलापों को मनमोहक ढंग से पेश करता है

2. प्रौढ़ों का बच्चों के प्रति एक कर्त्तव्य है। किसी समाज विशेष में बच्चों की देखभाल कितनी अच्छी तरह से होती है इसका पता इस बात से चल सकता है कि

A. विपदा के समय उनके लिए क्या किया जाता है

B. वे प्रौढ़ों का कितना ख्याल रखते हैं

C. प्रौढ़ उनके अधिकारों के प्रति कितने संवेदनशील हैं

D. समाज कितना समृद्ध है

3. लेखक की धारणा है कि

A. युद्धों के बावजूद बच्चे शान्तिपूर्वक रहने के अपने अधिकारों को प्राप्त कर लेते हैं

B. बच्चों के अधिकार सामाजिक दशाओं पर निर्भर होने चाहिए

C. बच्चों को शांति की भावना के साथ बड़ा होने का अधिकार है

D. राष्ट्रीय दर्शन बच्चों के अधिकारों का समर्थन करते हैं

4. युद्ध सम्बन्धी कार्यकलापों

A. का समाजों द्वारा परिहार किया जाता है

B. को समाजों द्वारा परिलक्षित किया जाता है

C. की समाजों द्वारा निन्दा की जाती है

D. को समाजों द्वारा स्वीकार किया जाता है

गद्यांश-36

हम सभी चिकित्सा विज्ञान के क्षेत्र में हुई कतिपय उल्लेखनीय खोजों से परिचित हैं। मिसाल के तौर पर, हम वेक्सीनों की खोज के बारे में जानते हैं। हम चेचक तथा पोलियो जैसे रोगों की रोकथाम को समझ सकते हैं। हम अनेक साधारण एंटीबायोटिक्स के बारे में भी जानते हैं। यह जानकारी कि हम उपदंश रोग पर पेनिसिलीन और तपेदिक पर आइसोनाइजिड से काबू पा सकते हैं, कुछ हद तक आश्वासनदायक है। हम इस विश्वास के आधार पर निश्चय ही अपने आपको झूठी तसल्ली दे सकते हैं कि संक्रामक रोग अब कोई खतरा नहीं रहे हैं। लेकिन यह सत्य नहीं है और समाचारों तथा मेडिकल जर्नलों में हाल में छपे समाचार हमें संक्रामक रोगों के विभिन्न तथा कभी-कभी 'नए' खतरों की याद दिलाते हैं।

ऐसे समाचारों में अपेक्षाकृत अधिक यथार्थवादी दृष्टिकोण को स्वीकार किया गया है। इस दृष्टिकोण का निहितार्थ यह

है कि संक्रामक रोग बने रहेंगे और यह कि उनके अन्दर कुछ ऐसी क्षमताएं हैं कि वे उन्हें खत्म कर देने की हमारी कोशिशों के खिलाफ लड़ सकते हैं। कतिपय मानव-व्याधियों, जैसे सुजाक रोग, तत्त्व-गुण (Strains) विकसित हो गए हैं जिन पर कतिपय एंटीबायोटिक्स का कोई असर नहीं होता।

1. चेचक तथा पोलियो जैसे रोगों की रोकथाम किसकी खोज के कारण संभव हो सकी है?

A. पेनिसिलीन B. आइसोनाइजिड

C. वेक्सीन D. एंटीबायोटिक्स

2. चिकित्सा विज्ञान के क्षेत्र में खोजों के द्वारा अब तक क्या संभव नहीं हो पाया है?

A. चेचक तथा पोलियो की रोकथाम

B. पेनिसिलीन की सहायता से उपदंश रोग के फैलाव पर नियंत्रण करने की संभावना

C. संक्रामक रोगों का उन्मूलन

D. आइसोनाइजिड की सहायता से तपेदिक के फैलाव पर नियंत्रण करने की संभावना

3. कुछ संक्रामक रोग उन्हें खत्म कर देने के हमारे प्रयासों के खिलाफ कैसे लड़ते हैं?

A. अन्य क्षेत्रों में अंतरित होकर

B. वेक्सीनों को प्रभावहीन बनाने की शक्ति विकसित करके

C. पहले की तरह भ्रांतिजनक बने रहकर

D. मानव-तंत्रिका में गहरे पैठ कर

4. यह अवतरण

A. सूचना देने वाला है B. वृत्तात्मक है

C. नाटकीय है D. प्रोत्साहक है

गद्यांश-37

प्रत्येक व्यवसाय अथवा व्यापार, कला और विज्ञान की अपनी तकनीकी शब्दावली होती है, जिसका कार्य अंशतः उन प्रक्रियाओं और वस्तुओं को दर्शाना होता है जिनके नाम सामान्य अंग्रेजी में नहीं मिलते और अंशतः पारिभाषिक शब्दावली में पूर्ण यथार्थता प्राप्त करना होता है। किसी भी प्रकार की तकनीकी बातचीत में ऐसी विशिष्ट भाषिका अथवा शब्दजाल की आवश्यकता होती है। विज्ञान अथवा कला विशेष के अध्येताओं के लिए सर्वविदित होने के साथ-साथ गणितीय सूत्र जैसी सूक्ष्मता रखते हैं। साथ ही, वे समय बचाते हैं, किसी प्रक्रिया का वर्णन करने की अपेक्षा उसका नाम लेना अधिक किफायती है। ऐसे हजारों पारिभाषिक शब्द बहुत अच्छी तरह इन शब्दकोशों में संकलित किए गए हैं, फिर भी, कुल मिलाकर, वे अंग्रेजी भाषा की मूल शब्दावली के बजाय उसके आस-पास ही ठहरते हैं। फिर भी विभिन्न व्यवसाय अपनी विशिष्ट शब्दावली की दृष्टि से पर्याप्त भिन्नता लिए हुए हैं। व्यापार, हस्तकला, कृषि और मछलीपालन जैसे अन्य व्यवसायों में जहाँ लम्बे समय से भारी संख्या में लोग लगे हैं, तकनीकी शब्दावली बहुत पुरानी है। इसमें अधिकतर स्थानीय शब्द मिलते हैं अथवा ऐसे आयातित शब्द हैं जो हमारी भाषा में घुल-मिल गए हैं। अतः अनेक रूपों में पूर्णतः तकनीकी होते हुए भी ये शब्दावलियां बोलने में अधिक परिचित-सी हैं और अन्य अधिकांश तकनीकीय तुलना में अधिक सहजता से समझी जाती हैं।

कानून, औषधि, धर्मविज्ञान और दर्शन की विशिष्ट भाषिका भी अपने प्राचीन रूप में परिष्कृत व्यक्तियों में पर्याप्त परिचित हो गई है, और प्रचलित शब्दावली में काफी योगदान कर चुकी है फिर भी प्रत्येक व्यवसाय आज भी ऐसी बहुत-सी तकनीकी शब्दावली लिए हुए है जो मूलतः विदेशी हैं। यह अनुपात पिछले पचास वर्षों में अधिक बढ़ा है विशेषतः यांत्रिक कलाओं, प्राकृतिक विज्ञान और राजनीति विज्ञान के विभिन्न क्षेत्रों में। यहाँ पूरी आजादी से नए शब्दों को शामिल कर लिया गया है और व्यर्थ हो जाने पर छोड़ दिया गया है। अधिकतर नए पद विशिष्ट बातचीत तक सीमित रहे हैं, कभी-कभी ही सामान्य बातचीत अथवा साहित्य जुड़ पाए हैं। पर आज कोई भी व्यवसाय, जैसा कि पहले सभी थे बंद निकाय नहीं हैं। वकील, चिकित्सक, वैज्ञानिक और पादरी अपने साथी सृजनकर्त्ताओं से जुड़ता है और ऐसा नहीं है कि मात्र व्यावसायिक रूप से ही मिलता है। बल्कि आज का प्रचलित विज्ञान प्रत्येक व्यक्ति को आधुनिक विचारों और खोजों से जोड़ता है। कोई भी महत्त्वपूर्ण प्रयोग चाहे वह दूर अथवा क्षेत्रीय प्रयोगशाला में किया गया हो, समाचार-पत्रों में तुरंत प्रकाशित हो जाता है और हर एक व्यक्ति उसके बारे में ऐसे ही बात करना शुरू कर देता है जैसे विकिरण किरणों और बेतारी तार-संचार के बारे में बात करता है। अतः हमारी सामान्य बोली सदैव नए तकनीकी शब्दों को अपना रही है और उन्हें प्रचलित कर रही है।

1. तकनीकी शब्दावली बढ़ाई जा सकती है :

A. नए शब्द बनाकर, विदेशी भाषाओं से शब्द ग्रहण करके और पुराने हुए शब्दों को निकालकर

B. नई अवधारणाओं के लिए नए शब्द गढ़कर

C. नए शब्द ढालकर और विदेशी भाषाओं से शब्द आयात करके

D. विदेशी शब्दों का अपनी भाषा में अनुवाद करके

2. प्रचलित विज्ञान, प्रत्येक व्यक्ति को परिचित कराता है

A. आधुनिक विचारों और नवीन खोजों से

B. नवीन खोजों और आविष्कारों से

C. आधुनिक विचारों, नवीन खोजों और तकनीक से

D. विज्ञान और तकनीक में नए विकास से

3. तकनीकी शब्दावली सभी की भाषा का अंग बन गई है :

A. व्यावसायिकों के प्रयासों द्वारा

B. विदेशी भाषा पढ़कर

C. प्रचलित वैज्ञानिक लेखों और समाचारपत्रों द्वारा

D. भाषा के परिवर्तनों द्वारा

4. तकनीकी शब्द हैं :

A. संक्षिप्त, किफायती और नामात्मक

B. नवीन, कठिन पर आवश्यक

C. भाषा की मूल शब्दावली से चुने हुए

D. सभी द्वारा सामान्य रूप से समझे जाने वाले

गद्यांश-38

मैं इस अंधविश्वास को जानता हूँ कि आत्म-ज्ञान जीवन की चौथी अवस्था में ही सम्भव है और वह है संन्यास। पर इस बात को सभी जानते हैं कि जो इस अमूल्य अनुभव को जीवन के अन्तिम क्षणों के लिए टालते हैं वे आत्म-ज्ञान प्राप्त नहीं करते बल्कि द्वितीय और दयनीय बचपन के समान बुढ़ापे को प्राप्त करते हैं और पृथ्वी पर एक भार की तरह जीते हैं। मुझे पूरी तरह याद है कि जब मैं 1911-12 में पढ़ाता था तब भी इसी विचार को मानता था भले ही इसी तरह की भाषा में उसे अभिव्यक्त न किया हो।

तब किस प्रकार यह आध्यात्मिक प्रशिक्षण दिया जाना था? मैंने बच्चों को भजन याद कराये और उनका अभ्यास कराया और उन्हें नैतिक शिक्षा की पुस्तकों से पढ़कर सुनाया। पर यह सब मेरे लिए संतोषजनक नहीं था। जब मैं उनके और अधिक निकट आया तो पाया कि अध्यात्म का प्रशिक्षण केवल पुस्तकों के माध्यम से नहीं कराया जा सकता। उसी प्रकार जैसे शारीरिक प्रशिक्षण व्यायाम के माध्यम से दिया जाता है और बौद्धिक अभ्यास के द्वारा, अतः अध्यात्म का प्रशिक्षण भी अध्यात्म के अभ्यास से संभव था। और अध्यात्म का प्रशिक्षण पूर्णतः अध्यापक के जीवन और चरित्र पर निर्भर करता है। अध्यापक चाहे विद्यार्थियों के बीच में है अथवा नहीं उसे सदैव अपने व्यवहार और चरित्र का ध्यान रखना है।

1. ऊपर उधृत पाठ सामग्री के लिए सर्वाधिक उपयुक्त शीर्षक है :
   A. बौद्धिक अभ्यास   B. अंधविश्वास
   C. आध्यात्मिक विकास   D. प्रशिक्षण

2. व्यापक स्तर पर आत्म-ज्ञान के बारे में लोगों के बीच अंधविश्वास है कि यह
   A. अनवरत प्रक्रिया है
   B. केवल संन्यास द्वारा संभव है
   C. केवल आरम्भिक जीवन में संभव है
   D. एक मिथक है

3. लेखक के अनुसार बच्चों का आध्यात्मिक प्रशिक्षण मुख्यतः किसके चरित्र पर निर्भर है?
   A. अभिभावकों के   B. अभिजात वर्ग के
   C. सामाजिक नेताओं के   D. अध्यापकों के

4. लेखक का बुढ़ापे के बारे में पहले विचार था कि यह
   A. एक गुण है   B. एक अभिशाप है
   C. विचारों की स्मृति है   D. संतोष है

गद्यांश-39

क्या विद्यार्थियों द्वारा प्राप्त किये गये परिणामों से अध्यापन-कार्य का मूल्यांकन किया जा सकता है? कुछ हद तक अध्यापकों को इसी प्रकार आँका जाता है, प्रायः सामूहिक रूप से, किसी संस्थान की ख्याति के रूप में। परन्तु इसमें कुछ कठिनाइयाँ हैं। विशेष रूप से उल्लेखनीय कठिनाई, जिसे स्क्राइवन (1988) ने 'हार्वर्ड फैलेसी (भ्रामकता)' के नाम से वर्णित किया है, इस प्रकार है :

...यह मान लेने की भ्रामकता कि हार्वर्ड में पढ़ाई अच्छी होती होगी क्योंकि यहां के स्नातक अपने बाद के जीवन में अच्छी तरक्की करते हैं ...इन आँकड़ों से यही परिणाम निकाला जा सकता है कि हार्वर्ड में मस्तिष्क को स्थायी हानि नहीं पहुँचाई जाती—सामान्यतया। बाकी की युक्ति केवल इतनी-सी है कि प्रतिभाशाली विद्यार्थियों का चयन कर कक्षाओं में भेजा जाए और उनके मार्ग में कोई रुकावट खड़ी न की जाए। उन्हें पुस्तकालय, प्रयोगशाला, पीयर ट्यूटरिंग और परिवार के प्रभाव या नाम के प्रति आदर का उपयोग करने दिया जाए। अध्यापकों का योगदान यदि कोई है तो वह अवशेष जो दूसरे कारणों से अलग करने के बाद बचता है जैसे कि ...'पुराने विद्यार्थियों के जाल' और नाम की मान्यता का नौकरी के लिए चयन और पदोन्नति पर प्रभाव। यद्यपि हार्वर्ड प्रमाण्यतः एक महान विश्वविद्यालय है तथापि निश्चित रूप से यह प्रमाण्यतः एक महान अध्यापन विश्वविद्यालय नहीं है बल्कि केवल एक भव्य रूप से सुसज्जित विश्वविद्यालय।

दूसरे देशों के विश्वविद्यालयों को स्पष्टतः हार्वर्ड के स्थान पर रखा जा सकता है। लेकिन फिर भी यदि एक जैसे संस्थानों के एक जैसे पाठ्यक्रमों के परिणामों की तुलना करना सम्भव हो तो भी सफलता का श्रेय दूसरे कारणों को देने की बजाय अध्यापन को देने के बारे में स्क्राइवन का तर्क विचारणीय रहेगा। किसी प्रकार के 'मूल्य-जुड़े' पैमाने से भी यह सम्भव नहीं होगा और ऐसे पैमाने या तो इतने अपक्व होंगे कि उनका कोई अर्थ ही नहीं होगा या फिर इतने जटिल होंगे कि जाँचने और आँकने के लिए पढ़ाने और सीखने की केन्द्रित गतिविधियों के मुकाबले में बहुत अधिक समय की आवश्यकता होगी। एक ही संस्थान में एक वर्ष के परिणामों की अगले वर्ष के परिणामों से तुलना करने में भी कठिनाइयाँ सामने आती हैं क्योंकि विभागों में और विद्यार्थियों में परिस्थितियाँ बदलती रहती हैं।

1. इस परिच्छेद का शीर्षक क्या हो सकता है?
   A. हार्वर्ड विश्वविद्यालय में अध्यापन
   B. विद्यार्थियों के परिणामों से अध्यापन-कार्य का मूल्यांकन
   C. संस्थानों की प्रतिष्ठा
   D. अध्यापकों के मूल्यांकन के लिए अवशिष्ट पद्धति

2. हार्वर्ड फैलेसी (भ्रामकता) का अर्थ है :
   A. यह मान लेना कि प्रतिष्ठित संस्थानों में पढ़ाई अच्छी होती है
   B. जो कुछ हार्वर्ड में भ्रामक रूप से किया जा रहा है
   C. कि हार्वर्ड में प्रतिभाशाली विद्यार्थियों को दाखिला दिया जाता है और अच्छे परिणाम प्राप्त किये जाते हैं
   D. कि हार्वर्ड में जो अध्यापन कार्य होता है उसमें बहुत-सी भ्रामकतायें हैं

3. विद्यार्थियों की उपलब्धियों में अध्यापकों के योगदान को स्क्राइवन के अनुसार किस बात से आँका जाना चाहिए?
   A. स्नातकों द्वारा बाद के जीवन में अर्जित उपलब्धियों से
   B. विद्यार्थियों के दाखिले के लिए संस्थानों द्वारा निर्धारित मानदण्डों से

C. बाकी सभी कारणों को निकालने के बाद बचे अवशिष्ट प्रभाव से
D. संस्थानों में उपलब्ध सुविधाओं से

4. स्क्राइवन के अनुसार हार्वर्ड की प्रतिष्ठा किस कारण से है?
A. इसका प्रचुर मात्रा में सुविधाओं से सम्पन्न होना
B. प्रतिभाशाली विद्यार्थियों को दाखिला और उनके मार्ग में रुकावट न डालना
C. इसका एक महान अध्यापन विश्वविद्यालय होना
D. इसके अपक्व और अर्थहीन तरीके जिनसे अध्यापन-कार्य की प्रभाविकता को माना जाता है

गद्यांश-40

संतान को बुढ़ापे की लाठी माना जाता है, परन्तु जब यह लाठी ही सहारा देने के बजाय मां-बाप को प्रताड़ना देने के लिए इस्तेमाल होने लगे तो संबंधों का क्या होगा? समाज और सरकार परम्पराओं को तोड़कर पैदा की जा रही विकृतियों की कब तक उपेक्षा कर सकते हैं? जाहिर है कि इन हालात में समाज व कानून के हस्तक्षेप की तैयारी पुख्ता हो जाती है। संसद द्वारा पारित द मेंटिनेन्स एंड वेलफेयर ऑफ पेरेंट्स एंड सीनियर सिटीजन बिल, 2007 एक प्रकार से ऐसा ही एक हस्तक्षेप है। बस देखना यही होगा कि इस हस्तक्षेप के लिए निर्धारित प्रावधानों का किस हद तक व कितना प्रभावी तरीके से इस्तेमाल होता है।

कानून तो बन गया है परन्तु इस पर अमल की चुनौतियां कम नहीं होंगी। कितने प्रताड़ित अभिभावक कानून के इस संरक्षण के प्रति जागरूक बन सकेंगे और कितने इस कानून के प्रावधानों के इस्तेमाल का संकल्प कर सकेंगे, उनका सचमुच इस्तेमाल कर न्याय हासिल कर सकेंगे? यहां पर समाज व सामाजिक एवं स्वयंसेवी संगठनों की भूमिका महत्त्वपूर्ण हो जाती है। उन्हें न केवल जागृति उत्पन्न करनी होगी बल्कि कानून के सदुपयोग के लिए सक्रिय भूमिका का निर्वाह भी करना होगा। यदि एक दफा इस कानून के अच्छे नतीजे सामने आने लगे तो ये मां-बाप की उपेक्षा की राह पर चलने वाली संतानों के लिए निषेधात्मक उपाय के रूप में भी प्रतिष्ठित हो सकेंगे।

1. सरकार को नया बिल संसद में क्यों लाना पड़ा?
A. इसके लिए सरकार पर दबाव डाला जा रहा था।
B. संसदीय समिति ने इस बारे में सुझाव सरकार के सामने रखे थे।
C. संतान द्वारा माता-पिता की उपेक्षा एक आम प्रचलन बनता जा रहा था।
D. A एवं C दोनों

2. नए कानून पर अमल के लिए सरकार को क्या करनी चाहिए?
A. न्यायिक प्रक्रिया में सुधार लानी चाहिए।
B. पुलिस कार्रवाई में तेजी लानी चाहिए।
C. जन-जागृति पैदा करनी चाहिए।
D. उपरोक्त सभी।

3. इस कानून को लागू करने में कौन-सी चुनौतियाँ हैं?
A. अभिभावकों को कानून के प्रति जागरूक बनाना।
B. कानून का सदुपयोग सुनिश्चित करना।
C. इससे जुड़े अपराध को रोकना।
D. A एवं B दोनों।

4. उपरोक्त उद्धरण के आधार पर सही कथन का चयन कीजिए।
A. संसद द्वारा पेरेंट्स एंड सीनियर सिटीजन बिल, 2008 में पारित किया गया।
B. यह कानून 65 वर्ष से अधिक उम्र के माता-पिता पर लागू होता है।
C. माता एवं पिता में से कोई भी इस कानून के तहत् अपना हक मांग सकता है।
D. इस कानून को सफल बनाने में स्वयंसेवी संगठनों को सक्रिय भूमिका निभानी होगी।

गद्यांश-41

भारत में नारी की स्तुति प्राचीनकाल से की जाती रही है "यत्र नार्यस्तु पूज्यन्ते रमन्ते तत्र देवता," इत्यादि के रूप में। यहाँ तक कि असुरों पर विजय प्राप्त करने हेतु भी देवताओं को नारी की शरण में जाना पड़ा था और देवी दुर्गा ने ही असुरों का संहार किया था। विद्या की देवी महासरस्वती, धन की देवी महालक्ष्मी और दुष्टों का नाश करने वाली महाकाली की आराधना की जाती है।

आधुनिक काल में भारत की आजादी की लड़ाई में महिलाओं ने पर्दा-प्रथा का त्याग कर देश को स्वतंत्रता दिलाने हेतु बढ़-चढ़कर हिस्सा लिया। आजाद भारत में महिलाओं को वोट देने का समान अधिकार दिया गया। हम सब जानते हैं कि आज की महिला जीवन के किसी भी क्षेत्र में पुरुषों से पीछे नहीं है। सर्वत्र अपनी विजय पताका फहरा रही है। माता-पिता ने भी समयानुसार आकाश छूने की आजादी दे दी है।

यह तो है महिला की तस्वीरों का एक पहलू। अब जरा दूसरे पहलू पर भी दृष्टि डालें। आज भी महिला शोषण का शिकार हो रही है। आश्चर्य की बात तो यह है कि यह शोषण अनपढ़, गाँव की महिलाओं के साथ ही नहीं, पढ़ी लिखी, ऊँचे पदों पर प्रतिष्ठित महिलाओं के साथ भी जारी है। फिर चाहे वह यौन शोषण हो, समाज द्वारा किया गया शोषण हो, अंधविश्वास के कारण हो या पुरुषों द्वारा अपना वर्चस्व बनाए रखने के कारण हो, महिलाएँ इसे सहने को अभिशप्त हैं। वैज्ञानिक शोधों को नकारते हुए संतानहीनता का दोष उसे ही भोगना पड़ता है। विधवा नारी को दी जाने वाली प्रताड़ना भले ही पहले जैसी कठोर न हो, पर वह एक सामान्य नारी न रहकर अशुभ का सूचक बन जाती है, इसलिए शुभ कार्यों में उसकी उपस्थिति वर्जित है। हालाँकि अब इस सोच में परिवर्तन आने लगा है, पर यदि वह निःसंतान है, तो परिवार के कार्यों में हाथ बंटाने के सिवाय उसका महत्व नही आंका जाता।

1. आज समाज में किन महिलाओं को प्रताड़ना झेलनी पड़ती है?
   A. विधवा
   B. निःसंतान
   C. अशिक्षित
   D. A एवं B दोनों
2. निम्न में से कौन महिलाओं के शोषण का सर्वाधिक प्रमुख रूप है?
   A. यौन शोषण
   B. संपत्ति में हिस्सेदारी न मिलना
   C. उन्हें घर के कामों तक ही सीमित रखना
   D. A एवं C दोनों
3. आजादी के बाद महिलाओं की स्थिति में क्या बदलाव आया है?
   A. महिलाओं को वोट का अधिकार मिला।
   B. सती प्रथा का निषेध किया गया।
   C. शिक्षा एवं जीवन के अन्य क्षेत्रों में भी उन्हें समानता मिली।
   D. A एवं C दोनों
4. उपरोक्त उद्धरण के आधार पर सही कथन का चयन कीजिए।
   A. प्राचीन काल में नारी को सम्मान की दृष्टि से देखा जाता था।
   B. आजादी की लड़ाई में महिलाओं ने बढ़चढ़कर भाग लिया।
   C. आज भी महिलाएँ यौन शोषण से सर्वाधिक पीड़ित हैं।
   D. उपरोक्त सभी

गद्यांश-42

साठ के दशक में ही कनाडा के दार्शनिक मार्शल मक्लूहन ने कहा था कि संचार व्यवस्था में अभूतपूर्व प्रगति के कारण दुनिया एक 'वैश्विक गांव' में बदल जायेगी। वर्तमान भूमंडलीकरण मक्लूहन की इस भविष्यवाणी का कार्यान्वयन लगता है। उल्लेखनीय है कि भूमंडलीकरण का वर्तमान प्रयोग मूलरूप से इंटरनेट से प्रेरित है और यही इसे अतीत में भूमंडलीकरण की दिशा में किये गये अन्य प्रयोगों से भिन्न कर देता है। वर्तमान भूमंडलीकरण एक ऐसी घटना साबित हुई है, जिसे समझने के लिए दुनिया की विभिन्न भाषाओं में अब तक कुल सात हजार पुस्तकें प्रकाशित हो चुकी हैं। हालांकि अभी भी इस परिघटना के बारे में अंतिम रूप से कुछ कहना मुश्किल माना जाता है। केवल एक ही बात पर आम सहमति है कि यह एक पेचीदा और बहुआयामी विकास प्रक्रिया है।

अर्थशास्त्र के आधुनिक विद्यार्थी इसे आर्थिक संसाधनों का सबसे सुंदर और प्रभावी विनियोजन मानते हैं और दुनिया में संपन्नता की वर्तमान लहर के लिए भी जिम्मेदार मानते हैं। इतना ही नहीं, कुछ लोगों की राय में तो भूमंडलीकरण के कारण दुनिया से युद्ध के खतरे भी मिट जायेंगे, क्योंकि देशों के बीच पारस्परिक व्यापार की जड़ें गहरी होने से उनमें युद्ध के प्रति आकर्षण खत्म हो जायेगा। दुनिया में प्रतिष्ठा हासिल करने के प्रतिमान बदल रहे हैं और देशों की पहचान सैनिक उपलब्धियों के बजाए आर्थिक सफलताओं से होने लगी है। युद्ध का स्थान आर्थिक प्रतियोगिता ने ले लिया है।

लेकिन भूमंडलीकरण के विरोधी इसे यूरोपीय अमेरिकी विकास मॉडल का महज एक आरोपण मानते हैं। उनका मानना है कि भूमंडलीकरण दुनिया को पश्चिमी देशों के हितों के अनुरूप ढालने की कोशिश है। पश्चिमी देशों द्वारा प्रतिपादित यह एक नयी किस्म की बाजार विचारधारा है जो निष्ठुर, सर्वग्रासी और निरंकुश है और जिसकी इतिहास में कोई मिसाल नहीं है। यह यूरोप और अमेरिका के दुनिया के संसाधनों पर स्थायी नियंत्रण स्थापित करने की पहल है।

1. भूमंडलीकरण है–
   A. एक पेचीदा और बहुआयामी विकास प्रक्रिया।
   B. इंटरनेट आधारित व्यापार संजाल।
   C. गरीब देशों के शोषण का एक नवीन आर्थिक तंत्र।
   D. उपरोक्त में से कोई नहीं।
2. भूमंडलीकरण के कारण दुनिया में युद्ध का खतरा कम हुआ है, कैसे?
   A. सभी देश आर्थिक उन्नति में लग गए हैं।
   B. पारस्परिक व्यापार की जड़ें गहरी होने से उनमें युद्ध के प्रति आकर्षण कम हो रहा है।
   C. युद्ध के खिलाफ अंतर्राष्ट्रीय जनमत गोलबंद हो रहा है।
   D. उपरोक्त सभी
3. भूमंडलीकरण को निष्ठुर एवं सर्वग्राही व्यवस्था क्यों कहा जा रहा है?
   A. इसके अंतर्गत दुनिया को पश्चिमी देशों के हितों के अंतर्गत ढालने की कोशिश की जा रही है।
   B. इसका लाभ सिर्फ अमेरिका और पश्चिमी देशों को मिल रहा है।
   C. भूमंडलीकरण के कारण अंतर्राष्ट्रीय वित्तीय संस्थाओं की भूमिका घटी है।
   D. उपरोक्त सभी
4. निम्न में से कौन भूमंडलीकरण का प्रभाव नहीं है?
   A. आर्थिक संसाधनों का बेहतर विनियोजन
   B. आर्थिक समृद्धि
   C. प्रतियोगी अर्थव्यवस्था
   D. नियोजित अर्थव्यवस्था

गद्यांश-43

तकनीकी रूप से भारतीय करेंसी परिवर्तनीय नहीं है। वह रेवेन्यू में परिवर्तनीय है, कैपिटल में नहीं। अगर आप विदेशों में जाकर बैंकों से कहें कि आप के पास भारतीय करंसी है, उसके बदले आपको डॉलर चाहिए तो ऐसा नहीं होगा। आपको डॉलर खरीदना पड़ेगा। इसका मतलब यह हुआ कि पूंजी में भारतीय करेंसी परिवर्तनीय नहीं है। इसी तरह हमें विदेशों में बैंक खाता खोलने के लिए डॉलर या पाउंड की जरूरत होगी। हमें पहले

रुपये को डॉलर या पाउंड में उसे बदलना होगा, तब जाकर हम उसे जमा करा सकते हैं। इसी तरह से विदेशों में शॉपिंग से लेकर किसी वस्तु की खरीदारी, आप किसी भी देश में डॉलर या पाउंड में कर सकते हैं। लोग उसे स्वीकार कर लेंगे, मगर वे रुपये को स्वीकार नहीं करेंगे। मगर रुपए का सिंबल बनने के बाद रुपए की कैपिटल में पूर्ण परिवर्तनीयता जल्द हो जाएगी। जिस तरह से भारत में आज डॉलर को लेने में कोई परहेज नहीं करता, वैसे अमेरिका में रुपये को लेने में कोई परहेज नहीं करेगा।

सवाल यह उठता है कि आखिर इसकी जरूरत क्या है। एक समय ब्रिटेन का कारोबार विश्व में काफी फैला था। कारोबार ब्रिटिश मुद्रा में होता था। ब्रिटेन ने इस विशिष्टता को कायम करने के लिए उसका प्रतीक चिह्न बनाया। अमेरिका ने भी यही रणनीति अपनाई। अपनी मुद्रा डॉलर की पहचान और वर्चस्व अंतर्राष्ट्रीय बाजार में स्थापित करने के लिए उसने अपनी मुद्रा का प्रतीक चिह्न बनाया। कई अन्य देशों में डॉलर मुद्रा का प्रचलन है, जापान के बाद 1999 में यूरोपीय देशों ने अपनी नई मुद्रा यूरो का प्रचलन शुरू किया, अपने खास प्रतीक चिह्न के साथ।

यह कारोबार के वर्चस्व की लड़ाई है। जिन-जिन देशों की मुद्रा के प्रतीक चिह्न हैं, उनके साथ कारोबार की पहली शर्त यह है कि कारोबार उनकी मुद्रा में होगा। एक्सपोर्ट से लेकर इंपोर्ट सब कुछ उनकी मुद्रा में होगा। अमेरिकी डॉलर ने विदेशी मुद्रा विनिमय बाजार में अपनी धुरी इस कदर बना ली है कि अन्य देशों की मुद्राओं की कीमत डॉलर के मुकाबले ही तय होती है। हालांकि यूरोपीय देश यूरो के द्वारा इस मिथ को तोड़ने की कोशिश में हैं, मगर अन्य देशों के साथ अमेरिका का कारोबार यूरोपीय देशों की तुलना में इतना अधिक है कि डॉलर का वर्चस्व बना हुआ है।

1. भारतीय करेंसी परिवर्तनीय है–
- A. अमेरिकी डॉलर के साथ
- B. राजस्व खाते पर
- C. पूँजी खाते पर
- D. सभी पर

2. देश की अपनी करेंसी का क्या लाभ है?
- A. इससे देश का कारोबार देश की मुद्रा में ही होगा।
- B. इससे देश का निर्यात बढ़ेगा।
- C. इससे देश का आयात प्रतिस्थापित होगा।
- D. इससे राष्ट्रीय उत्पाद में वृद्धि होगी।

3. दुनिया में अमेरिकी डॉलर के वर्चस्व का क्या कारण है?
- A. अमेरिकी डॉलर अन्य देशों की मुद्रा की तुलना में अधिक महँगा है।
- B. अमेरिकी डॉलर अन्य देशों द्वारा स्वीकृत मुद्रा है।
- C. अन्य देशों के साथ अमेरिका का कारोबार अधिक है।
- D. विदेशी विनिमय बाजार में डॉलर का कोई प्रतिस्थापन नहीं है।

4. पूँजी खाते पर रुपये के परिवर्तनीय होने का क्या लाभ है?
- A. इससे भारतीय रुपये को डॉलर एवं अन्य विदेशी मुद्राओं में बदलना आसान हो जाएगा।
- B. इससे देश में निवेश को बढ़ावा मिलेगा।
- C. भारतीय निर्यात में वृद्धि से व्यापार संतुलन देश के पक्ष में होगा।
- D. उपरोक्त सभी

गद्यांश-44

'आधार' से जुड़े विचार नए नहीं हैं। अमेरिका में काफी समय पहले सामाजिक सुरक्षा कार्यक्रमों से संबंधित लोगों को 'सामाजिक सुरक्षा नंबर' देने की सोच ने आकार लिया था और वहां पचास वर्षों से भी अधिक समय से ऐसे पहचान पत्र का इस्तेमाल हो रहा है। हाल ही में वहां पर सीनेट के कुछ सदस्यों ने यह प्रस्ताव रखा कि देश में बायोमेट्रिक सामाजिक सुरक्षा कार्ड शुरू किया जाए। इस प्रस्ताव को अमेरिका के नागरिक समूहों एवं निजता संबंधी वकीलों के जबर्दस्त विरोध का सामना करना पड़ा। आज से कुछ समय पहले ब्रिटेन सरकार ने भी बायोमेट्रिक राष्ट्रीय पहचान योजना शुरू की थी, लेकिन ब्रिटेन की नई सरकार इस योजना को खत्म करने, बल्कि एकत्रित बायोमेट्रिक आंकड़ों को ध्वस्त करने की सोच रही है। वहां कहा जा रहा है कि यह पूरी कवायद निरर्थक, नौकरशाही संबंधी और निजता में हस्तक्षेप करने वाली थी।

भारत में 'आधार' को सरकारी सेवाओं के समस्त रोगों की रामबाण दवा के रूप में पेश किया जा रहा है। अपेक्षा की जा रही है कि यह पहचान पत्र शिक्षा के अधिकार के तहत दाखिले की निगरानी करेगा। यह सार्वजनिक वितरण प्रणाली की दरारों को बंद कर देगा और वित्तीय समायोजन, ग्रामीण रोजगार गारंटी योजना, प्रस्तावित खाद्य सुरक्षा कानून तथा गरीबी-उन्मूलन से जुड़ी अन्य योजनाओं को लागू कराने में भी अचूक साबित होगा। फर्जी लाभार्थियों को छांट सकने वाली अनूठी पहचान संख्या की अवधारणा यकीनन आकर्षक है, लेकिन चिंता की बात यह है कि यह नंबर गलत पहचान या योजनाओं के क्रियान्वयन के रिसाव की समस्या को हल करने में कितना कारगर होगा। एक ऐसी व्यवस्था, जिसमें सरकारी अनुदान संबंधी ज्यादातर लाभ परिवार केंद्रित हैं, बल्कि बड़ा परिवार एक नेमत-सा हो, उसमें निजी सूचनाओं पर आधारित 'आधार' कैसे लाभप्रद हो सकता है?

1. सामाजिक सुरक्षा से जुड़ी राष्ट्रीय पहचान योजना निम्न में से किस देश में लागू की जा चुकी है?
- A. भारत
- B. ब्रिटेन
- C. संयुक्त राज्य अमेरिका
- D. उपरोक्त सभी

2. अमेरिका में बायोमेट्रिक सामाजिक सुरक्षा कार्ड योजना का विरोध किया जा रहा है, क्यों?
- A. इससे अमेरिका की राष्ट्रीय सुरक्षा खतरे में पड़ सकती है।
- B. इंटरनेट आधारित योजनाओं में इसके दुरूपयोग की संभावना बढ़ सकती है।
- C. इससे व्यक्ति की निजता प्रभावित होगी।

D. इससे अमेरिका की गोपनीय खुफिया रिपोर्ट सार्वजनिक हो सकती है।

3. उपरोक्त उद्धरण के आधार पर सही कथन का चयन कीजिए?

A. अमेरिका के कुछ सीनेटरों ने देश में बायोमेट्रिक सामाजिक सुरक्षा कार्ड का विरोध किया है।

B. अमेरिका के नागरिक समूह सुरक्षा कार्ड योजना का समर्थन कर रहे हैं।

C. ब्रिटेन की नई सरकार कुछ समय पहले शुरू की गई बायोमेट्रिक राष्ट्रीय पहचान योजना खत्म करने पर विचार कर रही है।

D. भारत सरकार ने भी इस योजना के खतरे को देखते हुए इसे स्थगित करने का निर्णय हाल ही में लिया है।

4. भारत में शुरू की गई आधार योजना का मुख्य लाभ क्या है?

A. इससे सार्वजनिक वितरण प्रणाली की खामियों को दूर करने में मदद मिलेगी।

B. इससे सरकारी खर्च पर नियंत्रण रखा जा सकेगा।

C. इससे रोजगार गारंटी योजना के लाभार्थियों को उचित लाभ मिल सकेगा।

D. A एवं C

गद्यांश-45

3जी मोबाइल सेवा टेलीकॉम जगत में क्रान्ति लेकर आई है। यह सेवा इन्टरनेट टेलीविजन, वीडियो ऑन-डिमांड, आडियो-वीडियो फोन कॉल और क्रांफ्रेंसिंग के साथ ही तीव्र गति डाटा आदान-प्रदान जैसे तेज सम्पर्क और एप्लीकेशन की सुविधा प्रदान करेगी। वीडियो फोन कॉल में एक-दूसरे को देखते हुए बातचीत की जा सकती है। कम्पनियों की योजना के अनुसार, शुरुआत में वे 100 चैनलों का लाइव टीवी शुरू करेंगी, जिसमें बाद में 100 और चैनल जोड़ दिए जाएंगे। तेज गति की ऑनलाइन गेमिंग, पिक्चर इन पिक्चर और फोटो अपलोडिंग भी सम्भव हो जाएगी। मोबाइल पर ईमेल एकाउंट या किसी वेबसाइट खुलने में देरी तब बीते जमाने की बात हो जाएगी। 2जी सेवाओं में फिलहाल प्रयुक्त किए जा रहे फोन सेटों में ईमेल एकाउंट का खुलना ज्यादा आसान हो जाएगा। चूंकि 3जी युक्त मोबाइल सेटों में सेवा प्रदाता कम्पनी से प्राप्त संकेत अधिक शक्तिशाली होंगे इसलिये सभी तरह की सेवाओं की गति अधिक होगी। जबकि 2जी सेवाओं में आडियो कॉल्स के साथ एमपीथ्री, एफएम, रिंगटोन और औसत गति का जीपीआरएस और टेक्स्ट मैसेजिंग (एसएमएस) का लाभ ही मिलता था। दूरसंचार विभाग के अनुसार, फिलहाल मोबाइल सेवा में उच्च श्रेणी के ब्रॉडबैंड इंटरनेट की गति 256 केबीपीएस होती है जबकि 3जी पर ब्रॉडबैंड की शुरुआत ही होगी 384 केबीपीएस से जो वर्तमान उपलब्ध संरचना में 3.2 एमबीपीएस तक जा सकती है। भारत में फिलहाल व्यापक रूप से जिस 3जी मोबाइल प्रौद्योगिकी की प्रतीक्षा की जा रही है, वह तीसरी पीढ़ी की है। इस समय बीएसएनएल और एमटीएनएल को छोड़कर सभी निजी मोबाइल ऑपरेटर कम्पनियाँ दूसरी पीढ़ी (2जी) प्रौद्योगिकी की सेवाएं उपलब्ध करा रही हैं।

1. 3जी मोबाइल सेवा को टेलीकॉम जगत में एक क्रान्ति के रूप में क्यों देखा जा रहा है?

A. इससे तीव्र गति से डाटा का आदान-प्रदान संभव हो पाएगा।

B. इससे ऑन लाइन टिचिंग संभव हो पाएगा।

C. मानसून की सटीक भविष्यवाणी की जा सकेगी।

D. उपरोक्त सभी

2. 3जी सेवा का प्रमुख लाभ क्या है?

A. डाटा का शीघ्र आदान-प्रदान।

B. टी.वी. चैनल सेवाओं का विस्तार।

C. पिक्चर इन पिक्चर एवं फोटो अपलोडिंग।

D. उपरोक्त सभी।

3. निम्न में से कौन-सी सुविधा 2जी सेवाओं पर आधारित नहीं है?

A. टेक्स्ट मैसेजिंग B. जीपीआरएस

C. एमपी थ्री D. वीडियो ऑन डिमांड

गद्यांश-46

बीपीओ के क्षेत्र में भारत जैसे देश की सफलता ने विकसित देशों को चौंका दिया। अमेरिका के राष्ट्रपति चुनाव में आउटसोर्सिंग एक बड़ा मसला बना। भारत के ज्ञान के आगे अमेरिका जैसा सशक्त देश सहम गया। अमेरिकी राष्ट्रपति बराक ओबामा कई बार अपने भाषण में भारत और चीन जैसे देश की उच्च स्तरीय बौद्धिक संपदा से खौफ जता चुके हैं। बराक ओबामा ने तो अमेरिकी कंपनियों को सख्त आदेश दिए कि बाहर नौकरी देने वाली कंपनियों को किसी तरह की सरकारी रियायत नहीं दी जाएगी, लेकिन विकसित देशों का यह खौफ आउटसोर्सिंग को रोक नहीं पाया, हां इसके लिए चुनौतियां जरूर बढ़ गई हैं। खासकर वैश्विक आर्थिक मंदी के बाद भारत की ओर जा रही नौकरियों को लेकर पश्चिमी देश अपनी भौहें टेढ़ी करने लगे, लेकिन एक बार वैश्विक कारोबार में अपने पांव जमाने के बाद भारतीय श्रम शक्ति को नजरअंदाज करना आसान नहीं है। फिर भी यह सच है कि आज चुनौतियां ज्यादा बढ़ गई हैं। जरूरत है इन चुनौतियों का मुकाबला कर, वैश्विक कारोबार में अपने पांव जमाए रखने की। आज के भारतीय युवा को इस क्षेत्र से काफी उम्मीदें हैं। भारत केपीओ का भी अगुआ बन रहा है। कल के सॉफ्टवेयर कुली आज के परामर्शदाता हैं। विकसित दुनिया की एक बड़ी जरूरत बन गए हैं। इस कामयाबी को बरकरार रखने और बढ़ाने की जरूरत है। आशा की जानी चाहिए कि भारत आने वाले दिनों में दुनिया का सबसे बड़ा केपीओ बाजार बन जाएगा।

1. भारत की कौन-सी सफलता विकसित देशों को चौंकानेवाली है?

A. एशिया में एक महत्वपूर्ण आर्थिक शक्ति के रूप में भारत का उभरना।

B. भारत द्वारा रुपये के नए चिह्न को अपनाना।
C. भारत में बीपीओ क्षेत्र की सफलता।
D. भारत का बढ़ता विदेशी मुद्रा भंडार।

2. अमेरिकी सरकार ने आउटसोर्सिंग को रोकने के लिए कौन-से कदम उठाए हैं?
A. आउटसोर्सिंग करनेवाली कंपनियों पर अतिरिक्त टैक्स
B. आउटसोर्सिंग करनेवाली कंपनियों को मिलने वाली सरकारी रियायत में कटौती
C. आउटसोर्सिंग पर पूर्ण प्रतिबंध
D. आउटसोर्सिंग रोकने के लिए यूरोपीय संघ के साथ समझौता

3. आनेवाले दिनों में भारत को दुनिया का सबसे बड़ा केपीओ बाजार बन जाने की संभावना व्यक्त की जा रही है, क्यों?
A. भारत को बीपीओ क्षेत्र की सफलता का लाभ मिलेगा।
B. भारत के पास उन्नत कोटि का मानव संसाधन उपलब्ध है।
C. केपीओ बाजार में भारत का कोई प्रतिद्वन्द्वी नहीं है।
D. उपरोक्त सभी

4. अमेरिका के राष्ट्रपति चुनाव का मुख्य मुद्दा क्या था?
A. इराक में शांति स्थापना
B. संयुक्त राष्ट्रसंघ की सुरक्षा परिषद् में सुधार
C. आउटसोर्सिंग
D. अमेरिकी राष्ट्रीय सुरक्षा

गद्यांश-47

विकास की दौड़ में देश का भीतरी संतुलन भी बहुत ही महत्वपूर्ण है। आज भारत के सन्दर्भ में परोक्ष रूप से संवैधानिक व्यवस्था के सामने समय की चुनौती है, परीक्षा है प्रजातन्त्र और गणतन्त्र की दुहाई देने वाले राजनीतिक दलों की, उनके निर्वाचित सदस्यों की और व्यवस्था का संचालन करने वाली शासकीय नौकरशाही की वे अपने कर्तव्यबोध में कितनी कर्मठता, पारदर्शिता, ईमानदारी और राष्ट्रीय भावना को तरजीह देते हैं।

हम कभी कर्ज से मुक्त और सम्पदा से युक्त एक राष्ट्र थे, हम समूचे विश्व को एक नई राह दिखाने की क्षमता वाले सक्षम राष्ट्र थे, परन्तु जो हुआ है और आज जो हो रहा है वह देश के हित में कम नेताओं के और उनके वंशजों के व पूँजीपतियों के हित में अधिक हो रहा है। देश का, जो विकास होना था वो हुआ या नहीं, न तो किसी को इसका ठीक-ठाक पता है और न ही किसी को यह सब देखने में रुचि है इतना तो अवश्य है कि नेताओं की स्वहितकारी पंचवर्षीय योजनाएं अच्छी तरह से बनती चली गई हैं और उनका भारी विकास होता चला गया है। एक अनुमान के अनुसार हमारे देश के नेताओं का एक लाख करोड़ रुपए से अधिक काला धन स्विस बैंकों में और छद्म सम्पत्तियों में रखा और निवेशित किया गया है। इतने धन से भारत की तस्वीर बदली जा सकती है, कुछ हद तक गरीबी दूर की जा सकती है, परन्तु यह धन आम जनता की गरीबी दूर करने के लिए नहीं है, बल्कि यही धन आम जनता से छीनकर उन्हें गरीब किया गया है इस देश को कर्जदार बनाया गया है और भारी विषमता की इस खाई को रचा गया है।

1. लेखक ने आम जनता की गरीबी का कारण किसे बताया है?
A. संसाधनों का सही उपयोग न हो पाने को।
B. धन के दुरूपयोग को।
C. जनता के धन के विदेशों में पलायन को।
D. उपरोक्त सभी।

2. लेखक ऐसा क्यों मानता है कि आज जो विकास हो रहा है वह देश का कम, नेताओं का ज्यादा है?
A. विकास का लाभ आम जनता को नहीं नेताओं को मिला है।
B. नेताओं ने विकास की प्रक्रिया को अपनी ओर मोड़ लिया है।
C. नेता ही विकास के सबसे बड़े नियंता हैं।
D. नेता देश का विकास नहीं चाहते।

3. भारत में विकास की सबसे बड़ी विसंगति क्या है?
A. देश में प्रजातंत्र की जड़ लगातार कमजोर हुई है।
B. संपदा से युक्त राष्ट्र आज सबसे बड़ा कर्जदार बन गया है।
C. देश का धन बड़ी मात्रा में विदेशों में भेजा जा रहा है।
D. A एवं C दोनों।

4. सवैधानिक व्यवस्था के सामने सबसे बड़ी चुनौती क्या है?
A. शासन में कर्तव्य बोध एवं पारदर्शिता का अभाव।
B. राष्ट्रीय भावना का कमजोर पड़ना।
C. नागरिकों में कर्मठता का अभाव।
D. उपरोक्त सभी।

गद्यांश-48

एक आर्थिक विचार के रूप में ब्रिक की धारणा का प्रतिपादन वर्ष 2001 में अमेरिका की वित्तीय कम्पनी गोल्डमैन सैच (Goldman Sachs) के अर्थशास्त्री जिम ओ नील (Jim O' Niel) ने किया था। नील ने इन चार देशों की उभरती अर्थव्यवस्थाओं को आगे आने वाले भविष्य के लिए महत्त्वपूर्ण माना था। इस धारणा का विधिवत् प्रतिपादन उनके द्वारा 2003 में लिखित रिपोर्ट 'Dreaming with BRICS : The path to 2050' में यह माना गया था कि इन चार देशों ने वैश्विक पूँजीवाद के आलोक में अपनी राजनीतिक व आर्थिक व्यवस्थाओं में परिवर्तन कर लिया है। इस रिपोर्ट के अनुसार वर्ष 2050 तक भारत व चीन विश्व में निर्मित वस्तुओं व सेवाओं के अग्रिम आपूर्तिकर्ता देश होंगे। इसी प्रकार रूस तथा ब्राजील

2050 तक विश्व में कच्चे माल के अग्रिम आपूर्तिकर्ता देश होंगे। इस प्रकार इन देशों की अर्थव्यवस्थाएं एक-दूसरे की पूरक होंगी। इसी प्रकार वर्ष 2005 में प्रकाशित गोल्डमैन सैच की एक अन्य रिपोर्ट में यह भविष्यवाणी की गई थी कि इन चारों देशों की अर्थव्यवस्थाएं इतनी तेजी से विकसित हो रही हैं कि वर्ष 2050 तक ये चारों अर्थव्यवस्थाएं वर्तमान विश्व के धनी देशों की अर्थव्यवस्थाओं से आगे निकल जाएंगी। लेकिन इस रिपोर्ट का तर्क यह नहीं था कि ये चारों अर्थव्यवस्थाएं एक आर्थिक सहयोग संगठन का निर्माण करेंगी।

वर्तमान में इन चारों देशों में विश्व की 40 प्रतिशत जनसंख्या निवास करती है तथा इन चारों का क्षेत्रफल विश्व के भौगोलिक क्षेत्रफल का 25 प्रतिशत है। साथ ही इन चारों का सकल राष्ट्रीय उत्पाद (GDP) 15.43 ट्रिलियन डॉलर है। इन चारों देशों में आपसी सहयोग की सम्भावना इसलिए अधिक है कि जहाँ रूस में तेल व प्राकृतिक गैस व ब्राजील में खनिज पदार्थों विशेषकर लौह अयस्क की अच्छी मात्रा है, वहीं भारत व चीन तकनीकी व निर्माण के क्षेत्र में आगे हैं।

1. लेखक ने किन अर्थव्यवस्थाओं को भविष्य के लिए महत्त्वपूर्ण माना है?
   A. ब्राजील, रूस भारत, चीन
   B. चीन, भारत, द. अफ्रीका, रूस
   C. ब्राजील, भारत, रूस, द. अफ्रीका
   D. रूस, भारत, चीन, जापान

2. 2050 तक किन देशों के निर्मित वस्तुओं एवं सेवाओं के अग्रिम आपूर्तिकर्ता होने की संभावना व्यक्त की गई है?
   A. भारत एवं ब्राजील   B. भारत एवं चीन
   C. ब्राजील एवं रूस   D. चीन एवं ब्राजील

3. निम्न में से कौन-सा कथन सही है?
   A. इस शताब्दी के अर्द्धांश तक ब्रिक राष्ट्रों की अर्थव्यवस्था विकसित देशों की अर्थव्यवस्था से आगे निकल जाएगी।
   B. ब्रिक राष्ट्रों के बीच आपसी व्यापारिक प्रतिस्पर्धा बढ़ेगी।
   C. ब्रिक राष्ट्र दुनिया के सर्वाधिक निर्यातक राष्ट्र के रूप में उभरेंगे।
   D. A एवं C दोनों

4. ब्रिक राष्ट्रों के बीच सहयोग की अधिक संभावना किस कारण से है?
   A. सभी राष्ट्र सहयोग के लिए प्रतिबद्ध हैं।
   B. इनकी अर्थव्यवस्था एक-दूसरे की पूरक है।
   C. इनकी अर्थव्यवस्था एक-दूसरे की प्रतिस्पर्धी है।
   D. सभी ने सीमा शुल्क रहित व्यापार का समर्थन किया है।

गद्यांश-49

भारत की सामाजिक संस्थाओं में जाति प्रणाली के घृणितम स्वरूप के दंश समाज के एक वर्ग ने शताब्दियों तक झेले हैं। जाति व्यवस्था से ही समाज में ऊँच-नीच की भावना पैदा हुई है। कर्म के आधार पर विकसित हुई वर्णव्यवस्था में बौद्धिक दृष्टि से श्रेष्ठतर तथा शिक्षा-दीक्षा का कार्य करने वाले लोग ब्राह्मण, समुदाय (राज्य) की रक्षा करने वाले लोग क्षत्रिय, कारोबारी लोग वैश्य तथा उत्पादन करने वाले लोग शूद्र कहलाए। यह वर्गीकरण जन्मगत न होकर कर्मगत था। कालान्तर में समाज में कर्म के ही आधार पर जातियाँ और उप-जातियाँ बनीं। बुद्धिबल, बाहुबल तथा धनबल के आधार पर कतिपय जातियों ने स्वयं को श्रेष्ठतम (ऊँचा) तथा अन्यों को निम्नतम (नीचा) मान लिया। तथाकथित नीची जातियों पर तरह-तरह की निर्योग्यताएं थोपी गईं यथा नीची जातियों के लोगों पर जूते पहनने, पगड़ी बाँधने पर प्रतिबन्ध लगा दिया गया। वे तथाकथित ऊँची जातियों के कुओं से पानी नहीं ले सकते थे; मन्दिरों में प्रवेश नहीं कर सकते थे; तथाकथित नीची जाति की महिलाएँ कमीज (ब्लाउज) नहीं पहन सकती थीं उन्हें साड़ी लपेट कर ही अपना शरीर ढंकना पड़ता था। तथाकथित नीची जातियों के लोग बराबरी के साथ चारपाई पर नहीं बैठ सकते थे। उनकी छाया तक पड़ जाने पर ब्राह्मण स्वयं को अशुद्ध मानकर स्नान करते थे। महाराष्ट्र में दलितों को सार्वजनिक स्थान, सड़क आदि पर थूकने के भी अधिकार नहीं थे। प्रताड़ना के विकृततम रूप में दलितों को अपने गले में कटोरा बाँधकर चलना पड़ता था ताकि यदि वे थूकें तो उसी कटोरे में थूकें और अपनी बस्ती में जाकर कटोरा साफ करें। कतिपय नीची जातियों के लोगों को अपनी कमर से एक झाड़ू बाँधकर चलना पड़ता था ताकि जिस रास्ते से वे चलें वह स्वतः ही साफ होता रहे। इस प्रकार की अमानवीय कुप्रथाओं तथा दलितों के सामाजिक उत्पीड़न के विरुद्ध उन्नीसवीं और बीसवीं शताब्दी में अनेक समाज सुधार आन्दोलन चले। महात्मा गांधी के अछूतोद्धार आन्दोलन तथा डॉ. बी.आर. अम्बेडकर के प्रयासों से स्वाधीनता आन्दोलन के दौरान ही जाति व्यवस्था पर कड़े प्रहार किए गए। भारतीय राष्ट्रीय कांग्रेस तथा अन्य समाज सुधारकों के प्रयास से जनगणना में जाति का उल्लेख किया जाना बन्द कर दिया गया। भारतीय जाति व्यवस्था की कुरीतियों को दास प्रथा, रंगभेद, सती प्रथा, बालिका भ्रूण हत्या के समकक्ष ही अमानवीय करार दिया गया। इन समस्त प्रयासों के चलते ही संविधान के मौलिक अधिकारों में समानता के अधिकार के तहत जाति, धर्म, लिंग, भाषा अथवा क्षेत्र के आधार पर किसी भी व्यक्ति के प्रति भेदभाव किए जाने को निषेध कर दिया गया। अस्पृश्यता को मौलिक अधिकारों के हनन की संज्ञा देते हुए एवं असंवैधानिक मानते हुए एक संज्ञेय अपराध भी माना गया।

1. समाज में ऊँच-नीच की भावना का मुख्य आधार क्या है?
   A. जाति व्यवस्था   B. वर्ण व्यवस्था
   C. सांप्रदायिक विभाजन   D. उपरोक्त सभी

2. निम्न में से कौन सामाजिक श्रेष्ठता का आधार है?
   A. बुद्धि   B. बाहुबल
   C. धन   D. उपरोक्त सभी

3. भारतीय समाज में निचली जाति पर कौन-सी निर्योग्यता आरोपित नहीं की गई थी?
A. ऊँची जाति के कुओं से पानी न भरना
B. पगड़ी बाँधना
C. जूते पहनना
D. मंदिरों में प्रवेश

4. जाति-व्यवस्था को असंवैधानिक माना गया है–
A. संविधान की प्रस्तावना में।
B. मौलिक अधिकार खंड में।
C. राज्य के नीति निदेशक भाग में।
D. उपरोक्त सभी में।

गद्यांश-50

भारत में प्राचीन काल से ही उत्तम कोटि के सूती वस्त्रों का उत्पादन होता आया है। यहाँ का मलमल अपनी विशेषता के लिए विश्वविख्यात रहा है। 17वीं शताब्दी तक भारत में उत्तम कोटि के सूती वस्त्रों का बड़े पैमाने पर उत्पादन होता था। अंग्रेजी साम्राज्य ने अपने देश के प्रभुत्व को स्थापित करने के उद्देश्य से ब्रिटेन में उत्पादित वस्त्र को भारतीय बाजार में उतार कर भारतीय वस्त्र उद्योग को नष्ट कर दिया था। इसके फलस्वरूप भारत यूरोपीय देशों के कच्चे माल की पूर्ति का केन्द्रमात्र बनकर रह गया। धीरे-धीरे भारतीय ग्रामों में फैला परम्परागत वस्त्र उद्योग नष्ट होने लगा।

राष्ट्रपिता महात्मा गांधी की दृष्टि लुप्तप्राय होते जा रहे ग्रामीण उद्योगों की ओर गई। उन्होंने स्वदेशी वस्त्र उत्पादन के कार्य को पुनर्जीवित करने के उद्देश्य को ध्यान में रखते हुए वर्ष 1925 में अखिल भारत चरखा संघ की स्थापना से खादी कार्य का सूत्रपात किया। गांधीजी का लक्ष्य खादी उद्योग के माध्यम से शोषण मुक्त समाज की रचना करना था। एक बार गांधीजी ने कहा भी था, ''यदि मुझे कोई हाथ-कताई से बेहतर सुविचारित व्यापक कार्यक्रम बतलाए तो मैं आज चरखा का त्याग कर दूँगा। परन्तु अभी तक न तो मैंने देखा है और न ही मुझे दिखाया गया है। यदि ऐसा कोई सुविचारित कार्यक्रम है, तो उसे जानने के लिए मैं उत्सुक हूँ।''

वर्ष 1947 तक यह उद्योग गांधीजी के मार्ग निर्देशन में रहा। स्वतंत्रता प्राप्त करने के पश्चात् सरकार ने इस उद्योग को आवश्यक संरक्षण प्रदान किया। खादी ग्रामोद्योग आयोग अधिनियम, 1946 द्वारा उद्योगों के विकास के लिए एक विशेष आयोग स्थापित किया गया। आयोग का काम खादी ग्रामोद्योग सम्बन्धी कार्यक्रमों की योजना बनाना तथा उनके कार्यान्वयन में सहायता देना है। खादी ग्रामोद्योग के क्षेत्र में काम करने वाले लोगों को प्रशिक्षण देने के अलावा आयोग ऐसी एजेंसियों के लिए वित्त की व्यवस्था करता है, जो इसकी पात्र होती हैं। उन्हें कच्चा माल जुटाता है तथा खादी ग्रामोद्योग के उत्पादों की बिक्री का प्रबन्ध करता है।

1. भारतीय वस्त्र उद्योग के नष्ट होने का मुख्य कारण क्या था?
A. भारतीय वस्त्र उद्योग की गुणवत्ता लगातार घटती जा रही थी।
B. भारतीय वस्त्रों की कीमत बाजार में लगातार बढ़ती जा रही थी।
C. भारतीय वस्त्र उद्योग को ब्रिटेन में उत्पादित सस्ते कपड़ों से मुकाबला करना पड़ रहा था।
D. B एवं C दोनों।

2. खादी उद्योग को बढ़ावा देने का गांधी का मुख्य उद्देश्य क्या था?
A. देशी उद्योग को बढ़ावा देना।
B. खादी को लोकप्रिय बनाना।
C. भारतीय उद्योग को आत्मनिर्भर बनाना।
D. शोषण मुक्त समाज की स्थापना करना।

3. 17वीं शताब्दी में भारत प्रसिद्ध था–
A. उन्नत कोटि के सूती वस्त्रों के लिए।
B. मलमल वस्त्र के लिए।
C. A एवं B दोनों के लिए।
D. रंगरेजी के लिए।

4. खादी ग्रामोद्योग आयोग का गठन किस उद्देश्य से किया गया?
A. खादी ग्रामोद्योग के विकास के लिए योजना बनाना।
B. इस उद्योग में काम करनेवाले लोगों को प्रशिक्षण देना।
C. इन उद्योगों में निर्मित वस्तुओं की बिक्री के लिए।
D. उपरोक्त सभी।

उत्तरमाला

गद्यांश-1

1	2	3
D	B	A

गद्यांश-2

1	2	3
C	D	D

गद्यांश-3

1	2	3	4
C	C	D	D

गद्यांश-4

1	2	3	4
A	D	B	D

गद्यांश-5

1	2	3	4
D	D	B	A

गद्यांश-6

1	2	3	4
A	A	D	A

गद्यांश-7

1	2	3	4
A	D	D	D

गद्यांश-8

1	2	3	4
B	D	D	A

गद्यांश-9

1	2	3	4	5
D	D	A	C	A

गद्यांश-10

1	2	3	4
D	B	D	B

गद्यांश-11

1	2	3	4	5
D	C	B	C	A

गद्यांश-12

1	2	3	4	5
C	A	B	D	A

गद्यांश-13

1	2	3	4	5
C	D	B	D	A

गद्यांश-14

1	2	3	4	5
A	C	D	C	B

गद्यांश-15

1	2	3	4	5
A	C	A	C	D

गद्यांश-16

1	2	3	4	5
B	B	C	C	C
6	**7**			
A	B			

गद्यांश-17

1	2	3	4	5
B	C	D	A	B

गद्यांश-18

1	2	3	4	5
D	B	A	A	C

गद्यांश-19

1	2	3	4	5
C	A	B	B	A

गद्यांश-20

1	2	3	4	5
B	B	D	C	A

गद्यांश-21

1	2	3	4	5
B	A	C	D	C

गद्यांश-22

1	2	3	4	5
B	A	C	A	C

गद्यांश-23

1	2	3	4	5
D	C	A	D	C

गद्यांश-24

1	2	3	4
C	A	A	A

गद्यांश-25

1	2	3	4
A	D	C	D

गद्यांश-26

1	2	3	4
B	D	B	A

गद्यांश-27

1	2	3	4
D	C	C	B

गद्यांश-28

1	2	3	4
D	D	A	D

गद्यांश-29

1	2	3	4
C	A	D	B

गद्यांश-30

1	2	3	4
D	C	A	D

गद्यांश-31

1	2	3	4
D	A	C	D

गद्यांश-32

1	2	3	4
B	D	B	A

गद्यांश-33

1	2	3	4
C	A	C	A

गद्यांश-34

1	2	3	4
A	B	D	C

गद्यांश-35

1	2	3	4
B	C	C	B

गद्यांश-36

1	2	3	4
C	C	B	A

गद्यांश-37

1	2	3	4
C	A	C	A

गद्यांश-38

1	2	3	4
C	B	D	B

गद्यांश-39

1	2	3	4
B	A	C	B

गद्यांश-40

1	2	3	4
C	C	D	D

गद्यांश-41

1	2	3	4
D	D	D	D

गद्यांश-42

1	2	3	4
A	B	A	D

गद्यांश-43

1	2	3	4
B	A	C	A

गद्यांश-44

1	2	3	4
D	C	C	D

गद्यांश-45

1	2	3
A	D	D

गद्यांश-46

1	2	3	4
C	B	B	C

गद्यांश-47

1	2	3	4
C	A	B	D

गद्यांश-48

1	2	3	4
A	B	A	B

गद्यांश-49

1	2	3	4
A	D	A	B

गद्यांश-50

1	2	3	4
C	D	C	D

भाषा बोध : काव्यांश

काव्यांश-1

चौ.–एक पिता के बिपुल कुमारा।
होहिं पृथक गुन सील अचारा।।
कोउ पंडित कोउ तापस ग्याता।
कोउ धनवंत सूर कोउ दाता।।
कोउ सर्बग्य धर्मरत कोई
सब पर पितहि प्रीति सम होई।।
कोउ पितु भगत बचन मन कर्मा।
सपनेहुँ जान न दूसर धर्मा।।
सो सुत प्रिय प्रान समाना।
जद्यपि सो सब भाँति अयाना।।
एहि बिधि जीव चराचर जेते।
त्रिजग देव नर असुर समेते।।
अखिल बिस्व यह मोर उपाया।
सब पर मोहि बराबरि दाया।।
तिन्ह महँ जो परिहरि मद माया।
भजै मोहि मन बच अरु काया।।

दिए गए काव्यांश के आधार पर निम्नलिखित प्रश्नों के उत्तर दें।

1. दिए गए पद्यांश का शीर्षक हो सकता है–
   A. पितृ वत्सलता B. पुत्र के गुण
   C. पुत्र का धर्म D. इनमें से कोई नहीं
2. दिए गए पद्यांश के आधार पर पिता का प्यार–
   A. ज्ञानी पुत्र को प्राप्त होता है
   B. धनी पुत्र को प्राप्त होता है
   C. पराक्रमी पुत्र को प्राप्त होता है
   D. सभी को प्राप्त होता है चाहे वह मूर्ख, निर्बल या निर्धन हो
3. 'तापस' शब्द का अर्थ होगा–
   A. सूर्य की गर्मी B. तपस्वी
   C. बुखार से पीड़ित D. गर्मी का मौसम
4. 'चराचर' शब्द का संधि-विच्छेद होगा–
   A. चरा + चर B. चर + आचर
   C. चर + अचर D. इनमें से कोई नहीं
5. 'असुर' शब्द का पर्यायवाची शब्द होगा–
   A. निशाचर B. दैत्य
   C. दानव D. ये सभी

काव्यांश-2

तेरा जन एक आध है कोई।
काम-क्रोध अरु लोभ विसर्जित, ये सब तेरी माया।।
राजस-तामस-सातिग तीन्यू, ये सब तेरी माया।
चौथे पद कौं जे जन चीन्हैं, तिनहिं परम पद पाया।।
असतुति-निंदा-आसा छाड़ै, तजै मान अभिमाना।
लोहा-कंचन समिकरि च्यंतामणि हरिपद रमै उदासा।
त्रिसनां अरु-अभिमान रहित है कहै कबीर सो दासा।।

दिए गए काव्यांश के आधार पर निम्नलिखित प्रश्नों के उत्तर दें।

1. प्रस्तुत पद्यांश के आधार पर ईश्वर का सच्चा भक्त वह है जो–
   A. ईश्वर की रात-दिन भक्ति करता है।
   B. गरीबों की सेवा करता है।
   C. तृष्णा व अभिमान से रहित है।
   D. इनमें से कोई नहीं
2. पद्यांश के आधार पर तीन गुण हैं–
   A. सात्विक, राजसी व तामसी
   B. लोभ, मोह, अहंकार
   C. काम, क्रोध, लोभ
   D. इनमें से कोई नहीं
3. सच्चे भक्त संसार में–
   A. पर्याप्त हैं।
   B. जंगलों में मिलते हैं।
   C. विरले पाए जाते हैं।
   D. एक मात्र कबीर थे।

4. 'कंचन' शब्द का अर्थ होगा–

A. कोयला B. हीरा

C. सोना D. काला

5. 'अभिमान' शब्द का विपरीतार्थक शब्द होगा–

A. सम्मान B. घमंड

C. विनम्रता D. दयालुता

काव्यांश-3

भा भादों दूभर अति भारी।
कैसे भरौं रैनि अँधियारी।।
मँदिर सून पिउ अनतै बसा।
सेज नागिनी फिरि-फिरि डसा।।
रहौं अकेलि गहे एक पारी।
नैन पसारि मरौं हिय फारी।।
चमक बीजु, घन गरजि तरासा।
बिरह काल होइ जीउ गरासा।।
बरसै मघा झकोरी झकोरी।
मोर दुइ नैन चुवै जस ओरी।।
धनि सखैं भरे भादौं माहाँ।
अबहुँ न आएन्हि सी चेन्हि नाहाँ।।
पुरबा लाग भूमि जल पूरी।
आक जवास भई तस झूरी।।
थल जल भरे अपूर सब, धरती गगन मिलि एक।
जनि जोबन अवगाह महँ, दे बूड़त पिउ टेक।।

दिए गए काव्यांश के आधार पर निम्नलिखित प्रश्नों के उत्तर दें।

1. पद्यांश द्वारा वर्णन किया गया है–

A. वर्षा ऋतु का

B. भादव महीने का

C. प्रकृति का

D. वियोगिनी के विरह वेदना का

2. पद्यांश के अनुसार वियोगिनी को प्रियतम की अनुपस्थिति में सेज कैसा लगता है?

A. काँटे के समान B. फूलों के समान

C. नागिन के समान D. इनमें से कोई नहीं

3. नायिका के आँखों से बहते आँसू की उपमा किससे दी गई है?

A. नदियों की धारा से

B. वर्षा की बूँदों से

C. मघा नक्षत्र में होने वाली वर्षा से

D. इनमें से कोई नहीं

4. 'घन' शब्द का अर्थ होगा–

A. बादल B. पानी

C. लोहा D. पत्थर

5. 'धरती' शब्द के पर्यायवाची हैं–

(*i*) तरनी (*ii*) अवनि

(*iii*) वसुन्धरा (*iv*) मेदिनी

A. (*i*), (*ii*) एवं (*iii*)

B. (*ii*), (*iii*) एवं (*iv*)

C. (*i*), (*iii*) एवं (*v*)

D. उपर्युक्त सभी

काव्यांश-4

अँखिया हरि-दरसन की भूखी।
कैसे रहैं रूप रसराची ये बतियाँ सुनि रूखी।।
अवधि गनत इक टक मग जोवत तव एती नहिं झूखी।
अब इन जोग-संदेस ऊधो अति अकुलानी दूखी।।
वारक वह मुख फेरि दिखाओ दुहि पय पिवत पतूखी।
सूर सिकत हरि नाव चलायो ये सरिता हैं सूखी।।

दिए गए काव्यांश के आधार पर निम्नलिखित प्रश्नों के उत्तर दें।

1. प्रस्तुत पद्यांश के आधार पर इसके रचयिता हैं–

A. तुलसीदास B. केशवदास

C. रसखान D. सूरदास

2. पद्यांश के अनुसार गोपियों की आँखें किसकी भूखी हैं?

A. प्रकृति दर्शन की B. कृष्ण के दर्शन की

C. देवताओं के दर्शन की D. इनमें से कोई नहीं

3. गोपियों की बातचीत किसके साथ हो रही है?

A. देवदूत के साथ

B. कृष्ण के साथ

C. कृष्ण सखा उद्धव के साथ

D. सूरदास के साथ

4. 'अवधि' शब्द का अर्थ होगा–

A. एक भाषा का नाम B. एक स्थान का नाम

C. समयान्तराल D. इनमें से कोई नहीं

5. 'दरसन' शब्द है–

A. तद्भव B. तत्सम

C. देशज D. विदेशज

काव्यांश-5

तपस्वी ! क्यों इतने हो क्लांत? वेदना का यह कैसा वेग?
आह ! तुम कितने अधिक हताश, बताओ यह कैसा उद्वेग!
हृदय में क्या है नहीं अधीर, लालसा जीवन की निश्शेष !
कर रहा वंचित कहीं न त्याग तुम्हें, मन में धर सुंदर वेश?
दुःख के डर से तुम अज्ञात जटिलताओं का कर अनुमान;
काम से झिझक रहे हो आज, भविष्यत् से बनकर अनजान।
कर रही लीलायम आनंद, महाचिति सजग हुई सी व्यक्त;
विश्व का उन्मीलन अभिराम इसी में सब होते अनुरक्त !

दिए गए काव्यांश के आधार पर निम्नलिखित प्रश्नों के उत्तर दें।

1. पद्यांश में किस रस की अभिव्यक्ति है?

A. वीर रस B. श्रृंगार रस

C. करुण रस D. वीभत्स रस

2. काव्यांश के अनुसार कौन नायक को जीवन से विमुख कर रहा है?
   A. हताशा B. वेदना
   C. लालसा D. त्याग
3. नायक काम (जीवन) की उपेक्षा क्यों कर रहा है?
   A. दुःख व जटिलताओं के भय से
   B. पीड़ा व वेदना के भय से
   C. निराशा और अधीरता के कारण
   D. मौत के भय से
4. 'अभिराम' शब्द का अर्थ होगा–
   A. राम का छोटा भाई B. सुन्दर
   C. अनन्त D. इनमें से कोई नहीं
5. 'निश्शेष' कौन-सी संधि होगी?
   A. दीर्घ स्वर संधि B. गुण स्वर संधि
   C. व्यंजन संधि D. विसर्ग संधि

काव्यांश-6

फिर मधुर दृष्टि से प्रिय कपि को खींचते हुये
बोले प्रियतर स्वर से अन्तर सींचते हुए–
"चाहिए हमें एक सौ आठ, कपि, इन्दीवर,
कम-से-कम, अधिक और हों, अधिक और सुंदर,
जाओ देवीदह, उषःकाल होते सत्वर,
तोड़ो, लाओं वे कमल, लौटकर लड़ो समर।"
अवगत हो जाम्बवान से पथ, दूरत्व, स्थान,
प्रभु - पद - रज सिर धर चले हर्ष भर हनुमान।
राघव ने विदा किया सबको जानकर समय,
सब चले सदय राम की सोचते हुए विजय !

दिए गए काव्यांश के आधार पर निम्नलिखित प्रश्नों के उत्तर दें।

1. काव्यांश में उल्लिखित पात्र हैं–
   A. राम कथा के B. कामायनी के
   C. महाभारत के D. इनमें से कोई नहीं
2. राम हनुमान को क्या लाने को कहते हैं?
   A. एक सौ आठ कपि
   B. एक सौ आठ नील कमल
   C. एक सौ आठ अनुचर
   D. इनमें से कोई नहीं
3. राम हनुमान को जाम्बवान से क्या जानने की आज्ञा देते हैं?
   A. स्थान B. रास्ता
   C. दूरी D. ये सभी
4. 'रज' शब्द का अर्थ है–
   A. पानी B. धूल
   C. गगन D. इनमें से कोई नहीं
5. 'राघव' शब्द के पर्यायवाची हैं–
   (i) राम *(ii)* वासुदेव
   (iii) मुरारी *(iv)* रघुनाथ
   A. *(i)* एवं *(ii)* B. *(ii)* एवं *(iii)*
   C. *(iii)* एवं *(iv)* D. *(i)* एवं *(iv)*

काव्यांश-7

चौ.–कहेउँ परम पुनीत इतिहासा।
सुनत श्रवन छूटहिं भव पासा।।
प्रनत कल्पतरु करुना पुंजा।
उपजई प्रीति राम पद कंजा।।
मन क्रम बचन जनित अघ जाई।
सुनहिं जे कथा श्रवन मन लाई।।
तीर्थाटन साधन समुदाई।
जोग बिराग ग्यान निपुनाई।।
कर्म धर्म द्विज गुर सेवकाई।
बिद्या बिनय बिबेक बड़ाई।।
जहँ लगि साधन बेद बखानी।
सब कर फल हरिभगति भवानी।।
सो रघुनाथ भगति श्रुति गाई।
राम कृपाँ काहूँ एक पाई।।
दो.–मुनि दुर्लभ हरि भगति नर पावहिं बिनहिं प्रयास।
जे यह कथा निरंतर सुनहिं मानि बिस्वास।।

दिए गए काव्यांश के आधार पर निम्नलिखित प्रश्नों के उत्तर दें।

1. काव्यांश के अनुसार व्यक्ति भव बंधन से कैसे मुक्त होता है?
   A. पावन राम कथा सुनकर
   B. योग, वैराग्य एवं ज्ञान द्वारा
   C. दरिद्रनारायण की सेवा कर
   D. इनमें से कोई नहीं
2. काव्यांश द्वारा बतायी गयी है–
   A. शिव भक्ति की महिमा
   B. योग वैराग्य आदि का महत्व
   C. राम भक्ति की महिमा
   D. उपरोक्त सभी
3. 'द्विज' शब्द में कौन-सा समास है?
   A. तत्पुरुष B. कर्मधारय
   C. अव्ययीभाव D. बहुब्रीही
4. 'पुनीत' शब्द का अर्थ होता है–
   A. पुराना B. पहला
   C. पवित्र D. इनमें से कोई नहीं
5. 'रघुनाथ' में शब्द भेद है–
   A. रूढ़ि B. यौगिक
   C. योगरूढ़ D. भाववाचक संज्ञा

काव्यांश-8

"मैया कबहि बढैगी चोटी।
किती बार मोहिं दूध पिवत भई, यह अजहूँ है छोटी।।
तू जो कहति बल की बैनी ज्यों, हवै हैं लांबी मोटी।
कांची दूध पिवावत पचि-पचि, देत न माखन रोटी।।"

दिए गए काव्यांश के आधार पर निम्नलिखित प्रश्नों के उत्तर दें।

1. बालक अपनी माँ से किसके बढ़ने के बारे में पूछ रहा है?
A. पहाड़ की चोटी B. कदम्ब के पेड़ की चोटी
C. अपने बालों की चोटी D. माँ के बालों की चोटी

2. बालक माँ से क्या पाने की इच्छा रखता है?
A. दूध-मिस्त्री B. माखन-रोटी
C. दुलार D. इनमें से कोई नहीं

3. 'पचि-पचि' शब्द का अर्थ होगा–
A. बार-बार B. पचा-पचा कर
C. पचने के बाद D. इनमें से कोई नहीं

4. 'दूध' शब्द का शब्द भेद है–
A. तत्सम B. तद्भव
C. देशज D. विदेशज

5. बनावट के आधार पर 'माखन' शब्द है–
A. रूढ़ि B. यौगिक
C. योगरूढ़ D. इनमें से कोई नहीं

काव्यांश-9

प्रकृति जोई जाके अंग परी।
स्वान-पूँछ कोटिक जा लागै सुधि न काहू करी।
जैसे काग मच्छ नहिं छांड़ै जनमत जोन धरी।
धोये रंग जात कहु कैसे ज्यों कारी कमरी?
ज्यों अहि उसत उदर नहिं पूरत ऐसी धरनी धरी।
सूर होउ सो होउ सोच नहिं तैसे है एउ री।।

दिए गए काव्यांश के आधार पर निम्नलिखित प्रश्नों के उत्तर दें।

1. काव्यांश के अनुसार व्यक्ति का स्वभाव–
A. बदला जा सकता है
B. अपरिवर्तनीय है
C. अन्य व्यक्ति से प्रभावित होता है
D. इनमें से कोई नहीं

2. कवि ने अपने कथन की पुष्टि के लिए कौन-कौन से उदाहरण दिए हैं?
(*i*) कुत्ता (*ii*) कौआ
(*iii*) बिल्ली (*iv*) साँप
(*v*) कम्बल
A. (*i*), (*ii*) एवं (*iii*) B. (*ii*), (*iii*) एवं (*iv*)
C. (*iii*), (*iv*) एवं (*v*) D. (*i*), (*ii*), (*iv*) एवं (*v*)

3. कम्बल का स्वभाव है कि–
A. वह काला होता है
B. वह गर्म होता है
C. उसका कालापन नहीं जाता
D. इनमें से कोई नहीं

4. 'स्वान' शब्द का अर्थ होता है–
A. मोर B. हंस
C. बगुला D. कुत्ता

5. 'अहि' शब्द का पर्यायवाची शब्द है–
(*i*) चक्षुश्रवा (*ii*) सर्प
(*iii*) भुजा (*iv*) विषधर
A. (*i*), (*ii*) एवं (*iv*) B. (*i*), (*ii*) एवं (*iii*)
C. (*i*), (*iii*) एवं (*v*) D. उपरोक्त सभी

काव्यांश-10

हिम गिरी के उत्तुंग शिखर पर,
बैठ शिला की शीतल छाँह।
एक पुरूष भीगे नयनों से
देख रहा था प्रलय प्रवाह।।

ऊपर जल था नीचे हिम था,
एक तरल था एक सघन।
एक तत्व की ही प्रधानता,
कहो उसे जड़ या चेतन।।

दिए गए काव्यांश के आधार पर निम्नलिखित प्रश्नों के उत्तर दें।

1. काव्यांश के अनुसार हिमगिरि के ऊँचे शिखर पर कौन बैठा था?
A. शीला नामक युवती B. एक पुरुष
C. एक देवदूत D. इनमें से कोई नहीं

2. 'तरल' शब्द का विपरीतार्थक शब्द होगा–
A. द्रव B. तैरता हुआ
C. सघन D. गर्म

3. व्यक्ति की आँखें थी–
A. भेंगी B. झुकी हुई
C. सुन्दर D. भींगी

4. 'हिमगिरि' के पर्यायवाची शब्द हैं–
(*i*) हिमालय (*ii*) हिमगह्वर
(*iii*) नगाधिराज (*iv*) हिमाद्रि
A. (*i*), (*ii*) एवं (*iii*) B. (*ii*), (*iii*) एवं (*iv*)
C. (*i*), (*iii*) एवं (*iv*) D. (*i*), (*ii*) एवं (*iv*)

5. 'चेतन' का विपरीतार्थक शब्द होगा–
A. जड़ B. तना
C. सचेत D. बेहोश

काव्यांश-11

"रूद्ध कोष है क्षुब्ध तोष,
अंगना-अंग से लिपटे भी
आतंक-अंक पर काँप रहे हैं
धनी वज्र-गर्जन से बादल!
त्रस्त नयन-मुख ढाँप रहे हैं।
जीर्ण बाहु, है शीर्ण शरीर
तुझे बुलाता कृषक अधीर,
ऐ विप्लव के वीर!
चूस लिया है उसका सार,
हाड़ मात्र ही हैं आधार,
ऐ जीवन के पारावार।"

दिए गए काव्यांश के आधार पर निम्नलिखित प्रश्नों के उत्तर दें।

1. काव्यांश के अनुसार अधीर कृषक किसे बुला रहा है?
A. वीर पुरुष को B. अपने बेटे को
C. बादल को D. इनमें से कोई नहीं

2. कृषक का क्या आधार मात्र बचा है?
A. केवल खेत B. केवल हड्डी
C. केवल घर D. केवल शरीर

3. शरीर शब्द का पर्यायवाची है–
A. देह B. गात
C. तन D. ये सभी

4. 'विप्लव' का अर्थ है–
A. महाविनाश B. परिवर्तन
C. सम्पन्नता D. इनमें से कोई नहीं

5. 'वीर' शब्द का विपरीतार्थक होगा–
A. कायर B. डरपोक
C. आलसी D. साहसी

काव्यांश-12

अति खल की संगति करने से,
जग में मान नहीं रहता है।
लोहे के संग में पड़ने से,
घन की मार अनल सहता है।।
सबसे नीतिशास्त्र कहता है,
दुष्ट-संग दुख का दाता है।
जिस पय में पानी रहता है,
वही खूब औंटा जाता है।।

दिए गए काव्यांश के आधार पर निम्नलिखित प्रश्नों के उत्तर दें।

1. 'पय' शब्द का अर्थ है–
A. पानी B. बर्तन
C. दूध D. इनमें से कोई नहीं

2. खल की संगति करने से–
A. मार सहना पड़ता है।
B. सम्मान नहीं मिलता।
C. प्रताड़ित किया जाता है।
D. खूब लाभ मिलता है।

3. उपरोक्त काव्यांश का केन्द्रीय भाव है–
A. अच्छी संगति के परिणाम
B. बुरी संगति के परिणाम
C. बुरी संगति से लाभ
D. इनमें से कोई नहीं

4. 'अनल' शब्द के पर्यायवाची हैं–
(*i*) पावक (*ii*) पय
(*iii*) अग्नि (*iv*) हुताशन
A. (*i*), (*ii*) एवं (*iii*) B. (*ii*), (*iii*) एवं (*iv*)
C. (*i*), (*iii*) एवं (*iv*) D. (*i*), (*ii*) एवं (*iv*)

5. किस दूध को खूब खौलाया जाता है?
A. जिसे पहले नहीं खौलाया गया हो
B. जिस दूध के फटने की आशंका हो
C. जिस दूध से दही बनाना हो
D. जिसमें पानी मिला हो

काव्यांश-13

गन्ध-विहिन फूल हैं जैसे चन्द्र चन्द्रिका-हीन।
यों ही फीका है मनुष्य का जीवन प्रेम-विहीन।।
प्रेम स्वर्ग है, स्वर्ग प्रेम है, प्रेम अशंक अशोक।
ईश्वर का प्रतिबिम्ब प्रेम है, प्रेम हृदय-आलोक।।

दिए गए काव्यांश के आधार पर निम्नलिखित प्रश्नों के उत्तर दें।

1. काव्यांश का केन्द्रीय भाव है?
A. मनुष्य का जीवन B. स्वर्ग में प्रेम
C. ईश्वर का प्रेम D. प्रेम का महत्त्व

2. प्रेम विहीन जीवन की उपमा किससे दी गई है?
(*i*) गंधहीन फूल से (*ii*) चाँदनी रहित चन्द्रमा से
(*iii*) मनुष्य के जीवन से
A. (*i*) एवं (*ii*) B. (*ii*) एवं (*iii*)
C. (*i*) एवं (*iii*) D. (*i*), (*ii*) एवं (*iii*)

3. 'स्वर्ग' का विपरीतार्थक शब्द होगा–
A. धरती B. पाताल
C. नरक D. आकाश

4. काव्यांश के अनुसार प्रेम है–
A. स्वर्ग B. ईश्वरीय प्रतिबिम्ब
C. हृदय की रोशनी D. ये सभी

5. 'प्रतिबिम्ब' शब्द में प्रयुक्त उपसर्ग है–
A. प्र B. बिम्ब
C. प्रति D. प्रतिबि

काव्यांश-14

भड़क भुला दो भूतकाल की,
सजिये वर्तमान के साज।
फैसन फेर इंडिया भर के,
गोरे गॉड बनो ब्रजराज।।
गौर वर्ण वृषभानुसुता का,
काले-काले तन पर तोप।
नाथ उतारो मोर मुकुट को,
सिर पै सजो साहिबी टोप।।
पौडर चंदन पोंछ लपेटो,
आनन की श्री ज्योति जगाय।
अंजन अंखियों में मत आंजो,
आला ऐनक लेहु लगाय।।
रवधर कानों में लटका लो,
कुंडल काढ़ मेकराफून।

तज पीताम्बर कम्बल काला,
डालो कोट और पतलून।।

दिए गए काव्यांश के आधार पर निम्नलिखित प्रश्नों के उत्तर दें।

1. दिया गया पद्यांश है–
   A. रीति-कालीन काव्यांश B. छायावाद युगीन काव्यांश
   C. हास्य-व्यंग्य रचना D. इनमें से कोई नहीं
2. पद्यांश में ब्रजराज को क्या बनने की सलाह दी गई है?
   A. अभिनेता B. गोरा गॉड
   C. अंग्रेजी वक्ता D. इनमें से कोई नहीं
3. कविता द्वारा मजाक उड़ाया गया है–
   A. विदेशी संस्कृति का
   B. अपनी संस्कृति
   C. पुराने विचारों का
   D. विदेशियों की नकल करने वालों का
4. 'वृषभानुसुता' में समास है–
   A. कर्मधारय B. द्विगु
   C. बहुव्रीहि D. अव्ययीभाव
5. 'पीताम्बर' का संधि-विच्छेद है।
   A. पीत + अम्बर B. पीता + म्बर
   C. पीला + अम्बर D. पी + ताम्बर

काव्यांश-15

सच्चा प्रेम वही है जिसकी,
तृप्ति आत्म-बलि पर हो निर्भर।
त्याग बिना निष्प्राण प्रेम है,
करो प्रेम पर प्राण निछावर।।
देश प्रेम वह पुण्य-क्षेत्र है,
अमल असीम त्याग से विलसित।
आत्मा के विकास से जिसमें,
मनुष्यता होती है विकसित।।

दिए गए काव्यांश के आधार पर निम्नलिखित प्रश्नों के उत्तर दें।

1. पद्यांश के अनुसार सच्चा प्रेम निर्भर है–
   A. आत्मोत्सर्ग पर B. सच्चे प्रेमी-प्रेमिका पर
   C. अच्छे पड़ोसियों पर D. विकसित समाज पर
2. त्याग के बिना प्रेम–
   A. बेकार है B. प्राण-रहित है
   C. मजाक है D. इनमें से कोई नहीं
3. मनुष्यता का विकास होता है–
   A. प्रेम से B. शिक्षा से
   C. आत्मा के विकास से D. शौर्य से
4. पद्यांश के अनुसार प्रेम का मूल तत्व है–
   A. सच्चाई B. उपहार
   C. आत्मा D. त्याग
5. 'निष्प्राण' में संधि भेद होगा–
   A. व्यंजन संधि
   B. स्वर संधि
   C. स्वर एवं व्यंजन संधि दोनों
   D. विसर्ग संधि

काव्यांश-16

क्या? देख न सकती जंजीरों का गहना?
हथकड़ियां क्यों? यह ब्रिटिश राज्य का गहना,
कोल्हू का चर्रक चूं? जीवन की तान,
गिट्टी पर लिक्खे अंगुलियों ने गान?
हूं मोट खींचता लगा पेट पर जूआ,
खाली करता हूं ब्रिटिश अकड़ का कूआं।

दिए गए काव्यांश के आधार पर निम्नलिखित प्रश्नों के उत्तर दें।

1. दिए गए काव्यांश में ब्रिटिश राज्य का गहना कहा गया है–
   A. कोल्हू को B. मोट को
   C. हथकड़ियों को D. इनमें से कोई नहीं
2. कोल्हू की आवाज को कहा गया है–
   A. जीवन का सत्य B. जीवन की तान
   C. चर्रक चूं D. इनमें से कोई नहीं
3. उपरोक्त काव्यांश को पढ़ने पर मानस पटल पर किसका चित्र उभरता है?
   A. भिखारी का B. कैदी का
   C. अंग्रजों का D. हथकड़ियों का
4. 'गहना' का पर्यायवाची शब्द है–
   A. आभूषण B. ग्रहण
   C. सघन D. चमकना
5. 'अकड़' शब्द का अर्थ होगा–
   A. अहंकार B. अत्याचार
   C. अंधविश्वास D. हठ

काव्यांश-17

एक बार बस और नाच तू श्यामा!
सामान सभी तैयार,
कितने ही असुर, चाहिए कितने तुझको हार?
कर मेखला मुंड-मालाओं से बन-बन अभिरामा–
एक बार बस और नाच तू श्यामा!
भैरवी मेरी तेरी झंझा
तभी बजेगी मृत्यु लड़ाएगी जब तुझसे पंजा;
लेगी खड्ग और तू खप्पर,
उसमें रुधिर भरूंगा माँ
मैं अपनी अंजलि भर-भर...

दिए गए काव्यांश के आधार पर निम्नलिखित प्रश्नों के उत्तर दें।

1. 'श्यामा' शब्द का अर्थ होगा–
   A. मेघ B. काली
   C. धरती D. इनमें से कोई नहीं

2. 'रुधिर' के पर्यायवाची शब्द हैं–
(i) दूध (ii) शोणित
(iii) रक्त (iv) अम्बुधि
A. (ii) एवं (iii) B. (ii) एवं (iv)
C. (iii) एवं (iv) D. (i) एवं (iv)

3. काव्यांश के आधार पर 'हार' शब्द का अर्थ होगा–
A. पराजय B. भय
C. माला D. इनमें से कोई नहीं

4. कवि ने किससे नाचने का आह्वान किया है?
A. नर्तकी से B. असुरों से
C. काली से D. मृत्यु से

5. कवि ने श्यामा को कैसे सुन्दर बनने को कहा है?
A. आभूषणों से B. अस्त्र-शस्त्रों से
C. पुष्पमाला से D. मुंडमाला से

काव्यांश-18

घुन खाये शहतीरों पर की बारहखड़ी विधाता बांचे,
फटी भीत है, छत चूती है, आले पर बिस्तुइया नाचे,
बरसा कर बेबस बच्चों पर मिनट-मिनट में पाँच तमाचे,
इसी तरह से दुखरन मास्टर गढ़ता है आदम के साँचे।

दिए गए काव्यांश के आधार पर निम्नलिखित प्रश्नों के उत्तर दें।

1. काव्यांश द्वारा किस व्यवस्था पर व्यंग्य किया गया है?
A. शिक्षा व्यवस्था पर B. शासन व्यवस्था पर
C. अर्थव्यवस्था पर D. इनमें से कोई नहीं

2. काव्यांश के अनुसार आदम को किस प्रकार ढाला जा रहा है?
A. अच्छी शिक्षा देकर B. दोषपूर्ण शिक्षा पद्धति द्वारा
C. उपदेश देकर D. इनमें से कोई नहीं

3. काव्यांश द्वारा विद्यालय की किस कमी को दिखाया गया है?
A. संसाधनों की कमी B. दोषपूर्ण पद्धति
C. अयोग्य शिक्षक D. उपरोक्त सभी

4. 'शहतीर' का अर्थ होता है?
A. लकड़ी का लम्बा लट्ठा जो नदी के किनारे पड़ा हो।
B. लकड़ी का लम्बा लट्ठा जो नदी में किनारे-किनारे बह रहा हो।
C. लकड़ी का लम्बा लट्ठा जिसका उपयोग गृह-निर्माण में किया जाता है।
D. इनमें से कोई नहीं

5. 'बिस्तुइया' का अर्थ होता है–
A. साँप B. छिपकली
C. मकड़ी D. चींटी

काव्यांश-19

चेहरे थे असंख्य
आँखें थीं
दर्द सभी में था
जीवन का दंश सभी ने जाना था
पर दो
केवल दो
मेरे मन में कौंध गयीं
मैं नहीं जानता किसी वे आँखें थीं
नहीं समझता फिर उनको देखूँगा
परिचय मन ही मन चाहा तो उद्यम कोई नहीं किया
किन्तु उसी को कौंध
मुझे फिर फिर दिखलाती है।
× × ×
वही परिचित दो आँखें ही
चिर माध्यम हैं
सब आँखों से सब दर्दों से
मेरे चिर परिचय का।

दिए गए काव्यांश के आधार पर निम्नलिखित प्रश्नों के उत्तर दें।

1. काव्यांश के अनुसार दर्द किसमें था?
(i) चेहरे में (ii) असंख्य आँखों में
(iii) मन में (iv) जीवन में
A. (i) एवं (ii) B. (ii) एवं (iii)
C. (iii) एवं (iv) D. (ii) एवं (iv)

2. 'आँख' का पर्यायवाची शब्द **नहीं** है–
A. चक्षु B. श्रवण
C. नयन D. लोचन

3. 'चिर' शब्द का अर्थ है–
A. कपड़ा B. चीरना
C. एक पेड़ D. पुराना

4. कवि के अनुसार दर्दों से परिचय का माध्यम है–
A. हृदय B. जीवन
C. आँखें D. ये सभी

5. काव्यांश में वर्णित वे आँखें किसकी थी?
A. कवि की
B. पाठक की
C. कवि नहीं जानता वह किसकी आँखे थी
D. इनमें से कोई नहीं

काव्यांश-20

मुझे भ्रम होता है कि प्रत्येक पत्थर में
चमकता हीरा है
हर एक छाती में आत्मा अधीरा है
प्रत्येक सुस्मित में विमल सदानीरा है
मुझे भ्रम होता है कि प्रत्येक वाणी में
महाकाव्य-पीड़ा है
पल भर में सबसे गुजरना चाहता हूँ
इस तरह खुद को दिये फिरता हूँ
अजीब है जिन्दगी :

दिए गए काव्यांश के आधार पर निम्नलिखित प्रश्नों के उत्तर दें।

1. कवि को क्या भ्रम होता है?
   A. प्रत्येक पत्थर के हीरा होने का
   B. प्रत्येक पत्थर में हीरा होने का
   C. प्रत्येक हीरे में पत्थर होने का
   D. इनमें से कोई नहीं
2. कवि के अनुसार प्रत्येक वाणी में–
   A. महाकाव्य की शक्ति है
   B. महाकाव्य की संभावना है
   C. महाकाव्य की पीड़ा है
   D. इनमें से कोई नहीं
3. कवि को हर छाती में–
   A. रोग होने की आशंका है
   B. अधीर आत्मा होने का भ्रम है
   C. विद्रोह सुलगने का डर है
   D. इनमें से कोई नहीं
4. 'पत्थर' का पर्यायवाची ***नहीं*** है–
   A. पाषाण B. उपल
   C. प्रस्तर D. इनमें से कोई नहीं
5. 'आत्मा' एक शब्द है–
   A. स्त्रीलिंग B. पुल्लिंग
   C. उभयलिंग D. नपुंसकलिंग

काव्यांश-21

"अन्दर बाहर धींगामुश्ती। परमारथ में भारी सुस्ती।
स्वारथ में तो बेहद चुस्ती।
एक-दूसरे की जड़ काटें तकरीरों से अग-जग पाटें।
अँग्रेजी की धकापेल है।
हिन्दी-उर्दू खतम खेल है। नौजवान के लिए जेल है।
सेठों से ही दिली मेल है..."

दिए गए काव्यांश के आधार पर निम्नलिखित प्रश्नों के उत्तर दें।

1. प्रस्तुत काव्यांश एक–
   A. व्यंग्य रचना है B. यथार्थ रचना है
   C. शोक गीत है D. इनमें से कोई नहीं
2. काव्यांश के अनुसार हिन्दी-उर्दू की क्या दशा है?
   A. विकासशील B. पतनोन्मुख
   C. स्थिर D. उन्नत
3. दी गई पंक्तियाँ आज के किस चीज का सटीक उल्लेख करती हैं?
   A. राजनीति B. शिक्षा
   C. धर्म D. समाज
4. 'तकरीर' शब्द का अर्थ है–
   A. भाषण B. विवाद
   C. लड़ाई D. इनमें से कोई नहीं
5. 'एक-दूसरे की जड़ काटना' मुहावरे का अर्थ है :
   A. परस्पर निन्दा करना B. परस्पर नुकसान करना
   C. परस्पर विचार करना D. इनमें से कोई नहीं

काव्यांश-22

"मुझे कल्पवृक्ष नहीं चाहिए
नहीं चाहिए कामधेनु
इस पृथ्वी पर जिन्दा रहने के लिए
मुझे इतना ही अन्न चाहिए
जितना चींटी अपनी चोंच में ले कर चलती है
उतनी ही जमीन चाहिए कि पसर सके लौकी की लतर
और उतनी की कपास कि ढक जाये लाज।"

दिए गए काव्यांश के आधार पर निम्नलिखित प्रश्नों के उत्तर दें।

1. काव्यांश के अनुसार कवि को क्या नहीं चाहिए?
   A. कल्पवृक्ष B. अन्न
   C. कपास D. जमीन
2. कवि को क्या-क्या चाहिए?
   (*i*) कल्पवृक्ष (*ii*) जमीन
   (*iii*) अन्न (*iv*) कपास
   (*v*) कामधेनु
   A. (*i*), (*ii*) एवं (*iii*) B. (*i*), (*ii*) एवं (*v*)
   C. (*ii*), (*iii*) एवं (*iv*) D. (*iii*), (*iv*) एवं (*v*)
3. कवि को कपास की जरूरत है–
   A. कपड़ा मिल के लिए B. लाज ढकने के लिए
   C. चरखा चलाने के लिए D. इनमें से कोई नहीं
4. 'चींटी' का पर्यायवाची शब्द है–
   A. तंतुवाय B. बिस्तुइया
   C. पिपीलिका D. इनमें से कोई नहीं
5. दिए गए काव्यांश का सबसे उपयुक्त शीर्षक हो सकता है–
   A. अभिलाषा B. जरूरत
   C. कटौती D. जीने का सामान

काव्यांश-23

ओ भिखमंगे, अरे पराजित, ओ मजलूम, अरे चिरदोहित,
तू अखंड भंडार शक्ति का, जाग अरे निद्रा-सम्मोहित!
प्राणों को तड़पाने वाली हुंकारों से जल-थल भर दे,
अंगारों के अंबारों में अपना ज्वलित पलीता धर दे।

दिए गए काव्यांश के आधार पर निम्नलिखित प्रश्नों के उत्तर दें।

1. दिए काव्यांश में किसको जगाने का प्रयास किया गया है?
   A. भिखमंगों को B. मज़लूमों को
   C. आम जनता को D. इनमें से कोई नहीं
2. अखंड शक्ति का भंडार किसके पास है?
   A. नेताओं के B. अधिकारियों के
   C. भिखमंगों के D. आम जनता के

3. कवि ने आम लोगों के लिए किन-किन शब्दों का प्रयोग किया है?

(*i*) पराजित (*ii*) अपमानित
(*iii*) मर्यादित (*iv*) भिखमंगे
(*v*) निद्रा-सम्मोहित

A. (*i*), (*iv*), (*v*) B. (*ii*), (*iii*), (*v*)
C. (*iii*), (*iv*) एवं (*v*) D. उपरोक्त सभी

4. 'मज़लूम' शब्द है–

A. तत्सम B. फारसी
C. अरबी D. तद्भव

5. 'जल' शब्द का पर्यायवाची है–

(*i*) नीड़ (*ii*) अम्बु
(*iii*) वारि (*iv*) सलिल

A. (*i*), (*ii*) एवं (*iii*) B. (*ii*), (*iii*) एवं (*iv*)
C. (*i*), (*iii*) एवं (*iv*) D. उपरोक्त सभी

काव्यांश-24

करेंगे क्या ले कर अपवर्ग,
हमारा भारत ही सुख-स्वर्ग।
नहीं है किसी लक्ष्य पर ध्यान,
चाहिए केवल स्वत्व समान।।
इसे तज कर क्या तरु निर्मूल,
करेंगे ले कर किंशुक फूल।
प्रकृत पुरुषों का जीवन-मूल,
चाहिए केवल घर का रूल।।

दिए गए काव्यांश के आधार पर निम्नलिखित प्रश्नों के उत्तर दें।

1. काव्यांश के आधार पर कवि को क्या चाहिए?

A. स्वर्ग-सुख B. किंशुकी फूल
C. स्वराज्य D. इनमें से कोई नहीं

2. काव्यांश का केन्द्रीय भाव है–

A. स्वहित B. देश प्रेम
C. सेवा D. इनमें से कोई नहीं

3. कवि के अनुसार प्रकृत पुरुषों का जीवन मूल क्या है?

A. स्वाभिमान B. उनका लक्ष्य
C. स्वर्ग-सुख की प्राप्ति D. स्वराज्य

4. "अपवर्ग" शब्द का अर्थ है–

A. मोक्ष B. परोपकार
C. देश प्रेम D. इनमें से कोई नहीं

5. 'निर्मूल' का संधि-विच्छेद होगा :

A. नीः + मूल B. निः + मुल
C. निः + मूल D. निर्मू + ल

काव्यांश-25

"मन करता है
मैं उस अगस्त्य सा पी डालू सारे समुद्र को अंजलि से
उस अतल वितल में तब मुझको
मुर्दा भगवान दिखाई दे
उस महामृतक को ले आऊँ फिर इस तट पर
अन्त्येष्टि करूँ, लकड़ी तो बेहद मंहगी है
इस बालू में दफना दूँ
नंगा करके"

दिए गए काव्यांश के आधार पर निम्नलिखित प्रश्नों के उत्तर दें।

1. पद्यांश के अनुसार कवि की इच्छा है कि–

A. वह समुद्र की पी जाय
B. भगवान का दर्शन करे
C. संसार में उथल-पुथल मचा दे
D. इनमें से कोई नहीं

2. कवि महामृतक को बालू में क्यों दफनाना चाहता है?

A. क्योंकि कवि मृतक से नाराज है
B. क्योंकि लकड़ी समुद्र के किनारे उपलब्ध नहीं है
C. क्योंकि लकड़ी महंगी है
D. इनमें से कोई नहीं

3. पद्यांश का मूलभाव किस पीड़ा की ओर इंगित करता है?

A. परतंत्रता B. सामाजिक विषमता
C. अभाव D. इनमें से कोई नहीं

4. इनमें से 'बालू' का पर्यायवाची शब्द है–

A. वीचि B. सिकता
C. कण D. इनमें से कोई नहीं

5. 'अन्त्येष्टि' का अर्थ है–

A. अंत्य परीक्षण B. अंतिम इच्छा
C. अंतिम संस्कार D. इनमें से कोई नहीं

काव्यांश-26

"अनोखी हवा हूँ बड़ी बावली हूँ
बड़ी मस्तमौला नहीं कुछ फिकर है
बड़ी ही निडर हूँ जिधर चाहती हूँ
उधर घूमती हूँ मुसाफिर अजब हूँ
न घर बार मेरा न उद्देश्य मेरा
न इच्छा किसी की न आशा किसी की
न प्रेमी न दुश्मन
जिधर चाहती हूँ उधर घूमती हूँ
हवा हूँ हवा मैं बसंती हवा हूँ"

दिए गए काव्यांश के आधार पर निम्नलिखित प्रश्नों के उत्तर दें।

1. पद्यांश के अनुसार बसंती हवा कहाँ घूमती है?

A. खेतों में B. बागों में
C. शहरों में D. जहां उसकी इच्छा हो

2. बसंती हवा की कौन-कौन सी विशेषताएँ हैं?

A. बावला B. मस्तमौला
C. निडर D. ये सभी

3. 'प्रेमी' शब्द का विपरीतार्थक शब्द होगा–

A. आशिक B. दोस्त
C. दुश्मन D. इनमें से कोई नहीं

4. 'आशा' शब्द का पर्यायवाची है?
A. इच्छा B. अभिलाषा
C. चाह D. उम्मीद

5. पद्यांश का केन्द्रीय भाव है?
A. मुक्ति की कामना B. चरित्र चित्रण
C. हास-परिहास D. इनमें से कोई नहीं

काव्यांश-27

"एक आदमी रोटी बेलता है
एक आदमी रोटी खाता है
एक तीसरा आदमी भी है
जो न रोटी बेलता है
न रोटी खाता है
वह सिर्फ रोटी से खेलता है
मैं पूछता हूँ यह तीसरा आदमी कौन है
मेरे देश की संसद मौन है।

दिए गए काव्यांश के आधार पर निम्नलिखित प्रश्नों के उत्तर दें।

1. पद्यांश के भावार्थ के अनुसार रोटी बेलने वाला कौन हो सकता है?
A. व्यवसायी B. रसोइया
C. मजूदर-किसान D. इनमें से कोई नहीं

2. पद्यांश के भावार्थ के अनुसार रोटी खाने वाला कौन है?
A. होटल का ग्राहक B. शोषक-वर्ग
C. आम आदमी D. इनमें से कोई नहीं

3. रोटी से खेलने वाला कौन हो सकता है?
A. शरारती बच्चे B. रसोइया
C. स्वार्थी नेता D. ये सभी

4. देश की संसद किस मुद्दे पर मौन है?
A. मजदूर-किसान के हितों को लेकर
B. शोषक वर्ग पर अंकुश लगाने को लेकर
C. रोटी से खेलने वालों को रोकने को लेकर
D. तीसरे आदमी के पहचान को लेकर

5. पद्यांश का केन्द्रीय भाव है–
A. सामाजिक कुव्यवस्था पर चोट
B. रोटी के महत्त्व पर प्रकाश
C. संसदीय व्यवस्था का वर्णन
D. इनमें से कोई नहीं

काव्यांश-28

चौ.–रहेउ एक दिन अवधि अधारा ।
समुझत मन दुख भयउ अपारा।।
कारन कवन नाथ नहिं आयउ ।
जानि कुटिल किधौं मोहि बिसरायउ।।
अहह धन्य लछिमन बड़भागी ।
राम पदारबिंदु अनुरागी।।
कपटी कुटिल मोहि प्रभु चीन्हा ।
ताते नाथ संग नहिं लीन्हा।।
जौं करनी समुझै प्रभु मोरी ।
नहिं निस्तार कलप सत कोरी।।
जन अवगुन प्रभु मान न काऊ ।
दीनबंधु अति मृदुल सुभाऊ।।
मोरे जियँ भरोस दृढ़ सोई ।
मिलिहहिं राम सगुन सुभ होई।।
बीतें अवधि रहहिं जौं प्राना ।
अधम कवन जग मोहि समाना।।

दिए गए काव्यांश के आधार पर निम्नलिखित प्रश्नों के उत्तर दें।

1. पद्यांश के भावार्थ के अनुसार इसका उपयुक्त शीर्षक होगा–
A. भरत का अनुताप B. राम वनगमन
C. लक्ष्मण का सौभाग्य D. इनमें से कोई नहीं

2. भरत ने लक्ष्मण को भाग्यवान क्यों माना है?
A. वन भ्रमण का अवसर मिलने के कारण
B. बड़े भाई राम की सेवा का अवसर पाने के कारण
C. लक्ष्मण की प्रशंसा करने के लिए
D. इनमें से कोई नहीं

3. भरत ने स्वयं को क्या-क्या कहा है?
(*i*) कपटी (*ii*) भाग्यवान
(*iii*) अपराधी (*iv*) कुटिल
A. (*i*) एवं (*ii*) B. (*ii*) एवं (*iii*)
C. (*iii*) एवं (*iv*) D. (*i*) एवं (*iv*)

4. भरत ने राम के क्या-क्या गुण बताये हैं?
(*i*) दीनबन्धु (*ii*) मृदुल स्वभाव वाला
(*iii*) अधम
A. (*i*) एवं (*ii*) B. (*ii*) एवं (*iii*)
C. (*i*) एवं (*iii*) D. ये सभी

5. 'दीनबन्धु' शब्द में कौन-सा समास है?
A. कर्मधारय B. अव्ययीभाव
C. तत्पुरूष D. द्विगु

काव्यांश-29

"मैया मोहि दाऊ बहुत खिझायौ।
मोसो कहत मोल को लीनो, तोहि जसुमति कब जायो"
कहा कहौ एहि रिस के मारे, खेलन हों नहिं जात।
पुनि-पुनि कहत कौन है माता, को है तुम्हरे तात।।
गोरे नंद जसोदा गोरी, तुम कत स्याम शरीर।
चुटकी दै दै हँसत ग्वाल सब, सिखै देत बलबीर।"

दिए गए काव्यांश के आधार पर निम्नलिखित प्रश्नों के उत्तर दें।

1. कृष्ण को कौन खिझाता है?
A. बड़े भैया B. गोपी
C. गोपियाँ D. यशोदा

2. बलराम कृष्ण को क्या कहकर खिझाता है?
A. कि उन्हें मोल खरीदा गया है, यशोदा ने उसे कब जन्म दिया?
B. कि उनका रंग सांवला है।
C. कि वह माखन चोर है।
D. कि उन्हें बाँसुरी बजाना नहीं आता।

3. ग्वालों को चुटकी दे-दे कर हँसने को कौन प्रेरित करता है?
A. एक ग्वाला B. स्वयं कृष्ण
C. बलराम D. यशोदा

4. 'रिस' शब्द का अर्थ होगा–
A. रिसना B. क्रोध
C. प्यार D. डर

5. कृष्ण क्यों खेलने नहीं जाते हैं?
A. लज्जा से
B. भय से
C. क्रोध से
D. क्योंकि खेलने का उनका मन नहीं है

काव्यांश-30

हरि बिनु कोऊ, काम न आयो।
यह माया झूठी प्रपंच लगि रतन सौ जनम गँवायो।
कंचन कलस विचित्र चित्रकारि रचि पचि भवन बनायो।
तेरे संग जरौगी यह कहि त्रिया पूत धनि खायो।
चलत रहे चित्त भोरि-भोरि मुख, एक न पग पहुँचायो।
बोलि-बोलि सुत स्वजन मित्र-जन, लीनों जी जेहि भायो।
परयो काज अब अंत की बिरियाँ, तिनही आनि बँधायो।

दिए गए काव्यांश के आधार पर निम्नलिखित प्रश्नों के उत्तर दें।

1. काव्यांश का स्थायी भाव है–
A. विरक्ति B. प्रेम
C. क्रोध D. शोक

2. काव्यांश के अनुसार अंत समय कौन काम आता है?
A. पुत्र B. पत्नी
C. ईश्वर D. इनमें से कोई नहीं

3. काव्यांश के अनुसार लोग कैसा घर बनाते हैं?
A. बहुमंजिली
B. सोने के कलश व चित्रकारी वाला
C. वातानुकूलित
D. इनमें से कोई नहीं

4. व्यक्ति किसके लिए अपना बहुमूल्य जीवन गवां देता है?
A. सत्कर्म B. समाज सेवा
C. माया और प्रपंच D. देश प्रेम

5. 'त्रिया' शब्द के पर्यायवाची है :–
(*i*) स्त्री (*ii*) दुहिता
(*iii*) कामिनी (*iv*) वनिता
A. (*i*), (*ii*) एवं (*iii*) B. (*ii*), (*iii*) एवं (*iv*)
C. (*i*), (*ii*) एवं (*iv*) D. (*i*), (*iii*) एवं (*iv*)

उत्तरमाला

काव्यांश-1

1	2	3	4	5
A	D	B	C	D

काव्यांश-2

1	2	3	4	5
C	A	C	C	C

काव्यांश-3

1	2	3	4	5
D	C	C	A	B

काव्यांश-4

1	2	3	4	5
D	B	C	C	A

काव्यांश-5

1	2	3	4	5
C	D	A	B	D

काव्यांश-6

1	2	3	4	5
A	B	D	B	D

काव्यांश-7

1	2	3	4	5
A	C	D	C	C

काव्यांश-8

1	2	3	4	5
C	B	A	B	A

काव्यांश-9

1	2	3	4	5
B	D	C	D	A

काव्यांश-10

1	2	3	4	5
B	C	D	C	A

काव्यांश-11

1	2	3	4	5
C	B	D	A	A

काव्यांश-12

1	2	3	4	5
C	B	B	C	D

काव्यांश-13

1	2	3	4	5
D	A	C	D	C

काव्यांश-14

1	2	3	4	5
C	B	D	C	A

काव्यांश-15

1	2	3	4	5
A	B	C	D	D

काव्यांश-16

1	2	3	4	5
C	B	B	A	D

काव्यांश-17

1	2	3	4	5
B	A	C	C	D

काव्यांश-18

1	2	3	4	5
A	B	D	C	B

काव्यांश-19

1	2	3	4	5
A	B	D	C	C

काव्यांश-20

1	2	3	4	5
B	C	B	D	A

काव्यांश-21

1	2	3	4	5
A	B	A	A	B

काव्यांश-22

1	2	3	4	5
A	C	B	C	C

काव्यांश-23

1	2	3	4	5
C	D	A	C	B

काव्यांश-24

1	2	3	4	5
C	B	D	A	C

काव्यांश-25

1	2	3	4	5
A	C	B	B	C

काव्यांश-26

1	2	3	4	5
D	D	C	D	A

काव्यांश-27

1	2	3	4	5
C	B	C	D	A

काव्यांश-28

1	2	3	4	5
A	B	D	A	C

काव्यांश-29

1	2	3	4	5
A	A	C	B	C

काव्यांश-30

1	2	3	4	5
A	C	B	C	C

English

COMPREHENSION

INTRODUCTION

Comprehension determines the ability of an examinee to grapple with abstract thoughts hidden in the text. It also judges his ability to draw conclusions from the given set of information that is in the form of running text. This test can be solved by reading the given paragraph and answering the questions that are given below it. Answers may be given either by ticking the right choices in the question paper or filling the relevant boxes (showing options) in the answer sheet with pencil. The passage can vary in length; it could be as small as a paragraph of 50 words or, it could be a type of small essay of nearly 500 words, conveniently divided into some paragraphs. Single paragraphs are also given in many a test. The topic of the paragraph generally deals with abstract subjects whereas figures or tables are generally avoided.

While treating the test from an artistic viewpoint, readers will have to develop the sense of making logical conclusions. These conclusions must be based on the text given in the passage; they cannot imagine phenomenon, conclusions or facts. They have to limit their imagination and the power to comprehend the abstract points (the "fine things" stated in the topic) to the passage only.

In order to solve this test in a scientific manner, readers will have to proceed according to the following steps:

(1) Read the passage and try to grasp the main theme of the story.

(2) Underline the important points.

(3) Read those words carefully that are in bold face letters. Try to connect them to the lines in which, they have been carefully embedded.

(4) Read the questions given below the passage and tick the relevant option in the answer sheet.

(5) Many passages have tests of antonyms and synonyms appended in the end of their questions. Do not imagine the antonym or synonym of the given word or the bold-faced word of the passage. Instead, link that word to the line in which, it is embedded. Try to find out what the author is saying in that line. Now, answer the question (antonym or synonym) keeping in mind the "true spirit" of the word in its sentence.

(6) In many tests, you may be asked to give a suitable title to the passage. Scan through the passage quickly and read the underlined phrases carefully. Give such a title to the passage as would encompass all the vital points of the passage. Do not go beyond the "real essence" of the given passage. Do not use difficult words in the title decided by you.

As an artist, you have to comprehend the fine aspects of the text that you will read. As a logician, you will be required to deduct and conclude.

PASSAGE–1

The villager has customarily been very conservative in his attitude and approach. He is reluctant to change his traditional way of thinking and doing things. His attitude, in many respects, is: "home-made is best". For instance, most cattle-farmers in the villages, prefer to feed their cows and buffaloes with a home-mix comprising local oil-cakes like mustard or cottonseed, pulses, jaggery, salt, etc. It takes numerous visits, hard-convincing, daily trials and experiments to convince the rural cattle-farmer that compound feeds, scientifically formulated, improve the yields of milk, without any incremental costs.

The age-old values and attitudes towards caste, creed, women, time and money take time to change. The villager has traditionally been a believer in the philosophy of 'Karma or fate. He has found it more convenient to blame his economic destitution, poor living conditions, and straitened social status on 'bhagya', 'Karma' or 'fate'. The security that the villagers find in the 'status quo', acts as a disincentive to change and experiment, in the short-run. Many of these antiquated attitudes, value-system and outlooks are changing, due to improved levels of awareness and education. However, the rate of change is sluggish. Attitudes that have fossilised over the centuries, do take time to change.

1. What does the phrase "home-made is best" imply?
   (*a*) The best should not be discarded.
   (*b*) Whatever is being practised is better than what is new.
   (*c*) People should go in for the Swadeshi because it is home-made
   (*d*) Change for the sake of change is no good.
2. Which one of the following is not the usual reason offered by an average Indian villager for his poverty?
   (*a*) It is God's will
   (*b*) It is a result of some of his bad deeds committed in this or the previous birth.
   (*c*) It is because of his resistance to new ideas.
   (*d*) It is his destiny
3. When will you call a person conservative in his attitude and approach?
   (*a*) When he sticks to old ways of thinking and doing.
   (*b*) When he would like to try out every new idea before accepting it.
   (*c*) When he imputes motives to change agents.
   (*d*) When he solves his problems through tried out methods.
4. Why does a villager feel secure in maintaining 'status quo'?
   (*a*) Because whatever is known should be the best.
   (*b*) Because change is seldom for the better.
   (*c*) Because too many people go about advising him.
   (*d*) Because of the imagined risk involved in trying a new approach.
5. What is the best method to convince the average Indian villager about the superiority of a new cattle-feed?
   (*a*) Discussion
   (*b*) Field demonstration
   (*c*) Distribution of related literature.
   (*d*) Home-visits.

PASSAGE-2

I do not suggest that the cultural side of education should be ignored. On the contrary, I think, it is essential to the production of the sort of adult who best fits the modern world. But I think that what is important in cultural education should be conveyed, at any rate in the early stages, by methods far more attrractive than those now usual. History and Geography should be taught at first by means of the cinema. When taught this way, they will give pleasure; attention will be spontaneous and therefore the impression will be less temporary. In spite of reforming movements, there is still among educators a feeling that what is enjoyed without effort cannot have much educational value. I would have children made aware of the manners and customs of tribes and nations utterly remote from their own. Education conducted on these lines would do more than many books to cure provincialism in space and time and to make children realise that actual human beings with actual feelings can be outwardly very different from the people among whom they live, but inwardly composed of the same human material. A Zulu would not appear strange, remote or savage but one like themselves.

1. The writer criticised traditional educators for not
   (*a*) using cinema as a method of teaching.
   (*b*) making learning an enjoyable activity.
   (*c*) imparting information about remote tribes.
   (*d*) imparting information about various cultures.
2. The writer thinks that the cultural side of education is needed to make man
   (*a*) appreciate one's heritage.
   (*b*) appreciate other civilisations.
   (*c*) suitable for modern civilisation.
   (*d*) admire his environment.
3. The expression "to cure provincialism in space and time" means to get rid of
   (*a*) regional feelings (*b*) obscure ideas
   (*c*) narrow views (*d*) selfish opinion
4. One of the goals of education should be to make children realise that
   (*a*) human culture is diverse.
   (*b*) regional cultures should not be ignored.
   (*c*) They must respect values of alien culture.
   (*d*) there is a unified system of human values underneath cultural diversity.
5. The response of the learners to teaching through cinema is
   (*a*) absorbing. (*b*) long-lasting.
   (*c*) enthusiastic. (*d*) superficial.

PASSAGE-3

In the technological systems of tomorrow — fast, fluid and self-regulating — machines will deal with the flow of physical materials; men with the flow of information and insight. Machines will increasingly perform tasks. Machines and men both, instead of being concentrated in gigantic factories and factory cities, will be scattered across the globe, linked together by amazingly sensitive, near-instantaneous communications. Human work will move out of the factory and mass office into the community and the home. Machines will be synchronised, as some already are, to the billionth of a second; men will be desynchronised. The factory whistle will vanish. Even the clock, "the key machine of the modern industrial age," as Lewis Mumford called it a generation ago, will lose some of its power over humans, as distinct from purely technological affairs. Simultaneously, the organisation needed to control technology will shift from bureaucracy to Ad-hocracy, from permanence to transience, and from a concern with the present to a focus on the future.

In such a world, the most valued attributes of the industrial age become handicaps. The technology of tomorrow requires not millions of lightly lettered men, ready to work in unison at endlessly repetitive jobs, it requires not men who take orders in unblinking fashion, aware that the price of bread is mechanical submission to authority, but men who can make critical judgments, who can weave their way through novel environment, who are quick to spot new relationships in the rapidly changing reality. It requires men who, in C.P. Snow's compelling terms, "have the future in their bones."

1. The type of society which the author has mentioned makes a plea for
   (*a*) a mind assimilative of modern scientific ideas
   (*b*) a critical mind having insight into future
   (*c*) a mind well-versed in cultural heritage
   (*d*) a mind with firm principles of life

2. The future man, according to this passage, must be
   (*a*) most adaptative and intelligent
   (*b*) most capable of dealing with the changing reality
   (*c*) more concerned with the present than the future
   (*d*) trained and obedient

3. Near-instantaneous communications' may be regarded as a symbol of
   (*a*) anachronisation
   (*b*) mischronisation
   (*c*) desynchronisation
   (*d*) synchronisation

4. If a person believes that 'the price of bread is mechanical submission to authority', he is
   (*a*) a believer in devotion to duty
   (*b*) a believer in taking things for granted
   (*c*) a believer in doing what he is told, right or wrong
   (*d*) a believer in the honesty of machines

5. The technological system of tomorrow will be marked by
   (*a*) dehumanisation (*b*) perfection
   (*c*) automation (*d*) unpredictability

PASSAGE-4

Education, particularly higher education is the obvious but crucially important instrument for nation building. As Confucious has said;

If you are thinking of one year, plant rice. If you are thinking of a decade, plant trees. If you are thinking of a century, educate the people.

When we set about the task of higher education, we should be absolutely clear in our perception of the goals of education in the specific context of our nation's development. No doubt, one of the important aims of education would be to create the required range and nature of trained manpower assessed to be needed by different sectors of national growth. The entire educational apparatus must be geared progressively to fulfill the requirements of different phases of our growth in every sector—primary, secondary and tertiary. The aim must be to ensure that our country does not experience either paucity, or a surfeit, of trained manpower in any specific segment of our economy. The requirements of our country, as a free, democratic, secular, socialist, nation, aspiring for rapid development, entail a specific recipe for our educational institutions. Today's educational institutions must therefore be developed accordingly and must regulate themselves to give the country the precise nature and quantum of trained manpower as projected by the requirements of our planned economy.

1. The author has quoted thoughts of Confucious to stress
   (*a*) importance of planting trees for human beings
   (*b*) the worthless efforts in planting rice
   (*c*) the benefits of investing in education
   (*d*) the need for assessing manpower requirement
   (*e*) None of these

2. Which statement cannot be made on the basis of the passage?
   (*a*) Higher education should keep in view the requirements of national economy
   (*b*) Higher education has not been employed for nation building

(*c*) All levels of education have a role to play in nation's growth
(*d*) In our country we need to have a specially planned educational system
(*e*) The educational system should be modified to suit to our country's needs

3. The writer believes that
(*a*) there are no problems related to higher education
(*b*) investment in education is of long-range
(*c*) higher education should be used to assess manpower needs
(*d*) aims of higher education in India are absolutely clear
(*e*) None of these

4. The author's expectations from higher education are essentially
(*a*) unrealistic (*b*) confusing
(*c*) critical (*d*) vague
(*e*) reasonable

5. The writer indicates that
(*a*) higher education did not play any role in national growth
(*b*) primary education did not play any role in national growth
(*c*) our nation experiences paucity of trained manpower in many sectors
(*d*) today's higher education has no precise goals to achieve
(*e*) None-of these

PASSAGE-5

Using infant mortality as a key indicator of the status of children, we now begin to have the broad features of a hypothesis as to the causes of higher or lower mortality rates. One aspect is the **complex** of factors involving the **access** of mothers to trained personnel and other facilities for child delivery, the nutritional status of pregnant and nursing mothers and the quality of health-care and nourishment which babies receive. The other aspect, indicated by rural-urban differentials, is the possible importance of human settlement patterns in relation to the availability of health-care and related facilities such as potable water, excreta disposal systems, etc. Thus, in a special sense it is much cheaper to make health and other basic services available to a community when it is densely settled rather than widely dispersed.

It is possible to argue, however, that both these sets of factors are closely related to a third one, namely income levels. Poorer mothers and babies have less access to health-care facilities and nourishment than those who are better-off, urban communities are on an average much better-off than rural communities. That economic conditions play a crucial role in determining the status of both mother and child is beyond dispute. But the question really is whether this is the only decisive factor or whether factors such as the availability of medical facilities, health-care programmes and nutritional programmes have an independent role. If so, then the settlement patterns which affect service delivery to the mother and child target groups become a relevant consideration. These are clearly issues of some importance for policy and programme planning.

1. Which of the following can be inferred from the passage?
(*a*) Infant mortality rate is higher in rural areas as compared to that of urban areas
(*b*) Income level alone can predict the infant mortality rate
(*c*) There, now, is more population in urban areas as compared to rural areas
(*d*) Delivery of services to the mother and child does not depend on the settlement pattern
(*e*) The rural areas have now become densely-populated

2. Which of the following is the issue of importance for policy?
(*a*) Relationship of mortality and income levels
(*b*) Growing rural-urban differentials
(*c*) Infant-mortality rate and mortality rate inter-dependence
(*d*) Dependence of education level of the mother and infant mortality rate
(*e*) Independence of factors other than income on infant mortality

3. Which, according to the passage, is the other main indicator of the status of children, besides infant mortality?
(*a*) Educational level
(*b*) Nourishment level
(*c*) Weight at birth
(*d*) Not mentioned
(*e*) None of these

4. What is the advantage of providing services in the urban areas, as compared to that of rural areas?
(*a*) The services are cheaply available
(*b*) Per-capita expenditure for setting up services is much less
(*c*) There is more awareness about availability of services
(*d*) The investment can be received in short duration
(*e*) It is much easier to set up services

5. Which of the following is the **same** in meaning as the word "**access**" as used in the passage?
(*a*) Passage (*b*) Outburst
(*c*) Surplus (*d*) Demand
(*e*) Reach

PASSAGE-6

To open up a field of study, draw attention to its vital elements, the lecture is invaluable. To listen to a lecture can be thrilling experience from which the student may gain ideas obtainable in no other way. But possibly to a greater degree than other forms of instruction, lecturing presumes a high order of intellectual competence on the part of learners. The purposes of the lecture are to summarize, to clarify, to stimulate and to humanize the materials of the course. It should synthesize, evaluate, criticise and compare ideas and facts with which students have come in contact through out-of-class assignments.

The effectiveness of lectures could be enhanced by introducing the lecture with a brief review of the work preceding. It should also be indicated how the day's lecture fits into the course pattern. A lecture should seldom be presented in one unbroken discourse. Unless exceptionally interesting, a long lecture **strains** the capacity for concentrated listening, causing intermittent wandering of attention and loss of continuity in thought. The lecture should therefore be organized in a few block or units. As a rule, the exposition should be concluded before the end of the class period so as to allow some time for general discussion.

For students to obtain maximum benefit from a lecture, individual participation in study both precede and follow it. On their own initiative, most students would not engage in preparatory study, hence formal assignments may be necessary. The lecture should be concluded on the assumption that the assignment has been fulfilled. It pays to explore the aids available for teaching a course particularly through lectures, since verbal exposition alone, however **lucid**, has its shortcomings.

1. Which of the following is the best suited title for the passage?
(*a*) Methods of Teaching
(*b*) Effective Learning
(*c*) Contrast Programmes
(*d*) Lecture-Method
(*e*) Teaching Without Tears

2. Which of the following is the **same** in meaning as the word "**strains**" as used in the passage?
(*a*) Spoils
(*b*) Damages
(*c*) Drains energy from
(*d*) Requires greater effort
(*e*) Puts premium on

3. An uninterrupted discourse type method results into.........
(*a*) loss of attention
(*b*) a thrilling experience
(*c*) stimulation of interest
(*d*) humanising the course material
(*e*) None of these

4. Which of the following is **not true** in the context of the passage?
(*a*) Students on their own take up assignments
(*b*) Lecture method humanises the course content
(*c*) There are many methods of teaching
(*d*) Improvements can be made in the traditional lecture method of instruction
(*e*) Various aids can be used with lecture method

5. Compared to other methods, lecturing requires ....
(*a*) more competent trainer
(*b*) bigger number of students
(*c*) higher level of learner
(*d*) a new field of study
(*e*) better presentation of ideas

PASSAGE-7

Among the several citrus fruits, acid lime is one of the most, prolific yielder, and this crop can be profitably grown in the tropical plains and hill slopes with scant water resources. It comes up well in sandy loam rich in organic residues and endowed with adequate drainage. Good quality grafts are ideal for raising a healthy and productive lime garden. The grafts yield true-to-parent plants of high yielding potential, and are early bearers. They also bear big fruits all through the year.

However, the longevity of the grafts is less as compared with the trees developed from the seeds, according to experts. Seeds extracted from healthy fruits from proven mother plants will develop into robust plants with longer life. The main field should be thoroughly tilled, and ripe farm-yard manure should be incorporated well with the final ploughing and land levelling. Green manuring will also help in increasing the soil's organic matter content, and in improving the soil structure. A spacing of 6 m by 6 m is recommended for raising acid lime plantation. Pits of 90 cm by 90 cm are to be dug, and filled up with adequate quantities of vermin-compost, coir-pith compost and small amounts of powdered neem cake and bio-fertilizers. About 250 plants can be accommodated in a hectare.

Regular irrigation is essential in the early stages of crop establishment. Drip irrigation, pitcher irrigation and micro-sprinklers have been found to give good results, besides saving considerable quantities of water and energy. In the initial months after planting, sufficient shade should be provided to protect the tender seedlings and grafts from harsh sun. Planting Sesbania (agathi) around the young plants will be effective in ensuring the required shade, besides enriching the soil. Several annual crops such as pulses and vegetables, can be raised as intercrops in the initial years. The plants should be trained to grow vertically by discouraging the lateral shoots and other growths.

Regular pruning to get the desired dome-shape should be done when the plants are still young. The field should be kept free of weed and other unwanted vegetation. Regular manuring should be done twice annually. The nutrients, mostly organic in nature, should be incorporated at the base of the plants, and watered immediately. The plants particularly respond well to liberal application of organic amendments. The micro-nutrient deficiencies will not be noticed in acid lime plantations raised with rich organic nutrients. Plant protection is an important aspect in acid lime cultivation. The plants should be sprayed with cow's urine, vermin-wash and other botanical insecticides to ward off leaf-munching caterpillars and other sucking and chewing pests.

Need-based application after monitoring the field for pest incidence will be rewarding. Spraying should be taken up at an interval of ten days, and it will also improve the fruit setting and fruit development. The plants will establish well and start yielding from the second year of planting. Though the fruits can be had all round the year, some major flushes can be harvested in December-January and July-August seasons. A well nurtured grown-up tree can yield as high as 3000 fruits a year. The profit for the growers depends on the season and the prevailing market rate. With an average price of Rs. 0.35 a fruit, a farmer can realize about Rs. 2.5 lakhs from a hectare of a healthy and well-tended acid lime garden.

1. It can be inferred from the passage that
   I. The quality and size of fruits depend upon the longevity of the plants.
   II. The yield of grafts is less as compared to the trees developed from the seeds.
   III. There is not much of a difference between grafts and the trees developed from the seeds, except in life.
   Which of the above statements is/are true?
   (*a*) Only III (*b*) Only II
   (*c*) I and II (*d*) I, II and III
2. For a good growth of acid-lime crop, all of the following are essential *except,*
   (*a*) water-logged tropical plains
   (*b*) good irrigation with adequate drainage
   (*c*) rich residues of orgainc nutrients
   (*d*) hill slopes with poor water resources
3. The author of the passage could be
   (*a*) an agricultural activist
   (*b*) an agricultural expert
   (*c*) a farmer
   (*d*) an analyst
4. Which of the following is necessary for the nascent crop?
   (*a*) Sufficient shade
   (*b*) Regular inrrigation
   (*c*) Regular manuring and application of organic nutrients
   (*d*) Both (*a*) and (*b*)
5. The most appropriate insecticide for acid-lime crop is
   (*a*) cow's urine
   (*b*) powdered neem
   (*c*) vermi-compost
   (*d*) organic residue

PASSAGE-8

We should preserve Nature to preserve life and beauty. A beautiful landscape, full of green vegetation, will not just attract our attention but will fill us with infinite satisfaction. Unfortunately, because of modernization, much of nature is now yielding to towns, roads and industrial areas. In a few places some Natural reserves are now being carved out to avert the danger of destroying Nature completely. Man will perish without Nature, so modern man should continue this struggle to save plants, which give us oxygen, from extinction. Moreover, Nature is essential to man's health.

1. What does "Nature" in the passage mean?
   (*a*) Countryside covered with plants and trees
   (*b*) Physical power that created the world
   (*c*) Inherent things that determine character
   (*d*) Practical study of plants and animals
2. Which one of the following is the correct statement?
   According to the passage
   (*a*) Beauty is only skin-deep
   (*b*) Everything is beautiful in its natural state
   (*c*) There is beauty in Nature
   (*d*) Nature is a moral teacher
3. What does the writer suggest?
   (*a*) We should not modernize, so that Nature can be preserved
   (*b*) While modernizing we should be careful not to destroy Nature completely
   (*c*) All Nature has been destroyed by modern living
   (*d*) Carving out Natural reserves will hamper the growth of industries
4. What does "Struggle" in the passage mean?
   (*a*) Man's Struggle to exist in the world
   (*b*) Man's Struggle to save Nature
   (*c*) Man's Struggle to catch up with modern trends
   (*d*) Man's Struggle to conserve oxygen

5. Why a beautiful landscape will fill us with infinite satisfaction'?
   (*a*) We love beauty
   (*b*) It is full of green vegetation
   (*c*) It will ensure our future existence
   (*d*) It will show our command over Nature

PASSAGE–9

Finally, there arises the question as to our leadership potential. Although the entire younger generation by the very definition is a potential storehouse of leadership, I feel that our universities provide the richest reservoir from which the future leaders of this country will be forthcoming. I have had occasion to travel fairly extensively and to visit a number of university centres in the country. It is deeply encouraging to see that despite the economic and other difficulties which these young men and women have to face they are full of energy and idealism. The real question is whether we have the ability and imagination to tap this reservoir, to fan the sparks of youthful idealism into bright flames that would illumine the future of India — the India of our dreams for the building of which countless generations have struggled and sacrifed; an India socially emancipated, economically prosperous, politically integrated, militarily strong and spiritually dynamic.

1. Which one of the following is correct?
   The writer believes that India is
   (*a*) socially emancipated
   (*b*) economically prosperous
   (*c*) spiritually dynamic
   (*d*) None of the above
2. What is the author's tone in the passage?
   (*a*) Optimistic (*b*) Autocratic
   (*c*) Pessimistic (*d*) Partisan
3. Where will the future leaders of the country mainly come from?
   (*a*) The families of present political leaders
   (*b*) The community of social scientists
   (*c*) The universities
   (*d*) The entire younger generation
4. Which one of the following is correct?
   For realizing the India of our dreams,
   (*a*) we should have the imagination to exploit our budding leadership potential
   (*b*) we should admire the sacrifices made by several generations
   (*c*) we should bring about more technological advancements
   (*d*) we should provide better facilities for sports
5. Which one of the following is correct?
   What is deeply encouraging about educated young men and women of India is that
   (*a*) they come from the richest reservoirs of potential leaders
   (*b*) they are full of energy and idealism because of quality education
   (*c*) they are full of youthful idealism and imagination
   (*d*) they are full of energy and idealism in spite of economic and other difficulties they face as students

PASSAGE–10

My own recollection is that I had not had any high regard for my ability. I used to be astonished whenever I won prizes and scholarships. But, I very assiduously guarded my character. The least little blemish drew tears from my eyes. When I merited, or seemed to the teacher to merit, a rebuke, it was unbearable for me. I remember having once received corporal punishment. I did not so much mind the punishment, as the fact that it was considered my desert. I wept piteously. That was when I was in the first or second standard. There was another such incident during the time when I was in the seventh standard. Dorabji Edulji Gimi was the Headmaster then. He was popular among the boys, though he was a disciplinarian. He was a man of method and a good teacher. He had made gymnastics and cricket compulsory for the boys of the upper standards. I disliked both. I never took part in any exercise, cricket or football, before they were made com-pulsory. My shyness was one of the reasons for this aloofness, which I now see as wrong. I then had the false notion that gymnastics had nothing to do with education. Today I know that physical training should have as much place in the curriculum as mental training.

1. Why did the author say that he did ***not*** have any high regard for his ability?
   (*a*) He was a dunce
   (*b*) He always used to miss his classes
   (*c*) He never did well in studies or sports
   (*d*) He was full humility
2. The author's idea that character is a treasure is revealed in which of the statements?
   (*a*) "I won prizes and scholarships"
   (*b*) "When I merited, or seemed to the teacher to merit, a rebuke, it was unbearable for me"
   (*c*) "I very assiduously guarded my character"
   (*d*) "I wept piteously"
3. Why did the author weep piteously?
   (*a*) He felt insulted
   (*b*) Punishment was considered his due
   (*c*) He felt the physical pain
   (*d*) He took the punishment to heart

4. Why did the author dislike gymnastics and cricket?
   (*a*) They cut into his study time
   (*b*) He had to spend money in buying bats, etc.
   (*c*) He felt that physical education could cause injury
   (*d*) He was shy

PASSAGE-11

According to the research findings of a team of American scientists published recently, the sea waves contain as much energy as the world is consuming at present. Scientists have found that through the application of two major devices called land-based systems and offshore devices, this source of energy can provide huge amount of electricity without cooling towers and pollution.

Land-based systems include tapered channels and fixed oscillating water column (OWC) devices whereas offshore devices include floating OWC devices, buoys, etc. Through these devices the mechanical energy of ocean waves is absorbed and converted into electrical energy. The wave power potential depends on numerous factors such as the device's capability to harness long wavelengths, period of waves and depth of water where they arise.

Compared to conventional power stations which require greater space and are difficult to maintain in critical situations, wave power devices are highly modular, cost effective and easier to upgrade. As the recent findings suggest, sea wave energy has much greater potential to be used for electricity generation than the hitherto known sources of renewable energy. Moreover, most of the renewable energy systems require hundreds of square acres of useful land for their installation. But in case of wave energy devices, space crunch' can never be a serious problem.

1. Which one of the following statements is correct?
   Harnessing energy from sea waves
   (*a*) undermines ecological balance.
   (*b*) requires huge capital.
   (*c*) requires high technical expertise.
   (*d*) results in saving of useful land area.
2. Which one of the following statements is correct?
   Wave power devices
   (*a*) convert wind energy into mechanical power.
   (*b*) convert mechanical energy of ocean waves into electrical energy.
   (*c*) require costly transmission mechanism
   (*d*) entail risk to human life.
3. Which one of the following statements is correct?
   (*a*) Fixed as well as floating oscillating water column devices are required to harness ocean wave energy.
   (*b*) Fixed oscillating water column devices are required for off shore based system.
   (*c*) Floating oscillating water column devices are required for land-based system.
   (*d*) Electricity generated from oceans is independent of the depth of water where waves arise.
4. Which one of the following statements is correct?
   The capacity of system to generate electricity from ocean waves
   (*a*) can be increased only at exorbitant cost.
   (*b*) can be easily upgraded.
   (*c*) can be increased but it requires a great space.
   (*d*) is only a few megawatts.
5. Which one of the following statements is ***not*** correct?
   (*a*) Conventional power stations require cooling towers.
   (*b*) Power generation from ocean waves also adds to pollution like conventional power stations.
   (*c*) Ocean wave energy can meet all the present energy of the world.
   (*d*) Period of waves is one of the relevant factors in power generation from ocean waves.

PASSAGE-12

The most important fact, which a leader who wishes to motivate others should bear in mind, is that an individual has an incessant and gnawing craving for importance. There is no exception to this psychological need. Barring his biological needs, practically all his actions are directed at satisfying his continuing need to feel important. According to William James, the deepest principle in human nature is the craving to be appreciated. The individual who can honestly satisfy this burning hunger for importance on the part of his fellow human beings can literally rule the world. He can motivate and influence any person, big or small, high or low, educated or uneducated, rich or poor, man or woman, provided he is capable of making the other person feel truly important. By discovering the special and particular gifts of an individual, by giving due recognition and sincere appreciation to that singular gift or talent, you can win him or her over to your side easily.

You have to create an eager want on the part of the other individual if you wish to motivate him. In other words, you have to make the horse feel thirsty if your aim is to make it drink. Fortunately for you, there is an inborn, ever-present, gnawing hunger on the part of every human being to gain recognition and appreciation. This want is already there and you don't have to create it. All you have to do is to satisfy this hunger. If you objectively analyse your own motives and needs you will find that this need for recognition is the strong driving factor behind your aspiration to become a leader. It was this urge for importance which made Alexander and Great embark on a world conquest, and made many emperors wage innumerable battles and wars. This urge has driven artists, authors, scientists, inventors and others to attain great heights in their chosen fields and produce the best results.

1. Which one of the following statements is correct?
(*a*) Many scientists and inventors have excelled because of the availability of research facilities.
(*b*) Artists and authors have made contribution to society because of their innate genius.
(*c*) Many athletes have won gold medals in the Olympics because of their coaches.
(*d*) People in different areas have been successful because of the need of recognition.

2. Which one of the following statements is ***not*** correct?
(*a*) Hunger for recognition has to be developed over the years in one's personality.
(*b*) Need to gain recognition is an inborn trait.
(*c*) Many wars have been waged to satisfy the need to get importance.
(*d*) Craving for importance is a natural psychological need of every human being.

3. Which one of the following statements is correct?
(*a*) A successful leader must be able to identify the need of importance of others.
(*b*) Need for recognition is a trait only of high professionals.
(*c*) To motivate a person, an increase of his salary is the best strategy.
(*d*) Monetary success is the driving force for a leader.

PASSAGE-13

Because goldfish can be kept easily in small ponds and aquariums, they make good pets, but like many other pets, they must have proper care and the right kind of place to live.

A two-inch fish requires a minimum of two gallons of water containing sufficient oxygen to support life. Some oxygen will make its way into the water of an aquarium from the air that touches the surface. Plants in an aquarium also help to furnish oxygen. Snails help to keep an aquarium clean. Thus, with plenty of plants and snails the water is an aquarium does not have to be changed frequently. A large lake may prove to be a quite unsuitable abode for goldfish.

It is important that goldfish not be overfed. They can be fed such things as dried insects in addition to commercially-prepared goldfish food, but they should never be fed more than once a day. Even then, they should not be given more food than can be consumed in about five minutes. This ensures prolonged life.

1. Which one of the following statements is correct?
(*a*) Snails eat up the goldfish in an aquarium
(*b*) A large lake may not be a suitable place for goldfish
(*c*) Plants provide food to the snails in an aquarium
(*d*) Goldfish come above the surface of water to get oxygen from air

2. Which one of the following statements is *not* correct?
(*a*) Goldfish can be made goods pets
(*b*) Plants in an aquarium provide oxygen to goldfish
(*c*) Goldfish must never be given too much food
(*d*) Snails make the aquarium clean by eating up goldfish

3. Which of the following helps supply goldfish with oxygen?
(*a*) Snails
(*b*) Dried insects
(*c*) Goldfish food
(*d*) Plants

4. Which one of the following statement is *not* correct?
(*a*) Water in an aquarium has to be changed frequently because of plants and snails
(*b*) Commercially-prepared goldfish is available
(*c*) The place for the goldfish should be selected with care
(*d*) Dried insects make good feed for goldfish

5. What is important to remember when feeding goldfish?
(*a*) Goldfish should be fed more than once a day at regular intervals
(*b*) Goldfish should be fed with plants and snails
(*c*) Goldfish should be fed only once a day
(*d*) Goldfish should be fed only in the evenings

PASSAGE-14

Ah ! whatever could be said was said. All held him guilty. Even his own mother who claimed to understand him the best. All had betrayed him in his hour of need. Yet, there he was, still with a sparkling hope and knew that the truth must prevail. In the cold, dark and damp cell he never for a moment lost faith in God and goodness and was waiting anxiously for an angel to come, plead non guilty for him and free him of his miseries.

1. Three of the following statements indicate that he had a sparkling hope. Which statement does not?
(*a*) He had never lost faith in God.
(*b*) He was sure there was goodness.
(*c*) He could have evidence in his favour.
(*d*) He knew that the truth must prevail.

2. Whatever others said about him, he
(*a*) betrayed no one.
(*b*) thought over the problem.
(*c*) never lost faith in goodness.
(*d*) raised his voice against injustice.

3. In the dark dungeon he always waited for
(*a*) his mother.
(*b*) the jailer.
(*c*) the verdict freeing him of his miseries.
(*d*) the angel to come and plead for him.

4. The truth must prevail means
(*a*) he was true.
(*b*) angel will reveal truth.
(*c*) truth always wins in the end.
(*d*) we must plead for the truth.

PASSAGE-15

Once while travelling by the local bus, I got a seat beside a very strange man. He seemed interested in every passenger aboard. He would stare at a person, scribble some odd mathematical notations on his long notebook and then move on to the next. Being quite interested in what he was doing I asked him what all those notations meant and then came the startling reply. He saw a man's face not as a single unit but as thousands of squares put together. He was in fact a statistical expert and a budding artist learning the art of graphics.

1. The man was scribbling down
(*a*) the figures of co-passengers.
(*b*) the details of thousands of squares put together.
(*c*) some mathematical formulae and calculations.
(*d*) some mathematical signs.

2. The man caught author's attention because
(*a*) he was sitting next to him.
(*b*) he was staring at every person in the bus.
(*c*) he would stare at every person and then scribble down some mathematical notation.
(*d*) he was a budding artist learning the art of graphics.

3. The author found that man's reply quite startling because
(*a*) a statistical expert cannot be a budding scientist.
(*b*) a budding artist cannot be a statistical expert.
(*c*) graphics is still a rare art form and he was learning it while travelling in a bus.
(*d*) the fact that "a man's face can be analysed as thousands of squares" was a strange concept.

4. From the passage we gather that
(*a*) the author is very inquisitive.
(*b*) the author tries to poke his nose in other people's business.
(*c*) the author is interested in mathematical notations.
(*d*) the author wants to talk to fellow passengers in the bus.

PASSAGE-16

With the inevitable growth of specialisation I see the universities facing two great dangers. First, it is very easy to get so involved in the technical details of education that the object of education is lost. And secondly, in an effort to condition a university to the needs of its students and to the needs of the state it may lose its power to make or mould those students into responsible men, capable of thinking for themselves and capable of expressing the results of their thoughts to others.

1. The author calls growth of specialisation 'inevitable'. Which one of the following statements is likely to be the most correct reason for this inevitability?
(*a*) Universities give grants only to do specialised work in different disciplines.
(*b*) The professors and researchers in universities are competent only for specialised work.
(*c*) Specialisation helps economic growth of the nation.
(*d*) In an age of science and technology specialisation becomes necessary.

2. Which one of the following statements most correctly suggests the central theme of the passage?
(*a*) The aim of education is specialisation.
(*b*) The aim of education is to mould the youth to work for the state.
(*c*) The aim of education is to make the youth capable of independent thought and expression.
(*d*) The aim of education is to enable the youth to earn a comfortable living.

3. Which one of the following statements most correctly suggests the warning implied in the passage?

(*a*) University education should not be concerned with technical details.
(*b*) Universities should not subordinate themselves to the interests of tile state.
(*c*) Universities should be concerned only with the needs of students.
(*d*) Universities should not go in for any specialisation.

PASSAGE-17

We shall go on to the end; we shall fight in France, we shall fight on the seas and oceans, we shall fight with growing confidence and strength in the air, we shall defend our island whatever the cost may be, we shall fight on the beaches, we shall fight on the landing grounds, we shall fight in the fields and in the streets, we shall fight in the hills. We shall never surrender, and even if this island or a large part of it were subjugated and starving, then our empire beyond the seas would carry on the struggle, untill the New World steps forth to the rescue and the liberation of the Old.

1. On the basis of the passage which of the following statements may be said to be correct?
(*a*) The speaker is encouraging his men for the conquest of France
(*b*) The speaker is aggressive and maniacal war-monger
(*c*) The speaker is not satisfied with the conquest of the island
(*d*) The speaker is a patriot urging the defence of his motherland

2. The speaker in the passage wants to go on fighting because
(*a*) he is a raving lunatic
(*b*) he is in a state of utter despair
(*c*) he expects help from other quarters
(*d*) he is the leader of a suicide squad

3. Which of the following pairs of the phrases helps best to bring out the intention of the speaker?
(*a*) "Go on to the end"; "shall never surrender"
(*b*) "Growing confidence"; "subjugated and starving"
(*c*) "Subjugated and starving"; "fight on the landing ground"
(*d*) "Fight in the streets"; "subjugated and starving"

4. The passage consists of repetitive patterns in syntax and vocabulary. The effect of this style is that it
(*a*) reveals the speaker's defects in giving a speech
(*b*) produces the impression of bad poetry
(*c*) conveys the speaker's helpless situation
(*d*) reinforces the speaker's basic intention

PASSAGE-18

It is said that once three old men set out on a Journey together. One of them was bald, the second was a philosopher and the third was a barber. At nightfall they decided that each one of them should sit for watch *turn* by turn. The *barber* was to keep watch first of all, the *philosopher* after that and the *bald* man last of all. So, the philosopher and the blad man went to sleep and the barber was on watch. For some time he kept awake but in the end, he felt tired of it and he thought of some *diversion* as otherwise it was difficult for him to *pass* time. Then he took out the razor from his box and shaved the head of the philosopher. At the fixed time he woke up the philosopher and himself went to sleep. when the philosopher got up and felt his head all over, he was startled and said in surprise, "It was my trun but this *wretched* fellow has *awakened* bald man."

1. Why did the philosopher get up?
(*a*) He realised that his head was being shaved off
(*b*) It was his turn to keep watch
(*c*) He was awakened by the barber
(*d*) he had a bad dream

2. Who went to sleep first?
(*a*) The philosopher and the barber
(*b*) The barber and the bald man
(*c*) The bald man and the philosopher
(*d*) The barber

3. Why did the barber shave off the head of the philosopher?
(*a*) The barber was jealous of the philosopher
(*b*) The barber wanted to indulge in some fun
(*c*) The barber wanted the philosopher to keep watch
(*d*) The barber was feeling drowsy

4. Which one of the following is the correct sequence decided upon the three to keep watch turn by turn?
(*a*) Barber – bald man – philosopher
(*b*) Bald man – philosopher – barber
(*c*) Barber – philosopher – bald man
(*d*) Bald man – barber – philosopher

5. Which one of the following statements is ***not*** correct?
(*a*) All the three men decided to keep watch one by one
(*b*) The barber woke up the bald man
(*c*) The head of the philosopher was shaved off
(*d*) The philosopher was startled on feeling his head all over

PASSAGE-19

There can be only two explanations why countries like UK, US, Germany and Japan are willing to spend up to 5.5 million to make the Next Generation Linear Collider (NGLC) : Intellectual snobbery or complete indifference to the problems of the real world. To plan a 20-mile-long tunnel merely to go about smashing atoms, so as to recreate the Big Bang, is a frightful waste of public money. The project has no foreseeable practical application. Already, cyber-savvy cosmologists are engaged in simulating the Big Bang, or the beginning of the universe, in the virtual world, through number crunching and reverse engineering. Thye have successfully created a black hole on the desktop. So why go in for prohibitively expensive experimentation, when the virtual world is just a mouse-click away? Scientific ingenuity, remember, is not confined to reallife experiments; many of today's break-throughs have been inspired by research conductd almost entirely in cyberspace. Moreover, virtual research is 'clean'— without such fallouts as lab accidents and chemical leakages—and costs next to nothing.

1. Countries like UK, US, Germany and Japan wish to spend lot of money.
   (*a*) to attend to the problems of humanity.
   (*b*) to control AIDS.
   (*c*) for defence research.
   (*d*) to carry out atomic research.
2. Virtual research is carried out
   (*a*) on computers.
   (*b*) by experimentation in the field.
   (*c*) by spending up billions of dollars.
   (*d*) by experimentation in space.
3. Scientific research is not prohibitively costly when conducted
   (*a*) by simulation in the virtual world.
   (*b*) smashing atoms in a tunnel.
   (*c*) making real-life models.
   (*d*) using satellites.
4. Reverse engineering
   (*a*) is commonly practised in research.
   (*b*) is prohibitively expensive experimentation.
   (*c*) is not used by cosmologists in the virtual world.
   (*d*) is independent of analysis using computers.

PASSAGE-20

Failure and success are the ways of life. Constant efforts despite initial setbacks have brought us from the chrysalis of failures into the bright opportunity of triumphs. The conquest of Everest is a fitting example. Success eluded men for nearly twenty-five years. The leader of an unsuccessful expedition started, "Everest cannot add to its height, but spirit of man heightens even under repulse." Subsequent conquest of Everest has proved the truth of this. Indeed every newborn day is in itself an opportunity teeming with splendid chances for those who are alert, wide awake and aspiring.

1. According to the writer, the conquest of Everest proves that
   (*a*) the spirit of man heightens under demanding circumstances.
   (*b*) man cannot attain the unattainable.
   (*c*) success is always elusive.
   (*d*) the nature is most potent.
2. In this passage, "chrysalis of failure" means that
   (*a*) failure involves a closed situation from which one cannot escape.
   (*b*) failure can be compared to the pupa of the gold-coloured butterflies.
   (*c*) failure is a transitional state.
   (*d*) as an insect emerges in a different shape from chrysalis, so a human being changes after every failure.
3. The very style of the prose suggests that the writer intends the last sentence of the passage to be
   (*a*) poetic
   (*b*) inspiring
   (*c*) vague
   (*d*) contradictory to the first sentence of the passage.
4. The expression "teeming with" in the passage can be replaced by
   (*a*) multiplying (*b*) abounding
   (*c*) fruitful (*d*) promising
5. Every new day brings fresh challenges for a person
   (*a*) who is young
   (*b*) whose head is teeming with bright ideas
   (*c*) who has come out of the chrysalis of failure
   (*d*) who is watchful and daring.

ANSWERS

PASSAGE-1

1	2	3	4	5
(*b*)	(*b*)	(*a*)	(*a*)	(*b*)

PASSAGE-2

1	2	3	4	5
(*b*)	(*a*)	(*c*)	(*d*)	(*b*)

PASSAGE-3

1	2	3	4	5
(b)	(b)	(d)	(c)	(c)

PASSAGE-4

1	2	3	4	5
(c)	(b)	(c)	(e)	(e)

PASSAGE-5

1	2	3	4	5
(a)	(b)	(b)	(b)	(e)

PASSAGE-6

1	2	3	4	5
(d)	(c)	(a)	(a)	(e)

PASSAGE-7

1	2	3	4	5
(a)	(a)	(d)	(a)	(a)

PASSAGE-8

1	2	3	4	5
(a)	(c)	(b)	(d)	(c)

PASSAGE-9

1	2	3	4	5
(d)	(a)	(c)	(a)	(d)

PASSAGE-10

1	2	3	4
(d)	(c)	(a)	(d)

PASSAGE-11

1	2	3	4	5
(d)	(b)	(a)	(b)	(b)

PASSAGE-12

1	2	3
(d)	(a)	(a)

PASSAGE-13

1	2	3	4	5
(b)	(d)	(d)	(a)	(c)

PASSAGE-14

1	2	3	4
(c)	(c)	(d)	(c)

PASSAGE-15

1	2	3	4
(a)	(c)	(d)	(a)

PASSAGE-16

1	2	3
(d)	(c)	(b)

PASSAGE-17

1	2	3	4
(d)	(c)	(a)	(d)

PASSAGE-18

1	2	3	4	5
(c)	(c)	(b)	(c)	(b)

PASSAGE-19

1	2	3	4
(d)	(a)	(a)	(a)

PASSAGE-20

1	2	3	4	5
(a)	(d)	(b)	(b)	(d)

❑❑❑

VOCABULARY

ONE WORD SUBSTITUTION

Ambiguous : (of a statement) having more than one meaning.

Ambidextrous : (of a person) who can write with both hands equally well.

Amphibian : an animal that can live both on earth and water.

Anaemia : deficiency of red blood cells or haemoglobin.

Andocracy : a social syctem dominated by men.

Anonymous : (of a person) of unknown name.

Anorexia : loss of appetite for food.

Anthology : a published collection of poems (from different poets).

Anthropophagy : the eating of human flesh by human beings.

Aquarium : a transparent bank of water in which the fish are kept.

Atheist : (of a person) who does not believe in the existence of God.

Archaeology : the study of science of historical relics or monuments.

Auditorium : a big hall, built for the gathering of people (audience).

Autograph : synatuses of an important person written as a memento for an admirer.

Bibliography : a list of books representing some scholarly work for reference.

Bibliomancy : the practice of foretelling the future with the help of the Bible.

Bibliomania : a great enthusiasm for collecting books.

Biblimetrics : a subject related to statistical analysis of books.

Bibliophile : a great lover of books.

Biography : life history of a person written by someone else.

Bioluminescence : the emission of light by an organism without producing heat.

Biology : the study of living organisms.

Botany : the science that deals with the study of plant life.

Bureaucracy : a government run by officials.

Cannibal : (a person) who eats human flesh.

Carnivorous : (of an animal) feeding on other animals.

Catalogue : a systematic complete list of items.

Catastrophe : an event that occurs suddenly causing a great damage or suffering.

Cavernows : cave-like shape or atmosphere.

Cholecystectomy : surgical removal of gall bladder.

Cholecystography : X-ray examination of the gall bladder.

Congenital : (of a physical abnormality) present from birth.

Contagious : (of a disease) spread from one person or organism to the other directly or in an indirect way.

Coprophagous : (of an organism) feeding on dung or faeces

Credulous : (of a person) easily ready to believe something.

Incredulous : (of a person) not ready to believe something or somebody.

Cruciform : having the shape of a cross.

Cryptology : art of writing and solving codes.

Cryptogram : a text written in codes.

Cacophony : a great discordant noise.

Cacography : bad handwriting.

Cosmology : the science of origin and development of universe.

Democracy : a government of people.
Dendrology : the scientific study of trees.
Deltiologist : a person having the hobby of collecting postcards.
Demonolatry : the worship of demons.
Diabolism : worship of the devil.
Ectomorph : a person with lean and delicate body.
Effulgent : shining brightly.
Egocentric : thinking only of oneself.
Endogamy : the practice or custom of marrying only within a local community.
Endomorph : a person with soft round body.
Epigraphy : the study and interpretation of ancient inscriptions.
Epilogue : a section or speech at the end of a book especially for giving the conclusion to what has been written.
Eponymous (of a person) giving his name to something.
Equinox : the time or date, when the day and night are of the same length.
Effervescent : giving off bubbles.
Fermentation : the chemical breakdown of a substance by yeasts or some bacteria, etc.
Fictitious : not real.
Folicide : the killing of one's son or daughter.
Floriferous : producing many flowers.
Fratricide : the killing of one's brother.
Fatal : a disease which ends in death.
Garrulous : excessively talkative.
Geophagy : the practice of eating earth.
Gigantic : of very big size.
Gluttonous : one who eats too much.
Gregarious : living in flocks or being fond of company.
Germicide : of something that kills germs.
Haemolysis : destruction of red blood cells.
Haemostasis : the stopping of flow of blood.
Hagiolatry : the worship of saints.
Homicide : the killing of human beings.
Horticulture : the art of garden cultivation.
Homogeneous : a combination of different elements.
Herbivorous : (of an animals) feeding on herbs.
Hypertension : pressure of blood more than normal.
Hypotension : pressure of blood less than normal.
Immiscible : (of a liquid) not forming a homogenous mixture with other liquids.
Immortal : never dying.
Impecunious : having little or no money.
Incorrigible : one which cannot be corrected.
Indolent : lazy; less active.
Kleptomania : a great desire of stealing things.
Loquacious : (a person) who talks excessively.
Lithography : the art of printing or drawing on stones.
Luxurious : extremely comfortable.
Matricide : killing of one's mother.
Misanthrope : a person who hates mankind.
Misogynist : a person who hates women.
Misogamist : a person who hates marriage.
Monogamy : the practice of marrying only one wife or husband.
Meticulous : a person who is very particular about every minute details.
Nepotism : the practice of providing opportunities to their friends or relatives by those who are in power.
Narcotic : a drug which is illegally sold and which causes addiction to the regular taker.
Nephrotoxic : destructive to the kidney.
Nascent : new and lacking in maturity.
Optimist : a person who looks at the bright side of things.
Omniscient : having unlimited knowledge.
Omnipotent : all powerful.
Omnipresent : present everywhere at the same time.
Opaque : a thing that cannot be seen through.
Polygamy : the practice of having more than one wife at the same time.
Pessimist : a person who always looks at the dark side of things.
Panacea : a remedy for all diseases.
Patricide : killing of one's father.
Regicide : killing of the king.
Remuneration : money paid for a work.
Simultaneous : an incident happening at the same time.
Scrupulous : (of a person or process) diligent and extremely attentive to details.
Sequacious : (of a person) lacking originality of thoughts.
Soliloqy : the act of speaking to oneself.
Teetotaller : a person who does not drink.
Theist : a person who believes in the existence of God.
Tenant : a person who stays in a house and pays rent for it.
Vociferous : (of a person) speaking loudly and vehemently.
Vivacious : (of a woman) attractive and sprightly.
Xenophobia : extreme fear from strangers.
Xylophagous *(of an insect)* : feeding on or boring into wood.

SYNONYMS & ANTONYMS

A. SYNONYMS

Ardent	eager, avid
Arduous	difficult, troublesome, tough
Aspire	hope, wish
Astonish	amaze, confound
Authentic	genuine, actual
Awesome	astonishing, amazing, awful, fearful
Ban	bar, debar
Bare	denuded exposed
Bear	carry, bring
Beautiful	attractive, charming
Becoming	attractive, graceful
Benchmark	model, example
Benevolent	bountiful, benign
Betwitch	attract, captivate
Boisterous	noisy, clamorous
Bonny	handsome, attractive, beautiful, healthy
Brave	bold, courageous
Break	crack, separate
Brief	laconic, curt
Bright	shining, flashing
Brisk	active, lively
Broad	generous, capacious
Build	assemble, construct
Busy	brisk, active
Cajole	Coax, dupe
Call	announce, shout
Calm	peaceful, mild
Candid	fair, frank
Capacious	spacious, roomy
Care	anxiety, concern
Catchy	attractive, captivating
Charming	attractive, appealing
Chief	main, key
Clean	pure, spotless
Clever	apt, intelligent
Clumsy	burgling, awkward
Colossal	giant, enormous
Compact	dense, condensed
Conspicuous	clear, apparent
Cordial	agreeable, cheerful
Credulous	trustful, unsuspicious
Cruel	atrocious, barbarous
Dangerous	alarming, hazardous
Dazzling	glorious, radiant
Deceive	cheat, betray
Deep	profound, bottomless
Delicate	fragile, weak, tender
Delight	ecstasy, happiness
Deny	disprove, rebuf
Eager	ardent, avid
Effective	active, capable
Elegant	beautiful, artistic
Emerge	arise, appear
Encouraging	cheerful, promising
Enormous	colossal, gigantic
Faded	dim, dull
Fair	clean, honest
Fascinating	attractive, bewitching
Foolish	imprudent, senseless
Frank	candid, ingenuous
Garrulous	chattering, gossiping
Generous	liberal, benevolent
Genuine	bonafide, authentic
Gloomy	dark, sad
Glorious	magnificent, excellent
Great	colossal, enormous
Haughty	assuming, arrogant
Hefty	big, robust
Humane	benign, gentle
Humble	modest, meek
Idle	lazy, inactive
Illogical	faulty, incorrect
Immense	enormous, colossal
Impudent	bold, brazen
Indolent	lazy, sluggish
Intelligent	clever, bright
Keen	ardent, arid
Kind	benevolent, benign
Laconic	brief, curt
Leading	dominating chief
Lively	agile, active
Lucid	evident, clear
Magnificent	excellent, glorious
Morose	gloomy, sad
Neglect	disdain, ignore
Obedient	submissive, amenable
Obscure	cloudy, vague
Obstinate	stubborn, firm
Opulent	lavish, affluent
Overnight	fault, mistake
Peaceful	harmonious, friendly
Polite	humble, civil
Prolific	teeming, bountiful
Radiant	bright, glorious
Rejoicing	delight, cheer
Sad	gloomy, depressed
Select	choose, opt
Silence	calm, peace

B. ANTONYMS

Abhor	Admire, love, adore
Adore	hate, abhor
Alert	listless, careless
Annex	remove, unfasten
Apex	bottom, nadir
Ban	allow, permit
Beautiful	awful, ugly
Benign	stern, harsh
Boisterous	quiet, peaceful
Brief	lengthy, extensive
Calm	stir, agitate
Careful	careless, unconcerned
Clear	cloudy, vague
Clever	clumsy, boring
Colossal	diminutive, small
Compatible	incompatible, inapt
Courageous	cowardly, timid
Damaging	useful, advantageous
Dangerous	safe, harmless
Deceit	honesty, candour
Delicate	harsh, indelicate
Deny	admit, accept
Dim	bright, clear
Eager	impassive, lazy
Efficient	inefficient, inept
Emerge	enter, fall
Encourage	deter, depress
Engaging	repulsive, unattractive
Fair	unfair, prejudiced
Fake	genuine, bonafide
Fascinating	unattractive, disgusting
Ferocious	mild, gentle
Gallant	cowardly, fearful
Gentle	aggressive, harsh
Gigantic	tiny, puny
Glorious	dull, dim
Handy	clumsy, inept
Happy	unhappy, gloomy
Hard	soft, flexible
Honset	dishonest, unfair
Huge	minute, puny
Idle	active, busy
Illogical	logical, coherent
Incorrect	correct, accurate
Indecent	decent, modest
Innocent	cunning, dishonest
Kind	unkind, cruel
Lazy	active, diligent
Like	unlike, diverse
Lovable	hateful, abhorrent
Major	minor, unimportant
Meek	arrogant, stubborn
Merry	sad, gloomy
Morose	happy, delightful
Nadir	bottom
Nonsense	sense, wisdom
Object	admire, accept
Obscure	clear, vivid
Overbearing	humble, modest
Peaceful	agitated, disturbed
Playful	gloomy, morose
Polite	impolite, ill-mannered
Proficient	incompetent, unskilled
Promising	unpromising, discouraging
Realistic	unrealistic, fanciful
Refined	unrefined, boorish
Reject	accept, select
Robust	feeble, frail
Secure	insecure, unsafe
Sensible	senseless, stupid
Sluggish	energetic, brisk
Tempting	untempting, unattractive
Tepid	zealous, eager
Timid	arrogant, bold
True	untrue, false
Ungainly	elegant, attractive
Unmannerly	mannerly, polite
Valid	invalid, illegal
Verbose	curt, brief
Violent	calm, quiet

IDIOMS AND PHRASES

1. **ABC** (basic principles) She does not know the ABC of photography.
2. **To cut a sorry figure** (present oneself in a bad way)
   She cut a sorry figure on the stage.
3. **Cut loose** (Keep away)
   India should cut loose from bad politics.
4. **To give a red carpet reception** (to give a warm welcome)
   The PM was given a red carpet reception in America.
5. **To dance one's tune** (to follow someone submissively)
   He always dances to his brother's tune.

6. **To turn a deaf ear to** (to disregard)
She turned a deaf ear to her parents' advice.
7. **To call a spade a spade** (to speak the truth)
Gandhiji always called a spade a spade.
8. **To bring to book** (to scold)
The naughty boy was brought to book by the teacher.
9. **From hand to mouth** (without any saving)
The poor factory worker is living from hand to mouth.
10. **Once in a blue moon** (seldom)
She visits her brother once in a blue moon.
11. **To cut short** (to reduce)
Smoking will cut short your life.
12. **By hook or by crook** (by any means fair or foul)
He wants to get money by hook or by crook.
13. **In the good books of** (be good in one's mind)
Jack is in the good books of his teachers.
14. **At sixes and sevens** (in disorder)
The drawing room articles were lying at sixes and sevens on the floor.
15. **To grease the palm of** (to bribe)
Rohit greased the palm of the clerk and got the file moved.
16. **Through thick and thin.** (under all circumstances)
We'll stand by you through thick and thin.
17. **At one's beck and call** (ready to obey)
He had a dozen men at his beck and call.
18. **To die by inches** (to die a painful death)
The old man died by inches.
19. **To eat one's words** (to retract one's statement)
You'll have to eat your words because you have spoken without thinking.
20. **To burn the midnight oil** (to work hard)
You'll have to burn the midnight oil if you want to get good marks.
21. **Fair and square** (clean)
One must be fair and square in one's dealing.
22. **To poke one's nose into** (to meddle with)
It is bad to poke your nose into others' affair.
23. **To fall flat** (to have no effect)
His father's advice fell flat on him.
24. **To make a clean breast of** (to confess)
He made a clean breast of his involvement in the bomb blast.
25. **To get the better of** (overcome)
Anger got the better of him.
26. **A wet blanket** (a discouraging person)
Don't allow Rakesh to accompany you to the hunting trip because he is a wet blanket.
27. **A big gun** (an important person)
Mr Smith is a big gun in our city.
28. **In black and white** (in written)
Don't give him anything in black and white.
29. **Neck and neck** (even)
There is a neck and neck fight between the two boxers.
30. **At a stone's throw** (at a short distance from)
My school is at a stone's throw from my house.
31. **Cut-throat competition** (a stiff competition)
There is a cut-throat competition among the publishers in the market.
32. **Black sheep** (a traitor)
Later on Mr XYZ proved a black sheep.
33. **By dint of** (by means of)
By dint of hard work, she earned a lot of money.
34. **A man of word** (a person who keeps his promise)
Mr Sharma is a man of word.
35. **A man of a few words** (a remarkable person)
Gandhiji was a man of a few words.
36. **In cold blood** (mercilessly)
The old woman was murdered in cold blood.
37. **At arm's length** (to keep away)
We should always keep bad boys at arm's length
38. **Keep the ball rolling** (to maintain the progress of some activity)
After the death of his father he had to take the charge of his office to keep the ball rolling.
39. **A bolt from the blue** (a sudden and unexpected event)
The news of my friend's death came to me like a bolt from the blue.
40. (i) **Break ones back** (to work hard to get something)
He broke his back to earn his livelihood.
(ii) **To break somebody's back** (to give too much work to him to do)
She broke his back by giving him so much hard work to do.
41. **Break the back of** (accomplish the hardest part of a certain job)
There is nothing to be worried about as we've already broken the back of the problem.
42. **Beat about the bush** (to go on talking on some worthless topic)
Stop this beating about the bush, come to the main task.
43. **Throw cold water on** (to discourage)
She tried to throw cold water on his plan but he was well-determined.
44. **Hard of hearing** (somewhat deaf)
She is a bit hard of hearing.
45. **Come what may** (no matter what happens)
I'll do it come what may.
46. **Beyond one's means** (beyond one's budget)
He is living beyond his means, therefore, he is sure to get ruined.

47. **A man of letters** (a scholar)
Radha Krishnan was a man of letters.
48. **Chips of the same block** (having the same taste)
They are the chips of the same block.
49. **The long and short of** (in brief)
The long and short of his lecture is that we should live like brothers.
50. **In full swing** (in full force)
The studies of the students are going on in full swing.
51. **To burn one's fingers** (to get oneself in trouble)
You have burnt your fingers by speaking against him.
52. **A hard nut to crack.** (a puzzling problem)
To get a win over American basket ball team is a hard nut to crack for India.
53. **To turn over a new leaf** (to change the course of life)
He has turned over a new leaf in his life.
54. **A yeoman's service** (service which is beneficial to the human beings)
He did yeoman's service through his life.
55. **To have one's own axe to grind** (to have vested interest)
He has his own axe to grind in this matter.
56. **To take to one's heels** (to run away)
The thief took to his heels as soon as he saw the policeman.
57. **A snake in the grass** (a hidden foe)
Beware of him because he seems to be a snake in the grass.
58. **To move heaven and earth** (to make too much effort)
The young man moved heaven and earth to find a job.
59. **To be caught red handed** (to be caught at the time of committing a crime)
The clerk was caught red handed when he was accepting bribe from Mr ABC.
60. **To receive with open arms** (to give a warm welcome)
The new president of the club was received with open arms by the members.
61. **Acid test** (hard test)
The election will be an acid test for the ruling party.
62. **A wolf in sheep's clothing** (a hypocrite)
You should not keep company with him because he is a wolf in sheep's clothing.
63. **To be born with a silver spoon in one's mouth** (to be born in a rich family)
Mr. J. L. Nehru was born with a silver spoon in his mouth.
64. **At the eleventh hour** (at the last moment)
The war was about to start but fortunately at the eleventh hour a messenger came to the PM with a message of peace.
65. **Drop someone a line** (send a letter, etc.)
Please drop me a line of your well-being.
66. **Dull the edge of** (reduce the intensity of)
Take this pill and it will dull the edge of pain.
67. **A fool of the first water** (one completely foolish)
Being a fool of the first water he could not solve even the simplest sum.
68. **To come to light** (to be known)
A new disease has recently come to light.
69. **To be the apple of one's eye** (be very dear)
He is the apple of his parent's eye.
70. **A bone of contention** (to be the cause of quarrel)
Kashmir is the bone of contention between India and Pakistan.
71. **To make fun of** (laugh at)
The children made fun of the waiter in the hotel.
72. **To let the cat out of the bag** (to divulge secret)
It was Sohan who let the cat out of the bag by telling the real matter.
73. **A great card** (an important person)
Mr Sood is a great card in the ministry of finance.
74. **To open a new chapter** (to start some habit, etc.
By drinking, you've opened a new chapter in your life.
75. **Under a cloud** (be in trouble or in a state of disgrace or suspicion)
His company seemed to be under a cloud as it had no funds to pay the wages to the workers.
76. **In a crack** (all of a sudden or rapidly)
The thief left the place in a crack.
77. **A green hand** (not very much experienced)
We shall pay a little to a green hand.
78. **To make the flesh creep** (to terrify)
The story made my flesh creep.
79. **To lose ground** (to retreat)
After fighting for some time the Pakistani army began to lose ground.
80. **All in all** (completely)
Rajesh is all in all in this office.
81. **An apple of discord** (to be the cause of)
Kashmir is an apple of discord between India and Pakistan.
82. **To bring to book** (to punish)
The student was brought to book by the teacher.
83. **A bed of roses** (a comfort)
Life is not a bed of roses.
84. **To show a clean pair of heels** (to run away)
The thief showed a clean pair of heels as soon as he saw the policeman approaching.

85. **A white elephant** (of no use)
This sort of glib talker always proves a white elephant in the end.

86. **In the twinkling of an eye** (quickly)
The monkey ate up grams in the twinkling of an eye.

87. **To gain ground** (to be established)
He gained ground in India in a few years.

88. **Slow and steady** (slowly but continually)
Slow and steady wins the race.

89. **A red letter day** (An important day)
15th August is a red letter day for the Indians.

90. **To get wind of** (to get information)
I got wind of his secret plans.

MULTIPLE CHOICE QUESTIONS

Directions (Qs. 1 to 50): *In the following questions choose the word which best expresses the meaning of the given word.*

1. INDICT
A. Condemn B. Reprimand
C. Accuse D. Allege

2. SCINTILLATING
A. Smouldering B. Gilittering
C. Touching D. Warming

3. REFECTORY
A. Restaurant B. Parlour
C. Living Room D. Dining Room

4. DISTINCTION
A. Diffusion B. Disagreement
C. Different D. Degree

5. IMPROVEMENT
A. Advancement B. Betterment
C. Promotion D. Preference

6. ADVERSITY
A. Failure B. Helplessness
C. Misfortune D. Crisis

7. TURN UP
A. Land up B. Show up
C. Crop up D. Come up

8. DEIFY
A. Flatter B. Challenge
C. Worship D. Face

9. ERROR
A. Misadventure B. Misgiving
C. Ambiguity D. Blunder

10. SHALLOW
A. Artificial B. Superficial
C. Foolish D. Worthless

11. MASSACRE
A. Murder B. Stab
C. Assissinate D. Slaughter

12. COMBAT
A. Conflict B. Quarrel
C. Feud D. Fight

13. VORACIOUS
A. Wild B. Hungry
C. Angry D. Quick

14. IMPROMPTU
A. Offhand B. Unimportant
C. Unreal D. Effective

15. RABBLE
A. Mob B. Noise
C. Roar D. Rubbish

16. TEPID
A. Hot B. Warm
C. Cold D. Boiling

17. MAYHEM
A. Jubilation B. Havoc
C. Excitement D. Defeat

18. TIMID
A. Fast B. Slow
C. Medium D. Shy

19. CANTANKEROUS
A. Quarrelsome B. Rash
C. Disrepectful D. Noisy

20. PRECARIOUS
A. Cautious B. Critical
C. Perilous D. Brittle

21. TACITURNITY
A. Dumbness B. Changeableness
C. Hesitation D. Reserve

22. INEBRIATE
A. Dreamy B. Stupefied
C. Unsteady D. Drunken

23. HARBINGER
A. Massenger B. Steward
C. Forerunner D. Pilot

24. INTIMIDATE
A. To hint B. Frighten
C. Bluff D. Harass

25. IRONIC
A. Inflexible
B. Bitter
C. Good-natured
D. Disguisedly sarcastic

26. STRINGENT
A. Tense B. Stringy
C. Strict D. Causing to shrink

27. ECSTATIC
A. Animated B. Bewildered
C. Enraptured D. Illful

28. COMMENSURATE
A. Measurable B. Proportionate
C. Beginning D. Appropriate

29. DESTITUTION
A. Humility B. Moderation
C. Poverty D. Beggary

30. ASCEND
A. Leap B. Grow
C. Deviate D. Mount

31. UNCOUTH
A. Ungraceful B. Rough
C. Slovenly D. Dirty

32. LYNCH
A. Hang B. Madden
C. Killed D. Shoot

33. LAUD
A. Lord B. Eulogy
C. Praise D. Extolled

34. CORRESPONDENCE
A. Agreements B. Contracts
C. Documents D. Letters

35. VENUE
A. Place B. Agenda
C. Time D. Duration

36. STERILE
A. Barren B. Arid
C. Childless D. Dry

37. SYNOPSIS
A. Index B. Mixture
C. Summary D. Puzzle

38. GERMANE
A. Responsible B. Logical
C. Possible D. Relevant

39. PONDER
A. Think B. Evaluate
C. Anticipate D. Increase

40. CANNY
A. Obstinate B. Handsome
C. Clever D. Stout

41. ABUNDANT
A. Ripe B. Cheap
C. Plenty D. Absent

42. CONSEQUENCES
A. Results B. Conclusions
C. Difficulties D. Applications

43. SHIVER
A. Shake B. Rock
C. Tremble D. Move

44. DILIGENT
A. Progressive B. Brilliant
C. Inventive D. Hard-working

45. DISTANT
A. Far B. Removed
C. Reserved D. Separate

46. FORAY
A. Excursion B. Contest
C. Ranger D. Intuition

47. FRUGALITY
A. Foolishness B. Extremity
C. Enthusiasm D. Economy

48. GARNISH
A. Paint B. Garner
C. Adorn D. Abuse

49. VIGOUR
A. Strength B. Boldness
C. Warmth D. Enthusiasm

50. CANDID
A. Apparent B. Explicit
C. Frank D. Bright

Directions (Qs. 51 to 100): *In the following questions choose the word which is the exact OPPOSITE of the given words.*

51. EPILOGUE
A. Dialogue B. Prelude
C. Post script D. Epigram

52. FRAUDULENT
A. Candid B. Direct
C. Forthright D. Genuine

53. LOQUCIOUS
A. Reticent B. Talkative
C. Garrulous D. Verbose

54. NIGGARDLY
A. Frugal B. Thrifty
C. Stingy D. Generous

55. PERTINENT
A. Irrational B. Irregular
C. Insistent D. Irrelevant

56. FAINT-HEARTED
A. Warm-hearted B. Full-blooded
C. Hot-blooded D. Stout-hearted

57. VIOLENT
A. Humble B. Harmless
C. Gentle D. Tame

58. STATIONARY
A. Active B. Mobile
C. Rapid D. Busy

59. HONORARY
A. Dishonourable B. Reputed
C. Paid D. Official

60. COMMON
A. Rare B. Small
C. Petty D. Poor

61. FRUGAL
A. Copious B. Extravagant
C. Generous D. Ostentatious

ENGLISH

62. MALICIOUS
A. Kind B. Boastful
C. Generous D. Indifferent

63. FAMILIAR
A. Unpleasant B. Dangerous
C. Friendly D. Strange

64. PRELIMINARY
A. Final B. First
C. Secondary D. Initial

65. DOUBTFUL
A. Famous B. Certain
C. Fixed D. Important

66. REMISS
A. Forgetful B. Watchful
C. Dutiful D. Harmful

67. INDISCREET
A. Reliable B. Honest
C. Prudent D. Stupid

68. FRESH
A. Faulty B. Sluggish
C. Disgraceful D. Stale

69. ANNOY
A. Praise B. Rejoice
C. Please D. Reward

70. TRANSPARENT
A. Semi-transparent B. Muddy
C. Opaque D. Dark

71. REVEALED
A. Denied B. Concealed
C. Ignored D. Overlooked

72. EXTRAVAGANCE
A. Luxury B. Poverty
C. Economy D. Cheapness

73. CROWDED
A. Busy B. Congested
C. Quiet D. Deserted

74. SHRINK
A. Contract B. Spoil
C. Expand D. Stretch

75. ENMITY
A. Important B. Unnecessary
C. Friendship D. Likeness

76. EXODUS
A. Influx B. Home-coming
C. Return D. Restoration

77. CULPABLE
A. Defendable B. Blameless
C. Careless D. Irresponsible

78. SUBSERVIENT
A. Aggressive B. Straightforward
C. Dignified D. Supercilious

79. AWARE
A. Uncertain B. Ignorant
C. Sure D. Doubtful

80. GRACEFUL
A. Rough B. Expert
C. Miserable D. Awkward

81. AUTONOMY
A. Slavery B. Subordination
C. Dependence D. Submissiveness

82. NADIR
A. Modernity B. Zenith
C. Liberty D. Progress

83. CONCEDE
A. Object B. Refuse
C. Grant D. Accede

84. SUPPRESS
A. Encourage B. Grow
C. Praise D. Permit

85. FAMOUS
A. Disgraced B. Notorious
C. Evil D. Popular

86. EXPAND
A. Contract B. Condense
C. Congest D. Conclude

87. ARROGANT
A. Polite B. Cowardly
C. Meek D. Gentlemanly

88. ENORMOUS
A. Soft B. Average
C. Tiny D. Weak

89. URBANE
A. Illiterate B. Backward
C. Discourteous D. Orthodox

90. HOSTILITY
A. Courtesy B. Hospitality
C. Relationship D. Friendliness

91. BELITTLE
A. Praise B. Flatter
C. Exaggerate D. Adore

92. HAPLESS
A. Cheerful B. Consistent
C. Fortunate D. Shapely

93. HAPHAZARD
A. Fortuitous B. Indifferent
C. Deliberate D. Accidental

94. GREGARIOUS
A. Antisocial B. Glorious
C. Horrendous D. Similar

95. VALUABLE
A. Invaluable B. Worthless
C. Inferior D. Lowly

96. ABSOLUTE
A. Deficient B. Faulty
C. Limited D. Scarce

97. CONFESS
A. Deny B. Refuse
C. Contest D. Contend

98. GULLIBLE
A. Incredulous B. Fickle
C. Easy D. Stylish

99. HIRSUTE
A. Scaly B. Bald
C. Erudite D. Quiet

100. HINDRANCE
A. Aid B. Persuasion
C. Cooperation D. Agreement

Directions (Qs. 101 to 150): *In questions given below out of the four alternatives choose the one which can be substituted for the given words/sentence.*

101. Something that relates to everyone in the world.
A. General B. Common
C. Usual D. Universal

102. An expression of mild disapproval.
A. Warning B. Denigration
C. Impertinence D. Reproof

103. One who is not easily pleased by anything.
A. Maiden B. Mediaeval
C. Precarious D. Fastidious

104. Murder of a king
A. Infanticide B. Matricide
C. Genocide D. Regicide

105. A remedy for all diseases.
A. Stoic B. Marvel
C. Panacea D. Recompense

106. A dramatic performance
A. Mask B. Mosque
C. Masque D. Mascot

107. Study of birds
A. Orology B. Optology
C. Ophthalmology D. Ornithology

108. Ready to believe
A. Credulous B. Credible
C. Creditable D. Incredible

109. Incapable of being seen through.
A. Ductile B. Opaque
C. Obsolete D. Potable

110. One who eats everything—
A. Omnivorous B. Omniscient
C. Irresistible D. Insolvent

111. A place where bees are kept is called
A. An apiary B. A mole
C. A hive D. A sanctuary

112. One who cannot be corrected.
A. Incurable B. Incorrigible
C. Hardened D. Invulnerable

113. One who is in charge of a museum.
A. Curator B. Supervisor
C. Caretaker D. Warden

114. Continuing fight between parties, families, clans, etc.
A. Enmity B. Feud
C. Quarrel D. Skirmish

115. A voice loud enough to be heard.
A. Audible B. Applaudable
C. Laudable D. Oral

116. A paper written by hand.
A. Handicraft B. Manuscript
C. Handiwork D. Thesis

117. Habitually silent or talking little.
A. Serville B. Unequivocal
C. Taciturn D. Synoptic

118. To slap with a flat object.
A. Chop B. Hew
C. Gnaw D. Swat

119. A person who speaks many languages.
A. Linguist B. Monolingual
C. Polyglot D. Bilingual

120. A light sailing-boat built specially for racing.
A. Canoe B. Yacht
C. Frigate D. Dinghy

121. A fixed orbit in space in relation to earth.
A. Geological B. Geo-synchronous
C. Geo-centric D. Geo-stationary

122. A style in which a writer makes a display of his knowledge.
A. Pedantic B. Verbose
C. Pompous D. Ornate

123. A religious discourse.
A. Preach B. Stanza
C. Sanctorum D. Sermon

124. A place that provides refuge.
A. Asylum B. Sanatorium
C. Shelter D. Orphanage

125. Detailed plan of a journey.
A. Travelogue B. Travelkit
C. Schedule D. Itinerary

126. A person who insists on something.
A. Disciplinarian B. Stickler
C. Instantaneous D. Boaster

127. A drawing on transparent paper
A. Red print B. Blue print
C. Negative D. Transparency

128. One who believes that all things and events in life are predetermined is a
A. Fatalist B. Puritan
C. Egoist D. Tyrant

129. A school boy who cuts classes frequently is a
A. Defeatist B. Sycophant
C. Truant D. Martinet

130. The act of violating the sanctity of the church is

A. Blasphemy B. Heresy
C. Sacrilege D. Desecration

131. A place where monks live as a secluded community.
A. Cathedral B. Diocese
C. Convent D. Monastery

132. One who is fond of fighting
A. Bellicose B. Aggressive
C. Belligerent D. Militant

133. Tending to move away from the centre or axis.
A. Centrifugal B. Centripetal
C. Axiomatic D. Awry

134. Words inscribed on tomb.
A. Epitome B. Epistle
C. Epilogue D. Epitaph

135. Leave or remove from a place considered dangerous.
A. Evade B. Evacuate
C. Avoid D. Exterminate

136. Malafide case is one
A. which is undertaken in good faith
B. which is undertaken in bad faith
C. which is undertaken after a long delay
D. which is not undertaken at all

137. The *raison d'etre* of a controversy is
A. the enthusiasm with which it is kept alive
B. the finesse with which partici-pants handle it
C. the reason or justification of its existence
D. the unending hostility the parties con-cerned have towards each other

138. A prima facie case is such
A. as it seems at first sight
B. as it is made to seem at first sight
C. as it turns out to be at the end
D. as it seems to the court after a number of hearings

139. A person of good understanding, knowledge and reasoning power.
A. Expert B. Intellectual
C. Snob D. Literate

140. One absorbed in his own thoughts and feelings rather than in things outside.
A. Scholar B. Recluse
C. Introvert D. Intellectual

141. One who does not marry, especially as a religious obligation
A. Bachelor B. Celibate
C. Virgin D. Recluse

142. A person who tries to deceive people by claiming to be able to do wonderful things.
A. Trickster B. Impostor
C. Magician D. Mountebank

143. To take secretly in small quantities
A. Robbery B. Pilferage
C. Theft D. Defalcation

144. Policemen riding on motorcycles as guards to a VIP.
A. Outriders B. Servants
C. Commandos D. Attendants

145. The part of a government which is concerned with making of rules.
A. Court B. Tribunal
C. Bar D. Legislature

146. That which cannot be corrected-
A. Unintelligible B. Indelible
C. Illegible D. Incorrigible

147. A child born after the death of its fater-
A. Posthumous B. Orphan
C. Bastard D. Progenitor

148. Something that can be heard-
A. Auditory B. Audio-visual
C. Audible D. Audition

149. One who dabbles in fine arts for the love of it and not for monetary gains:
A. Connoisseur B. Amateur
C. Professional D. Dilettante

150. To accustom oneself to a foreign climate.
A. Adapt B. Adopt
C. Accustom D. Acclimatise

Directions (Qs. 151 to 170): *Some proverbs/idioms are given below together with their meanings. Choose the correct meaning of the proverb/idiom. If there is no correct meaning given, E i.e. 'None of these' will be the answer.*

151. To beg the question
A. To refer to
B. To take for granted
C. To raise objections
D. To be discussed
E. None of these

152. To drive home
A. To find one's roots
B. To return to place of rest
C. Back to original position
D. To emphasise
E. None of these

153. To hit the right nail on the head
A. To do the right thing
B. To destroy one's reputation
C. To announce one's fixed views
D. To teach someone a lesson
E. None of these

154. To pick holes
A. To find some reason to quarrel
B. To destory something

C. To criticise someone
D. To cut some part of an item
E. None of these

155. To smell a rat
A. To see signs of plague epidemic
B. To get bad smell of a dead rat
C. To suspect foul dealings
D. To be in a bad mood
E. None of these

156. A black sheep
A. An unlucky person
B. A negro
C. An ugly person
D. A partner who takes no share of the profits
E. None of these

157. To catch a tarter
A. To trap wanted criminal with great difficulty
B. To catch a dangerous person
C. To meet with disaster
D. To deal with a person who is more than one's watch
E. None of these

158. To be above board
A. To have a good height
B. To be honest in any business deal
C. To have no debts
D. To try to be beautiful
E. None of these

159. To keep one's temper
A. To become angry
B. To be in good mood
C. To preserve one's energy
D. To be aloof from
E. None of these

160. To have an axe to grind
A. A private end to serve
B. To fail to arouse interest
C. To have no result
D. To work for both sides
E. None of these

161. To cry wolf
A. to listen eagerly
B. to give false alarm
C. to turn pale
D. to keep off starvation
E. None of these

162. A man of straw
A. a man of no substance
B. a very active person
C. a worthy fellow
D. an unreasonable person
E. None of these

163. To make clean breast of
A. to gain prominence
B. to praise oneself
C. to confess without reserve
D. to destroy before it blooms
E. None of these

164. To end in smoke
A. to make completely understand
B. to ruin oneself
C. to excite great applause
D. to overcome someone
E. None of these

165. To leave someone in the lurch
A. to come to compromise with someone
B. constant source of annoyance to someone
C. to put someone at ease
D. to desert someone in his difficulties
E. None of these

166. To play second fiddle
A. To be happy, cheerful and healthy
B. To reduce importance of one's senior
C. To support the role and view of another person
D. To do back seat driving
E. None of these

167. To set one's face against
A. To oppose with determination
B. To judge by appearance
C. To get out of difficulty
D. To look at one steadily
E. None of these

168. To put one's hand to the plough
A. To take up agricultural farming
B. To take a difficult task
C. To get entangled into unnecessary things
D. Take interest in technical work
E. None of these

169. To join issue with
A. To cooperate with others for a cause
B. To join any voluntary organisation for good purpose
C. To resolve dispute and restore peace
D. To enter into argument over any issue
E. None of these

170. To do oneself justice
A. To dispense justice on our own
B. To treat others with due respect
C. To defend one's point of view
D. To follow the path of truth and justice
E. None of these

ENGLISH

ANSWERS

1	2	3	4	5	6	7	8	9	10
C	B	D	C	B	C	B	C	D	B
11	12	13	14	15	16	17	18	19	20
D	D	B	A	A	B	B	D	A	B
21	22	23	24	25	26	27	28	29	30
D	D	C	B	D	C	C	B	C	D
31	32	33	34	35	36	37	38	39	40
A	C	C	D	A	A	C	D	A	C
41	42	43	44	45	46	47	48	49	50
C	A	C	D	A	A	D	C	A	C
51	52	53	54	55	56	57	58	59	60
B	D	B	D	D	D	C	B	C	A
61	62	63	64	65	66	67	68	69	70
B	C	D	A	B	C	C	D	C	C
71	72	73	74	75	76	77	78	79	80
B	C	D	D	C	A	A	C	B	A
81	82	83	84	85	86	87	88	89	90
C	B	B	B	B	B	A	C	C	D
91	92	93	94	95	96	97	98	99	100
C	C	C	A	B	C	A	A	B	A
101	102	103	104	105	106	107	108	109	110
D	D	D	D	C	C	D	A	B	A
111	112	113	114	115	116	117	118	119	120
A	B	A	B	A	B	C	D	A	B
121	122	123	124	125	126	127	128	129	130
D	A	D	A	D	B	D	A	C	C
131	132	133	134	135	136	137	138	139	140
D	A	A	D	B	B	C	A	B	C
141	142	143	144	145	146	147	148	149	150
B	A	B	A	D	D	A	C	B	D
151	152	153	154	155	156	157	158	159	160
B	D	A	C	C	E	B	B	B	A
161	162	163	164	165	166	167	168	169	170
B	A	C	E	D	C	A	B	B	E

❑❑❑

FUNCTIONAL GRAMMAR

ARTICLES

Articles are a kind of demonstrative Adjectives. Also being determiners, they precede nouns.

Kinds of Articles

There are two kinds of articles.

(a) Indefinite Articles
(b) Definite Article

(a) Indefinite Articles (a, an)

'A' and 'an' are called indefinite articles because they point out inanimate or animate objects in general. They do not particularize objects.

(i) A cat mews. (ii) An owl hoots.

(b) Definite Article (the)

'The' is called definite article because it points out (a) particular object/objects.

(i) A cat mews. **The cat** is black in colour.
(ii) Dogs are barking. **The dogs** are running after a beggar.

A and An Distinguished

(a) 'A' is used before a noun or adjective etc. which begins with a consonant sound, *e.g.,* a lion, a book, a table, a black cat, a brown bag, a university, a year, etc.

(b) 'An' is used before a noun or adjective etc which begins with a vowel sound, *e.g.,* an honest boy, an hour, an umbrella, an egg, an elephant, an MA, an MBBS, an FDR, etc.

Uses of Indefinite and Definite Articles

Definite and Indefinite articles are used,

1. Before a countable noun: **A cow** is grazing in the field. **A rhinoceros** can run as fast as man.
2. To convey the numerical value 'one'
   (i) Once there was a lion.
   (ii) She bought an umbrella.
3. To denote a whole class
   (i) A crow caws. (Every crow caws.)
   (ii) The camel is a beast of burden. (Every camel is a beast of burden.)
4. (i) He is a boy. (general use of an article)
   (ii) He is **the boy** who met us in the circus. (A particular boy)
   (iii) **The boys** who met us at the Paul Cafe were my classmates. (Particular boys)
5. A Proper name does not take an article.
   (i) His name is Jack. (ii) I am Girish.

   But when a proper noun is used as a common noun, it takes an article.
   (i) We need **a Kapil Dev** to win the match. (a player who can play well as Kapil Dev did.)
   (ii) Sohan is **the Kalidas** of our school. (He writes the plays well as Kalidas did.)
6. An abstract noun does not take an article
   (i) Give me more oil.
   (ii) Give me a litre oil.
   (iii) Milk is essential for health.
   (iv) She drank a little water.

   But 'the' is sometimes used with abstract nouns to give a particular sense.
   (i) **The Milk** of this cow is sweet.
   (ii) **The Water** in this jug seems to be contaminated.
7. To lay emphasis
   (i) Ashoka, **the Great** was kind and wise.
   (ii) Gandhi **the** peace lover, was the foremost freedom fighter.
8. An article is not used before the name of a disease, sport, subject, etc.

(i) Measles is not a fatal disease.

(ii) She died of cancer.

(iii) I like football. (sport)

(iv) He kicked the football. (an object to play)

(v) I have no taste for music/mathematics.

But sometimes an article is used before a disease to give a particular sense.

Corruption is **a** cancer in society

9. Definite Article is used before the superlatives:
   (i) He is **the** strongest boy in our class.
   (ii) Rohit is **the** tallest boy in our street.
10. The Germans usually speak in their mother tongue. (the people of Germany)
11. Sometimes an article is not used before a common noun when it is used in its widest sense.
   (i) Man is mortal.
   (ii) Woman is the creator of all mankind.

Definite Article is used in the followings manners:

1. Before the names of monuments
   (i) The Taj
   (ii) The Red Fort
2. Before the names of rivers, gulfs, mountain ranges, oceans, channels, etc.
   (i) The Himalayas (ii) The Alps
   (iii) The Ganga (iv) The Yamuna
   (v) The Bay of Bengal (vi) The Indian Ocean
   (vii) The Pacific Ocean
   (viii) The English Channel
3. Before the names of the newspapers, magazines & journals
   (i) The Hindu (ii) The Times of India
   (iii) The Sun (iv) The Sunday.
4. Before the names of the Holy Books
   (i) The Gita (ii) The Bible
   (iii) The Ramayana
5. Before the names of trains, ships, aeroplanes, missile etc.
   (i) The Rajdhani Express
   (ii) The Vikrant (iii) The MIG-22
   (iv) The Agni - II (v) The Prithvi
6. Before the names of musical instruments
   (i) The guitar (ii) The piano
   (iii) The violin (iv) The flute
7. Before the names of imaginary geographical lines and directions
   (i) The Longitude
   (ii) The Latitude
   (iii) The Tropic of Cancer
   (iv) The Tropic of Capricorn
   (v) The Equator
   (vi) The East
   (vii) The West
8. Before the names of races, political parties, movements, etc.
   (i) The Sikhs
   (ii) The Jews
   (iii) The BJP
   (iv) The Indian National Congress
   (v) The Quit India Movement
9. Before a comparative degree
   (i) The more you laugh, the more you look foolish.
   (ii) The more you work, the more you gain.

MODALS

A verb which is used to help the finite verb in a sentence is called an Auxiliary Verb.

You **should** help the poor.

In the aforesaid sentence 'help' is the finite verb whereas 'should' has been used as a helping verb so 'should' is an auxiliary.

The auxiliary verbs can be classified into two categories.

I Primary Auxiliaries

II Modal Auxiliaries

I. Primary Auxiliaries

The primary auxiliaries can be used either finite verbs or helping verbs. They are three in number.

Be = be, is, am, are, was, were, being, been

Do = do, does, did, done, doing

Have = have, has, had, having.

Be / Do / Have as helping verbs

(i) She is singing a song.

(ii) He does not know how to swim.

(iii) John has painted the pictures.

Be / Do / have as finite verbs

(i) She is an intelligent girl.

(ii) Anu will be doing her homework.

(iii) I have an exotic pen.

Modals Auxiliaries

The following are the commonly used modal auxiliaries:

Can, could, shall, should, will, would, may, might, must, mustn't, need, needn't, dare, daren't, ought to, used to, have to, had to.

Can

Can is used:

1. To express present ability
   (i) I can count upto 1000.
   (ii) I can speak French.
2. To make a request
   (i) Can I open the door?
   (ii) Can I switch on the light?
3. To give permission
   (i) You can go now.
   (ii) You can sit down now.
4. To express an impossibility
   (i) Who can defeat death?
   (ii) Who can reject God?

Could

Could is used:

1. As the past tense of 'can'.
   (i) She said that she could understand French.
   (ii) The boy said that he could solve all the sums.
2. To make polite requests
   (i) Could I use your bike?
   (ii) Could you help me?
3. To express past ability
   (i) Seema could work for ten hours a day at a stretch when she was young.
   (ii) He could read and write well when he was a student.

Shall

Shall is used:

1. To express a simple future tense with first person pronouns
   (i) I shall bring you something to eat.
   (ii) We shall buy a new house next year.
2. Used in questions indicating suggestions/offers
   (i) Shall I make you a cup of tea?
   (ii) Shall we play the piano in the evening?

Note: Shall is used with the second and third person as under:

(A) To express a strong assertion, determination, promise or intention
   (i) You shall have your will.
   (ii) He shall have his due.

(B) To express a threat
   (i) You shall be punished soon.
   (ii) He shall be taken to task by the officer.

(C) To express a legal obligation
   (i) All the candidates shall submit their resumes at time of interview.
   (ii) You shall return all your loans by the end of this year.

(D) To express a prohibition
   (i) You shall not stick bills on this wall.
   (ii) You shall not litter the room with the pieces of paper.

Should

Should is used:

1. As Past Tense of 'Shall'
   (i) She said she should not invest in that project.
   (ii) The old man said that he should try to bring round his son to his idea.
2. To express moral duty/obligation
   (i) We should love our countrymen.
   (ii) We should look after our elders.
3. To give a piece of advice or suggestion
   (i) Should you find something suspicious, phone me at once.
   (ii) Should you need something, call me without hesitation.
4. To express purpose with 'lest'
   (i) Walk fast lest you should miss the train.
   (ii) Work hard lest you should get poor marks.
5. To express assumption
   (i) It should be about I am.
   (ii) This book should be somewhere between a hundred and hundred fifty.

Will

Will is used:

1. To express plans for the future, when used with second and third persons
   (i) You will go to the station to receive the guests.
   (ii) They will join the army.
2. To express a request
   (i) Will you allow me to use your phone?
   (ii) Will you lend me some money?
3. To express determination
   (i) He will not open his mouth against you.
   (ii) She will do or die.
4. To express an invitation
   (i) Will you have some snacks?
   (ii) Will you dine at ours tonight?
5. To express a universal or habitual truth
   (i) The sun will set in the west.
   (ii) My brother will take a cup of tea after dinner.

Note: 'Will' is used with the First Person to express:

(A) A Promise

(i) I will suggest your name at today's meeting.

(ii) I will recommend your name to the manager.

(B) A threat

(i) I won't allow you to cross this road again.

(ii) I will pay you back in your own coin.

(C) A refusal

(i) I won't support you.

(ii) I won't lend you any money.

Would

Would is used:

1. as a Past Tense of 'will'

(i) She said that she would complete her post graduation.

(ii) He said that his uncle would start the sale and purchase of computers in America.

2. To express a wish

(i) Would that I were rich!

(ii) Would that I were the PM!

3. To make a polite offer

(i) Would you take a cup of tea?

(ii) Would you like to eat apples or oranges?

4. To express unreal condition in the past

(i) Had you run fast you would have won the match ?

(ii) Had she told us before, it would not have happened ?

5. To give advice

(i) I wouldn't bicker with you if I were you.

(ii) I wouldn't let him go if I were you.

6. To express consequence

(i) He would be dismissed if he was caught red handed.

(ii) He would be punished if the teacher saw him laugh.

7. To express willingness

(i) I would leave these premises if you wish so.

(ii) I would not come here again if you say so.

May

May is used:

1. To express wish/prayer

(i) May you live long!

(ii) May God help you!

2. To express possibility

(i) It may snow today.

(ii) It may rain today.

3. To seek permission

(i) May I come in, sir?

(ii) May I go now?

4. To give permission

(i) You may go in (come in).

(ii) You may go now.

Might

Might is used:

1. To express the past tense of 'may'

(i) He asked me if I might help him.

(ii) She asked him if she might lead him to the railway station.

2. To express remote possibility

(i) It might rain today.

(ii) It might snow tonight.

Note: Might expresses less possibility than 'may'.

3. To seek permission

(i) Might I come in, sir?

(ii) Might I go now?

4. To give permission

(i) You might come in.

(ii) You might go now.

Note: 'Might' is a softer word than 'may' but it is less frequently used than 'may'.

Must

Must is used:

1. To express compulsion

(i) You must learn this lesson.

(ii) You must work hard.

2. To express obligation

(i) You must speak the truth.

(ii) You must obey your teachers.

3. To express strong possibility

(i) It must rain today.

(ii) It must snow tonight.

4. To express determination

(i) I must win the match.

(ii) I must stand first in the class.

5. To give advice

(i) You must go to office in car.

(ii) You must take a bath daily.

Ought to

'Ought to' is used:

1. To express advice

(i) You ought to see a doctor.

(ii) You ought to reach the station in time.

2. To express moral obligation

(i) You ought to obey your teachers.

(ii) You ought to pay your taxes.

3. To express guess

(i) This food ought to be enough for three persons.

(ii) Four lakh ought to be money enough for buying a car.

Used to

'Used to' is used:

1. To depict existence of something in the past
   (i) There used to be a palace in this city.
   (ii) There used to be a zoo at that place.
2. To express some habit in the past
   (i) She used to eat some sugar after lunch.
   (ii) He used to smoke whenever he felt tense.

Note: 'used to' is always used in past tense. It does not have a present form.

Have to and Had to

'Have to' is used to express a compulsion in present time whereas 'had to' is used to express a compulsion in past time.

(i) She has to prepare a speech for the chair person.
(ii) You had to go to Shimla to meet the manager.
(iii) They have to sign the documents.
(iv) Deepak had to resign his job.

Note: A few modal auxiliaries like used to, had to, etc are always used in past tense but others may be used in present or past tense, *e.g.,*

(i) He can solve all the sums. (Present Tense)
He could solve all the sums. (Past tense)
(ii) She will sing a song. (Present Tense)
She would sing a song. (Past Tense).
(iii) I shall talk to you later on. (Future Tense)
I should talk to you later on. (Present or Past Tense).
(iv) You may go there. (Present tense)
(v) You might go there. (Present or past tense).

NOUN

A noun is the name of a person place or thing, *e.g.,*

(a) He is a boy. (Person)
(b) Let us go to the library. (Place)
(c) Where is my bag? (Thing)

All animals, insects and birds are also nouns.

Kinds of Noun

There are the following kinds of Noun:

1. Common Noun
2. Proper Noun
3. Collective Noun
4. Material Noun
5. Abstract Noun

1. Common Noun

A common noun begins with a small letter but if it is the sentence starting word then its first letter should be written capital. A common noun is the name of a person, place or thing, *e.g.,*

(i) A **crow** is black.
(ii) This **table** is expensive.

Some other common nouns:

(a) Persons: Man, woman, father, mother, cousin, postman, doctor, teacher, policeman
(b) Animals: Cow, sheep, elephant, tiger, lion, rabbit, etc.
(c) Birds: Peacock, sparrow, dove, pigeon, parrot, etc.
(d) Insects: Ant, mosquito, cockroach, wasp, etc.
(e) Sea Creatures: Dolphin, shark, starfish, octopus, snail, cod, etc.
(f) Places: School, hospital, office, bus stop, railway station, etc.

2. Proper Noun

A proper noun is the name of a particular person, place or thing. It always starts with a capital letters.

(a) **Mohit** is my classmate. (Person)
(b) **Delhi** is the capital of **India**. (Places)
(c) **Jacky**, my pet, seldom barks. (Animal)

When an article is used before a proper noun, it changes into a common noun, *e.g*

(a) Rohit is **the Kalidas** of our class. (He writes plays as nicely as Kalidas wrote).
(b) We need a Gandhi to establish peace in the world. (A person who is as impressive as Gandhi was.)

3. A Collective Noun

A collective noun is the name of a group of persons, animals, birds, places or things taken together and regarded as one entity, *e.g.,*

(a) a bunch of grapes/keys
(b) a bouquet of flowers
(c) a fleet of ships/cars
(d) a galaxy of stars
(e) a class of students
(f) a block of birds/sheep
(g) a herd of cattle
(h) a swarm of bees/mosquitoes/flies
(i) an army of ants
(j) a band of musicians
(k) a gang of robbers
(l) a clutch of eggs
(m) a gaggle of geese
(n) an army of ants
(o) a troupe of dancers/actors/singers

4. Material Noun

The raw materials which are obtained from nature and the other things are made from them are known as material nouns, *e.g.,*

(a) **Cotton** is used to make cloth.
(b) **Honey** contains sugar and minerals.
(c) **Milk** is good for health.
(d) Woollen clothes are made of **wool**.
(e) **Wheat** is the staple food of the Punjabis.

We usually do not use an article with a material noun but when a material noun is used in a particular sense, the article 'the' is used e.g.,

(a) **Water** is essential for life.
The **water** of this well is sweet.
(b) **Milk** is a complete food.
The **milk** of this cow is full of fats.

5. An Abstract Noun

An abstract noun introduces us to some abstract idea, subject, action, state of being, etc. An abstract noun does not have a concrete shape.

(a) State of being: death, sleep, soundness, sickness, sadness, wilderness, calmness childhood, boyhood, etc.
(b) Quality: A person may either possess a good quality or, a bad one.
(i) Good qualities: bravery, gentleness, kindness, sincerity, faithfulness, etc.
(ii) Bad Qualities: laziness, cunningness, meanness,
(iii) Action: completion, objection, theft, recreation, meditation, etc.
(iv) Result of an action : excitement, punishment, etc.
(v) Ability: encourage, wisdom, intelligents, etc.
(vi) Names of various branches of science, arts, professions, etc: Physics, chemistry, zoology, botany, music, pharmacy, engineering, cooking, singing, dancing, yachting, etc

An abstract noun usually does not take an article, except sometimes when it is used before it to give a particular sense e.g.,

(a) **Love** begets love.
He is **the love** of her dreams. (A person whom she loves in the dreams.)
(b) **The love** of Laila for Majnu was immortal.
(c) She has a lack of **sensitivity**.
He has a **sensitivity** to citrus fruits.

Noun as a Subject

A noun can be used as a subject. A subject has a quality. It may be in a state of being; it may do some action or it may sometimes show an action taking place on it when the passive verb is used.

(i) Sumit plays the flute well. (Subject with an active verb.)
(ii) The boy was ill. (Subject in a state of being.)
(iii) The culprit was brought to book (Action taking place on the Subject.)

Noun as an Object of a Verb

A noun can be used as an object when the action of the subject passes over to it.

(i) He plucked flowers.
(ii) She sings a song.

Noun as an Indirect Subject (Dative Case)

Sometimes a noun is used as an Indirect Subject. Then it is said to be in the Dative Case.

(i) She gave John a purse.
(ii) She made Jack a cup of tea.
(iii) Mohit bought Ravi a bicycle.

Nouns in Apposition

When in order to explain a noun, another noun is used, the latter is said to be in apposition to the former:

(i) Mr Joshi, our neighbour, suffered a heart attack.
(ii) Sheila, my darling aunt, made me an Italian dish.

PRONOUN

The word which is used in place of a noun is known as a pronoun, *e.g.,*

(i) Rohit is my classmate. **He** is an intelligent boy.
(ii) Raveena is my neighbour. **She** sings well.

In sentence no. (i) 'He' is a pronoun because it stands for **Rohit** (a masculine noun).

In sentence no (ii) 'She' is a pronoun because it stands for **Raveena** (a feminine noun).

Kinds of Pronoun

There are following kinds of Pronoun :

I. Personal Pronouns
II. Reflexive Pronouns
III. Emphatic Pronouns
IV. Indefinite Pronouns
V. Demonstrative Pronouns
VI. Distributive Pronouns
VII. Reciprocal Pronouns
VIII. Interrogative Pronouns
IX. Relative Pronouns

I. Personal Pronouns

The personal pronouns stand for persons. Like nouns these pronouns also have their singular and plural forms and also have genders like nouns.

They can be read in the following ways:

Personal Pronoun: Subject of Sentences

The following pronouns can be used as subjects in sentences:

I, We, You, He, She, They.

Singular	Plural
(i) **I** am going to school.	(i) **We** are going to the market.
(ii) **He** is my best friend.	(ii) **You** are my best friend/friends.
(iii) (a) **He** knows how to swim.	(iii) (a) **They** know how to fly kites.
(b) **She** writes a letter.	(b) **They** sing songs.

Note: 'You' always takes a plural verb. It may stand for one person or more than one person.

I and we are known as the first person pronouns.

'I' is used by the speaker to describe himself.

'We' is used by more than one speaker to describe themselves.

'You' stands for one or more than one person close to the speaker.

'He' stands for a male singular noun usually not present at the place of speaking or who may be at a distance.

Note: 'You' is also used as object for one or more than one person close to the speaker.

Objective Case

Masculine	Feminine	Masculine	Feminine
me	me	us	us
you	you	him	her
them	them		

Personal Pronouns - Possessive Case

The following pronouns are used as possessive pronouns:

mine, ours, yours, his, hers, theirs

Singular	Plural
(i) This book is **mine**.	(i) Those shirts are **ours**.
(ii) It is **your** pen.	(ii) These pens are **yours.**
(iii) (a) The friend of **his** does not look active.	(iii) (a) Those pencils are **theirs**.
(b) This cat is **hers**.	(b) These dogs are **theirs**.

Note: 'Yours' is used to show the possession of one or more than one person.

'She' stands for a female singular noun usually not present at the place of speaking or who may be a distance.

Plural of 'He' and 'She' is 'They'.

For a small bird or animal 'It' word is used and the plural form of 'It' is 'They'.

Nominative Case

Masculine	Feminine	Masculine	Feminine
I	I	We	We
You	You	He	She
They	They		

Personal Pronouns:- Objects of Sentences

The following pronouns can be used as objects in sentences: **me, us, you, him, her, them**

Singular	Plural
(i) She is known to **me**.	(i) Don't try to cheat **us**.
(ii) I know **you**.	(ii) I know **your** parents.
(iii) (a) Somebody threw a stone at **him**.	(iii) (a) Nobody likes **them**.
(b) He promised **her** a grand birthday gift.	(b) Everybody loves **them**.

Possessive Case

Masculine	Feminine	Masculine	Feminine
mine	mine	ours	ours
yours	yours	his	hers
theirs	theirs		

II. Reflexive Pronouns

When the action of the subject reflects upon itself we have to use a reflexive pronoun, *e.g.,*

(i) I hurt myself.

(ii) She is sewing a dress for herself.

(iii) He baked a cake for himself.

(iv) They put by some money for themselves.

(v) We got a house built for ourselves.

Formation of Reflexive Pronouns

The suffix 'self' is added to some simple pronouns to make singular reflexive pronouns whereas the addition of 'selves' to some pronouns makes plural reflexive pronouns.

Reflexive Pronouns

Singular	Plural
my + self = myself	our + selves = ourselves
your + self = yourself	your + selves = yourselves
him + self = himself	them + selves = themselves
her + self = herself	them + selves = themselves

III. Emphatic Pronouns

When a reflexive pronoun is used to lay emphasis, it is known as an Emphatic Pronoun.

(i) I **myself** white washed the fence.

(ii) We **ourselves** repaired the bike.

(iii) You **yourself** wrote the poem. (one person)

(iv) You **yourselves** painted the doors of your house. (more than one person)

(v) She **herself** told the matter to her father.

Note: An Emphatic Pronoun cannot be used as the subject of a sentence.

(i) Myself oiled the old locks. (incorrect)
I myself oiled the old locks. (correct)

(ii) Himself prepared lunch. (incorrect)
He himself prepared lunch. (correct)

IV. Indefinite Pronouns

A pronoun which is not used for a particular person or thing but is instead used for a person or thing in a general way, it is called an Indefinite Pronoun, *e.g.,*

(i) **One** must obey one's parents.
(ii) **Nobody** is going to Switzerland this summer vacation.
(iii) **Somebody** told me about his bad health.
(iv) **All** are not kind to animals.
(v) **Few** know His way of working.
(vi) **Anyone** can solve this sum. It's so simple.
(vii) Look around for **anybody** who may help us.
(viii) **No one** has the right to stop him from going abroad.
(ix) **Something** is better than nothing.
(x) What do you want to eat? **Anything** will do.
(xi) **Some** have wisdom to live a good life.
(xii) **Everybody** advises him efforts.

Note: There are some indefinite pronouns which can be used as determiners when they are followed by nouns, *e.g.,*

(i) Some boys do not understand their teachers.
(ii) All people should work for mankind.

Most of the Indefinite Pronouns stand for persons. Only a few stand for things.

V. Demonstrative Pronouns

The pronouns which point out the objects are known as Demonstrative Pronouns:

This, That, These, Those.

(i) **This** is my purse.
(ii) **That** is your gun.
(iii) **These** are her shoes.
(iv) **Those** are his books.

The pronoun 'this' is used when an object close at hand is referred 'to' but for more than one object close at hand we should use 'these'.

The pronoun 'that' is used when an object at a distance is referred 'to' but for more than one object at a distance we should use 'those'.

VI. Distributive Pronouns

The following pronouns which are used to refer to persons or things are known as Distributive Pronouns:

either, neither, each, both, none, any

(i) **Either** of you can tell us a story.
(ii) **Neither** of you can be allowed to ramble over the fields.
(iii) **Each** of the girls was given a prize.
(iv) **Both** of you can come in.
(v) **None** of your schemes worked.
(vi) **Any** of you can recite this lesson.

Either and neither are used only when two persons have to be referred to. Neither is the opposite of either and is used to make a negative statement. To refer more than two persons none, or 'any' should be brought into use.

VII. Reciprocal Pronouns

These are :

each other, one another

'Each other' is used to refer to two persons/ things.

'One another' is used to refer to more than two persons/things.

(i) Two boys are quarrelling with **each other**.
(ii) All the candidates began to fight with **one another**.

VIII. Interrogative Pronouns

The pronouns which are used to ask questions, are known as Interrogative Pronoun, *e.g.,* **who, whose, whom, which, what**.

Such pronouns are used to ask direct as well as indirect questions.

(i) **Who** broke the windowpane?
(ii) **Whose** is this watch?
(iii) **Whom** do you want to see?
(iv) **Which** is your dog?
(v) **What** are you looking for?

The Interrogative Pronouns can denote persons, birds, animals, and things.

Who, whose, and **whom** are most often used for persons.

(i) **Who** is there on the roof?
(ii) **Whose** is this bike?
(iii) **Whom** did you see walking across the road?

'What' is used for things.

(iv) **What** is behind the curtain?
(v) **What** is there over the fields?

'What' sometimes is used for birds, animals and for persons' prefession.

(i) **What** is your brother? 'He is a teacher.'
(ii) **What** is bigger than a sparrow?
(iii) **What** is stronger than an elephant?

'Which' is used for both persons and things.

(i) **Which** is your book?
(ii) **Which** of the boys broke the chair?
(iii) **Which** of the girls is going to join the club?

IX. Relative Pronouns

A pronoun which refers to a preceding noun is called a Relative Pronoun. It acts as both a pronoun and a conjunction which joins the two clauses.

Relative Pronoun introduces us with Relative Clauses. Important Relative Pronouns are:

Who, Whose, Whom, Which, That, What (such) as, (same) as

Relative Pronoun 'who' has three forms

Nominative case : Who

Genitive case : Whose

Accusative case : Whom

ADJECTIVES

An Adjective is a word which qualifies a noun or pronoun. It adds something to its meaning, *e.g.,*

(i) Jyoti is an **intelligent** girl.

(ii) Somesh has a **black** dog.

In sentence no. (i) the word 'intelligent' shows the quality of the girl. So, it is an adjective.

In sentence no (ii) 'black' is the quality of the dog (which is a noun). So, 'black' is an adjective.

Kinds of Adjectives

I Adjectives of Quality

II Adjectives of Quantity

III Adjectives of Number

IV Demonstrative Adjectives

V Distributive Adjectives

VI Possessive Adjectives

VII Interrogative Adjectives

VIII Exclamatory Adjectives

IX Emphatic Adjectives

I. Adjectives of Quality

The adjectives which add some qualities to nouns and pronouns are known as Adjectives of Quality. Such adjectives supply the answer to the question: of what kind?

Examples

(i) This box is **big**.

(ii) That basket is **small**.

(iii) Rakesh is a **clever** boy.

(iv) John is **tall**.

(v) Riya is **fat**.

(vi) Mohit is a **brilliant** boy.

Note: When a noun or pronoun has more than one quality of the same kind, usually the conjunction 'and' is used to join them. If these qualities are contrasting, then the conjunction 'but' is used.

(i) Rajesh is **tall** and **handsome**.

(ii) Aman is **fat** but **active**.

(iii) Renu is **rich** and **kind**.

(iv) Sohan is **intelligent** but **rude**.

II. Adjectives of Quantity

The adjectives which show the quantity of a noun are known as Adjectives of Quantity. Such adjectives answer the question: How much?

(i) There is **a little** water in the pot.

(ii) There is **much** sugar in the box.

(iii) We do not have **enough** money to buy a car.

(iv) The child drank **some** milk and walked out of the house to play.

(v) Is there **any** ink in the pot?

(vi) There isn't **any** water in the jug.

(vii) There is **little** juice in the jug.

(viii) **The little** coffee in the cup has been drunk by Seema.

(ix) **All** the boys were singing a song.

Note:

(a) 'Any' is used in interrogative sentences or negative sentences.

(b) 'Some' is used to express a positive sense.

(c) 'Little' means near about nil.

(d) 'A little' means small in quantity.

(e) 'The little' means the consumption of the whole quantity of some thing which was not much.

(f) 'Enough' refers to something in a quantity which meets the demand.

(g) 'Much' refers to something abundant or in good quantity which may be more than necessary to meet the immediate demand.

Note: Most of the Adjectives of Quantity are used as adverbs and pronouns. It is important for a student to know their uses as different parts of speech.

III. Adjectives of Number

The adjectives which show the number of persons, things etc, are known as Adjectives of number. They answer the question: How many?

(i) There are **many** cows in the field.

(ii) There were only **a few** students in the class.

(iii) **Few** persons work honestly.

(iv) **The few** eggs on the shelf have been eaten by Rohit.

(v) **Some** oranges were sour.

(vi) Are there **any** mangoes in the basket?

(vii) There are **no** birds in the nest.

Note: The adjectives which refer to the exact numbers are known as Cardinals, *e.g.*, one, two, three........

But: First, second, third ...... are known as Ordinals.

IV. Demonstrative Adjectives

The Adjectives which straight away point out the things are known as Demonstrative Adjectives, *e.g.*,

(i) **This** pen is yours.

(ii) **That** book is hers.

(iii) **These** shirts are mine.

(iv) **Those** shoes are his.

The Demonstrative Adjectives can also be used as Demonstrative Pronouns.

Demonstrative Adjectives	Demonstrative Pronouns
1. This pen is hers.	1. This is her pen.
2. That bike is mine.	2. That is my bike.
3. These socks are his.	3. These are his socks.
4. Those shoes are yours.	4. Those are your shoes.

Note: 1. 'This' is used to refer to one object close to the speaker and 'these' is the plural form of 'this'.

2. 'That' is used to refer to one object at a distance from the speaker and 'those' is the plural form of 'that'.

V. Distributive Adjectives

These adjectives refer to each one of a number.

(i) **Neither** boy is intelligent.

(ii) On **either** side of the road there is a bed of flowers.

(iii) **Each** boy will be given a prize.

(iv) **Every** line he quoted was incorrect.

VI. Possessive Adjectives

The Adjectives which are used to show possession are known as Possessive Adjectives.

(i) This is **my** jacket.

(ii) That is **our** house.

(iii) These are **your** shoes.

(iv) This is **her** purse.

(v) That is **his** watch.

(vi) These are **their** pants.

Note: Mine, ours, yours, his, hers, theirs are possessive pronouns. But 'his' can be used both as a Possessive Adjective and a Possessive Pronoun.

(i) This is **his** book. (Possessive Adjective).

(ii) This book is **his.** (Possessive Pronoun).

VII. Interrogative Adjectives

The Adjectives which are used to ask questions are known as Interrogative Adjectives.

(i) Which bike is yours?

(ii) What kind of machine is this ?

(iii) Whose name is Tony?

VIII. Exclamatory Adjectives

In the following sentences 'what' has been used as an exclamatory adjective.

(i) What a bird! (ii) What luck!

(iii) What folly!

IX. Emphatic Adjectives

The Adjectives which are used to lay emphasis are known as Emphatic Adjectives.

(i) This is the **very** watch. I was looking for.

(ii) I saw him with my **own** eyes.

(iii) You have **every** reason to dismiss him.

ADVERBS

An Adverb modifies the meaning of an Adjective, a Verb or some other Adverbs. e.g.

(i) She sang **sweetly**.

(ii) The horse ran **fast**.

(iii) It was **extremely** cold outside.

(iv) She lived in a **very** big house.

Kinds of Adverbs

The following are Adverbs:

I Adverbs of Time

II Adverbs of Manner

III Adverbs of Place

IV Adverbs of Frequency

V Adverbs of Degree, Extent or Quantity

VI Adverbs of Reason

VII Adverbs of Assertion

VIII Interrogative Adverbs

IX Relative Adverbs

I. Adverbs of Time

The Adverbs which answer the question 'when'

(i) She gets up **early** in the morning.

(ii) You always come to school **late**.

(iii) I have **already** read this book.

(iv) Have you met him **before**?

(v) She was ten years old **then**.

II. Adverbs of Manner

The Adverbs which answer the question 'How?' are known as Adverbs of Manner.

(i) She speaks Hindi **fluently**.

(ii) The fire spread around **rapidly**.

(iii) He hit the child **violently**.

(iv) He works **diligently**.

(v) She knocked at/on the door **gently**.

III. Adverbs of Place

The Adverbs which answer the question 'where?' are known as Adverbs of Place.

(i) Come **here**, please.

(ii) Sit **there**.

(iii) **Everywhere** you will find these birds.

(iv) A violent mind never gets peace **anywhere**.

(v) He walked **forward**.

IV. Adverbs of Frequency

The Adverbs which answer the question 'How often?' are known as Adverbs of Manner.

(i) She **never** tells lies.

(ii) He **always** speaks the truth.

(iii) Jack **often** comes here to see his brother.

(iv) They **frequently** visit the Taj.

(v) I saw him **once**.

V. Adverbs of Degree, Extent or Quantity

The Adverbs which answer the question 'What degree?' are known as the Adverbs of Degree, Extent or Quantity.

(i) He was **completely** convinced.

(ii) She is rich **enough** to buy a car.

(iii) The box was **too** heavy to carry.

(iv) It was **extremely** hot outside.

(v) Gama was a **very** strong wrestler.

VI. Adverbs of Reason

The Adverbs which show the reason are known as Adverbs of Reason.

(i) He fell down **therefore** unable to win the race.

(ii) She was hence not allowed to enter the hall.

VII. Adverbs of Assertion

(i) He was **certainly** not involved in the conspiracy.

(ii) John is **actually** looking for a big deal.

(iii) I do **not** have any idea of his wherabouts.

VIII. Interrogative Adverbs

The Adverbs which are used to ask questions are known as Interrogative Adverbs.

(i) **How** many students are there in your class? (Number)

(ii) **How** long was the snake? (Degree)

(iii) **How** did you manage to escape from that house?

(iv) **Why** are you late? (Time)

(v) **When** will you visit England? (Time)

(vi) **Where** did you find a 'cow'? (Place)

IX. Relative Adverbs

The Adverbs which modify some words and also refer back to the Antecedent are known as Relative Adverbs. The Relative Adverbs may refer to the place, time and cause.

Relative Adverbs referring to Place.

(i) I do not remember the place **where** we met last year.

(ii) You may go to the place **wherever** you like.

Relative Adverbs referring to Time.

I dont know the time when the earthquake struck the place.

Relative Adverb referring the Cause.

I do not know the reason **why** he hates you.

Placement of Adverbs

The placement of the Adverbs takes place as follows:

I. Adverbs of Manner

These Adverbs more often are preceded by verbs.

(i) She knocked on/at the door **softly**.

(ii) Hema laughed **heartily**.

(iii) John looked at her **contemptuously**.

(iv) She smiled **sweetly**.

Note 1: But most often they are followed by past participles.

(i) The doctor gave the patient a **sweetly** scented syrup.

(ii) I got a **badly** written letter.

(iii) The laboratory of our school is **fully** equipped.

Note 2: Sometimes Adverbs of Manner in phrases are put at the start of the sentences as to lay emphasis.

(i) **A sweetly** scented syrup is liked by the children.

(ii) **A badly** written letter, sometimes fails to convey the real message.

(iii) **A fully** equipped laboratory is the backbone of a school.

Note 3: Sometimes they are sandwiched between the helping verb and the finite verb.

(i) I shall **happily** carry this message. (It means: willingly)

(ii) We shall **merrily** play the pianos.

Note 4: Sometimes they are used before the finite verb.

(i) He **ceremoniously** folded his hands and greeted the guests.

(ii) The car **abruptly** turned away.

II. Adverbs of Time

Most of these adverbs follow the verbs.

(i) What do you say **now**?

(ii) Who opened the door **now**?

(iii) I'll inform you **then**.

(iv) He was strong **then**.

Note 1: Phrases containing adverbs of time sometimes are used to start sentences.

(i) **From now on** you won't sit in his company.

(ii) **Now then**, who wants to sit indoors?

(iii) **Just then**, a snake shot its head.

Note 2: Adverbs of time are sometimes used to start the sentence.

(i) **Now**, you should take some rest.

(ii) **Presently**, there was a knock on the door and he stood to open it. (**Presently** here shows that something happened after a short time.)

Note 3: Some phrases containing adverbs of time or those behaving as an adverb phrases follow the verbs.

(i) The firemen reached **late**. Everything was changed into ashes **by then**.

(ii) You want to see Mr Jack. He is in his dressing room. You may please stay in my room until then.

(iii) That's all **for now**.

(iv) She'll be in America **by now**.

(v) **At present** we should not tell the secret to anybody.

III. Adverbs of Place

Most often these adverbs follow the verbs.

(i) Please come **here**.

(ii) Don't go **there**.

(iii) Put this bag **here**.

Note 1: Sometimes these adverbs are used to start sentences:

(i) **Here** is the book you were looking for.

(ii) **There** lies the bag.

IV. Adverbs of Frequency

Most often these adverbs are used just after the subject when the sentence does not have any helping verb.

(i) He **always** speaks the truth.

(ii) She **sometimes** comes to see her ailing brother.

(iii) We **often** go to the municipal park in the evening.

Note 1: These adverbs are usually sandwiched between a helping verb and a finite verb.

(i) I've **always** wished you good luck.

(ii) We've **often** tried to bring him round to this view but in vain.

Note 2: End Position

(i) Try to solve puzzles more **often**.

(ii) She commits errors **sometimes**.

Note 3: Starting Position

(i) **Sometimes**, hunter misses his target.

(ii) **Rarely**, have you seen such a charming sight.

V. Adverbs of Degree or Extent

These adverbs are in fact used to lay emphasis..

Most of the adverbs of degree or extent precede an adjective.

(i) There was a **very** beautiful dress in the wardrobe.

(ii) The sum was **extremely** tough.

(iii) Their efforts are **highly** appreciable.

Note 1: Sometimes these adverbs take the end position.

The fire destroyed the crops **extensively**.

NARRATION

(Direct Speech and Indirect Speech)

The words spoken by the speaker are in Direct Speech.

The words spoken by somebody expressed by someone else with some modification are known as Indirect Speech.

(a) Rohit says to me, "You do not understand me."

(b) Rohit tells me that I do not understand him.

The sentence no. (a) shows the words spoken by Rohit. So, it is a sentence of direct speech.

The sentence no. (b) shows the words spoken by Rohit and they have been reported with certain modification. So, it is a sentence of Indirect Speech.

Important Rules Regarding the change of Direct Speech into Indirect Speech

(A) In the sentence of direct speech the verb outside the inverted commas is known as the Reporting Verb.

(B) The words inside the inverted commas are known as direct speech.

(C) When the sentence is indirect speech, it won't take a sign of exclamation or a sign of interrogation.

(D) The Reporting Verb can be given in Present, Past or Future Tense.

(E) When the Reporting Verb is in Present or Future Tense, there will be no change in the tense of direct speech while converting it into indirect speech.

(F) When the Reporting Verb is in Past Tense the tense of direct speech will be changed while converting it into Indirect Speech.

(G) The following adverbs and possessives should be changed as given:

(a) This into that

(b) These into those

(c) Here into there

(d) Now into then

(e) Today into that day

(f) Last night into the previous night

(g) Tomorrow into the next day

(h) The next day/week into the following day/week

(i) Hence into thence.

I. When the Reporting Verb is in Present or Future Tense

II. When the Reporting Verb is in Past Tense

I. When the Reporting Verb is in Present or Future Tense:

1. (a) Ajay says, "My brother lives in Australia."

(b) Ajay says that his brother lives in Australia.

2. (a) Vikas says to Amit, "We shall see a movie today."

(b) Vikas tells Amit that they shall see a movie today.

3. (a) Mohit will say, "My aunt died last night."

(b) Mohit will say that his aunt died last night.

4. (a) Sonu will say to Anu, "We have completed the first phase of the project."

(b) Sonu will tell Anu that they have completed the first phase of the project.

II. When the Reporting Verb is in Past Tense

Tensewise change. (Affirmative and Negative Sentences)

(A) When the Direct Speech is in Present Indefinite Tense it will change into Past Indefinite Tense.

1. (a) Rakesh said, "I write a letter to my friend."

(b) Rakesh said that he wrote a letter to his friend.

2. (a) Harish said to Mohan, "My brother does not take interest in studies."

(b) Harish told Mohan that his brother did not take interest in studies.

(B) When the Direct Speech is in Present Continuous Tense, it will change into Past Continuous Tense.

1. (a) Amar said to Sohan, "The dogs are barking at the stranger."

(b) Amar told Sohan that the dogs were barking at the stranger.

2. (a) Nina said to Pinki, "My father is not typing letters."

(b) Nina told Pinki that her father was not typing letters.

(C) When the Direct Speech is in Present Perfect Tense, it will change into Past Perfect Tense

1. (a) Mohit said to Krishan, "The workers have completed the construction work."

(b) Mohit told Krishan that the workers had completed the construction work.

2. (a) Gopal said, "I have not read this novel."

(b) Gopal said that he had not read that novel.

(D) When the direct speech is in Present Perfect Continuous, it will change to Past Perfect Continuous Tense.

1. (a) Meena said to Kuldeep, "It has been raining since morning."

(b) Meena told Kuldeep that it had been raining since morning.

2. (a) Hari said to Amarjeet, "The birds have not been chirping for three hours."

(b) Hari told Amarjeet that the birds had not been chirping for three hours.

(E) When the direct speech is in Past Indefinite Tense it will change into Past Perfect Tense.

1. (a) Vinod said to Deepak, "My cousin sold his old car yesterday".

(b) Vinod told Deepak that his cousin had sold his old car the previous day.

2. (a) Anil said, "I did not go to Mumbai to see my ailing aunt."

(b) Anil said that he had not gone to Mumbai to see his ailing aunt.

(F) When the direct speech is in Past Continuous Tense, it will change into Past Perfect Continuous Tense.

1. (a) Seema said to Tina, "Rita was rowing in the moonlight."

(b) Seema told Tina that Rita had been rowing in the moonlight.

2. (a) Ashok said, "My uncle was not telling a story to us."

(b) Ashok said that his uncle had not been telling a story to them.

(G) When the direct speech in Past Perfect Tense, there will be no change in its tense in Indirect Speech.

(H) When the direct speech is in Past Perfect Continuous Tense, there will be no change in its tense in Indirect Speech.

(I) When the direct speech is in, future tense, usually 'shall' and 'will' are changed into 'would'. (Sometimes 'shall' can be changed into should.)

1. (a) The officer said to Veena, "I shall grant you leave for three days."

(b) The officer told Veena that he would grant her leave for three days.

2. (a) Ali said, "My aunt will be sewing a table cloth."

(b) Ali said that his aunt would be sewing a table cloth.

3. (a) Tina said, "The boys will have been flying kites for three hours."

(b) Tina said that the boys would have been flying kites for three hours.

Interrogative Sentences

(A) Starting with Modals (Primary Auxiliary)

When the Interrogative Sentences start with modals, usually ask and 'if' are brought into with use in Indirect Speech. Can is changed into could, shall into should/would, and will into would, may into might.

1. (a) The army officer said to the soldier, "Can you climb up that wall?"

(b) The army officer asked the soldier if he could climb up that wall.

2. (a) The head-clerk said to the officer, "Could I use your pen?"

(b) The head-clerk asked the officer if he could use his pen. or him.

3. (a) The student said to the teacher "May I come in, sir?"

(b) The student asked the teacher respectfully if he might go in.

4. (a) Tina said to Hema, "Does your brother have a close association with this political group?"

(b) Tina asked Hema if her brother had a close association with that political group.

5. (a) Dinesh said to Kavita, "Are you joining the evening classes?"

(b) Dinesh asked Kavita if she was joining the evening classes.

6. (a) Jaswinder said to Ravinder, "Have you applied for this vacancy?"

(b) Jaswinder asked Ravinder if he had applied for that vacancy.

7. (a) Anju said, "Has the bee been humming around the flowers for three hours?"

(b) Anju asked somebody if the bee had been humming around the flowers for three hours.

8. (a) The bank officer said to the customer, "Did you get the cash yesterday?"

(b) The bank officer asked the customers if he had got the cash the previous day.

9. (a) Priya said to Preeti, "Was the cat prowling around the building?"

(b) Priya asked Preeti if the cat had been prowling around the building.

10. (a) The shopkeeper asked the customer, "Had you purchased a mineral water bottle before going to Shimla?"

(b) The shopkeeper said to the customer if he had purchased a mineral water bottle before going to Shimla.

(B) Interrogative Sentences starting with wh-words

When an interrogative sentence in Direct speech starts with any of the follwing words: What, Which, When, Why, Who, Whose, Whom, How in Indirect speech, we should not use if or whether clause with 'ask' e.g.

1. (a) Amit said to Sumit, "What do you like to drink?"

(b) Amit asked Sumit what he liked to drink.

2. (a) Pradeep said to Surendra, "Whom are you waiting for?"

(b) Pradeep asked Surendra whom he was waiting for.

3. (a) Anita said to Kavita, "Who has mistakenly left her purse in my room?"

(b) Anita asked Kavita who had mistakenly left her purse in her room.

4. (a) Sangeeta said to Anita, "Why have you been so sad since morning?

(b) Sangeeta asked Anita why she had been so sad since morning.

5. (a) Akash said to Veena, "Why didn't you dance at the party yesterday?"

(b) Akash asked Veena why she did not dance at the party the previous day.

Imperative Sentences

(a) As we know, these sentences do not begin with any subject. The subject 'you' is understood, therefore, these sentences usually start with verbs in a Direct Speech.

These sentences most often denote request, advice, suggestion, order, command, instruction, permission, etc.

(b) In order to change these sentences into the Indirect Speeches the following words are needed to be introduced in place of "said":

Order	Request	Suggest	Beg
Prompt	Command	Warn	Forbid
Plead	Instruct	Inform	Propose
Threaten	Entreat	Pardon	Persuade

Some Examples

1. (a) The officer said to the clerk, "Read the file once again."

(b) The officer ordered the clerk to read the file once again.

2. (a) The peon said to the Principal, "Please grant me leave for two days."

(b) The peon requested the Principal to grant him leave for two days."

3. (a) The teacher said to the students, "Work hard."

(b) The teacher advised the students to work hard.

4. (a) The convict said to the judge, "Please take mercy on me."

(b) The convict begged the judge for mercy.

5. (a) The gardener said to the children, "Don't pluck flowers."

(b) The gardener forbade the children to pluck flowers.

Note: With 'forbid' the word 'not' should not be used because it itself conveys the negative sense.

6. (a) Hari said to his friend, "Let us take a cup of tea."

(b) Hari suggested that they should take a cup of tea.

or

Hari Proposed that his friend and he should have a cup of tea.

Exclamatory Sentences

(a) These sentences are used to express sudden emotions like joy, sorrow, contempt, regret, surprise, etc. These sentences take the mark of exclamation at the end.

(b) In order to convert these sentences into Indirect Speech the following expressions are most often introduced in place of said: exclaimed with, toy, exclaimed with surprise, exclaimed with contempt, exclaimed with sorrow.

The sign of exclamation is also replaced with the full stop.

Some examples

1. (a) The child said, "What a beautiful flower it is!"

(b) The girl exclaimed with joy that the flower was extremely beautiful.

2. (a) The girl said, "How wonderful these insects are!"

(b) The girl exclaimed with surprise that those insects were extremely wonderful.

3. (a) The coach said, "What a bad shot it is!"

(b) The coach exclaimed with disappointment that the shot was extremely bad.

4. (a) Hari said, "Hurrah! I have won the match!"

Hari exclaimed with joy that he had won the match.

Optative Sentences

(a) These sentences are used to express a wish, prayer, desire or a curse. These sentences take the sign of exclamation at the end.

(b) In order to convert them in Indirect Speech the following expressions are introduced in place of 'said': wished that, prayed that, cursed that, bade good night, etc.

Some examples

1. (a) The old woman said to me, "May God bless you!"

(b) The old woman wished/prayed that God might bless me.

2. (a) The old man said, "O for a glass of water!"

(b) The old man wished for a glass of water.

3. (a) I said to my mother, "Good morning, mom."

(b) I wished good morning to my mother.

Note: (a) With "good morning" and "good evening" use ..... wished good morning–evening to my mother/father, etc.

(b) With 'good night' and 'good bye' use ..... bade good night to my father/mother, etc.

(c) Some grammarians prefer to place the optative sentences in the category of exclamatory sentences.

Universal Truth, Habitual Truth, Historical Truth

In Sentences containing the idea of any universal truth, habitual truth or historical truth, the tense of the Indirect Speech remains the same as in Direct Speech.

1. (a) The teacher said to the students, "The sun rises in the east." (Universal truth).

(b) The teacher told the students that the sun rises in the east.

But when there is a general talk a change in the tense takes place in the Indirect Speech.

2. (a) Rohit said to Narender, "The sun will set soon."

(b) Rohit told Narender that the sun would set soon. (Don't use 'will)

3. (a) Sonu said to Amar, "My father daily walks five kilometres."

(b) Sonu told Amar that her father daily walks five kilometres.

(The sentence shows the daily routine of Sonu's father).

4. (a) The Principal said to the students, "India got its freedom in 1947." (Historical Truth)

(b) The Principal told the students that India got its freedom in 1947.

PREPOSITIONS

Read the following sentences:

(i) She is employed **in** a bank.

(ii) I daily get up **at** 6 o'clock.

In sentence no. (i) the word 'in' joins the noun phrase 'a bank' with the rest of the sentence.

In sentence no. (ii) the word 'at' joins '6 o'clock' with the rest of the sentence.

Both these words are prepositions.

A preposition is a word which joins a noun, a pronoun or their equivalents with the rest of the sentence.

Classification of Prepositions

The prepositions can be classified in the following ways.

I Prepositions pertaining to Place.

II Prepositions pertaining to Time.

III Prepositions expressing cause, reason, purpose, etc.

IV Prepositions expressing manner.

V Prepositions expressing method, intrumentality.

VI Prepositions expressing measure, quantity, rate.

I. *Prepositions Pertaining to Place*

The following are a few prepositions which pertain to place: In, at, on, behind, under, in front of, above, below, beneath, over, from Examples:

(i) He lives **in** Russia.
(ii) I live **at** Rampur.
(iii) There is an oak tree **in front** of my house.
(iv) The dog was lying **under** the table.
(v) She raised her hand **above** the head.
(vi) She was lying asleep **behind** a cart.
(vii) There was a red patch of mark **below** his left eye.
(viii) He hailed **from** Africa.
(ix) I saw a hawk flying **over** the hill.

Note: The preposition 'in' is used when somebody is living in a big city or a country, etc. But the preposition 'at' is used when somebody is living in a small town, village, etc.

II. *Preposition Pertaining to Time*

The following prepositions pertain to time:

at, on, in, from, by, after, before, within between. Examples

(i) She got up **at** 9 o'clock.
(ii) The train reached the station **on** time.
(iii) I reached the airport **before** time.
(iv) We'll go back home **after** the sun sets.
(v) You are **in** time.
(vi) I'll return **within** an hour.
(vii) He'll be here **by** the evening.
(viii) She lived in American **from** 1980 to 2000.
(ix) I went to England twice **between** 1980 to 1999.

Note: 'On time' means on the time which was scheduled. 'In time' means before the scheduled time. The Preposition 'from' in sentence no (viii) shows the continuity of an action whereas the preposition 'between' in sentence no (ix) shows that I visited England twice during the period given without specifying when either visit took place.

III. *Preposition Expressing Cause, Reason, Purpose, etc.:* to, with, of, from, for

(i) Drinking is injurious **to** health.
(ii) She died **of** cancer.
(iii) The boy was trembling **with** fear.
(iv) His uncle died **from** overwork.
(v) She is struggling **for** her livelihood.

IV. *Preposition Expressing Manner:* with, by

(i) The old woman was dying **by** inches.
(ii) The soldiers moved forward with great courage.

V. *Preposition Expressing Method, Instrumentality:* with, from, by, of

(i) She killed the snake **with** a rod.
(ii) I caught him **by** the collar.
(iii) I heard it **from** him.

VI. *Prepositions Expressing Measure, Rate, Quantity:* at, by

(i) This shirt is dirt cheap **at** fifty rupees.
(ii) The cloth is sold **by** metre.

TENSES

Tenses tell us the time of actions.

There are three kinds of Tenses.

I Present Tense II Past Tense

III Future Tense

I. Present Tense

The tense which shows action in the present time is known as the present tense. It is of the following kinds :

(A) Present Indefinite Tense or Simple Present Tense
(B) Present Continuous Tense
(C) Present Perfect Tense.
(D) Present Perfect Continuous Tense.

(A) *Present Indefinite Tense or Simple Present Tense*

This tense is used:

1. To show an action in the present time without referring to its finishing time
   (i) I write a letter to my friend.
   (ii) She helps the old man lift the bag.

Note: With I, we, you, they or Plural Noun the first form of the Verb is used. But with He, She, It, or Singular Noun, first form of the verb + s/es is used.

2. To show a habit or liking or disliking in the present time
   (i) She hates meat.
   (ii) We like singing and dancing.
   (iii) I daily go out for a walk.
   (iv) My uncle daily drinks a cup of tea after dinner.
3. To refer to a universal truth
   (i) The sun rises in the east.
   (ii) A bat flies better when it is dark around.
   (iii) The stars twinkle at night.

Negative and Interrogative Sentences

With I, we, you, they or Plural Nouns: do not + 1st form of the verb is used.

In case of interrogative sentences Do + subject + 1st form of the verb + object is used.

With He, She, It, or a Singular Noun does not + 1st form of the verb is used.

In case of interrogative sentences Does + Subject + 1st form of the verb + object is used.

(i) He does not borrow anything from anybody.
(ii) I do not advise you to do this job.
(iii) Do they know how to write business letters?
(iv) Does she understand French?

(B) *Present Continuous Tense*

It is used to show the continuity of an action in the present time.

Affirmative Sentences

(i) I am sending a telegram to Jack.
(ii) You are admiring my opponent.
(iii) She is speaking for the manager.

Note: When 'I' is the Subject of the sentence use an + present participle.

When 'we, you, they or a Plural Noun is the Subject of sentence 'are + present participle' is used. But if 'he, she, it or a Singular Noun' is the Subject of the sentence 'is + present participle' is used.

Negative and Interrogative Sentences

(i) I am not trying to find out errors in your essay.
(ii) Am I trying to find out errors in your essay?
(iii) He is not creating any problem to the children.
(iv) Is he creating any problem to the children?
(v) They are not decorating the room.
(vi) Are they decorating the room?

(C) *Present Perfect Tense*

The tense which shows the completion of an action in the present tense is known as the Present Perfect Tense.

Affirmative Sentence

(i) I have eaten/ taken breakfast.
(ii) She has mixed up the ingredients to bake a cake.

When the subject of the sentence is I, we, you, they or a plural noun use have + past participle.

When the subject of the sentence is 'he, she, it or a singular noun, use has + past participle.

Negative and Interrogative Sentences

(i) The officer has not granted leave to the clerk.
(ii) Has the officer granted leave to the clerk?
(iii) They have not shovelled snow on to the truck yet.
(iv) Have they shovelled snow on to the truck?

(D) *Present Perfect Continuous Tense*

The tense shows a part of an action having been completed and another part of it still being done in the Present Tense.

(i) He has been mending the shoes since morning.
(ii) We have been flying kites for three hours.

Note: Preposition 'since' is used when the point of time is given *i.e.* since 1965, since 5 o'clock, since morning, since evening etc.

Preposition 'for' is used when the period of time is given, e.g. for two weeks, for three days, for five years, etc.

Negative and Interrogative Sentences

(i) The peon has not been ringing the bell for two hours.
(ii) Have the firemen been trying to extinguish fire since morning?

II. Past Tense

The tense which shows action in the past time is known as Past Tense. It is of the following kinds.

(A) Past Indefinite Tense or Simple Past Tense
(B) Past Continuous Tense
(C) Past Perfect Tense
(D) Past Perfect Continuous Tense

(A) *Past Indefinite or Simple Past Tense*

It is used:

Affirmative Sentences

1. To show an action in the past time without referring to its finishing time
   (i) The scientist found the food contaminated with bacteria.
   (ii) The calves frisked in the courtyard.
   (iii) He typed three letters this morning.

Note: Subject + IInd form of verb + Object is used.

2. To show a habit in the past time
   (i) She used to go to temple daily.
   (ii) He daily prayed to God before going to office.
   (iii) They most often took a long walk in the morning.
3. To show historical truth
   (i) India got its freedom on 15 August, 1947.
   (ii) Mr. J.L. Nehru was elected the first Prime Minister of India.

Negative and Interrogative Sentences

(i) She did not attend the meeting.
(ii) We did not allow the children to play in the lawn.
(iii) Did he complain to the officer against you?

With 'did' first form of the verb is used.

With some Adverbs e.g. yesterday, ago, etc. Past Indefinite Tense is used.

(i) My father bought me a new bicycle five days ago.
(ii) A thief broke into my neighbour's last night.
(iii) We saw a movie yesterday.

(B) *Past Continuous Tense*

This tense shows the continuity of an action in the past.

Affirmative Sentences

(i) He was driving a car.
(ii) I was memorizing the lesson.
(iii) The workers were building the flyover.

Subject + was/were + Present Participle + object (if any)

Negative and Interrogative Sentences

(i) They were not planning to go to Sweden in Summer.
(ii) Was he advising his friends to help the poor?
(iii) Were the mechanics repairing the machines?
(iv) She was not any taking any interest in houshold chores.

(C) *Past Perfect Tense*

This tense shows the completion of an action in the past time.

Affirmative Sentences

(i) She had finished painting the pictures.
(ii) We had planted the saplings of mango plants.
(iii) The doctor had operated upon the patient.

Subject + had + Past Participle + Object.

Negative and Interrogative Sentences

(i) Had she applied for the past of a clerk?
(ii) He had not reserved a berth in the Rajdhani Express.

(D) *Past Perfect Continuous Tense*

This tense shows the part completion of an action/work when the other part of the action/work is still continuing in the Past Tense.

Affirmative Sentences

(i) She had been working in that office for five years.
(ii) They had been living in that house since 1968.

Negative and Interrogative Sentences

(i) Had the gardener been watering the plants since morning?
(ii) The birds had not been chirping on the branches of the tree for three hours.

III. Future Tense

The tense which used to express the actions in future time is known as the future tense. It is of the following kinds:

(A) Future Indefinite Tense or Simple Future Tense
(B) Future Continuous Tense.
(C) Future Perfect Tense.
(D) Future Perfect Continuous Tense.

(A) *Future Indefinite Tense*

It is used to indicate the actions planned for future.

Affirmative Sentences

(i) I shall write a letter to my mother.
(ii) The maid will wash the clothes after the sunrise.
(iii) They will varnish the chairs.

Subject + Will/Shall + 1st form of the verb + Object

Note: For the usage of 'shall and will' read the chapter "Modals."

Negative and Interrogative Sentences

(i) He will not associate with those boys.
(ii) We shall not walk over the slippery snowy path.

(B) *Future Continuous Tense*

It is used to show a continuous action in the future time.

Affirmative Sentences

(i) She will be planning to meet the P.M.

The policeman will be standing on guard at the check post.

Negative and Interrogative Sentences

(i) They will not be carrying coal to the city from the mine.
(ii) Will you be singing on radio the next month?

(C) *Future Perfect Tense*

It is used to show the completion of an action in the future.

Affirmative Sentences

(i) You will have got admission in the new school by then.

(ii) He will have joined the army by then.

Negative and Interrogative Sentences

(i) She will not have told you the story of a lion and a mouse.

(ii) Shall we have reserved two berths in the Janata Express by then?

(D) *Future Perfect Continuous Tense*

It is used to show the part completion of a work/ action and the continuity of the other part in the Future Tense.

Affirmative Sentences

(i) He will have been working in the office for five years.

(ii) They will have been painting the pictures since morning.

Negative and Interrogative Sentences

(i) She will not have been discussing the matter with her friends for two hours.

(ii) Will they have been begging for food since morning ?

TRANSFORMATION OF SENTENCES

By 'Transformation' we usually means the following grammatical drills.

- Removal of "too".
- Insertion of "too".
- Change of Voice.
- Change of Narration.
- Change of Degrees of Comparison.
- Interchange of Kinds of Sentence.
- Interchange of Principal and Subordinate Clauses.
- Interchange of Different Parts of Speech in Sentences.
- Expression of Condition.
- Expression of Contrast or Conversion.
- Conversion of Simple, Compound and Complex Sentences from one to the other.
- Completion of Incomplete Sentences.
- Use of Modals, Conjunctions, Preposition, Articles etc. for specific purposes.

Explanation

1. Removal of 'too'

(i) He is too weak to walk.
He is so weak that he cannot walk.

(ii) She is too proud to listen to you.
She is so proud that she will not listen to you.

(iii) He was too poor to buy a house.
He was so poor that he could not buy a house.

(iv) It is too cold outside.
It is cold outside beyond the proper limit.

Or

It is extremely cold outside.

2. Insertion of "too".

(i) She is so lazy that she will not do any work.
She is too lazy to do any work.

(ii) He is so weak that he cannot lift this box.
He is too weak to lift this box.

(iii) He ran so slowly that he could not catch the train.
He ran too slowly to catch the train.

3. Interchange of Kinds of Sentence

(i) Change of Affirmative Sentences into Negative Sentences:

(a) He is a dull boy.
He is not an intelligent boy.

(b) He told the truth.
He did not tell a lie.

(c) He runs fast.
He does not run slowly.

(ii) Change of Negative Sentences into Affirmative Sentences:

(a) The earth is not flat.
The earth is round.

(b) No sooner did the train arrive then the passengers rushed towards it.
As soon as the train arrived, passengers rushed towards it.
This glass is so hot that I cannot touch it.
This glass is so hot for me to touch it.

(iii) Change of Assertive Sentences into Interrogative Sentences:

(a) He is not lazy.
Is he lazy?

(b) Everybody wants peace.
Doesn't everybody want peace? **Or** Who does not want peace?

(iv) Change of Interrogative Sentences into Assertive Sentences:

(a) Where can peace be found?
Peace can't be found anywhere.
Or Peace can be found nowhere.

(b) What if we lose the match? **Or** What does it matters if ......?
Or Does it matter if ....?
It does not matter if ....

(v) Change of Assertive Sentences into Imperative Sentences:

(a) You are advised to Work hard.

(b) You are requested to sit down.

Sit down, please.

4. Interchange of Principal and Subordinate Clauses:

(i) I like him because he is a good person.

He is a good person for which I like him.

(ii) The bus was moving fast such that I couldn't alight from it.

I couldn't alight from the bus as it was moving fast.

(iv) As I love my country, I'm ready to die for it.

I'm ready to die for my country because I love it.

(v) If you work hard, you'll pass.

Work hard lest you should fail.

5. Interchange of Different Parts of Speech

(i) He likes to see clouds. (verb)

He has a great liking for seeing clouds. (noun).

(ii) His face expresses that he is happy. (Adj.)

There is an expression of happiness on his face. (noun).

(iii) One who is cruel can be punished.

Cruelty can lead one to punishment.

6. Conversion of Simple, Compound and Complex Sentences from one to the other.

(i) (a) In spite of working hard, he failed. (Simple)

(b) He worked hard, still or but he failed. (Compound).

(ii) (a) Unless you work hard, you cannot pass. (Complex).

(b) You should work hard and then you will pass. (Compound).

(c) You cannot pass without working hard. (Simple)

7. Completion of Incomplete Sentences:

(i) (a) .... is a happy child.

He is a happy child.

(b) **He** helped ....

He helped **me**. (by supplying subject/object).

(ii) The book ....

The book **lies on the table**. (by supplying Predicate).

(iii) She is ....

She is **happy**. (by supplying complement).

(iv) They are ....

They are **busy**. (by supplying a word).

(v) I love ....

I love **animals**. (by supplying a noun).

(vi) The stars are very ....

The stars are very **beautiful**. (by supplying an adjective).

(vii) She .... to God.

She **prays** to God. (by supplying a verb)

(viii) You .... I are friends.

You **and** I are friends. (by supplying a conjunction).

(ix) He runs ....

He runs **fast**. (by supplying adverb).

(x) He inserted .... going with me.

He inserted **on** going with me. (by supplying a preposition)

8. Interchange of non-finites in sentences:

(i) I love **writing** (books). (gerund).

(ii) The pen is to **write** with. (Infinitive).

(iii) The pen is **used** for writing purposes. (Participle).

VOICE

A sentence is said to be active when its subject does some action. e.g.

Ajay flies a kite.

The subject 'Ajay' is doing the action of flying a kite. So, it is a sentence in the active voice.

But if the subject is being acted upon then the sentence is said to be in the passive voice e.g.

A kite is flown by Ajay.

The subject 'A kite' is being acted upon by Ajay's act of flying it.

A. Tense wise (Active to Passive Voice)

I. Present Indefinite Tense

1. (a) Meena bakes a cake.

(b) A cake is baked by Meena.

2. (a) They do not invest money in business.

(b) Money is not invested in business by them.

3. (a) Does he scrape some carrots?

(b) Are carrots scraped by him?

II. Present Continuous Tense

1. (a) She is plucking vegetables.

(b) Vegetables are being plucked by her.

2. (a) They are not pricking holes in the paper.

(b) Holes in the paper are not being pricked by them.

3. (a) Is he whitewashing the fence?

(b) Is the fence being whitewashed by him?

III. Present Perfect Tense

1. (a) She has learnt her lesson.

(b) Her lesson has been learnt by her.

2. (a) The maid has not removed the dust from the sill.

(b) The dust from the sill has not been removed by the maid.

3. (a) Have you greased the bike?

(b) Has the bike been greased?

IV. Persent Perfect Continuous Tense

No Passive Voice

V. Past Indefinite Tense

1. (a) The carpenter shaved a plank.

(b) A plank was shaved by the carpenter.

2. (a) He did not read the new law book.

(b) The new law book was not read by him.

3. (a) Did they prepare an Italian sauce?

(b) Was an Italian sauce prepared by them?

VI. Past Continuous Tense

1. (a) She was consulting a physician.

(b) A physician was being consulted by her.

2. (a) The workers were not building a tower.

(b) A tower was not being built by the workers.

3. (a) Were the farmers harvesting the crops?

(b) Were the crops being harvested by the farmers?

VII. Past Perfect Tense

1. (a) He had already taken the measurements of the room.

(b) The measurements of the room had already been taken by him.

2. (a) The workers had not shovelled snow.

(b) Snow had not been shovelled by the workers.

3. (a) Had Leena admitted her mistake?

(b) Had her mistake been admitted by Leena?

VIII. Past Perfect Continuous Tense

No Passive voice

IX. Future Indefinite Tense

1 (a) The teacher will draw circles and parallel lines on the blackboard.

(b) Circles and parallel lines will be drawn on the blackboard by the teacher.

2. (a) Seema will not compile a dictionary.

(b) A dictionary will not be compiled by Seema.

3. (a) Will the police conduct a raid on his premises?

(b) Will a raid be conducted by the police on his premises?

X. Future Continuous Tense

No Passive Voice

XI. Future Perfect Tense

1. (a) Rohit will have decorated the room.

(b) The room will have been decorated by Rohit.

2. (a) We shall not have boiled the potatoes.

(b) The potatoes will not have been boiled by us.

XI. Future Perfect Continuous Tense

No Passive Voice.

B. Double Object

The sentences which have two objects can be written in passive voice in the following two ways.

1. (a) She gave me a book.

(b) I was given a book by her.

(c) A book was given to me by her.

2 (a) He did not tell a story to us.

(b) We were not told a story by him.

(c) A story was not told to us by him.

C. Infinitives

1. (a) It is time to open the gate of the museum.

(b) It is time for gate of the museum to be opened.

2. (a) She is a girl to trust.

(b) She is a girl to be trusted.

D. Imperative Sentences

1. (a) Do it.

(b) Let it be done or It should be done.

2. (a) Don't pluck flowers.

(b) You are forbidden to pluck flowers.

Or

(c) You are advised not to pluck flowers.

3. (a) Post letter at once.

(b) You are ordered to post this letter at once.

4. (a) Kindly help me.

(b) You are requested to help me.

5. (a) Let us take some rest.

(b) It is proposed that we should take some rest.

6. (a) Let him come in.

(b) You are ordered to let him come in.

E. Quasi–Passive Verbs

Intransitive verbs usually cannot be converted into passive verbs but there are some sentences (as given below) that can be written in their passive forms.

1. (a) Quinine tastes bitter

(b) Quinine is bitter when tasted.

MULTIPLE CHOICE QUESTIONS

Directions (Qs. 1 to 50): *Read each sentence to find out whether there is any grammatical error in it. The error, if any, will be in one part of the sentence. The letter of that part is the answer. If there is no error, the answer is 'D'. (Ignore the errors of punctuation, if any).*

1. (A) The brakes and steering failed/(B) and the bus ran down the hill/(C) without anyone being able to control it./(D) No error.
2. (A) The polling was marred/(B) at many a place/(C) by attempts at rigging./(D) No error.
3. (A) He wanted to work all right/(B) but we saw that he was completely worn/(C) and so we persuaded him to stop./(D) No error.
4. (A) When a whale is washed ashore by the tide,/(B) the people flock together to see it./(C) wondering how so huge an animal can swim about in the water./(D) No error.
5. (A) Few scientists changed/(B) people's ideas as much as/(C) Darwin with his Theory of Evolution./(D) No error.
6. (A) Were he/(B) to see you,/(C) he would have been surprised./(D) No error.
7. (A) The number of marks carried by each question/(B) are indicated/(C) at the end of the question./(D) No error.
8. (A) An animal/(B) can be just as unhappy in a vast area/(C) or in a small one/(D) No error.
9. (A) It is time/(B) we did something/(C) to stop road accidents./(D) No error.
10. (A) A free press is not a privilege/(B) but the organic necessity/(C) in a free society./(D) No error.
11. (A) The Indian radio./(B) which was previously controlled by the British rulers./(C) is free now from the narrow vested interests./(D) No error.
12. (A) Because of the emergency help/(B) that the patient received./(C) he would have died/(D) No error.
13. (A) At present juncture,/(B) however, the supercomputer/(C) would be a costly toy./(D) No error.
14. (A) Students should not take part/(B) in party politics and political demonstrations/(C) as they interfere in serious study./(D) No error.
15. (A) Wherever they go/(B) Indians easily adapt to/(C) local circumstances./(D) No error.
16. (A) According to the Bible/(B) it is meek and humble/(C) who shall inherit the earth./(D) No error.
17. (A) I was there/(B) many a time/(C) in the past./(D) No error.
18. (A) As much as I admire him for his sterling qualities./(B) I cannot excuse him for/(C) being unfair to his friends./(D) No error.
19. (A) Were you/(B) given a choice/(C) or you had to do it?/(D) No error.
20. (A) When he was asked what is wrong with him,/(B) he said that he was not well,/(C) and asked for leave of absence for one day./(D) No error.
21. (A) At the end of the year/(B) every student who had done adequate work/(C) was automatically promoted./(D) No error.
22. (A) Many times the news has been published/(B) in the papers that the end of the world will be certain/(C) if a nuclear war breaks out./(D) No error.
23. (A) Happily, zoos were/(B) unwilling to cooperate/(C) in a scheme that was potentially harmful to animal welfare./(D) No error.
24. (A) We discussed about the problem so thoroughly/(B) on the eve of the examination/(C) that I found it very easy to work it out./(D) No error.
25. (A) She reluctantly said that/(B) if nobody else was doing it/(C) she will do it./(D) No error.
26. (A) He will end up his work/(B) in the city/(C) by the end of the year./(D) No error.
27. (A) Though child marriage/(B) has been banned,/(C) the custom still prevailed among some groups in India./(D) No error.
28. (A) Supposing if/(B) there is no bus,/(C) how will you get there?(D) No error.
29. (A) At the moment the house/(B) was burgled the family/(C) attended a night party in the neighbourhood./(D) No error.
30. (A) On a holiday/(B) Sudha prefers reading/(C) than going out visiting friends/(D) No error.
31. (A) Neither he/(B) nor his father is interested/(C) in joining the party./(D) No error.
32. (A) A group of friends/(B) want to visit/(C) the new plant as early as possible./(D) No error.
33. (A) May I/(B) know who you want/(C) to see please/(D) No error.
34. (A) Myself and Gopal/(B) will take care of/(C) the function on Sunday./(D) No error.
35. (A) I could not put up in a hotel/(B) because the boarding and lodging charges/(C) were exorbitant./(D) No error.

36. (A) He is not coming tomorrow/(B) as he is having a pain in the chest/(C) and has to see a doctor./(D) No error.

37. (A) They have been/(B) very close friends/(C) until they quarrelled./(D) No error.

38. (A) Since India has gained Independence/(B) 49 years ago,/(C) much progress has been made in almost every field./(D) No error.

39. (A) The party chief made it a point to state that/(B) the Prime Minister and the Union Home Minister should also come/(C) and they see what his party men had seen./(D) No error.

40. (A) Due to me being a newcomer/(B) I was unable to get a house/(C) suitable for my wife and me./(D) No error.

41. (A) The reason why/(B) he was rejected/(C) was because he was too young./(D) No error.

42. (A) The scientist must follow/(B) his hunches and his data/(C) wherever it may lead./(D) No error.

43. (A) Firstly you should/(B) think over the meaning of the words/(C) and then use them./(D) No error.

44. (A) Scarcely had/(B) I arrived than/(C) the train left./(D) No error.

45. (A) Unless you stop to make noise at once/(B) I will have no option but to/(C) bring the matter to the attention of the police./(D) No error.

46. (A) He couldn't but help/(B) shedding tears at the plight of the villagers/(C) rendered homeless by a devastating cyclone./(D) No error.

47. (A) Since it was his first election campaign, the candidate was confused;/(B) none could clearly understand/(C) either the principles he stood for or the benefits he promised./(D) No error.

48. (A) It is an established fact that the transcendental American poets and philosophers,/(B) who lived in the latter half of the nineteenth century,/(C) were more influenced by Indian philosophy, in particular by Upanishadic Philosophy./(D) No error.

49. (A) The crew were on board/(B) and they soon busied themselves/(C) in preparing to meet the storm./(D) No error.

50. (A) One of the members/(B) expressed doubt if/(C) the Minister was an athiest./(D) No error.

Directions (Qs. 51 to 70): *Pick out the most effective word(s) from the given words to fill in the blank to make the sentence meaningfully complete.*

51. A woman came in with a baby who, she said, ... a safety pin.
A. was just swallowing
B. swallowed
C. had just swallowed
D. just swallowed

52. The telephone ..... several times before I answered it.
A. was ringing B. has rung
C. had rung D. would ring

53. An employment advertisement should ..... the number of vacancies.
A. provide B. specify
C. contain D. declare

54. A crescendo of metallic thuds arose from the market, where the iron-smiths were ..... the pieces of metals.
A. flattening B. striking
C. hammering D. thrashing

55. Ambition is one of those ..... which are never satisfied.
A. ideas B. fancies
C. passions D. needs

56. The new education policy provides a useful ..... for the planners to remove illiteracy.
A. breakup B. breakthrough
C. breakaway D. break-in

57. The family gave father a gold watch on the ..... of his fiftieth birthday.
A. time B. event
C. occasion D. celebration

58. The passengers were afraid but the captain ..... them that there was no danger.
A. promised B. assured
C. advised D. counselled

59. It's very kind of you to ..... to speak at the meeting.
A. accept B. agree
C. comply D. concur

60. I haven't seen you ..... a week.
A. within B. since
C. for D. from

61. Besides other provisions, that shopkeeper deals ..... cosmetics too.
A. with B. in
C. at D. for

62. That rule is applicable ..... everyone.
A. to B. for
C. about D. with

63. I shall take revenge ..... you.
A. from B. with
C. on D. at

64. The ruling party will have to put its own house ..... order.
A. in B. on
C. to D. into

65. ..... all intents and purposes, the manager is the master of the firm.

A. in B. upon
C. with D. to

66. Like any other country India has its ..... share of superstitions.
A. proper B. abundant
C. fair D. peculiar

67. The miser gazed ..... at the pile of gold coins in front of him.
A. avidly B. admiringly
C. thoughtfully D. earnestly

68. The pilot had been warned about the storm before he .....
A. took away B. took up
C. took over D. took off

69. On account of the dearth of grass on the arid plains the cattle became .....
A. flippant B. jubilant
C. agitated D. emaciated

70. I saw a ..... of cows in the field.
A. group B. herd
C. swarm D. flock

Directions (Qs. 71 to 100): *Find the correctly spelt word.*

71. A. Survaillance B. Surveillance
C. Survellance D. Surveilance

72. A. Sepulchral B. Sepulchrle
C. Sepalchral D. Sepalchrle

73. A. Eflorescene B. Eflloresccnce
C. Efflorescence D. Efflorascence

74. A. Itinarery B. Itinerary
C. Itenerary D. Itinarary

75. A. Bouquete B. Bouquette
C. Bouquet D. Boquet

76. A. Renaisance B. Renaissance
C. Rennaissance D. Rennaisance

77. A. Lckadaisicle B. Lackdaisical
C. Lackadisical D. Lackadaisical

78. A. Entrepreneur B. Entrapreneur
C. Entrepraneur D. Entreprenuer

79. A. Vetarinary B. Veteninary
C. Vetniary D. Veterinary

80. A. Gaurantee B. Guarantee
C. Garuntee D. Guaruntee

81. A. Equanimity B. Equannimity
C. Equanimmity D. Equinimity

82. A. Parallelled B. Parralleled
C. Paralleled D. Paralelled

83. A. Puerrile B. Puerille
C. Purrile D. Puerile

84. A. Velnerable B. Vulnarable
C. Vulnerable D. Valnerable

85. A. Inoculation B. Innoculation
C. Inocculation D. Inocullation

86. A. Schedule B. Schedeule
C. Schdule D. Schedule

87. A. Treachrous B. Trecherous
C. Trechearous D. Treacherous

88. A. Acommodation B. Accomodation
C. Accommodation D. Acomodation

89. A. Satelite B. Sattelite
C. Satellite D. Sattellite

90. A. Excessive B. Exccessive
C. Exccessive D. Excesive

91. A. Dammage B. Damaige
C. Dammege D. Damage

92. A. Hindrance B. Hinderrance
C. Hindrence D. Hinderence

93. A. Klaptomania B. Kleptomonia
C. Kleptemonia D. Kleptomania

94. A. Exaggerate B. Exeggerate
C. Exagerate D. Exadgerate

95. A. Simpal B. Bannar
C. Pattren D. Modern

96. A. Chancelary B. Chancellary
C. Chancelery D. Chancellery

97. A. Palete B. Palet
C. Palate D. Pelate

98. A. Indipensable B. Indipenseble
C. Indispansible D. Indispensable

99. A. Rigerous B. Rigourous
C. Regerous D. Rigorous

100. A. Occured B. Occurad
C. Ocurred D. Occurred

Directions (Qs. 101 to 120): *In each question below a sentence is broken into five or six parts. Join these parts to make a meaningful sentence. The correct order of parts is the answer.*

101. a. do b. today
c. you d. must
e. it
A. cdaeb B. bedac
C. abedc D. eacbd
E. debac

102. a. I b. help
c. not d. you
e. did
A. bdcea B. aecbd
C. debca D. dcaeb
E. ebdca

103. a. tea b. have
c. that d. some
e. before
A. dcbea B. bdcae
C. bdaec D. ebdca
E. dacbe

104. a. seen b. going
c. you d. him
e. have
A. cebad B. ceadb
C. cbead D. ceabd
E. ecabd

105. a. of b. capable
c. he d. mean
e. anything f. is
A. edfcba B. cfdbae
B. cfebad C. cdfbae
E. cfbaed

106. a. make b. others
c. weak d. fun
e. of f. people
A. fadfcb B. cbadfe
C. fdebac D. cfadeb
E. cfadbe

107. a. killed b. a
c. Jaswant d. bear
e. wild
A. cabed B. ecabd
C. bcade D. dcabe
E. aebcd

108. a. medicine b. a
c. Neeta d. given
e. was
A. eadbc B. bedca
C. aedbc D. dbeca
E. cedba

109. a. him b. the
c. to d. charge
e. handover
A. dbeca B. eacdb
C. daceb D. debca
E. ebdca

110. a. at b. it
c. take d. once
e. away
A. bcead B. adceb
C. cbead D. ecbad
E. dbcae

111. a. you b. this
c. ready d. are
e. do f. to
A. dacfeb B. adcebf
C. dcafeb D. adbcfe
E. febadc

112. a. get b. meet
c. soon d. to
e. him f. we
A. eadbfc B. cfadbe
C. cfbdea D. adbcfe
E. dbecaf

113. a. bag b. you
c. seen d. have
e. my
A. eadcb B. dceab
C. dbcea D. dbaec
E. badce

114. a. of b. we
c. heard d. him
e. had
A. dbcea B. ebcda
C. becda D. bedca
E. becad

115. a. perfection b. the
c. take d. step
e. first f. to
A. bafced B. cbedfa
C. cabedf D. fedcba
E. cfbdea

116. a. left b. the
c. house d. he
e. suddenly
A. adbce B. baced
C. deabc D. ebcda
E. bdace

117. a. not b. Hari
c. away d. run
e. did
A. acedb B. cedab
C. ebdca D. beadc
E. bacde

118. a. I b. immediately
c. salary d. my
e. want
A. dcaeb B. aedcb
C. beadc D. dbcea
E. deacb

119. a. not b. hotel
c. comfortable d. was
e. the
A. cdeba B. ecdab
C. cdaeb D. daceb
E. ebdac

120. a. was b. and
c. Satish d. kind
e. loving
A. cadbe B. ebdac
C. cdbea D. aebdc
E. abcde

Directions (Qs. 121 to 140): *Which of the phrases given below each sentence should replace the phrase printed in* **bold** *type to make the sentence grammatically correct? If the sentence is correct as it is, mark 'E' as the answer.*

121. The research study is an eye-opener and **attempts to acquaint** us with the problems of the poor nations.
A. attempted to acquaint
B. attempts at acquainting

C. attempt to acquaint
D. attempting to acquaint
E. No correction required

122. The man who has committed such a serious crime must **get the mostly severe** punishment.
A. be getting the mostly severely
B. get the most severe
C. have got the most severely
D. have been getting the severemost
E. No correction required

123. Acquisition of certain specific skills **can be facilitated from** general awareness, education and exposure to novel situations.
A. can be facilitated by
B. may facilitate through
C. can be felicitated with
D. may be felicitated with
E. No correction required

124. He confidently asked the crowd if they thought he was right and the crowd shouted **that they did.**
A. that he did
B. that they had
C. that he is
D. that he didn't
E. No correction required

125. If he has to spend five hours in the queue, it **was really a wastage.**
A. is a really wastage
B. is real a wastage
C. has really a wastage
D. is really a wastage
E. No correction required

126. Why **did you not threw** the bag away?
A. did you not throw
B. had you not threw
C. did you not thrown
D. you did not thrown
E. No correction required

127. They **are not beware of** all the facts
A. are not aware for
B. are not aware of
C. are not to be aware
D. must not to be aware for
E. No correction required

128. **If I would have** realised the nature of the job earlier, I would not have accepted it.
A. If I have had
B. In case I would have
C. Had I been
D. Had I
E. No correction required

129. The moment they saw me, they **were delight**
A. had delighted
B. were delighted
C. are delighted
D. have been delighted
E. No correction required

130. The small child does whatever his father **was done.**
A. has done
B. did
C. does
D. had done
E. No correction required

131. It was unanimously resolved that the parties **should unitedly undertook** launching of popular programmes–
A. should be united undertook
B. should be unitedly undertaken
C. should be unitedly undertake
D. should unitedly undertake
E. No correction required

132. One of my drawbacks is that **I do not have to** tolerance of ambiguity.
A. do not have
B. cannot have to
C. am not
D. did not have to
E. No correction required

133. They **should have calmly thought of** the advantages that would accrue to them.
A. should have been calm in thinking about
B. should be calmly thought of
C. shall have to calmly thought of
D. should have calmly think of
E. No correction required

134. Their earnings are such that they find it difficult **to make both ends to meet**.
A. to making both ends meet
B. to make both ends for meeting
C. to make both ends meet
D. for making both ends to meet
E. No correction required

135. They **were all shocked at** his failure in the competition.
A. were shocked at all
B. had all shocked at
C. had all shocked by
D. had been all shocked on
E. No correction required

136. He is too impatient **for tolerating** any delay.
A. to tolerate
B. to tolerating
C. at tolerating
D. with tolerating
E. No correction required

137. Why **should the candidates be** afraid of English Language is not clear.
A. the candidates should be

B. do the candidates be
C. should be the candidates
D. are the candidates
E. No correction required

138. Ramesh is **as tall if not,** taller than Mahesh.
A. not as tall but
B. not so tall but as
C. as tall as, if not
D. as if not
E. No correction required

139. The easiest **of the thing to do** is to ask the address to the postman.
A. of the things to do
B. among the things did
C. of the thing to be done
D. of all the things done
E. No correction required

140. The player was asked **that why he had not** attended the prayer.
A. why had he not
B. that why had he not
C. why he was not
D. is hesitated to listen to
E. No correction required

ANSWERS

1	2	3	4	5	6	7	8	9	10
C	D	B	D	A	A	B	C	D	B
11	**12**	**13**	**14**	**15**	**16**	**17**	**18**	**19**	**20**
C	A	A	C	B	B	A	A	A	A
21	**22**	**23**	**24**	**25**	**26**	**27**	**28**	**29**	**30**
D	D	C	A	C	A	C	A	A	C
31	**32**	**33**	**34**	**35**	**36**	**37**	**38**	**39**	**40**
D	B	B	A	A	C	A	A	C	A
41	**42**	**43**	**44**	**45**	**46**	**47**	**48**	**49**	**50**
C	C	A	B	A	A	D	C	C	B
51	**52**	**53**	**54**	**55**	**56**	**57**	**58**	**59**	**60**
C	C	B	C	C	B	C	B	B	C
61	**62**	**63**	**64**	**65**	**66**	**67**	**68**	**69**	**70**
B	A	C	A	D	C	A	D	D	B
71	**72**	**73**	**74**	**75**	**76**	**77**	**78**	**79**	**80**
B	A	C	B	C	B	D	A	D	B
81	**82**	**83**	**84**	**85**	**86**	**87**	**88**	**89**	**90**
A	C	D	C	A	D	D	C	C	A
91	**92**	**93**	**94**	**95**	**96**	**97**	**98**	**99**	**100**
D	A	D	A	D	B	C	D	D	D
101	**102**	**103**	**104**	**105**	**106**	**107**	**108**	**109**	**110**
A	B	C	B	E	D	A	E	E	C
111	**112**	**113**	**114**	**115**	**116**	**117**	**118**	**119**	**120**
A	B	C	E	B	C	D	B	E	A
121	**122**	**123**	**124**	**125**	**126**	**127**	**128**	**129**	**130**
B	B	A	E	D	A	B	D	B	C
131	**132**	**133**	**134**	**135**	**136**	**137**	**138**	**139**	**140**
D	A	E	C	E	A	A	C	A	D

❑❑❑

WRITING ABILITY

FACTUAL DESCRIPTION

EXAMPLE-1

The two great epics of ancient India—The Ramayana and the Mahabharata—probably took shape in the course of several hundred years, and even subsequently additions were made to them. They deal with the early days of the Indo-Aryans, their conquests and civil wars, when they were expanding and consolidating themselves, but they were composed and compiled later. I do not know of any books anywhere which have exercised such a continuous and pervasive influence on the mass mind as these two Dating back to a remote antiquity, they are still a living force in the life of the Indian people, not in the original Sanskrit, except for a few intellectuals, but in translations and adaptations, and in those innumerable ways in which tradition and legend spread and become a part of the texture of a people's life. They represent the typical Indian method of catering all together for various degrees of cultural development, from the highest intellectual to the simple unread and untaught villager. They make us understand somewhat the secret of the old Indians in many ways and graded in castes, in harmonizing their discords, and giving them a common background of heroic tradition and ethical living. Deliberately they tried to build up a unity of outlook among the people which was to survive and overshadow all diversity

----- J.L. Nehru

Factual Description

The Ramayana and the Mahabharata

The two great epics of ancient India are the Ramayana and the Mahabharata. Their subject matter is the Indo-Aryan exploits for conquest, expansion and consolidation, though the books were compiled later. They are the unique books written in Sanskrit which has had such a forceful influence on the Indian mass mind since antiquity. They are available in several translations and adaptations. They express the unity in diversity of the Indian culture in all its graded forms.

EXAMPLE-2

Habits of idleness once firmly fixed cannot be suddenly thrown off. The man who has wasted precious hours of life's seed–time finds that he cannot reap a harvest in life's autumn. Lost wealth may be replaced by industry, lost knowledge by study, lost health by temperance or medicine, but lost time is gone for ever. In the long list of excuses for neglect of duty, there is none which drops oftener from men's lips, which is founded on more of self-delusion than the want of leisure. People are always cheating themselves with the idea that they would do this or that desirable thing 'if only they had time'. It is thus that the lazy and the selfish excuse themselves from a thousand things which conscience dictates to be done. Remember that the men who have done the most for their own and the general good are not the wealthy, leisurely people who have abundance of time to themselves and nothing to do. They are the men, who are in ceaseless activity from January to December – men, however, pressed with business, are always found capable of doing a little more. You may rely on them in their fullest seasons with ten times more assurance than on idle men.

Factual Description

Idleness is a Curse

Habits of idleness once formed cannot be easily got rid of. Lost wealth, knowledge and health can be retrieved but not the lost time. Many people make the excuse of want of leisure to neglect their duty. It is not the lazy rich who have done any good to society, but the busy, active ones. It is the men of the latter kind who are more reliable ones.

EXAMPLE-3

There is no doubt that pollution is playing havoc with environment. Almost always man himself is responsible for this criminal act. Tonnes of slag or waste generated when the iron scrap is melted in the foundries, is dumped at random on roadsides, open grounds and drains.

Even a monument of the stature of the Taj is not spared from being polluted. Those who visit the Taj tell a story of their own. If the multi–coloured plastic bags behind the eastern walls of the great mausoleum are an eyesore, the non–biodegradable slag is bound to contaminate the soil and the already highly–polluted water of the Yamuna. Like the ash from the thermal plants, the slag is everywhere.

The problem of flash ash is being tackled in certain states, no doubt. The brick kiln owners are being asked by the state governments to use it in the moulding of bricks, so that it does not choke the rivers, canals and other water channels. But the brick kiln owners too have a point. They say that the use of fly ash in brick making is very uneconomical. It pushes up the labour cost and hence of the prices of bricks, such that the consumers are the sufferers in the long run. The owners of factories might be asked to pay for this usage so that prices of bricks have not to be raised. But will the government do so? As the matter stands today, the consumers are destined to suffer.

Factual Description

Environmental Pollution

Environmental pollution is a big problem. Wastes from factories can be seen on roadsides, open grounds and drains. Plastic bags and slag can be seen everywhere even around the Taj. Thus, the Yamuna is also getting polluted.

Similarly, there is the problem of the disposal of fly ash released by factories. It chokes the water channels. The government have ordered that it should be used in brick making. But that increases costs and the consumers are the sufferers.

EXAMPLE-4

Forest fires should be taken up with all the seriousness they deserve. Particularly, in the forest tracts where pine trees have a growth, forest fires are frequent. It has been reported that just in one state, 4500 cases of forest fires were there in four years. It is mostly in the dry season of summer when these fires take place.

It is very important to take proper precautions to prevent these fires. Many of these fires take place because of human negligence. According to the Forest Department instructions, a fire near or in a forest should not be lighted, especially during summer. This fact should be brought to the notice of those who are ignorant of it. Whenever a fire in a forest is noticed, it should be beaten down at once. The brooms used for the purpose should be made of brushwood having green leaves.

It becomes the duty of all concerned to report the matter to the nearest officials of the department whenever a forest fire is noticed. All concerned should also consider it their sacred duty to cooperate with forest officials in preventing and extinguishing forest fires. It becomes the particuler duty of those who own a piece of land on the periphery of a forest to be extremely careful in the use of fire for the disposal of the waste material on their plot. It should be borne in mind that such an action of theirs can cause a major forest fires. Particularly, when a strong wind is blowing, the lighting of fire should be avoided.

Factual Description

Preventing Forest Fires

Forest fires are frequent, particularly in areas where there is dense growth of pine trees and that mostly during summer. To a great extent, these fires can be prevented by conscious efforts. The lighting of a fire in or near a forest, especially in summer should be avoided. If still a fire is noticed, it should be beaten down immediately. If need be, it should be reported to the nearest forest authorities. Those owning land near a forest should avoid lighting a fire there especially on a windy day.

EXAMPLE-5

According to a specialist in international affairs, both global terrorism and weapons of mass destruction pose a danger to humanity. At the same time, the use of force by a super power in the garb of fighting global war against terrorism without U.N. Security Council's express authorisation is of doubtful legality. It is hard to challenge this view.

According to the said specialist, war is also strategically counter–productive. There is no denying the fact that global terrorism poses a great danger to mankind. But it has to be fought somehow. The best way to fight global terrorism for all nations of the world is to unite under the hammer of U.N. Security Council. After all, global terrorism has been making more and more countries its targets in the recent past. This is what is now being witnessed in many parts of India, in Russia, West Asia, Saudi Arabia etc.

After 9/11, the world seemed to have waken up to reality. It appeared that the world might after all unite vigorously and whole-heartedly to fight with this dangerous menace. Then the world witnessed train bombing in Madrid and certain happenings in Chechneya, Indonesia, Saudi Arabia and Nepal and even Pakistan.

Neither Afghanistan nor Iraq has so for recovered from the after-effects of war. Nobody can even claim that these countries have been ridden of the menace of terrorism. It means there is something wrong in choosing war as a means for eradicating terrorism. Some other ways and means will have to be found out to get rid of this menace.

Factual Description

Fighting Global Terrorism

Global terrorism and weapons of mass destruction pose a great danger to mankind. But meeting the challenge of terrorism is not possible through war especially when it is not authorized by the U.N. security council.

After 9/11, the world seemed to have united for eradicating this menace. But the events in several countries have belied the hopes of the international community.

Even after Afghanistan and Iraq wars, there seems to be no improvement in the situation. So, war is not the solution to this problem.

EXAMPLE-6

If someone were inclined to know what the all-time favourite drink with most Indians is, of course, one would name tea. Tea is of several varieties. It is said that tea of all varieties is beneficial to human health if taken in moderation, but green tea is said to be the best for the heart.

India is one of the largest tea producers of the world and that is good for India as well as the whole world. In the matter of exporting tea, she has to compete with countries like Sri Lanka and China mainly. In India, the Assam hill region is the largest tea producing area. The Assam tea is said to be very pungent in taste.

As far as the point of flavour of tea is concerned, the Darjeeling tea is the most famous all over the world. Tea plantations are there in the Brahmputra valley, in Himachal Pradesh, in the southern parts of the Western Ghats and in some parts of South India.

Now, tea tasting is a skill for which there are specific institutions. Each tea company employs tea tasters to obtain high standards of their product. These tea tasters can tell the kind and quality of tea just by tasting. They can tell the region to which the tea they have tasted belongs. Tea tasters are not required to have high essential educational qualification, perhaps not higher than 10 + 2, but they must have the required aptitude and inclination to acquire the skill.

It is said that slower growth of tea plants improves tea flavour. Not only tea tasting but also tea growing as well as tea plucking is now considered an art which is beyond the approach of anybody and everybody.

Factual Description

Tea As a Drink

Tea is the favourite drink with most Indians. It is a health beverage. In India, tea is planted in several regions, but the Darjeeling tea is considered to be the best in flavour.

Tea tasting is now considered an important skill which is taught in several institutions. Tea tasters are employed by all the tea companies to maintain the quality of their products. Tea tasters don't have high educational qualifications but they can tell much about the kind, quality and region of the tasted tea. Like tea tasting, tea growing and plucking are also skilful arts.

EXAMPLE-7

A giant tsunami struck South Asia after a high intensity earthquake of 9 degree magnitude on Richter scale on 26th December, 2004. The tsunami struck several countries including Indonesia, India, Maldives, Mayanmar, Thailand, Malaysia, Sri Lanka etc. Some people were killed even in Bangladesh, Kenya, Tanzania and some other countries. A total number of about 1,60,000 were said to have died in the tsunami and thousands of people were reported missing.

The maximum number of casualities took place in Indonesia where about 1,10,000 people were said to have been killed as high sea waves struck the country at an incredibly high speed. Not to speak of human beings even tall concrete buildings which were both builders' and owners' pride fell like houses of cards.

The Indonesians called it "Mata'ie" which in Indonesian means "tears". It was the Aceh province in Indonesia which was the most affected area in the entire region. According to a report published in "The Independent", "When an earthquake and tidal waves destroyed vast swaths of the Indonesian province on Boxing Day, survivors from coastal areas near Banda Aceh, the capital, fled to higher ground and found themselves in Mata' ie, in the shadow of Aceh's hills."

"The Independent" further reported, "Now 3,000 homeless and destitute people are living in a crowded camp on the outskirts of the town, where they spend their days reliving the nightmare unleashed by the tsunami and searching fruitlessly for relatives and friends."

"The camp's front fence has become a wall of despair, where hundreds of messages scrawled on fragments of cardboard beg for information on missing people. Many of them are children, washed to oblivion by the giant walls of water that swept away their flimsy homes."

It was rightly described by many as the greatest human tragedy in history. Although massive aid from various sources arrived within a few days, the loss to human life and property could never be accurately measured, much less repaired.

Factual Description

Tsunami in South Asia

On December 26, 2004, a powerful tsunami struck several countries of South Asia after a massive earthquake in the Indian Ocean. About 1,60,000 were reported dead and thousands were missing.

Indonesia bore the brunt of tsunami with about 1,10,000 casualities. In Indonesia, the province of Aceh was the most seriously hit. The Indonesians called it "Matai' ie" which in Indonesian means "tears."

"The Independent" reported the condition of 3000 homeless people in Aceh who led a miserable life in a relief camp on the outskirts of the capital. They are searching fruitlessly for their lost friends and relatives. But the total loss to life and property will ever remain inestimable.

EXAMPLE-8

In the matter of eating habits, animals can be divided into two broad kinds. Animals who eat flesh are known as carnivores. Those who eat grass, leaves of plants, etc. are called herbivores.

Carnivores usually have long canine teeth. They use these teeth for catching and tearing up their prey. These animals belong to the category of hunters among the mammals.

Basically, lions, leopards and tigers belong to the same family as the domestic pussy cat. This may seem strange but it is true. In our daily life, we frequently come across cats. They are carnivores and belong to the category of hunters. They often run after their prey such as mice, sparrows, pigeons, etc. from dawn to dusk.

It is commonly believed that cats can see in darkness. This is only partly true. It is true that their eyes are especially designed by nature to enable them to see in darkness. But even cats may not see quite well in total darkness.

Cats have an excellent way of hunting. They indulge in this activity as if they were pursuing consciously and vigorously some art. They can be seen lazily sitting at a shady place under an undergrowth or near a terrace with their eyes half-closed. But this laziness is only on the surface. They may be inwardly as alert as ever. It is their way of allowing their prey to come and sit close to them without being alarmed. They make no noise even while walking. They go close to the prey, say a sparrow, creating the least stir or disturbance. As they reach within the pouncing distance, they pounce upon the prey in one swoop and capture the prey. Often their grip is so strong that the poor prey cannot escape it. The prey flutters and writhes in their mouth but within minutes the matter is over with it. Soon, what one can find at the place is a heap of feathers and claws.

Factual Description

Cats as Hunters

Cats are among the mammals. They belong to the category of hunters. They are relentless, but cleve hunters. They hunt their prey from morning to evening. They can see in darkness, though not quite well in total darkness.

They have the art of hunting their prey. Often they sit lazily at a vantage place. They give no clue of their presence to their prey. Their unsuspecting prey comes to a place close to where a cat is sitting.

As a cat walks towards the prey, it makes no noise or disturbance. Slowly it comes very close to the prey, and pounces upon it and captures it.

ESSAY WRITING

INTRODUCTION

The term 'essay', for examination purposes, can be applied to a composition in which the writer states his knowledge of, and gives his opinions about, a certain topic. An essay, in this sense, will contain narrative and descriptive elements as well as comments and criticism representing the writer's own point of view. Thus, an essay becomes a test, not only of knowledge, but of thought and imagination. It reflects the writer's personality as well as his or her ability to weave disintegrated bits of information into a thread of unity.

Essentials of a Good Essay

1. An essay must be a unity, developing one theme with a definite purpose.
2. The essay should follow a certain ordered line of thought and come to a definite conclusion. The matter— the ideas/facts,— should be arranged into an attractive design.

3. The presentation of the matter should be clear. Language and sentence construction should be simple and lucid.
4. An essay should reveal the personal feelings and opinions of the writer.

However, idiosyncrasies had better not be expressed. Nor should extreme or dangerous opinions be expressed.

TOURISM

Tourism is a growing industry in India. Hoteliering and tourism account for major foreign revenues of our nation. The declining value of the rupee and a good image of India as an exotic tourist destination have boosted the tourism and hotel industry in India during the last decade.

It is surprising to note that small nations like Thailand, Hongkong, Malaysia, Seyshells, Mauritius, and Indonesia have been able to do very well on the tourism front. India is the ancient cultural cradle of the world. It has fascinating tourist destinations like the Taj (Agra), Khajuraho Temples (Khajuraho), Marble mountains (Jabalpur), Gateway of India (Mumbai), Red Fort and Qutab Minar (New Delhi), Amar Vilas Palace (Jaipur), Bharatpur Bird Sanctuary (Bharatpur), the city of canals (Alleppey), and many attractive hill spots in the North. We Indians are also not aware of the beauty of our nation. Our ancient cities, lakes, mountains, palaces, temples, mosques, minarets and gardens are thrilling experiences for all the visitors. Almost every foreign tourist longs for a tryst with the beauty of India and loves to visit each and every corner of this vast nation.

Goa, Khajuraho, New Delhi, Mumbai, Kolkata, north-eastern states, and Pondicherry are the most popular tourist destinations. Rajasthan is a paradise for the foreingers and this state offers a wide range of cultural and ethnic diversities to the visitors.

Foreign tourists are appalled at the state of Indian roads, hotels, motels, guide services, catering services, transportation services and environment of the Indian subcontinent. We would have to provide four-star amenities to the tourists at the prices of three-star standards. If we do not follow this norm, we would lose tourists, who would move to the USA, Europe, Japan, Hongkong, Thailand, Singapore, Mauritius, and Seychells. These nations offer good quality rooms, food, liquor, entertainment, and transportation at the most competitive prices. They follow international tourism norms in terms of hygiene, hospitality and catering. We do not follow these norms and this leads to apathetic attitudes of tourists towards India.

It is fortunate to note that tourism and hotel management have become serious subjects and vocations. The government and private institutions have launched many courses in hotel management and tourism. Tourism professionals are required by tour operators and airlines. The airlines and sea cruisers also need hospitality staff. Finally, chefs are required around the world. Hotel professionals are also in great demand. This would boost the hotel industry and hence the economy.

The services of telecommunications, sea ferries sanitation, air travel, roads, catering and tourist guides would have to be operated on professional grounds. The international agency, the IATA, is doing well to promote and regulate air travel around the world. Government of India is also doing its best. Participation of the private firms has also increased. However, a lot needs to be done in this crucial area. We can earn the much coveted foreign exchange through tourism and hotel industries. Our outlook and approach would have to be made professional, if we want to achieve concrete results in this fastest growing industry.

UNEMPLOYMENT

Unemployment is actually a global problem but it is most serious in India. We have here in our country unemployment of various kinds and varying degrees. There is white-collar and blue-collar unemployment. Many highly educated degree holders in electronics, engineering, management and other disciplines are also unemployed or only semi-employed. Nearly 5 crore educated people of our country are fully unemployed; this number is growing at a fast pace.

There are both skilled and unskilled workers who are unemployed on a large scale. There are unemployed people both in rural and urban areas. There are both agricultural and industrial unemployed workers. The more serious thing is that the problem is being aggravated day by day.

On the surface of it there seem to be many jobs available through Business Process Outsourcing (BPO) and overseas, but that are available only to a handful of highly skilled personnel and a vast majority of people remains unemployed. Jobs available through BPO, though welcome, are mostly concerned with such disciplines as financing, accounting, designing, medical transcription etc. These are not so many in number, considering the vastness of our country and the mammoth population and gigantic problem of unemployment that we are facing. These jobs touch only the tip of our problem. Our government and private sectors must try to answer the problem adequately to check the growing number of tables, which is rising among all sections of society.

Unemployment is, no doubt, a serious problem all over the world. Says an analyst:

"The worst victims of the marketisation rush have been the lower strata of the population. Competition and efficiency, the two hallmarks of the neo-capitalism, essentially mean job cuts." Europe is reeling under the anachronism of more investment, more production and more loss of employment. Upgradation of the quality of labour has been an inseparable aspect of the efficient production line. So, less intelligent ones fall by the way side.

In India, globalisation and modernisation have taken their toll. Now, few jobs are there only for the highly skilled ones and they are given to those people who have some recommendation and, better still, if they can cough up a considerable amount as hush money. The VRS has further added to vows of some people. Many, particularly the illiterate, unskilled people take recourse to the weird route of crime and not only they themselves suffer but also cause suffering to many others.

The jobless are being offered various schemes to combat the menace. The JRY was in vogue recently. In rural areas, the new employment guarantee scheme is bring implemented (read about it in this volume). The private sector does not take unskilled poorly trained personnel. Hence, job reservation in the private sector is nothing but a Utopian dream. Even the government cannot force the private sector firms to accept poorly performing people in its fold. If that is done, the efficiency and profit–making prowess of the corporate sector firms would be reduced. That is what we do not want at any cost, for the private sector is the primary growth engine of our economy now-a-days.

The situation is even worse now when with the advent of multinational giants like LG, Samsung, etc. Several Indian companies including some quite prestigious ones as Voltas, Crompton Greaves, Glaxo Pharma etc. have virtually closed shop. Lakhs of workers have been thrown in the streets. As the President CITU pointed out:

"Post-liberalisation has seen workers lose jobs on a daily basis in the textiles, coal, manufacturing and steel industry. No safety nets have been put in place, and there is a sense of desperation and fear in the homes of all the workers we visit today. There are no regular salaried jobs available in these sectors anymore."

A very dismal position was depicted by the President of the federation of 750 Maharashtra based trade, transport and small scale industries associations:

"Land in and around Mumbai has become a prised commodity. Most of the industrialist groups have sold their units at whopping profits to land sharks. They pocket all that money without giving workers any compensation. They then borrow crores of rupees from institutional lending groups at concessional rates to set up alterative industries in places like Gujarat etc, where workers are being hired at Rs. 2,000 per month. They are akin to slaves toiling in sweetshops. The government has just turned a blind eye to all these goings on."

Surely, the situation is very explosive and if some concrete steps are not taken expeditiously, there can arise some serious socio-economic and political upheaval. No doubt there are some schemes like Nehru Rozgar Yojna and others on paper. But they are not enough and are not implemented sincerely.

Most state-controlled enterprises and corporation are being privatised now-a-days. So, the number of jobs is less in the government-run departments and companies. The youth are advised to be on their own and start small enterprises, they would certainly do well in their own firms. They will be the masters of their destiny. They will earn more that way. Moreover, self-employment would also help them realise their cherished dreams. They can also export their goods.

In sum, unemployment is a major challenge for our planners and the youth alike. We must meet this challenge with zest and determination if we want to become a high-performing economy of the new century.

HUMAN RIGHTS

The concept of Human Rights lays stress on respect for the human-beings, regardless of the considerations of colour, race, sex, religion, etc. These are fundamental rights to which, every man or women is entitled merely by virtue of having been born as a human being. The preamble to the Universal Declaration of Human Rights (1948) states, "recognition of the inherent dignity and of the equal and inalienable rights of all the members of the human family is the foundation of freedom, justice and peace in the world."

Human rights are categorized as civil, political, economic, social and cultural. Sometimes, their particular components are specified as the right to live, right to liberty and security of person and so on but all sets of rights, irrespective of categorization, constitute one indivisible whole. Denial of one specific right impinges upon the fulfilment of other rights.

Most of the violations of human rights take place in the management of law and order, either by police or by armed forces. So, the State may be held responsible for violation of human rights when the State, by its acts of omission and commission, allows human rights to be violated. There may also be situations in which, breach of human rights takes place for reasons that cannot be said to originate due to actions of the State.

The terrorist activities in various parts of the world, which take innocent lives, presecution of undertrial POWs (Prisoners of War), incarceration of national leaders fighting for Independence (for example, Nelson Mandela in South Africa and Aung San Suu Kyi in Burma), use of child labour at low wages, atrocities inflicted by the police on liberal authors like Taslima Nasreen in Bangladesh are some types of human rights violations.

India is the only Asian nation in which, the Parliament passed the Human Rights Act in 1993 which had only a few amendments since March 1, 1994. The National Human Rights Commission of India is headed by retired Chief Justice K.G. Balakrishnan. The head office of the Commission is in New Delhi. The other members of the Commission are the dignitaries who had held the positions of the Judges of High Courts and who are well versed with issues related to human rights.

Thus, it is not the executive of the country but the judiciary, which controls the Human Rights Commission. In addition to a National Commission, there is a provision in the Act for the Constitution of State Human Rights Commissions. These are headed by the Judges of State High Courts or the Supreme Court. Such a person has the status of the secretary of a state. Human rights violation cover, in general, acts of unprovoked violence against a person, persecution, molestation, public insult, etc. Although these seem to overlap the Fundamentals Rights granted under Article (21), yet the Human Rights Act is specific about those acts, which ultimately culminate in the violation of human rights. The Commission has powers to investigate those acts, which have been mentioned in the Indian Criminal Procedure Code. The Commission has become popular and a large number of cases is being brought to the human rights courts. These courts try cases of police atrocities and the maltreatment of undertrial prisoners. These courts, supported by the judicial system, have been asked to deliver justice in many a case.

On the global level, human rights violation pivots on the issue of atrocities committed by terrorists. Terrorism is now prominent in a number of countries including Britain, the USA, Canada, India, Spain, Sri Lanka and many developing nations. In India, terrorism with financial and material support from abroad, seeks to decimate her secular, democratic and pluralistic civil order.

At its meeting in Geneva in March 1994 the UN finally recognized that terrorism poses a major threat to human rights. The UN Human Rights Commission unequivocally described terrorism as a heinous activity, aimed at destroying human integriy. The historic resolution called upon all the States to take all necessary and effective measures to "prevent, combat and eliminate terrorism." However, it also stipulated a controversial clause, stating that measures taken against terrorists must conform to international standards of human rights. This is viewed by many experts as a weak clause; while the terrorist outfit employs all available means of warfare, the target State will have to abide by constitutional guarantees. Thus, the militant group will use the alibi human rights to promote her nafarious designs!

However, containing of terrorism by State-sponsored acts of official terrorism would only suppress the problem and may not solve it. Freedom is man's most prized possession. The Human Rights Declaration was drafted by the Nobel Prize Laureate Rene Cassin in 1968 and is the hallmark of the civilized society, which guarantees freedom from fear to everyone. Pragmatists find such an idealist interpretation slightly irrational and demand logical thinking and pragmatic steps in this regard. Terrorist states, aided by petro-Dollars and lucrative trafficking activities in narcotics, have resources at their disposal. Thus, they can easily harm the targeted State if it has to observe human rights standards. Further, every burst of fire has to be justified in a court of law. When an emergency occurs, fundamental rights of the common citizens are suspended. Why cannot it be done in the case of regions dominated by terrorists? All these questions make the UNHRC controversial and debatable.

While a democratic government system is vital for the protection of human rights, the fact remains that human rights are essentially the rights of the people, both as individuals and as groups. Hence, persistent vigilance of people themselves, to safeguard their right has to be developed as the guiding tenet. In this connection, the roles of media and free Press are also important.

Free market forces would lead to exploitation of poor masses. The role of the national and international human rights agencies would be to protect the interests of the common man. The tasks is Herculean, but the common man cannot be left at the mercy of those who are cruel, influential, and rich beyond imagination.

SPREADING TENTACLES OF TERRORISM

The new century has taken the legacy of terrorism from the previous one. In the new century, the forces of terrorism have taken all democratic forces for a ride. Sadly, there seems to be no solution in sight and the war against terrorism is likely to be bitter in the years to come. Let us take a look at the nefarious designs of the forces of terrorism that are a threat to the peoples of most nations, law-enforcing agencies and judicial systems alike.

Aum Shinrikyo was a cult set up in 1987 in Japan. It was started by Aum Asahara. It wanted to take over Japan and later, the entire world. On March 20, 1995, the members of this cult released a chemical nerve agent (called Sarin) in many suburban trains of Tokyo. Twelve people were killed in these trains and more than 6,000 people were injured. This cult mainly operates in Japan. The name of the LTTE is well-known. It was founded in 1976. It wants to set up a separate Eelam (State) within the boundary of Sri Lanka. The LTTE cadres are ruthless to the core. Their suicide bombers are called Black Tigers. The LTTE uses bombs and human bombs to kill and terrorise people, politicians and security forces. The Late Rajiv Gandhi was the victim of a human bomb. He was killed on May 21, 1991 by a human bomb when he was addressing an election rally in Sriperambadur (Tamil Nadu). The LTTE is also responsible for killing many political leaders and heads of previous governments of Sri Lanka. It has been alleged that it has been receiving the support from some politicians of Tamil Nadu.

Another organisation to be carefully monitored is the Basque Fatherland and Liberty. It was founded in 1959. Its objective is to establish an independent homeland for those people who nurture the Marxist ideology. It operates in northern Spain and south-western France. In one major incident, this organisation killed 38 people and injured several others. The Basques are a powerful entity in Spain. The Irish Republican Army (IRA) was created in 1998. Its aim is to remove the British from Ireland. It aims to unite Ireland. This group is famous for its car bomb attacks and building explosions. On August 15, 1998, it attacked through a car bomb in Omagh and killed 29 people, injuring 220 others. In 2000 and 2001, it resumed its spate of violence. The British government is trying to chalk out a peace plan in consultation with the IRA cadres. However, the situation is not fully under control. Bobby Sands, an IRA cadre, gave his life for the cause of free Ireland when he went on hunger strike. This organisation is active in Britain and Ireland.

The National Liberation Army of Colombia is a Marxist insurgent group. It was created in 1965. The chief supporters and promotors of this group were Fidel Castro (of Cuba) and Che Guevara. It kidnaps people for getting ransom. It often targets foreign employees of large corporations. It operates in Colombia. Another organisation, the National Liberation Army of Colombia, is also an active organisation of Colombia. In February, 2003, it was responsible for killing 30 persons through a car-bomb attack in Bogota.

Further, there are many other organisations operating in Europe and South America that attack people and security personnel off and on. We have mentioned the names and activities of only important organisations in this text.

The rebels of Chechnya are hell-bent upon making Chechnya a free State. They are Muslim guerillas and have give enough tantrums to the Russians. Recently, they took over a theatre in Moscow and held several hundred people as hostages. The Russian armed forces swiftly moved in and killed 41 of these insurgents. However, 128 hostages were also killed. The problem of Chechen rebels is proving to be a great headache for Mr. Putin and his colleagues. The Russian government has imprisoned many top-line leaders of this rebel group and a few of them have died in prison. However, the Chechens are not in a mood to shed their claim. The head of Chechen rebels is Mr Mousar Basayev.

Al-Qaeda is a baby of Osama-bin-Laden. His most trusted deputy is Aimaan-al-Zawahiri. Both of them are at large and could not be traced by the forces of the UK and USA operating in Afghanistan. Osama bin Laden was a stooge of the Americans during the time when Russia had occupied Afghanistan (during the eighties). He was trained by the Americans to put up fight against the Russian forces operating in Afghanistan. Ironically, the same Osama has become a headache for the Americans. He is always elusive, thanks to his well-created and finely maintained intelligence network. Osama was responsible for the 9/11 carnage that had shaken America and the world. A war against terrorists ensured in 2001. It was won by the US-led forces. The Taliban is another organisation that was working in collusion with Al-Qaeda. The Taliban was wiped out from Afghanistan. However, we have many reasons to believe that the Taliban is down but not out. That is why, Mr Hamid Karzai and his cohorts are being incessantly protected by the forces led by the Americans. Karzai has also won the first ever democratic election held in Afghanistan. Her population is based on several tribes that operate and kill to survive in the tough terrain of the wild cold mountaions. Although Afghanistan is trying to become fully democratic, Al-Qaeda and the Taliban can strike back at any point of time. In a video released by Al Jazeera TV, Mr Laden announced that he would repeat the incident of 9/11 time and again. He was seen in perfect health which means that he is fit enough to fight and lead his cadres against Uncle Sam. Mr Barak Obama would find it difficult to contain Al-Qaeda because the latter is not in a mood to compromise. If an incident like 9/11 is repeated, the USA may retaliate with an untold vigour against Al-Qaeda. This organisation operates in Afghanistan and Pakistan, although it has supporters and deadly links in many countries. Experts aver that Osama may be hiding in Kashmir or in a border district of Pakistan. The Pakistani government denies that it has links with this organisation. However, the world refuses to accept this logic. In the past, the Pakistani army was hands in glove with the Taliban and Al-Qaeda. It cannot shift its stand in a few years. The Pakistani army has launched many campaigns to capture Al-Qaeda cadres and also succeeded in some of its campaigns. However, there may be a covert understanding between the Pakistani army (and its generals) and the cadres of Al-Qaeda. Pakistan was directly responsible for supporting and protecting many terrorist groups. The Taliban is the brainchild of the Pakistani army. In fact, the Taliban was created because the Pakistani army could not overtly fight the forces of the West. Hence, it created a pawn to unleash a wave of terror on the Afghan people and security forces. The Taliban and Al-Qaeda consider India as their opponent. This fact has brought the USA and India closer than ever.

The Indonesian *Jehadi* group is a close associate of Al-Qaeda. In October, 2002, it attacked two night clubs in Bali, killing 200 people. Most of the victims were Australians. In August, 2003, it struck again. It attacked Hotel Jakarta Marriott in Jakarta.

Finally, the latest spate of violence was observed when Chechen rebels had attacked a school near the Russian border. Several children and their teachers were killed. This bloodbath stunned the world. The total toll of the dead was 338. The school was located in Beslan, near the border of Russia. The incident took place on September 1, 2004. On September 9, 2004, a car bomb exploded near the Australian embassy in Jakarta. Eleven persons were killed in this attack while 160 persons were wounded.

In Kashmir, several terrorist organisations are operating. The Hizbul Mujahiddeen (HM) was founded by Sayyed Salahuddin. He was released by the Indian government in exchange for the hostages taken by Kashmiri militants in 1999. They had hijacked an Air India aircraft and taken it to Kandahar. The then foreign minister of India had to intervene and personally visit Kandhar to ensure a smooth exchange of hostages with the terrorists released from Indian jails. The other militant organisations of Kashmir are Dukhtaran-e-Millet and Lashkar-e-Taiyyaba. Besides, many other Kashmiri militant organisations are also operating on a small scale. They are demanding the liberation of Kashmir. Most of Kashmiri militant groups are operating from Muzaffarabad, which is located in Pak-Occupied-Kashmir (POK). India has time and again told Pakistan to demolish terrorist training camps operating on her soil but to no avail. The Kashmir imbroglio could not be resolved because of this very reason. The Kashmiri terrorist cadres cross the border from some points in POK and attack civilians and military forces in the Indian part of Kashmir. Since the eighties, this spate of violence has continued.

The logical, justified demands of every terrorist organisation should be accepted and that organisation should be allowed to join the mainstream. However, the unjustified polarised demands of any organisation must be rubbished. The PLO was once a terrorist organisation but it is a peaceful group now. Its demands and suggestions are heard by the world community. The Israelis are leaving no stone unturned to decimate the Palestinian masses and rebels. The message is clear—killing innocent people cannot help any person or group achieve his or its goals, howsoever pious they may be. Solutions can be found through across-the-table negotiations, not through car bombs, attacks on civilians and guerilla wars.

EMPOWERMENT OF WOMEN

Women are the companion of man, gifted with equal mental capabilities. She has the right to participate in every minute detail of the activites of man and she has an equal right of freedom and liberty with him. She is entitled to a supreme place in her own sphere of activity as men is in his. The Constitution of India ensures a place of dignity and honour for all women.

The last five decades have witnessed some basic changes in the status and the role of women in our society. Today this processes has been further accelerated with some women becoming increasingly self-conscious of discrimination against them in several areas of family and public life. Unlike the pre-independence period, a girl is sent to school right from the nursery class. She even studies in a boarding school and thus stays away from her parents. Even after her education is complete, she does not stay back home but looks forward for a bright career. By doing so she even helps her parents financially. She walks shoulder to shoulder with her male counterpart. She is no more illiterate, backward, ignorant or suppressed in the urban areas. But still a large section are still not literate and the government is doing its best to educate and uplift them. Inspite of all these the mentality of the parent has changed. In most countries of the world, there are approximately 105 female births for every 100 males. But in India there are less than 93 women for every 100 men in the population. The accepted reason for such disparity is the practice of female infanticide in India.

According to UNICEF, the problem is getting worse as scientific methods of detecting the sex of a baby and of performing abortions are improving.

These methods are becoming increasingly available in rural areas of India, fuelling fears that the trend towards the abortion of female foetuses is on the rise. According to a report in Asian Age, there are atleast 70,000 women sex workers in Delhi, Chennai, Kolkata, Bangalore and Hyderabad. Majority of these women are from the weaker sections of the society.

Women have played a silent, self effacing role to sustain Indian civilization down the ages. But since independence her image has changed. All our political and social leaders have always insisted on education and equal rights for women. Because of their education and advancement, women today accompany the exploration team to Antartica. Kalpana Chawla proved that women were in no way inferior to men even in space shuttle area. Today women are competing with men in each and everysphere, be it politics, armed forces, police force, management, banking or the judicial sector. Our country has seen one of the most intelligent lady–Smt. Indira Gandhi during whose Prime Ministership the country flourished. The whole world became aware of Indra's capability. Women are also excelling in sports like P.T. Usha and in beauti contests like Sushmita Sen and Aishwarya Rai.

The Constitution has not only provided for equal rights and privileges for both men and women but has also made special provisions for women. Inspite of so many laws, the female still lives under great stress and strain under the male dominated society.

With the process of industrialisation, globalisation and modernisation showing its deep import on the human society all over the world, the role and responsibility of women has attained a new dimension. The educational and occupational patterns have also changed and widened with women entering the domains, which till decade back was considered to be dominated by men. Unless women throw off shackles which ignore their talent, their skill and their spirit, women cannot be empowered. And unless they are empowered to take a decisive part in the social political and economic life of the country, the very development of the country may be adversely affected.

SECULARISM

Before Independence, Nationalist leaders of India envisaged a nation which must be democratic, socialist, republic in which all sections of the society and people of all caste, creed and region should enjoy freedom, equality and justice and shall have the equal opportunity in government jobs and private enterprises. To turn this commitment that India should be secular state, the government established a legislation in the Parliament and added the word 'secular' in the constitution through 42nd Amendment act.

India as a nation shall have no religion, however, the Constitution confers religious freedom to all and shall have no religion be given priority over others vis-a-vis state promulgamations. In fact, India shall have no state religion which means no particular religion will be given preference. The framers of our Constitutions the intellectual elite and the political stalwarts keeping in mind the diversity of the country, proposed and created a nation which has no religion.

The state considers religion as individual's private belief and faith wherein the state shall have no objection in following propagating and organising religious assemblies. No individual shall be discriminated or favoured because of his or her religion and that an Indian identity will not be a religious identity. However Indian identity is the first and fore-most identity.

Secularism has always been a subject of debate among leaders, intellectuals and clerics. Fundamentalist group and narrow-minded demagogues vehemently oppose India being called a secular state. There has been hue and cry over this issue but as a concept of a healthy nation, securlism is widely accepted principle. And the people of this country, the masses and the youths inspect of their religious affiliations are all secular by nature.

Not only this bold and wise step of making India a secular state, the great Indian leaders have placed this country on a very higher and honourable position among the democratic states in the world. Such is the superiority of secularism that a demagogue like 'Jinnah', the chief architect of the division of this country, proposed Pakistan as a secular state, though the fundamentalist could not swallow this idea.

The constitution of India provided enough security and safety to the minorities of this country secularism is the best ideal to safeguard the interest of such communities.

This is an outstanding feature of India that a nation which has the most number of religious followers and the people most religious and pious that not a single country in the world has this honour. Even though the state is under the influence of no single religion.

Here Muslims enjoy full rights of the citizens as their Hindu brothers; a Buddhist, a Jain, a Christian or a Sikh a Marxist or Heathen—all enjoy the rights provided by the constitution.

In a world full of ideological strifes and conflicts, India stands tall as it honours all religious but favours none and to be a strong nation it is a wise move to have the state free from religious narrow-mindedness. And to be the most powerful nation, the people of this country must maintain this ideal which can hold the nation in one binding code emits many discodes.

ROLE OF MEDIA IN EDUCATION

The media scenario in India has undergone spectacular changes since independence. From the era of the ubiquitous bullock cart, we have travelled to the modern age of satellite technology, Internet and digital devices. Ever since the beginning of planned development in the country, the role of the media in the process of development has been recognized. The growth of media means the development of society as a whole and of all of its economic, social and political engines. It calls for the improvement in the standards of the poor masses through an equitable distribution of resources. Education is an important weapon in the hands of poor, which can be used for reaching new heights in life.

As per 2011 census, India had a literacy rate of only 74.04 per cent for the entire population. As compared to the situation at the time of Independence, India has made rapid progress in the field of education for her citizens. But increased population and a lack of the resources and voluntary organisations during the initial periods have been the major limitations. The major initiative to eradicate illiteracy began during the 1980s. The Human Resource Development ministry was constituted to harmonize all the inputs required for proper education of Indian masses. The national Adult Education Programme was launched by many voluntary agencies, educational institutions, local bodies and government departments for adult education. In 1988 the National Literacy Mission was constituted to tackle with the challenge of achieving complete literacy, *i.e.*, this mission launched the total literacy campaign. Indian Census (2011) has shown us good percentages of literacy. Now, the government plans to make the nation fully literate by the end of Eleventh Five year Plan.

The National Educational Policy (1986) reinforced the importance of media for perpetuating and supporting educational processes. The diffused, inflexible and hackneyed structures in villages provided immense communication barriers with the outside world. Realising the problem, SITE (Satellite Instructional Television Experiment) programme was launched during 1970s. It was the most advanced technological experiment ever conducted for such a large population which utilized community television sets for teaching modern methods of production, process of fertilization and technologies, soil and water conservation methods, crop patterns, seeds, dairy development and animal husbandry. The brain behind the experiment, Dr Vikram Sarabhai, commented, "Mass media is an indispensable condition for rural development in modern times. Through the process of communication, the new ideology of equality, human dignity, social justice, etc., had to be spread across." The BJP government launched schemes like Sankhya Vahani and TRYSEM. These essentially involved the use of modern training tools and computers.

The number of journals and newspapers has multiplied since the dawn of independence. Newspapers are being brought out in 96 languages and dialects. The combined circulation of the Press is several crore per day. An educated person can go through the newspaper and inform the illiterates. Since the message is in black and white, the communicator has the option of reading in detail. However, the newspapers and other print media have the limitation, which cannot communicated directly to the illiterate masses. Most of these papers are sold in large towns and cities. However, local and vernacular papers have a great utility in rural areas.

Radio is by far the most extensive network of communication for our people. Technically, the radio signals cover almost the whole country. According to an estimate, there are about 8 crore radio sets in the country. The message is conveyed directly and in a spoken language. Radio has been broadcasting educational programmes including news-bulletins, talks, panel discussions, quiz contests, commentaries, classroom lectures, discussions and face-to-face interviews with the audience. It is a participative medium and can be used for educating and developing the masses in general and for primary education. FM channel has revolutionized the entertainment scenario. In the four metropolises, one-way information exchanges regarding traffic, national news and leisure are effected through the radio.

The relevance of media in imparting education is quite obvious. However, proper choice of the medium, framing of strategy, designing of message and effective utilization of resources are vital for success. Huge sums of money are wasted because the beneficiaries were not aware of the literary campaigns. In the field of education, it is necessary to estimate their requirements, decide the media to convey the message and implement the media strategy. Finally, media can only prepare suitable conditions and inspire people but ground realities must meet the promises and projections otherwise the credibility of the media would go down. The media will have to play an important role for achieving the coveted target.

PANCHAYAT SYSTEM IN INDIA

The village Panchayat system has been an integral part of the Indian administration since times immemorial. A village is a self-contained social microcosm, a composite peasant society representing different communities and rural cultural hues. It does not have irritant elements but represents an integrated composite culture, free to a greater extent from the penetration of urban cultural patterns into village life.

The importance of village with its headman, called *Gramani*, can be traced to the Rig Vedic times; and this headman figures in later Vedic literature as one of the jewels of *Ratnas* of State administration. The decimal system of classification of villages into units of ten, twenty, hundred and thousand is well-known. According to Vinaya, the heads of villages (*Gramikas*) are stated to be meeting in an assembly of their own.

Narada supervised the appointment of five officials in each village. The State took full responsibility for rural development, particularly for constructing roads for traffic, setting up of markets, etc. References were also made village elders — *Gamma-vriddhas and Grama-mahattaras* — who were the prominent persons of a village and were associated with the village administration.

An account of the Panchayat system comparing five persons (official and non-official) in districts as well as in subdivisions is afforded by the inscriptions of the Gupta period. At the district level, the *Vishayapati* or its head had a non-official advisory council representing different interests in the locality. These included the *Nagara-sresthin*—the chief banker representing the commercial interests; the *Sarthavaha* or caravan—the chief of the leader of the trading community; the *Prathama Kulika* —the chief of the heads of the families or the community head; and the *Prathama Kayastha*— the chief scribe or the official administrator.

The assistance of the council was sought in matters of alienation of lands and other allied matters of community interest. At the subdivision (*Vithi*) and village level, there was a council of those persons who were not officials. Such a council comprised *Vithi-mahattaras* and *Kutumbins*, representing the elders and the agricultural households, respectively. The *Kulikas* represented the unofficial elements in advisory capacity.

At the village level, the *Gramika* or the headman and his council settled land disputes by fixing boundaries; they also maintained law and order. His advisory council comprised the *Mahattaras* — the village elders and the *Astha-kuladhikaranas* — the eight heads of the families and other leading men of good experience and high social status. The village elders in Southern India were known as the *Mahajanas.* They used to regulate the socio-economic activities in the village and assisted equally in administration. Their concurrence was necessary before the completion of the alienation procedure. There are evidences of reference to charters of rights and responsibilities of the *Mahajanas*.

The Panchayat system was prevalent in the urban context as well. The local body was called *Uttara-sabha, Goshthi, Panchakula* and a board of *Sauvayika*. The *Panchakula* signified a body of five persons who were appointed by the provincial head. They deliberated in the townhall, called *Mandapika*. The committee looked after proper realization of grants and rent from the endowed property. An inscription of the period from Gwalior mentions a *Sresthin* — the headman in the city with the caravan trader and other leading members of the board lof *Sauvayikas* administering the city. There are also evidences of references to the constitution of the *Sabhas* comprising both official and unofficial elements.

The election procedure of the Panchayats is recorded in the *Utaramalure* inscription of Rajaraja Chola of Tamil Nadu. In the South, the Panchayat body was known as *Sabha* or *Ur*. It functioned in the village as the most important elective body, entrusted with the task of administering the village at all the levels. The Panchayat also managed temples and other assets as well as their funds.

The local bodies constituting the Panchayats varied in nature and functions in Tamil Nadu and Karnataka. In Tamil Nadu, 20-30 members in the council were elected by people, unlike the whole of adult population in Karnataka or just a few in Maharashtra and Gujarat. There was a number of subcommittee in charge of different departments.

The popular element in the village councils was the uniform feature of all the village councils in the South. Property qualifications, academic acumen and experience were the prerequistes for membership of this body of councillors (*Variyam*) of the assembly. The election procedure, as described in the famous *Uttaramalure* inscription, is very interesting. A small boy picked up names from the basket and the election officer announced the result at the spot. The eligibility qualifications of membership further demanded that the person would have a break for a period of ten years before seeking re-election. He had to be of plus forty years of age, learned and impartial and none of his relatives was to be found guilty convicted of any crime, including robbery or involved in any case of bribery.

There are reference to 36 *Pariharas*, the types of levies which, these village bodies could impose. These included marriage tax as well. The duties and remunerations of members of the local bodies were fixed by the assembly itself, which worked in close harmony with the central administration.

The village panchayats have a long history. It was pointed out by Munro in 1815 that any attempt to restrain the Panchayat, by rules unknown to their ancient forms, would render them as redundant. Nothing can tend more strongly to raise men in their own estimation than to make them act according to it and no motives can be more poweful than the consciousness that they are not neglected by the administration and form a vital part of the same.

On May 15, 1989 the then Prime Minister Rajiv Gandhi introduced a Constitutional Amendment Bill in the Lok Sabha. This was introduced to make the Panchayati Raj in India a truly representative and effective system. For the last four decades, Panchayat elections were not being held regularly. Therefore, the neglected rural population was unable to exercise their rights. The Bill could not become a law as it was not passed by the Rajya Sabha. The Congress party had a majority in Lok Sabha and so, the Bill was cleared easily. In the Upper House, the opposition stalled the Bill. The Bill was again introduced in the new Parliament by the Narasimha Rao government.

This Bill, the Seventy-third Amendment Act, 1992 passed by Parliament, was made effective on April 24, 1993. It elaborates the Constitution of Panchayats. It also delineates the election procedure for Chairpersons of Panchayats and their powers. It stipulates proportionate reservation of seats for Scheduled Castes, Scheduled Tribes and women. The Act further outlines the financial powers, authorities of the panchayats, Constitution of Finance Commission to review and audit their financial position and terms and powers of State Election Commissioners.

Madhya Pradesh was the first state in the country to comply with the letter and spirit of the act. Elections were held to the Panchayati Raj bodies and powers and responsibilities were conferred upon them to undertake the economic and social upliftment of the area. Other state followed suit. With the exception of a couple of states, most of them constituted the laws governing the Panchayati Raj bodies. The central government used carrot and stick policy to make the state conform to the Seventy-third Amendment Act.

There are 2.20 lakh village Panchyats, 5,500 Panchayat Samitis and 375 Zila Parishads. These institutions have been granted statutory authority in many states for raising of finance through taxation, cess, land and fairs. The Ninth Five Year Plan has ambitious plans for Panchayati system reforms. These bodies would take into account local aspirations, resources and recommend programmes and methodologies to match them.

CONSUMERS' RIGHTS

It has been rightly said that today, we are living in a consumer age. Never before in man's social life, have supermarkets and business centres been so dominant with their consumer food items and durables. Some 'malls' or markets of Western countries have arrived in multi-storeyed buildings of our cities. You get everything from pins to paste, household appliances to machine parts under one roof. There could be a whole floor dedicated to different types of perfumes, books and music systems.

While the manufacturers cater to every palate and taste, the consumer finds himself inundated with so much products that his powers of discrimination are challenged. It is obvious that many manufacturers take consumers for a ride. By advertising aggressively through media such as TV, the manufacturers almost hypnotize consumers into buying their brands. The goods are presented in such an artistic style as to suggest everything a consumer wants to make his life worthwhile — economy, grace, elegance and luxury. Life seems to be miserable for a housewife unless she buys "ultra-whiteners" for her husband's clothes. For the working woman or man, fast food has arrived as a boon. "Two minute noodles" is a blessing when the mother is exhausted and all the children demand food! There lies the trap. The consumer does not take the trouble to ascertain various facts about the food he or she buys. A consumer has the following rights : *(a)* right to choose; *(b)* right to accept or reject the offer; *(c)* right to complain in an appropriate court of law for settlement of a dispute; *(d)* right to get information about the product / service; and *(e)* right to get good quality products.

Consumer awareness cells of the government have laid down guidelines to save the innocent and unwary consumer as follows:

(1) Always ask for a bill for goods, which you have bought. This should mention properly the date, the name of the product and the price paid. You can use this bill to report a case of food-poisoning or of overcharging which you could discover later.

(2) Look at the expiry date of a product marked on the tin or on the packet. Do not buy anything — drugs, foods, etc. — for which, the expiry date is almost near the date of your purchase.

(3) You must ask for the guarantee card for the consumer durables you buy. You can claim for damage or can ask for a replacement later if need be.

(4) Note the ingredients of a food item. Do they suit your health? In Western countries, it is mandatory to mention salt, sugar and fat contents on the label. Are the artificial colours used in the food item permitted? Quite often, artificial colours cause vomiting and stomach upsets. Certain types of ghee and some vegetable oils contain high contents of fats and salts which could harm heart patients.

Consumer courts all most active in the Indian subcontinent today, thanks to the efforts of the State and NGOs. Today, our consumers can go to a consumer court to seek compensation for financial losses incurred by them, if any particular product or service (purchased by them) ever led to such losses.

In the West, not only is there very strict quality check on manufactured items but, also the compensation for damage could be exorbitant. A mother of a child, who eats a chewing gum which chokes the child, can sue the gum manufacturing company and can claim heavy compensation. We are lenient in India about such incidents. If we discover a spurious item or a food that was stale, we consume it as we are short on time or we grumble a little and forget. This has encouraged unscrupulous manufacturers and sellers to work in collusion and dupe the buyers. Consumer Cells remind you to bring every such case to their notice. Even collective protests by housewives or consumers can prevent such types of crimes.

Consumer courts have been set up in almost all the towns to redress such grievances. Usually, they have senior or retired judges and listen to pros and cons of each case and penalize the guilty manufacturer. Cases at those courts are decided summarily within a one and two years. Constituted both at the state and district levels, these fora have statutory powers and legal status.

The agencies of the government like the Departments of Health, Food Agriculture, Social Welfare, etc., support consumers and protect their interests indirectly. These agencies have comparative rates of products advertized regularly in the newspapers. Consumers can read them, compare them and decide the product quality, price and the place of purchase. The print media include newspapers, magazines, handbills, pamphlets, etc., Radio and TV have a special roles to play in educating the illiterate masses. These awareness cells also build awareness about foods by pointing out age-old misconceptions about fast foods and dieting. Thus, costly foods are not necessarily the most nutritious ones. The humble sprouted gram and the soyabean are far more nutritious than costly almonds and fruits. Seasonal fruits, which are usually cheap, are the best to eat. Mother's milk is the best for the baby and it does not spoil mother's health but improves it if she suckles her baby quite often. Certain food items like betelnut and other mouth freshners are carcinogenic. Some soft drinks are habit-forming. All these facts help to make the consumer aware about the products that flood the markets and are advertized by multinationals and Indian corporate houses.

The Prevention of Food Adulteration Act (1954) makes the usage of harmful additives and preservatives a legal offence. Such additives cause chemical reactions in the foodstuffs. The cumulative effect of small doses of these additives may lead to serious debilitating diseases. There is no restriction on traditional preservatives like salt, sugar or spices but there is a restriction on the usage of sulphur dioxide which makes food toxic and may lead to vitamin deficiency. Sulphur dioxide is also the leading cause of rising number of cases of asthma. Too much of nitrites in food find their way into the bloodstream, which may prove to be fatal. Anti-oxidants like Butylated Hydroxy Toluene (BHT) in ghee and butter are banned in many countries as they lead to asthma or dermatitis. However, they are allowed in India. Such types of adulteration have serious implications for the masses on the health front. Artificial sweeteners like saccharine have lethal effects on the digestive system and cause several abnormalities. So, care has to be taken while buying processed foods. Consumer rights must be exercised in case of TVs, food items, clothes, toys, petroleum products and medicines as these products affect our lives everyday.

LETTER/APPLICATION

The following points should be borne in mind while writing a letter.

1. A letter should contain all the necessary parts which normally and formally it is required to contain.
2. It should follow the pattern according to the nature of the letter whether it is personal, impersonal, to the editor, to some official, customer, etc.
3. It should contain no irrelevant matter.
4. Normally it should indicate the date of writing.
5. In English most of the letters start in a direct way and there is not much scope for introductory words except in letters of particular nature.

Personal Letters

The following are commonly accepted parts of a personal letter:-

1. The Heading.
2. The Salutation.
3. The Body
4. The Subscription.
5. The Superscription.

Explanation

1. The Heading

It has two sub-parts.

(i) Address of the writer.

(ii) Date.

In traditional way of writing the Heading is written in the right hand top corner of the letter, but nowadays it is increasingly being written on the left hand top corner. In business and commercial letter-writing, this is generally the practice.

2. The Salutation

(i) It is written on the left hand starting from near the margin on a line or little below the Heading.

(ii) Generally, the salutation is written in the following way.....

(a) My dear Father/ Mother/Brother/Sister/ Uncle....(Relatives).

(b) My dear Umesh/Rani/Ali/Gopi, ...(Friends).

(c) Dear Sonu/Guleri/Mukherjee/Murthy ....(Acquaintances)

(d) Dear Sir/Madam,

(those not well-acquainted)

(Also to government and other officials)

(e) Sir/Madam (To Editor), Principal, Teachers, etc.)

(iii) In the traditional way of writing we put a comma after the salutation, but it is generally omitted in the modern style of letter-writing.

3. The Body

There are no hard and fast rules for the Body. Still, the following points should be borne in mind -----

(i) There should be a direct start and no beating about the bush.

(ii) The language used must be simple, interesting, idiomatic, clear and easily intelligible.

(iii) There may be one or more than one paragraph depending on the nature of message to be conveyed.

(iv) There should be no unnecessary details and digressions unless required by the nature of the letter.

(v) The language in the letter must be natural, spontaneous, sincere and logical.

(vi) Each paragraph must contain a substantial idea which leads spontaneously to the next.

4. The Subscription

In traditional letters it is written on the right hand side just below the body. However, in modern style of letter writing, it is being written increasingly on the left hand side.

In this connection, the following points should be borne in mind:

(i) Yours affectionately, (To relatives) or we may write.........

Your loving son/daughter/nephew/niece, etc.

(ii) Yours sincerely, (To friends) or we write.......

Your friend, or Yours ever, etc.

(iii) Yours faithfully, (to officials or strangers)

(iv) Yours truly, or Yours faithfully, (To editors)

(v) Yours obediently, (or faithfully) (To Principal)

Note: Generally, after the subscription we write a comma, but it is being omitted increasingly in the modern style of letter writing.

5. The Superscription

It comprises the name and address of the addressee and is written on the envelope below the postage stamp.

Other Letters

Other kinds of letters are written in slightly modified form. Some other kinds of letters (including applications) are ------

1. Applications to the Principal.
2. Business Letters.
3. Letters to officials.
4. Letters to the Editor, etc.

1. Write a letter to your friend congratulating him on his grand success in the matriculation examination.

Examination Hall
x y z
6 April.....

My dear Rohit,

I have just received a letter from your father. He has written that you have got 90% marks in your matriculation examination. You stand first in your town. Please accept my heartiest congratulations.

No doubt, you have always been an intelligent student. Your father has written that this year you studied much harder than usual. It is a true saying that hard work is the key to success.

I request you to write to me at the earliest about your future plans.

Please convey my best wishes to respectable uncle and aunt.

Yours sincerely,

ABC.

2. Write a letter to your friend describing the value of sports.

Examination Hall,
PQR
14 December, ...

My dear Anurag,

It will make you happy to learn that I have just understood the real value of sports. Sports are not only for entertainment and improving health, but also for development of personality and infusing the spirit of cooperation. They teach us discipline and brotherhood. While playing a match no one is asked to tell his, caste or religion.

Playing one or the other sport regularly keeps us fit. It is a true saying that health is wealth. Only a healthy person enjoys himself in life. He can do more work than a weak person. Therefore, he can earn a lot.

What I am going to say–take it as a request or a piece of advice that you should also start to play one or the other sport.

Convey my compliments to your revered parents.

Yours sincerely,

STU.

3. Write a letter to your younger brother advising him to take part in games.

Examination Hall,
PQR City
15 October, ...

My dear Satnam,

Today I received your first House Examination Report from the Principal of your college. I am very glad to learn that you have stood first in the aggregate in your class.

One thing, however, has greatly pained me. It is that you do not take part in any game and have become very weak. It is clear from a remark given by the Principal in the "Remarks" column.

Dear Satnam, I am your elder brother. So, I can give you a piece of sound advice and I hope you will take it seriously. It is that studies are all right, but health is no less important. It is rightly said that a sound mind lives only in a sound body. If you are not physically strong, you will not be able to face the world as you grow up.

So, please start playing one or the other game right from today and write to me as you start it.

Love from father and mother.
Yours affectionately,
(Gurnam)

4. Write a letter to your uncle thanking him for the birthday gift.

Examination Hall,
TUV.
6 July, ...

My dear uncle,

I thank you very much for the watch that you have just sent as my birthday gift. It is really a beautiful watch. It keeps correct time. I will never be late for college now. My friends also like it very much.

I request you to attend my birthday party in person the next year. Don't forget to bring aunt and kids.

Your affectionate nephew

ABC.

5. Write a letter to your father requesting him to allow you to join a historical tour of your college.

Examination Hall,
ABC city
September 15, ...

My dear Father,

A historical tour of our college is going to visit historical places of north India during the first week of the next month. It is being led by our teacher of history, Mrs. Sujata Kulkarni, who is a great scholar. She will explain the real historical importance of every historical building.

The tour will go to Amritsar, Kurukshetra, Delhi, Mathura and Agra. It will include thirty students in all. One who wants to join it has to deposit Rs. 1000/- before 25th instant. This amount includes boarding, lodging and travelling expenses.

Dear father, it is a golden opportunity. So, please allow me to join this tour and send Rs. 1000/– as early as possible. Love to dear mother and naughty Kittu.

Yours affectionately,

(Sangeeta).

6. Write a letter to your younger brother advising him to give up bad company and take more interest in studies.

Examination Hall,

XYZ city

18 November, ...

My dear Deepak,

Yesterday, I received the report of your first house examination from the Principal of your college. I was shocked to read that you have failed in almost every subject.

Some of your friends have also told me that you take no interest in studies but keep moving in bad company. It is a pity to learn that you have started drinking, gambling and smoking. You frequently see movies and just loiter on roads with your friends.

Dear Deepak, if you waste your precious youth time in this manner, you will have to repent your whole life. I therefore, advise you to give up bad company right from today and start taking more interest in your studies. I wish to get a much letter report from your college Principal in future.

Love from papa and mamma.

Yours affectionately,

(Gurdip)

7. Write a letter to your mother describing the Annual Prize Distribution in your college.

Examination Hall,
XYZ city
12 February, ...

My dear Mother,

The Annual Prize Distribution function was celebrated in our college yesterday. Mrs. Triveni Goyal, the Deputy Commissiner, was the Chief Guest.

The function was held in the college hall. Preparation had started a few days earlier. The hall was well-decorated. The Chief Guest arrived at 10 am sharp. The function started soon thereafter.

At first, the President of the Managing Committee read out the welcome address. Then the cultural show started. It included songs, hymns, skits, jokes, bhangra, giddha and a fancy dress show.

Then the prizes were distributed by the Chief Guest. I got the first prize for standing first in English in the house test. The Principal read out the Annual Report. It highlighted the achievements of the college during the year. During his speech, the Chief Guest appreciated them. The President of the Students' Committee thanked the Chief Guest. Then the function was over at about 12 : 30 pm. Thereafter, the Chief Guest took tea with the members of the staff and the prize winners.

Regards to papa and love to little Dipu.

Your loving daughter,
(Simpy).

8. Write a letter to your uncle telling him what profession you want to choose after completing your studies.

Examination Hall,
XYZ
17 March, ...

My dear Uncle,

In your last letter, you asked me what I want to do after completing my studies. The completion of my studies will take a number of more years. It is because I want to do M.A. (English).

After completing my studies, I intend to become a college teacher. For this, I'll have to clear the UGC test NET. I hope I'll be able to do so. If for any reason I fail to become a college lecturer, then I shall like to become a school lecturer.

Teaching is a noble profession. Teachers are nation builders. Students are future leaders and the best service for anyone is to give proper guidance to students and that is what I want to do.

Convey my regards to dear aunt.

Your loving nephew,

(Kuldip)

9. Write a letter to your friend inviting him to the marriage of your sister.

Examination Hall,
XYZ
15 May, ...

My dear Pankaj

You will be glad to know that the marriage of my sister comes off on 5th June this year.

You are invited to attend the marriage of my sister. You should come at least a week earlier. It is because I have to seek your advice at every step.

Convey my regards to your parents.

Yours sincerely,

(Ravinder)

10. Place an order for books with a book-seller.

15, Boy's Hostel – II,
A.P. Convent School,
Mayur Vihar, Phase I, Delhi.
Date ....

To

ABC Booksellers,
44/E, Daryaganj,
New Delhi

Dear Sirs,

Please send us the following books one copy each via V.P.P. All the books must be in a good condition. Send us the books of the latest editions. We are your old customer. So, please offer us the maximum possible discount.

1. 'Treasure Island' by R.L. Stevenson.
2. 'Gulliver's Travels' by Jonathan Swift.
3. 'The Gitanjali' by R.N. Tagore
4. 'The Discovery of India' by J.L Nehru.

Thank you.
Yours faithfully
(Avinash Ghosh).

11. Write a letter to a book-seller informing him of the wrong supply of books and asking him to take back the books at his own cost and supply the correct ones.

15, Boy's Hostel II,
A. P. Convent School
Mayur Vihar Phase–I
Delhi
(Dt) ....

To

ABC Booksellers,
44/E Daryaganj,
New Delhi.

Sir,

Please refer to our order for books dated -------------------. I am sorry to bring to your kind notice that in your registered parcel dated ------------------ you have supplied wrong books.

It appears books ordered by some other customer have been wrongly despatched to me. You are requested to take back books at your own cost and supply to me the books ordered by me in my order mentioned above at an early date.

Yours faithfully,
(Avinash Ghosh).

12. Write an application for the position of manager in a hotel.

758, Gola Park,
Lawrence Road,
Amritsar
Date ....

To

The ITC Hotels
Malcha Marg
New Delhi.

Sir,

With reference to your advertisement in The Tribune of 30 January I wish to apply for the position of manager in your hotel. I did degree course in hotel management in 1980. I have been working in a reputed hotel as manager for a few years. I did my matric in 1955 with 95% marks. I am good at spoken and written English. Besides I can speak Hindi, Punjabi and French well. I have a pleasing personality and have the decision-making quality. My employers are happy with me.

If appointed, I promise to work sincerely. Wish you all the best.

Yours faithfully
(PP ARORA)
Contact Number
Phone No. 2456901
Mobile Phone : 98104/49797.

13. Write a letter to the Editor of a newspaper bringing to the notice of the public the hazards of rash driving.

To

The Editor
The Hindustan Times
Chandigarh

Sir,

I shall feel obliged if you publish the following lines in your newspaper for the benefit of the public.

Now-a-days so many road accidents are reported daily in newspapers. These accidents in many cases result in loss of precious human life.

Most of these accidents take place because of rash driving. In many cases, the drivers are dead drunk.

It is very important that the speed limit for driving on all important roads is fixed. Those who cross this limit should be heavily fined and even imprisoned.

Yours faithfully,
(xyz)

14. Write a letter to the editor of a newspaper expressing your views against the menace of dowry system.

To

The Editor
The Indian Express
Mumbai

Sir,

Kindly publish the following lines in your newspaper to make the people aware about the menace of dowry system.

Dowry system has created a big problem for the people these days. Particularly, the poor people are at a great disadvantage. In order to arrange the marriage of their daughters, many of them have to incur heavy debts.

Most of the boys and their parents are greedy. They want a rich dowry even when the girl is beautiful and is highly educated. Sometimes, the girls who fail to bring a rich dowry are tortured and even burnt alive.

Young boys and girls in all educational institutions should be taught to reject dowry. Mass media should start a compaign against this menace.

Yours truly,
(xyz)
Date ....

15. Write a letter to the SHO of your town complaining him about the theft of your motorbike.

Examination Hall
xyz ....
Date ....

To

The SHO

Sadar Police Station

xyz

Sir,

I wish to draw your attention towards the theft of my black motorbike bearing number plate 48E 4949. Yesterday I parked it outside the Plaza Shopping Complex. I locked it properly and went inside the Plaza to make some purchases. I spent not more than fifteen minutes there and as I went outside the Plaza I found my motorbike missing. I asked many persons around if they could tell me anything about its whereabouts. But none of them seemed to have any useful information about it.

I request you to look into the matter and solve my problem at your earliest.

Yours faithfully

(PK KAPOOR)

16. Write a letter to the Post Master complaining against the Post man.

18, Krishan Nagar,
Ludhiana

Date ....

To

The Post Master,

The Main Post Office,

Ludhiana

Dear Sir,

It is a matter of deep concern that the postman of our locality is not worthy of the job he has been appointed for. Either he is absent–minded or he enjoys harassing others. He most often delivers the dak on the wrong addresses. When he is requested to mend his way of working he talks rudely.

We shall be thankful to you if you appoint a responsible person in our locality in his place.

Yours faithfully,

Arun Sharma.

17. Write a letter to the Editor of a newspaper expressing your views on the harm being done by cell phones to students.

To

The Editor,

The Tribune,

Chandigarh

Sir,

Subject: Harm being done by cell phones to the students

Kindly allow me to a ventilate through your esteemed daily my views regarding the harm being done by the cell phones to the students.

There is no denying the fact that twenty first century is an age of information technology. India has not lagged behind to ride this wave. Though it is a boon for the society, certain aspects of it are decidely harmful. Take the case of cell phones. This revolution of telecommunications has made communication very easy, but it also has harmed our society. It has taken the students community in its grip. We can see students of all ages flaunting their cell phones at every pertext. This evil has even entered the class rooms. The students do not give attention to their lectures and are often found absorbed in their cell phone talks. Even while driving they are busy in their cell phone talks. So it invites many accidents.

Excessive use of cell phones is not good for students. The parents and teachers should take quick remedial steps before it is too late.

Yours faithfully,

XYZ

Date ....

18. Write a letter to an old customer of yours explaining to him the reason for delay in executing his order and asking for extension of period for the purpose.

Zobog Plastic Agency
15, Esplanade Road
Kolkata,

Date ....

To

M/S Lovely Toy House,

89, Mukherjee Mar,

Hawrah.

Dear Sirs,

Reg.: Extension of Delivery Period for goods.

Ref: Your order for supply of goods dated ......

Please refer to your order for supply of goods mentioned above.

We are grateful to you for the said order but at the same time we regret to point out that we are not in a position to meet the dead line set by you for the execution of the order. It is because the supply of raw material to us has been unduly delayed by the supplier.

Today we have received the raw material and we are going to start the manufacturing of goods ordered by you right from today.

We shall, therefore, be thankful if you extend the delivery period of goods by seven days and inform us telegraphically in this regard.

Thank you.

Yours faithfully,

(Baldev Raj)

Manager

19. Write a circular letter to your customers asking them to make bulk purchases of some goods as you are offering a grand clearance sale at a big discount for a specified period.

Soloman Textile Manufacturers
11, Industrial Estate
Panipat
Date ....

Circular Letter

To

M/S ....

....

Dear Sirs,

Reg.: Grand Clearance Sale of Cotton Goods.

You will be glad to know that we are offering a special discount of 20% besides the usual discount on all cotton goods till the end of the current month.

You are, therefore, advised to make a bulk purchase of all such goods as the prices of such goods may be greatly enhanced during the next month.

Thank you.

Yours faithfully,

Sales Manager.

20. Application for the position of English Teacher.

62, Trilok Nath Street
Jajpur Road
Bhavnagar
(Gujarat)
(Dt.)

To

The Director
Institute for Destitute Women
Lakhya Ram Trust,
Ahmedabad

Dear Madam

With reference to your advertisement in the Times of India of ...., I hereby apply for the post of an english teacher for middle classes.

As regards my academic and other qualification, I may mention that I'm a young, energetic B.A. B.Ed. of 23 years with an experience of about one year as an English teacher in a local primary school here.

My date of birth is 15 March 1982. I passed my Matriculation examination in the first division from the local Shiv Shakti High School in 1997. Then I shifted to the local D.A.V. School from where I passed the 10 + 2 examination with English as an elective subject in 1999.

I did B.A. from the Gujarat University in 2002. I had again English as an elective subject. Then I passed B.Ed. from Sewagram National College of Education, Surat in 2004 and soon got appointment as a primary teacher in the local Purshottam Das Primary School.

At present I am getting a salary of Rs. 4000/- per month. I expect an enhancement of the least 3000/- at your end.

If appointed, I would work most diligently. I'm sure of delivering the goods as a I find my students and their parents and school authorities here fully satisfied with my work.

I'm enclosing photostat copies of my testimonials.

Yours sincerely

(Kirti Bhardwaj)

21. Application for the position of Vice Principal.

24, Sir Chhotu Ram Street
Saraswati Mohalla
Johana
(Haryana)
(Dt.)

To

The Director
Holy Angels Playway School
Mehrauli
Delhi

Respected Madam

I am writing in response to your advertisement in the Patriot of .... for the position of Vice-Principal in your school.

I am a young, energetic trained postgraduate with a pleasing personality. I'm about 26 years, my date of birth being..........

I did my post-graduation in English in the second division in .... from Delhi University. Earlier I did graduation from the same university in first division in .... I did B.Ed. from Desh Bhagat Institute of Education, Ambala in ....

Besides B.Ed. I also did the Nursery Teacher's Training (NTT) Course from Guru Agarsen Nursery Training School, Karnal in ....

I've got about two year teaching experience as a teacher in a nursery school here. At present I'm getting a salary of Rs. 8000/- per month but expect an enhancement of an equal amount if I'm selected for the post at your end.

I'm enclosing copies of testimonials for persual.

Hoping early hearing from you.

Yours faithfully

(Rita Kulkarni)

22. Application for the position of a Company Legal Advisor.

27A, Megha Appartments
Near Darpan Photos
Hoshiarpur (Pb.)
(Dt.)

To

M/s Canda Cycle Parts Ltd.
G.T. Road, Shispur Chowk
Ludhiana (Pb.)

Dear Sirs

With reference to your advertisement in 'The Tribune' of 22nd May, I hereby apply for the post of a 'Company Legal Advisor'. Please find enclosed a copy of my CV.

I am currently employed in a small company. I've a rich experience in the field. My employers are all praise for me.

If appointed, I promise to work sincerely.

I look forward from a hearing from you.

Yours faithfully

Jagroop Arora.

23. Application for the position of School Cashier.

43, Sutlej Avenue
Peshawari Mohalla
Noor Mahal
(Dt.)

To

The Principal
Doaba Model School
Nakodar
Jalandhar

Dear Sir

With reference to your advertisement in Tribune of .... for the position of cashier, I hereby apply for the same.

I was born at Noot Mahal in .... After passing matric and 10 + 2 from PSEB in .... and .... respectively, I joined B.Com. classes at DAV College Jalandhar. I passed B.Com. from GNDU in ....

Thereafter, I joined the famous Punjab Accountancy & Finance Institute, Capurthala, run by Punjab Technical University. I completed the Accountance & Finance course last year and got the appointment of a cashier in a local bank here on purely temporary basis. The appointment was for on year only.

So, it ended on .... I was, however, called again by the bank for the same job at few days later. But since the appointment is only on adhoc basis, I want some job where I can find stability, continuity and confirmation after the due probationary period. Since your advertisement holds a promise in this regard, I'm applying for the same.

I'm adept in all accounts matters, especially cash and financial matters. I hope I'll prove an asset to your institution.

Please find enclosed photocopies of all the relevant testimonials. Hoping to get an early response.

Yours faithfully

(Samita Trikha)

24. Application for the position of Supervisor for old age home.

12, Santosh Nagar
Ganguli Marg
Jamshedpur
(Dt.)

To

The President
Dowell Old Age Home Society
53 Gurudev Colony
Bhagalpur

Dear Sir

With reference to your advertisement in the Horizon of .... for the position of supervisor for an old age home in Bhagalpur, I hereby apply for the same.

I was born on .... at Jamshedpur. It was here that I passed matric and 10 + 2 from WB School Education Board in .... and .... respectively.

Then I joined the army and served the country for many years. I retired from service last month. I've no liability, my children having well-settled. Thus, I can look after an old age home with a spirit of dedication and service.

I'll feel satisfied with a reasonable remuneration as I will also get pension from the government.

I hope I'll given an opportunity to serve the old people for whom I have great regard and affection. Moreover, I'd find my own self in them as I'm myself fast approaching the same silver state.

Please find enclosed photocopies of my matric, 10+2 and other relevant certificates for persual.

Yours faithfully

M.T. Chatterjee

❑❑❑

MAIN LANGUAGE (ENGLISH)

(For English Language Teacher)

Comprehension

Comprehension is a very important part of English paper. The questions on comprehension lay particular stress on understanding a given passage. You are required to read a passage or poem and answer a few questions based on it. Various comprehension questions are set solely with the objectives named below:

1. To test your ability to detect the central idea or the focal point in the given passage.
2. To test your ability to understand and interpret the given passage or poem.
3. To judge your capability to pick out the various arguments put forward by the writer for or against something.
4. To test your accuracy and richness of vocabulary.
5. To test your academic ability to understand the implied and the clearly and fully expressed ideas of the writer of the passage or poem.
6. To test, occasionally, your power of appreciating critically the views contained in the given passage or poem.

While answering comprehension questions, you must comply with the following important points:

1. First, read the whole passage or poem attentively, carefully and quickly.
2. Read it for the second time, slowly but steadily.
3. Work out the probable meaning of new words, from the context in which they have been used.
4. Underline and look for transitional words and phrases as an aid to comprehension.
5. The process of elimination should be used while selecting the correct answer.
6. Your answers should be brief and to the point, where-ever required.

I. CLOZE TEST

A cloze test is a procedure in which a person is asked to supply words that have been removed from a passage as a test of his ability to comprehend text. Practise it regularly to score well.

Directions: *In each of the following passages some numbered blank spaces are given. For each numbered blank space answer choices are given. Pick out the one which is the most appropriate for that blank space. Keep the trend of the passage in mind.*

PASSAGE-1

A drug which has been ....(1).... promoted here for fever and pain ....(2).... has invited medical ....(3).... over its ....(4).... side-effects following adverse reactions and its ....(5).... withdrawal in certain European countries. The scientific advisory committee has issued a ....(6).... advice on the ....(7).... of the drug ....(8).... some serious ....(9).... in the liver. While most doctors in India ....(10).... there is not need to ....(11).... yet, they also admit that they ....(12).... ....(13).... about it as most studies on the drug are industry .... (14).... .

QUESTIONS

1. A. aggressively B. astonishingly C. surprisingly D. immensely

2. A. treatment B. relief C. cure D. removal

3. A. concern B. criticism C. discussion D. debate

4. A. probable B. probably C. possible D. possibly

5. A. unconditional B. immediate C. consequent D. subsequent

6. A. precautionary B. preliminary C. formal D. informal

7. A. sell B. purchase C. recommendation D. marketing

8. A. reminding B. following C. thinking D. caring

9. A. complications B. problem C. complexity D. consequences

10. A. suggest B. insist
C. lay D. say

11. A. worry B. react
C. panic D. exorbitant

12. A. think B. know
C. knew D. known

13. A. a bit B. a little
C. a few D. little

14. A. based B. sponsored
C. surveyed D. experimented

PASSAGE-2

I believe the biggest challenge ....(1).... the world is that of ....(2).... poverty across a large ....(3).... of the ....(4).... population and the continued ....(5).... between the rich and poor nations. The globalisation ....(6).... of the Nineties was ....(7).... to change all that and it has not made a significant impact as yet. Indeed, poverty today is the single biggest ....(8).... of place and democracy. It is high time that even the most ....(9).... rich citizen or indeed all of us ....(10).... people, realise that the only way to ....(11).... prosperity is to defeat poverty.

QUESTIONS

1. A. confronting B. facing
C. spoiling D. destroying

2. A. acute B. continued
C. general D. common

3. A. proportion B. share
C. portion D. fraction

4. A. universal B. en bloc
C. entire D. global

5. A. disputation B. disparity
C. discrimination D. tensile

6. A. struggle B. efforts
C. wave D. air

7. A. considered B. perpetually
C. supposed D. perhaps

8. A. curse B. enemy
C. hurdle D. obstruction

9. A. complacent B. compliant
C. fatuous D. inconsiderate

10. A. well-to-do B. cultured
C. privileged D. developed

11. A. defend B. debilitate
C. protect D. save

PASSAGE-3

What the daily newspapers nowadays ....(1).... carry are the reports of ...(2).... murders, killings, genocides and ....(3).... cleansing all over the world. India is not an exception ...(4).... . For a moment one is sure ....(5).... the principle of religious tolerance, peace and ....(6)...., which were the ....(7).... of Indian society, that are now slowly but steadily ....(8).... hatred, anger, distrust and religious intolerance. Making things worse are the divisive practices being ....(9).... by some ....(10).... minds that have led to the rise of religious fundamentalism. And this is a ....(11)...., which is ....(12)..... in the form of hundreds of innocent lives being lost in all corners of the country.

QUESTIONS

1. A. usually B. generally
C. regularly D. casually

2. A. huge B. massive
C. brutal D. mass

3. A. ethnic B. ethical
C. evasive D. eventual

4. A. to it B. in it
C. for it D. on it

5. A. of thinking B. to think about
C. to think of D. thinking about

6. A. conscientious B. compassion
C. rapacity D. sagacity

7. A. heart B. core
C. cornerstones D. milestones

8. A. are replaced with
B. replaced by
C. being replaced by
D. being replaced with

9. A. precluded B. precipitated
C. predisposed D. fabricated

10. A. perverted B. scrupulous
C. nefarious D. ruthless

11. A. calumny B. bane
C. crass D. denouncement

12. A. visible B. coming
C. taking its toll D. resulting its toll.

PASSAGE-4

The outstanding ....(1).... of the development of science and technology can neither be realised nor enriched in an atmosphere with disturbed ....(2).... balance, ...(3).... to pollution hazards. The ....(4).... of pollution and conservation of the natural ecosystems in all the development efforts are ....(5).... not merely for the growth of our ....(6).... but for our very existence on this earth. It demands the ....(7).... that it deserves. Although ....(8).... is expressed in various circles for ....(9).... the environmental balance and ....(10).... of forests, but at the same time there is a large scale ....(11).... of forests, as ....(12).... evidenced in several river valley projects ....(13).... at the national level.

QUESTIONS

1. A. capacity B. potential C. possibility D. advancement
2. A. economical B. natural C. ecological D. polluting
3. A. susceptible B. adversely C. salubrious D. pernicious
4. A. removal B. eradication C. discarding D. evolution
5. A. imperil B. imminent C. impulsive D. imperative
6. A. status B. sociability C. economy D. environment
7. A. importance B. attention C. value D. care
8. A. interest B. enthusiasm C. deep concern D. anxiety
9. A. maintaining B. evolving C. developing D. rising
10. A. growing B. maintaining C. maintenance D. regeneration
11. A. degeneration B. degradation C. deprivation D. dereliction
12. A. blatantly B. vitally C. vividly D. indiscreetly
13. A. executed B. planned C. organised D. undertaken

PASSAGE-5

India is a country where women ....(1).... worshipped and ....(2).... at the same time. If mantras have been chanted to ....(3)... the Goddesses, ...(4).... have also been hurled at a domestic wife questioning her devotion and ....(5).... . Their position has remained more or less the same ....(6).... . Though women have taken ....(7).... since the country achieved independence, they still are a ....(8).... of political, socio-economic and legal neglect. The current year has seen a number of government ....(9).... to empower women. Though these are ....(10)...., much will depend on the ....(11).... implementation of these schemes or else they ....(12).... achieve the targets, they have set for themselves.

QUESTIONS

1. A. are B. were C. has been D. have been
2. A. cursed B. blamed C. crucified D. insulted
3. A. placate B. please C. plead D. respect
4. A. curses B. expletives C. obscenity D. objurgation
5. A. virginity B. purity C. chastity D. fecundity
6. A. till date B. over time C. till now D. until now.
7. A. remarkable progress B. advancement C. rapid strides D. important steps
8. A. object B. subject C. matter D. victim
9. A. machinery B. initiatives C. project D. plannings
10. A. laudable B. languor C. lascivious D. lassitude
11. A. efficient B. thorough C. appropriate D. effective
12. A. would not B. should not C. will not D. cannot

PASSAGE-6

We are ....(1).... about our success and failure in every field. No doubt, we start our actions with ....(2).... but still in a corner of our mind ....(3).... about success and failure and ....(4).... makes us tense. And this tension sometimes ....(5).... that it effects our efficiency and performance. So, we ....(6).... remember that the mind is efficient ....(7).... it is cool, not hot or tense. The tease or excited mind ....(8).... produce rational concepts or ....(9).... thought processes. A calm person has his senses fully ....(10).... with the environment ....(11).... he places himself. A restless person ....(12).... notice anything, consequently he gets into trouble with himself and others and ....(13).... everything.

QUESTIONS

1. A. always worried B. anxious always C. curious always D. in doubt-always
2. A. over-confidence B. full confidence C. full enthusiasm D. full effort
3. A. a doubt remains still B. remains a doubt C. still remians a doubt D. a doubt still remains
4. A. intentionally B. unnecessarily C. necessarily D. unconsciously
5. A. become so intense B. grow so much C. become so intensive D. become so serious

6. A. must B. have to
C. will have to D. shall have to

7. A. when B. when only
C. only then when D. only when

8. A. can never B. could not
C. connot D. possibly

9. A. obnoxious B. obligatory
C. objective D. orderly

10. A. engrossed B. paralleled
C. identified D. sunk

11. A. on which B. in which
C. at which D. where

12. A. do not B. does not
C. did not D. cannot

PASSAGE-7

Great books do not spring from something ....(1).... in the great men who wrote them. They are the ....(2).... of their very core, the ....(3).... of the life itself of the authors. And literature cannot be said to ....(4).... its true purpose. Until it ....(5).... translated into the actual life of him who reads. Literature is the ....(6).... of true ideas and high emotions and life is ....(7).... of ideas and emotions. In a world ....(8).... of literature, the intellectual and emotional activity of all ....(9)... exceptionally gifted men would quickly sink and ....(10).... to a narrow circle. The broad, the noble, the generous would tend to disappear ....(11).... accessible storage. And life would be ....(12).... degraded, because the ....(13).... idea and the pretty emotion would never feel the upward pull of the ideas and emotions of genius.

QUESTIONS

1. A. accidental B. remarkable
C. strange D. superficial

2. A. affluence B. effluence
C. excellence D. magnificence

3. A. outcome B. offspring
C. flow D. expression

4. A. have served B. done
C. achieve D. accomplished

5. A. is B. has been
C. gets D. has

6. A. store B. stock
C. vast reservoir D. huge collection

7. A. expression B. expansion
C. storage D. constituted

8. A. devout B. devolve
C. deterrent D. deprived

9. A. but few B. except
C. but a few D. people

10. A. die B. spoil
C. dissolve D. retract

11. A. for want of B. desiring
C. searching D. for

12. A. altogether B. correspondingly
C. contrarily D. actually

13. A. beautiful B. ornamental
C. stupid D. fallacious

PASSAGE-8

Patriotism is one of the qualities that touches the heart of the ....(1).... countrymen. When a soldier fights and dies in saving his country from the enemy, his sacrifice in this way is termed as ....(2).... and attains the ....(3).... worthy of worship. Thus in a war the soldier gets ....(4).... without surrendering, by which he ....(5).... saved his life, ...(6).... the hearts of his fellow being. This situation is true not only in ....(7).... an enemy but anyone who struggles to acheive a ....(8).... aim without surrendering and ....(9).... his life. He ....(10).... succeeded but he leaves a ....(11).... for others to follow who will definitely win and attain the victory ....(12).... the adversaries..

QUESTIONS

1. A. humble B. rustic
C. fellow D. sophisticated

2. A. intelligent B. virtuous
C. supreme D. courageous

3. A. death B. martyrdom
C. end D. goal

4. A. vanquished B. vanguard
C. reward D. award

5. A. would have had B. would be able to
C. would have D. could have

6. A. attracting B. winning
C. taking D. getting

7. A. struggling B. killing
C. winning D. fighting

8. A. esteemed B. high
C. patriotic D. laudable

9. A. offers B. sacrifices
C. lays D. present

10. A. could have B. could not have
C. may have D. may not have

11. A. trail B. trial
C. goal D. situation

12. A. upon B. over
C. on D. against

PASSAGE-9

Our beautiful sunbright ....(1).... is being systematically damaged by industrial pollution ....(2).... into rivers like the Ganga and Jamuna, ...(3).... wastes from atomic plants ....(4).... into-the world's oceans, and poisonous gases ....(5).... with the ozonosphere. ....(6)...., tropical rain forests and green pastures are ....(7).... under the pressure of a ....(8).... population. Rivers like the Narmada are being dammed to change nature's ....(9).... surface ....(10).... between flora and fauna, and sloping mountain terrain is being ....(11).... into mini oceans to supply electricity to the ....(12).... industrial stomach of our age.

QUESTIONS

1. A. ecology
   B. ecosystem
   C. environment
   D. physical phenomena
2. A. directed B. channelled
   C. scattered D. accumulated
3. A. atomic B. scientific
   C. nuclear D. bumptious
4. A. diverted B. routed
   C. outstretched D. overflown
5. A. channelled B. routed
   C. scattered D. mixed
6. A. Besides B. Instead
   C. Addition to D. Above all
7. A. diminishing B. reducing
   C. minimising D. disappearing
8. A. proliferating B. profiting
   C. projecting D. pronounceable
9. A. smooth B. well balanced
   C. rough D. unequal
10. A. equilibrium B. equality
    C. equation D. equity
11. A. contracted B. convulsed
    C. conjured D. converted
12. A. hungry B. greedy
    C. vacant D. ever starving

PASSAGE-10

Only ....(1)...., people find a long journey by motor-car ....(2)... . Mostly a long journey by train is much more comfortable and ....(3).... . The tracks, the coaches and the smooth though swift motion ....(4).... the pleasantness of the train journey. ....(5).... at the beautiful countryside from a window seat in a fast moving train has a ....(6).... of its own. A night journey ....(7).... its pleasures too. One can experience a sense of adventure ....(8).... a restful sleep. Modern railway travel being ....(9)... comfortable than in the past, ...(10).... the childhood excitement of ....(11).... the train and its engine as ....(12).... of visual and imaginative delight.

QUESTIONS

1. A. exceptionally B. ordinarily
   C. unusually D. abnormally
2. A. disagreeable B. unenjoyable
   C. strange D. agreeable
3. A. enjoyable B. suitable
   C. appropriate D. enjoying
4. A. hike B. jolt
   C. contribute D. all add to
5. A. Observing B. Enjoying
   C. To look D. Looking
6. A. comfort B. complacence
   C. delight D. satisfaction
7. A. had B. has
   C. have D. has have
8. A. alongwith B. together with
   C. addition to D. adding to
9. A. highly B. extensively
   C. exceptionally D. so much more
10. A. revives B. vibrates
    C. regenerates D. enliven
11. A. fancying B. enjoying
    C. feeling D. dreaming
12. A. subjects B. objects
    C. centre D. focus

PASSAGE-11

Women were earlier considered as the kitchen keepers and house keepers – that was ....(1).... as their ....(2).... field of activity. ....(3)... women began to get educated and came out ....(4).... the social and potitical field and today they are there in all fields and are ....(5).... equal emloyment as the menfolk. Not only this they are ....(6)... themselves in those fields. Two important reasons behind the changed ....(7).... are : firstly, Womens are ....(8).... themselves duly qualified and want to use-their talents to seek an employment; and secondly, with the price-index ....(9).... everyday it is found necessary for the middle class families that the wife having ....(10).... academic qualifications working and ....(11).... the family income. This while giving them a social status, also helps the family to have a better standard of living, which everyone ....(12).... for and rightly too.

QUESTIONS

1. A. recognised B. realized
   C. regarded D. looked
2. A. exclusive B. only
   C. working D. one

3. A. Day by day B. Slowly
C. Later D. Gradually

4. A. on B. in
C. at D. to

5. A. finding B. seeking
C. enjoying D. sharing

6. A. distinguishing B. proving
C. mastering D. struggling

7. A. scenario B. circumstances
C. society D. culture

8. A. thinking B. finding
C. educating D. proving

9. A. excelating B. intensifying
C. changing D. escalating

10. A. registered B. recognised
C. requisite D. minimum

11. A. substituting B. segment
C. influencing D. suplement

12. A. do crave B. does crave
C. starve D. do starve

PASSAGE-12

Importance of music especially in today's hum drum life cannot be ....(1).... . Today man is surrounded by ....(2).... worries and listening to music ....(3).... his nerves. Music acts as a ....(4).... and soothes the nerves. It is a fine art and groups of all ages ....(5).... to its sweet sound. A person gifted with aesthetic ....(6).... finds music as a food for his soul. Some of the great musicians of the world ....(7).... in high esteem ....(8).... of the kind of they produce western, oriental, classical, pop or light. These musicians ....(9).... concerts which attract people from all walks of life. If people are ....(10).... to balming music, they will definitely find life a rich and healthy ....(11)..... In this way, the importance of music is really ....(12).... .

QUESTIONS

1. A. overstated B. understated
C. irrelevant D. relevant

2. A. varied B. innumerable
C. different D. variegated

3. A. calm B. cure
C. soothe D. please

4. A. stimulant B. catalyst
C. machinery D. device

5. A. are attracted B. get attracted
C. are pleased D. feel pleasure

6. A. beauty B. blessing
C. capabilities D. knowledge

7. A. were held B. are held
C. are taken D. are received

8. A. no matter B. considering
C. respectively D. irrespective

9. A. popularize B. organize
C. form D. propagate

10. A. forced B. brought
C. introduced D. exposed

11. A. stage B. experience
C. achievement D. thing

12. A. considerable B. unavoidable
C. imimense D. recognisable

PASSAGE-13

There are groups of people in ....(1).... developing countries who are in poverty line and who became the victims and ....(2).... in a self-fulfilling vicious of poverty. ....(3).... of the parents in the society ....(4).... afford to send their children to school. ....(5)...., the children often go to the labour force ....(6).... in order to ....(7).... the family income and to help the economic ....(8).... of the family. The Indian Government and educational ....(9).... are taking adequate steps for their standard of living and ....(10).... opportunities for schooling with full day food and other required ...(11)... .

QUESTIONS

1. A. each B. all
C. whole D. every

2. A. engulfed B. surrounded
C. trapped D. fall

3. A. line B. circle
C. frame D. structure

4. A. can't B. couldn't
C. cannot D. can never

5. A. Though B. Despite
C. Instead D. Even so

6. A. at an early age
B. in his growing stage
C. in his childhood
D. at his childhood

7. A. add B. supplement
C. hike D. improve

8. A. servility B. survivality
C. conditon D. situation

9. A. activist B. executives
C. planners D. propagonist

10. A. approving B. alloting
C. distributing D. providing

11. A. privileges B. facilities
C. necessities D. factors

PASSAGE-14

What is urgently, ...(1).... in our country is a proper survey and a planned assessment of what sort of jobs ....(2).... demand both in the public as well as in the private sector and there ....(3).... a controlled enrolment in institutes and institutions which should be training young men in such needed jobs. It is a ....(4).... task, no doubt, but when the government and the private agencies ....(5).... make large scale survey for so many other problems of the country why cannot this grave problem of unemployment be ....(6).... at a priority basis and money and manpower be invested and ....(7).... to make an assessment of the requirements and then the process of their fulmilment ....(8).... . What is actually needed is not only scheming and planning but actually to have a ....(9).... to find the root of the ....(10).... . Only then can the ....(11).... be found out.

QUESTIONS

1. A. demanded B. needed
   C. prevalent D. lacking
2. A. are of B. are at
   C. are most in D. currently
3. A. needs to be B. is
   C. are D. shall be
4. A. labourious B. Herculean
   C. time taking D. stupendous
5. A. can B. could
   C. are out to D. readily
6. A. noticed B. surveyed
   C. treated D. observed
7. A. used B. employed
   C. organised D. treated
8. A. be worked out B. be taken up
   C. be decided D. be developed
9. A. spirit B. will
   C. motive D. strength
10. A. malady B. grievances
    C. curse D. paradox
11. A. treatment B. cure
    C. remedy D. solution

PASSAGE-15

A sudden flood of ....(1).... dangerous toys like swords and bow and arrow make their ....(2).... in the market during the Dussehra festival. ....(3)...., eyes can and do get injured ....(4).... by these toys and ....(5)...., the victims aare innocent children. ....(6).... by the Ram Lila and similar television serials, children ....(7).... swords at each other or fire arrows from bows which ....(8).... to permanent blindness if ....(9).... to hit the eye. This happens ....(10).... if the injury is servere and not managed properly. Any injury in and around the eye ....(11).... taken seriously land managed on an emergency basis.

QUESTIONS

1. A. potentially B. instantly
   C. constantly D. inevitably
2. A. arrival B. appearance
   C. place D. position
3. A. unknowingly B. undoubtedly
   C. undauntedly D. unfortunately
4. A. advertently B. inadvertently
   C. unfortunately D. unknowingly
5. A. almost B. almost always
   C. all the time D. very often
6. A. Motivated B. Inspired
   C. Encouraged D. Taught
7. A. attack B. take out
   C. brandish D. home
8. A. can lead B. could lead
   C. would lead D. lead
9. A. it targets B. it comes
   C. they happen D. they are
10. A. usually B. generally
    C. commonly D. more often
11. A. are to be B. is to be
    C. shall be D. may be

PASSAGE-16

The scientist of today is a man of ....(1).... ambition. He is not contented with ....(2).... he has achieved, but wants to be a creator of new and surprising things so that the common people may ....(3).... at the marvels of his ....(4)...., feel thrilled and go away ....(5).... by his superior wisdom and his ....(6).... inventiveness. The new and challenging scientific forces now ....(7).... by him in the universe will continue to work ....(8).... in ever increasing numbers, to lead mankind to ....(9).... material progress, and to ....(10).... in its hand unlimited power for conquering ....(11).... territories of knowledge and experience.

QUESTIONS

1. A. increasing B. elevating
   C. soaring D. diversing
2. A. what B. whatever
   C. those D. that
3. A. broad B. work
   C. gape D. deride
4. A. invention B. genius
   C. life D. achievement
5. A. impressed B. dejected
   C. attracted D. motivated
6. A. enviable B. reliable
   C. unavoidable D. considerable

7. A. brought B. given
C. let loose D. realised

8. A. fruitfully B. miracles
C. magic D. wonders

9. A. unscathed B. unrelenting
C. unmitigated D. unprecedented

10. A. keep B. allot
C. load D. place

11. A. greater B. varied
C. unknown D. more and more

PASSAGE-17

Education of the future has to ....(1).... human values and see that the human factor is not neglected. The task of education is to help the individual to know himself. ....(2).... as the individual is ignorant of his ....(3)...., his potentialites and his mission of life, he ....(4).... contribute in a creative manner ....(5).... his own growth and development of the society. It is often said that, as education is the ....(6).... of the thinking elite of the nation, ...(7).... the nation's future depends on its system of education. This is true to some ....(8).... .But ....(9)...., the general outlook of society has also a strong ....(10).... on education itself so that education can only be reformed when a ....(11).... change has already begun in society.

QUESTIONS

1. A. consider B. protect
C. care D. preserve

2. A. Till then B. So long
C. Uptill then D. Till that time

3. A. own B. credibilities
C. nature D. real self

4. A. can't B. could not
C. could never D. cannot

5. A. in B. throughout
C. to D. towards

6. A. developing process B. development
C. building up D. guidance

7. A. much of B. many of
C. mostly D. mainly

8. A. limit B. horizon
C. context D. extent

9. A. conversely B. alternately
C. actually D. outwardly

10. A. hearing B. relation
C. opposition D. affinity

11. A. consequent B. corresponding
C. subsequent D. similar

PASSAGE-18

Every action we perform ....(1).... a result. And, naturally, we lay claim ....(2).... the results or fruits ....(3).... from that action in the ....(4).... that it is we who perform the action. This is .....(5).... ignorance because ....(6).... is it the Lord who ....(7).... the result of any action, it is by His will ....(8).... that even the action is accomplished. The will of the Lord ....(9).... whether we cooperate with His will or strive ....(10).... If God wills that an action takes place, he arranges for the ....(11).... for it to happen. It is ....(12).... experience that sometimes despite our best efforts we ....(13).... achieve the results we desire, and at other times the seemingly most ....(14).... situations mysteriously get ....(15).... . ....(16).... way man chooses to act, both the act and the outcome of the cost are dependent ....(17).... on the will of the Lord.

QUESTIONS

1. A. produce B. produces
C. causes D. undergoes

2. A. on B. at
C. to D. for

3. A. occuring B. obtaining
C. deriving D falling

4. A. belief B. hope
C. fantasy D. folly

5. A. sheen B. keen
C. sheer D. sheathe

6. A. alone B. only that
C. not only D. for only

7. A. declares B. decides
C. ordains D. ornate

8. A. completely B. entirely
C. only D. alone

9. A. prevails always
B. prevails everywhere
C. is prevalent
D. always prevails

10. A. alone B. always
C. constantly D. independently

11. A. wherewithal B. whereabouts
C. whatsoever D. wherefore

12. A. usual B. general
C. universal D. common

13. A. does not B. may not
C. do not D. might not

14. A. intractable B. intangible
C. internecine D. intricate

15. A. subsided B. resolved
C. solved D. converted

16. A. Whatever B. All the
C. All those D. Whichever

17. A. mainly B. actually
C. entirely D. generally

PASSAGE-19

For centuries, women not only in India but all over the world ....(1).... treated as ....(2).... secondary position to men. ....(3).... human history men ....(4).... far greater power then women to name, classify, and order the worlds in which they both live. ....(5).... studies in various parts of the world point out to a wide ....(6).... in male and female roles ....(7).... cultures and demonstrate the possibility of change in these sex-determined roles. The 20th century in particular ....(8).... the cause of gender justice by internationalizing struggles for equality ....(9).... women and other oppressed people. Women's struggles against their ....(10).... were interwined in ....(11).... degrees with ideologies and movements based on the values of freedom, self-determination, equality, democracy and justice.

QUESTIONS

1. A. has been B. have been
C. had been D. were

2. A. occupying B. taking
C. possessing D. serving

3. A. All through B. Throughout
C. Since D. From

4. A. have B. had
C. have had D. enjoy

5. A. Sociological B. Anthropological
C. General D. Practical

6. A. concord B. repulsion
C. disagreement D. variation

7. A. among B. across
C. between D. of

8. A. developed B. envolved
C. promoted D. entertained

9. A. for B. to
C. among D. by

10. A. subsidiary B. subsequent
C. subservience D. subordination

11. A. various B. varying
C changing D. differeing

PASSAGE-20

What is required today in our country is ....(1).... of a new political culture based on full respect for human liberty, on pluralism and on a better social deal for all. The major ....(2).... facing us today is to carry out democratic transformation in all the ....(3)...., social, cultural, economic and political. The events of the 20th century ....(4).... one thing absolutely clear that human ....(5)...., everywhere, specially in countries whose political structures were ....(6).... to reflect the revolutionary aspirations of the people ....(7).... not only under stress and strain but are ....(8).... vast upheavals because of the ....(9).... of democracy. At the same time it has also to be understood that democracy cannot be ....(10).... into a static mould.

QUESTIONS

1. A. growing B. developing
C. creating D. creation

2. A. development B. crisis
C. challenge D. drawback

3. A. corners B. context
C. realm D. spheres

4. A. have made B. has made
C. had made D. made

5. A. travails B. traverse
C. trapse D. transverse

6. A. supposed B. meant
C. caused D. forced

7. A. were B. was
C. are D. have been

8. A. developing B. evolving
C. experiencing D. faced with

9. A. denial B. rebuff
C. rebuttal D. absence

10. A. shaped B. flex
C. frozen D. caused

PASSAGE-21

We are living in very exciting ....(1).... . The ....(2).... change is dizzying and the impact this progress is having on our present and – more importantly – on our future is difficult to ....(3).... in its ...(4).... . This is the age of ....(5).... micro processors, sophisticated software, new hardware technology and high bandwith, high-speed networks. The PC gave us a new way to work, play and ....(6).... . In fact, it brought ....(7).... our desktops computing power, which until a few years ....(8).... had only been available to corporates. With the ....(9).... of the internet, the PC ....(10).... us the most convenient and flexible way to head on to the Net.

QUESTIONS

1. A. periods B. days
C. phase D. times

2. A. phase B. pace
C. sphere D. drastic

3. A. guess B. forecast
C. comprehend D. approximate

4. A. whole B. entirety
C. fruition D. fullness

5. A. strong B. changing
C. powerful D. sonorous

6. A. convey B. communicate
C. entertain D. enjoy

7. A. onto B. to
C. on D. at

8. A. back B. earlier
C. behind D. before

9. A. addendum B. adherence
C. afoot D. advent

10. A. allowed B. privileged
C. brought D. offered

PASSAGE-22

Visualisation is a strong ....(1).... to memory. Those persons who ....(2).... a powerful memory cannot do so without taking the help of visualisaton. Such persons have developed the skills to ....(3).... visualisation even in such ....(4).... tasks as remembering names and numbers. These persons have the names and numbers ....(5).... in their brain even after hearing those names and figues only once. On the other hand those who take the help of revising to memorise ....(6).... to forget it once they have ....(7).... the practice of revising ....(8).... the ones who have applied visualisation to memorise. Psychologists ....(9).... in visualisation a powerful tool for personality development. The more you visualise, the more you are ....(10).... your attitude and behaviour to the blue prints of your vision and ....(11).... more you are inching towards success.

QUESTIONS

1. A. way B. path
C. aid D. symptom

2. A. command B. master
C. rule D. enjoy

3. A. use B. apply
C. put D. place

4. A. trivial B. difficult
C. mundane D. unscrupulous

5. A. impress B. imprinted
C. impinge D. store

6. A. bent B. incline
C. prone d. tend

7. A. dropped B. left
C. gave up D. given up

8. A. unlike B. opposite
C. contrary D. not like

9. A. found B. have found
C. sees D. finds

10. A. shaping B. moulding
C. making D. attuning

11. A. actually B. factually
C. subsequently D. consequently

PASSAGE-23

....(1).... people today remember the war that was fought after China invaded India in 1962. Not because the war was never really ....(2).... . Nor because it was ....(3).... almost before it began. The reason is ....(4).... that most of us were yet to be born. The main reason for the Chinese attack seems to ....(5).... to establish the ....(6).... order, expose our ....(7)...., put us in our place. The official reason, ...(8)...., was the territorial dispute, ...(9).... more than 100,000 square kilometres. ....(10).... speaking, India borders Tibet, not China. The McMohan Line ....(11).... the border with Tibet in what is now Arunachal Pradesh was the result of a 1914 treaty ....(12).... British India and Tibet. This was not ....(13).... to the Chinese the result was a .....(14)..... nose. The Chinese attack was ....(15).... fast and furious. ....(16).... brave soldiers ....(17).... down their lives, but India was simply unable to halt the ....(17).... . Panic quickly ....(18)....

QUESTIONS

1. A. A few B. Few
C. Fewer D. A little

2. A. joined B. combined
C. acted D. approved

3. A. finished B. ceased
C. over D. stopped

4. A. simple B. simply
C. common D. commonly

5. A. had been B. have
C. had D. have been

6. A. pecking B. unavoiding
C. powerful D. selfish

7. A. projections B. pretensions
C. presumption D. pretending

8. A. more over B. probably
C. perhaps D. however

9. A. effecting B. causing
C. affecting D. influencing

10. A. Formally B. Informally
C. Broadly D. Technically

11. A. relating B. dividing
C. defining D. laying

12. A. among B. between
C. of D. by

13. A. favourable B. favoured
C. acceptable D. accepting

14. A. angry B. bloody
C. honed D. blitz

15. A. quick B. prick
C. sudden D. unassuming

16. A. Some B. Few
C. Many D. A lot of

17. A. onrush B. onset
C. omnipotence D. omen

18. A. come in B. gone in
C. set in D. set out

PASSAGE-24

Man has always been ....(1).... with flying because it ....(2).... a sense of freedom, of romance and thrill-something too ....(3).... to resist. It is the task of the ....(4).... of the skies to safeguard Indian air-space from unwelcome ....(5)..... . The Indian Air Force ....(6).... a chequered and glorious history. From its ....(7).... days of single-engine aeroplanes like Tempests and Spitfires to the state of the art multi-engine, supersonic MIG and Sukhoi fighters, the Indian Air Force ....(8).... a long way. In addition to the already existing ....(9).... of aircraft and weapon systems, plans are ....(10).... to enhance its air defence power and ....(11).... capability through upgradation and ....(12).... .

QUESTIONS

1. A. fascinated B. moved
C. inspired D. fancied

2. A. generates B. cultivates
C. reaps D. evokes

3. A. envisaging B. impressing
C. enchanting D. laudable

4. A. sentiness B. sedulous
C. venturous D. fervid

5. A. emigrants B. intruders
C. foreigners D. tourists

6. A. had B. have
C. have had D. has had

7. A. early B. undeveloped
C. growing D. embryonic

8. A. had come B. has come
C. have come D. came

9. A. invention B. inventory
C. mechanism D. technique

10. A. progressive B. afresh
C. afoot D. affluent

11. A. combat B. increase
C. intensify D. ensure

12. A. acquistion B. acknowledgement
C. acquiescence D. accumulation

PASSAGE-25

Libraries were never ....(1).... the place to ....(2).... They never will be. But those who've visited libraries for the ....(3).... pleasure of it will testify to the feeling of ....(4).... on entering the labyrinth ....(5).... high with books. Suddenly, a ....(6).... spent reading seems the ideal. It's a similar experience to ....(7).... in a bookshop. The difference : in the second situation, despair ....(8).... you as your eyes zoom ....(9).... on the price; in the first there is the ....(10).... that all these books are yours for the asking. Today, ...(11)...., liberary use is almost ....(12).... necessity-based. The reading room is ....(13).... full with students poring ....(14).... their books..

QUESTIONS

1. A. realised B. seen
C. recognised D. considered

2. A. hung out B. hang out
C. hang out in D. hung out in

3. A. mere B. sheer
C. trivial D. trifle

4. A. exhilaration B. exhaustion
C. expedition D. extrapolation

5. A. going B. moving
C. pik D. towering

6. A. long time B. whole life
C. life time D. life long

7. A. browsing B. move about
C. move D. stroll

8. A. swamps B. swab
C. swoon D. swoop

9. A. at B. on
C. in D. upon

10. A. idea B. surity
C. certainty D. knowledge

11. A. although B. however
C. in fact D. moreover

12. A. wholly B. partially
C. outwardly D. purely

13. A. tight B. completely
C. over crowded D. cramped

14. A. into B. onto
C. over D. upon

PASSAGE-26

The ....(1).... of a country does not depend on the abundance of its revenue but more ....(2).... by its citizens; its men of education, enlightenment and character. It is for the ....(3).... of higher learning to ....(4).... an academic environment of equity, justice and fair play where those ....(5).... in the ....(6).... task of nation building can ....(7).... their responsibilities in a spirit of sincerity, dedication and commitment. Higher education in India ....(8).... great strides after independence. The ideal of education is to ....(9).... for self-preservation but which also prepares us to recognise and ....(10).... the rights of others and to shoulder our ....(11).... as responsible citizens.

QUESTIONS

1. A. prospects B. fortune C. protrusion D. gaiety
2. A. illustrated B. emancipated C. defined D. apprehended
3. A. institute B. centre C. college D. university
4. A. encourage B. embark C. promote D. polish
5. A. employed B. recruited C. held D. engaged
6. A. paramount B. ardous C. lucrative D. laudable
7. A. dispense B. disburse C. carry D. discharge
8. A. have taken B. had taken C. has taken D. is taking
9. A. evoke B. prepare C. encourage D. cultivate
10. A. concede B. preserve C. coddle D. clung
11. A. obligations B. obduracy C. obsequiousness D. portfolio

PASSAGE-27

Observation is one of the key ....(1).... of modern corporate behaviour. Indeed it has long been the ....(2).... for humans and animals generally. It is essential for every corporate citizen to be able to taste the ....(3).... of what is happening around him all the time, not merely to survive but to ....(4)..... ....(5).... the corporate corridors to check which way the wind is blowing ! Know when it is appropriate to get your ....(6).... in and when it is ....(7).... to maintain a low profile. To ....(8).... a career with the ease and ....(9).... of a winner, you need to be able to ....(10).... a disaster before it happens! You need to take an advantage before someone else ....(11)..... You need to be at the right place before someone else ....(12).... there. Observation or paying attention to what's happening around us is essential ....(13)..... We need to take the time to ....(14).... the habit of paying attention so that we can make our work ....(15).... and so that we can stand at ease! Career ....(16).... will be the happy outcome!

QUESTIONS

1. A. approach B. method C. tactics D. means
2. A. rule B. norm C. convention D. technique
3. A. presence B. essence C. events D. problem
4. A. thrive B. throb C. fare D. blow
5. A. Sniff B. Snuffle C. Spin-off D. Splutter
6. A. shore B. oar C. objective D. ogle
7. A. correct B. right C. prudent D. prudish
8. A. carry B. initiate C. continue D. conduct
9. A. caprice B. comfort C. over-confidence D. aplomb
10. A. forecast B. apprehend C. guess D. foretell
11. A. do B. does C. takes D. gets
12. A. come B. comes C. get D. gets
13. A. everytime B. alltime C. everywhere D. forever
14. A. reap B. sow C. cultivate D. grow
15. A. easy B. easier C. easiest D. simple
16. A. advancement B. progression C. achievement D. cultivation

PASSAGE-28

The ....(1).... Euphoria over the ....(2).... fall in the cost of domestic air travel has ....(3).... to a more realistic appraisal of what is on offer. The aggressive ....(4).... schemes offered since the beginning of July have certainly been good news for certain categories of passengers who probably value ....(5).... above anything else. For them, the heavily discounted fare ....(6).... enables them to afford air travel for the first time. In fact, the ....(7).... of the fare cut ....(8).... such that in specific instances air travel compares ....(9).... to the fares charged by the Railways for upper class travel. Obviously, it ....(10).... for a change in mindset to switch to air travel in ....(11).... to, say, rail transport in India. Economy and affordability will certainly be key ....(12).... but they must be made available ....(13).... a fairly long period. To put it differently, cheaper air travel or at least a ....(14).... fare structure ....(15).... institutionalised in the country.

QUESTIONS

1. A. embryonic B. early C. ending D. initial
2. A. casual B. sudden C. surprising D. dramatic
3. A. raised B. caused C. given way D. gave way
4. A. lucrative B. lofty C. laudable D. promotional
5. A. expenses B. affordability C. comfort D. time
6. A. scheme B. structure C. system D. circular
7. A. portion B. ratio C. magnitude D. proportion
8. A. are B. is C. has been D. have been
9. A. very slightly B. very favourably C. specifially D. generally
10. A. causes B. calls C. invites D. lures
11. A. choice B. favour C. preference D. alternative
12. A. determinants B. detrimenetals C. performers D. issues
13. A. over B. for C. to D. through
14. A. different B. distinctive C. reducing D. differential
15. A. must be B. has to be C. ought to be D. have to be

PASSAGE-29

"I need a break" is a common ..... (1) ..... among the ....(2).... middle and elite classes – under ....(3).... pressure to perform, to live up to their own artificial standards, to earn, and earn some more and ....(4).... some more. But in this vortex, time is at a ....(5)...., and the much needed break ....(6).... materialises because harried professionals are unable to stay away from work long enough ....(7).... from the city and breathe in some fresh air—metaphorically and literally. And weekends? They are ....(8).... lazing at home, ...(9).... on chores, or may be watching some mind numbing television programme. Because it would be hard to think of a place you ....(10).... escape to that was far enough from the city to be ....(11).... and yet close enough to ....(12).... as a weekend break.

QUESTIONS

1. A. restrain B. refrain C. remark D. saying
2. A. hurried B. harried C. worried D. busy
3. A. continuous B. consequent C. constant D. stable
4. A. even B. add C. farther D. then
5. A. premium B. minimum C. limitation D. restriction
6. A. never often B. often never C. although never D. sometimes do not
7. A. to stay away B. to escape C. to go away D. to get moved
8. A. there B. for C. those D. some
9. A. getting B. catching C. catching up D. catching down
10. A. can B. ever C. would D. could
11. A. refreshed B. refreshing C. resting D. rejoining
12. A. consider B. anticipate C. contemplate D. meditate

PASSAGE-30

Every monsoon I'm reminded of an incident that ....(1).... many years ago when I was a young man ....(2).... my first job in Mumbai. I was staying with my sister in those days. On one wet and windy night I ....(3).... with friends, and as it happens when you are in pleasant company, the ....(4).... . It was past ten when I finally bid goodby to my companions and moved towards my sister's house. It had rained the whole day, and it ....(5).... to drizzle again. The rain had ....(6).... people indoors earlier than usual and the dimly-lit street I was walking along was ....(7).... . I had heard that the road was ....(8).... . They said one could hear a woman calling for help on some nights. As I proceeded, I suddenly saw a figure walking ....(9).... me. A bandicoot chose to ....(10).... across my path, just then she seemed to have ....(11).... into thin air. Then I heard a faint ....(12).... for help. This frightened me and as such I turned and fled. The next morning I came to know from my sister that the bandicoot was no other but her friend who had mistakenly thought she was being ....(13).... . Out of fear she was looking behind and walking when she ....(14).... into a ditch. Now every monsoon, I'm reminded of my ....(15).... on that wet night.

QUESTIONS

1. A. happened B. occured
   C. took place D. had taken place
2. A. in B. on
   C. working at D. working with
3. A. had been out B. went for outing
   C. had gone D. was out
4. A. time passes B. time runs
   C. time flies D. time files
5. A. has B. was
   C. began D. had begun
6. A. pushed B. sent
   C. send D. driven
7. A. calm B. peace
   C. lonely D. deserted
8. A. mysterious B. ghostly
   C. haunted D. devilish
9. A. before B. in front of
   C. a head D. near
10. A. scuttle B. scurry
    C. scuff D. scrouge
11. A. faded B. vanished
    C. vaporised D. melted
12. A. sound B. voice
    C. cry D. whisper
13. A. followed B. chased
    C. pursued D. caught
14. A. fall B. stumbled
    C. threw D. jumped
15. A. foolishness B. ignorance
    C. confusion D. cowardice

PASSAGE-31

Most of India's educational institutions, ...(1).... by hiring people who are ....(2).... qualified to be teachers. They are ....(3).... an unhappy group, which is ill-paid and which commands ....(4).... respect. Sadly, it is these men and women who have the enormous duty of ...(5).... tomorrow's society, a responsibility that remains ...(6).... Children are ....(7).... in this terrifying circle : they are ....(8).... into submission, their innocence is destroyed and their lives become ....(9).... joyless. What follows is still ....(10).... . A violent childhood ....(11).... a violent adulthood. A child who faces the ....(12).... of an adult grows up ....(13).... that violence is the answer to all problems. They become ....(14).... individuals and often their intellectual development ....(15).... in the absence of congenial peace.

QUESTIONS

1. A. get away B. manage
   C. run D. go away
2. A. not really B. really not
   C. virtually not D. not actually
3. A. commonly B. mainly
   C. specifically D. usually
4. A. scant B. scanty
   C. scarce D. rare
5. A. forming B. moulding
   C. framing D. making
6. A. unsatisfied B. unprecedented
   C. unfulfilled D. unrequited
7. A. taught B. caught
   C. captured D. chained
8. A. battered B. split
   C. squeezed D. shaped
9. A. universally B. utterly
   C. wholly D. complete
10. A. unfavourable B. bad
    C. not good D. worse
11. A. may lead to B. may grow to
    C. may reach to D. would develop to
12. A. consequences B. wrath
    C. grief D. wretch
13. A. thinking B. supposing
    C. infering D. believing
14. A. complex B. complicated
    C. rough D. sanguine
15. A. slows down B. moves slowly
    C. hampers D. brakes

PASSAGE-32

Men ....(1).... the maker of their own destinies and they ....(2).... make the destiny of the society and the nation. Life is a great gift of God to men and man ....(3).... making constant efforts to live a ....(4).... life right from the stone age to the modern one. But it is man who ....(5).... to think out how to live well. The ....(6).... before mankind today is between self-preservation and self-destruction. Science has given men all the powers that they need but the new millennium ....(7).... new challenges. We are ....(8).... what nature has given us—forests are being cut down, slums are being ....(9)...., rivers are being polluted. Medical science has made great ....(10)....; but the population is growing in a geometrical ....(11).... . Our natural resources like coal and oil are being ....(12).... . Atomic energy is our only hope. The ....(13).... welcome of the new millennium lies in our determination and hope for self-preservation ....(14).... self-destruction.

QUESTIONS

1. A. are B. have been
   C. being D. had been
2. A. unitedly B. ultimately
   C. conjointly D. co-exist to
3. A. have been B. are
   C. has been D. have had been
4. A. congenial
   B. cordial
   C. congregational
   D. congruent
5. A. have B. is
   C. are D. has
6. A. optional B. choice
   C. possibilities D. probabilities
7. A. presents B. places
   C. offers D. puts forth
8. A. destroying B. ignoring
   C. neglecting D. wasting
9. A. developed B. constructed
   C. created D. manufactured
10. A. advancement B. advances
    C. achievement D. inventions
11. A. dimension B. angle
    C. index D. proportion
12. A. deported B. deplored
    C. depleted D. disposed
13. A. actual B. real
    C. warm D. innate
14. A. upon B. over
    C. on D. above

II. PASSAGES

Directions: *Read each of the following passages carefully and choose the best answer to each question out of the four alternatives and mark it in the Answer Sheet.*

PASSAGE-1

Cyber crime is the branded stigma defacing the culture and magnanimity of computer technology. It is up keeping the flag with indomitable triumph against developing computer technology worldwide.

Modern age is striding with marching steps of technology revolution beating the past decade of ancestral belief with ultimate care. Computer invention has unfolded the mystery of quick access with the objective of minimum manpower and cutting the time consumption parameters.

As each coin has dual face of its portrait, likewise computer technology is sick of creeping virus. Synthetic manmade dilemma of site hackers activation is causing setback to the expanding anchor of revolutionary device with great loss of time, economy and data profile as suffered by consumers. A recent report from Internet security firm Websense estimates that 85.6 per cent of all the unwanted e-mails contained links to spam sites. The company's data suggests that the number of malicious sites grew 233 per cent in the last six months and saw 671 per cent growth in the number of malicious sites during the last year. In June alone, the total number of e-mails detected as containing viruses increased by 600 per cent compared to May.

Chat rooms, blogs and message boards where the users post comments have been identified as the top targets of hackers and spammers due to the high traffic these attract. According to Websense, 95 per cent of user-generated comments to blogs, chat rooms and message boards during the first half of 2009 were malicious.

It is advisable not to click on spurious links and stay away from keying in passwords at unknown sites as they are most likely to be spammed. Hackers can steal your passwords and log in to your account and access critical information like account numbers and contact details among other things.

QUESTIONS

1. The above passage is:
   A. an advisory for the computer users.
   B. an advisory for the Internet users.
   C. a warning against possible threat to the Internet users.
   D. related to chat rooms, blogs and message boards.
2. People who use chat rooms and blogs,
   A. are safe and have no threats from spam.
   B. are more prone to malicious e-mails.
   C. create virus and hack the accounts of others.
   D. are unsafe.
3. According to the writer, it is not safe to:
   A. log on to spurious links.
   B. access one's own account frequently.
   C. have essential information stored in a computer.
   D. include data-stealing code.
4. Hackers and spammers, according to the writer, are:
   A. a new threat to the Internet users and the economy.
   B. only pranksters and not serious threat to the system.
   C. trained, professional technocrats who are an asset.
   D. not expert professionals.

5. Which word in the passage is synonym of *weblog*?
A. blog B. password
C. site D. e-mail

6. Which agency has assessed the data record with spam sites?
A. Microsoft
B. Internet security from Google
C. Websense
D. Spammers

7. Which month dominates the e-mails detection data record?
A. May B. June
C. Last six months D. Last year

PASSAGE-2

South Asian tropical weather reels valuable geographical aesthetic beauty surrounded by wildlife, mountains, steep elevations with dense forest. Human sapiens has been old and innocent victim of natural calamities branded as flood, hurricane, storm, earthquake and tsunami since ages.

Biological data depicts the loss of valuable men and material suffered by mankind owing to the chain reaction by such fatal natural incidents. Global warming has turned an eyesore to the rapid glory of rising civilsation with great mystery yet to be unfolded. UNO data reveals the rate of mortality owned due to natural disaster with great sway of cruel time factor.

Of the 245 natural disasters in the first 11 months of 2009, 224 or 91.4 per cent were due to weather, a UN study has found.

Of the 58 million people affected, 55 million were affected by weather-related disasters, which accounted for $15 billion (₹ 7,05,000 crore) spent in coping with these disasters.

A study has found that half of these disasters, mainly storms and floods, have taken place in Asia, Debarati Guha Sapir of Brussels-based CRED said.

And this data does not include the loss due to drought because that takes longer to account for. Guha Sapir said, "We have found that this is due to global warming, weak political systems, urbanisation, weak infrastructure, population increase and deforestation."

"We have to cap the emissions of greenhouse gases because they produce greater risk of disasters," WMO head Michel Jerraud said. Greenhouse gases, mainly carbon dioxide, are causing the climate change that is already affecting farm output, making droughts, floods and storms more frequent and more severe, and raising the sea level.

QUESTIONS

1. Mark the correct statement(s).
1. Weather is responsible for most of the natural disasters.
2. There is no need to worry about the climatic changes.
3. All the nations are trying to have a common pact to tackle natural disasters.

A. 1 is correct
B. Only 2 is correct
C. Only 3 is correct
D. 1 and 2 are correct

2. Which one of the following statements is not true?
A. More than 58 million people have been affected by natural disasters.
B. $15 billion have been spent in coping with these disasters.
C. Most of the natural disasters have taken place in Asia.
D. The report does not include the loss caused by droughts.

3. The main cause of natural disasters is :
A. global warming
B. weak political system
C. deforestation
D. all of these

4. The first priority before the nations and the scientists across the world is :
A. to cap the emission of greenhouse gases.
B. to reach an agreement on the nuclear weapons.
C. to help one another when natural disasters occur.
D. to find out the causes of natural disasters.

5. Which word in the passage means the same as *serious*?
A. Reduce B. Severe
C. Underlined D. Underscore

6. Which region is mainly affected by these disasters?
A. United Nation B. Africa
C. Asia D. Brussels

7. Which statement is true?
A. Sea level rise is an alarming incident.
B. Rapid urbanisation is a curse to the global warming.
C. Deforestation with climatic change is responsible for green house gaseous effect.
D. All of these.

PASSAGE-3

Time has brought forth different classical and instrumental range of device that serves healing element to the aweful and mentally distressed state of affair. Temperament compatibility matching is a reasonable trend of motion adhered with the ,concept of body movement termed as dance therapy.

Dance has mobilised different acknowledgement of its noted culture proclaimed by experts and sensational aspirants. Vedas describe the dance origin from aryan culture to the creeping span of modern India. Archaeological Survey of India has claimed the civilsation existence issue owing to excavation of past events traced in the stone idols displayed in dance "mudra".

Dance is an art form that generally refers to movement of the body, usually rhythmic and to music, used as a form of expression, social interaction or presented in a spiritual or performance setting. Gymnastics, figure skating and synchronised swimming are sports that incorporate dance, while martial arts Kata are often compared to dances. Motion in ordinarily inanimate objects may also be described as dances (the leaves dance in the wind). Every dance, no matter what style, has something in common. It not only involves flexibility and body movement, but also physics. If the proper physics is not taken into consideration, injuries may occur. Choreography is the art of creating dances. The person who creates (*i.e.* choreographs) a dance, is known as the choreographer. Dance has certainly been an important part of ceremony, rituals, celebrations and entertainment since the birth of the earliest human civilisations. Archaeology delivers trace of dance from prehistoric times such as the 9,000 years old Rock Shelters of Bhimbetka painting in India and Egyptian tomb painting depicting dancing figures from circa 3300 BC. One of the earliest structured uses of dance may have been in the performance and in the telling of myths. Before the production of written languages, dance was one of the methods of passing these stories down from generation to generation.

QUESTIONS

1. Dance does not necessarily involve:
A. movement of the body.
B. face expression.
C. rhythmic movements.
D. costumes.

2. According to the passage, which one of the following sports does not incorporate dance?
A. Figure skating B. Gymnastics
C. Chess D. Swimming

3. Which one, according to the passage, is not common in all the dances?
A. Flexibility B. Body movement
C. Music D. Physics

4. Physics in every dance is an important element to:
A. master the art of dance.
B. to perform it scientifically.
C. to save oneself from injury.
D. to get an award.

5. In prehistoric times dance was:
A. a substitute of written language.
B. a source of entertainment.
C. a necessary ritual.
D. not allowed in royal palaces.

6. Choreographer is a term addressed to:
A. a sports trainer B. a gym coach
C. a painting teacher D. a dance teacher

7. What does the term 'the telling of myths' refer to?
A. Telling the beads B. Vedic convention
C. Spiritual recitation D. Protest march

PASSAGE-4

Personal sentiments exposure portray in sober class of distinct feature with fair and pleasant expression. As the cruelty can be overpowered by the amicable terms likewise, impossible review let with expression can be publically announced by either electronic device or diary writing habit. On line conversation such as chattering, message convey are the rampant tool of the time to manage in communication congestion.

Blogs, online versions of personal diaries, have been a craze for quite some time now. Some of us, before the Internet age, used to maintain a small diary to jot down random thoughts, reflections, sayings, poems and other such stuff. Their online versions, however, are much more than that. The biggest difference between a blog and a personal diary is while the latter was a very private affair accessible not even to family members, a blog is a public account. In fact the whole world connected to the internet gets to read its contents if they come across it.

What a blogger should keep in mind while blogging is that by displaying our thoughts, emotions, opinions and personal life in full public glory, we are revealing a part of our private life. We are giving outsiders, strangers, friends, colleagues and relatives a full view of what's happening inside us and without lives, something we would hesitate to do in real life. Once blogging begins, it's difficult to control, and we end up sharing our personal thoughts and emotions that we would otherwise have kept to ourselves. The blog entices us, and we fall to be bait.

Blogs don't preserve our anonymity. They let us publish our pictures, professional and personal details, physical address and locations, etc. The biggest precaution to be observed therefore is to think twice before publishing anything, and ask oneself if one would like to make such matters public. The blog readers try to judge us, understand us, get information about us and take pleasure while peeping into our private lives without realising it.

QUESTIONS

1. Blogs are __________.
A. diaries B. personal diaries
C. online diaries D. official diaries

2. Earlier the personal diaries were not available even to family members but blog can be read by:
A. family and friends
B. friends only

C. anyone who connects to the Internet
D. relatives

3. Which one of the following statements is not true?
A. Blogging does not affect our privacy.
B. Blogging displays our private life in public.
C. Blogging cannot be controlled easily.
D. Blogging allows outsiders to peep into our personal life.

4. The writer in the above passage:
A. favours blogging.
B. criticises the practices.
C. does not want the reader to become a victim of blogging.
D. favours blogging but with some precautions.

5. Which word in the passage stands for *an account from on point of view*?
A. version B. block
C. affair D. account

6. The word Anonymity in the passage refers to:
A. hostility B. friendship
C. unacknowledged D. differences

7. What precaution is stressed by the narrator while releasing personal information?
A. Suggest Comprehensive issue only
B. Reader friendly blog appreciation
C. Hiding personal facts
D. Diary maintenance

PASSAGE-5

Pleasure and sorrow being twin face of a coin suffers the sign of commend and condemn since long before the historic ages. Warriors outcry with victory decorated with deep throat laugh has marked the sentimental coverage of battle filed victory. Baffled war victims, war widows, dependents are the oppressed classes. They seek relief against those causing sabotage to their established settlement.

The history of literature really began long before man learned to write. Dancing was the earliest of the arts. Man danced for joy round his primitive camp fire after the defeat and slaughter of his enemy. He yelled and shouted as he danced and gradually the yells and shouts became coherent and caught the measure of the dance and thus the first war song was sung. As the idea of God developed, prayers were framed. The song and prayers became traditional and were repeated from one generation to another, each generation adding something of its own. As man slowly grew more civilsed, he was compelled to invent some method of writing by three urgent necessities. There were certain things that were dangerous to forget and which, therefore, had to be recorded.

It was often necessary to communicate with persons who were some distance away and it was necessary to protect one's property by making tools and so on, in some distinctive manner. So man taught himself to write and having learned to write purely for utilitarian reasons, he used this new method for prescrving his songs and his prayers. Of course, among these ancient people, there were only a very few individuals who learned to write, and only a few could read what was written.

QUESTIONS

1. Liguistic comment and condemn refers to:
A. physical grudge against sorrows
B. a temporary verbal communication
C. slip of tongue with praise and denounce
D. a communal fury against the joys

2. Which one of the following statements is true?
A. Study reveals the historic onslaught with cruelty only.
B. Suffers pledge to reform the existing tyranny.
C. A permanent code of sympathetic temper is sought by the suffers.
D. Language dominates with great passion during mental aggression.

3. Before man invented writing, _____.
A. literature was passed on by word of mouth
B. prayres were considered literature
C. literature was just singing and dancing
D. all of the above

4. According to the passage, dance originated from
A. literature
B. yelling and shouting
C. prayers
D. war

5. Writing was invented because
A. there were certain things which had to be remembered.
B. there were certain things which had to be communicated to the people who were away.
C. there were certain rituals which had to be preserved.
D. all of the above

6. Which one of the following statements is not true?
A. Since only a few individuals had learnt to write and a few could read what was written.
B. Prayers were developed after the idea of god developed.
C. People learned writing for utilitarian reasons.
D. Dancing was the earliest form of art.

7. Which one of the following words in the passage stands for *ancient*?
A. primitive B. traditional
C. coherent D. utilitarian

PASSAGE-6

Quality dominates the world ahead of its spherical, classical, racial or any undue discrimination ever exercised by any individual. Physical characteristics of a produce differs its structural attribution in quality from substandard produce with richness of prolong usage features declared by the claimant. Talent Hunt initiated by quality seekers have turned the table of established brand on account of innovative additions presented by their hardships.

The simple message that quality matters because it is cheaper to do things right the first time is yet to sink into the thinking of Indian managers and workers who seem quite content to live in their cloistered world where mediocrity reigns supreme. It is only the ignorant who believe that quality consciousness is a cultural trait. Barely half a century back no one associated Japan with high quality, but today 'Made in Japan' is a symbol of assured quality. The daily drill at school is far more important than the seasonal seminar and an obsession with quality at home is the best way of convincing the world that we value good quality. Indian exports will never be recognised for quality unless Indians are known to insist on good quality at home.

Global appreciation surrounds the exceptional brand by keeping up the physical standard neatly and efficiently. It is designed to meet the international standards' numerous logos and certificates to upkeep the label of quality consciousness. It has prime motto of swaying clean chit observation to the sanctioned produce without any objection. Modern age has been proved a turning point to the old established traditional belief. They are using tiring house hold produce to industrial device responsible to deface the status of rapid development. We breath into the cool and fresh air of healthy surrounding devised by mankind monitored by quality management with rigorous span or struggle tackled with due care.

QUESTIONS

1. The theme of the passage is:
A. quality consciousness
B. export promotion
C. quality management
D. promoting Indian culture

2. According to the passage, the Indian exports will never be recognised for quality:
A. unless there is technical advancement.
B. unless there is competition.
C. unless the Indians are known to insist on good quality.
D. unless government supports the exporters.

3. Which one of the following statements is true?
A. Indians are known for their insistence on quality.
B. Indians are not quality conscious.
C. Japan is not known for its quality product.
D. 'Made in Japan' is not a symbol of assured quality.

4. The best way to convince the world about quality is:
A. to conduct seminars on quality control.
B. to advertise the products.
C. to value for quality products at home.
D. all of the above

5. According to the passage, the main fault with the Indian managers is that:
A. they are not hard-working.
B. they are not quality conscious.
C. they are not well trained in quality control.
D. they lack technical knowledge.

6. How quality consciousness is termed as a cultural trait with the ignorant?
A. The mature opinion of quality.
B. Quality dominates ahead of traditional belief.
C. Cultural trait justifies any quality standard.
D. Quality consciousness leads to management growth.

7. Why 'Made in Japan' is a symbol of assured quality?
A. Traditional belief
B. Quality consciousness
C. Age old negligence suffering
D. High export offer

PASSAGE-7

Creamy outlook with soft speech presentation is a prima facie attraction that brings joy on the withering faces with a mixture of sensational touch. Smile with grace is the ultimate boon to the mankind keeping away any melancholy at bay. Old age is often miscalculated as liability with little attention paid to them. Their talents and learned potential is buried alive with undue care by oblivious approach due to disfigured or deformed physical structure taken over by aged talents of the society.

It happens to us all, however hard we may try to delay the process. We grow old. Cosmetic surgery may remove the wrinkles, skin which has sagged may be tightened by means of a facelift and hair dresser may dye grey hair a more youthful colour, but we cannot remain young forever.

However, what is important is the quality of life. Some people are lucky to be taken care of at home whereas others may have to move to residential homes. The worst part of ageing is that often the mind becomes less alert. As people grow older, they experience short term memory. Later some may suffer from dementia, often in the form of Alzheimer's disease.

By no means all people are in this category. Many senior citizens are in the possession of all their faculties and see retirement as a time of freedom. Not only that if they have a generous retirement pension, they are likely to be quite well off with money to be spent on a holiday and other luxuries. Because of this, both businesses and government have a new respect for what is known as grey power.

It is unfortunate that many people regard old people as geriatrics who have one foot in the grave. Someone should remind them that they too would be old one day!

They are honoured with senior citizen label granted by the authority with due regard paid from distinct possession of living cadres. One should always bear in mind the old saying "Tit for Tat". Which denotes its symbolic regulation of periodical sufferings. The aforesaid misdoings of emotional disparity, done by striding steps is a curse to the mankind.

QUESTIONS

1. Cosmetic surgery :
A. helps in the retention of youth forever.
B. cannot stop the natural process of ageing.
C. is the solution to ageing.
D. is the fancy of the rich.

2. While ageing man's greatest worry is :
A. his growing wrinkles.
B. his short term memory.
C. his quality of life.
D. moving to a residential home.

3. The government considers grey power as :
A. a liability
B. an asset
C. neither an asset nor a liability
D. a spent force

4. Retirement is seen as a time of freedom because people:
A. no longer have to go to office.
B. can enjoy their earnings.
C. can spend time with their families.
D. finally move into residential homes.

5. *geriatrics* in the passage refers to :
A. handicapped people
B. doctors for the aged
C. a branch of medicine
D. aged people

6. What is the theme of the passage?
A. Old is gold
B. The grey power
C. Youth domination in the society
D. Aged suffering

7. What does the phrase 'suffer from dementia' refer to?
A. Harmful
B. Short term memory loss
C. Lunacy
D. Paralysis

PASSAGE-8

1. The world is teemed with different continents and oceans surrounded with settled and manless island as declared by the geographical experts of the world.
2. Pacific island dominates amongst the oceans escorted with wildlife, ecosphere and mana-geable resources with identified culture of scientific explorations. Man hunt for unseen spheres remains a landmark occasion yearning for lavish search with instrumental approach. Galapagos Islands remind us of such human efforts noted for spherical search with wildhunt.
3. The Galapagos Islands in the Pacific Ocean are a rocky, lonely spot, but they are also one of the most unusual places in the world. The reason is that they are the home of some of the last giant tortoises left on earth.
4. Weighing hundreds of pounds, these tortoises wander slowly around the rocks and sand of the islands. Each of these islands has its own particular kind of tortoise. There are seven different kinds of tortoises on the eight islands.
5. Hundreds of years ago, thousands of tortoises wandered around these islands. All that changed when people started landing there. When people first arrived, their ships had no refrigerators. This meant that fresh food was always a problem for the sailors on board. The giant tortoises provided a solution to his problem.
6. Ships would anchor off the islands, and crew would seize as many tortoises as they could. Once the animals were aboard the ship, the crew would roll the tortoises onto their backs and use them for soups and stews.
7. Human search never ends with seeking variable resources sustainable to their growth-oriented programme. Man hunt with crew supported by voyage turns the pages of historical map to best transformation regions discovered by his hardcore practice. How long 'wants' arrest his peace of mind with the dream of next destination is yet to know with.

QUESTIONS

1. The author calls the Galapagos Islands an unusual place because :
A. they are in the Pacific Ocean.
B. the endangered giant tortoises are found there.
C. they are rocky and lonely spots.
D. they are located off the western coast of South America.

2. Which statement is correct?
A. There is one kind of tortoise found on the seven islands.
B. There are eight kinds of tortoises found on the eight islands.
C. There are seven kinds of tortoises found on the eight islands.
D. All the tortoises are on one island.

3. The giant tortoises provided a solution to the problem of not having refrigerators because :
A. the sailors went looking for refrigerators as they were starving.

B. fresh food was available in plenty as the sea was vast.
C. the fresh giant tortoise could be killed and eaten whenever the sailors were hungry.
D. the sailors seized the tortoise to store in refrigerators.

4. *Ships would anchor off the islands* means that Ships:
A. would go off
B. would be near the shore
C. would be off to another land
D. would go to another island

5. In paragraph 6 the word crew means :
A. the new settlers.
B. the men arriving on Galapagos Islands.
C. the men working on the ships.
D. the men catching the tortoises.

6. Mark the True statement which best suits the passage.
A. Galapagos is the unusual island due to regular plains.
B. People landed at Island duely in search of tortoises.
C. Lack of refrigerators made crew turn to tortoises.
D. Tortoises numbered more than crews on the Island.

7. Soups and stews refers to :
A. soup apart with flesh.
B. soup extracted out of tortoise cooking.
C. tortoise fat.
D. a synthetic process of vegetation.

PASSAGE-9

The goal of the fair, to be held at the Cervantes Institute in the Indian capital, is to attract the largest number of students in order to present them with information on the educational programmes Spain has to offer, primarily postgraduate. Studying in Spain gives students an added advantage of living and studying in one of the world's most important economies that also aims for an internationalisation of its university system, which plays a decisive role in knowledge-based economy.

In this context, the Spanish universities, both private and public, numbering 77 in total, offer Master degrees and PhD programmes adapted to the European Higher Education Area; a harmonised space between all European countries that have opted to participate in this model. This implies that any student that obtains a postgraduate degree in a Spanish university will automatically have their studies recognised in any participating country and may continue their doctoral studies without needing to validate their degree. In addition, Spanish universities are offering more and more postgraduate degrees in English in order to attract international students. Nevertheless, it is also very common for students to come to Spain intending to complete postgraduate studies in Spanish as well. Students are offered a double advantage from, first, studying in high quality university programmes, and second, studying in a rapidly growing language, that will soon reach 500 million speakers. Spanish is also the official language in more than 20 countries and a second language in important economies such as the United States and Brazil, which gives graduates and edge when entering the workforce.

These are just a few reasons why studying in Spain is such a unique opportunity. On February 19 and 20th, Indian students are invited to visit the Cervantes Institute where they can directly ask the universities any and all questions about studying in Spain as well as get information about programmes that the universities offer.

Another incentive for students to attend will be the prize drawing for six intensive Spanish courses at Spanish universities in summer 2011. The six big winners will have air fare, accommodations, and tuition paid for while attending the month-long course.

QUESTIONS

1. The objective of the fair is __________.
A. to tell about Spain
B. to tell about the courses being started in India
C. to impart information about education in Spain
D. none of the above

2. Decisive role means __________.
A. taking decisions
B. important role
C. key role
D. minor role

3. Spanish Universities are offering programmes in English because __________.
A. English is a global language
B. it wants to get students from all over the world
C. English is easy to understand
D. it is easy to get professors to teach in English

4. One of the advantages of studying in Spain is that __________.
A. it is a beautiful country
B. education there is cheap
C. courses are easy
D. Spanish is the second language in some important countries

5. Those who attend the fair __________.
A. will get to participate in a prize draw
B. will be given free air ticket to Spain
C. will get fee waiver for one term
D. none of the above

PASSAGE-10

An incandescent bulb lights up when electrical power heats a metal filament wire to a high temperature until it glows. You usually get them rated between 15 and 100 watts. Meanwhile, fluorescent lamps (tubes and their newer compact versions, known as CFLs) use inert gases inside to fluoresce and produce light. There are also lamps that use an array of light-emitting diodes (LEDs) working in the way electrons behave, a phenomenon called electro luminescence. Because LED lamps are costly, very few homes use them—and it's best to wait a while before buying for their prices to come down, just as you did with CFLs over the past years.

At about ₹ 20 a piece, incandescent bulbs may look cheap, but they are not. They waste some 90 per cent of the power consumed—as heat. Consumers preferred them to energy-efficient fluorescent tubes not just because they are cheaper, but also because you may place them in choice lamp shades. Or because the bluish-white illumination from tubes can seem harsh and unnatural, and may contribute to glare and eyestrain.

If you don't like the way tube lights look in the hall or bedroom, use them only in passages, verandas and the kitchen.

QUESTIONS

1. Bulbs light up when ______.
A. metal filament burns
B. electricity heats up metal filament
C. electric current is in excess
D. metal comes in contact with heat

2. CFLs use ______.
A. gases like Argon, Krypton, etc.
B. mercury
C. thin metal strips
D. any of the above

3. Electro luminescence is the process where ______.
A. electrons and protons react to emit light
B. diodes function as electrons and emit light
C. light is generated by water
D. light is generated by sun

4. Incandescent bulbs are costly because ______.
A. they cost ₹ 20 a piece
B. they break easily
C. their power consumption is high
D. none of the above

5. Bulbs are used because they ______.
A. are cheap
B. conserve energy
C. you can place them in choice lamp shades
D. none of the above

PASSAGE-11

Conservation of water in the agricultural sector is essential since water is necessary for the growth of plants and crops. A depleting watertable and a rise in salinity due to overuse of chemical fertilisers and pesticides have made matters serious. Various methods of water harvesting and recharging have been and are being applied all over the world to tackle the problem. In areas where rainfall is low and water is scarce, the local people have used simple techniques that are suited to their region and reduce the demand for water. In India's arid and semi-arid areas, the 'tank' system is traditionally the backbone of agricultural production. Tanks are constructed either by bunding or by excavating the ground and collecting rainwater.

Rajasthan, located in the Great Indian Desert, receives hardly any rainfall, but people have adapted to the harsh conditions by collecting whatever rain falls. Large bunds to create reservoirs known as khadin, dams called johads, tanks and other methods were applied to check water flow and accumulate run-off. At the end of the monsoon season, water from these structures was used to cultivate crops. Similar systems were developed in other parts of the country. These are known by various local names *jal talais* in Uttar Pradesh, the *haveli* system in Madhya Pradesh, *ahar* in Bihar, and so on.

QUESTIONS

1. There is an increase in water salinity due to ______.
A. conservation of water
B. depletion of water
C. overuse of chemical fertilisers and pesticides
D. water harvesting

2. 'Depleting watertable' means ______.
A. reduction in the groundwater level
B. measurement of water level
C. recharging of water level
D. usage of fertilisers and pesticides

3. In arid and semi-arid regions, rainwater is collected by ______.
A. using industrial methods
B. constructing tanks
C. harvesting of water
D. adapting to the harsh conditions

4. How much rainfall does Rajasthan, the state in the Great Indian Desert, receive?
A. plenty of rainfall B. no rainfall
C. moderate rainfall D. scanty rainfall

5. Where do farmers of Rajasthan get water from to cultivate their crops after the monsoon season?
A. from tanks, bunds, dams and reservoirs
B. from whatever rain that falls
C. from excess rainwater
D. from the rivers

PASSAGE-12

Every family with two or more children often experiences sibling rivalry at one time or the other. Children in general, fight with each other for their parents' attention. They fight among themselves mostly on trivial issues. If it does not get excessive, this kind of rivalry can, in fact, be a healthy competition that trains children to share, respect one another.

They will learn to deal with frustration and displeasures in the maturing process.

The firstborns generally feel that they don't have to share their parents' love and attention. But when the next baby or siblings come along, they feel neglected and that changes everything. The first child starts to feel that he/she is no longer the centre of attraction and that he/she is being sidelined because of the new one. Some children might develop negative feelings and emotional imbalance, which may lead to regressive behaviour.

Such problems could be averted if right moves are taken. One way is to explain the firstborns about the arrival of a new child. They need to establish a connection with the new baby before it is born. Older children should be trained to show a positive attitude towards their siblings. They should be involved, along with their parents, in teaching their siblings social and manual skills, which in turn, helps them to accept them. Sometimes personality differences and parental conflicts too have an impact on the children. Parents have to show patience, understand these issues and should openly communicate with their children to resolve them.

QUESTIONS

1. Sibling rivalry means fight between ______.
   A. firstborn and second child
   B. children of same parents
   C. children born to different parents
   D. cousins and relatives
2. 'Why do firstborns feel neglected by the arrival of a new child in the family?
   A. because they have to share their parents' love and attention
   B. because of their negative attitude
   C. because they hate their siblings
   D. because parents do not love them
3. What does the word 'regressive' in para 2 mean?
   A. emotional imbalance
   B. withdraw or shy away
   C. negative feeling
   D. harsh or rude
4. How can older children develop a positive attitude towards their siblings?
   A. by developing sibling rivalry
   B. by keeping away from their siblings
   C. by their involvement in matters related to the young ones
   D. by dominating their siblings
5. What should parents do to control sibling rivalry?
   A. allow children to fight among themselves
   B. do not allow any communication between children
   C. punish the children
   D. openly communicate with children to resolve issues

PASSAGE-13

Music can have strong consequences on our feelings. One should try to gain benefits from the power of music. Music, in general, helps one to calm down and feel revitalized. It helps to beat a bad mood or to continue a good state of mind. To cheer up or to enhance vitality, one should listen to music with beats, lots of drumming and a fast tempo. When one wants to relax after a busy day, instrumental music with less percussion and a slower rhythm can help. Listening to soothing music before stressful activities has a lot of benefits and so is always advised. A collection of preferred relaxing tunes help to combat stress at work. One can change one's frame of mind by switching from one kind of music to another. To feel refreshed, it is better to start with something tranquil and soothing and to slowly pick up the pace and the beat. But when one prefers to settle down after a busy schedule, follow the reverse style.

Music is an incredible means that people can use to communicate things, especially their feelings and emotions. When added to speech in a song, it becomes a powerful device of communication. Music generally needs special aptitude, inborn talent and rigorous practice. Also, a person needs to have fine muscular strength in order to sing in tune or play a musical instrument. Recollection of the notes demands good memory power. Besides, many people feel that music and love are connected to each other. A person tries to make an impression on his/her love by way of selecting appropriate music.

QUESTIONS

1. Music with fast beats and lots of drumming __________.
   A. boosts up one's energy
   B. calms down one's mind
   C. is less beneficial
   D. leads to stress
2. What does 'percussion' mean?
   A. stressful condition
   B. tranquil mood
   C. thumping or fast beat
   D. inborn talent
3. What kind of music is preferred when a person wants to settle down?
   A. music with lots of percussion
   B. first upbeat music and then soothing music
   C. music of string instruments
   D. first gentle music and then fast music
4. Why is music considered to be a powerful means of communication?
   A. because it helps people to express their emotions
   B. because it is an incredible tool
   C. because it reduces stress at work
   D. because it enhances energy in people

5. What qualities are needed for a person to sing or play a musical instrument?
   A. love, talent, speech and memory
   B. aptitude, emotion, strength and love
   C. knowledge, emotion, love and talent
   D. aptitude, talent, practice and strength

PASSAGE-14

In order to heal your emotional baggage and prevent it from possibly costing you yet another relationship, you must recognise the roots of your emotional pain or fears and acknolwedge your accountability in them.

According to psychologists, one should review the event or experience that you think caused you to be hurt and identify your role in the experience. "Allow yourself to learn from that and forgive yourself—often misplaced guilt can be the cause for fear. Acknowledge that your past does not have to dictate your future. Release all the emotional hurt and fears that were weighing you down and standing in the way of your seeing each individual relationship for its own merit and potential. It can be difficult to let go of the security blanket of past behaviours but assure yourself that you no longer need them. Sometimes one may require professional help to be able to identify, draw links, acknowledge, accept and forgive themselves. In the end, it all comes down to trust. Want to leave that baggage behind? Allow yourself to trust again," concludes a psychologist.

QUESTIONS

1. It is important to understand ________.
   A. pain
   B. emotions
   C. cause of emotional pain
   D. effect of emotional pain
2. It is advised that we should ________.
   A. stop feeling the pain
   B. review the event
   C. take rest
   D. all of the above
3. We should not allow the past ________.
   A. to guide our future
   B. to bother us
   C. actions to make today's decision
   D. to affect our present
4. We should learn to let go ________.
   A. pain
   B. negative emotion
   C. fear
   D. the security of the past
5. The most important thing in life is ________.
   A. trust B. love
   C. compassion D. fear

PASSAGE-15

Maintaining work-life balance is necessary because imbalance wreaks chaos in life. Increased pressure on one side will affect the other side too.

After all, the two cannot be completely dis-connected! The first step towards this is finding the cause for the imbalance.

Some of the potential causes are—you are genuinely overloaded with work, you are incompetent, your time management skills are poor or you chase conflicting goals.

Once you identify the problem, you should admit it and work towards overcoming it. When you are better organised, your efficiency increases. Make a list of activities and prioritise them. This should be done on daily, weekly and monthly basis.

Plan in advance how you will deal with impending additional responsibilities. If you have to spend extra time at the office, inform your family about it and seek their support. If you have to take leave, inform your boss.

When your organisation is going through a change, there is a crisis or you are vying for a promotion, it can be inevitable to spend more time at work. So explore alternative ways to show your loved ones that you care. When you are with your family and friends, make the most of the time. Do not think about work at least during the 'special' time you allotted for them.

Pay attention to your health. Sleep well. Spend time on activities that can help beat fatigue. Allot time for physical exercises, yoga or sports.

QUESTIONS

1. Chaos here means ________.
   A. disturbance B. confusion
   C. happiness D. calmness
2. As soon as we identify the problem we should ________.
   A. work towards overcoming it
   B. forget it
   C. overcome it
   D. none of the above
3. When there is extra work one should ________.
   A. stay up at night B. work from home
   C. plan in advance D. all of the above
4. When one is spending time with family ________.
   A. one should carry work also
   B. one should relax and sleep
   C. one should keep thinking about work
   D. one should not think about work
5. It is important to take care of one's health because ________.
   A. it helps to be positive and chargeable

B. one can do more work
C. work is worship
D. none of the above

PASSAGE-16

You are at a party and want to watch your weight and health. However when the appetisers are served you notice nothing looks healthy. The next thing you know, you go ahead and eat those decorative little morsels and blow your eating plan. Stop!

Those little delicious nuts in that bowl are chock-full of nutrition. They will improve your cardio-vascular health; hold cancer prevention properties and help you lose weight. It's hard to believe but it's true!

The idea that something from nuts may actually help weight control seems a little counter-intuitive at first; bearing in mind the reputation nuts have for being both fatty and fattening. Nuts are nutrient-packed, healthy 'primal' food, and something that experience shows satisfy the appetite and prevent overeating at meal time. High in proteins, unsaturated fats may aid in weight loss and other disease-fighting properties.

What do nuts have that is heart-healthy? Nuts are an intensely fatty food, with about 80 per cent of the calories they offer coming from fat. But bear in mind that the type of oils found in nuts such as almonds, cashews, walnuts is predominantly the healthy monounsaturated and polyunsaturated type.

Researchers found that people who eat nuts regularly have lower risk of heart disease. In 1998, a study conducted by the Harvard School of Public Health found that women who ate nuts less than four times a week were 40 per cent less likely to die of heart disease. Further, potential heart health benefits of nuts were also found among men. In 2002, the Physician's Health Study found that men who consumed nuts two or more times per week had reduced risk of sudden cardiac death.

QUESTIONS

1. Nuts possess ________.
A. nutritive value   B. fattening properties
C. oil   D. all of the above

2. During meal time nuts __________.
A. add taste to the food
B. satisfy appetite
C. should not be consumed
D. create an urge for water

3. Nuts contain ________.
A. unhealthy oils   B. cholesterol
C. healthy oils   D. none of the above

4. People who consume nuts regularly _______.
A. are not prone to heart attacks
B. are prone to heart attacks
C. are not prone to kidney failure
D. are prone to kidney failure

5. Sudden cardiac death means death due to _________.
A. kidney failure
B. sudden heart failure
C. sudden brain malfunction
D. increase in lung pressure

PASSAGE-17

Acupuncture is an ancient form of healing that dates back to Stone Age. It is a technique of inserting and manipulating fine needles into specific points on the body to relieve pain or for therapeutic purposes. Acupuncture originated in China and is most commonly associated with traditional Chinese medicine. As per the traditional Chinese medical theory, acupuncture points are situated on meridians along which 'Qi' (pronounced as 'chee'), the vital energy, flows. Apparently, there is no known histological basis for the existence of acupuncture meridians. Different types of acupuncture such as Classical Chinese, Japanese, Tibetan, Vietnamese and Korean are practised throughout the world.

The practice of acupuncture is based on the understanding that a vital energy flows along channels or meridians throughout our bodies. When this energy becomes blocked or does not flow freely, it causes disharmony or disease. In order to correct this disharmony, the vital force must be stimulated so that it moves freely again. A set of very fine needles are used to stimulate peculiar points located on the flow of energy and the actions of the various acupuncture points to treat diseases and disharmonies in the body. Quite significantly, acupuncture is not usually painful. Acupuncture needles are tiny and are quickly inserted through the skin, where the nerves that transmit pain are located. The sensation of the insertion is like a "quick pinch". In general, there is an agreement that acupuncture is safe when administered by well-trained practitioners using sterile needles and that further research is appropriate.

QUESTIONS

1. Where does vital energy flow through in human bodies?
A. through muscle cells
B. through blood cells
C. through meridians
D. through sense organs

2. How are acupuncture points stimulated?
A. by inserting find needles into specific points on the body
B. by knowing the histological basis
C. by flow of vital energy
D. by going to China

3. A person specialising in the technique of Acupuncture is called ________.

A. a practitioner B. an acupuncturist
C. a classical Chinese D. a medical doctor

4. How is a disease caused as per the traditional Chinese medical theory?
A. when one feels a quick pinch
B. when blood does not flow through the vessels
C. when needles are inserted into specific points
D. when vital energy does not flow freely through meridians

5. Where are the acupuncture needles inserted?
A. in the nerve cells where vital energy flows
B. on the upper part of the right or left hand
C. in the skin where the nerves transmitting pain are found
D. in the muscular part of the hip region

PASSAGE-18

While many of India's parks have been developed from the hunting preserves of princely India, Keoladeo, popularly known as Bharatpur Wildlife Sanctuary, is perhaps the only case where the habitat has been created by a maharaja. In earlier times, Bharatpur town used to be flooded regularly every monsoon. In 1760, an earthen dam, called the Ajam Dam, was constructed, to save the town from this annual vagary of nature. The depression created by extraction of soil for the dam was cleared and this became the Bharatpur Lake.

At the beginning of this century, this lake was developed and divided into several portions. A system of small dams, dykes, sluice gates, etc., was created to control the water level in different sections. This became the hunting preserve of the Bharatpur royalty and also one of the best duck-shooting wetlands in the world. But hunting was prohibited by mid-60s and the area was then declared a national park on 10 March 1982. This was later accepted as a World Heritage site in December 1985.

The major attractions of tourists visiting this park are the numerous migratory birds, which come from as far away as Siberia and Central Asia to spend their winters in Bharatpur, before returning to their breeding grounds. The migratory birds at this bird sanctuary include several species of Cranes, Pelicans, Geese, Ducks, Eagles, Hawks, Shanks, Stints, Wagtails, Warblers, Wheatears, Fly catchers, Buntings, Larks and Pipits, etc.

QUESTIONS

1. Bharatpur Wildlife Sanctuary was developed ________.
A. from the hunting preserves of princely India
B. by constructing Ajam dam
C. by the Maharaja of Bharatpur Royalty
D. from the floods of every monsoon

2. What is the reason behind the construction of Ajam dam?
A. to develop a hunting preserve
B. to develop a wildlife sanctuary
C. to bring an end to floods
D. to save the town from being flooded

3. One of the best duck-shooting wetlands of the world is ________.
A. Princely India B. Bharatpur lake
C. Ajam dam D. Bharatpur royalty

4. When was Bharatpur Lake given the status of a national park?
A. 10 March 1982 B. 10 January 1982
C. 10 December 1985 D. 10 October 1985

5. What are migratory birds?
A. birds from Siberia and Central Asia
B. birds that travel long distances during some seasons
C. birds from Bharatpur Wildlife Sanctuary
D. birds from the hunting preserves of India

PASSAGE-19

Lexicographer : a writer of dictionaries, a harmless drudge, that busies himself in tracing the original, and detailing the signification of words. Thus said Samuel Johnson in his Dictionary, with an ironic swipe at his own work. It wasn't the first dictionary of the English language, but it continued to be regarded as an authoritative if quirky icon of language for more than two centuries. In two volumes and 2,300 pages, Johnson tried to tidy up a notoriously untidy and promiscuous language, though he knew at the same time that it was futile to attempt to straitjacket it. We tend to think of dictionaries as "anonymous" productions, but Johnson's personality is all over the work. In his bitter definition of a patron, "commonly a wretch who supports with insolence, and is paid by flattery", Johnson took care of his own patron, Lord Chesterfield, who had promised to help financially but had not delivered till too late. Since Johnson's Dictionary, which has been reprinted, abridged, and is still written about, there have been books too numerous to count on the English language: Melvyn Bragg's The Adventure of English: The Biography of a Language, the most recent (2004), Raymond Williams' Keywords: A Vocabulary of Culture and Society (1985), one of the most respected. But there are hundreds of others.

QUESTIONS

1. Samuel Johnson made an ironic remark at his own work by calling a lexicographer ________.
A. a harmless drudge
B. a writer of dictionaries
C. one who is busy in tracing the original
D. all the above

2. Johnson's Dictionary __________.
   A. continues to be regarded as an authority on icons
   B. was one of the first dictionaries of English language
   C. was regarded a quirky icon of language
   D. has been printed for more than two centuries

3. Tick the correct statement.
   A. Since Johnson's dictionary many have been reprinted.
   B. Johnson's dictionary has been reprinted and abridged.
   C. Johnson abridged his dictionary many times.
   D. Johnson abridged Melvyn Bragg's 'The Adventure of English'.

4. Which of the following statements are true?
   (1) Johnson's dictionary has two volumes.
   (2) His dictionary defines 'patron' as commonly a wretch who supports with insolence, and is paid by flattery.
   (3) Lord Chesterfield was Johnson's patron.
   (4) Lord Chesterfield did not help Johnson financially.
   A. (1) and (3) are True, (2) and (4) are False.
   B. All are True.
   C. (1), (2) and (3) are True and (4) is False.
   D. (2), (3) and (4) are True and (1) is False.

5. Find a word in the passage that means the same as 'unsuccessful'.
   A. swipe B. insolence
   C. straitjacket D. futile

PASSAGE-20

Swaminathan went to school feeling that he was the worst perjurer on earth. His conscience bothered him : he wasn't at all sure if he had been accurate in his description of Samuel. He could not decide how much of what he had said was imagined and how much of it was real. He stopped for a moment on the roadside to make up his mind about Samuel.... His cane skinned people's hands. Swaminathan cast his mind about for an instance on this. There was none within his knowledge. Years and years ago he was reputed to have skinned the knuckles of a boy in the First Standard and made him smear the blood on his face. No one had actualy seen it. But year after year the story persisted among the boys.... Swaminathan's head was dizzy with confusion in regard to Samuel's character—whether he was good or bad, whether he deserved the allegations in the letter or not.... he felt an impulse to run home and beg his father to take back the letter. But Father was an obstinate man.

As he approached the yellow building he realised that he was perjuring himself and was ruining his teacher. Probably the Headmaster would dismiss Samuel and then the police would chain him and put him in jail. For all this disgrace, humiliation and suffering who would be responsible? Swaminathan shuddered. The more he thought of Samuel, the more he grieved for him. As he felt the bulge of the letter in his pocket, he felt like an executioner.

As he entered the school gate an idea occurred to him, a sort of solution. He wouldn't deliver the letter to the Headmaster immediately, but at the end of the day—to that extent he would disobey his father and exercise his independence. There was nothing wrong in it, and Father would not know it anyway. If the letter was given at the end of the day there was a chance that Samuel might do something to justify the letter.

Swaminathan stood at the entrance to his class. Samuel was teaching arithmetic. He looked at Swaminathan for a moment, Swaminathan stood hoping that Samuel would fall on him and tear his skin off. But Samuel merely asked, 'Are you just coming to the class?'

QUESTIONS

1. Swami was not comfortable going to school that day because __________.
   A. he was not well
   B. he had lied about his teacher Samuel
   C. he had not done his home work
   D. his friend was not there

2. He was not sure about Samuel's character because __________.
   A. what he knew was all hearsay
   B. what he knew was his imagination
   C. other teachers had told him so
   D. none of the above

3. Swami's father was not likely to take back the letter because __________.
   A. he believed that Samuel was a good teacher
   B. his father wanted to help Swami and other children
   C. he was a very stubborn man
   D. all of the above

4. Swami decided to __________.
   A. give the letter to the Headmaster
   B. give the letter directly to Mr. Samuel
   C. tear off the letter
   D. give it to the Headmaster at the end of the school

5. As Swami was late to the school he expected __________.
   A. Mr. Samuel to hit him
   B. Mr. Samuel will allow him into the class
   C. to be shouted at by Mr. Samuel
   D. none of the above

PASSAGE-21

Leadership does not exist without followership. A leader has to be accepted by the group which the former is supposed to lead. To gain acceptability the leader should cause an emotive impact on the group members. The character exhibited by leaders make them dear to their followers. A leader is one who effectively inspires employees to achieve worthwhile goals. What character of the leader motivates the followers? It is not pomp and show or flattery or sanctioning more incentives.

Pomp and show creates a sense of awe and the leader is defied rather than emulated. Flattery is unrealistic and cannot serve as a long-term motivational tool.

A leader's style should be one that can be emulated by all irrespective of cadre, class or calibre. Simplicity in one's day-to-day conduct is the only thing that can be adopted by all. When the leader is simple, he is counted as one belonging to the group of which he is the leader. That's to motivate the people. Motivation is the innate quality that enables an individual or group to contribute unlimitedly with limited means. It is the proud prerogative of enlightened human beings.

QUESTIONS

1. Leadership co-exists with ________.
A. obedience B. followership
C. discipline D. incentives

2. The pre-requisite for the success of a leader is ________.
A. obedience by the group
B. simplicity of the leader
C. acceptability by the group he is supposed to lead
D. strict discipline of the group

3. The leader should cause an emotive impact on the group members as ________.
A. to ensure obedience
B. to enforce discipline
C. to control the group
D. to gain acceptability

4. To inspire employees to achieve long term goals, a leader should not use ________.
A. sanctioning more incentives
B. flattery
C. pomp and show
D. all of the above

5. Find a word having the same meaning as 'emotive' from the words given below:
A. Prerogative B. Enlightened
C. Sensitive D. Proud

PASSAGE-22

We first became aware that something unusual was happening when one of the ship's officers came up to the Chief Engineer, who sat at one table and spoke to him on a low voice. The Chief Engineer at once stood up and with a brief excuse which told us nothing, left the dining room. At first we thought that there had been an accident or that a fire had broken out on board ship, but soon the word went round that a man had been floating in the sea. Then we noticed that the ship had slowed down and was beginning to turn round, with a rather violent motion. Some of the passengers did not wait to finish their meal, but at once rushed upon deck. Others crowded round the portholes, making it impossible for us to eat in comfort. There was such confusion in the dining room that we decided to join those who had come up on deck.

There we learnt that one of the crew had seen a man in the sea some distance from the ship. He had informed the captain who at once ordered the ship to be turned round. We were now only two hundred yards or so from the man and a life boat had already been lowered into the sea. In it there were four sailors, who were sitting ready at the oars, an officer and the ship's doctor. The officer shouted an order and the sailors began to row away the ship. But looking in the same direction as the boat was going, we were able to make out the position of the man in the water. He was clinging to a large piece of wood. At last, after what seemed to us an age the life boat reached the man and two of the sailors pulled him on the boat. This was not at all easy for the sea was rather rough. Then the sailors began to row back to the ship again. The life boat was raised out of the water and the rescued man, wrapped in a blanket was helped out on the deck. Leaning on the arm of the ship's doctor, but still able to walk, in spite of his terrible experience he was led off to the ship's hospital. As he passed along the deck everyone cheered loudly.

QUESTIONS

1. 'We' here refers to ________.
A. the crew members
B. the sailors
C. the passengers of the ship
D. all of the above

2. The Passengers rushed to the back of the ship because ________.
A. the ship was drowning
B. a fire had broken out on board ship
C. a fight had broken up
D. the crew was trying to save a drowning man

3. It was tough for the crew to save the drowning man as ________.
A. the weather was rough
B. the sea was rough
C. the man was unwilling to come along with the sailors
D. the ship had moved ahead

4. Everyone cheered the man loudly as ________.
A. he had saved the drowning man
B. he had informed about the drowning man
C. he had survived a terrible experience
D. he was the doctor who treated the drowning man

5. The words or the phrase in the passage that means 'it came into knowledge' is ________.

A. seem to us an age
B. with a rather violent motion
C. in comfort
D. the word went round

PASSAGE-23

In this world there is no worse nuisance than a boy at the age of fourteen. He is neither ornamental nor useful. It is impossible to shower affection on him as a smaller boy; and he is always getting in the way. If he talks with a childish lisp he is called a baby, and if in a grown-up way he is called impertinent. In fact, talk of any kind from him is resented. Then he is at the unattractive, growing age. He grows out of his clothes with indecent haste: His voice grows hoars and breaks and quivers; His face grows suddenly angular and unsightly. It is easy to excuse the shortcomings of early childhood, but it is hard to tolerate even unavoidable lapses in a boy of fourteen. He becomes painfully self-conscious, and when he talks with elderly people is either unduly forward, or else so unduly shy that he appears ashamed of his own existence.

Yet, it is at this age that in his heart of hearts, a young lad most craves recognition and love; and he becomes the devoted slave of any one who shows him consideration. But none dare openly love him, for that would be regarded as undue indulgence and therefore bad for the boy. So, what with scolding and chiding, he becomes very much like a stray dog that has lost its master.

His own name is the only paradise that a boy of fourteen can know. To live in a strange house with strange people is little short of fortune; while it is height of bliss to receive the kind looks of women and never to suffer their slights.

QUESTIONS

1. The expression 'he is always getting in the way' means that he is __________.
   A. found/seen everywhere you go
   B. behaving in a different way from expected/desired
   C. always troubling others with his undesired ways
   D. he goes where he is asked to
2. A lad of fourteen years of age is resented because __________.
   A. he behaves too childishly
   B. he acts like a grown-up
   C. his behaviour becomes neither of a child nor of a grown-up
   D. he looks troublesome
3. A fourteen-year-old boy becomes self-conscious when __________.
   A. when he is regarded neither as a young nor a grown-up
   B. when he is slighted by elders
   C. when he is not appreciated for his good actions
   D. none of the above
4. The great bliss for such a boy is __________.
   A. to be rewarded for his achievements
   B. to receive the kind glances of women
   C. to have the company of jolly friends
   D. to do what he likes to do
5. The writer's own attitude towards the fourteen-year-old boy is __________.
   A. satirical
   B. sympathetic
   C. indifferent
   D. none of the above

PASSAGE-24

For years, Fukuoka was widely known as the closest city that Japan had to Venice. It might not have enjoyed the splendid architecture, piazzas or the Basilica San Marco of the Italian city, but the people of the largest metropolis on Kyushu, Japan's most southerly main island, prided themselves on the carefully maintained network of rivers that emptied into the graceful curve of Hakata Bay and gave Fukuoka its blue credentials. Today, however, the capital of Kyushu is forging a new identity for itself as green complements the blue.

Not satisfied with pioneering a method of semi-aerobic landfill known the world over as "The Fukuoka Method", the city has gone on to implement some highly exacting rubbish-segregating standards for both homes and businesses. And it has ambitious plans to turn itself into the world's first city to be powered by hydrogen, a project that is under way and will eventually evolve into a "corridor" of homes and businesses linking Fukuoka with the larger cities of Osaka, Nagoya and eventually, the mammoth Tokyo, some 900 kilometres to the rest.

All that and yet Fukuoka is still regarded as the most pleasant place to live in Japan and among the best in the world. In its annual quality of life survey in July 2010, Britain's *Monocle* magazine ranked Fukuoka the 14th "most liveable" city on the planet, thanks in part to its air connections with the rest of Asia, its low crime rate, sub-tropical climate, excellent public transport services and cultural opportunities.

City authorities also received high marks for subsidising local residents who want to install solar-energy systems in their homes to the tune US$1.2 million. Elsewhere, funds have been invested in the creation of green spaces.

QUESTIONS

1. The city of Fukuoka is considered ________.
   A. closest to Venice
   B. different from Venice
   C. Peaceful city
   D. close to Rome
2. Green complements the blue means ________.
   A. green and blue do not go together
   B. green and blue go well with each other

C. If we have green in a place, it is auspicious to have blue there
D. none of these

3. Fukuoka has set very high standards for
A. cleanliness
B. keeping city green
C. separating bash at home as well as work place
D. maintaining clean air

4. Fukuoka is high on the list of the most liveable cities in the world because ________.
A. there is less crime
B. environment is clean
C. excellent connectivity, within and outside the city
D. all of the above

5. Residents of Fukuoka who wish to install solar powered system ________.
A. Know the advantages of the same
B. will be subsidised by the state
C. are encouraged by the government
D. none of these

PASSAGE-25

A tiger relies on stealth to catch its prey. It has excellent eyesight and hearing, which help it track animals in the dark. Tigers hunt large animals such as deer and wild pigs, which will provide food for a few days. They slink up on their prey unseen, only charging when they are within about 20m (65 ft). Tigers kill their prey by biting the back, its neck or throat, then dragging it away into thick cover to feed. When they have eaten enough, they conceal the carcass with leaves so they can return to it later on. Male tigers can eat up to 40 kg (85 lb) of meat in one meal.

Tigers love water and often bathe or cool off in rivers and pools during the heat of the day. They usually hunt at night and rest during the day. Most tigers live alone, although mothers with cubs or young siblings sometimes hunt together. A male tiger roams a territory of up to 100 sq km (60 sq. miles) in area, defining its boundaries with scent markings, droppings and scratch marks on boulders or trees. These signals tell other tigers about its sex and size as well as its territory. Tigers also communicate by roaring and moaning. They defend their territory fiercely against rival males, but will tolerate some overlap with the smaller territories of females.

QUESTIONS

1. Stealth means ________.
A. by cheating
B. secret way
C. attacking from front
D. jumping at the prey

2. Tigers hunt big animals because ________.
A. it is easy to hunt them
B. their meat is tasty
C. the meat will last them a few days
D. they are easily available

3. Tigers drag their prey into the bush ________.
A. so that nobody can disturb them
B. it is cool under a bush
C. other animals may snatch their prey
D. to conceal it

4. During the hot summer season ________.
A. tigers like to cool by staying in water
B. tigers go off to sleep
C. tigers stay under the bush
D. tigers move to cooler areas

5. Tigers prefer to ________.
A. stay in small groups
B. stay alone
C. stay as a family
D. take care of their young one

PASSAGE-26

The Kidneys of nearly five per cent of people under the age of 20 are not functioning normally, a study shows. The youngsters have albumin in the urine, which indicates that they could develop a serious kidney disease later in their lives. Doctors say that more youngsters today are at a risk of kidney malfunction due to lifestyle changes, which includes smoking, consumption of junk food and less physical activity from desk-bound jobs. On the eve of World Kidney Day, doctors are stressing on the early detection of Kidney malfunction as the only way to reduce serious complications and chronic kidney disease.

For the pilot study, the institute of nephrology at a hospital used a home detection kit that is dipped in urine to show presence of protein in the sample. During the study, 1,000 people were given the kits. A total of 265 returned them with feedback. Of this, 5% of the young population had urinary protein.

Doctors say that the main issue with kidney disease is the lack of early detection. If detected early, patients can avoid reaching the stage of dialysis, which indicates irreversible and serious kidney damage. "Simple health screening test comprising urine tests, blood test and ultrasounds are important. Early diagonsis and treatment for kidney disease can significantly delay and even prevent kidney failure and need for dialysis." said doctors. One doctor said home detection kits would help in early detection, and added that they were targeting young people in colleges and IT firms to use this kit.

QUESTIONS

1. As many as ________ of youngsters have kidney problem.
A. 20% B. 5%
C. 22% D. 12%

2. This problem is mainly due to ________.
   A. obesity in youngsters
   B. change in lifestyle
   C. poor intake of water
   D. none of the above
3. The main problem with kidney related disease is ________.
   A. it is fatal
   B. it cannot be treated
   C. it cannot be detected early
   D. it is painful
4. Simple tests will help in ________.
   A. preventing and delaying kidney failure
   B. giving treatment
   C. relieving pain
   D. all of the above
5. Hospitals are targeting colleges and IT firms because ________.
   A. youngsters need it the most
   B. these places have only youngsters
   C. they want to bring down kidney issue among youngsters
   D. all of the above

PASSAGE-27

Global warming this century could trigger a run away thaw of Greenland's ice sheet and other abrupt shifts such as a dieback of the Amazon rainforest, scientists say.

They urged governments to be more aware of "tripping points" in nature, tiny shifts that can bring big and almost always damaging changes such as a melt of Arctic summer sea ice or a collapse of the Indian monsoon.

"Society may be lulled into a false sense of security by smooth projections of global change," the scientists at British, German and American institutes wrote in a report saying there were many little-understood thresholds in nature.

"The greatest and clearest threat is to the Arctic with summer sea ice loss likely to occur long before, and potentially contribute to, Greenland ice sheet melt", they wrote in the journal "Proceedings" of the National Academy of Sciences. "Tipping elements in the tropics, the boreal zone, and west Antarctica are surrounded by large uncertainty", they wrote, pointing to more potential abrupt shifts than seen in a 2007 report by the UN Climate Panel.

A projected drying of the Amazon basin, linked both to logging and to global warming, could set off a dieback of the rainforest. Many of these tipping points could be closer.

Other sudden changes linked to climate change, stoked by human use of fossil fuels, included a dieback of northern pine forests, or a stronger warming of the Pacific under EI Nino weather events that can disrupt weather world-wide, they wrote.

A possible greening of parts of the Sahel and the Sahara, if monsoon rains in West Africa were disrupted, was one of the few positive abrupt shifts identified by the scientists.

Even a moderate warming could set off a thaw of Greenland's ice sheet that could then vanish in 300 years—raising sea levels by 20ft, or 2 meters a century and threatening coasts, Pacific islands and cities from Bangkok to Buenos Aires. The UN Climate Panel foresees a rise in world sea level ranging up to about 80 cms this century and reckons that a thaw of Greenland would take hundreds of years longer.

The new study said a disappearance of Arctic sea ice in summer time could happen in coming decades—earlier than projected by the UN panel. That could stoke further global warming as dark water soaks up more heat than ice and snow.

QUESTIONS

1. Global warming can cause ________.
   A. thawing of green land
   B. excess rain
   C. severe draught
   D. a green earth
2. Nations should be sensitive to small changes that can cause ________.
   A. famine
   B. melting of Arctic ice
   C. decrease in sea level
   D. chill in polar regions
3. There could be a die-back of the rainforest because of ________.
   A. drying of Amazon Basin
   B. water level
   C. ses level
   D. melting glaciers
4. As a result of rains in West Africa ________.
   A. Sahara will turn into desert
   B. Sahara will turn green
   C. flood will come
   D. none of these
5. According to a UN panel report ________ in this century.
   A. sea level will decrease
   B. sea level will remain same
   C. sea level will rise
   D. none of these

PASSAGE-28

1. Music constitutes mood with variable notes of rhythm transformed from any corner to the destination with a view point of sowing seeds of mental relief with sensational pleasure. It allows generations to bear the

pleasure of routing melody of listening lyrics challenging aweful ruckus of mental distress with sweet and melodious voice into individual ears.

Renowned musicians have earned landmark, attribution to the theme of music therapy, woven with classical and orchestral beat of drum sound shakes beat with thrill and pleasure. Music allotes identity to host and listener with keen interest of sweeping away boring and stranded congestion of monotony.

2. A folk singer from Bengal who sings spiritual Baul songs, on hearing a snatch of Blues music remarked, 'That sounds so much like our kind of singing.' Indeed it is possible to hear Baul, Blues and folk rhythms one after another, without feeling any strangeness. Any kind of good music rejuvenates and moves a person and knows no geographical boundaries.

3. This is also the case with instrumental music. A person listening to a Latin American flute could easily be reminded of a plaintive raga composition. The guitar recital of the Latin American guitarist Paco de Lucia could be just as thrilling as a recital by an Indian sitarist playing in full flow. As for percussion, imagine the dance the gods would break into, if African drums were to play alongside the mridangam, tabla and the dholak!

4. There are scores of music lovers around the world who like Elvis Presley's singing as much as the singing of Subbalakshmi. Even in the very interior of India it would not be surprising if someone were to talk of the Las Vegas legend with as much feeling, for it is possible to feel comfortable with specific cultures and yet like the music one has been associated with.

5. Since music allows latitude, it encourages an exhilarating exchange of genres and people. In ancient days Muthuswamy Dikshitar introduced many North Indian ragas into Carnatic music. The late John Higgins 'Bhagavatar', an American, was a distinguished scholar of Carnatic music. Similarly, Kadri Gopalan, an exponent of Carnatic music, plays it on the western saxophone. The Beatles produced some wonderfully popular numbers, such as 'Norwegian Wood', and 'Girl', by infusing elements of Hindustani classical music. Suman Kabir uses the tabla to great effect with his trademark solo guitar. Indeed many Indian musicians and groups display comfort in playing a western melodic rhythm in their music. Bollywood has matured in the nineties to mix melodic traditions. A R Rahman pioneered this new trend. In most of his music he uses African beats and the tabla to good effect.

6. Music has promoted the fusion of genres without compromising the identity of any form. Really good musicians around the world like their creative counterparts in other fields to shuttle into each other's traditions while being rooted in their own. That is what the richness of music really means. That is the kind of music that elevates.

QUESTIONS

1. On the basis of your reading of the passage answer the following questions. Write your answers against the correct blank numbers.

(*i*) List two qualities mentioned by the writer about good music.

(*ii*) What is unique about the music of John Higgins and Kadri Gopalan?

(*iii*) What is A R Rahman's contribution to Indian music?

2. Answer the following notes appropriately. Do not add extra information. Write your answers against the correct blank numbers.

(*i*) Folk music of Bengal __________

(*ii*) Las Vegas legend __________

(*iii*) Latin American guitarist __________

(*iv*) Norwegian wood __________

3. On the basis of your reading the passage answer the following. Write your answers against the correct blank numbers.

(*i*) geographical boundaries refer to (Para 2) __________

(*ii*) latitude in this paragraph means (Para 5) __________

(*iii*) a fusion of genres means (Para 6) __________

PASSAGE-29

1. Mind management is a way to control one's mind. To do this, we need to be cautious about our thinking process and also need a high level of understanding and meditation as well. Understanding is wisdom – 80 per cent of people are knowledgeable, while 20 per cent are wise. Knowledgeable men take sides without reason. They feel sad seeing deprived people but jealous when they see happy people. They work in the guidance of others' inspiration, take unnecessary responsibility to keep themselves disturbed.

2. A wise person does not stand for or against any idea without concrete reason. He works according to the situation and capacity. He looks at everything intellectually. To him, failure is a stepping stone for future success. So depression and conflict are not seen. Like the phrase 'Stop, Look, Go', first one should see, and this needs patience. Meditation is necessary to control and manage mind which then becomes an easy task.

3. Unless we control or manage our mind, it is difficult to achieve success and peace. Psychologists say every interest is first born in the mind as a seed. Then it continues to grow. Later it takes its real form which

everybody can see. The interest that first appears in the mind remains weak for the first three minutes and it becomes strong within the next five minutes. All the negative aspects should be deleted within the first three minutes. If not taken out, they would become stronger later and you can never throw them out. After taking control over the mind, we can control passion, interest and unrest. Mind management is essential for a peaceful, successful and healthy life.

4. The age of computers has thrown us on the escalator of aspirations but has robbed us of simple charms like falling asleep. The compulsions of hectic schedules burden the mind and cause stress. However, the joys that elude us can be regained by practising power meditation. It creates tranquility, simplifies life and cleanses the mind. It helps control indolence, ego and anger and builds confidence and patience. With power meditation, negative thoughts get dissipated and a sense of happiness is achieved.

5. With happiness and spiritual knowledge, one can relearn the meaning of life. The picture of life's journey also becomes clearer. Osho said, "As science is not based on orthodox and blind beliefs and functions only on the principle of cause and effect, similarly power meditation doesn't function on age-old theories or communal thoughts but originates from rational and divine experience. It strives to make an individual free from the confining pressures of daily life".

6. The beauty of meditation is that it is independent of religion. According to modern medical science, combinations of factors like pollutants, imbalanced diet and high aspirations have rendered the human mind restless, thereby making the body perpetually ill.

7. Here is a meditation method, which will enable you to control stress. Sit in the padmasan or sukhasan, cross-legged and erect. Keep your back, spine and neck straight. Keep your eyes closed. Sit in this position for 10 minutes. The method has two stages: for the first five minutes, breathe in slowly, hold it and then release it very slowly. Again, for the next five minutes, breathe and release your breath slowly.

QUESTIONS

1. Answer the following questions briefly:
   (*i*) What is mind management?
   (*ii*) What are the character traits of wise person?
   (*iii*) Why should all negative aspects be deleted within the first three minutes?
   (*iv*) Why do we feel stress in this age of computers?

2. What do the following statement mean :
   (*i*) 'Failure is a stepping stone for future success'.
   (*ii*) 'Mind management is essential for a peaceful, successful and healthy life.'

3. Find words from the passage whose opposites are given below :
   (*i*) to let free [para 1]
   (*ii*) peaceful and calm [para 2]
   (*iii*) strong [para 3]
   (*iv*) complex [para 4]

PASSAGE-30

1. A youngster quit Facebook in December after spending over three years on the social networking site. With that one act, he bid a silent adieu to more than 300 contacts that he had added to his account during the period. Like almost everyone from his "friends' circle," the 20-year-old was a regular on the service; visiting it everyday to post photos and status updates. But last week, a new feature on Facebook called Timeline forced him to reconsider the pros and cons of being on the networking site.

2. 'Everyone has some skeletons in their closet and I am just not comfortable with Facebook digging up and displaying all the facets of my life on a bulletin board,' says this youngster who joined the network in July 2007 while he was in Class11.

3. Facebook, you see, had compressed the time he spent on the site and arranged it in chronological order. And while he initially liked the new, neatly organised scrapbook-like feature, he wasn't happy to reveal posts from the past, those that, until recently, were hidden under layers and layers of recent updates. Just clicking on a date on the timeline could transport his friend back in time and enable them to 'view every embarrassing comment, link or photo he had posted on his profile'.

4. "I think it's a recipe for disaster," he says. "In 2007, I had some wall posts, which seemed appropriate at the time, but now after a lapse of four years, I have moved on and don't want them to be openly displayed for all to see."

5. And he is not alone. Many users, worried about how Facebook activity could possibly affect their offline lives, are choosing to commit 'Facebook suicide'. While some have privacy concerns, others feel that the site that was meant to bring them closer to their friends actually does the opposite – it reduces their friendship to something superficial.

6. "Poking and liking are not enough to keep a friendship going," says a business analyst. Having quit Facebook three years ago, she prefers meeting her 'real' friends face-to-face, instead of reading their trite posts online.

7. "On Facebook, people hype everyday issues including what they ate and where they went on a daily basis," says this analyst who continues to use Twitter.

8. Similarly, an engineering student, quit Facebook last December four years after joining it. One find day, he exported all the data from his account into a little zip file and hit the delete button.

9. "I realised that when it came to my friends who really mattered, I could actually keep in touch with them over the phone or by meeting them in real life," he wrote on his blog.

10. "Facebook had become a time sink and it could not justify the time I spent on it," he says, "I spend more time calling up friends or relatives over the phone now.... I also go out and meet people whenever possible and have a good offline life. I do not regret the change." Today, Facebook has 800 million users of which 37 million are Indian. The site has become an online identity for most, and many of those who decide to quit cannot overcome the withdrawal symptoms and return. Facebook, fully aware of its addictive powers, facilitates this return by allowing users to 'deactivate' their accounts. The option allows members to temporarily disable their accounts, but continues to store their information on its servers so that they can return from their 'break', whenever they wish.

QUESTIONS

1. Answer the following questions briefly.

(*i*) What did this youngster do with his Facebook account and why?

(*ii*) What was this youngster upset about?

(*iii*) Why are people generally not comfortable about their past being revealed?

2. Complete the statements given below.

(*i*) In a period of four years people ________ on.

(*ii*) Facebook suicide means ________.

(*iii*) Instead of bringing friends closer ________.

(*iv*) We generally keep ________ who matter to us.

3. Find words from the passage which mean the same as:

(*i*) the advantages and disadvantages [Para 1]

(*ii*) various aspects of one's life. [Para 2]

(*iii*) complete details of a person [Para 3]

(*iv*) to remove [Pare 4]

III. POETRY

Directions: *Read the following poems carefully and choose the best answer to each question out of the four alternatives and mark it in the Answer Sheet.*

POEM-1

It is an ancient Mariner,
And he stoppeth one of three.
'By thy long grey beard and glittering eye,
Now wherefore stopp'st thou me?
The Bridegroom's doors are opened wide,
And I am next of kin;
The guests are met, the feast is set:
May'st hear the merry din.'

He holds him with his skinny hand,
'There was a ship,' quoth he.
'Hold off! unhand me, grey-beard loon!'
Eftsoons his hand dropt he.

He holds him with his glittering eye —
The Wedding-Guest stood still,
And listens like a three years' child:
The Mariner hath his will.

— *ST Coleridge*

QUESTIONS

1. What is the most potent factor with the Ancient Mariner that enables him to hold the wedding guest?

A. His glittering eye

B. His skinny hand

C. His long grey-beard

D. His starting words.

2. What is the significance of comparing the wedding guest to a three years' child?

A. A three years' child is innocent.

B. He is afraid of a strange man.

C. He is fond of listening to stories.

D. He cannot run away from a grown-up man.

3. Which among the following is not an argument presented by the wedding-guest?

A. The wedding-guest is a close relative of the Bridegroom.

B. His participation in some ceremonies is essential.

C. Merry-making is already going on.

D. Other guests have already arrived.

4. The Ancient Mariner is:

A. A young man

B. A middle-aged man

C. An old man

D. It is not clear from the text

5. The Mariner's story is related to:

A. A ship B. Giants

C. Fairies D. A forest

POEM-2

Shall I hear the lament of the nightingale, submissively lending my ear?

Am I the rose to suffer its cry in silence year after year?

The fire of verse gives me courage and bids me no more to be faint.

With dust in my mouth, I am abject: to God I make my complaint.

Sometimes You favour our rivals then sometimes with us You are free,

I am sorry to say it so boldly. You are no less fickle than we.

(Iqbal: 'Complaint to God')

QUESTIONS

1. What fault does the poet find in God?
   A. God causes misery to people.
   B. He opposes the poet and his companions and favours their opponents.
   C. He is fickle.
   D. He does not care for the poor.
2. What gives courage to the poet?
   A. The song of the nightingale.
   B. The power of poetry.
   C. The sweet smell of the rose.
   D. God's mercy.
3. What is the present mood of the poet?
   A. He is distraught.
   B. He is in a happy mood.
   C. He is in a contemplating mood.
   D. He is talking only frivolously.
4. Why does the poet use the word "lament" for the song of the nightingale?
   A. The nightingale is sad at poet's miserable condition.
   B. It is only teasing the poet.
   C. It seems sad to the poet only.
   D. Proverbially, the nightingale is said to sing sweet but sad songs.
5. In what situation is the rose placed in the poem?
   A. Very advantageous situation.
   B. Helpless situation.
   C. Confusing situation.
   D. Situation of expectation.

POEM-3

'In vain to me the smiling mornings shine,
And reddening Phoebus lifts his golden fire;
The birds in vain and amorous descant join,
Or cheerful fields resume their green attire.
These ears, alas! for other notes repine;
"A different object do these eyes require;
My lonely anguish melts no heart but mine;
And in my breast the imperfect joys expire;"
Yet morning smiles the busy race to cheer,
And new-born pleasure brings to happier men;
The fields to all their wanted tribute bear;
To warm their little loves the birds complain.
"I fruitless mourn to him that cannot hear,
And weep the more because I weep in vain."

— Thomas Gray

QUESTIONS

1. The poet's object in the given poem cannot hear him because:
   A. He has gone deaf.
   B. He does not care for him.
   C. He is awfully busy.
   D. He is dead.
2. What does nature bring to the poet?
   A. A sense of loss
   B. A feeling of joy
   C. A sense of satisfaction
   D. A feeling of charm
3. Why does the poet use the phrase "in vain" so many times?
   A. To tell about the uselessness of his existence.
   B. To tell about the uselessness of beauties of nature and his wails.
   C. To tell about the uselessness of birds' love.
   D. To tell about waste of morning time.
4. What feeling can a keenly observant reader get from a study of the first twelve lines and the last two lines?
   A. A feeling of harmony.
   B. A feeling of amplitude.
   C. A feeling of dichotomy of sense.
   D. A sense of overall satisfaction.
5. What does the morning bring to the "happier men"?
   A. A sense of loss.
   B. A new joy.
   C. A feeling of sorrow.
   D. A feeling of sympathy.

POEM-4

'Turn on the prudent Ant thy heedless eyes,
Observe her labours, Sluggard, and be wise;
No stern command, no monitory voice,
Prescribes her duties, or directs her choice;
Yet, timely provident, she hastes away
To snatch the blessings of a plenteous day;
When fruitful Summer loads the teeming plain,
She crops the harvest, and she stores the grain.
How long shall sloth usurp thy useless hours,
Unnerve thy vigour, and enchain thy powers?
While artful shades thy downy couch enclose,
And soft solicitation courts repose,
Amidst the drowsy charms of dull delight,
Year chases year with unremitted flight,
Till Want now following, fraudulent and slow,
Shall spring to seize thee, like an ambush'd foe.

— Dr Samuel Johnson

QUESTIONS

1. What can be said to be the overwhelming quality of an ant?
   A. Industriousness
   B. Dutifulness
   C. Time-consciousness
   D. Regular routine
2. What will finally overtake a sluggard?
   A. Sloth B. Waste of time
   C. Loss of energy D. Want
3. What does the Ant do in summer?
   A. It enjoys the beauties of nature.
   B. It sits in the shade of trees.
   C. It fills its stores with grain.
   D. It spends time eating summer fruits.
4. Which among the following is not the characteristic of Want?
   A. Fraudulence
   B. Ambush
   C. Springing over the enemy.
   D. Abusing the enemy.
5. What is the main characteristic of summer?
   A. It is a very hot season.
   B. It is a fruitful season.
   C. It expects all to do their duties.
   D. It always comes on time.

POEM-5

On their own feet they came, or on shipboard,
Camel-back, horse-back, ass-back, mule-back,
Old civilisations put to the sword.
Then they and their wisdom went to rack;
No handiwork of Callimachus,
Who handled marble as if it were bronze,
Made draperies that seemed to rise
When sea-wind swept the corner stands:
His long lamp-chimney shaped like the stem
Of a slender palm, stood but a day;
All things fall and are built again,
And those that build them again are gay.

— WB Yeats

QUESTIONS

1. Which of the following means of transport was not used by the destroyers of old civilizations?
   A. By sea
   B. By air
   C. On the backs of animals
   D. On foot
2. What is the eternal law of life?
   A. Destruction and recreation
   B. Destruction
   C. Creation
   D. Failure of art
3. Which of the following could Callimachus do?
   A. Make a long thin lamp-chimney last long.
   B. Engrave in bronze.
   C. Make metallic artefacts.
   D. Work with marble without breaking it.
4. Is there no hope for civilizations?
   A. Yes, there is.
   B. No, there's none.
   C. The poet gives no clue to it.
   D. There is only a little hope.
5. Who get real happiness from their activity?
   A. The destroyers. B. The builders.
   C. The observers. D. The sea-creatures.

POEM-6

I lay in sorrow, deep *distressed*:
My *grief* a proud man heard;
His looks were cold, he gave me gold
But not a kindly word,
My sorrow passed—I paid him back
The gold he gave to me;
Then stood *erect* and spoke my thanks
And blessed his *Charity.*
I *lay* in *want,* in grief and pain:
A poor man passed my way;
He bound my head, he gave me *bread*
He watched me night and day.
How shall I pay him back again,
For all he did to me?
Oh, gold is great, but greater far
Is *heavenly* Sympathy!

—Charles Mackey

QUESTIONS

1. The proud man heard the poet
   A. crying in sorrow B. sing in joy
   C. lying in misery D. crying due to pain
2. The proud man helped the poet by
   A. giving him comfort
   B. assisting him to lie down
   C. his cold looks
   D. giving him gold
3. The poet thanked the proud man by
   A. speaking nicely to him

B. giving him money
C. praising him
D. blessing his large-heartedness

4. The poor man helped the poet by
A. giving him comfort
B. binding his body
C. giving him food
D. serving him like his own

5. The word 'heavenly' means
A. relating to paradise
B. like that of heaven
C. like angels
D. like gods

POEM-7

The earth was green, the sky was blue;
I saw and heard one sunny *morn*
A *skylark hang* between the two,
A singing *speck* above the corn.
A stage below in gay *accord*,
White butterflies danced on wing,
And still the singing skylark *soared*,
And silent sank and soared to sing.
The *cornfield stretched* a *tender* green
To right and left beside my walks;
I knew he had a nest unseen
Somewhere among the million *stalks*.
And as I *paused* to hear his song
While swift the sunny moments *slid*,
Perhaps his *mate* sat listening long,
And listened longer than I did.

—Christina Rossetti

QUESTIONS

1. The skylark sang when
A. it rained
B. the sun shone
C. the earth was green and the sky without clouds
D. there were clouds

2. The skylark while singing looked like
A. a star B. an insect
C. an eagle D. a small dot

3. The skylark rose upwards and upwards
A. while flying B. while singing
C. as it sang D. as it flew

4. The nest of the skylark was
A. in the fields below
B. among the numberless stems of corn
C. beside other nests
D. among trees

5. The word 'paused' means
A. stopped B. stood erect
C. flew across D. went straight

POEM-8

The Forst *performs* its secret *ministry*,
Unhelped by any wind. The owlet's cry
Came loud—and *hark*, again! loud as before.
The *inmates* of my cottage, all at rest,
Have left me to that *solitude*, which suits
Abstruser musings : save that at my side
My *cradled infant slumbers* peacefully.
Tis calm indeed! so calm, that it disturbs
And *vexes meditation* with its strange
And extreme silentness ......

—S.T. Coleridge

QUESTIONS

1. The 'secret ministry' of the frost is that
A. it is falling on the ground
B. it ministers the earth
C. it has a secret deal with the nature
D. it deals with the air

2. There is silence all round. This is seen in the phrase
A. and hark, again B. all at rest
C. that solitude D. Abstruser musings

3. Who is sleeping in the cradle?
A. the poet's son B. the poet's child
C. the poet's nephew D. a stranger baby

4. What disturb(s) the calm?
A. the surroundings B. nature
C. weather D. calmness

5. The word 'meditation' means
A. prayers B. thought
C. deep thought D. deep ideas

POEM-9

She *dwelt* among the *untrodden* ways
Beside the springs of Dove,
A Maid whom there were none to praise
And very few to love :
A *violet* by a *mossy* stone
Half hidden from the eye!
—*Fair* as a star, when only one
Is shining in the sky.
She lived unknown, and few could know
When Lucy *ceased* to be;
But she is in *grave*, and, oh,
The difference to me!

—William Wordsworth

QUESTIONS

1. Lucy lived a lonely life because
A. no person loved her
B. no one praised her
C. there was no human population
D. she was born in nature

2. Lucy was like a
A. rose flower B. a star
C. a violet flower D. a daffodil

3. She died on unknown death because
A. no one knew her
B. no one could tell where she died
C. she was never known
D. no one knew when she died

4. That the poet is sad over Lucy's death is clear in the words :
A. she is in grave
B. oh
C. the difference to me
D. Lucy ceased to be

5. The word 'untrodden' means
A. not covered B. unwalkable
C. not walked over D. hard to walk

POEM-10

I wandered lonely as cloud
That *floats* on high o'er *vales* and hills,
When all at once I saw a crowd,
A *host* of golden daffodils ;
Beside the lake, beneath the trees,
Fluttering and dancing in the breeze.
Continuous as the stars that shine
And *twinkle* in the milky way,
They *stretched* in never-ending line
Along the *margin* of a *bay* :
Ten thousasnd saw I at a *glance*,
Tossing their head in *sprightly* dance.
The waves beside them danced; but they
Outdid the *sparkling* waves in *glee* :
A poet could not but be gay,
In such a *jocund* company;
I *gazed*—and gazed—but little thought
What wealth the show to me had brought.
For oft, when on my couch I lie
In vacant or in *pensive* mood,
They *flash* upon that inward eye
Which is the bliss of *solitude*;
And then my heart with pleasure fills
And dances with the daffodils.

—William Wordsworth

QUESTIONS

1. The poet compares himself with
A. a cloud that is rainy
B. a cloud
C. a floating cloud
D. a daffodil

2. The daffodils danced
A. like stars
B. beside the lake
C. like twinkling stars
D. in lake water

3. The daffodils made the waves shy in their
A. dancing B. shining
C. sparkling D. shaking

4. The poet's wealth from daffodils is
A. the bliss of solitude
B. their dancing
C. their bright colour
D. his joyful heart

5. The word 'sprightly' means
A. happy B. blissful
C. joyful D. playing

POEM-11

Is this a holy thing to see
In a rich and fruitful land,
Babes reduc'd to *misery,*
Fed with cold and *usurous* hand?
Is that *trembling* cry a song?
Can it be a song of joy?
And so many children poor?
It is a land of poverty?
And their sun does never shine,
And their fields are *bleak and bare,*
And their ways are fill'd with thorns :
It is *eternal* winter there.
For where'er the sun does shine,
And where'er the rain does fall,
Babes can never hunger there,
Nor poverty the mind *appall.*

—William Blake

QUESTIONS

1. 'Rich and fruitful land' stands for
A. U.S.A. B. England
C. India D. China

2. Babies there sing a song with
A. joy B. trembling hands
C. a trembling cry D. sadness

3. If the babies live a miserable life, that country is indeed a country of
   A. sick children   B. happy children
   C. poor children   D. hungry children
4. 'It is eternal winter there' means
   A. children's life is not happy
   B. children's future is bleak
   C. winter is all the year around
   D. winter is at the peak
5. The word 'usurous' means
   A. of zamindar
   B. very cruel
   C. of money lender
   D. of trader

POEM-12

There was a family of rabbits
who lived near a *pack* of wolves.
The wolves *announced* that they did
not like the way the rabbits were
living. One night several wolves were
killed in an earthquake and this was
blamed on the rabbits, for it
is well known that rabbits *pound*
on the ground with their *hind*
legs and cause earthquakes. On
another night one of the wolves was
killed by a bolt of *lightning*
and this also was blamed on the
rabbits. The wolves *threatened* to *civilise* the
rabbits if they didn't behave, and
the rabbits decided to run away
to a desert island. But the other
animals, who lived at a great distance,
shamed then saying, "You must stay where
you are and be brave. This is no world
for escapists. If the wolves attack you,
we will come to your aid, in all
probability." So the rabbits continued
to live near the wolves. And one day
there was a *terrible* flood which
drowned a great many wolves. This was
blamed on the rabbits, for it is
well known that they with long
ears cause floods. The wolves *descended* on
the rabbits for their own good,
and imprisoned them in a dark *cave,*
for their own protection.
When nothing was heard about
the rabbits for some weeks, the other
animals demanded to know what
had happened to them. The wolves
replied that the rabbits had been
eaten and since they had been
eaten the affair was a purely
internal matter.
"They were trying to escape" said
the wolves, "and, as you know, this
is no world for escapists."

—James Thurber

QUESTIONS

1. Rabbits do an activity that is similar to earthquakes. It is
   A. moving the soil
   B. causing earthquakes
   C. shaking their hind legs
   D. striking the ground
2. The second time wolves died due to
   A. electricity   B. lightning
   C. floods   D. earthquakes
3. The other animals advised the rabbits not to go away because
   A. they shouldn't be affraid of wolves
   B. there was no fear
   C. they must be brave
   D. they should oppose the wolves
4. The lesson of the incident is that those who escape
   A. can't live
   B. can't progress
   C. shall be free from danger
   D. shall lag behind
5. The word 'announced' means
   A. went away   B. spoke
   C. whistled   D. declared

POEM-13

The countryside must *preserved*
(Preferably miles away from me.)
Neat hectares of the *stuff* reserved
For those in need of flower or tree.
I'll make do with *landscape* painting
Film *documentaries* on TV
And when I need to escape, *panting,*
Then open-mouthed I'll head for the sea.

Let others *stroll* and take their *leisure,*
In grasses wade upto their knees.
For I *derive* no earthly pleasure
From the green green *rash* that makes me *sneeze.*

—Roger McGough

QUESTIONS

1. The poet feels that the countryside should look
A. green
B. covered with vegetation
C. full of flowers
D. good with trees

2. The poet would like to satisfy himself of his desire to see nature from
A. films B. documentaries
C. TV D. cable TV

3. The poet gets immense pleasure when he is far from
A. natural beauty
B. countryside
C. villageside
D. film documentaries

4. The poet hates the greenery because it makes him
A. sick B. dissatisified
C. a nature lover D. sneeze

5. The word 'landscape' means
A. a scene of nature
B. physical scene of a place
C. nature beauty
D. vegetation

POEM-14

One infant grows up and becomes a *jockey;*
Another plays basketball or hockey,
This one the prize ring hates to enter
That one becomes a *tackle or center,*
I am just as glad as glad can be
That I'm not them, that they're not me.
With all my heart do I admire
Athletes who *sweat* for fun or hire,
Who take the field in *gaudy pomp,*
And *maim* each other as they *romp,*
My *limp and bashful spirit* feeds
On other people's *heroic deeds.*
Now A runs ninety yards to score,
B knocks the champion to the floor.
C risking *vertebrae and spine,*
Lashes his steed across the line,
You'd think my *ego* it would please
To *swap* positions with one of these.
Well, ego might be pleased enough,
But zealous athletes play so rough,
They do not ever, in their dealings
Consider one another's feelings.
I'm glad that when my struggle begins
Twixt prudence and ego, prudence wins.
Athletes, I'll drink to you
Or eat with you,
Or anything except compete with you,
Buy tickets worth their weight in *radium,*
To watch you *gambol* in a stadium.
And reassure myself anew
That you're not me and I'm not you.

—Ogden Nash

QUESTIONS

1. The poet admires the sportspersons who
A. win the game
B. perspire for goals
C. beat other participants
D. enjoy playing

2. The poet's spirit enjoys
A. the great sport feats of the players
B. seeing them getting injured
C. knocking one another of sportspersons
D. their fighting for the goal

3. What makes the poet not to be a sportsperson?
A. hatred to be a player
B. wisdom to avoid playing
C. fear of injuries
D. careless playing leading to injuries

4. The poet will do anything
A. to see the players playing
B. to go to the stadium
C. for the sportspersons
D. for the well-being of the players

5. The word 'prudence' means
A. athletics B. wisdom
C. skill D. bravery

POEM-15

The *fair breeze* blew, the white foam flew,
The *furrow* followed free;
We were the first that ever burst
Into that silent sea.
Down dropt the breeze, the sails *dropt* down,
T was sad as sad could be;
And we did speak only to break
The silence of the sea!

All in a hot and copper sky,
The bloody Sun, at noon,
Right up above the mast did stand,
No bigger than the Moon.
Day after day, day after day,
We *struck*, nor breath nor motion;
As *idle* as a painted ship
Upon a painted ocean.

—S.T. Coleridge

QUESTIONS

1. The weather became fine and this is clear from
   A. the wind blowing very fast
   B. the wind blowing leisurely
   C. the furrow being free
   D. the white foam
2. But soon the weather became very bad as
   A. the ship couldn't move
   B. the sails couldn't gather wind
   C. they became sad
   D. they couldn't speak
3. The sky became
   A. very hot
   B. bloody
   C. hot and copper like
   D. very perspiring
4. The ship looked like a painted one because it
   A. couldn't run B. couldn't move
   C. got fully aground D. got anchored
5. The word 'mast' means
   A. a pillar
   B. sailing prop
   C. upright post in a ship
   D. upright post of wood in a ship

POEM-16

The old priest Peter Gilligan
Was *weary* night and day;
For half his *flock* were in their beds,
Or under green *sods* lay.
Once while he *nodded* on a chair,
At the *moth-hour* of *eve*,
Another poor man sent for him,
And he began to *grieve*.
"I have no rest, nor joy, nor peace,
For people die and die";
And after cried he, "God forgive!
My body *spake,* not I!"
He knelt, and *leaning* on the chair
He prayed and fell asleep;
And the moth-hour went from the fields,
And stars began to *peep*.
"*Mavrone,* mavrone! The man has died
While I slept on the chair";
He *roused* his horse out of its sleep,
And rode with little care.
He rode now as he never rode,
By rocky *lane and fern*;
The sick man's wife opened the door :
"Father! You come again!"
"And is the poor man dead?" he cried.
"He died an hour ago."
The old priest Peter Gilligan
In grief *swayed to and fro*.
"When you were gone, he turned and died
As merry as a bird."
The old priest Peter Gilligan
He knelt at that word.

—W.B. Yeats

QUESTIONS

1. Peter Gilligan was very tired because he
   A. had not slept for long
   B. had been serving the people day and night
   C. nursed the sick
   D. cared much for his own people
2. He worried much because
   A. his people were dying
   B. he had had no sleep
   C. his own people were sad
   D. the poor man came to him
3. He regretted that the man died
   A. when he had slept
   B. when it was midnight
   C. when no one was near him
   D. when he slept
4. Father Gilligan found when he visited the poor man's house that
   A. God had visited in his place
   B. God had excused him
   C. he was not wanted
   D. he couldn't do anything
5. The word 'moth-hour' means
   A. late evening B. midnight
   C. morning D. mid-day

POEM-17

It takes much time to kill a tree,
Not a simple *job* of the knife
Will do it. It has grown
Slowly *consuming* the earth,

Rising out of it, feeding
Upon its *crust, absorbing*
Years of sunlight, air, water,
And out of its *leprous hide*
Sprouting leaves.
So *hack and chop*
But this alone won't do it.
Not so much pain will do it.
The bleeding *bark* will heal
And from close to the ground
Will rise *curled green twigs,*
Miniature boughs
Which if unchecked will expand again
To former size.
No,
The root is to be pulled out
Out of the *anchoring* earth;
It is to be roped, tied,
And pulled out—*snapped out*
Or pulled out *entirely,*
Out from the earth-cave,
And the strength of the tree *exposed,*
The source, white and wet,
The most sensitive, hidden
For years inside the earth.
Then the matter
Of *scorching* and *choking*
In sun and air,
Browning, hardening,
Twisting, withering,
And then it is done.

—Gieve Patel

QUESTIONS

1. The tree has come out of the earth after
   A. taking breath in the atmosphere
   B. using the soil
   C. feeling the heat of the sun
   D. absorbing the crust.
2. If the tree is chopped, it will still
   A. live B. wither
   C. stand D. heal
3. If the tree is chopped, its leaves will
   A. glisten
   B. grow to their former size
   C. will rise from the ground
   D. shine beautifully
4. The 'white and wet' part of a tree when uprooted is its
   A. source B. sensitive part
   C. life D. important part
5. The word 'hidden' means
   A. clear B. obscure
   C. safe D. concealed

POEM-18

The quality of mercy is not *strain'd*;
It droppeth as the gentle rain from heaven
Upon the place beneath. It is twice blest.
It blesseth him that gives and him that takes.
T is *mightiest* in the mightiest; it *becomes*
The *throned monarch* better than his *crown*;
His *sceptre* shows the force of *temporal* power,
The *attribute* to *awe* and *majesty,*
Wherein doth sit the *dread* and fear of kings;
But mercy is above this sceptred *sway,*
It is enthroned in the hearts of kings,
It is an attribute to God himself;
And earthly power doth then show likest God's
When mercy *seasons* justice.

QUESTIONS

1. Mercy is compared with
   A. rain B. king
   C. monarch D. gentle rain
2. Mercy adds more glory to a
   A. king
   B. monarch
   C. monarch's crown
   D. monarch sitting in his throne
3. When does mercy becoem God-like?
   A. when it enters a king's heart
   B. when it mixes with the king's grace
   C. when it is seasoned with justice
   D. when mercy seasons a king's justice
4. What shows the temporal power of a monarch?
   A. his throne B. his mercy
   C. sceptre D. his crown
5. The word 'attribute' means
   A. quantity B. quality
   C. absolute D. feature

POEM-19

Whose *woods* these are I think I know,
His house is in the village thought,
He will not see me stopping here
To watch his woods fill up with snow.
My little horse must think it *queer*

To stop without a farmhouse near
Between the woods and frozen lake
The darkest evening of the year.
He gives his *harness bells* a shake
To ask if there is some mistake.
The only other sound's the sweep
Of easy wind and *downy flake.*
The woods are lovely; dark and deep,
But I have promises to keep,
And miles to go before I sleep,
And miles to go before I sleep.

QUESTIONS

1. The poet is standing
A. in a village
B. on the bank of a river
C. in a forest
D. by the side of a lake

2. When the poet stands, the horse
A. shakes its harness bells
B. shakes the bells
C. stands silently
D. asks a question

3. What kind of a weather is it?
A. wet and cloudy
B. cold and snowy
C. very cold and windy
D. cold and windy

4. '... before I sleep' means here
A. before I sleep on my bed
B. before I die
C. before I go home and sleep
D. before I 'sleep' at one level and before I 'die' at another

5. The words 'downy flake' mean
A. soft particles of snow
B. soft snow
C. fluffy snow
D. soft and fluffy

POEM-20

The little creature
with a hundred feet
was on its journey
to where
only it knew.
My civilised foot
dressed in polished leather
came down upon it
even so gently
there was only a soft sound
signifying
the end
of a creature of God
my Maker
I looked to see
if my *sole* was *spoiled*
and walked away

QUESTIONS

1. '... with a hundred feet' actually means
A. a hundred feet
B. many feet
C. about a hundred feet
D. near about a hundred feet

2. The poet calls his foot 'civilised' because he
A. means it otherwise
B. is civilised
C. is wearing polished shoes
D. looks civilised

3. This poem can be classified as
A. humorous
B. religious
C. satirical
D. romantic

4. The poet walked away. It means he
A. didn't bother about the death of the centipede
B. remained indifferent towards the centipede's death
C. regetted the centipede's death
D. felt pity for the insect

5. The word 'signifying' here means
A. displacing
B. indicating
C. making it important
D. proving

POEM-21

I take it you already know
Of tough and bough and cough and dough?
On hiccough, thorough, laugh and through?
Well done! And now you wish perhaps.
To learn of these familiar traps?
Beware of heard, a dreadful word,
That looks like beard and sounds like bird,
And dead : it's said like bed, not bead
For goodness'sake, don't call it deed!
Watch out for meat and great and threat,
They rhyme with suite and straight and debt.
A moth is not a moth in mother
Nor both in bother, broth in brother,
And here is not a match for there,
Now dear and fear for bear and pear,
And then there's does and rose and lose—
Just look them up and goose and choose,...

QUESTIONS

1. Below is a summary of the poem. Complete it by writing the missing word/phrase against the correct blank numbers.

   The poet is talking about the (*i*) ________ of words in English. He concludes that the reader knows how to say certain words and wants to learn the familiar words in the language. He takes up words like 'heard'; 'dead' 'meat'; great; and (*ii*) ________ in the same way. He points out that the word 'moth' is said in the same way in (*iii*) ________ and (*iv*) ________ does not match the sound of there. Finally he asks the reader to look up (*v*) ________.

2. On the basis of your reading the poem, fill in the pronunciations mentioned, against the blank. Write your answers against the correct blank numbers.

   (*i*) ________ is pronounced as in bed broth is not pronunced as in (*ii*) ________. While dear and fear sound as ________.

POEM-22

Will no one tell me what she sings?
Perhaps the plaintive numbers flow
For old, unhappy, far-off things,
And battles long ago:
Or is it some more humble lay,
Familiar matter of to-day?
Some natural sorrow, loss, or pain,
That has been, and may be again?

—William Wordsworth

QUESTIONS

1. Why does the poet seem to be so much puzzled?
2. What type of song is the girl singing according to the poet?
3. About what can the girl's song be?
4. What is the rhyme scheme of the given lines?
5. Do you think the poet really enjoyed the girl's song even if he couldn't understand it?
6. What title would you like to give to poet's such enjoyment of a song without its dialect and theme?

POEM-23

Death be not proud, though some have called thee
Mighty and dreadfull, for, thou art not soe,
For, those, whom thou think'st, thou dost overthrow,
Die not, poore death, nor yet canst thou kill mee;
From rest and sleepe, which but thy pictures bee,
Much pleasure, then from thee, much more must flow,
And soonest our best men with thee doe goe,
Rest of their bones, and soules deliverie.
Thou art slave to Fate, chance, kings, and desperate men,
And dost with poyson, warre, and sicknesse dwell,
And poppie, or charmes can make us sleepe as well,
And better than thy stroake; why swell'st thou then?
One short sleepe past, wee wake enternally,
And death shall be no more, Death thou shalt die.

—John Donne

QUESTIONS

1. What have some called death?
2. Why does the poet say that those whom death claims to kill, actually do not die?
3. What are the pictures of death?
4. To whom is death a slave?
5. With whom does death dwell?
6. How does a person seem to die?

POEM-24

I am silver and exact. I have no preconceptions.
Whatever I see I swallow immediately
Just as it is, unmisted by love or dislike.
I am not cruel, only truthful.
The eye of a little god, four-cornered.
Most of the time I meditatie on the opposite wall.
It is pink, with speckles. I have looked at it so long.
I think it is a part of my heart. But it flickers.
Faces and darkness separate us over and over.
Now I am a lake. A woman bends over me,
Searching my reaches for what she really is.
Then she turns to those liars, the candles or the moon.
I see her back, and reflect it faithfully.
She rewards me with tears and an agitation of hands.
I am important to her. She comes and goes.
Each morning it is her face that replaces the darkness.
In me she has drowned a young girl, and in me an old woman
Rises toward her day after day like a terrible fish.

Directions : *Read the given lines of poem in each question-set and answer the questions that follow.*

1

I am silver and exact. I have no preconceptions.
Whatever I see I swallow immediately
Just as it is, unmisted by love or dislike.

Multiple Choice Questions

Q.1. The poetic device used in these lines is
A. Simile
B. Metaphor
C. Irony
D. Personification

Ans. D. Personification

Q.2. 'I am silver and exact' means
A. I stand for truth only
B. I am only truthful
C. I am like a silver
D. I am precious like silver

Ans. B. I am only truthful

Q.3. 'I have no preconceptions' means
A. I have no pre-thoughts
B. I am not biased
C. I stand for nobody
D. I am myself

Ans. A. I have no pre-thoughts

Comprehension Questions

Q.1. Explain : 'I have no preconceptions'.

Ans. It means that the mirror has no pre-thoughts or biased attitude about anything. It is simply exact, truthful and only truthful and nothing else.

Q.2. Which figure of speech is used in 'I swallow'?

Ans. It is 'personification'.

Q.3. Who is the speaker?

Ans. The speaker is the mirror.

2

I am not cruel, only truthful.
The eye of a little god, four-cornered.

Multiple Choice Questions

Q.1. The poetic device used in these lines is
A. Personification B. Metaphor
C. Alliteration D. Simile

Ans. A. Personification

Q.2. 'I am not cruel ......' means
A. I am not mercy
B. I have the capacity to pity
C. I am pitiless
D. I am not indifferent

Ans. B. I have the capacity to pity

Q.3. 'The eye of a little god' means
A. the speaker acts like a god
B. the speaker can be a god
C. the mirror sees things like a little god
D. the god's presence

Ans. C. the mirror sees things like a little god

Comprehension Questions

Q.1. Who does the 'I' refer to?

Ans. 'I' refers to the mirror.

Q.2. Do you think that the mirror is cruel?

Ans. No, the mirror is not cruel but it is only truthful and reflects what it sees.

Q.3. Why has the mirror been called a 'four-cornered god'?

Ans. It has been called so because like a god it watches one fairly. Also it watches one without any preeconceptions.

3

Most of the time I meditate on the opposite wall.
It is pink, with speckles. I have looked at it so long.
I think it is a part of my heart. But it flickers.
Faces and darkness separate us over and over.

Multiple Choice Questions

Q.1. 'It is pink, with speckles' stands for
A. the mirror B. the wall
C. the woman D. the housekeeper

Ans. B. the wall

Q.2. The mirror doesn't meditate actually but
A. is fixed on the wall
B. has become a part of the wall
C. is shown as meditating impliedly
D. looks at things

Ans. C. is shown as meditating impliedly

Q.3. 'Faces and darkness' separate the mirror from
A. the other wall B. the lady
C. the little girl D. the housewife

Ans. A. the other wall

Comprehension Questions

Q.1. How does 'I' meditate on the opposite wall?

Ans. 'I', the mirror, is fixed permanently on the wall. So it rests there day and night and it seems that to be in this state it is involved in deep thinking.

Q.2. How has the wall become a part of the speaker?

Ans. The wall and mirror have become a single thing because the mirror has been fixed permanently on it.

Q.3. Explain : 'But it flickers'.

Ans. By 'it' the mirror means the wall on which the mirror has been fixed. When it moves from this to that side, it shows the wall shaking showing that it flickers it.

4

Now I am a lake. A woman bends over me,
Searching my reaches for what she really is.
Then she turns to those liars, the candles or the moon.
I see her back, and reflect it faithfully.

Multiple Choice Questions

Q.1. The mirror is 'a lake' as it
A. is deep and acts like it
B. reflects the objects and is deep
C. shows the objects
D. reflects the water

Ans. B. reflects the objects and is deep

Q.2. The woman looking at the mirror searches for
A. her beauty that once she had
B. her own identity
C. the reflection of the wall
D. her own body

Ans. A. her beauty that once she had

Q.3. 'The candles or the moon' stand for
A. objects giving out dim light
B. objects showing the beauty of things
C. objects seen by the woman
D. those things that enhance beauty.

Ans. A. objects giving out dim light

Comprehension Questions

Q.1. How is the mirror 'a lake'?

Ans. The mirror is 'a lake' in its action. When the old woman looks at her face into the mirror, she is amazed to look at her old face. She moves this or that way to see her youthful face that she once had. But it has now 'swallowed' or 'drowned' that face.

Q.2. How does the woman behave before the mirror?

Ans. The woman is wonderstruck to see that now she has grown old and she doesn't want to see it. So she searches the mirror to see her young face with the help of the candle or moonlight.

Q.3. How are 'candles or the moon' liars?

Ans. 'Candles and the moon' are liars in the sense that in their misted light the woman can't see her old age. Besides, they help the woman in hiding the wrinkles etc, from her face in the mirror.

5

She rewards me with tears and an agitation of hands.
I am important to her. She comes and goes.
Each morning it is her face that replaces the darkness.

Multiple Choice Questions

Q.1. 'She' here is
A. the woman who looks into the mirror
B. the house owner
C. the young girl
D. the old woman

Ans. A. the woman who looks into the mirror

Q.2. 'She' is in tears over
A. her lost youthfulness
B. her lost youth and her helplessness in it
C. her growing mature
D. her loss of strength

Ans. B. her lost youth and her helplessness in it

Q.3. The mirror is important to her because
A. by it she can look at her face
B. she can see her figure in it
C. she can evaluate her beauty and appearance
D. it can tell how she looks

Ans. C. she can evaluate her beauty and appearance

Comprehension Questions

Q.1. Who is the speaker here and who is 'She'?

Ans. The mirror is the speaker here. 'She' is the woman who looks at her reflection in it.

Q.2. Why does she come there often?

Ans. She comes there often to see her face reflected in the mirror.

Q.3. What is her reaction on seeing her image?

Ans. Her reaction is of showing her sadness at her growing old. Once she was beautiful and young. Now she has grown old and tries to see that reflection of a beautiful woman that once she was.

6

In me she has drowned a young girl, and in me an old woman
Rises toward her day after day like a terrible fish.

Multiple Choice Questions

Q.1. 'In me she has drowned a young girl' means
A. she was once beautiful
B. once she had a girl-like figure
C. once she looked like a girl
D. a young girl in her has become a woman

Ans. D. a young girl in her has become a woman

Q.2. The mirror shows that the young girl has now become
A. an old woman
B. a woman

C. a mature lady
D. the owner of the house

Ans. A. an old woman

Q.3. The old woman looking at the mirror behaves like a terrible fish. It means she is angry at
A. her growing mature
B. her becoming old
C. her losing beauty
D. her becoming wrinkled

Ans. C. her losing beauty

Comprehension Questions

Q.1. Who is 'me' here?

Ans. 'Me' here is the mirror.

Q.2. Who are 'a young girl' and 'an old woman'?

Ans. 'A young girl' and 'an old woman' are the same woman who in her young age was a young girl. But now she has become old.

Q.3. How is she 'a terrible fish'?

Ans. She behaves like 'a terrible fish' because she is now old, always wanted to be 'young'. Now that she is actually old, she agitates her hands in anger and sadness at her age.

Textual Questions

Q.1. On the basis of your understanding of the poem, answer the following questions by ticking the correct choice.

(*i*) When the mirror is being described as being 'unmisted by love or dislike' we understand that the mirror is
A. not misted B. nor prejudiced
C. four angles D. silver in colour

Ans. B. not prejudiced

(*ii*) The other word for 'contemplation' is ......
A. contempt B. meditation
C. mediation D. thoughtful

Ans. B. meditation

(*iii*) When the mirror says 'it has no precon-ceptions' it means that :
A. it reflects back an image objectively
B. it modifies an image as it reflects it
C. it beautifies an image as it reflects it
D. it gives a biased view of a person/object

Ans. A. it reflects back an image objectivley

(*iv*) The mirror has been called 'a four-cornered god' because :
A. it is square shaped
B. like God it watches you unbiased and fair from all four angles
C. it reflects back all that it sees
D. it never stops reflecting

Ans. B. like God it watches you unbiased and fair from all four angles

(*v*) The 'speckles' refer to :
A. a pink object
B. the opposite wall which has spots on it
C. a person with pink pimples
D. pink spots in general

Ans. D. pink spots in general

(*vi*) The phrase 'agitation of the hand' suggests that the person is :
A. very ill B. very upset
C. very angry D. very happy

Ans. B. very upset

(*vii*) By saying 'Now I am a lake' the narrator wants to show that
A. the poem is not only about external beauty but also the inside of a person
B. the lake can also reflect surfaces
C. the depth of the lake is important
D. the lake does not show as exact an image as a mirror.

Ans. A. the poem is not only about external beauty but also the inside of a person.

Q.2. Answer the following questions briefly.

(*i*) What is the poetic device used when the mirror says 'I swallow'?

Ans. The poetic device used in it is 'person-ification'. The mirror is shown as a human being which he is not. 'Swallow' shows the use of 'metaphor' in it.

(*ii*) How does the mirror usually pass its time?

Ans. It passes its time 'meditating', or 'contemplating'.

(*iii*) What distrubs the mirror's contemplation of the opposite wall?

Ans. What disturbs the mirror is the opposite wall that has been painted pink.

(*iv*) Why does the mirror appear to be a lake in the second stanza? What aspect of the mirror do you think is being referred to here?

Ans. The mirror appears to be a lake in the second stanza because like the lake it reflects back the images objectively. The dispassionate and objective reflection of the mirror is intensified in it.

(*v*) What is the woman searching for in the depths of the lake?

Ans. The woman is searching for the beauty of her face in the depths of the lake. Once she was beautiful but now she has grown old and is not what she was earlier. Now she doesn't want to see her old face. So she searches for her old face of her youthful days.

(*vi*) How does the narrator convey the fact that the woman looking at her reflection in the lake is deeply distressed?

Ans. The narrator conveys the fact that the woman looking at her reflection in the lake is deeply distressed by showing her agitating hands. Secondly, she weeps and behaves like 'a terrible fish'.

(*vii*) What makes the woman start crying?

Ans. The wrinkled old face without beauty makes the woman start crying. She wanted to see her face always youthful. But now it is not so as she has grown old.

(*viii*) What do you think the 'terrible fish' in the last line symbolizes? What is the poetic device used here?

Ans. The 'terrible fish' symbolizes the woman agitating at the loss of her youthful beauty. She is now old and behaves like 'a terrible fish' at the loss of her youth. The poetic device used here is 'simile'.

Q.3. Find the various instances of personification used in this poem.

Ans. Various instances of personification :

1. I am silver—as a human being
2. I am the eye of a little god—as a god
3. I am 'a part' of the wall—now a wall
4. 'Now I am a lake'—as a lake.

Brief Answer Type Questions

Q.1. How is the mirror *'exact'* and *'only truthful'*?

Ans. The Mirror is the speaker in this poem and says that it is 'silver and exact' and has no preconceptions. It is just 'truthful' and not less or not more than that. Nor is it affected by love, dislike or any other human emotion. It tells how the woman reacts to her reflection when she looks into it. She searches for what she once was. She has wrinkles and she looks for hiding these truthfully and exactly.

Q.2. Give out the theme of the poem *"Mirror"*.

Ans. The theme of the poem "Mirror" is clear. It is that there is always a change in everything. It is, therefore, the principle of life and every one must understand it. One must not create false ego or illusions as these will never stand permanent. Everything shall change. The woman who looks into the mirror behaves like a terrible fish because she wants to be beautiful always. But it is against the law of nature. Everyone should be like the mirror-exact, truthful and without any previous conceptions.

Q.3. How is the mirror *'the eye of a little god'* and *'a lake'*?

Ans. The mirror is described as 'the eye of a little god' as it is impartial and truthful like a little god. Its judgement is not misled by love or dislike. Like god, it gives a true reflection of the objects that appear before it.

The mirror is also a 'lake' in its action. A woman looks into the mirror. She moves this way or that way to see her face more intently as she wants to see her young face. However, she agitates at her growing old age.

Q.4. Describe the symbolic significance of the comparison between the woman and the terrible fish as given in *'Mirror'*.

Ans. The woman given in the poem was once beautiful. But now she has grown old and her face is getting wrinkled. As the age has grown she had not changed mentally as she still wished to be beautiful as earlier she was. So when she has to face the reality of her fading beauty, she agitates. She cries and cries and hunts for some dim light which might hide her wrinkles. So she looks for the candlelight and the moonlight which may not show her withering face clearly. Thus the symbolic camparison is apt.

Essay Type Questions

1. What do you mean by *'Personification'*? How is *'Mirror'* an example of personification?

Ans. 'Personification' means 'personifying' a thing, an object or some non-living thing with human-like qualities. It makes that thing like a human thing. It also means to make a non-living thing invested with the qualities of living human beings. For this 'Mirror' is a beautiful example of 'personification'. The Mirror assumes the personality of a living human being and becomes itself the speaker. It behaves like a human being and describes itself like him. It tells what it is and where it lives. It also tells what are the reactions of the woman who looks into it. It 'sees', 'swallows', 'meditates', 'thinks', 'is a lake', etc. All these things are had by the human beings. The Mirror relates how it looks at things occuring before it. It doesn't add anything from its side. It beautifully describes the emotions and reactions of the woman who looks into it and behaves like a terrible fish. It doesn't add anything about itself except the truth. It is only truthful.

2. Describe the feeling of the woman as she looks into the mirror.

Ans. The mirror beautifully records the actions and reactions of the woman who looks into it. The woman was once very beautiful. It was in her youth. But now she has grown old. But she has wanted to be beautiful always. She had thought that she would always look young and beautiful. She never thought that time brings a change. Any one born shall degenerate and die one day. Beauty is of the mind and physical beauty shall degenerate one day. However, she is not so now and wants to be beautiful. She turns to 'the candles or the moon'. These dim her face so that the wrinkles are hidden and she looks beautiful. The mirror has shown her grow into an old woman from a young girl as it is truthful only.

3. *"In one she has drowned a young girl"*. Why does the mirror say this?

Ans. The mirror says this because the woman seeing at her face into the mirror was once a pretty young girl. She had thought that she would always look young and beautiful. She never thought that time brings a change. Any one born shall degenerate and die one day. Beauty is of the mind and physical beauty shall degenerate one day. Now this 'girl' is growing into an old woman. She has lost her youthful beauty but she wants to be always beautiful. She turns to candles and the moon. These become 'liars' because they help to hide the wrinkles by adding their lights on her face. The mirror reflects the woman's face truthfully which is growing old. But she behaves like a terrible fish because of her growing old. She in her old age doesn't want to face the reality of life. She has always desired to look young. But the mirror can't help her at all. It shows her what she is at present. It doesn't tell a lie. It is the woman who herself is responsible for this kind of sadness and depression. She must know the truth of life.

POEM-25

Not marble, nor the gilded monuments
Of princes, shall outlive this powerful rhyme;
But you shall shine more bright in these contents
Than unswept stone, besmear'd with sluttish time.
When wasteful was shall statues overturn,
And broils root out the work of masonry,
Nor Mars his sword nor war's quick fire shal burn
The living record of your memory.
'Gainst death and all oblivious enmity
Shall you pace forth; your praise shall still find room,
Even in the eyes of all posterity
That wear this world out to the ending doom.
So, till the judgment that yourself arise,
You live in this, and dwell in lover's eyes.

Directions : *Read the given lines of poem in each question-set and answer the questions that follow.*

1

Not marble, nor the gilded monuments
Of princes, shall outlive this powerful rhyme;
But you shall shine more bright in these contents
Than unswept stone, besmear'd with sluttish time.

Multiple Choice Questions

Q.1. 'This powerful rhyme' here is
A. the rhyme scheme
B. music of the sonnet
C. this very sonnet
D. rhyme having power

Ans. C. this very sonnet

Q.2. 'You shall shine more bright in these contents' means
A. the poet's beloved will shine like a star
B. the poet's beloved shall shine brightly in this sonnet
C. the poet's beloved shall shine more than the monuments
D. the poet's beloved shall be like a star

Ans. B. the poet's beloved shall shine brightly in this sonnet

Q.3. 'Time' here has been personified to
A. give more meaning
B. show its supreme power
C. compare with a slut
D. elaborate the idea of immortality

Ans. B. show its supreme power

Comprehension Questions

Q.1. Why are monuments made?

Ans. Monuments are made by princes, kings etc, to perpetuate their memories till posterity.

Q.2. Who is 'you' in the third line here? How will 'you' shine?

Ans. 'You' here is the poet's beloved or friend. His beloved or friend shall shine more brightly than these monuments.

Q.3. Why has time been called 'sluttish'?

Ans. Time has called 'sluttish' because it spoils these monuments like a slut spoils her virtue.

2

When wasteful was shall statues overturn,
And broils root out the work of masonry,
Nor Mars his sword nor war's quick fire shall burn
The living record of your memory.

Multiple Choice Questions

Q.1. The war has been described as 'wasteful' because it
A. destroys everything
B. destroys the monuments
C. doesn't let anything live
D. spoils everything

Ans. A. destroys everything

Q.2. The work of masonry here is
A. historical buildings
B. old buildings now neglected
C. monuments built in memory of princes etc
D. what is rooted out by wars

Ans. C. monuments built in memory of princes etc

Q.3. The poet's beloved has been immortalised here in the form of
A. art B. literature
C. this sonnet D. books

Ans. C. this sonnet

Comprehension Questions

Q.1. What do the wars and fights do to the monuments?

Ans. The wars and fights destroy the monuments.

Q.2. How is Mars recognised? Why has it been referred to here?

Ans. Mars is recognised by his sword. It has been referred to here because of its capacity to destroy everthing.

Q.3. How has the poet's beloved been described here?

Ans. The poet's beloved has been described as a living record in the form of this sonnet.

3

'Gainst death and all oblivious enmity
Shall you pace forth; your praise shall still find room,
Even in the eyes of all posterity
That wear this world out to the ending doom.

Multiple Choice Questions

Q.1. What will pace forth against death and enmity?
A. poet's beloved
B. living memory of poet's beloved
C. this sonnet
D. poet's beloved's memory

Ans. B. living memory of poet's beloved

Q.2. Till when shall the 'praise' live?
A. till next generations
B. till the doomsday
C. till the beloved lives
D. till the edge of ending doom

Ans. D. till the edge of ending doom

Q.3. The poet through this sonnet wants to prove that
A. time is all powerful
B. his beloved is immortal
C. his beloved shall live till the end
D. all has to die soon

Ans. B. his beloved is immortal

Comprehension Questions

Q.1. Which kind of enmity is it?

Ans. The enmity mentioned here is that enmity which forgets everything and seeks to destroy everything.

Q.2. How does the poet immortalise his beloved's memory here?

Ans. The poet immortalizes his beloved's memory by saying that it will find some space even in the eyes of posterity.

Q.3. What will happen to the world when the poet's beloved's praise shall face it?

Ans. The world will be outlived by the beloved's praise even to the edge of doom.

4

So, till the judgment that yourself arise,
You live in this, and dwell in lover's eyes.

Multiple Choice Questions

Q.1. The poet expects that his beloved shall arise
A. till the judgment
B. even after the judgment day
C. when God will command
D. when she will be examined in her actions.

Ans. B. even after the judgment day

Q.2. 'You live in this' means
A. you shall live in this world
B. you shall live in your lover's eyes
C. you shall live for ever
D. you shall never die

Ans. A. you shall live in this world

Q.3. The poet through this sonnet immortalises
A. time B. wars
C. his friend D. his beloved

Ans. D. his beloved

Comprehension Questions

Q.1. Till when will the poet's beloved live?

Ans. The poet's beloved will live till the judgement day.

Q.2. Explain '...till the judgment'.

Ans. 'Till the judgment' means the poet's beloved shall live till the judgement day. On the judgement day, it is believed, one's good and bad deeds are examined and one gets reward or punishment from God accordingly.

Q.3. How does the poet look at his beloved when he calls her 'you live in this...'?

Ans. The poet looks at his beloved as a personified being, that is, human being, though till now she has been living in his memory only.

Textual Questions

Q.1. On the basis of your understanding of Shakespeare's sonnet, answer the following questions by ticking the correct options.

(*i*) The rich and powerful get ornate monuments made in order to ______

A. show off their wealth
B. display their power
C. show their artistic talent
D. be remembered till posterity

Ans. D. be remembered till posterity

(*ii*) The poet addresses his sonnet to ______.

A. time
B. war
C. the person he loves
D. powerful rulers

Ans. C. the person he loves

(*iii*) In the line 'The living record of your memory', living record refers to ______

A. the sonnet the poet has written for his friend
B. an existing statue of his friend
C. his friend who lives in the poet's memory
D. the autobiography of the poet's friend

Ans. C. his friend who lives in the poet's memory

(*iv*) The poet's tone in the poem is ______

A. despairing B. optimistic
C. loving D. admiring

Ans. C. loving

(*v*) The poem is set in ______

A. the place where the poet meets his friend
B. a battlefield where Mars is fighting a battle
C. a city ravaged by war
D. the poet's study where he is writing.

Ans. D. the poet's study where he is writing.

Q.2. Answer the following questions briefly.

(*i*) Why do you think the rich and powerful people get monuments and statues erected in their memory?

Ans. The rich and powerful people get monuments and statues erected in their memory for being remembered till posterity.

(*ii*) Describe how the monuments and statues brave the ravages of time.

Ans. The monuments and statues brave the ravages of time. In doing so they get spoiled, disfigured and broken, if they are not taken care of.

(*iii*) Why does the poet refer to Time as being sluttish?

Ans. The poet refers to Time as being sluttish because Time spoils the marbled or gilded monuments. It discolours them, breaks them or makes them dirty through its agencies. These agencies are like air, rain, natural vegetation etc.

(*iv*) The poet says that neither forces of nature nor wars can destroy his poetry. In fact, even godly powers of Mars will not have a devastating effect on his rhyme. What quality of the poet is revealed through these lines?

Ans. The quality of the poet is clearly revealed through these lines. It is the immortality of his verse and the permanence of his poetic or literary art. It is true that like Time or Nature, literary art is also permanent and immortal. That's why, we have poets and artists through their works who had lived thousands of years before.

Brief Answer Type Questions

1. How according to the poet, will his beloved outlive monuments and time?

Ans. According to the poet, his beloved being in this sonnet shall outlive the marbled and gilded monuments built by princes etc. These monuments spoiled by time shall not out-live her being in this sonnet.

2. How does the poet call his beloved in the second quatrain? What will not affect her in it? What is her present status?

Ans. The poet calls his beloved 'the living record of your memory'. Wasteful wars, fights, Mars' sword and war's quick fire shall not be able to burn this 'memory' of his beloved. So she is immortal in being in this sonnet.

3. How will the poet's beloved sustain herself against death etc?

Ans. The poet's beloved shall walk forth against death and all oblivious enmity which is forgetful of everything and seeks to destroy everthing. Her praise shall be there in all posterity. She will wear out this world to the ending doom.

4. How does the poet immortalize his beloved?

Ans. The poet immortalizes his beloved by stating that his beloved shall ever live in this sonnet and in the eyes of posterity. Also she will wear out this world till the judgement day and shall outlive it. In this way, she will be immortal.

5. What is the moral of the poem *'Not Marble, nor the Gilded Monuments'*?

Ans. The moral of the poem is that literary art is not affected by time, though marbled and gilded monuments are. They are ravaged by time but it will have no effect on his beloved who is a living record in this sonnet. Time is shown a great leveller and destroyer here.

Essay Type Questions

1. How does the poet describe his beloved in this poem?

Ans. The poet describes his beloved or friend in this poem beautifully. He says that princes, kings etc, build marbled and gilded monnuments to perpetuate their memories. But wars, fights and time destroy them. But his beloved has been immortalized in this sonnet. These monuments shall not outlive 'this powerful rhyme'. On the other hand, his beloved being so will shine more brightly than these monuments spoiled by sluttish time. Wasteful wars, fights and even Mars' sword or war's quick fire shall not destroy her living memory in this sonnet. His beloved shall pace forth agaisnt death and enmity. She will live in the eyes of all posterity and wear out this world to the ending doom. This way she shall always live in this sonnet and dwell in her lover's eyes.

2. As a reader of *'Not Marble, nor the Gilded Monuments'* write out what you learn about the poet's beloved.

Ans. After reading *'Not Marble, nor the Gilded Monuments'* I learn that the poet has immortalized his beloved or friend through this poem. He says that his beloved or friend lies immortalized in 'this powerful rhyme'. She has become a living memory in this literary art. Marbled or gilded monuments of princes etc, shall not outlive her. Nor will these and sluttish time affect her immortality. Wars and fights destroy even the most beautiful works of masonry. But these will not affect her. Mars sword or war's quick fire will not burn this living record in this sonnet. On the other hand, his beloved shall walk against death and enmity. Her praise shall find a place in the eyes of all posterity. This all will wear this world out even to the ending doom. Thus his beloved shall arise even after the judgement day. She shall ever live in this sonnet and consequently in her lover's eyes.

POEM-26

I met a traveller from an antique land
Who said : Two vast and trunkless legs of stone
Stand in the desert. Near them, on the sand,
Half sunk, a shattered visage lies,
whose frown,
And wrinkled lip, and sneer of cold command,
Tell that its sculptor well those passions read
Which yet survive, stamped on these lifeless things,
The hand that mocked them, and the heart that fed ;
And on the pedestal these words appear :
"My name is Ozymandias, king of kings :
Look upon my works, ye Mighty, and despair!"
Nothing beside remains. Round the decay
Of that colossal wreck, boundless and bare
The lone and level sands stretch far away.

Directions : *Read the given lines of poem in each question-set and answer the questions that follow.*

1

I met a traveller from an antique land
Who said : Two vast and trunkless legs of stone
Stand in the desert. Near them, on the sand,
Half sunk, a shattered visage lies,

Multiple Choice Questions

Q.1. When did the narrator meet the traveller?
A. after they had gone to the ancient land
B. after the traveller had visited the ancient land
C. when the traveller was coming from the ancient land
D. when they met in the ancient land

Ans. B. after the traveller had visited the ancient land

Q.2. What had happened to the trunk of the statue?
A. It had fallen down
B. Time had claimed it
C. The wind had swept it
D. The desert had claimed it

Ans. B. Time had claimed it

Q.3. How did the human face look?
A. broken and shattered
B. half sunk
C. in pieces
D. separate from the body

Ans. A. broken and shattered

Comprehension Questions

Q.1. Where has the traveller travelled?

Ans. The traveller has travelled the ancient land.

Q.2. What kind of statue is it that the traveller sees?

Ans. The human statue is vast and big but the trunk of this statue has broken.

Q.3. What has become of the human face?

Ans. The human face is broken and has fallen though the legs still stand.

2

whose frown,
And wrinkled lip, and sneer of cold command,
Tell that its sculptor well those passions read

Multiple Choice Questions

Q.1. '...... whose frown' was it?
A. traveller's B. narrator's
C. sculptor's D. Ozymandias's

Ans. D. Ozymandias's

Q.2. What suggested that Ozymandias was a cruel and dictatorial ruler?
A. his wrinkled lip
B. his sneer of cold command
C. his wrinkled visage
D. his shattered face

Ans. B. his sneer of cold command

Q.3. What does the statue of Ozymandias tell about the sculptor?
A. that he was a great sculptor
B. that he was very intelligent
C. that he had beautifully carved Ozymandias's face
D. that he was a real sculptor

Ans. A. that he was a great sculptor

Comprehension Questions

Q.1. What lies in the sands and how?

Ans. A broken human face lies half sunk in the sands.

Q.2. How does the shattered visage look?

Ans. The 'shattered visage' looks very cruel and pitiless with a 'wrinkled lip' and sneer of cold command.

Q.3. What does the face tell of the sculptor?

Ans. The face tells that the sculptor was a great artist and imitated well the real expressions of the king's face in stone.

3

Which yet survive, stamped on these lifeless things,
The hand that mocked them, and the heart that fed ;

Multiple Choice Questions

Q.1. What is 'which' here in the first line?
A. sneer of cold command
B. wrinkled lip
C. passions of the king
D. feelings of Ozymandias

Ans. C. passions of the king

Q.2. The 'hand that mocked ......'. Whose 'hand'?
A. Ozymandias's B. king's
C. sculptor's D. narrator's

Ans. C. sculptor's

Q.3. What did the 'hand' do?
A. It sculpted the expressions of the king.
B. It made fun of Ozymandias by sculpting him as such.
C. It laughed at the king's passions.
D. It ridiculed the king.

Ans. B. It made fun of Ozymandias by sculpting him as such.

Comprehension Questions

Q.1. Which things of the king survive still?

Ans. Two legs and broken human face with its expressions survive still.

Q.2. What are 'these lifeless things'?

Ans. 'These lifeless things' are two vast legs, broken human face with its expression and the sculptor's art.

Q.3. What did the sculptor actually do in sculpting the king's statue?

Ans. The sculptor actually showed his real art in carving the true and genuine feelings of the king in stone.

4

And on the pedestal these words appear :
"My name is Ozymandias, king of kings :
Look upon my works, ye Mighty, and despair!"

Multiple Choice Questions

Q.1. 'My name is Ozymandias, king of kings' shows the
A. despair of the king
B. despair of the king and repentance of his pride
C. uselessness of sneer, frown and hatred
D. futility of life

Ans. B. despair of the king and repentance of his pride

Q.2. The king asks the readers to 'despair' because
A. life is as such
B. pride, arrogance and contempt lead one nowhere
C. time is a great healer
D. time levels all

Ans. B. pride, arrogance and contempt lead one nowhere

Q.3. The poem conveys the moral that
A. pride and sneer are useless emotions
B. one should recognize the power of time
C. pride and cold command take one nowhere
D. pride hath a fall.

Ans. A. pride and sneer are useless emotions

Comprehension Questions

Q.1. What has become of the statue of Ozymandias?

Ans. The statue of Ozymandias was in ruins because of the claim of time on it.

Q.2. What is the underlying thought of the writing on the pedestal?

Ans. The underlying thought of the writing is that time claims everything howsoever powerful it may be. Once Ozymandias was a king of kings but now his statue tells his worth.

Q.3. Why one looking upon Ozymandias's work should despair?

Ans. One should despair that time is all powerful. Even the sneer and cold command are nothing before it. Secondly, these passions are meaningless.

5

Nothing beside remains. Round the decay
Of that colossal wreck, boundless and bare
The lone and level sands stretch far away.

Multiple Choice Questions

Q.1. 'Nothing beside remains'. 'Beside what'?
A. two vast and trunkless legs
B. two vast and trunkless legs and shattered visage
C. sneer of cold command
D. sands

Ans. B. two vast and trunkless legs and shattered visage

Q.2. 'Boundless and bare' symbolise
A. the vastness of sands
B. limitless sand stretches meaning death
C. sands
D. destruction

Ans. B. limitless sand stretches meaning death

Q.3. The last line here refers to
A. nature
B. the capacity of sand to destroy everything
C. the total destruction of things by nature and time
D. the capacity of time to destroy all things.

Ans. C. the total destruction of things by nature and time

Comprehension Questions

Q.1. What does the broken statue symbolise?

Ans. The broken statue symbolises the futility of pride and command and the great power of time.

Q.2. What is the intention of the poet here?

Ans. The poet's intention is clear. He means to say that pride, command and cruelty are nothing before good human values. Time is all powerful.

Q.3. What do the 'colossal wreck' and 'sands' symbolise?

Ans. The 'colossal wreck' and 'sands' symbolise the nature's and time's all pervading power.

Textual Questions

1. Answer the following questions by ticking the correct options.

(i) The poem is set in ________
A. the wilderness B. an ancient land
C. a palace D. a desert

Ans. D. a desert

(ii) The expression on the face of the statue is one of ________
A. admiration B. anger
C. despair D. contempt

Ans. D. contempt

(iii) This poem throws light on the ________ nature of Ozymandias.
A. cruel B. arrogant
C. boastful D. aggressive

Ans. B. arrogant

(iv) The sculptor was able to understand Ozymandias' ________
A. words B. expression
C. feelings D. ambition

Ans. C. feelings

(v) The tone of the poem is ________
A. mocking B. nostalgic
C. gloomy D. gloating

Ans. A. mocking

2. Answer the following questions briefly.

(i) "The hand that mocked them, and the heart that fed." Whose hand and heart has the poet referred to in this line?

Ans. The poet has referred to the hand of the sculptor and the heart of the king Ozymandias.

(ii) "My name is Ozymandias, king of kings:" Why does Ozymandias refer to himself as King of Kings? What quality of the king is revealed through this statement?

Ans. Ozymandias refers to himself the king of kings out of sneer, arrogance, haughtiness and contempt for other kings. It is so as he heads them all in these qualities.

(iii) "Look on my works, ye Mighty, and despair!" Who is Ozymandias referring to when he speaks of ye Mighty? Why should they despair?

Ans. He is referring to the mighty kings. They should despair at seeing the end of his haughtiness, contempt, pride, arrogance and cruelty.

(iv) Bring out the irony in the poem.

Ans. The irony in the poem is that it shows the arrogance, haughtiness, contempt and cruelty of Ozymandias but what is the result. The broken statue and the vastness of the sands symbolise the uselessness of these emotions.

(v) 'Nothing beside remains'. What does the narrator mean when he says these words?

Ans. The narrator means that there is no other thing of the king who once was mighty, powerful, ruthless and cruel.

(vi) What is your impression of Ozymandias as a king?

Ans. My impression about Ozymandias is that he was a ruthless and contemptible king. He was stupid also and lacked even an iota of wisdom, farsightedness and humility. He was simply a bundle of cruelty and inhumanness.

(*vii*) What message is conveyed through this poem?

Ans. The message conveyed through the poem is the futility of these qualities of arrogance, sneer and cruelty and all the powerfulness of Time and Nature. These qualities meet an end as it comes to this arrogant king.

Brief Answer Type Questions

1. What did the traveller tell the narrator about what he saw in the ancient land?

Ans. The traveller told the narrator that he travelled to an ancient land. There he saw a strange scene in desert. There he saw two vast and trunkless legs of stone standing in the desert. Near them on the sand there lay half sunk a human face.

2. What kind of expression did the human face have? What did it tell of the sculptor and the human being after whom he had carved that statue?

Ans. The human face had the expression of frown and sneer of cold command. The wrinkled lip indicated the feeling of arrogance. These told indirectly that the sculptor who carved this statue had read those passions of the person whose statue he had carved. He had also mocked these.

3. What was written on the pedestal of the statue? What does it indicate?

Ans. On the pedestal of the statue was written: 'My name is Ozymandias, king of kings: Look upon my works, Ye Mighty, and despair'. It indicates that the king wanted to tell the on-lookers that his works, arrogance, pride, cruelty, brutality etc, proved useless against Time.

4. What else remained there beside the broken statue? What does it signify?

Ans. Beside that broken statue there spread sands and sands far away. The desert was limitless, lonely and levelling. This desert indicates vastness of decay and death which claims everything.

5. What is the message given indirectly in the poem?

Ans. The message of 'Ozymandias' is clear. It is that nothing of human emotions like pride, arrogance, sneer, frown, haughtiness etc, guarantee immortality and permanence against all powerful Time or Nature. The broken statue symbolises the destruction caused by Time. The sands, lone, boundless and bare symbolise the power of the elements.

Essay Type Questions

1. What does the traveller tell the narrator of what he saw in a desert?

Ans. The traveller tells the narrator that he saw in an ancient land a strange spectacle. He saw two vast and trunkless legs of stone standing in the desert. Near them there lay a broken human face. It was half sunk in the sand. It had the expressions of frown, scorn and sneer of cold command. The lip was wrinkled. All these suggested that the sculptor had studied these expressions well and had carved them skilfully in the stone. However he had mocked at these in carving on the stone. On the pedestal of his statue were written the words : My name is Ozymandias, king of kings : Look upon my works and despair. Besides this nothing remained there. However, vast, boundless, bare and lonely and level sands stretched away far and wide.

ANSWERS

I. Cloze Test

Passage-1

1	2	3	4	5	6
A	B	A	C	D	A
7	8	9	10	11	12
A	B	A	B	C	B
13	14				
D	B				

Passage-2

1	2	3	4	5	6
B	B	A	D	B	C
7	8	9	10	11	
C	B	A	C	A	

Passage-3

1	2	3	4	5	6
C	D	A	A	B	B
7	8	9	10	11	12
C	D	B	A	B	C

Passage-4

1	2	3	4	5	6
B	C	A	B	D	C
7	8	9	10	11	12
B	C	A	D	B	A
13					
D					

Passage-5

1	2	3	4	5	6
D	C	A	B	C	B
7	8	9	10	11	12
C	D	B	A	D	C

Passage-6

1	2	3	4	5	6
A	B	D	B	A	B
7	8	9	10	11	12
D	C	D	C	B	B

Passage-7

1	2	3	4	5	6
A	B	D	A	B	C
7	8	9	10	11	12
D	D	C	D	A	B
13					
D					

Passage-8

1	2	3	4	5	6
C	C	B	A	D	B
7	8	9	10	11	12
D	D	C	D	A	B

Passage-9

1	2	3	4	5	6
B	B	C	B	D	A
7	8	9	10	11	12
D	A	B	C	D	D

Passage-10

1	2	3	4	5	6
A	D	A	D	D	C
7	8	9	10	11	12
B	B	D	A	A	B

Passage-11

1	2	3	4	5	6
C	B	D	A	B	A
7	8	9	10	11	12
A	B	D	C	A	B

Passage-12

1	2	3	4	5	6
A	B	C	A	B	C
7	8	9	10	11	12
B	D	B	D	B	C

Passage-13

1	2	3	4	5	6
D	C	B	C	C	A
7	8	9	10	11	
B	B	C	D	B	

Passage-14

1	2	3	4	5	6
B	C	A	D	C	C
7	8	9	10	11	
D	A	B	A	C	

Passage-15

1	2	3	4	5	6
A	B	D	B	D	B
7	8	9	10	11	
C	A	C	D	B	

Passage-16

1	2	3	4	5	6
C	A	C	B	A	A
7	8	9	10	11	
C	B	D	D	D	

Passage-17

1	2	3	4	5	6
D	B	D	D	D	C
7	8	9	10	11	
A	D	A	A	B	

Passage-18

1	2	3	4	5	6
B	C	B	A	C	C
7	8	9	10	11	12
C	D	D	D	A	D
13	14	15	16	17	
C	A	B	D	C	

Passage-19

1	2	3	4	5	6
B	A	B	C	B	D
7	8	9	10	11	
B	C	D	D	B	

Passage-20

1	2	3	4	5	6
D	C	D	A	A	B
7	8	9	10		
C	C	A	C		

Passage-21

1	2	3	4	5	6
D	B	C	B	C	B
7	8	9	10		
A	D	D	D		

Passage-22

1	2	3	4	5	6
C	A	B	C	B	D
7	8	9	10	11	
A	A	B	D	D	

Passage-23

1	2	3	4	5	6
B	A	C	B	A	A
7	8	9	10	11	12
B	D	C	A	C	B
13	14	15	16	17	18
C	B	C	C	A	C

Passage-24

1	2	3	4	5	6
A	D	C	A	B	D
7	8	9	10	11	12
D	B	B	C	A	A

Passage-25

1	2	3	4	5	6
D	C	B	A	D	C
7	8	9	10	11	12
A	A	C	D	B	D
13	14				
D	A				

Passage-26

1	2	3	4	5	6
A	C	B	C	D	B
7	8	9	10	11	
D	C	B	A	A	

Passage-27

1	2	3	4	5	6
C	B	B	A	A	B
7	8	9	10	11	12
C	A	D	D	B	D
13	14	15	16		
C	C	B	B		

Passage-28

1	2	3	4	5	6
D	D	C	D	B	B
7	8	9	10	11	12
C	C	B	B	C	A
13	14	15			
A	D	C			

Passage-29

1	2	3	4	5	6
B	B	C	D	A	B
7	8	9	10	11	12
A	B	C	D	B	C

Passage-30

1	2	3	4	5	6
B	C	A	A	D	D
7	8	9	10	11	12
D	C	C	B	B	C
13	14	15			
A	B	D			

Passage-31

1	2	3	4	5	6
A	B	D	A	B	C
7	8	9	10	11	12
B	A	B	D	A	B
13	14	15			
D	A	A			

Passage-32

1	2	3	4	5	6
B	C	C	A	D	B
7	8	9	10	11	12
C	A	C	B	D	C
13	14				
B	B				

II. Passages

Passage-1

1	2	3	4	5	6	7
A	D	A	A	A	C	B

Passage-2

1	2	3	4	5	6	7
A	A	D	A	B	C	D

Passage-3

1	2	3	4	5	6	7
D	C	D	C	A	D	B

Passage-4

1	2	3	4	5	6	7
C	C	A	D	A	D	C

Passage-5

1	2	3	4	5	6	7
B	D	D	B	D	C	A

Passage-6

1	2	3	4	5	6	7
A	C	B	C	B	C	B

Passage-7

1	2	3	4	5	6	7
B	C	C	B	D	B	C

Passage-8

1	2	3	4	5	6	7
B	C	C	B	B	C	A

Passage-9

1	2	3	4	5
C	C	B	D	A

Passage-10

1	2	3	4	5
B	A	B	C	C

Passage-11

1	2	3	4	5
C	A	B	D	A

Passage-12

1	2	3	4	5
A	A	B	C	D

Passage-13

1	2	3	4	5
A	C	B	A	D

Passage-14

1	2	3	4	5
C	B	A	D	A

Passage-15

1	2	3	4	5
B	A	C	D	A

Passage-16

1	2	3	4	5
A	B	C	A	B

Passage-17

1	2	3	4	5
C	A	B	D	C

Passage-18

1	2	3	4	5
B	D	B	A	B

Passage-19

1	2	3	4	5
D	C	B	C	D

Passage-20

1	2	3	4	5
B	A	C	D	A

Passage-21

1	2	3	4	5
B	C	D	D	C

Passage-22

1	2	3	4	5
C	D	B	C	D

Passage-23

1	2	3	4	5
A	C	D	B	A

Passage-24

1	2	3	4	5
A	D	A	D	B

Passage-25

1	2	3	4	5
B	C	D	A	B

Passage-26

1	2	3	4	5
B	B	C	A	D

Passage-27

1	2	3	4	5
A	B	A	B	C

Passage-28

1. (i) Good music has mood with variable notes of rhythm and provides mental relief with sensational pleasure.

(ii) Both of them practised Carnatic music.

(iii) He pioneered the use of African beats and tabla in his music.

2. (i) Baul songs (ii) Elvis Presley

(iii) Paco de Lucia (iv) The Beatles

3. (i) limits (ii) freedom

(iii) mixing of styles

Passage-29

1. (i) Mind management is a method to control one's mind.

(ii) A wise person does not accept or oppose any idea without valid reason. He works as per the situation and his capacity. He is always optimistic.

(iii) Because if kept any longer in mind they become stronger and difficult to remove later.

(iv) Because our aspirations are raised. The compulsions of hectic work-schedules burden the mind and cause stress.

2. (i) When one fails, he works hard and strives to achieve success with increased vigour. Hence, his failure acts as stepping stone for future success.

(ii) When we manage our mind, we have patience, peace and calmness which pave the way to success, and a successful and peaceful life is a healthy life.

3. (i) control (ii) disturbed, unrest

(iii) weak (iv) easy

Passage-30

1. (i) The youngster closed his facebook account after using it for three years. He did not like the Timeline feature of the facebook that was recently introduced.

(ii) He was upset because his friends will be able to see his old post on facebook easily with the help of the new feature. Until now those were buried under heaps of recent posts.

(iii) Every one commits some mistake or foolishness while posting online comments or photos which are almost forgotten by the time but if the same is easily accessible to all. The situation will be embarrassing and may cause more harm than good.

2. (i) moved (ii) deactivating it

(iii) separates (iv) friends

3. (i) pros and cons (ii) facets of life

(iii) profile (iv) to delete

III. Poetry

Poem-1

1	2	3	4	5
A	C	B	C	A

Poem-2

1	2	3	4	5
C	B	A	D	B

Poem-3

1	2	3	4	5
D	A	B	C	B

Poem-4

1	2	3	4	5
B	D	C	D	B

Poem-5

1	2	3	4	5
B	A	D	A	B

Poem-6

1	2	3	4	5
C	D	D	D	B

Poem-7

1	2	3	4	5
C	D	B	B	A

Poem-8

1	2	3	4	5
A	B	A	D	C

Poem-9

1	2	3	4	5
A	C	D	B	C

Poem-10

1	2	3	4	5
C	B	A	A	C

Poem-11

1	2	3	4	5
B	C	C	B	C

Poem-12

1	2	3	4	5
D	B	C	B	D

Poem-13

1	2	3	4	5
B	B	A	D	B

Poem-14

1	2	3	4	5
A	A	D	A	B

Poem-15

1	2	3	4	5
B	B	C	C	D

Poem-16

1	2	3	4	5
B	A	D	A	A

Poem-17

1	2	3	4	5
B	A	B	A	D

Poem-18

1	2	3	4	5
D	D	C	C	B

Poem-19

1	2	3	4	5
C	A	C	D	A

Poem-20

1	2	3	4	5
B	A	C	B	B

Poem-21

1. (i) Pronunciation (ii) threat
(iii) mother (iv) here
(v) them

2. (i) dead (ii) brother
(iii) bear and pear

Poem-22

1. It is because nobody is telling him what a particular girl (the Highland lass) is singing. She seems to be singing in a strange dialect which the poet does not know.

2. The girl is singing a sad song.

3. The poet makes several guesses:

(*i*) His first guess is that the girl is singing about some old and unhappy things which happened in bygone days and, may be, at some distant place.

(*ii*) The poet's second guess is that the girl is singing about some battles which were fought long long ago.

(*iii*) The poet's third guess is that the girl's sad song perhaps pertains to some routine day-to-day matter.

(*iv*) From this, the poet derives the idea that the girl's melancholy song might pertain to some natural sorrow, loss or pain. Such things can happen at any time and to anybody. Once having happened to somebody, they may happen again.

4. It is ab ab cc dd.

5. Yes, it appears he did.

6. It may be titled: "The Power of Music."

Poem-23

1. They have called it mighty and dreadful.

2. It is because they actually wake eternally, and it is, in reality, death itself that dies.

3. Rest and sleep.

4. Death is a slave to fate, chance, kings and desperate men.

5. It dwells with poison, war and sickness.

6. He just sleeps for sometime (after his death) and then he wakes up for ever in heaven.

Functional Grammar and Vocabulary

TENSES

1. Tense indicates a point in time or period of time in the past, present, or future tense.
2. The verb may consist of a single word, or a main verb and one or more auxiliary words.
   A. The verb can indicate a state of being (What the subject is) or location.
   Bhaskar is intelligent.
   Mahesh is at work.
   B. A verb can indicate what the subject is like or becomes.
   That child **seems** frightened.
   C. A verb can indicate an action. (What the subject is doing).
   The students **will finish** in time.

The key point is that tense is related to the form of verb. There are normally three forms of the verb, say, V_1, V_2, V_3 and for convenience a fourth form V_4 as verb+ing may be assumed.

Forms of Verb

V_1	V_2	V_3	V_4
Write	Wrote	Written	Writing
Read	Read	Read	Reading
Go	Went	Gone	Going
...	...	...	...

A Comparative Chart Regarding Tenses and Verbs

Simple Present	**Simple Past**	**Simple Future**
V_1	V_2	shall/will + V_1
Present Continuous	**Past Continuous**	**Future Continuous**
is/am/are + V_4	was/were + V_4	shall/will + be + V_4
Present Perfect	**Past Perfect**	**Future Perfect**
has/have + V_3	had + V_3	shall/will + have + V_3
Present Perfect Cont.	**Past Perfect Cont.**	**Future Perfect Cont.**
has/have + been + V_4	had + been + V_4	shall/will + have been + V_4

SIMPLE PRESENT:

A. A present state of affairs. — A. My sister lives in Kashmir.
B. A general fact. — B. The sun rises in the east.
C. Habitual actions. — C. I listen to the radio in the mornings.
D. Future time-tables. — D. My flight leaves at 10:00.

PRESENT CONTINUOUS:

A. A specific action that is occurring. — A. Arvind is watching TV (right now).
B. A general activity that takes place. — B. These days, I'm taking it easy.
C. Future arrangements. — C. I'm inviting Hari to the party on Friday.

SIMPLE PAST:

A. An action that began and ended at a particular time in the past. — A. The mail came early this Morning.

B. An action that occurred over a period of time but was completed in the past. — B. Dad worked in advertising in the past.

C. An activity that took place regularly in the past. — C. We jogged every morning before class.

PAST CONTINUOUS:

A. Interrupted Actions. — A. I was sewing when the telephone rang.

B. A continuous state over a period of time but was completed in the past. — B. She was looking very ill. I was meeting lots of people at that time.

C. Events planned in the past. — C. Neetu was leaving for Jammu but had to make a last minute change

D. Expressing a future intent. — D. Jyoti is going to bring her sister tonight.

E. Predicting an event. — E. You are going to pass the test. Don't worry.

SIMPLE FUTURE:

A. Making a future decision. — A. I will call you after lunch.

B. Predicting a future event. — B. You will pass the test. Don't worry.

C. Indicating willingness to do something. — C. If I don't feel better soon, I will go to the doctor.

FUTURE CONTINUOUS:

A. An action that will be going at a particular time in the future. — A. At noon tomorrow, I will be taking the children to their piano lessons.

B. Future actions which have already been decided. — B. I will be wearing my black dress to the dinner.

PRESENT PERFECT:

A. An action that happened at an unspecified time. — A. She has never climbed a mountain. I'm sorry. I have forgotten your Name.

B. An action that has recently occurred. — B. He's just gone to sleep.

C. An action that began in the past and continues up to the present (often used with "for" or "since"). — C. Jack has lived in Shri Nagar all his life. I have been here since Monday. He has known her for two weeks.

D. An action that happened repeatedly before now. — D. We have flown across the Pacific four times. I've failed my driver's test twice.

PRESENT PERFECT CONTINUOUS:

A. An action that began in the past and has just recently ended. — A. Have you been ringing the Bell?

B. An action that began in the past and continues in the present. — B. Lokesh has been studying for two hours.

C. An action repeated over a period of time in the past and continuing in present. — C. Suresh has been smoking since he was fifteen.

PAST PERFECT:

A. An action that occurred before another past action. — A. Tarun had left hours before we got there.

B. An action that was expected to occur in the past. — B. I had hoped to know about the job before now.

PAST PERFECT CONTINUOUS:

A. An action that occurred before another past action. — A. His eyes hurt because he had been reading for eight hours.

B. An action that was expected to occur in the past. — B. I had been expecting a change in his attitude.

FUTURE PERFECT:

A. An action that will be completed before a particular time in the future. — A. By next July, my parents will have been married for fifty years.

FUTURE PERFECT CONTINUOUS:

A. Emphasizing the length of time that has occurred before a specific time in the future. — A. By May, my father will have been working at the same job for thirty years.

MULTIPLE CHOICE QUESTIONS

Directions: *Find the correct word(s) that completes the sentence according to tenses.*

1. The manner in which bombs ...... in five trains within a short span of time suggests that it is a part of a conspiracy.
A. explode B. exploding
C. exploded D. has been exploding

2. What ..... the postage for an airletter?
A. are B. am
C. is D. be

3. I don't really know how to ..... the problem.
A. tackle B. tackling
C. do tackle D. did tackle

4. ...... a two-inch margin on each page for the teacher's remarks.
A. Leave B. Has left
C. Leaves D. Left

5. We ..... such a wonderful time at the party last night.
A. has B. have
C. had D. are having

6. Due to a failure of some traffic lights, traffic ...... very slowly.
A. move B. is moving
C. has moved D. had moved

7. ...... the earlier train will give us the chance to do some shopping.
A. Catch B. To catch
C. Having caught D. Catching

8. 'Please' and 'Thank you' are the little courtesies by which we ...... the machine of life oiled and running smoothly.
A. keep B. keeps
C. keeping D. were keeping

9. The French ..... reputed to have a very good sense of humour.
A. is B. was
C. are D. will be

10. Life ...... to death as pleasure is to pain.
A. is B. was
C. are D. will be

11. Do you know ..... ?
A. where she comes from
B. where does she come from
C. where from she comes
D. from where does she come

12. Few works of reference ..... so valuable as the Encyclopaedia Britannica.
A. is B. was
C. are D. will be

13. The paths of glory ..... but to the grave.
A. leads B. lead
C. leading D. have lead

14. ..... at three o'clock, I heard the rumble of thunder.
A. Walk B. Walks
C. Walking D. Walked

15. The thief ..... all the money.
A. made up B. made off with
C. made do with D. made good

16. Pakistan lost a crucial wicket just when they ..... to be doing so well, and that led to their eventual defeat.
A. seem B. seems
C. have seemed D. seemed

17. In high school many of us never realised the importance that grammar would ..... in later life.
A. plays B. played
C. play D. have played

18. I was ...... at his colossal lack of knowledge about the Continent of Africa.
A. astounded B. astounding
C. have astounded D. had astounded

19. The veracity of the Minister's statement cannot be ...... by people who have no access to official records.
A. verify B. verifies
C. verified D. have verified

20. You haven't had your lunch yet, ... you?
A. are B. aren't
C. have D. haven't

21. A woman came in with a baby who, she said, ... a safety pin.
A. was just swallowing
B. swallowed
C. had just swallowed
D. just swallowed

22. The telephone ..... several times before I answered it.
A. was ringing B. has rung
C. had rung D. would ring

23. An employment advertisement should ..... the number of vacancies.
A. specifies B. specify
C. be specifying D. have specified

24. A crescendo of metallic thuds arose from the market, where the iron-smiths were ..... the pieces of metals.
A. hammers B. to hammer
C. hammering D. having hammered

25. Ambition is one of those passions which are never ..... .
A. satisfy B. satisfies
C. satisfying D. satisfied

26. Like any other country India ...... its fair share of superstitions.
A. has B. have
C. had D. having

27. The miser ..... avidly at the pile of gold coins in front of him.
A. gaze B. gazes
C. gazed D. has gazed

28. The pilot ..... about the storm before he took off.
A. has been warned B. have been warned
C. had been warned D. was warned

29. On account of the dearth of grass on the arid plains the cattle became ..... .
A. amaciated B. amaciating
C. amaciate D. amaciates

30. I ..... a herd of cows in the field.
A. sees B. saw
C. seeing D. has seen

31. Besides other provisions, that shopkeeper ..... in cosmetics too.
A. deals B. deal
C. dealing D. has deal

32. That rule ..... applicable to everyone.
A. be B. were
C. is D. are

33. I ...... revenge on you.
A. take B. taking
C. shall take D. takes

34. The ruling party ..... its own house in order.
A. put B. shall have to put
C. will have to put D. have to put

35. To all intents and purposes, the manager ..... the master of the firm.
A. be B. is
C. are D. were

ANSWERS

1	2	3	4	5	6	7	8	9	10
C	C	A	A	C	B	D	A	C	A
11	12	13	14	15	16	17	18	19	20
A	C	B	C	B	D	C	A	C	C
21	22	23	24	25	26	27	28	29	30
C	C	B	C	D	A	C	C	A	B
31	32	33	34	35					
A	C	C	C	B					

MODALS

AUXILIARY VERBS

Modals are actually helping verbs. They help the finite verbs in framing sentences:

She **was** cooking food.
I **shall** guide you.

Kinds of Auxiliary Verbs

Auxiliary verbs are of two kinds:

A. Primary Auxiliaries (Modals)
B. Modal Auxiliaries (Auxiliary Modals)

A. Primary Modals

Primary modals work both as Helping Verbs and Finite Verbs.

Be = is, am, are, was, were, being, been
Have = has, have, had, having
Do = do, does, did, done, doing

(*a*) **Usage of be/have/do as Helping verbs:**
She **is** making a cane basket.
I **have** finished my homework.
She **does** know French.

(*b*) **Usage of be/have/do as Finite verbs:**
She **was** happy.
I **have** an expensive pen.
She **is doing** her homework.

B. Modal Auxiliaries

Shall, should, will, would, can, could, may, might, must, ought to, used to, have to, had to, dare, daren't, need needn't, mustn't are modal Auxiliaries.

Shall

'Shall' is used in the following ways:

(*a*) **With first Person Pronouns (I/we)**
I shall lend you my book.
We shall go to school together.

(*b*) **to express a suggestion**
Shall we go out for a walk?
Shall we meet the officer tomorrow?

Sometimes 'Shall' is used with Second and Third Person Pronouns as under:

(*a*) **to express a command**
You shall not tell a lie.
You shall not disturb us.

(*b*) **to express prohibition**
You shall not smoke here.
You shall not drink here.

(*c*) **to express a legal obligation**
You shall submit your sales tax return before the end of this month.

Should

'Should' is used in the following ways:

(*a*) **As Past Tense of 'shall'**
She said that she **should** settle in America.

(*b*) **to express duty and obligation**
You should do your duty honestly.

(*c*) **to express advice**
You should reach the station before time.

(*d*) **to express guess**
It should be 9 o'clock now.

(*e*) 'Should' is used with lest to express purpose.
Walk fast lest you should miss the train.

Will

'Will' is used in the following ways:

(*a*) **With Second and Third person Pronouns:**
You will dance at the party.
He will sing a song.

(*b*) **to express (Invitation/offer)**
Will you dine with me tonight?

(*c*) **to express an order**
Will you shut your big mouth?

(*d*) **to express probability**
He will come to see me tomorrow.

Sometimes 'Will' is used with 'I'

(*a*) **Determination**
I will win the first position.

(*b*) **A threat**
I will punish you.

(*c*) **A promise**
I will lend you Rs. 500/- tomorrow.

Would

'Would' is used in the following ways:

(*a*) **As Past Tense of 'will'**
He said that they would be attending the meeting the next day.

(*b*) **to express a desire or wish**
Would that I were a king!

(*c*) **to express a polite invitation**
Would you like some biscuits?

(*d*) **The usage of would in conditional sentences**
You would get good marks if you worked hard.
You would have won the race if you had run fast.

(*e*) **to express a piece of advice**
I would not meet him if I were you.

Can

'Can' is used in the following ways:

(*a*) **to express ability**
He can speak English fluently.

(*b*) **to grant permission**
You can go now.

(*c*) **to express impossibility**
Who can defeat his fate?

(*d*) **to make a request**
Can I use your motorbike?

Could

'Could' is used in the following ways:

(*a*) **As Past Tense of 'can'**
She said that she could see the sun rising.

(*b*) **to express past ability**
I could sing and dance when I was young.

(*c*) **to express a request**
Could I use your phone?

May

'May' is used in the following ways:

(*a*) **to express a request**
May I use your bicycle?

(*b*) **to seek and allow permission**
May I come in, sir?
Yes, you may.

(*c*) **to express possibility**
It may rain tonight.

(*d*) **In optative sentences**
May you live long!

Might

'Might' is used in the following ways:

(*a*) **As past tense of 'may'**
She said that her brother might come back home.

(*b*) **to express less possibility**
It might rain tonight.

(*c*) **to give and seek permission**
Might I come in, sir?
You might go home now.

Must

'Must' is used in the following ways:

(*a*) **to express duty**
You must serve your motherland.

(*b*) **to express obligation**
We must obey our elders.

(*c*) **to express advice**
You must take an umbrella before going to office.

(*d*) **to express probability**
'Must' expresses a stronger probability than may.
It must rain tonight.

Ought to

'Ought to' is used in the following ways:

(*a*) **to express obligation**

We ought to respect our teachers.

(*b*) **to express advice**

You ought to help the poor.

Used to

'Used to' is used in the following ways:

(*a*) **to express past habits**

He used to smoke.

(*b*) **to express past existence of something**

There used to be a five star hotel in this city.

Have to

'Have to' expresses compulsion in the present tense.

You have to sign the documents.

Had to

'Had to' expresses compulsion in the past time.

She had to join the office again.

Dare

'Dare' is used as a Modal only in Interrogative sentences.

How dare you touch my bag?

Dare not (Daren't)

'Dare not (Daren't)' is used in negative sentences.

She daren't complain against me.

Need

'Need' expresses an obligation/compulsion. It is used in Interrogative Sentences.

Need I say more?

Need not (Needn't)

'Need not (Needn't)' is used in negative sentences.

You needn't come here again.

Must not (Mustn't)

'Must not (Mustn't)' is the negative form of must.

You mustn't follow us.

MULTIPLE CHOICE QUESTIONS

Directions: *In the following questions choose the correct options to fill in the blanks:*

1. .... that I were rich!
A. Should B. Would
C. Could D. Ought to

2. .... you like some snacks?
A. Should B. Would
C. Could D. Ought to

3. .... I open the window?
A. Should B. Would
C. Could D. Ought to

4. Read carefully lest you .... fail in the examination.
A. should B. would
C. could D. ought to

5. You ...... love your countrymen.
A. should B. would
C. could D. ought to

6. You ...... stand first if you worked hard.
A. should B. would
C. could D. ought to

7. Had you sung well you ...... have won the first prize.
A. should B. would
C. could D. ought to

8. It ...... be 6 pm now.
A. should B. would
C. could D. ought to

9. .... that I were an actor!
A. Should B. Would
C. Could D. Ought to

10. Work hard lest you ..... get poor marks.
A. should B. would
C. could D. ought to

11. I ...... jump over this wall when I was young.
A. can B. could
C. may D. might

12. ...... I come in, sir?
A. Can B. Could
C. May D. Might

13. .... you progress by leaps and bounds!
A. Can B. Could
C. May D. Might

14. You ..... go home now.
A. can B. could
C. may D. might

15. Can I drink here? Yes, you ..... .
A. can B. could
C. may D. might

16. Can I smoke here? No, you ..... .
A. cannot B. could
C. may D. might

17. There are only small patches of clouds in the sky. It .... rain today.
A. can B. could
C. may D. might

18. Who .... win God?
A. can B. could
C. may D. might

19. .... I use your bike?
A. Can B. Should
C. May D. Might

20. She said that she .... solve all the sums in no time if she got a Parker Pen.
A. can B. would
C. may D. might

21. If I were you I ... not attend the meeting.
A. would B. should
C. could D. will

22. She ...... smoke in those days.
A. ought B. should
C. would D. used to

23. You ...... take the child to an intelligent doctor.
A. would B. ought to
C. shall D. will

24. ..... I sit here for some time?
A. Shall B. Will
C. Can D. Would

25. I .... sing a song but I can not dance.
A. can B. should
C. would D. could

26. I think you .... not mind my reciting the poem loudly.
A. should B. could
C. may D. would

27. Work fast lest you ...... not finish it before the sunset.
A. could B. should
C. may D. would

28. .... that I were a cricket player of great-fame!
A. Would B. Should
C. Could D. Was

29. ...... you like some more coffee?
A. Should B. Could
C. Would D. May

30. ...... I borrow your bicycle for a day?
A. Should B. Could
C. Would D. Might

31. No one ...... be allowed to make a noise here.
A. will B. shall
C. need D. dare

32. You ...... take care of your kids.
A. need B. dare
C. ought to D. would

33. He ..... have a walk daily when he was young.
A. ought to B. used to
C. need D. dare

34. ...... God bless you!
A. May B. Should
C. Must D. Might

35. He ...... be at the hotel now.
A. used to B. ought to
C. need D. should

ANSWERS

1	2	3	4	5	6	7	8	9	10
B	B	A	A	D	B	B	A	B	A
11	**12**	**13**	**14**	**15**	**16**	**17**	**18**	**19**	**20**
B	C	C	C	C	A	D	A	A	B
21	**22**	**23**	**24**	**25**	**26**	**27**	**28**	**29**	**30**
A	D	B	C	A	D	B	A	C	B
31	**32**	**33**	**34**	**35**					
A	C	B	A	D					

DETERMINERS & ARTICLES

Determiners are actually Adjectives. They are always followed by nouns.

Determiners are of the following kinds:

(A) Demonstrative Determiners
this, that, these, those etc.

(B) Possessive Determiners
my, our, your, his, her, its, their etc.

(C) Quantitative Determiners
some, any, much, enough, sufficient, whole, a little, the little, little, all, both etc.

(D) Numerical Determiners
a few, some, few, the few, any, several, many, no, etc.
One, two, three .... (Cardinals)
First, second, third .... (Ordinals)

(E) Distributive Determiners
either, neither etc.

(F) Articles
Indefinite: a, an
Definite: the

MULTIPLE CHOICE QUESTIONS

Directions: *In the following questions choose the correct options to fill the blanks.*

1. Give me .... rice.
   A. some B. few
   C. a few D. any
2. .... sheep grazing on the slope of the hill had gone away.
   A. Any B. The few
   C. This D. Much
3. Have you got .... magazines to read?
   A. all B. much
   C. some D. little
4. I have .... money that I want to spend on shares.
   A. any B. much
   C. less D. some
5. There is .... owl on the branch of the tree.
   A. a B. the
   C. an D. some
6. My brother is .... MBA.
   A. a B. an
   C. the D. any
7. Have you got .... cheese?
   A. some B. many
   C. a few D. few
8. No, I haven't got .... cheese.
   A. many B. few
   C. any D. some
9. There is only .... milk left in the bottle.
   A. enough B. few
   C. much D. a little
10. There is .... hope of his recovery.
    A. any B. little
    C. many D. few
11. .... dogs were barking at the strangers.
    A. some B. any
    C. much D. less
12. The girl bought her father .... juice.
    A. few B. some
    C. any D. many
13. You should take .... honey everyday.
    A. any B. many
    C. a little D. a few
14. .... boy was punished by the teacher.
    A. Either B. All
    C. Any D. Many
15. .... girl was asked to join the army.
    A. None B. Neither
    C. All D. Any
16. .... water in the jug has been drunk by Mohan.
    A. The little B. The few
    C. A few D. Few
17. I shall play .... piano at the party.
    A. some B. any
    C. the D. few
18. .... labourers were found dead in the mine.
    A. Any B. Fewer
    C. Many D. Less
19. Could I borrow .... umbrella?
    A. our B. your
    C. yours D. my
20. My brother is standing in the .... row.
    A. any B. many
    C. some D. first
21. Do you want .... tea?
    A. any B. more
    C. much D. few
22. He can fly .... aeroplane.
    A. a B. an
    C. some D. many
23. .... students were asked to bring their birth certificates.
    A. Many B. Any
    C. Much D. Less
24. .... gun needs oiling.
    A. It B. This
    C. These D. Those
25. .... shirts are mine.
    A. These B. This
    C. It D. That
26. .... child was allowed to enter the kitchen.
    A. The B. All
    C. Many D. A few
27. I have been waiting for you for .... hour.
    A. a B. an
    C. the D. a few
28. You must pay .... visit to your brothers.
    A. the B. an
    C. a few D. a
29. Why are you making .... noise?
    A. your B. enough
    C. a D. whole
30. He is .... honourable man.
    A. a B. the
    C. an D. much
31. .... shirts are mine.
    A. These B. That
    C. This D. It
32. .... glasses belong to Mr. Jack.
    A. This B. That
    C. Those D. It
33. .... birds have colourful wings.
    A. That B. These
    C. This D. It
34. I want a car. I'll get ....one.
    A. these B. this
    C. those D. it

35. I need a camera. I'll get .... now.
A. it B. these
C. this D. those

36. His conduct is bad, and his honesty is not ..... suspicion.
A. above B. beyond
C. under D. in

37. I hate sitting ..... him as he always smells of garlic.
A. besides B. along
C. at D. beside

38. The English schemed to continue their rule in India by playing off one community ..... the other.
A. before B. upon
C. against D. with

39. He lives near a lovely ...... of countryside.
A. length B. piece
C. section D. stretch

40. We had a ..... of warm weather in February.
A. time B. spell
C. length D. phase

ANSWERS

1	2	3	4	5	6	7	8	9	10
A	B	C	D	C	B	A	C	D	B
11	12	13	14	15	16	17	18	19	20
A	B	C	A	B	A	C	C	B	D
21	22	23	24	25	26	27	28	29	30
B	B	A	B	A	A	B	D	C	C
31	32	33	34	35	36	37	38	39	40
A	C	B	B	A	A	D	C	D	B

NARRATION

Direct Speech and Indirect Speech

The words spoken by a speaker are in Direct Speech.

The words spoken by somebody and expressed by someone else with some modification are known as Indirect Speech.

(*a*) Rohit says to me, "You do not understand me."
(*b*) Rohit tells me that I do not understand him.

The sentence (*a*) shows the words spoken by Rohit. So, it is a sentence of direct speech.

The sentence (*b*) shows the words spoken by Rohit and they have been reported with certain modification. So, it is a sentence of Indirect Speech.

Important Rules Regarding the change of Direct Speech into Indirect Speech

A. In a sentence of direct speech the verb outside the inverted commas is known as the Reporting Verb.

B. The words inside the inverted commas are known as Direct Speech.

C. When the sentence is indirect speech, it won't take a sign of exclamation or a sign of interrogation.

D. The Reporting Verb can be given in Present, Past or Future Tense.

E. When the Reporting Verb is in Present or Future Tense, there will be no change in the tense of direct speech while converting it into indirect speech.

F. When the Reporting Verb is in Past Tense the tense of direct speech will be changed while converting it into Indirect Speech.

G. The following adverbs and possessives should be changed as given:

(*i*) This into that
(*ii*) These into those
(*iii*) Here into there
(*iv*) Now into then
(*v*) Today into that day
(*vi*) Last night into the previous night
(*vii*) Tomorrow into the next day
(*viii*) The next day/week into the following day/week
(*ix*) Hence into thence.

Change of Tense

Reporting Verb	*Reporting Speech*	*Change of Tense*
Present Tense	Any Tense	No change
Future Tense	Any Tense	No change
Past Tense	Present/ Future Tense	Change into corresponding Past Tense
Past Tense	Past Indefinite Tense	Change into Past Perfect Tense

Past Tense	Past Continuous Tense	Change into Past Perfect Continuous Tense
Past Tense	Past Pefect/Perfect Continuous Tense	No change
Past Tense	Universal Truth	No change
Past Tense	Proverb	No change

Transformation Based on Special Rules

1. Rule Related to Interrogative Sentence

- If the answer of an interrogative sentence is possible in yes-no manner.

Illustration.

M.S. Dhoni told Rahul Dravid, "Will you help me?"
M.S. Dhoni asked Rahul Dravid whether he would help him.
(**Note :** The answer of Reporting Verb is possible in yes-no manner)

Rule of Transformation from Direct to Indirect speech

Step I : Change R.V. into ask.
Step II : In place of comma use 'if/whether'.
Step III : Change interrogative sentence into assertive sentence.

- If the answer of an interrogative sentence is not possible in yes-no manner.

Illustration:

Rahul Dravid told Dhoni, "What do you want?"
Rahul Dravid asked Dhoni what he wanted.
(**Note :** Only in Step II, you have to avoid comma and inverted comma and rest will be same as mentioned above).

2. Rule related to Imperative Sentence

- Imperative sentence is a sentence which shows Order/ Advice/Request

Illustration:

My father said to me, "Go there".
My father ordered me to go there.

Rule of Transformation from Direct to Indirect Speech

Step I : Change R.V. as per meaning/sense of R.S. into order/request/advise.
Step II : In place of comma, use 'to'.
Step III : Rest portion will be same.

3. Rule related to Optative Sentence

- Optative sentence is a sentence which exposes the feeling of bless/curse/pray/wish.

Illustration:

Mother said to me, "May you live long!"
Mother blessed me that I might live long.

Rule of Transformation from Direct to Indirect Speech

Step I : Change R.V. as per meaning/sense of R.S. into bless/curse/pray/wish.
Step II : In place of comma, use 'that'.
Step III : Change optative sentence into assertive sentence.

4. Rule related to Exclamatory Sentence

- Exclamatory sentence is a sentence which takes note of exclamatory (!) mark in that sentence showing inner feeling.

Illustration:

She said, "Alas! I am ruined".
She exclaimed with sorrow that she was ruined.

Rule of Transformation from Direct to Indirect Speech

Step I : Change R.V. as per meaning/sense of R.S. into exclaim/exclaims/exclaimed/will or shall exclaim + joy/sorrow/anger/surprise/applause/ contempt.
Step II : Change comma into that.
Step III : Change note of exclamation (!) into full (.)
Step IV : Change exclamatory sentence into assertive sentence.

MULTIPLE CHOICE QUESTIONS

Directions: *Each sentence in direct speech is followed by four options in indirect speech, only one is correct. Spot the correct answer.*

1. She said, "Shall I thread the needle?"
A. She asked if she should thread the needle.
B. She asked if she shall thread the needle.
C. She requested if she should thread the needle.
D. She says that if she would thread the needle.

2. We said, "What a place it is!"
A. We said that it was a very fine place.
B. We said that is a very fine place.
C. We said that the place is fine.
D. We exclaimed with joy that the place was very fine.

3. My father said, "The earth is round".
A. My father said that the earth was round.
B. My father says that the earth is round.
C. My father said that the earth is round
D. My father ordered that the earth is round.

4. The teacher said, "Don't make a noise".
A. The teacher says to us not to make a noise.
B. The teacher asked us not to make a noise.
C. The teacher requested us not to make a noise.
D. The teacher asked us not to made a noise.

5. He said, "Bring a chair at once".
A. He ordered to bring a chair at once.
B. He requested to bring a chair at once.

C. He told to bring a chair at once.
D. He says to bring a chair at once.

6. I said to my sister, "Please, give me more money".
A. I requested my sister to give me more money.
B. I ordered my sister to give me more money.
C. I advised my sister to gave me more money.
D. I requested my sister to give her more money.

7. Baby said, "I will go".
A. Baby said that she will go.
B. Baby said that she could go.
C. Baby say that she will go.
D. Baby said that she would go.

8. The teacher says, "Two and two makes four".
A. The teacher says that two and two made four.
B. The teacher wishes that two and two makes four.
C. The teacher advises that two and two makes four.
D. The teacher says that two and two makes four.

9. He told me, "Shall I go to the picture?"
A. He asked that he should go to the picture.
B. He asked me if he shall go to the picture.
C. He asked me if he should go to the picture.
D. He requested me to go to the picture.

10. I told Ravi, "Do have a cup of tea".
A. I ordered Ravi to have a cup of tea.
B. I advised Ravi to had a cup of tea.
C. I requested Ravi to have a cup of tea.
D. I said Ravi to have a cup of cold tea.

11. She said, "I am an early-riser".
A. She regretted that she was an early-riser.
B. She said that she is an early-riser.
C. She said that she was an early-riser.
D. She regretted that she is an early-riser.

12. The police officer said to the criminal, "Speak as I tell you".
A. The police officer directed the criminal to speak as he told him.
B. The police officer told the criminal to speak as he told him.
C. The police officer advised the criminal to speak as he told him.
D. The police officer requested the criminal to speak as he told him.

13. The preacher said to me, "May God help you!"
A. The preacher prayed that God might help me.
B. The preacher prayed that God might help him.
C. The preacher requested that God might help me.
D. The preacher requested the God might help them.

14. She said to me, "Happy Diwali!"
A. She blessed me a happy Diwali.
B. She wished me a happy Diwali.
C. She prayed a happy Diwali.
D. She said to me a very happy Diwali.

15. He said, "Shall I open the gate?"
A. He asked that he should open the gate.
B. He asked if he should open the gate.
C. He ordered that he should open the gate.
D. He requested that he should open the gate.

16. She said to me, "Keep quite and listen to my words".
A. She requested me to keep quite and listen to her words.
B. She ordered me to keep quite and listen to her words.
C. She entreated me to keep quite and listen to her words.
D. She told me to keep quite and listen to her words.

17. My brother said to me, "What are you doing here?"
A. My brother asked me that what I was doing there.
B. My brother asked me what I was doing there.
C. My brother asked me that what was I doing there.
D. My brother asked me what I was doing here.

18. Ravi said, "My father lived in this city two years ago."
A. Ravi said that his father had lived in that city two years before.
B. Ravi said that his father had lived in that city two years ago.
C. Ravi told that his father had lived in that city ago two years.
D. Ravi asked that his father had lived in that city before two years.

19. My brother said to me, "When I was young, I used to play cricket".
A. My brother told me that when I was young, I used to play cricket.
B. My brother told me that when I was young, I used to play cricket.
C. My brother told me that when he was young, I used to play cricket.
D. My brother told me that when he was young, he used to play cricket.

20. The student said, "Sir, I am not guilty".
A. The student said with respect that he was not guilty.
B. The student pleaded that he was not guilty.
C. The student pleaded with respect that he was not guilty.
D. The student said respectfully that he was not guilty.

21. Mohini said to me, "Trust in God."
Mohini advised me:
A. that I should trust in God.
B. should trust in God.
C. trusted in God.
D. to trust in God.

22. I said to him, "Let us go to school."
I told him:
A. we would go to school.
B. we shall go to school.
C. that we would go to school.
D. that we should go to school.

23. Rajni said, "May God bless you?"
Rajni:
A. exclaimed with wish that God might bless me.
B. expressed a wish that God might bless me.
C. asked God to bless me.
D. shouted with joy to bless me.

24. My mother said to me, "Do not have so many friends."
My mother forbade me:
A. to have so many friends.
B. not to have so many friends.
C. to have been so many friends.
D. to possess so many friends.

25. Ram said, "Pay attention to me."
Ram asked:
A. pay attention to him.
B. paid attention to him.
C. having paid attention to him.
D. to pay attention to him.

ANSWERS

1	2	3	4	5	6	7	8	9	10
A	D	C	B	A	A	D	D	C	C
11	**12**	**13**	**14**	**15**	**16**	**17**	**18**	**19**	**20**
C	A	A	B	B	B	B	A	D	C
21	**22**	**23**	**24**	**25**					
A	D	B	A	D					

ACTIVE & PASSIVE VOICE

An active sentence focuses on the person or thing doing the action. A passive sentence focuses on the person or thing affected by the action.

e.g., The tower was built. (Active voice)
Someone built the tower. (Passive voice)

Transformation of Voice

i.e., Active voice to Passive voice & vice versa.

- Voice and Tense are closely associated with each other.
- Tense plays an important role while transforming the voice.

MULTIPLE CHOICE QUESTIONS

Directions: *In these questions, the sentences have been given in Active/Passive voice. From the given options, choose the one which best expresses the given sentence in Passive/Active voice.*

1. Help the poor.
A. The poor should be helped.
B. The poor would be helped.
C. The poor must be helped.
D. The poor will be helped.

2. Bring a glass of water.
A. A glass of water will be brought.
B. A glass of water should be brought.
C. Let a glass of water be brought.
D. Let a glass of water will be brought.

3. He gave me a beautiful flower pot.
A. A beautiful flower pot was given to me by him.
B. A beautiful flower pot had given to me by him.
C. A beautiful flower pot had been giving by him.
D. I was giving him a beautiful flower pot.

4. Is he answering the question?
A. The question is answered by him.
B. The question is being answered by him.
C. Is the question being answered by him?
D. Is the question being answering by him?

5. Who gave you this letter?
A. This letter was given to you by whom?
B. This letter had given to you by whom?
C. Was this letter given to you?
D. By whom was this letter given to you?

6. The professor teaches students.
A. Students are being taught by the professor.
B. Students are taught by the professor.
C. The professor is being taught by students.
D. Students being taught by the professor.

7. M.S. Dhoni has created a world record.
A. A world record has been created by M.S. Dhoni.
B. A world record has created by M.S. Dhoni.
C. A world record is created by M.S. Dhoni.
D. A world record is being created by M.S. Dhoni.

8. Srishti sings a lovely song.
A. A lovely song had sung by Srishti.
B. A lovely song was sung by Srishti.

C. A lovely song is sung by Srishti.
D. A lovely song is sang by Srishti.

9. He was drawing a picture.
A. A picture was drawn by him.
B. A picture was being drawn by him.
C. A picture was drawing by him.
D. A picture was drew by him.

10. We made him leader.
A. He was made leader by us.
B. He was maded leader.
C. He made leader by us.
D. He was made leader.

11. There is no time to waste.
A. There is no time to be wasted.
B. No time to be wasted there.
C. No time to be wasted by there.
D. No time is to be wasted.

12. Take medicine in time.
A. In time medicine to be taken.
B. Medicine should be taken in time.
C. Medicine in time will be taken.
D. Medicine has to be in time taken.

13. He reads a novel.
A. A novel was read by him.
B. A novel has read by him.
C. A novel is being read by him.
D. A novel is read by him.

14. They had cleared the dues.
A. The dues had been cleared by them.
B. The dues had cleared by them.
C. The dues are being cleared.
D. The dues is cleared.

15. I invite you on the dinner.
A. On the dinner you have been invited.
B. On the dinner you are inviting.
C. You are inviting by me on the dinner.
D. You are invited by me on the dinner.

16. We chose him our leader.
A. He was chosen our leader.
B. He has been chosen our leader.
C. He had chosen our leader.
D. He have been chosen our leader.

17. Who made a maiden century?
A. By whose was a maiden century made?
B. By whom was a maiden century make?
C. By whom was a maiden century made?
D. By whom had a maiden century made?

18. I may help her in her project.
A. She might be helped by me in her project.
B. She may be helped by me in her project.
C. She might be helped in her project by me.
D. In her project, she may be help by me.

19. Take medicine in time.
A. Medicine should be taken in time.
B. Medicine will be taken in time.
C. Medicine will be took in time.
D. Medicine shall take in time.

20. I am solving the questions.
A. The questions are being solved by me.
B. The questions have been solved by me.
C. The questions are to be solved by me.
D. The question are solved by me.

21. May I take this pen?
A. May this pen will be taken by me?
B. May this pen shall be taken by me?
C. May this pen should be taken by me?
D. May this pen be taken by me?

22. Can we send it by air?
A. Can this be sent by air?
B. Can it be sent by air?
C. Can it go by air?
D. Can it be send by air?

23. Who wrote this book?
A. By whom was this book written?
B. By whom is this book written?
C. By whom was this book being written?
D. By whom is this book being written?

24. What did you buy?
A. What is bought by you?
B. What is being bought by you?
C. What was bought by you?
D. What was being bought by you?

25. Whom do you want?
A. Who is wanted by you?
B. Who is being wanted by you?
C. You are wanted by whom?
D. You are being wanted by whom?

ANSWERS

1	2	3	4	5	6	7	8	9	10
A	C	A	C	D	B	A	C	B	A
11	**12**	**13**	**14**	**15**	**16**	**17**	**18**	**19**	**20**
A	B	D	A	D	A	C	B	A	A
21	**22**	**23**	**24**	**25**					
D	B	A	C	A					

CLAUSES

THE CLAUSE AND THE SENTENCE

1. **The Sentence** is a group of words that makes complete sense. As such it contains a subject and a predicate containing a finite verb. Sometimes, it has one or more objects. It is independent and grammatically self-contained.
2. **The Clause** is a part of the predicate and has a finite verb. It also has a subject but it is dependent on the Principal (or the main) clause.

Kinds of Clauses

The following are the kinds of clauses:

1. Principal clause
2. Coordinate clause
3. Subordinate clause

There are three kinds of subordinate clauses:

I. Adjective clause
II. Adverb clause
III. Noun clause

A. Adjective Clause

A clause which acts as an adjective is known as Adjectives clause. Most often it can replace an adjective or adjective phrase e.g.

(*i*) Mrs Sharma has a **black** purse. (Adjective)
(*ii*) Mrs Sharma has a purse of **black colour.** (Adjective Phrase)
(*iii*) Mrs Sharma has a purse **which is black in colour**. (Adjective clause)

In sentence no. (*i*) 'black is an adjective and in sentence no. (*ii*) 'of black colour' is an adjective phrase. Both of these can be replaced with an adjective clause 'which is black in colour.'

All Relative clauses are the examples of the adjective clauses.

A clause which follows a Noun or Pronoun is known as an Adjective clause. The said Noun or Pronoun is called 'Antecedent'.

Relative clauses are made by the Relative Pronouns and Relative Adverbs.

Relative Pronouns which make Adjective clauses
who whose whom which that, as what, whatsoever
Relative Adverbs which make Adjective clauses
when, why, how, whenever, where, wherever

B. Adverb Clause

An Adverb clause is the clause which does the function of an Adverb. Most often it replaces an Adverb or an Adverb Phrase. It may modify a verb, an adjective or another adverb, *e.g.*

(*i*) Amar is taller **than you** (are).
(*ii*) **As soon as the boy saw the snake**, he cried loudly.
(*iii*) If you work hard, you'll get good marks.

Classification of Adverb Clauses

Adverbs clauses can be classified as under:

I. Adverb clauses of Place.
II. Adverb clauses of Time.
III. Adverb clauses of Manner.
IV. Adverb clauses of Comparison.
V. Adverb clauses of Condition.
VI. Adverb clauses of Cause or Reason.
VII. Adverb clauses of Purpose.
VIII. Adverb clauses of Result or Consequences.
IX. Adverb clauses of Extent or Degree.
X. Adverb clauses of Contrast or Concession.

I. Adverb Clauses of Place

A clause which shows the place of an action is know as Adverb Clause of Place.

(*i*) This is the place **where** I found a coin.
(*ii*) I'll follow you **wherever** you go.

II. Adverb clauses of Time

A clause which is related to time is called an Adverb clause of Time.

(*i*) Stay here until I come back.
(*ii*) I was reading my book when somebody called out my name.

III. Adverb Clauses of Manner

The clause which indicates the manner of an action is known as the Adverb clause of Manner.

(*i*) Do as you are instructed.
(*ii*) He talks as if he were a prince.

IV. Adverb Clauses of Comparison

The clause which indicates the comparison is known as the Adverb clause of comparison.

(*i*) She is fatter than you.
(*ii*) He is as wise as he.

V. Adverb Clauses of Condition

A clause which indicates the condition imposed on the action of the verb is called the Adverb Clause of condition.

(*i*) If you work hard you may get good marks.
(*ii*) In case you need my help, please call me out loudly.

VI. Adverb Clauses of Cause or Reason

The clause which indicates the cause or reason of an action is known as the Adverb Clause of Cause or Reason.

(*i*) He could not run fast because he was injured.
(*ii*) I do not like him as he lacks in manners.

VII. Adverb Clauses of Purpose

The clause which indicates the purpose of an action is known as the Adverb clause of Purpose.

(*i*) Walk carefully lest you should fall.

(*ii*) She cried loudly so that she might be heard.

VIII. Adverb Clauses of Result or Consequence

The clause which indicates the result or consequence of an action is known as Adverb Clause of Result or Consequence.

(*i*) She is so weak in studys that she cannot read anybook.

(*ii*) He runs so fast that you cannot catch him.

IX. Adverb Clauses of Extent or Degree

The clause which indicates the extent or degree of an action is known as the Adverb Clause of Extent or Degree.

(*i*) As far as I know, he is a good man.

(*ii*) The more, the marrier.

X. Adverbs Clauses of contrast or concession

(*i*) Although he ran fast, he could not catch the train.

(*ii*) Howsoever busy he may be, he'll attend to you.

C. Noun Clauses

The clause which does the function of a Noun is known as a Noun Clause.The Noun Clause can act in the following ways:

1. As Subject to a verb.
2. As Object to a participle.
3. As Object to an infinitive.
4. As Object to a preposition.
5. As Object to a verb.
6. As Complement to a verb.
7. Case in Apposition to a noun or pronoun.

1. As the Subject to a verb

(*i*) **Why you are crying** we fail to understand.

(*ii*) **Where he will go,** nobody cares.

(*iii*) **How he earned money** is known to all.

(*iv*) **When he will wake up** is not sure.

2. As Object to a participle

(*i*) **Knowing that his father will not rebuke him,** he starts disturbing his sister.

(*ii*) **Finding that the necklace lying on the ground** was of gold, he picked it up.

(*iii*) **Saying that he did not know French** he started singing English songs.

(*iv*) They started playing in the ground thinking that nobody will object to it.

3. As Object to an infinitive

(*i*) I would like to know **whether you are going** to the USA or Russia.

(*ii*) He wants to say whether his brother will come back or not.

(*iii*) She wants to inform why she did not attend the meeting.

4. As Object to a preposition

(*i*) He stuck to **what he believed.**

(*ii*) Listen to **what she says.**

(*iii*) She Objected to what you said.

5. As Object to a verb

(*i*) I do not understand **why he behaves like this.**

6. As complement to a verb

(*i*) His fear is that he will be asked about the murder.

(*ii*) It seems that he would catch the train.

7. Case in Apposition to a noun or a pronoun

(*i*) The fact that he is honest is known to all.

(*ii*) The reason why he failed in the examination is not far to seek.

MULTIPLE CHOICE QUESTIONS

Directions: *Tick the correct alternative for each of the following italicised clauses:*

1. I like the dog *which has black soft fur.*

A. Noun clause B. Adjective Clause
C. Adverb clause D. None of these

2. This is the boy *who met us in Shimla.*

A. Adverb Clause B. Adjective Clause
C. Noun Clause D. None of these

3. Here is the pen *which you gave me.*

A. Adjective Clause B. Adverb Clause
C. Noun clause D. None of these

4. The reason *why he didn't attend the meeting is not known.*

A. Noun Clause B. Adverb Clause
C. Adjective Clause D. None of these

5. She wears the same clothes *as her brother wears.*

A. Adjective clause B. Adverb Clause
C. Noun Clause D. None of these

6. I have such relatives *as will support me in bad times.*

A. Adverb Clause B. Adjective Clause
C. Noun Clause D. None of these

7. I know *that he is a good boy.*

A. Adverb Clause B. Noun Clause
C. Adjective Clause D. None of these

8. *What you think* is good.

A. Noun clause B. Adjective Clause
C. Adverb clause D. None of these

9. Who can say *where he lives?*

A. Adjective clause B. Adverb clause
C. Noun clause D. None of these

10. Listen to *what the teacher says.*
A. Adjective clause B. Noun clause
C. Adverb clause D. None of these

11. She is not *what she seems.*
A. Noun clause B. Adjective clause
C. Adverb clause D. None of these

12. I want to know *where you have put my watch.*
A. Adverb Clause B. Adjective Clause
C. Noun Clause D. None of these

13. It is known to all of us *that he is a stupid fellow.*
A. Adjective Clause B. Adverb Clause
C. Noun clause D. None of these

14. I went to my father finding *that none of us could open that box.*
A. Adverb Clause B. Noun Clause
C. Adjective Clause D. None of these

15. She came back *before it was morning.*
A. Adjective clause B. Adverb Clause
C. Noun Clause D. None of these

16. We looked *where mush-rooms were growing.*
A. Adjective Clause B. Noun Clause
C. Adverb Clause D. None of these

17. *Where there is a will* there is a way.
A. Adverb Clause B. Adjective Clause
C. Noun Clause D. None of these

18. You may go *wherever you like.*
A. Adjective Clause B. Noun clause
C. Adverb clause D. None of these

19. *As soon as the thief saw a policeman,* he ran away.
A. Adjective clause B. Adverb clause
C. Noun clause D. None of these

20. Wait here *until I come.*
A. Adjective clause B. Noun clause
C. Adverb clause D. None of these

21. He walked out of the house *when the rain stopped.*
A. Noun clause B. Adjective clause
C. Adverb clause D. None of these

22. Her brother danced *while she sang.*
A. Adverb Clause B. Adjective Clause
C. Noun Clause D. None of these

23. You must listen to me *whenever you have finished your home work.*
A. Adjective Clause B. Adverb Clause
C. Noun clause D. None of these

24. We had returned home *before the storm started.*
A. Noun Clause B. Adverb Clause
C. Adjective Clause D. None of these

25. *As long as I'm here* you needn't get afraid of anybody.
A. Adjective clause B. Noun Clause
C. Adverb Clause D. None of these

26. I haven't seen him since I *met him five years ago.*
A. Adverb Clause B. Adjective Clause
C. Noun Clause D. None of these

27. *Just as I was getting out of my car,* I saw a monkey jumping over the wall of the orchard.
A. Adjective Clause B. Adverb Clause
C. Noun Clause D. None of these

28. *As I went out into the courtyard of my house,* I saw a snake in the grass.
A. Adjective Clause B. Noun clause
C. Adverb clause D. None of these

29. She was happy *because she had won a jackpot.*
A. Adjective clause B. Adverb clause
C. Noun clause D. None of these

30. *Since/As you are not going to office,* let's play hockey.
A. Adjective clause B. Noun clause
C. Adverb clause D. None of these

31. I take antihypertensive drugs *that my blood pressure may remain in control.*
A. Noun clause B. Adjective clause
C. Adverb clause D. None of these

32. He is running fast *so that he may catch the train.*
A. Adverb Clause B. Adjective Clause
C. Noun Clause D. None of these

33. Walk fast *lest you should miss the train.*
A. Adjective Clause B. Adverb Clause
C. Noun clause D. None of these

34. I don't let him run a race *in case he is ill.*
A. Noun Clause B. Adverb Clause
C. Adjective Clause D. None of these

35. We've arranged her a tutor *in order that Mshe may continue her studies.*
A. Adjective clause B. Noun Clause
C. Adverb Clause D. None of these

36. He walks *as if or as though he were a king.*
A. Adjective Clause B. Adverb Clause
C. Noun Clause D. None of these

37. Do *as I tell you.*
A. Adverb Clause B. Adjective Clause
C. Noun Clause D. None of these

38. He can do *as he wishes.*
A. Adjective Clause B. Noun clause
C. Adverb clause D. None of these

39. He *is wiser than you.*
A. Adjective clause B. Adverb clause
C. Noun clause D. None of these

40. She will work *as fast as she can.*
A. Adjective clause B. Noun clause
C. Adverb clause D. None of these

41. He likes to sit calmly *rather than work.*
A. Adverb clause B. Adjective clause
C. Noun clause D. None of these

42. *Although he had worked* hard, he failed in the examination.
A. Noun Clause B. Adjective Clause
C. Adverb Clause D. None of these

43. *Even if/even though/although you don't like him,* you should greet him in the party.
A. Adjective Clause B. Adverb Clause
C. Noun clause D. None of these

44. *However hard you work* you'll not (or won't) get success.
A. Adverb Clause
B. Noun Clause
C. Adjective Clause
D. None of these

45. *If you call him,* he will come to see you.
A. Adjective clause B. Adverb Clause
C. Noun Clause D. None of these

46. *If the weather is not good,* the flight may be cancelled.
A. Adjective Clause B. Noun Clause
C. Adverb Clause D. None of these

47. If *I had the magazine Sun,* I would show you the picture of Madonna in it.
A. Adverb Clause B. Adjective Clause
C. Noun Clause D. None of these

48. *If anybody threatened me,* I would call the police.
A. Adjective Clause B. Noun clause
C. Adverb clause D. None of these

49. I would not tell him this *if I were you.*
A. Adjective clause B. Adverb clause
C. Noun clause D. None of these

50. You would have won the race *if you had run fast.*
A. Adverb clause B. Noun clause
C. Adjective clause D. None of these

ANSWERS

1	2	3	4	5	6	7	8	9	10
B	B	A	C	A	B	B	A	C	B
11	**12**	**13**	**14**	**15**	**16**	**17**	**18**	**19**	**20**
A	C	C	B	B	C	A	C	B	C
21	**22**	**23**	**24**	**25**	**26**	**27**	**28**	**29**	**30**
C	A	B	B	C	A	B	C	B	C
31	**32**	**33**	**34**	**35**	**36**	**37**	**38**	**39**	**40**
C	A	B	B	C	B	A	C	B	C
41	**42**	**43**	**44**	**45**	**46**	**47**	**48**	**49**	**50**
A	C	B	A	B	C	A	C	B	A

IDIOMS & PHRASES

An idiom is a group of words established by usage as having a meaning different from the individual words. A phrase is a small group of words standing together as an idiomatic expression.
Learn and practise as many as you can.

IDIOMS AND IDIOMATIC PHRASES

1. **ABC** (basic principles)
   She does not know the ABC of photography.
2. **To cut a sorry figure** (present oneself in a bad way)
   She cut a sorry figure on the stage.
3. **Cut loose** (Keep away)
   India should cut loose from bad politics.
4. **To give a red carpet reception** (to give a warm welcome)
   The PM was given a red carpet reception in America.
5. **To dance one's tune** (to follow someone submissively)
   He always dances to his brother's tune.
6. **To turn a deaf ear to** (to disregard)
   She turned a deaf ear to her parents' advice.
7. **To call a spade a spade** (to speak the truth)
   Gandhiji always called a spade a spade.
8. **To bring to book** (to scold)
   The naughty boy was brought to book by the teacher.
9. **From hand to mouth** (without any saving)
   The poor factory worker is living from hand to mouth.
10. **Once in a blue moon** (seldom)
    She visits her brother once in a blue moon.
11. **To cut short** (to reduce)
    Smoking will cut short your life.

12. **By hook or by crook** (by any means fair or foul) He wants to get money by hook or by crook.
13. **In the good books of** (be good in one's mind) Jack is in the good books of his teachers.
14. **At sixes and sevens** (in disorder) The drawing room articles were lying at sixes and sevens on the floor.
15. **To grease the palm of** (to bribe) Rohit greased the palm of the clerk and got the file moved.
16. **Through thick and thin.** (under all circumstances) We'll stand by you through thick and thin.
17. **At one's beck and call** (ready to obey) He had a dozen men at his beck and call.
18. **To die by inches** (to die a painful death) The old man died by inches.
19. **To eat one's words** (to retract one's statement) You'll have to eat your words because you have spoken without thinking.
20. **To burn the midnight oil** (to work hard) You'll have to burn the midnight oil if you want to get good marks.
21. **Fair and square** (clean) One must be fair and square in one's dealing.
22. **To poke one's nose into** (to meddle with) It is bad to poke your nose into others' affair.
23. **To fall flat** (to have no effect) His father's advice fell flat on him.
24. **To make a clean breast of** (to confess) He made a clean breast of his involvement in the bomb blast.
25. **To get the better of** (overcome) Anger got the better of him.
26. **A wet blanket** (a discouraging person) Don't allow Rakesh to accompany you to the hunting trip because he is a wet blanket.
27. **A big gun** (an important person) Mr Smith is a big gun in our city.
28. **In black and white** (in written) Don't give him anything in black and white.
29. **Neck and neck** (even) There is a neck and neck fight between the two boxers.
30. **At a stone's throw** (at a short distance from) My school is at a stone's throw from my house.
31. **Cut-throat competition** (a stiff competition) There is a cut-throat competition among the publishers in the market.
32. **Black sheep** (a traitor) Later on Mr XYZ proved a black sheep.
33. **By dint of** (by means of) By dint of hard work, she earned a lot of money.
34. **A man of word** (a person who keeps his promise) Mr Sharma is a man of word.
35. **A man of a few words** (a remarkable person) Gandhiji was a man of a few words.
36. **In cold blood** (mercilessly) The old woman was murdered in cold blood.
37. **At arm's length** (to keep away) We should always keep bad boys at arm's length.
38. **Keep the ball rolling** (to maintain the progress of some activity) After the death of his father he had to take the charge of his office to keep the ball rolling.
39. **A bolt from the blue** (a sudden and unexpected event) The news of my friend's death came to me like a bolt from the blue.
40. **Break one's back** (to work hard to get something) He broke his back to earn his livelihood.
41. **Break the back of** (accomplish the hardest part of a certain job) There is nothing to be worried about as we've already broken the back of the problem.
42. **Beat about the bush** (to go on talking on some worthless topic) Stop this beating about the bush, come to the main task.
43. **Throw cold water on** (to discourage) She tried to throw cold water on his plan but he was well-determined.
44. **Hard of hearing** (somewhat deaf) She is a bit hard of hearing.
45. **Come what may** (no matter what happens) I'll do it come what may.
46. **Beyond one's means** (beyond one's budget) He is living beyond his means, therefore, he is sure to get ruined.
47. **A man of letters** (a scholar) Radha Krishnan was a man of letters.
48. **Chips of the same block** (having the same taste) They are the chips of the same block.
49. **The long and short of** (in brief) The long and short of his lecture is that we should live like brothers.
50. **In full swing** (in full force) The studies of the students are going on in full swing.

VERBAL PHRASES

Back

Back up (to make a queue) The vehicles began to back up.

Back down (withdraw claim in the presence of opposition) The leader backed down from his previous statement.

Back off (draw back some plan or action)
They backed off from building a flyover.
Back out (withdraw from a promise, etc.)
The government backed out of its promise.

Break

Break down (stop working) My car broke down on the highway.
Break into (enter in certain premises by breaking the door, etc.)
Last night a thief broke into my neighbour's.
Break off (stop all of a sudden)
She broke off and began to think over about her/his hand.
Break out (spread)
Cholera has broken out in the town.
Break out of (escape from)
A prisoner broke out of the prison last night.
Break up (disperse)
The cloud of fog began to break up as the sun rose.
Break something up (Cause something to break into small pieces)
She broke up the chewing gum to distribute it among the girls.
Break with (Cut off connection after quarrelling with someone)
He has broken with his brother.

Call

Call on (pay a visit to somebody)
I'll call on Mohan's today.
Call out (to start)
The workers have called out a strike.
Call off (to stop the strike etc.)
The workers have called off the strike.
Call at (to visit someone's house)
I called at his house yesterday.
Call in (send for)
Please call in the doctor.

Carry

Carry on (continue)
Please carry on your work.
Carry something out (perform a task)
Our company is carrying out a big deal with a foreign company.
Carry something over (postpone)
The fancy dress competition had to be carried over till Monday)
Carry someone off (kill somebody)
Cancer carried her off on the day of her 20th birthday.

Come

Come of age (get established)
As our company has come of age, so, there is no problem in selling our goods.
Come of (belong to)
She comes of a royal family.
Come over (surmount)
We at last came over all our problems.
Come off (to take place)
The marriage of my brother comes off in the next month.
Come round (agree)
At last he came round to my views.
Come under (fall in the category of)
All these animals come under the same species.
Come down with (suffer from)
She came down with whopping cough.
Come from (be the nature of)
She came from London.
Come about (happen)
The explosion came about when the worker struck the match to light a cigarette.

Cut

Cut off (die)
The princess was cut off in the prime of her life.
Cut down (reduce)
The prices of consumer goods should be cut down.
Cut someone out (exclude someone)
His father cut him out of his will.

Fall

Fall in
She fell in love with the prince.
Fall down (fail)
The deal fell down for lack of transparency.
Fall out (quarrel)
She fell out with his elder brother.
Fall through (fail)
The project fell through for lack of funds.

Get

Get away (escape)
She got away with her life.
Get by (to accomplish something with great difficulty)
She is not rich. She has just enough to get by.
Get on (perform)
How are you getting on with your studies?
Get out (become known)
The news got out that the PM was paying a visit to Russia.

Get over (overcome)
At last I got over all obstacles.
Get up (rise)
When do you get up in the morning?

Give

Give up (stop)
He gave up smoking.
Give out (emit)
Garlic gives out a pungent smell.
Give in (collapse)
The bridge gave in under the heavy load.
Give away (distribute)
The Principal gave away the prizes.
Give out (announce)
It was given out that the President of India would visit the place soon.

Go

Go off (explode)
The gun went off suddenly.
Go on (continue)
She went on about how she flew the aeroplane.
Go through (examine)
I'll go through this book later on.
Go up (be built)
The construction of the house is going up.

Grind

Grind on (continue for a long time in a tedious way)
The discussion over political issues ground on.
Grind something out (produce something a tedious way)
She will grind some more short stories.

Look

Look out (be careful)
Look out! there is a snake.
Look down upon (hate)
We should not look down upon the poor.
Look at (watch)
Look at the blackboard.
Look after (take care of)
We ought to look after our old parents.
Look into (investigate)
The new police inspector will look into the matter.
Look up (rise)
The prices of consumer goods are looking up.
Look back (think of the past)
It made her feel disolate when she looked back on things of the past.

Make

Make up (to fulfil)
I'll make up my deficiency in Mathematics.
Make out (understand)
I could not make out what she said.
Make up one' mind (to resolve)
I have made up my mind to settle in the USA.
Make off (leave hurriedly)
She made off without informing anybody.
Make something over (transfer)
She should make her property over to her sons.
Make over (hand over)
He made over the charge of the file to Mr Robert.

Pull

Pull back (retreat)
The government has pulled back from its previous policy.
Pull something down (demolish)
The authorities concerned pulled down a few building which were illegally built on government land.
Pull out (pluck)
The child pulled out a few petals of the flower.
Pull through (recover)
The patient will pull through.

Push

Push on (continue a journey)
It was getting darker but we pushed on.
Push at (exert force)
He pushed at the bell, but it did not ring.
Push for (demand persistently)
The workers have been pushing for the installation of new machines since 2003.

Put

Put out (extinguish)
She put out the light.
Put on (wear)
He put on an overcoat.
Put off (postpone)
The plan had to be put off.
Put by (spare something for future)
We must put by some money for future.
Put up with (stay)
Your aunt is out of town for a couple of days, you may put up with us till she comes.
Put something down (record something)
She put a new idea down on the paper.

Take

Take after (resemble)
He takes after his father.
Take off (remove)
He took off his shoes.
Take something out (obtain)
You may take out some money from Rohit if you want to purchase this car.
Take to (fall into the habit of)
He took to gambling.

Turn

Turn something down (reject something)
The judge turned down his appeal.
Turn on (attack)
The thief turned on him with a knife.

MULTIPLE CHOICE QUESTIONS

Directions: *Some idioms/phrases are given below with their meanings. Choose their correct meanings.*

1. To beg the question
A. To refer to B. To take for granted
C. To raise objections D. To be discussed

2. To drive home
A. To find one's roots
B. To return to place of rest
C. Back to original position
D. To emphasise

3. To hit the right nail on the head
A. To do the right thing
B. To destroy one's reputation
C. To announce one's fixed views
D. To teach someone a lesson

4. To pick holes
A. To find some reason to quarrel
B. To destory something
C. To criticise someone
D. To cut some part of an item

5. To smell a rat
A. To see signs of plague epidemic
B. To get bad smell of a dead rat
C. To suspect foul dealings
D. To be in a bad mood

6. A black sheep
A. An unlucky person B. A negro
C. An ugly person D. None of these

7. To catch a tarter
A. To trap wanted criminal with great difficulty
B. To catch a dangerous person
C. To meet with disaster
D. To deal with a person who is more than one's watch

8. To be above board
A. To have a good height
B. To be honest in any business deal
C. To have no debts
D. To try to be beautiful

9. To keep one's temper
A. To become angry
B. To be in good mood
C. To preserve one's energy
D. To be aloof from

10. To have an axe to grind
A. A private end to serve
B. To fail to arouse interest
C. To have no result
D. To work for both sides

11. To cry wolf
A. to listen eagerly B. to give false alarm
C. to turn pale D. to keep off starvation

12. A man of straw
A. a man of no substance
B. a very active person
C. a worthy fellow
D. an unreasonable person

13. To make clean breast of
A. to gain prominence
B. to praise oneself
C. to confess without reserve
D. to destroy before it blooms

14. To end in smoke
A. to make completely understand
B. to ruin oneself
C. to excite great applause
D. None of these

15. To leave someone in the lurch
A. to come to compromise with someone
B. constant source of annoyance to someone
C. to put someone at ease
D. to desert someone in his difficulties

16. To play second fiddle
A. To be happy, cheerful and healthy
B. To reduce importance of one's senior
C. To support the role and view of another person
D. To do back seat driving

17. To set one's face against
A. To oppose with determination
B. To judge by appearance
C. To get out of difficulty
D. To look at one steadily

18. To put one's hand to the plough
A. To take up agricultural farming
B. To take a difficult task
C. To get entangled into unnecessary things
D. Take interest in technical work

19. To join issue with
A. To cooperate with others for a cause
B. To join any voluntary organisation for good purpose
C. To resolve dispute and restore peace
D. To enter into argument over any issue

20. To do oneself justice
A. To dispense justice on our own
B. To treat others with due respect
C. To defend one's point of view
D. None of these

21. Once in a blue moon
A. Once in a while B. Often
C. At a short interval D. At a particular time

22. Crocodile tears
A. Big tears B. Cry in a huge voice
C. To fee sorry D. Hypocritical tears

23. To beat about the bush
A. To do something wrong
B. To beat somebody badly
C. To open some secret
D. To talk meaninglessly or in a roundabout way

24. To be at sixes and sevens
A. To be in a proper order
B. To be in an improper order
C. To be in a good mood
D. Something in abundance

25. A big mouth
A. A man having a large mouth
B. A strong man
C. A boastful person
D. A heavy cannon

26. French leave
A. A leave without permission
B. A leave for a long time
C. A leave for a short period of time
D. A leave forever

27. To cool one's heals
A. To run away
B. To stand in comfort
C. To keep (to be kept) waiting for someone
D. To stand firmly

28. Chips of the same block
A. Persons of the same caste
B. Persons of the same taste
C. Persons from the same family
D. Foolish persons

29. To kick the bucket
A. To fall unconsciously
B. To hate someone
C. To beat someone
D. To die

30. To make out
A. To prepare something
B. To understand
C. To guess
D. To complete something

31. To call a spade a spade
A. To speak the truth
B. To tell a lie
C. To open the secret
D. To say something on somebody's face

32. To bank upon
A. To go to bank
B. To depend upon
C. To sit on the bank of a lake
D. To say something in a quick manner

33. To spread like wild fire
A. To spread in a large area
B. To spread rapidly
C. To spread at a great height
D. To be very colourful or shining

34. Burn the candles at both ends
A. A wealthy person
B. A lazy person
C. Treat as important
D. Use up too much energy

35. To be cut out
A. To be fit for
B. To fight
C. To get a deep wound
D. To be a great enemy of

36. Dark horse
A. Unexpected winner B. To be indifferent
C. Natives of Africa D. Decide for good reasons

37. Yeoman service
A. To do something in a mysterious way
B. Good commendable service
C. Service to the peasants
D. A religious service

38. Through thick and thin
A. To pass through a narrow passage
B. In all circumstances
C. To be in a great trouble
D. To become weak

39. Of the first water
A. Of high order B. Of a foreigner
C. Of a strong person D. Of an elder one

40. To go to the wall
A. A cold welcome
B. To be pushed to the worst position
C. To be in a cheerful mood
D. To move towards the wall

ANSWERS

1	2	3	4	5	6	7	8	9	10
B	D	A	C	C	D	B	B	B	A
11	12	13	14	15	16	17	18	19	20
B	A	C	D	D	C	A	B	B	D
21	22	23	24	25	26	27	28	29	30
A	D	D	B	C	A	C	B	D	B
31	32	33	34	35	36	37	38	39	40
A	B	B	D	A	A	B	B	A	B

SYNONYMS & ANTONYMS

Synonym: A word or phrase that means the same as another word or phrase.

Antonym: A word or phrase that means the opposite of another word or phrase.

SYNONYMS

Ardent	eager, avid
Arduous	difficult, troublesome, tough
Aspire	hope, wish
Astonish	amaze, confound
Authentic	genuine, actual
Awesome	astonishing, amazing, awful, fearful
Ban	bar, debar
Bare	denuded exposed
Bear	carry, bring
Beautiful	attractive, charming
Becoming	attractive, graceful
Benchmark	model, example
Benevolent	bountiful, benign
Betwitch	attract, captivate
Boisterous	noisy, clamorous
Bonny	handsome, attractive, beautiful, healthy
Brave	bold, courageous
Break	crack, separate
Brief	laconic, curt
Bright	shining, flashing
Brisk	active, lively
Broad	generous, capacious
Build	assemble, construct
Busy	brisk, active
Cajole	Coax, dupe
Call	announce, shout
Calm	peaceful, mild
Candid	fair, frank
Capacious	spacious, roomy
Care	anxiety, concern
Catchy	attractive, captivating
Charming	attractive, appealing
Chief	main, key
Clean	pure, spotless
Clever	apt, intelligent
Clumsy	burgling, awkward
Colossal	giant, enormous
Compact	dense, condensed
Conspicuous	clear, apparent
Cordial	agreeable, cheerful
Credulous	trustful, unsuspicious
Cruel	atrocious, barbarous
Dangerous	alarming, hazardous
Dazzling	glorious, radiant
Deceive	cheat, betray
Deep	profound, bottomless
Delicate	fragile, weak, tender
Delight	ecstasy, happiness
Deny	disprove, rebuf
Eager	ardent, avid
Effective	active, capable
Elegant	beautiful, artistic
Emerge	arise, appear
Encouraging	cheerful, promising
Enormous	colossal, gigantic
Faded	dim, dull
Fair	clean, honest
Fascinating	attractive, bewitching
Foolish	imprudent, senseless
Frank	candid, ingenuous
Garrulous	chattering, gossiping
Generous	liberal, benevolent
Genuine	bonafide, authentic
Gloomy	dark, sad
Glorious	magnificent, excellent
Great	colossal, enormous
Haughty	assuming, arrogant

Hefty	big, robust
Humane	benign, gentle
Humble	modest, meek
Idle	lazy, inactive
Illogical	faulty, incorrect
Immense	enormous, colossal
Impudent	bold, brazen
Indolent	lazy, sluggish
Intelligent	clever, bright
Keen	ardent, arid
Kind	benevolent, benign
Laconic	brief, curt
Leading	dominating chief
Lively	agile, active
Lucid	evident, clear
Magnificent	excellent, glorious
Morose	gloomy, sad
Neglect	disdain, ignore
Obedient	submissive, amenable
Obscure	cloudy, vague
Obstinate	stubborn, firm
Opulent	lavish, affluent
Overnight	fault, mistake
Peaceful	harmonious, friendly
Polite	humble, civil
Prolific	teeming, bountiful
Radiant	bright, glorious
Rejoicing	delight, cheer
Sad	gloomy, depressed
Select	choose, opt
Silence	calm, peace

ANTONYMS

Abhor	Admire, love, adore
Adore	hate, abhor
Alert	listless, careless
Annex	remove, unfasten
Apex	bottom, nadir
Ban	allow, permit
Beautiful	awful, ugly
Benign	stern, harsh
Boisterous	quiet, peaceful
Brief	lengthy, extensive
Calm	stir, agitate
Careful	careless, unconcerned
Clear	cloudy, vague
Clever	clumsy, boring
Colossal	diminutive, small
Compatible	incompatible, inapt
Courageous	cowardly, timid
Damaging	useful, advantageous
Dangerous	safe, harmless
Deceit	honesty, candour
Delicate	harsh, indelicate
Deny	admit, accept
Dim	bright, clear
Eager	impassive, lazy
Efficient	inefficient, inept
Emerge	enter, fall
Encourage	deter, depress
Engaging	repulsive, unattractive
Fair	unfair, prejudiced
Fake	genuine, bonafide
Fascinating	unattractive, disgusting
Ferocious	mild, gentle
Gallant	cowardly, fearful
Gentle	aggressive, harsh
Gigantic	tiny, puny
Glorious	dull, dim
Handy	clumsy, inept
Happy	unhappy, gloomy
Hard	soft, flexible
Honset	dishonest, unfair
Huge	minute, puny
Idle	active, busy
Illogical	logical, coherent
Incorrect	correct, accurate
Indecent	decent, modest
Innocent	cunning, dishonest
Kind	unkind, cruel
Lazy	active, diligent
Like	unlike, diverse
Lovable	hateful, abhorrent
Major	minor, unimportant
Meek	arrogant, stubborn
Merry	sad, gloomy
Morose	happy, delightful
Nadir	bottom
Nonsense	sense, wisdom
Object	admire, accept
Obscure	clear, vivid
Overbearing	humble, modest
Peaceful	agitated, disturbed
Playful	gloomy, morose
Polite	impolite, ill-mannered
Proficient	incompetent, unskilled
Promising	unpromising, discouraging
Realistic	unrealistic, fanciful
Refined	unrefined, boorish
Reject	accept, select
Robust	feeble, frail

Secure	insecure, unsafe
Sensible	senseless, stupid
Sluggish	energetic, brisk
Tempting	untempting, unattractive
Tepid	zealous, eager
Timid	arrogant, bold
True	untrue, false
Ungainly	elegant, attractive
Unmannerly	mannerly, polite
Valid	invalid, illegal
Verbose	curt, brief
Violent	calm, quiet

MULTIPLE CHOICE QUESTIONS

Directions: *In the following questions choose the word which best expresses the meaning of the given word.*

1. INDICT
A. Condemn B. Reprimand
C. Accuse D. Allege

2. SCINTILLATING
A. Smouldering B. Gilittering
C. Touching D. Warming

3. REFECTORY
A. Restaurant B. Parlour
C. Living Room D. Dining Room

4. DISTINCTION
A. Diffusion B. Disagreement
C. Different D. Degree

5. IMPROVEMENT
A. Advancement B. Betterment
C. Promotion D. Preference

6. ADVERSITY
A. Failure B. Helplessness
C. Misfortune D. Crisis

7. TURN UP
A. Land up B. Show up
C. Crop up D. Come up

8. DEIFY
A. Flatter B. Challenge
C. Worship D. Face

9. ERROR
A. Misadventure B. Misgiving
C. Ambiguity D. Blunder

10. SHALLOW
A. Artificial B. Superficial
C. Foolish D. Worthless

11. MASSACRE
A. Murder B. Stab
C. Assissinate D. Slaughter

12. COMBAT
A. Conflict B. Quarrel
C. Feud D. Fight

13. VORACIOUS
A. Wild B. Hungry
C. Angry D. Quick

14. IMPROMPTU
A. Offhand B. Unimportant
C. Unreal D. Effective

15. RABBLE
A. Mob B. Noise
C. Roar D. Rubbish

16. TEPID
A. Hot B. Warm
C. Cold D. Boiling

17. MAYHEM
A. Jubilation B. Havoc
C. Excitement D. Defeat

18. TIMID
A. Fast B. Slow
C. Medium D. Shy

19. CANTANKEROUS
A. Quarrelsome B. Rash
C. Disrepectful D. Noisy

20. PRECARIOUS
A. Cautious B. Critical
C. Perilous D. Brittle

21. VENUE
A. Place B. Agenda
C. Time D. Duration

22. STERILE
A. Barren B. Arid
C. Childless D. Dry

23. SYNOPSIS
A. Index B. Mixture
C. Summary D. Puzzle

24. GERMANE
A. Responsible B. Logical
C. Possible D. Relevant

25. PONDER
A. Think B. Evaluate
C. Anticipate D. Increase

Directions: *In the following questions choose the word which best expresses the opposite of the given word.*

26. DEAR
A. Priceless B. Free
C. Worthless D. Cheap

27. FLAGITIOUS
A. Innocent B. Vapid
C. Ignorant D. Frivolous

28. LIABILITY
A. Property B. Assets
C. Debt D. Treasure

29. VIRTUOUS
A. Wicked B. Corrupt
C. Vicious D. Scandalous

30. ENCOURAGE
A. Dampen B. Disapprove
C. Discourage D. Warn

31. MORTAL
A. Divine B. Immortal
C. Spiritual D. Eternal

32. LEND
A. Borrow B. Cheat
C. Pawn D. Hire

33. COMIC
A. Emotional B. Tragic
C. Fearful D. Painful

34. ADDITION
A. Division B. Enumeration
C. Subtraction D. Multiplication

35. MINOR
A. Big B. Major
C. Tall D. Heavy

36. REPEL
A. Attend B. Concentrate
C. Continue D. Attract

37. ARTIFICIAL
A. Red B. Natural
C. Truthful D. Solid

38. CAPACIOUS
A. Limited B. Caring
C. Foolish D. Changeable

39. PROVOCATION
A. Vocation B. Pacification
C. Peace D. Destruction

40. METICULOUS
A. Mutual B. Shaggy
C. Meretricious D. Slovenly

41. ABLE
A. Disable B. Inable
C. Unable D. Misable

42. COMFORT
A. Uncomfort B. Miscomfort
C. Discomfort D. None of these

43. GAIN
A. Loose B. Fall
C. Lost D. Lose

44. SYNTHETIC
A. Affable B. Natural
C. Plastic D. Cosmetic

45. ACQUITTED
A. Freed B. Burdened
C. Convicted D. Entrusted

46. FLIMSY
A. Frail B. Filthy
C. Firm D. Flippant

47. BUSY
A. Occupied B. Engrossed
C. Relaxed D. Engaged

48. ADAPTABLE
A. Adoptable B. Flexible
C. Yielding D. Rigid

49. LOVE
A. Villainy B. Hatred
C. Compulsion D. Force

50. BALANCE
A. Disbalance B. Misbalance
C. Debalance D. Imbalance

ANSWERS

1	2	3	4	5	6	7	8	9	10
C	B	D	C	B	C	B	C	D	B
11	**12**	**13**	**14**	**15**	**16**	**17**	**18**	**19**	**20**
D	D	B	A	A	B	B	D	A	B
21	**22**	**23**	**24**	**25**	**26**	**27**	**28**	**29**	**30**
A	A	C	D	A	D	A	B	C	C
31	**32**	**33**	**34**	**35**	**36**	**37**	**38**	**39**	**40**
B	A	B	C	B	D	B	A	B	D
41	**42**	**43**	**44**	**45**	**46**	**47**	**48**	**49**	**50**
C	C	D	B	C	C	C	D	B	D

SPOT THE ERROR

The most common errors in English are of spellings, grammar and usage of words. By regular practice, the errors can be easily spotted and minimised.

COMMON ERRORS WITH NOUNS AND NOUN-PHRASES

Incorrect	Correct
1. I have bought new *furnitures.*	I have bought new *furniture.*
2. The wages of sin *are* death.	The wages of sin *is* death.
3. She told these *news* to her mother.	She told her mother this *news.*
4. He took *troubles* to do his work.	He took *trouble* (or pains) over his work.
5. The *cattles* were grazing.	The *cattle* were grazing.
6. He showered *many abuses* on me.	He showered *much abuse* on me.
7. I spent the holidays with my *family members.*	I spent the holidays with my *family.*
8. There is no *place* in this compartment.	There is no *room* in this compartment.
9. Write this new *poetry* in your *copy.*	Write this new *poem* in your *note-book.*
10. He took *insult* at this.	He took *offence* at this.
11. Put your *sign* here.	Put your *signatures* here.
12. She is my *cousin sister.*	She is my *cousin.*
13. *Sunil's* my *neighbour's* house was burgled.	*Sunil* my *neighbour's* house was burgled.
14. I lost a *ten-rupees* note.	I lost *a ten-rupee* note.
15. Road closed for *repair.*	Road closed for *repairs.*
16. His house is out of *repairs.*	His house is out of *repair.*
17. What is the *reason* of an earthquake?	What is the *cause* of an earthquake?
18. This building is made of *stones.*	This building is made of *stone.*
19. I disapprove of *these kinds* of games.	I disapprove of *this kind* of games.
20. Veena's and Sheela's father is ill.	Veena and Sheela's father is ill.

COMMON ERRORS WITH PRONOUNS

Incorrect	Correct
1. Both did not go.	Neither went.
2. We all did not go.	None of us went.
3. Each of these boys play.	Each of these boys plays.
4. Whoever does best he will get a prize.	Whoever does best will get a prize.
5. One should not waste his time.	A man should not waste his time.
6. I and she are sisters.	She and I are sisters.
7. He is wiser than me.	He is wiser than I.
8. Between you and I, Anil is not to be trusted.	Between you and me, Anil is not to be trusted.
9. Nobody was there but I.	Nobody was there but me.
10. Who is there ? It is me.	Who is there ? It is I.
11. Only he and me can use this card.	Only he and I can use this card.
12. Let you and I go now.	Let you and me go now.
13. Everyone got one's pay.	Everyone got his pay.
14. Everyone is frightened when they see a tiger.	Everyone is frightened when he sees a tiger.
15. These two friends are fond of one another.	These two friends are fond of each other.

Incorrect	Correct
16. I did not like him coming at that hour.	I did not like his coming at that hour.
17. Who do you think I met?	Whom do you think I met?
18. You should avail this opportunity.	You should avail yourself this opportunity.
19. When you have read these books, please return the same to me.	When you have read the books, please return them to me.
20. They that are humble need fear no fall.	Those that are humble need fear no fall.

COMMON ERRORS WITH ADJECTIVES

Incorrect	Correct
1. These all oranges are good.	All these oranges are good.
2. He held the book in the both hands.	He held the book in both hands.
3. Both men have not come.	Neither man has come.
4. That man should do some or other work.	That man should do some work or other
5. He is elder than I.	He is older than I.
6. Shakespeare is greater than any other poets.	Shakespeare is greater than any other poet.
7. He is a coward man.	He is a cowardly man.
8. Many villagers cannot write his own name.	Many villagers cannot write their own name.
9. Each of us loves our home.	Each of us loves his home.
10. Much efforts bring their reward.	Much effort brings its reward.
11. He found hundred rupees.	He found a hundred rupees.
12. He had leave of four days.	He had four days leave.
13. This is a worth seeing sight.	This is a sight worth seeing.
14. He will spend his future life here.	He will spend the rest of his life here.
15. There is a best teacher in that class.	There is a very good teacher in that class.
16. Of the two plans this is the best.	Of the two plans this is the better.
17. He is becoming strong every day.	He is becoming stronger every day.
18. He is worst than I.	He is worse than I.
19. Jaipur is hot than Delhi.	Jaipur is hotter than Delhi.
20 In our library the number of books is less.	In our library the number of books is small.

COMMON ERRORS WITH VERBS

Incorrect	Correct
1. He asked had we taken our luggage.	He asked if we had taken our luggage.
2. She asked what are you doing.	She asked what we were doing.
3. Rama asked to Anil why he is angry.	Rama asked Anil why he was angry.
4. He does not care for his money.	He does not take care of his money.
5. He does not care for his work.	He takes no care over his work.
6. No one cared for him after his mother died.	No one took care of him after his mother died.
7. He got angry before I said a word.	He got angry before I had said a word.
8. I met a man who was my tutor 20 years ago.	I met a man who had been my tutor twenty years ago.
9. I had been for walking yesterday.	I went for a walk yesterday.
10 If I shall do this I shall be wrong.	If I do this I shall be wrong.
11. I have left trekking.	I have given up trekking.
12. I came to know as to how he did this.	I learnt how he did this.

Incorrect	Correct
13. I came to know why he was sad.	I found out why he was sad.
14. He knows to swim.	He knows how to swim.
15. The criminal's head was cut.	The criminal's head was cut off.
16. I said to him to go.	I told him to go.
17. I told the teacher to excuse me.	I asked the teacher to excuse me.
18. He is troubling me.	He is giving me trouble.
19. I have got a hurt on my leg.	I have hurt my leg.
20. She gave a speech.	She made a speech.
21. From the three he is more clever.	He is the cleverest of the three.
22. India is the first peace-loving country in the world.	India is the foremost peace-loving country in the world.
23. Verbal instruction will not do.	Oral instruction will not do.
24. Her command over French is most excellent.	Her command over French is excellent.
25. He has not some money with him.	He has not any money with him.
26. I have visited Bombay many a times.	I have visited Bombay many a time.
27. Death is more preferable to dishonour.	Death is preferable to dishonour.
28. I gave him a few books I had.	I gave him the few books I had.
29. If he wants farther help send him to me.	If he wants further help, send him to me.
30. She is so cunning as a fox.	She is as cunning as a fox.

COMMON ERRORS IN SUBJECT-VERB AGREEMENT

Incorrect	Correct
1. The owners of this factory *is* very rich.	The owners of this factory *are* very rich.
2. The pleasures of nature that one can experience at Shimla *is* beyond description.	The pleasures of nature that one can experience at Shimla *are* beyond description.
3. There *is* no street lights in our colony.	There *are* no street lights in our colony.
4. He and I *am* entrusted with the job.	He and I *are* entrusted with the job.
5. Rice and curry *are* his favourite dish.	Rice and curry *is* his favourite dish.
6. The honour and glory of our country *are* at stake.	The honour and glory of our country *is* at stake.
7. Time and tide *waits* for none.	Time and tide *wait* for none.
8. All the passengers with the driver *was* killed.	All the passengers, with the driver, *were* killed.
9. The teacher, with her students, *were* going out	The teacher, with her students, *was* going out.
10. I as well as they *am* tired.	I as well as they *are* tired.
11. Not only the soldiers but their captain also *were* captured.	Not only the soldiers but their captain also was captured.
12. Neither you nor I *were* selected.	Neither you nor I *was* selected.
13. Either of these two applicants *are* fit for the job but neither want to accept it.	Either of these two applicants *is* fit for the job but neither wants to accept it.
14. One of these students are sure to stand first.	One of these students *is* sure to stand first.
15. Everyone of these workers want a raise.	Everyone of these workers wants a raise.
16. None of these letters has been answered so far.	None of these letters *have* been answered so far.
17. None of the girls were present at the party.	None of the girls *was* present at the party.
18. Many a battle were fought on Indian soil.	Many a battle *was* fought on Indian soil.
19. A lot of work remain to be done.	A lot of work *remains* to be done.
20. The majority of these girls likes music.	The majority of these girls *like* music.
21. The number of admissions are encouraging.	The number of admissions *is* encouraging.

	Incorrect	Correct
22.	A large number of boys was present.	A large number of boys *were* present.
23.	A variety of books was on display.	A variety of books *were* on display.
24.	Variety are the spice of life.	Variety *is* the spice of life.
25.	If my estimates are correct. I will need another hundred rupees.	If my estimate is correct, I will need another hun dred rupees.
26.	Mathematics *are* my favourite subject.	Mathematics *is* my favourite subject.
27.	'Gulliver's Travels' *are* written by Swift.	'Gulliver's Travels' *is* written by Swift.
28.	Ten miles *are* a long distance to cover on foot.	Ten miles *is* a long distance to cover on foot.
29.	A new pair of shoes *are* to be purchased.	A new pair of shoes *is* to be purchased.
30.	The Committee *have* issued its report.	The Committee *has* issued its report.

COMMON ERRORS IN USE OF WILL, SHALL, WOULD, SHOULD, MAY, MIGHT, MUST

	Incorrect	Correct
1.	When I shall see him I shall tell him this.	When I *see* him, I shall tell him this.
2.	If I should do wrong, he would punish me.	If I *did* wrong, he would punish me.
3.	Until he will have confessed his fault, he will be kept in prison,	Until he *has* confessed his fault, he will be kept in prison.
4.	She will obey me.	She *shall* obey me.
5.	You would work hard.	You *should* work hard.
6.	You shall find him in the garden.	You *will* find him in the garden.
7.	He must have died of exposure, but we cannot be certain.	He *might* have died of exposure, but we cannot be certain.
8.	You might not show disrespect to your elders.	You *must* not show disrespect to your elders.
9.	You may take exercise in order to maintain good health,	You *must* take exercise in order to maintain good health.
10.	He must be a crook for all we know.	He *may* be a crook for all we know.

COMMON ERRORS IN THE USE OF ADVERBS

(Very, Much, Too, Enough, Quite, Hardly, Scarcely, Before, Ago, Since, Yet, Still, etc.)

	Incorrect	Correct
1.	He is very much angry.	He is *very* angry.
2.	She was very good enough to help me.	She was *good enough* to help me.
3.	She runs much fast.	She runs *very* fast.
4.	She runs very faster than Seema.	She runs *much* faster than Seema.
5.	It is bitter cold today.	It is *bitterly* cold today.
6.	He is a much learned man.	He is a very learned man.
7	She is thinking very hardly.	She is thinking very hard.
8.	To tell in brief the film was boring.	*In short* the film was boring.
9.	He told the story in details.	He told the story *in detail.*
10.	I did it anyhow.	I *managed to do* it somehow.
11.	Aeroplanes reach Europe soon.	Aeroplanes reach Europe quickly.
12.	Before long there were dinosaurs on the earth.	*Long ago,* there were dinosaurs on the earth.
13.	This book is too interesting.	This book is *very* interesting.

Incorrect	Correct
14. He lives miserly.	He lives in *a miserly* way.
15. Just I had gone when she came.	I had just gone when she came.
16. He sings good.	He sings *well.*
17. He sings good than I.	He sings *better* than I.
18. Really speaking it is cold.	*As a matter of fact* it is cold.
19. He is enough tall to reach the ceiling.	He is *tall enough* to reach the ceiling.
20. He went directly to his college.	He went *direct* to his college.

COMMON ERRORS IN THE USE OF CONJUNCTIONS

Incorrect	Correct
1. As he is fat so he runs slowly.	As he is fat *he* runs slowly.
2. If he is fat then he will run slowly.	If he is fat, he will run slowly.
3. Though he is fat still he runs fast.	Though he is fat, *he runs* fast.
4. *As* I pulled the trigger at the sametime he shook my arm.	As I pulled the trigger, he shook my arm.
5. No sooner I had spoken than he left.	No sooner *had* I spoken than he left.
6. Not only he will go, but also he will stay there.	Not only *will he* go, but he *will also* stay there.
7. Neither he comes nor he writes.	Neither *does he* come nor *does he* write.
8. Scarcely he entered the room than the telephone rang.	Scarcely *had* he entered the room *when the* telephone rang.
9. Hardly she had left the house than it began to rain.	Hardly *had she* left the house *when* it began to rain.
10. He is the fastest runner and he comes last.	He is the fastest runner *but* he comes last.
11. She is as innocent as if she looks.	She is as innocent as she looks.
12. Until he does not try he must be punished.	He must be punished unless he tries
13. I want to know as to why you are late.	I want to know why you are late.
14. I am fond of Chinese food as for example sweet and sour prawns.	I am fond of Chinese food, for example, sweet and sour prawns.
15. He was angry therefore I ran away.	He was angry so I ran away.
16. I was trying to work, at that time he was disturbing me.	While I was trying to work, he was disturbing me.
17. Supposing if he is late, what will happen?	Supposing he is late (or if he is late) what will happen?
18. He asked me that why I was late.	He asked me why I was late.
19. Let us catch a taxi lest we should not get late.	Let us catch a taxi lest we should get late.
20. She dresses herself like the teacher does.	She dresses herself as the teacher does.
21 Wait while I come.	Wait *until* (or *till)* I come.
22. Until, there is corruption in India, there can be little progress.	*As long* as there is corruption in India there can be little progress.
23. I have never told a lie nor cheated anybody.	I have never told a lie *nor have I* cheated any body.
24. Both Mohan as well as Arun are responsible for this action.	Both Mohan *and* Arun are responsible for this action.
25. Hindus and Muslims both are to blame for the riots.	*Both Hindus* and Muslims are to blame for the riots.
26. I have bought paintings, books, records, and etc.	I have bought paintings, books *and records etc.*
27. He as well as you is a fool.	He as well as you *are* a fool.
28. He is so poor and he cannot save anything.	He is so *poor that* he cannot save anything.
29. Such a' book that you want is not available.	Such a book *as* you want is not available.
30. Such was her condition as everyone was moved to pity.	Such was her condition that everyone was moved to pity.

COMMON ERRORS IN THE USE OF PREPOSITIONS

Incorrect	Correct
1. I will not listen him.	I will not listen *to* him.
2. Copy this word by word.	Copy this word *for* word.
3. He enquired from her where she lived.	He enquired *of* her where she lived.
4. Sign here with ink.	Sign here *in* ink.
5. Has she come in train or by foot?	Has she come *by* train or *on* foot?
6. She said this at his face.	She said this *to* his face.
7. Open the book on page one	Open the book *at* page one.
8. I was invited for lunch.	I was *invited to* lunch.
9. I am ill since three months.	I have been *ill for* three months.
10. This paper is inferior than that.	This paper is inferior *to* that.
11. This resembles to that.	This *resembles* that.
12. My brother is superior than you in strength.	My brother is superior *to* you in strength.
13. He wrote me	He wrote *to* me.
14. I shall explain them this.	I shall explain this *to* them.
15. Send this letter on my address.	Send this letter *to* my address.
16. He suggested me this.	He suggested this *to* me.
17. He goes *on his* work.	He goes *to his* work.
18. He *reached to* Nagpur.	He *reached* Nagpur.
19. He told *to me* to go.	He told *me* to go.
20 The term begins *from* July 1st.	The term begins *on* July 1st.
21. There are many advantages *from* this.	The advantages *of* this are many.
22. We waste much time *in* trifles.	We waste much time *on* (or *over)* trifles.
23. He sat *on* a tree.	He sat *in* a tree.
24. This is a comfortable house to *live*.	This is a comfortable house to *live in*.
25. This is the road to *go*.	This is the road to *go by*.
26. He married *with* an Indian lady.	He *married an Indian* lady.
27. He accompanied *with* his friend.	He *accompanied his* friend.
28. He went *for doing some* business.	He went away *on* business.
29. He went for *riding*.	He went *for a ride*.
30. I *pitied on* him.	I *pitied* him.

MISCELLANEOUS ERRORS

(Including Ambiguities and Indianisms)

Incorrect	Correct
1. Many *homes* are lying vacant.	Many *houses* are lying vacant.
2. It is cool in the *shadow* of the tree.	It is cool in the *shade* of the tree.
3. She *keeps* good health.	She *enjoys* good health.
4. My leg is *paining*.	*I am feeling pain* in my leg.
5. *See* this word in the dictionary.	*Look up* this word in the dictionary.
6. The train will arrive *just now*	The train will arrive *shortly*.
7. They are *pulling* on well.	They are *getting* on well.
8. The river has *over flown* its bank.	The river has *over flown* its banks.
9. He was appointed *on* the post.	He was appointed *to* the post.

Incorrect	Correct
10. Last but not *the least,* we have to discuss the problem of over population.	Last but not *least,* we have to discuss the problem of over population.
11. *Cities* after *cities* fell.	*City* after *city* fell.
12. What is the use Munir going there?	What is the use of Munir going there?
13. He *did many mischief.*	He *made much mischief.*
14. It is exact five *in* my watch.	It is exact five *by* my watch.
15. I will dine with them on *next Sunday.*	I will dine with them *Sunday next.*
16. Misfortunes when faced bravely and *manly* become less troublesome.	Misfortunes when faced bravely and *manfully* become less troublesome.
17. I am *laid down* with fever.	I am *laid up* with fever.
18. He is habituated to smoking.	He is *addicted* to smoking.
19. *According to my opinion* he is right.	*In my opinion* (or according *to me)* he is right.
20. Could you please *open* this knot?	Could you please *untie* this knot?

MULTIPLE CHOICE QUESTIONS

Directions: *In the following questions some of the sentences have errors and some are correct. Find out which part of a sentence has an error, the number of that part is your answer. If a sentence is free from errors, then your answer is D i.e., No error.*

1. (A) Either Ram or/(B) you is responsible/(C) for this action./(D) No error.

2. (A) The student flatly denied/(B) that he had copied/(C) in the examination hall./(D) No error.

3. (A) By the time you arrive tomorrow/(B) I have finished/(C) my work./(D) No error.

4. (A) The captain with the members of his team/(B) are returning/(C) after a fortnight./(D) No error.

5. (A) After returning from/(B) an all-India tour/(C) I had to describe about it./(D) No error.

6. (A) The teacher asked his students/(B) if they had gone through/(C) either of the three chapters included in the prescribed text./(D) No error.

7. (A) Do you know/(B) how old were you/(C) when you came here?/(D) No error.

8. (A) Beware of/(B) a fair-weather friend/(C) who is neither a friend in need nor a friend indeed./(D) No error.

9. (A) Copernicus proved/(B) that Earth/(C) moves round the Sun./(D) No error.

10. (A) The property/(B) was divided/(C) among the two brothers./(D) No error.

11. (A) I am quite certain/(B) that the lady is not only greedy/(C) but miserly./(D) No error.

12. (A) The brilliant success in the examination/(B) as well as his record in sports/(C) deserves high praise./(D) No error.

13. (A) I cannot find/(B) where has he gone/(C) though I have tried may best./(D) No error.

14. (A) If I was/(B) the Prime Minister of India/(C) I would work wonders/(D) No error.

15. (A) If it weren't/(B) for you,/(C) I wouldn't be alive today./(D) No error.

16. (A) He looked like a lion/(B) baulked from/(C) its prey./(D) No error.

17. (A) Widespread flooding/(B) is affecting/(C) large areas of the villages./(D) No error.

18. (A) If we really set to/(B) we can get the whole house/(C) cleaned in an afternoon./(D) No error.

19. (A) It's arrogant for you/(B) to assume you'll/(C)win every time./(D) No error.

20. (A) The two books are the same/(B) except for the fact that this/(C) has an answer in the back./(D) No error.

21. (A) Your husband doesn't/(B) believe that you are older/(C) than I./(D) No error.

22. (A) I could not/(B) answer to/(C) the question./(D) No error.

23. (A) Two years passed/(B) since/(C) my cousin died./(D) No error.

24. (A) I am learning English/(B) for ten years/(C) without much effect./(D) No error.

25. (A) Ramesh has agreed/(B) to marry with the girl/(C) of his parent's choice./ (D) No error.

26. (A) When he was arriving./(B) the party was/(C) in full swing./(D) No error.

27. (A) The most studious boy/(B) in the class/(C) was made as the captain./(D) No error.

28. (A) I am participating/(B) in the two-miles race/(C) tomorrow morning./(D) No error.

29. (A) When the boy committed a mistake/(B) the teacher made him to do/(C) the sum again./(D) No error.

30. (A) Whenever a person lost anything/(B) the poor folk around/(C) are suspected./(D) No error.

31. (A) It is time/(B) we did something/(C) to stop road accidents./(D) No error.

32. (A) I was there/(B) many a time/(C) in the past./(D) No error.

33. (A) Were you/(B) given a choice/(C) or you had to do it?/(D) No error.

34. (A) At the end of the year/(B) every student who had done adequate work/(C) was automatically promoted./(D) No error.

35. (A) She reluctantly said that/(B) if nobody else was doing it/(C) she will do it./(D) No error.

36. (A) He will end up his work/(B) in the city/(C) by the end of the year./(D) No error.

37. (A) Supposing if/(B) there is no bus./(C) how will you get there?(D) No error.

38. (A) At the moment the house/(B) was burgled the family/(C) attended a night party in the neighbourhood./(D) No error.

39. (A) On a holiday/(B) Sudha prefers reading/(C) than going out visiting friends./(D) No error.

40. (A) Neither he/(B) nor his father is interested/(C) in joining the party./(D) No error.

41. (A) A group of friends/(B) want to visit/(C) the new plant as early as possible./(D) No error.

42. (A) May I/(B) know who you want/(C) to see please?/(D) No error.

43. (A) Myself and Gopal/(B) will take care of/(C) the function on Sunday./(D) No error.

44. (A) He is not coming tomorrow/(B) as he is having a pain in the chest/(C) and has to see a doctor./(D) No error.

45. (A) They have been/(B) very close friends/(C) until they quarrelled./(D) No error.

46. (A) The reason why/(B) he was rejected/(C) was because he was too young./(D) No error.

47. (A) Scarcely had/(B) I arrived than/(C) the train left./(D) No error.

48. (A) The students/(B) returned back/(C) home well in time./(D) No error.

49. (A) English should/(B) be make/(C) the national language./(D) No error.

50. (A) Ravi is a/(B) intelligent student/(C) of my school./(D) No error.

ANSWERS

1	2	3	4	5	6	7	8	9	10
B	D	B	B	C	C	D	D	B	C
11	**12**	**13**	**14**	**15**	**16**	**17**	**18**	**19**	**20**
C	D	B	A	C	C	C	A	A	C
21	**22**	**23**	**24**	**25**	**26**	**27**	**28**	**29**	**30**
C	B	A	A	B	A	C	B	B	A
31	**32**	**33**	**34**	**35**	**36**	**37**	**38**	**39**	**40**
D	A	A	D	C	A	A	A	C	D
41	**42**	**43**	**44**	**45**	**46**	**47**	**48**	**49**	**50**
B	B	A	C	A	C	B	B	B	A

PREPOSITIONS

A Preposition is a word which comes before a Pronoun or a Noun and expresses the relationship between Noun or Pronoun and some part of the remaining sentence.

(*a*) He is busy **with** his work.

(*b*) The boy jumped **into** the river.

(*c*) The birds are chirping *in* the trees.

In these sentences the words **with, into** and **in** show the relationship between the verbs **busy, jumped** and **chirping** with the nouns **work, river** and **trees** respectively.

Position of the Preposition

1. A Preposition usually precedes its object.

(*i*) He laughs **at** the poor.

(*ii*) He is angry **with** you.

(*iii*) She agrees **with** me.

2. In the case of Relative Pronouns it comes after the subject.

(*i*) This is the boy whom I was looking **for**.

(*ii*) That is the pen whose mention I was making **of**.

3. In the following cases, the Preposition comes after its object.

(*i*) Where is the boy you were complaining **against**?
(*ii*) What things are there you are looking **for**?
(*iii*) Who is there, you are waiting **for**?

Omission of the Preposition

In many cases when the sentences contain Nouns of Time or Place, the Prepositions **from, in** and **for** are often omitted.

(*i*) He walked many kilometres.
(*ii*) He came to see me last year.
(*iii*) As I could not find my puppy anywhere, I looked here and there.

Prepositions are small words that show the relationship between one word and another. Prepositions in the following sentences show the position of the paper in relation to the desk, the book, his hand and the door.

The paper is **on** the desk.
The paper is **under** the book.
The paper is **in** his hand.
The paper is **by** the door.

Common Prepositions

about	at	by
in	onto	toward
above	before	concerning
inside	out	under
across	behind	despite
into	over	until
after	below	down
like	since	up
against	beneath	during
near	through	upon
along	beside	except
of	throughout	with
amid	between	for
off	till	within
among	beyond	from
on	to	without

MULTIPLE CHOICE QUESTIONS

Directions: *Tick the correct Preposition for the blank in each of the following sentences.*

1. He applied ...... the manager.
A. for B. to
C. with D. by

2. Trust ...... God and do the right.
A. in B. for
C. to D. with

3. She is worthy ...... a prize.
A. with B. for
C. to D. of

4. Mr. Gomes has no taste ...... music.
A. of B. for
C. with D. to

5. You are hard ...... hearing.
A. at B. of
C. with D. for

6. He is sure ...... his success
A. for B. with
C. on D. of

7. Preeti was warned ...... the danger ahead.
A. for B. at
C. of D. about

8. I am thankful ...... you for a good advice.
A. for B. with
C. to D. from

9. Deepak would not surrender ...... the police.
A. with B. to
C. for D. on

10. The small plant in your lawn is very sensitive ...... touch.
A. on B. with
C. to D. for

11. Divya was sure to succeed ..... the examination.
A. for B. in
C. to D. with

12. Geeta was jealous ...... Ravina's beauty.
A. to B. with
C. for D. of

13. He was ignorant ..... what was happening there.
A. for B. of
C. to D. with

14. Your pen is inferior ...... mine.
A. than B. with
C. from D. to

15. Reenu is no match ...... Meenu.
A. to B. for
C. with D. upon

16. It is necessary ...... you to apply for this job.
A. on B. with
C. for D. to

17. Be loyal ...... your country.
A. for B. to
C. on D. with

18. Mukesh is junior ...... me.
A. than B. to
C. from D. of

19. Deepika was innocent ...... the crime.
A. of B. with
C. from D. to

20. I am desirous.... joining the Indian cricket team.
A. for B. of
C. to D. on

21. Pradeep is not eligible ...... the post.
A. to B. on
C. upon D. for

22. Does she believe ...... God?
A. to B. for
C. in D. over

23. Mr. Posh was charged..... the murder of his aunt.
A. for B. with
C. on D. to

24. Tagore is famous (or popular) ...... Indians.
A. for B. with
C. to D. towards

25. Kalidasa is famous ...... his drama the *Shakuntalam*.
A. for B. with
C. on D. about

26. He applied ...... the post of a teacher.
A. to B. on
C. for D. at

27. I differ ...... you in this matter.
A. from B. with
C. for D. above

28. My pen differs ...... yours.
A. with B. from
C. for D. upon

29. The air escaped out ...... the balloon.
A. from B. of
C. to D. under

30. I am confident ...... success.
A. of B. to
C. from D. about

31. He was deprived ...... his share and property.
A. of B. with
C. from D. about

32. He complains ...... headache.
A. about B. to
C. of D. in

33. My father deals ...... sugar.
A. with B. to
C. in D. about

34. His services were dispensed ......
A. for B. to
C. with D. of

35. Mohinder was born ...... a noble famly.
A. with B. about
C. towards D. in

36. He was born ...... poor parents.
A. of B. to
C. in D. on

37. A son was born ...... him.
A. to B. for
C. in D. upon

38. I was aware ...... the matter.
A. to B. of
C. in D. upon

39. He was absorbed ...... study.
A. in B. into
C. of D. under

40. The boy jumped ...... the river.
A. in B. under
C. below D. into

41. I agree ...... you.
A. upon B. to
C. with D. None of these

42. Wolves abound ...... this forest.
A. for B. in
C. with D. to

43. She did not agree ...... your proposal.
A. with B. in
C. to D. None of these

44. I was angry ...... his misconduct.
A. with B. to
C. at D. on

45. He is bent ...... mischief.
A. on B. of
C. to D. for

46. I put ..... the light and slept.
A. up B. down
C. in D. out

47. I shall call ..... you tomorrow.
A. at B. on
C. with D. by

48. Fate smiles ..... those who untiringly grapple with stark realities of life.
A. with B. over
C. on D. round

49. Those who persist in their endeavour at long last triumph ..... the odds of life.
A. over B. on
C. upon D. about

50. The parliament invested the new organisation ..... judicial authority.
A. by B. with
C. from D. through

51. She has an aversion ..... taking even onion and garlic.
A. with B. at
C. against D. to

52. Brothers must live in harmony. They must never fall .....
A. off B. out
C. apart D. away

53. He was accused ..... stealing his aunt's necklace.
A. for B. with
C. of D. [illegible]

54. He became enamoured ..... her grace when he first saw her dance.

A. with B. of
C. buy D. in

55. My first lesson .... forgiveness came from my father

A. upon B. about
C. in D. on

ANSWERS

1	2	3	4	5	6	7	8	9	10
B	A	D	B	B	D	C	C	B	D
11	**12**	**13**	**14**	**15**	**16**	**17**	**18**	**19**	**20**
B	D	B	D	B	D	B	B	A	B
21	**22**	**23**	**24**	**25**	**26**	**27**	**28**	**29**	**30**
D	C	B	B	A	C	B	B	A	A
31	**32**	**33**	**34**	**35**	**36**	**37**	**38**	**39**	**40**
A	C	C	C	D	A	A	B	A	D
41	**42**	**43**	**44**	**45**	**46**	**47**	**48**	**49**	**50**
D	B	C	D	A	D	C	C	A	B
51	**52**	**53**	**54**	**55**					
D	B	C	B	D					

REORDERING SENTENCES

The words form a sentence and sentences form a paragraph but they convey their meaning only when they are arranged in a proper order. You must study and practise it regularly.

TYPE A

Directions: *Each of the following passages contains five sentences marked a, b, c, d and e. Rearrange the sentences in proper sequence in order to form a meaningful paragraph. Answer the questions given below each of the passages.*

PASSAGE-1

a. Both of them are human beings.
b. They have the same desires, passions, emotions and sentiments.
c. Both of them are made of five elements.
d. Both men and women are created by the same God.
e. They are made of the same flesh and blood.

Questions

1. Which of the following will be the FIRST sentence?

A. a B. b
C. c D. d
E. e

2. Which of the following will be the SECOND sentence?

A. a B. b
C. c D. d
E. e

3. Which of the following will be the THIRD sentence?

A. a B. b
C. c D. d
E. e

4. Which of the following will be the FOURTH sentence?

A. a B. b
C. c D. d
E. e

5. Which of the following will be the FIFTH sentence?

A. a B. b
C. c D. d
E. e

PASSAGE-2

a. All of them are very dedicated to the institute.
b. It was started with only four faculty members.
c. It is one of the reasons for its recognition in such a short period.
d. Now it has a team of fifty highly qualified persons.
e. This institute is only four years old.

Questions

1. Which of the following should be the FIRST sentence?

A. a B. b

C. c D. d
E. e

2. Which of the following should be the SECOND sentence?
A. a B. b
C. c D. d
E. e

3. Which of the following should be the THIRD sentence?
A. a B. b
C. c D. d
E. e

4. Which of the following should be the FOURTH sentence?
A. a B. b
C. c D. d
E. e

5. Which of the following should be the FIFTH sentence?
A. a B. b
C. c D. d
E. e

PASSAGE-3

a. She came back wet and with a cold.
b. It was raining in torrents.
c. Ram had been sick for some days.
d. Many things were needed in the house.
e. Despite it, Ram's wife went out to market.

Questions

1. Which sentence should come FIRST in the passage?
A. a B. b
C. c D. d
E. e

2. Which sentence should come SECOND in the passage?
A. a B. b
C. c D. d
E. e

3. Which sentence should come THIRD in the passage?
A. a B. b
C. c D. d
E. e

4. Which sentence should come FOURTH in the passage?
A. a B. b
C. c D. d
E. e

5. Which sentence should come FIFTH in the passage?
A. a B. b
C. c D. d
E. e

PASSAGE-4

a. The patient became helpless.
b. The patient went to the doctor.
c. He wanted to give him some present.
d. The doctor totally refused to do so.
e. He requested him to accept it.

Questions

1. Which of the following should be the FIRST sentence?
A. a B. b
C. c D. d
E. e

2. Which of the following should be the SECOND sentence?
A. a B. b
C. c D. d
E. e

3. Which of the following should be the THIRD sentence?
A. a B. b
C. c D. d
E. e

4. Which of the following should be the FOURTH sentence?
A. a B. b
C. c D. d
E. e

5. Which of the following should be the FIFTH sentence?
A. a B. b
C. c D. d
E. e

PASSAGE-5

a. Children sat listening to him for almost an hour.
b. All the stories were full of crime and mystery.
c. Ramesh conceded to their request.
d. That hour was fascinating for them.
e. Children requested Ramesh to tell them stories.

Questions

1. Which of the following will be the First sentence?
A. a B. b
C. c D. d
E. e

2. Which of the following will be the SECOND sentence?
A. a B. b
C. c D. d
E. e

3. Which of the following will be the THIRD sentence?
A. a B. b
C. c D. d
E. e

4. Which of the following will be the FOURTH sentence?
A. a B. b
C. c D. d
E. e

5. Which of the following will be the FIFTH sentence?
A. a B. b
C. c D. d
E. e

ANSWERS

PASSAGE-1

The proper sequence of the sentences is:

Both men and women are created by the same God. They are made of the same flesh and blood. Both of them are made of five elements. They have the same desires, passions, emotions and sentiments. Both of them are human beings.

1	2	3	4	5
D	E	C	B	A

PASSAGE-2

The proper sequence of the sentences is:

This institute is only four years old. It was started with only four faculty members. Now it has a team of fifty highly qualified persons. All of them are very dedicated to the institute. It is one of the reasons for its recognition in such a short period.

1	2	3	4	5
E	B	D	A	C

PASSAGE-3

The proper sequence of the sentences is:

Ram had been sick for some days. Many things were needed in the house. It was raining in torrents. Despite it, Ram's wife went out to market. She came back wet and with a cold.

1	2	3	4	5
C	D	B	E	A

PASSAGE-4

The proper sequence of the sentences is:

The patient went to the doctor. He wanted to give him some present. He requested him to accept it. The doctor totally refused to do so. The patient became helpless.

1	2	3	4	5
B	C	E	D	A

PASSAGE-5

The proper sequence of the sentences is:

Children requested Ramesh to tell them stories. Ramesh conceded to their request. Children sat listening to him for almost an hour. All the stories were full of crime and mystery. That hour was fascinating for them.

1	2	3	4	5
E	C	A	B	D

TYPE B

Directions: *The first and last sentences of each question named S_1 and S_6 are given. Four other sentences named M, N, O and P are jumbled up and not in their proper order. From the alternatives, pick up the one which gives the correct order.*

1. S_1 : Some people seem to have a compulsive need to work continually; they may be called work-addicts.

M : However they never quite reach the top.

N : There are companies which expect everyone to be at work early and stay back late.

O : Because of their diligence, they tend to get rapid promotions at first.

P : Work-addicts generally end up in such organisations.

S_6 : For, they make excellent salesmen, they would be terrible managing directors.

A. PNMO B. MOPN
C. OMNP D. NPOM

2. S_1 : There is one important aspect of food problem.

M : Multiplicity of courses at meals is out of place.

N : This implies maximum economy in its use.

O : Hotels should exercise restraint.

P : Waste should be avoided.

S_6 : Some of these steps are necessary.

A. MNOP B. NOMP
C. PNMO D. PNOM

3. S_1 : India led the battle of freedom against British imperialism.

M : That technique brought success.

N : We championed the cause of other countries.

O : We fought it with a special technique.

P : We are happy that they achieved freedom.

S_6 : Some countries are still slaves.

A. OMNP B. MNPO
C. PNMO D. MNOP

4. S_1 : Mahatma Gandhi had a way of life.

M : He did not believe in theoretical ideology.

N : His principles mainly lay in action.

O : So we must keep them.

P : He gave much that suits our tradition.

S_6 : That will be our homage to Gandhiji.

A. MNPO B. PNMO
C. MPNO D. NMPO

5. S_1 : It is our policy that the regional language should prosper.

M : Rather they should be medium of instruction.

N : They would never be replaced by some other language.

O : Such an arrangement would give diversity.

P : The official language should be regional language.

S_6 : India's unity lies in diversity.

A. PNMO B. MNOP
C. NMPO D. OMPN

6. S_1 : There is a kind of war hysteria in India.

M : We are sure to feel upset.

N : In fact, these are discussions and not protests.

O : Why should others accuse us of protesting?

P : There has been aggression on our country.

S_6 : Being democratic we have the right to discuss.

A. NMOP B. MNOP
C. PMON D. OPMN

7. S_1 : Corruption is a difficult and delicate task.

M : It is difficult to prove the charge.

N : Those conventions must be respected.

O : The law is not effective in dealing with it.

P : So some conventions will have to be built up.

S_6 : This is possible if we are men of integrity having honesty of purpose.

A. PNMO B. OMPN
C. MPNO D. OPNM

8. S_1 : Planning in India is a difficult problem.

M : So planners cannot decide the size of the plan.

N : The gap between what people want and what can be done is big.

O : Moreover resources are limited.

P : Plan can be drawn on the basis of actual resources.

S_6 : But without planning no nation can progress.

A. NMOP B. MNOP
C. MONP D. PONM

9. S_1 : The public sector has to expand.

M : But private sector should not be allowed to die.

N : It is in accordance with our policy.

O : Moreover the government can enter into collaboration.

P : Equally important is the incapacity of the investors to invest.

S_6 : Incentives must be given to keep them alive.

A. MOPN B. PNOM
C. NPOM D. PNMO

10. S_1 : Efforts should be made to reduce imports, and to stimulate exports.

M : We have another source of foreign exchange.

N : But people are reluctant to part with it.

O : I mean the hoarded gold.

P : It is necessary to increase our foreign exchange reserve.

S_6 : In order to get it, gold bond will be issued.

A. NPMO B. MNOP
C. PMON D. MNPO

ANSWERS

1	2	3	4	5	6	7	8	9	10
C	C	A	C	A	C	B	A	A	C

Writing

ESSAY

CLEAN INDIA DRIVE

Prime Minister Narendra Modi launched the Swachch Bharat sanitation programme on October 2, 2014. It was a befitting tribute to the Father of the Nation who was concerned about sanitation issues. The proposed sanitation programme will reframe the social and economic face of India and prove to be a great game changer. Sanitation has a direct link with the spread of communicable diseases which are prevalent in India. As a matter of fact, the initiative "Health for All by 2000 A.D." flopped because an effective sanitation programme was not launched simultaneously. The basic cause of frequent epidemics in India is insanitation. The country can attain Health for All by October 2, 2019, if the programme is implemented in totality.

Quality of Life

Living in an insanitary environment, like poverty, degrades the quality of human life and it is a curse and a social stigma as well. Therefore, the accomplishment of the total Sanitation Programme (TSP) will improve the living standard of the poorest of the poor on the one hand and improve the Human Development Index (HDI) of India on the other. Presently, India is positioned 134 in the UN's HDI. Poverty is less painful if one gets a chance to live in a sanitary environment. In fact, a sanitary environment is the basic necessity of human life like air, water and food for its aesthetic and psychological development. That is why we say, "Cleanliness is next to godliness". If India ensures total sanitation by 2019, our stock will rise in the comity of nations.

According to the proposed Swachh Bharat scheme, the government will build individual toilets in 1.04 crore households and 5 lakh community/public toilets in urban areas. Around 8.8 crore toilets will be built in rural areas and a majority of these are to be provided in individual households. The total sanitation programme includes programmes that are to be executed under the umbrella programme.

Steps Towards Total Sanitation

Provision of 100 per cent sewerage and a drainage system in all urban towns together with innocuous disposal or recycling of the finally treated effluent for irrigation with a total ban on discharge into the drains or rivers. An effective sewerage and drainage system forms the backbone of urban sanitation.

There is need for 100 per cent solid waste management, both in urban and rural areas and recycling of the final waste product. Around 100 per cent coverage of rural households and slum areas with sanitary latrines. All the open areas in urban and rural communities will be either paved or grassed. All the streets to be paved with concrete blocks or paver blocks. There should be zero tolerance to dumping or littering of solid waste matter (mostly paper and plastic matter) in open spaces, both in urban and rural areas. It should be the same for stagnation of sullage or any other waste water in urban or rural areas. There should be daily sweeping of streets, roads or public places both in rural and urban areas. The vacant plots should be provided with boundary walls and kept neat, clean and green.

Each element is more important than the other. The accomplishment of this programme by 2019 is a onerous task and will require huge amount of funds. Execution of the TSP will be done by the state agencies. The Central Government will only facilitate and monitor the progress of the programme with partial funding. Therefore, it will be appropriate if the Centre prepares a blueprint and then calls a meeting of state chief ministers to hand over the blueprint to them to prepare rough cost estimates. Considering the amazonian size of the project, it will be essential to set up a separate ministry to prepare a financial and administrative model and give a go-ahead to the states to implement this programme by October, 2019.

The campaign faces formidable financial and implementation challenges. Financially, the government will easily need 2-3% of GDP annually till the target date. There are only four avenues to mobilising such vast resources: increases in revenues made possible by accelerated growth; cuts in middle-class subsidies such as for cooking gas; elimination of enormous leakages in the myriad social schemes by replacing them with cash transfers; and accelerated disinvestment including outright privatisation. All roads to Swachh Bharat pass through the thicket of reforms.

Pursuit of Swachh Bharat also requires strengthening public health services. Services such as good drainage systems, absence of swamps and ponds that are home to stagnant water, and the supply of safe drinking water—all of which reduce exposure to and spread of diseases—are classic examples of public goods and require effective government intervention.

Swachh Bharat would do well to encourage each state to restart a separate public health department, accountable for the delivery of public health services.

NAXALISM : A THREAT TO INTERNAL SECURITY

On May 25, 2013 naxalites made a violent attack on some congress leaders returning from the 'Parivartan Yatra' at Darba Valley of district Sukma in Chhattisgarh. In this attack 29 people, including state's Ex-Home Minister Mahendra Varma, Congress leader Nand Kumar Patel and ex-MLA Uday Mudaliar, were killed. On June 29, 2010 at least 26 CRPF jawans were killed in a massive attack by naxalites near Narayanpur Camp in Chhattisgarh.

This was a most coordinated and successful operation carried out by the Naxalites against the paramilitary forces. It was the third big attack by Naxals against the police and paramilitary forces. It shows some security lapses in operation against Naxals.

Earlier, on April 6 last year the Maoists launched biggest attack in the history of naxal movement and killed 76 paramilitary forces in Dantewada district in Chhattisgarh. Within a few days they killed 35 people in the same district. In the summer of 2009, Maoist largely captured the Lalgarh area of West Bengal and posed a serious threat to security forces. Their strength lies in ambushing, mining the road and other guerrilla tactics. These incidents exposed the chinks in the armour of security forces.

As its historical evolution indicates, the naxal movement in India, in last few years shown the tendency of expanding its support base as well as intensification of violent activities. It has assumed regional and international orientation in view of the success of Maoist in the neighbouring Nepal. This has emboldened Naxal groups in India. They are at present well entrenched in worst affected areas of West Bengal, Chhattisgarh, Jharkhand, Andhra Pradesh and Odisha. Their guerrilla tactics have surprised the security forces. Besides, their wide support in rural and tribal areas of these states, they have generated certain amount of sympathy among certain urban educated and intellectual sections.

On the contrary, government forces are not acquinted with the jungle and terrains where maoist have control. Neither they are trained to face the guerrilla tactics of the maoist. The state police forces are under-manned, poorly trained and ill-equipped.

To counter the Naxal threat, military action is not enough alone. Work should be done on multi-dimensional fronts. Surrender and resettlement schemes should be launched by the state governments in the affected areas, where naxals surrendering to the government are given financial incentives and facilities for their resettlement. The other component is a long term measure of expanding the development process in the affected areas. Due to lack of effective implementation of various development schemes, the naxals are able to co-opt the marginalised sections of rural poor and tribals. The corruption and administrative inefficiency have further compounded the development process.

In the view of the above discussion, it is clear that naxal violence is not a law and order problem in India. It is serious security threat to India with international and regional dimensions. The need of the hour is to adopt both social and administrative measures to tackle the threat posed by the naxal groups. Besides, the better training of security forces, planning and coordination is must for the success of government measures.

NITI AAYOG

The government on January 1, 2015 replaced the 65-year-old Planning Commission—a relic of the Socialist era—with a Niti Aayog or National Institution for Transforming India, marking a major shift in policy making by involving states. The Aayog will recommend a national agenda, including strategic and technical advice on elements of policy and economic matters. It will also develop mechanisms for village-level plans and aggregate these progressively at higher levels of government. To be headed by PM Narendra Modi, the new body will have a governing council comprising CMs of all states and Lt Governors of Union Territories and will work towards fostering co-operative federalism for providing a national agenda to the Centre and states. The membership of states has rendered the National Development Council, a body of CMs that approves five-year Plans, defunct. Former secretary of Defence Research and Development Organisation (DRDO) VK Saraswat and economist Bibek Debroy are appointed as full-time members. The Aayog will have finance minister Arun Jaitley, home minister Rajnath Singh, railway minister Suresh Prabhu and agriculture minister Radha Mohan Singh as ex-officio members. Union ministers Nitin Gadkari, Thawar Chand Gehlot and Smriti Irani are special invitees to the panel.

Birth of a New System

Prime Minister Modi has declared that his government will dissolve the Planning Commission in his first Independence Day speech in 2014. He substantiated his decision with former PM Manmohan Singh's opinion, who felt India has lacked foresight after introducing reforms. He has put forward a new idea called 'Cooperative Federalism'.

The NDA government has started its discussion with experts, right after it came into power. The first Independent Evolution Office (IEO) Assessment Report was submitted to the PM on May 29, three days after he was sworn in. The report had categorically recommended the replacement of Planning Commission with a Control Commission.

The NDA government has minimised the funds and functions of Planning Commission as a first step towards its annihilation. It directed the important central ministries and departments to submit their planned budget estimation to the Central Government directly.

On January 1, 2015 the new body named NITI Aayog has replaced the Planning Commission with immediate effect.

Structure of NITI Aayog

The NITI Aayog was established by a resolution of the central government. It will be governed by the Governing Council and will have a team chaired by the Prime Minister.

Governing Council : Governing Council is the highest body of NITI Aayog. It consists of following members:

1. Prime Minister of India as the Chairperson
2. A Vice-Chairperson and a CEO, nominated by the Prime Minister
3. The Chief Ministers of all the states and Lieutenant Governors of Union Territories
4. Members: Two (Full-time)
5. Part-time members: Maximum of two from leading universities research organizations and other relevant institutions in an ex-officio capacity. Part-time members will be on a rotational basis
6. Ex Officio members: Maximum of four members of the Union Council of Ministers to be nominated by the Prime Minister

Aims and Objectives

NITI Aayog will seek to provide a critical directional and strategic input into the development process by consulting the states, Centre and different stakeholders. Its aims and objectives are as following:

- The top-down centre-to-state one-way flow of policy, that was the hallmark of the Planning Commission era, is now sought to be replaced by a genuine and continuing partnership of states.
- NITI Aayog will emerge as a think-tank that will provide Governments at the central and state level with relevant strategic and technical advice across the spectrum of key elements of policy.
- The body will also seek to put an end to slow implementation of policy, by fostering better Inter-Ministry coordination and better Centre-State coordination. It will help evolve a shared vision of national development priorities and foster cooperative federalism, recognizing that strong states make a strong nation
- The NITI Aayog will develop mechanisms to formulate credible plans to the village level and aggregate these progressively at higher levels of government. It will ensure special attention to the sections of society that may be at risk of not benefitting adequately from economic progress.
- The NITI Aayog will create a knowledge, innovation and entrepreneurial support system through a collaborative community of national and international experts, practitioners and partners. It will offer a platform for resolution of inter-sectoral and inter-departmental issues in order to accelerate the implementation of the development agenda.

In addition, the NITI Aayog will monitor and evaluate the implementation of programmes, and focus on technology upgradation and capacity building.

INDIA AND THE NSG

Recently, India rejected China's contention that it must sign the NPT to get membership of the Nuclear Suppliers Group, saying France was included in the elite group without signing the Non-Proliferation Treaty.

What is NSG?

Nuclear Suppliers Group (NSG) is a multinational body concerned with reducing nuclear proliferation by controlling the export and re-transfer of materials that may be applicable to nuclear weapon development and by improving safeguards and protection on existing materials.

Interestingly, the NSG was set up in 1974 as a reaction to India's nuclear tests to stop what it called the misuse of nuclear material meant for peaceful purposes. Currently, it has 48 members.

Background

India sought membership of the NSG in 2008, but its application hasn't been decided on, primarily because signing the NPT or other nuclear moratoriums on testing is a pre-requisite. However, India has received a special waiver to conduct nuclear trade with all nuclear exporters.

India, Pakistan, Israel and South Sudan are among the four UN member states which have not signed the NPT, the international pact aimed at preventing the spread of nuclear weapons.

Recent Controversy

China had opposed India's bid to get NSG membership on the ground that it was yet to sign the NPT. It had said all the multilateral non-proliferation export control regime including the NSG have regarded NPT as an important standard for the expansion of the NSG. And hence, members of the Nuclear Suppliers Group should be party to NPT.

Benefits Associated with NSG Membership:

- Timely information on nuclear matters
- Contributes by way of information
- Has confirmed credentials
- Can act as an instrument of harmonization and coordination
- Is part of a very transparent process.

NSG membership cannot be linked with NPT. But, it can be linked with International Atomic Energy Agency (IAEA). And India has closely cooperated with IAEA. Therefore, India's case should be judged independently without prejudice or on requests to block it following lobbying from other countries. In 2008, China was among the last few countries to lift its objection to clean waiver by NSG to India. During American President Barack Obama's visit to India in January 2015, the US had announced that India was ready to join the NSG.

India's nuclear doctrine is non-proliferation-oriented and is both sensible and responsible. Having accepted IAEA safeguards and Additional Protocol and having effectively subscribed to and practised the principles of non-proliferation, it is immaterial if India has formally signed the NPT, CTBT or any other such treaty. India has already acquired high-level expertise in the peaceful use of nuclear energy in industry, power, agriculture and health care. India's membership of the NSG shall not only benefit it but also encourage civil nuclear trade globally without compromising on world peace and harmony.

Why India Should be Granted NSG Membership?

In this game of developing nuclear weapons India has not indulged in any dubious/clandestine activity and its programme has been developed solely by years of hard work indigenously. By this single act India has shown that developing a credible nuclear weapons programme through honest and civilian means is possible for any country having high-level scientific manpower and materials.

Besides, by declaring a voluntary moratorium on further underground nuclear tests India has effectively acted in sense and spirit of NPT/CTBT provisions. By steering its programme only as a minimum deterrence and pledging NFU unless faced with an attack of weapons of mass destruction (WMD), India has established itself as a responsible nuclear state.

SMART CITIES IN INDIA

A 'smart city' is an urban region that is highly advanced in terms of overall infrastructure, sustainable real estate, communications and market viability. It is a city where information technology is the principal infrastructure and the basis for providing essential services to residents. There are many technological platforms involved, including but not limited to automated sensor networks and data centres. Though this may sound futuristic, it is now likely to become a reality as the 'smart cities' movement unfolds in India. In a smart city, economic development and activity is sustainable and rationally incremental by virtue of being based on success-oriented market drivers such as supply and demand. They benefit everybody, including citizens, businesses, the government and the environment.

The concept of smart cities originated at the time when the entire world was facing one of the worst economic crises. In 2008, IBM began work on a 'smarter cities' concept as part of its Smarter Planet initiative. By the beginning of 2009, the concept had captivated the imagination of various nations across the globe. Countries like South Korea, UAE and China began to invest heavily into their research and formation. Today, a number of excellent precedents exist that India can emulate, such as those in Vienna, Aarhus, Amsterdam, Cairo, Lyon, Málaga, Malta, the Songdo International Business District near Seoul, Verona etc.

The cities with ongoing or proposed smart cities include Kochi in Kerala, Ahmedabad in Gujarat, Aurangabad in Maharashtra, Manesar in Delhi NCR, Khushkera in Rajasthan, Krishnapatnam in Andhra Pradesh, Ponneri in Tamil Nadu and Tumkur in Karnataka. Many of these cities will include special investment regions or special economic zones with modified regulations and tax structures to make it attractive for foreign investment. This is essential because much of the funding for these projects will have to come from private developers and from abroad.

The concept is not without challenges, especially in India. For instance, the success of such a city depends on residents, entrepreneurs and visitors becoming actively involved in energy saving and implementation of new technologies. There are many ways to make residential, commercial and public spaces sustainable by ways of technology, but a high percentage of the total energy use is still in the hands of end users and their behaviour. Also, there is the time factor—such cities can potentially take anything between 20 and 30 years to build.

What is the Scope of Smart Cities in India?

India is drawing on the development of smart cities at the global level. Prime Minister Narendra Modi's vision 'Digital India', has a plan to build 100 smart cities across the country. Modi in his speech said, "Cities in the past were built on riverbanks. They are now built along highways. But in the future, they will be built based on availability of optical fiber networks and next-generation infrastructure."

Digital India envisages making India a leader in digitally delivering services in the health, education, banking sectors. Modi announced an investment of $1.2 billion in smart cities with more funding coming from private sectors and abroad.

What Needs to be Done?

The smart city project needs to be designed wisely, considering the local population as the key point. Also, it has to be careful as to not widen the already present gulf between the rural and the urban class. A nation should progress taking all its citizens along, irrespective of class differences, and catering to everyone's need equally.

As much as the vision of smart cities is incredible and rational, its implementation on India at the given socio-economic condition, might be a bit difficult. However, as a fast developing economy, the country needs to keep up with the global standards. Hence, the execution of this plan could make India take a major leap in the race of development.

Across the world, the stride of migration from rural to urban areas is increasing. By 2050, about 70 per cent of the population will be living in cities, and India is no exception. It will need about 500 new cities to accommodate the influx.

Interestingly, urbanisation in India has for the longest time been viewed as a by-product of failed regional planning. Though it is inevitable, and will only change when the benefits of urbanisation overtake the costs involved, it is an opportunity for achieving faster growth.

With increasing urbanisation and the load on rural land, the government has now realised the need for cities that can cope with the challenges of urban living and also be magnets for investment. The announcement of '100 smart cities' falls in line with this vision.

START-UP INDIA PROGRAMME

"Start-up India program" announced by the PM on his Independence Day speech in 2015 is a program to provide financial support to young entrepreneurs to kick start their initiatives. The main objective of this programme is to provide financial support to atleast 1.25 lakhs start-ups via 1.25 lakh bank branches in India. With an objective to encourage self-employment and job opportunities, governments time and again encourage entrepreneurs.

The entrepreneurial spirit of the underprivileged is often nipped in the bud due to lack of finances. To tackle this, the Govt of India has announced "Start-up India" program. The program calls upon 1.25 lac bank branches in the country to finance start-ups by at least one tribal and dalit entrepreneur and one woman entrepreneur.

Advantages of the Scheme:

1. *Social empowerment:* Dalits, tribals and women are still the most discriminated population in India. The scheme would enable them to strengthen their social position by building capacity in them.
2. *Fillip to Pradhan Mantri Jan Dhan Yojana:* The program will incentivise the financially excluded people to open accounts under PMJDY to avail credit facility.
3. India is facing crunch of entrepreneurs now. The scheme would help in increasing the number.

Criticisms of the Scheme

1. *A blow to Indradhanush program:* The program will conflict with the recent attempts to deal with the bad assets of the Public sector banks.
2. *Increase apathy to the poor:* The program will add to the reluctance of banks officials to admit the poor as their clients as has been happening under PMJDY.
3. *A kind of affirmative action:* The program ignores the poor lying outside the targetted population.
4. *Against the spirit of economic reforms:* The govt should restrict itself to providing conducive business environment.

The initiative of Start-up India to lead to Stand-up India is a good one but needs modification given the rising bad assets of banks. The dalits, tribals and women will not come forward with their ideas unless they are socially empowered which will come only when they are looked up with respect in the society. This can better happen through education.

The Start-up programme to boost new means of production as well as employment is a welcome step. In addition to raising productivity and employment elasticity of growth, the start-ups will provide consumers with better services, competitive products for export, taxes to the state and innovation to people at large.

However, there are certain steps that need to be taken for this programme to be a success:

1. Start-up programme can deliver best results when proper implementation of Skill India as well as Digital India takes place.
2. Regulation of this sector must be inter-ministerial with proper coordination framework.
3. Industry-educational institution collabora-tion needs to be ramped up as students in top-notch universities are eager as well as able to drive innovations.
4. There is a need for diversification of start-ups to leverage potential of youth in sectors other than IT and software.
5. Overall financial health of banks and corporates must be good so as to promote the start-ups as credit is needed for almost every start-up.

If all these are taken care of, Start-up India can surely be a road to Step-up India.

Such a programme, if implemented has the following positive implications:

1. It will be a support for the young Indian entrepreneurs who migrate to other countries like the USA to find angel investors to fund their projects.
2. It will boost the research programmes in India. Not only the research, such a programme will also result in shaping the research output into a successful product in the global market, which is missing now in India.
3. Already Indians are at the top most levels of big MNCs such as Google and Microsoft. Such a financial initiative with expert guidance from people like Sam Pitroda and Sundar Pichai would definitely yield good results.

Overall "Start up India" is a good programme which can revolutionise Indian economy and even may result in an "Indian google", "Indian apple" or Indian Microsoft.

MANGALYAAN : THE MARS ORBITER MISSION

India made history on September 24, 2014 when its ₹ 450 crore *Mars Orbiter Mission (MOM)* or *Mangalyaan* was successfully placed in the Red Planet's (Mars') orbit on the very first attempt. The tryst with the Red Planet came 10 months after the ISRO launched its first orbiter to Mars on November 5, 2013. But the final critical moment was on September 24, when the main Liquid Apogee Motor and the eight small thrusters ignited simultaneously and enabled the manoeuvre. All the engines fired flawlessly for 24 minutes and reduced the spacecraft's velocity by 1.09 km per second; this contained the spacecraft in an orbit around Mars. PM Narendra Modi was present at the command centre of Indian Space Research Organisation (ISRO) in Bengaluru to witness the space history in the making by India. With this grand success, India joined the US, European Space Agency and the former Soviet Union in the elite club of Martian explorers. Later, the colour camera on board the spacecraft beamed back about 10 pictures of 'good quality' of the Red Planet's surface which show some craters.

The mission is a "technology demonstrator" project to develop the technologies for design, planning, management, and operations of an interplanetary mission. It carries five instruments that will help advance knowledge about Mars to achieve its secondary scientific objective.

The Mars Orbiter Mission probe lifted-off from the First Launch Pad at Satish Dhawan Space Centre (Sriharikota Range SHAR), Andhra Pradesh, using a Polar Satellite Launch Vehicle (PSLV) rocket C25 on 5 November 2013.

The launch window was approximately 20 days long and started on 28 October 2013. The MOM probe spent about a month in geocentric, low-Earth orbit, where it made a series of seven altitude-raising orbital manoeuvres before trans-Mars injection on 30 November 2013 (UTC). After a 298-day transit to Mars, it was successfully inserted into Mars orbit on 24 September 2014.

It is India's first interplanetary mission and ISRO has become the fourth space agency to reach Mars, after the Soviet space program, NASA, and the European Space Agency. It is also the first nation to reach Mars orbit on its first attempt, and the first Asian nation to do so.

The spacecraft is currently being monitored from the Spacecraft Control Centre at ISRO Telemetry, Tracking and Command Network (ISTRAC) in Bangalore with support from Indian Deep Space Network (IDSN) antennae at Byalalu.

Objectives

The primary objective of the Mars Orbiter Mission is to showcase India's rocket launch systems, spacecraft-building and operations capabilities. Specifically, the primary objective is to develop the technologies required for design, planning, management and operations of an interplanetary mission, comprising the following major tasks:

- design and realisation of a Mars orbiter with a capability to perform Earth-bound manoeuvres, cruise phase of 300 days, Mars orbit insertion / capture, and on-orbit phase around Mars;
- deep-space communication, navigation, mission planning and management;
- incorporate autonomous features to handle contingency situations.

The secondary objective is to explore Mars' surface features, morphology, mineralogy and Martian atmosphere using indigenous scientific instruments.

History

The MOM mission concept began with a feasibility study in 2010, after the launch of lunar satellite Chandrayaan-1 in 2008. The government of India approved the project on 3 August 2012, after the Indian Space Research Organisation completed 125 crore (US$20 million) of required studies for the orbiter. The total project cost may be up to 454 crore(US$74 million). The satellite costs ₹ 153 crore (US$25 million) and the rest of the budget has been attributed to ground stations and relay upgrades that will be used for other ISRO projects.

The space agency had planned the launch on 28 October 2013 but was postponed to 5 November 2013 following the delay in ISRO's spacecraft tracking ships to take up pre-determined positions due to poor weather in the Pacific Ocean. Launch opportunities for a fuel-saving Hohmann transfer orbit occur every 26 months, in this case, 2016 and 2018. The Mars Orbiter's on-orbit mission life is six-to-ten months.

Assembly of the PSLV-XL launch vehicle, designated C25, started on 5 August 2012. The mounting of the five scientific instruments was completed at ISRO Satellite Centre, Bangalore, and the finished spacecraft was shipped to Sriharikota on 2 October 2013 for integration to the PSLV-XL launch vehicle. The satellite's development was fast-tracked and completed in a record 15 months. Despite the US federal government shutdown, NASA reaffirmed on 5 October 2013 it would provide communications and navigation support to the mission. During a meeting in 30 September 2014, NASA and ISRO officials signed an agreement to establish a pathway for future joint missions to explore Mars. One of the working group's objectives will be to explore potential coordinated observations and science analysis between MAVEN orbiter and MOM, as well as other current and future Mars missions.

THE ERA OF CYBER CRIMES

Cyber Crimes are committed mainly on those computers that are connected to Internet. A computer, which is connected to Internet, can be used to surf through the information and facts loaded on other computers, which are also connected to Internet. If we get some codes, which help us to get the secret information of a particular website, then we can manipulate the data and information loaded on that website. These codes or passwords are not difficult to get. Eccentric young boys, computer programmers and greedy computer users get these codes to manipulate the information loaded on websites. In order to carry out such activities, software programme are needed. After getting the password (or code) of a website, people exchange money or information by manipulating that website. This is known as Cyber Crime in technical language.

Crimes like this can be of several types. Firstly, any person can send ugly and obscene messages through the E-mail service. Due to this action, the receiver of the E-mail message receives a setback. Secondly, if a person, who knows only a little bit of computers, can spread Internet viruses on the Net. Normally, E-mail services are used to carry out such heinous tasks. Viruses enter that computer to which, these E-mail messages are sent; thus they destroy that computer. Both the machine and its information can be seriously decimated. Only recently, the Phillippines Police had arrested the creator of the virus "I Love You". This young man had jammed the computer systems of the American Department of Defence by spreading this virus on Internet. Thirdly, persons with malafide intentions collect information about the numbers or access codes of bank accounts. They get the money transferred from these banks into their own bank accounts and the banks in question are do not even know about these transactions. There is only the need for some deftness and the criminals walk away with millions. Fourthly, some persons wreak havoc on the websites owned by the private sector firms. They send viruses on such websites, collect highly sensitive information from the same or use the tools of defamation and try to foil the image of any person or firm on a website. Fifthly, the system of electronic signature is in vogue on the Net. Some eccentric people steal the electronic signatures of others and use them to earn money. Such types of crimes take place in transactions related to E-cash and global business operations.

It has become very important to check cyber crimes, because in the times to come, all the activities would be carried out through Internet. Some crazy criminals or youth make Internet a toy in their hands and surf through it all the times to achieve their base ends. They had better become alert because IT Act (2000) has been passed to deal with cyber criminals. Under the aegis of this Act, there is a provision to give harsh punishment to cyber criminals. Even in the United States, where cyber crimes are high in number, such tough laws have already been made.

Cyber crimes are like a blot on the mankind. If these were to continue, then man would not be able to make progress in the arena of Information Technology. In the times to come, computers, Internet and electronic techniques would rule the roost. Cyber crimes would successfully make these (three) their easy targets. The governments of nations, people connected with the field of Information Technology and the private sector firms are responsible for controlling such crimes.

Cyber laws is that branch of law, which checks cyber crimes and regulates Information Technology. In this context, the President of India has given his consent to the first cyber law of the country—Information Technology Act, 2000. The objective of this Act is to give legal recognition to electronic data interchanges or transactions done through electronic communication modes. In its other objectives, some others are—use of alternatives of paper-based communication and information gathering, making electronic filing of documents easier in government organisations and making amendments in Indian Evidence Act (1872), Bankers' Book Evidence Act (1891) and RBI Act (1934). The objective of this Act is to provide such a type of infrastructure with which, the legal sanctity may be maintained in the context of activities being carried out through the modes of electronic processing. According to the provisions of this Act, E-mail would be deemed a legal form of communication and it would also be recognised by courts. On the basis of the legal framework given by the Act, firms can now continue E-mail activities. It can be hoped that this law would play an important role in checking cyber crimes.

CONSUMER PROTECTION

A consumer is a person who buys a good or service. The meaning of consumer protection is — protection of the rights of the consumer. In the present era of free trade system, the private enterpreneurs are capable of exploiting consumers because of their economic strength. Hence, the government is required to make such laws and acts (through planned means) as could enable the consumer to escape the wrath of the private entrepreneur. Besides, he can also make full use of the products and services provided by that private entrepreneur. The issue of consumer protection was raised for the first time in Europe and the United States. Slowly, the grip of the law in both these nations became so strong that the supremacy of the consumer was established in every field. There was only one reason for this phenomenon— individual freedom in the western nations has already touch unseen peaks and the individual has a higher status than the society and the nation. Hence, a terrified and exploited consumer has great legal protection. It is a victory of democracy on all the issues. It is a direct evidence of the supremacy of human rights. If we try to learn the meaning of consumer protection in real sense, then we would learn that consumers have many rights. Some of these rights are as follows:

1. The right to state one's viewpoint
2. The right to select a product or service of one's choice
3. The right to know the price
4. The right to know the details of quality
5. The right to learn about the chief components (or parts) of the product
6. The right to make one's complaint
7. The right to file a complaint before an official or judicial chair and get the compensation for the loss incurred due to the use of the product/service.

Most of the Indians are not even aware of consumer rights. After 1980 our consumers came to know about their rights after the initiation of the free market system of the West in India. By the arrival of the year 1990 some laws and Acts were passed. Consumer protection cells were also set up. Some magazines were also published, in which, the rights of consumers were described in the context of purchase and use of products, small and large. Many consumers also won legal battles and they were also given appropriate compensation by private firms. These firms manufacture products to earn money. Hence, they would have to ensure that the products: (a) should be available at a reasonable price; (b) its quality/measure should be accurate; (c) in the event of the product being defective, it should be taken back and the consumer should be given a new product in lieu of the same; and (d) the complaints of the consumer should be heard.

With the advent of the free market system into its full force, the concept of consumer protection would get more strength. In order to protect the interests of consumers, government institutions (like telephone, electricity, water and housing authorities) have started many a scheme to listen to the grievances of the common man and solve his problems. The consumer should contact the manufacturer or company if he has been cheated due to its product, or if he has been given wrong information with respect to its product. If that firm or producer does not attend to his complaint, then the consumer can file a complaint in the consumer protection cell. It should be remembered that the government of India has given many powers to these institutions. If one cannot get justice even in these institutions, then there is no harm in taking a legal action.

It is hoped that consumer protection front would become powerful and active in all aspects in the modern era.

DIRECT BENEFIT (CASH) TRANSFER SCHEME

The government has launched the Direct Benefit (Cash) Transfer Scheme on January 1, 2013 with the objective of providing the government subsidy directly through the bank accounts of the beneficiaries. The DBT programme aims that entitlements and benefits to people can be transferred directly to them through biometric based Aadhaar linked bank accounts, thus reducing several layers of intermediaries and delays in the system. The system will allow actual disbursements to take place at the doorstep of the beneficiaries through a dense, interoperable network of business correspondents (BCs) using biometric micro ATM machines. Thus, the yardstick of success is not going to be that the money has reached a bank account, but that it has reached the hands of the intended beneficiary—a student, a pensioner, a widow, an elderly person, a disabled person, or a poor family.

According to a study by National Institute of Public Finance & Policy (NIPFP) substantial benefits would accrue to the government by integrating Aadhaar with schemes such as PDS, MNREGS, Fertilizer & LPG subsidies, as well as housing, education and health programmes. The benefits arise from the reduction in leakages that occur due to identification and authentication issues. The study estimates the leakages due to identification and authentication errors, i.e. the existence of duplicates and "ghost" beneficiaries. Any reduction in leakages is considered a benefit, the money can then be utilized for its real purpose, that is for the targeted beneficiaries, or if the reduction in leakages leads to a reduction in the overall government expenditure required for the respective scheme, it is a benefit because the money can then be utilized in other programs.

What is the Scheme

It is a poverty reduction measure in which government subsidies and other benefits are given directly to the poor in cash rather than in the form of subsidies. The government transfers the subsidy or the financial help to the poor through companies, corporations or customer centres. It is then indirectly reaches the beneficiaries. There is a big scope of diversion and pilferage of subsidy money in the current system. But this will not happen now. The subsidy will be directly transferred to the bank accounts of the beneficiaries. There will be no one in between. The beneficiary can withdraw the subsidy-money from his/her bank account or through ATM. The main schemes covered under it are: The scholarship granted to the students belonging to scheduled castes, scheduled tribes and other backward classes for the post-matric education; Indira Gandhi Awas Yojana, Janani Suraksha Yojana, the insurance cover for the daughter of scheduled castes; and the Dhanlakshmi Scheme.

Having announced the transfer of subsidy to poor on the basis of Aadhar numbers, the government will have to provide ATM card to all account holders. Alongwith this, the government will ensure ATM facility in all the branches of banks. The central government has directed all the public sector banks and regional rural banks to establish ATMs at their all branches.

The new scheme has great economic importance. If it succeeds, then it will be a decisive turning point for the Indian Economy. Whenever any scheme is launched, it is obviously welcomed and opposed as well. The same is happening with this scheme also, but it is a fact that it is not possible for any scheme to be flawless. It should be viewed on the basis whether it is better in comparison of the current system, or worse. If it has some flaws then certainly those can be removed in future. It is not that there will be no place at all for corruption, red-tapism and biase, but it will be lesser than in the current system and it will be easy to reduce them with time. The reason for this is that the technology used in it is modern and there is more possibility of improvement in it. The way, by the computerization of reservation of railway tickets their black-marketing has not stopped completely but it has reduced considerably and there is further scope to reduce it even more; the same way Aadhar Card based system may not be free from the possibilities of corruption and fraud, still it is better than the Ration Card based system. It is easy to improve the system based on Aadhar Card, and it is expected that its flaws will go on reducing in future.

INTERNET

Internet is the logical conglomeration of computer systems that are spread around the world. It has been created with the help of optical cable networks, modem devices, telephone lines, LAN and WAN networks and satellites. Information is displayed on various web sites on Internet. This information is related to almost every area of human endeavour, including environment, space and facts related to the cosmos.

In Internet jargon, if a person opens Internet web sites on his computer (or surfs through the web sites), then he is called Netizen. Presently, there are nearly 45,00,000 Internet connections in India. But vis-a-vis 1.5 million connections operating in the West, this number is very timid. Internet is a boon for a nation like India. It helps us exchange vital information and data and our readers know that in the present information technology age, information is everything. Almost all the govern-ments of the world, private firms, non-government organisation and professionals either want to get their web sites developed or surf through various Internet web sites. Many of them have got their web sites developed and also got them uploaded on this wonderful information super-highway. Not only this, there are web sites of many newspapers, magazines and technical journals as well.

This method of information exchange is very efficient and fast. E-mail can be used by Netizens to send information to any part of the world. Voice, data, video information and information in the form of text can be sent from one computer to another with ease. Besides, Internet has put man on the peak of the business world. This concept is called Electronic Commerce (E-com). Electronic Commerce is related to the exchange of goods and services through the Net and in this system, money is not physically transferred. It is transferred through a new system, which is called Electronic Cash (E-cash). We can buy and sell practically anything through Internet; exchange of data for engineering projects is also included in this system

There are three levels of connectivity of Internet. The first level is T1 in which, the user can only see the information/data put on various web sites. The second level is T2 in which, he can create his own web sites as well as collect information from the Net. The third level is T3 in which, he himself becomes a part of the Internet System. Nowadays, VSNL, Mantra Online and Satyam Online are the three major Internet Service Providers (ISPs). Many other firms are entering the vast markets related to Internet services. VSNL has been privatised now. Internet affects all the areas of human endeavour. It has been successful in earning valuable achievements in fields like education, entertainment, sports and games, science and technology, Electronic Commerce and social interactions (like marriage alliances). This world has already taken the shape of a small village. The prices of Internet services are falling. Internet connectivity can be obtained by paying just Rs. 525 on an annual basis. But in addition to this, we would need a computer (Pentium-800 system), software for running programs of Internet, one telephone line and a modem device. The government has provided local dial-up service in all the districts of the country. A user, who is located within the 100-kilometer radius of an ISP, can use Internet services through a local telephone line. In order to surf through Internet, we have to connect our computer system to the main information gateway of the ISP through a telephone line and modem. We use Internet navigation software to surf through Internet. These programs are provided by Microsoft Corporation (Internet Explorer) or Netscape (Netscape Navigator). Dialling is automatic over the telephone and if a connection is made, then we arrive at the main menu of the ISP. We can surf through any web site if we feed its correct URL on the computer's screen at the command line. We can surf through various web sites, send and receive E-mail, read magazines and even listen to music.

There is also a lot of garbage—like information on the Net, which is related to obscene photographs and movies. It is sad to note that the youth of today do not use Internet for educational purposes, or for enhancing their professional capabilities. This tendency ought to be given a U-turn.

In sum, Internet would become a dominant force in the areas related to professional, social, business and entertainment activities of all the people in this century.

MAKE IN INDIA CAMPAIGN

Prime Minister Narendra Modi launched the 'Make in India' campaign at a high-profile event on September 25, 2014. Unveiling the campaign PM Modi said FDI should be understood as 'First Develop India' along with 'Foreign Direct Investment' while encouraging investors not to just look at India as merely a market but also as an opportunity. The Prime Minister pointed out that it was crucial to increase the purchasing power of the common man to boost demand and thus spur development.

Key thrust of the programme would be on cutting down in delays in manufacturing projects clearance, develop adequate infrastructure and make it easier for companies to do business in India. The 25 key sectors identified under the programme include automobiles, auto components, bio-technology, chemicals, defence manufacturing, electronic systems, food processing, leather, mining, oil & gas, railways, ports and textile.

The national programme aims at time-bound project clearances through a single online portal which will be further supported by the eight-member team dedicated to answering investor queries within 48 hours and addressing key issues including labour laws, skill development and infrastructure.

The objective of the mega programme is to ensure that manufacturing sector which contributes around 15% of the country's Gross Domestic Products is increased to 25% in next few years.

However, for making India an investment hub, the first and foremost important step would be to create an efficient administrative machinery which would cut down on delays in project clearances. Economists say that India has been very stringent when it comes to giving procedural and regulatory clearances. Besides a time bound clearance from all regulatory authority would create a conducive environment for business.

Delay in getting regulatory clearances lead to rise in cost of production. A leading multinational automobile major said, "costs of production in India increase because of various government policies, procedures, regulations and the way some of the laws are implemented." The quicker the government addresses these challenges its better for the industry to set up facilities in the country.

For providing better infrastructure for the industry, there has been a big constraint in term of land acquisition. Often land acquisition for the industrial purpose run into trouble at the local level. Economists have noted that with the globalization becoming a reality, Indian manufacturers will have to compete with the best and cheapest the rest of the world has to offer even in the domestic market.

They urged for providing tax concessions to any industry which would set up manufacturing facility in the country. Besides a critical aspect is the country's huge small and medium-sized industries which could play a big role in making the country take the next big leap in manufacturing.

Besides the skill development, labour law flexibility is a key element for the success of this campaign for increasing manufacturing in the country. Economists say that "labour law flexibility does not imply 'hire and fire' policy, it's about providing a sound social safety net to workers."

Notwithstanding the challenges faced in making India a manufacturing hub, the country is poised to reap rich dividend for being one of the youngest nations in the world. According to reports by 2020, India is set to become the world's youngest country with 64% of its population in the working age group.

Although a sound beginning has been made for the Make in India campaign, now the ball is in the government's court to ensure its success.

THE BLACK SHADOW OF BLACK MONEY

Money earned through illegal means or by way of covert activities is called Black Money. This money remains deposited with people. As it is earned through corrupt methods and income tax is not paid on it, it is very important to hide it. In the public jargon, it is also called "dirty money". The chief sources of black money are thefts and misappropriations in income tax, excise duty, property tax, death tax and customs duty. Money earned through smuggling is also deemed black money. Money earned through the activities of black-marketing is also falls under this category. Funds received through the acts of bribery are also a part of black money. We have defined the sources of black money in the preceeding text. On the basis of these sources, one can easily conclude who are the people who could be having black money. In the category of such people, indus-trialists, owners of factories, traders, shopkeepers (both wholesalers and retailers), owners of buildings, landlords, individuals engaged in businesses of imports and exports, politicians and government officials on high posts. But this list is not exhaustive; many more names can be added to it.

Today, the activity of collecting and hoarding black money is flowering at a very fast pace. According to the broad estimates of the National Institute of Public Finance and Policy, people in India have black money deposits of Rs 37,000 crore with them. Remember that this amount can be larger than this figure too, it is based on an estimate because those who have black money do not give its accounts to anyone. The International Monetary Fund (IMF) has also estimated the amount of black money of many nations. It has been stated in its estimate that the amount of black money is 50 per cent of her Gross Domestic Product (GDP). According to the estimate of IMF, the amount of black money in India ranges from Rs. 80,000 crore to Rs. 90,000 crore.

Why is the business of black money growing by leaps and bounds in our country? Some genuine reasons in this context are as follows:

1. Lust for money,
2. Too much of materialism,
3. Weak laws,
4. Complex procedures to earn money with honesty
5. Awareness of the fact that money can buy everything and all types of good or bad deeds can be got done from any person through its use.

The fact that this has become an uncurable disease is not a hyperbole. However, some suggestions can be given to check the spread and effect of black money:

1. The government should control its expenses and these should be monitored,
2. High-deficit budgets should not be made,
3. Expenses being incurred on the government projects should be strictly monitored,
4. In the government administration, the self-discretionary rights of senior officials in Industrial licensing department, income tax department, company law department or any other department should be either made defunct or minimised. Bias, corruption and black money are created because of the perpetuation of these very rights.
5. The taxation system should be pragmatic; the rates should not be very high because if they are moderate, people would not resort to acts of tax evasion.
6. The departments that collect taxes should be efficient and honest.
7. There should be a provision for harsh punishment for the acts of tax-evasion.
8. In the Institutions like state legislatures, government departments, financial institutions, judiciary, etc., the work should be of high quality.

All their tasks should be done at the right time and the administrative machinery should be transparent (which means that actions and data should not be kept secret). If this is done, then the possibilities of corrupt practices and bias behaviours would be lessened. We can expect that the production of black money would be at least reduced due to the aforesaid remedies.

RIGHT TO INFORMATION

The term 'inform' has been derived from the Latin word 'informare', which means giving shape to something.

Information adds something new to our awareness and removes the vagueness of our ideas. It equips us with necessary knowledge to help us in our pursuits. Be it material or spiritual. This can be a handy tool in bringing about transparency and accountability in public life thus serving a larger interest.

Article 19(1) (a) of the Indian Constitution guarantees the fundamental rights to free speech and expression. The prerequisite for enjoying this right is knowledge and information. The absence of authentic information on matters of public interest leads to administrative corruption and decadence, which India is witnessing on a scale so large that it has become one of the most corrupt countries in the world. This is hampering development and growth of the country. The only way to tackle this problem is to equip citizens with Right to Information so that the bureaucracy, police and local government bodies become more responsive and accountable.

The Right to Information has, in fact, received judicial recognition as a part of the fundamental right to free speech and expression in a Supreme Court judgment in 1975. Again in 1982, the court declared that the concept of an open government is the direct emanation from the right to know which seems to be implicit in the right of free speech and expression guaranteed under article 19 (1) (a). An open government is the new democratic culture of an open society towards which every liberal democracy is moving and our country should be no exception. In a country like India, right to know becomes a necessity for the poor, ignorant and illiterate masses. Information is indispensable for the functioning of a true democracy.

Despite such pronouncements, the Indian government did little to confer on its citizens this inalienable right. It is only after decades of concerted campaigning by several grass-root organizations, NGOs and noted activists like Aruna Roy, Prashant Bhushan, Bharat Dogra etc. that the government finally relented and enacted the Right to Information Act 2005. The salient features of the law are as follows:

The Act confers a right to "information" rather than just "records" or "documents". Information has broadly defined to permit the inspection of public works including taking samples of materials. The definition also includes "information relating to a private body which can be accessed by a public authority under any law".

The Act explicitly states that it "shall be a constant endeavour...to provide as much information suo moto...so that the public have minimum resort [to the Act]".

Public Information Officers (PIOs) are required to be appointed "in all administrative units/office...as may be necessary to provide information to persons requesting it". Assistant PIOs are also to be appointed at each sub-divisional or sub-district level, and these Assistants are tasked with receiving applications and passing them on to the relevant PIO. These provisions combined are designed to bring access closer to the people, by ensuring that applicants can submit requests in their local area, rather than having to rely on the post or travel to the city.

A time limit of thirty days for normal applications and 40 days where a third party submissions is to be called for has been set. In a novel approach, these time limits are reduced to a mere 48 hours where the information sought "concerns the life and liberty of a person".

All of the exemptions under the Act (except the exemption for information which is subject to copyright) are subject to a public interest override, whereby information may be disclosed "if public interest in disclosure outweighs the harm to the protected interests".

Every PIO can be fined ₹ 250 per day up to a maximum of ₹ 25,000 for not accepting application; delaying information release without reasonable cause; denying information in bad faith; knowingly giving incomplete, incorrect, misleading information; destroying information that has been requested and obstructing furnishing of information in any manner.

Despite such progressive provisions, the Act still retains a number of restrictive measures, which could be abused to deny information. A proviso is added that decisions of the Council of Ministers, their reasons and the materials on the basis of which the decisions were made will be published after a decision is taken and the matter is complete. This would only defeat the very purpose of the law, as it would never be possible to know the conduct of the ministers and the interests they may be serving. A range of Central intelligence and security agencies are specifically and entirely exempted from the Act.

Third parties are permitted to make representations where a PIO intends to disclosure information supplied by the third party and "treated as confidential by the third party". There is some concern that this provision could be abused in practice to improperly delay responses to requests, particularly because the Act defined third parties to include other public authorities.

The final form of the Act removed references to imprisonment for serious acts of non-compliance with the Act. It is notable in this respect that while the Act now allows for a fine for "denying information [in bad faith]; knowingly giving incomplete, incorrect, misleading information; destroying information that has been requested and obstructing furnishing of information in any manner". It is not clear how this provision will apply in practice.

The original Bill required that Information Commissioners would be selected by a Committee comprising the Prime Minister, leader of the Opposition and Chief Justice of India. The Bill was amended, however, to replace the Chief Justice by a Cabinet Minister chosen by the PM. This would render the selection process partisan.

Whatever may be the shortcomings of the law, it's undoubtedly, a landmark legislation of modern India. Its avowed aim is to bring about transparency in administration and public life that would ultimately lead to openness, accountability and integrity. Going by the way the citizens have started using this law to expose corruption in government departments, it can be concluded that it would certainly help achieve that aim.

LETTER WRITING

Write an E-mail Message to the editor, giving your views about the rising number of terrorist activities in the country.

From : raj@sify.com
To : editor@times.com

Sub : Rising Number of Terrorist Activities

Sir

I would like to express my views on the rising number of terrorist activities in India. I hope these would find space in the columns of your esteemed daily (in section Readers' Thoughts, appearing every Sunday).

The incidents of Kaluchak, Doda, Srinagar and other areas of Jammu and Kashmir have put the Indian police and security forces on the state of maximum alert. Pakistan is perpetuating the reign of terrorism. She is also resorting to heavy shelling along the LoC in Punjab and Jammu and Kashmir. Under the cover of this shelling, the Pakistani army and the ISI send terrorists into the Indian territory. These terrorists use the locally based agents as platforms. They indulge in the acts of bomb blasts, killing of innocent people and attacks on important buildings. The assassination of Mr. Abdul Gani Lone (of APHC) and the bomb blast outside the J&K assembly are the grim reminders of a bloody war that has been continuing for the past twenty years. Innocent Kashmiris and security forces are the helpless victims of these terrorist attacks.

A dialogue with Pakistan would not put out the fire of terrorism. We must rise to the occasion and meet this challenge with courage. We are with the people of Jammu and Kashmir during this critical phase of time. We shall also give all type of moral and financial support to innocent Kashmiri brothers and sisters.

Yours truly
....

Write a letter to the Principal of your native school informing him that you have got a good job and thanking him for all that the school has done for you.

The Principal
Govt. Boys Sr. Sec. School
Gulabi Bagh
Delhi-110007

Respected Sir

Perhaps you remember that I was a student of Commerce Course in your school during the sessions .... and .... I passed my Senior School Certificate Examination in .... I had topped the list of all the successful candidates in the concerned course. Thereafter I busied myself in Chartered Accountancy Course.

Now I have been selected as an officer in the General Insurance Corporation. My present posting is at Kirti Nagar, New Delhi. I am getting a handsome salary and lucrative perks. My job has a wide scope. There are ample promotional avenues in it. I am fully satisfied with my job.

I was just a mediocre student when I had sought admission in class XI. The main inspiration behind my glaring and enviable success at the examination and in seeking the job can be attributed to the teachers of the school. They are qualified, experienced and painstaking. I learnt the lesson of hardwork from my teachers. Your kindness and guidance helped in showing us the right path.

Kindly accept my sense of gratitude and pass it on to all the teachers of the school. I shall ever remain indebted to the school.

With profound regards,

Yours faithfully
Tarun Sharma

Dated: 7th May, *(year)*

Write a letter to your father describing a road accident witnessed by you.

1457, Deep Nagar, Ludhiana
7th June, *(year)*

Respected Father

Yesterday, I was travelling from Ludhiana to Jalandhar by bus. My seat was in the fourth row. The driver of our bus was very rash. He was driving the bus madly at the flying speed, not caring to stop it at all the bus stops. The aged passengers felt alarmed and asked him to behave himself. But he did not listen to their requests or threats. Some young people felt thrilled and urged him to drive the bus his way.

In the meantime, another bus blowed the horn from behind and tried to overtake our bus. Our stupid driver took it as a challenge and dared not make way for him. The other driver was also brainless and hot-headed. He drove still faster. As a result, both the buses began to run neck-to-neck on the road.

Just then a truck came from the opposite side at a great speed. The driver of the overtaking bus tried to apply brakes but it was too late. The overtaking bus and the truck had a head-on collision. We requested our driver to apply brakes. He did it unwillingly. All the passengers of the bus held him guilty of the accident and gave him a good thrashing. Then they got down the bus and ran to the spot of accident. We saw that the drivers of both the vehicles died on the spot. Ten other persons also had lost their lives. Four persons were injured seriously and the remaining passengers received minor injuries. Women and children were crying in pain. It was a heart-rending sight.

Somebody rang up the police. The police party reached there with a team of doctors. The injured were rushed to Civil Hospital, Jalandhar. The police party took snaps and sent the dead persons for post-mortem.

Thank God, the passengers of our bus were saved from meeting with a fatal accident.

You need not worry. I am safe and healthy. However, I feel pained whenever I am reminded of the accident.

Please pay my compliments to mother and love to Mukul and Nikunj.

With profound regards,

Your loving son
Rohit

Write a letter to your mother describing your visit to an Exhibition.

378, Patel Nagar II
Ghaziabad, U.P.
8th January, *(year)*

Dear Mother

Yesterday, I visited an exhibition which is being held at Pragati Maidan, Delhi. The maidan is spread over many kilometres. It is fenced all around by a wall. There was a great hustle and bustle near the main gate. Hundreds of people were standing in queues to buy tickets. I also bought a ticket and entered the main gate. I enjoyed soft music which was being played just inside the entrance.

People from all walks of life had come to see the exhibition. They were moving leisurely in the stalls. Some people were making purchases while others were passing by various stalls. The exhibition was arranged in four sections. The tricks and feats displayed by clowns, jugglers and magicians attracted a large crowd of people.

Almost all the states of India had set-up their stalls or pavilions inside the exhibition ground. They had displayed their peculiar products in order to show their progress. The Himachal pavilion displayed its honey, woollen shawls and blankets. The Punjab pavilion displayed the hosiery products and latest agricultural implements. The Haryana pavilion displayed cycles and its parts. The Jammu and Kashmir pavilion exhibited the embroidery work.

The Soviet and American pavilions displayed their scientific technological and electric goods. The latest type of radars and missiles were the major source of attraction.

An international exhibition promotes understanding and fraternity. It adds to our knowledge in the fields of industry, science, technology, agriculture and commerce.

I feel much enlightened, amused and benefitted by this visit. God willing and time permitting I would like to show you this exhibition when you return home from your brother's house.

Pay my regards to my maternal uncle and aunt and love to kiddies.

Yours affectionately
Sunder

Write a letter to your uncle informing him of a strange happening at your home.

Jindal Bhavan
17/21, Panchsheel Colony
Nagpur
15th March, *(year)*

Dear Uncle

Recently my sister-in-law was in the family way. We were expecting a glimmer of light in the form of a blossoming baby. Yesterday she gave birth to a child. The baby was dead before it was born. But whatever happened, it was for the good.

You must not wonder because the baby had no limbs. It was supposed to be the result of some gynaecological defect in its mother. I am afraid to tell you that the baby had neither legs nor arms. It was like a doll of cloth, stuffed with cotton. Its belly was as hard as stone. Its nose, eyes and ears were all deformed. It was frightful to look at it.

I thought, my sister-in-law was going to cry a lot, having lost her baby. But she did not cry at all. She rather pitied her own lot and pressed the baby to her heart. The silent tears rolling down her cheeks showed her maternal affection for her still-born baby. She also kept on running her fingers through its hair. My mother saw the baby. She was terribly frightened. She shrieked aloud before bursting into a loud scream. She kept gesticulating wildly all the while. The doctors pacified all of us.

I was also shocked to see the dead baby. Everything has become normal now. However, I'm pining to meet you. Rest, when we meet. Convey my sincere regards to dear auntie and love to Peeyush and Ayush.

Yours affectionately
Rohit

Write a letter to your younger sister telling her about the role of the press in a democratic country.

4345, Sector 18
Chandigarh-19
August 23, *(year)*

Dear Sister,

In my present letter, I would like to tell you about the role of the press in a democratic country.

Democracy depends on public opinion. The press is a link between the government and the people. It apprises the people of the omissions and commissions of the government. It reflets public opinion by placing the people's view before the government. The press arouses national consciousness among the masses on important issues. The press also serves as a social reformer. Social abuses are exposed and criticised through the columns of the press.

A newspaper has different uses for different persons. An illiterate person regards it as a wrapper. Some persons go through the newspapers and tear them into bits. Some people preserve their cuttings for future information. The silly people ill-treat a newspaper but the civilized people value it highly.

They do not take their breakfast unless they have read the daily newspaper. Newspapers give us fresh and valuable information. They also express their opinion about the social and political problems facing the country from time to time. They mould the readers into their own way of thinking.

Some newspapers excite the readers by publishing sensational news. A popular newspaper identifies itself with the best interests of the people. A newspaper should defend the cause which is just and expose the wrong doers frankly and fearlessly. It should be neutral in its approach.

An earnest reader enriches his knowledge, gets entertainment and makes proper use of his leisure by reading it line by line. It widens his intellect and updates his knowledge.

I hope you will also start reading a newspaper every morning without fail.

Yours sincerely
Protima Arora

Write a letter to your friend telling him what you would do if you were the Prime Minister of India.

4444, Pahari Dhiraj
Near Sadar Bazar, Delhi
December 23, *(year)*

Dear Suraj,

You may laugh heartily at my wish to become the Prime Minister of India. But anyone may become the Prime Minister in a democratic country, like India. Prime Ministership is both a bed of roses and a bed of thorns.

If I happen to become the Prime Minister of India, I would bring about great many changes in my country. I would launch the scheme of E.F.A. (Education for All) earnestly. I feel annoyed at the present slow pace in the spread of education. I shall direct the Chief Ministers of all the states to give top priority to education. I shall wage a war against black-marketing, hoarding, undue profiteering, corruption, adulteration, casteism and untouchability.

Additionally, I shall get the bribery seekers punished. I shall never spare those who are found guilty of feeding fat at the cost of others and have a hand in scams.

I would see that unemployment and under-employment are weeded out from the country. I would get all the key industries nationalised. I would get the surplus land distributed among the landless labourers of the country. I would build a huge and strong army equipped with modern weapons. Atom bombs will also be manufactured to defend our country from aggressive designs of hostile countries.

I am hopeful that all these steps taken by me would place the country on a strong footing.

Above all, I shall make you the Home Minister of India.

Rest, when we meet.

Yours sincerely
Madhup

Write a letter to the Editor of a newspaper about the rise in prices of essential goods.

Village P.O. Kangan Heri
New Delhi
17th September, *(year)*
The Editor
The Times of India
New Delhi

Sir

Through the columns of your esteemed paper I want to voice my feelings on the rise in prices of essential goods.

The problem of rising prices of essential commodities has become a matter of great concern for the salaried people. The plight of the poor is becoming more and more pitiable day by day.

The labourers, lower classes and salaried persons find it difficult to make both ends meet. Their children remain ill-fed, ill-clad and ill-housed. The enormous increase in the prices of flour, coal, kerosene oil, gas cylinders, cement, steel and petroleum products is adversely affecting the lower middle class. They cannot buy even a small piece of land to build their hut.

It has become difficult for the poor to buy edible oil, pulses, fuel, wheat and rice in sufficient quantity. The sharp rise in the prices of fertilizers and agricultural implements has broken the backs of the petty farmers. They can hardly get the reasonable return for their produce.

The tendency of hoarding, blackmarketing and profiteering, increasing population, defective system of distribution, black money and the policy of deficit financing by the government are solely responsible for the price hike.

The government should declare hoarding as a capital crime. The shopkeepers should be made to display the prices of the goods they sell. You are requested to take stern steps to control the menace of rise in prices or it would definitely lead to some alarming situations.

Yours faithfully
Garib Das

Write a letter to the Health Minister drawing his attention towards the problems caused by increasing population in India.

Village & P.O. Mundela Kalan
New Delhi
8th December, *(year)*
The Health Minister
Ministry of Health
New Delhi

Honourable Sir

May I have the liberty to bring to your kind notice the problems caused by increasing population in India.

Population in India is increasing at a very fast rate. We have reached a stage of population explosion. Due to progress in medical sciences the death rate has been remarkably reduced here. The eradication of epidemics has enlarged the rate of survival. The ignorant and superstitious people think that the children are born through God's will and they have no right to interfere in his will. Early marriages are also responsible for the growth of population in India. The poor people find recreation only in sexual indulgence which leads to increase in population. Moreover, the poor do not find an additional child a burden. For, every child in a poor family is an earner and a helper.

India is quite a poor and developing country. She has very limited sources. The increasing population is sure to threaten her very existence. It will add to our problems. The progress in our production is not as much as the progress in population. It brings starvation and misery.

This problem cannot be solved so easily. It can only be solved if the government takes drastic measures to control the population. The family planning programme should be enforced in right earnest. Spread of education can also make people understand the gravity of this problem. The government should fix 26 years in case of boys and 23 years in case of girls as the marriageable age. A law should be enacted to limit the number of children. The married couples should be educated about the use of contraceptives.

Kindly look into the matter seriously and find out some meaningful remedy to this malady because our country cannot prosper without planning the population.

Yours faithfully
Hans Raj

Write a letter to the Home Minister drawing his attention to the problem of unemploy-ment in India.

1506/21E Daya Nand Park
Nangloi Road, Najaf Garh, New Delhi-110043
8th February, *(year)*
The Home Minister
Ministry of Home Affairs
New Delhi

Sir

May I draw your kind attention towards the problem of unemployment in India? Unemployment is a major human problem which is unnerving all sections of Indian society.

It has to be kept in mind that merely giving some kind of nominal occupation to a large number of people does not ultimately lessen unemployment or increase employment. Employment is generated by newer and more effective means of wealth production or through the growth of technological methods. It is not at all possible for us to grapple with the problem of unemployment without technological advancement. India's poverty is solely due to her backwardness in science and technology. We can create both wealth and employment by uprooting backwardness.

Millions of educated and skilled persons are without a meaningful job in India. Many professionals like engineers and technicians are without a job. Even the labourers and peasants are either unemployed or semi-employed.

Overpopulation results in acute unemployment because there is excess in the supply of labour than its demand. Low purchasing power of the people leads to retrenchment of labour leading to unemployment. Another cause of unemployment is the demand for 'white collar job'. The educated people dislike the jobs involving physical labour. The pace of economic development is slow due to industrial backwardness of our country. Therefore our industries fail to provide employment to the increasing numbers. Poor agriculture is also a hurdle. Even the peasants suffer from starvation and misery. The hungry are angry. They become dishonest, corrupt and criminals.

Kindly give a serious thought to this problem and find out some unfailing and lasting remedy.

Yours faithfully
Naresh Kumar

Write a letter to the Editor of a newspaper about the problem of corruption in India.

361, Civil Lines
Patiala
March 27, *(year)*
The Editor
The Statesman
New Delhi

Dear Sir

Through the esteemed columns of your daily newspaper, I wish to draw the immediate attention of the government towards the problem of corruption in India.

Corruption has entered every department of Indian society. Corruption means bribery or illegal gratifications. It is the root of all evils. It has eaten up our values of life and is debasing the social, economic and political structure of the country.

In India of today, most of the government officials, politicians and even ministers have become corrupt. Files in offices do not move without bribe. In the materialistic age every person wants to become rich overnight. He wants to earn money by hook or by crook because a person's worth and position are measured by the amount of money he possesses. The higher authorities have set a bad example and the officials of lower rank follow suit fearlessly. Moreover, the salaries of the government servants are quite meagre. As a result they have to take bribe to make both ends meet.

Poverty, lavish expenditure on social customs, rising prices and vast powers in the hands of officers promote corruption. Businessmen are the worst perpetrators of corruption through hoarding, adulteration, blackmarketing and profiteering. The smugglers and manufacturers of spurious goods are the worst corruption mongers.

I hope the authorities concerned would take necessary steps to root out the deep-rooted corruption.

Yours faithfully
Ram Dayal

Write a letter of complaint to the General Manager of Mahanagar Telephone Nigam Ltd. about overcharging in telephone bill.

2074, Gulabi Bagh
Delhi-110007
26th December, *(year)*
The General Manager
Mahanager Telephone Nigam Ltd.
Darya Ganj, Delhi

Subject : Complaint about overcharging in telephone bill.

Sir

I was shocked to receive the telephone bill for the month of October and November, ... against telephone No. 734783 installed in my name. It shows an impossible and undue amount of ₹ 7248 as payable by me.

I must not hesitate in informing you that we use telephone mainly for a few calls for domestic purposes to talk to a few friends and relatives now and then. We have kept a diary in which we record all the calls made by us. As per entries in our diary we have made only one STD call to Rohtak during the aforesaid period. Moreover, during this period our telephone remained dead for three weeks (8th October to 28th October) which is also on your record through our complaints. Therefore, it is quite evident that there is a gross discrepancy in billing.

In this connection, I may add that there are general complaints from many other residents of our colony of similar inflated bills due to the malafide intentions of the billing clerk. He is hell-bent on harassing the consumers and grabbing money from them. It is also rumoured that STD is being misused by the telephone staff.

Therefore you are requested to get the matter investigated; otherwise a public hue and cry is bound to result.

Thanking you,

Yours faithfully
S.B. Sharma

General Knowledge, Reasoning Ability and Numerical Ability

GENERAL KNOWLEDGE

1. Match List-I with List-II and select the correct answer from the codes given below the lists:

List-I	List-II
(*a*) Napoleon Bonaparte	1. 'A history is contemporary history'
(*b*) Jean Jacques Rousseau	2. 'Liberty what crimes are committed in thy name'
(*c*) Croce	3. 'Man is born free but everywhere he is in chains.'
(*d*) Madame Roland	4. 'I am the Child of Revolution'

Codes :

	(*a*)	(*b*)	(*c*)	(*d*)
A.	1	2	3	4
B.	4	3	1	2
C.	3	4	2	1
D.	3	4	1	2

2. Abraham Lincon was elected the President of United States in:
A. 1862 B. 1860
C. 1875 D. 1855

3. Who was known as the 'Prince of Humanists'?
A. Francisco Petrarch B. Dante
C. Boccacio D. Erasmus

4. D-Day is the day when:
A. Germany declared war on Britain
B. US dropped the atom bomb on Hiroshima.
C. Allied Troops landed in Normandy
D. Germany surrendered to the allies

5. Whose teachings inspired the French Revolution?
A. Locke B. Rousseau
C. Hegel D. Plato

6. At a time when empires in Europe were crumbling before the might of Napoleon which one of the following Governor-Generals kept the British flag flying high in India?
A. Warren Hastings B. Lord Cornwallis
C. Lord Wellesley D. Lord Hastings

7. Which one of the following statements regarding Fascism in Italy is *not* true?
A. The Fascists came to power as a result of popular uprising
B. In 1926, all political parties except Mussolini's party were banned
C. The Fascists suppressed the Socialist movement
D. The Fascists were hostile to the Communists

8. The fall of Czar Nicholas-II is known as:
A. Bloody Sunday
B. Bolshevik Revolution
C. February Revolution
D. October Revolution

9. Industrial Revolution took place first in:
A. France
B. Germany
C. United Kingdom
D. Japan

10. The British Prime Minister at the outbreak of World War II was :
A. Churchill B. Baldwin
C. Attlee D. Chemberlain

11. The 'Great Depression' (1929) economic crisis was met by adopting the policy of
A. Stimulus B. Marshall Plan
C. New Deal D. Open Door

12. The slogan "No taxation without representation" was raised during the:
A. American War of Independence
B. Russian Revolution
C. French Revolution
D. Indian Freedom struggle

13. In the nineteenth century the people of Europe started moving from the villages to the cities due to the impact of :
A. Epidemics
B. War
C. Industrialisation
D. Population explosion in villages

14. The important cause of the Civil War in America was:
A. Abolition of slavery
B. Quest for freedom
C. Industrialisation
D. Rebellion by the native Americans

15. Industrial Revolution could not have come about without:
A. Merchant capitalism
B. The Enclosure Movement
C. The services of the proletariat class
D. An agricultural revolution

16. Consider the following statements :
The French Revolution came about mainly due to the :
1. Extreme poverty of the people
2. Impact of the works of great writers
3. Cruelty of the rulers
4. Impact of impulsive reaction
Which of the above statements are correct?
A. 1, 2 and 4 B. 2 and 3
C. 1, 3 and 4 D. 1, 2, 3 and 4

17. Asia's oldest and largest Buddhist monastery is situated in :
A. Tawang (Arunachal Pardesh)
B. Lhasa (Tibet)
C. Trincomallee (Sri Lanka)
D. Ulan Bator (Mongolia)

18. Who was the main architect of the Russian Revolution?
A. Karl Marx B. Lenin
C. Stalin D. Tolstoy

19. V.I. Lenin is associated with :
A. Russian Revolution of 1917
B. Chinese Revolution of 1949
C. German Revolution
D. French Revolution of 1789

20. Which one of the following statements is *not* correct?
A. Voltaire believed in Natural Religion
B. Rousseau wrote *Social Contract*
C. Montesquieu authored *The Spirit of Laws*
D. Necker believed in 'General Will'

21. 6th April, 1930 is well known in the history of India because this date is associated with..........
A. Dandi March by Mahatma Gandhi
B. Quit India Movement
C. Partition of Bengal
D. Partition of India

22. Which ruler enforced the system of 'Price Control' in India?
A. Mohammad Tughlak
B. Razia Begum
C. Alauddin Khilji
D. Sher Shah Suri

23. The concept of 'Din-e-Elahi' was founded by which king?
A. Dara Shikoh B. Akbar
C. Sher Shah Suri D. Shahjahan

24. Who are supposed to be the earliest inhabitants of India? Where did they come from?
A. Aryans from Central Asia
B. Dravidians from Mediterranean
C. Negroids from Africa
D. Bhils and the Santhals from West Asia

25. The one chief characteristic of temple architecture of the Gupta Age was :
A. Absence of dome
B. Huge size
C. Beautiful carvings
D. Absence of a covered courtyard for the gathering of worshippers

26. The Rigveda consists of :
A. 1000 hymns B. 2028 hymns
C. 1028 hymns D. 1038 hymns

27. The central point in Ashoka's dharma was :
A. royalty to kings
B. peace and non-violence
C. respect to elders
D. religious tolerance

28. The social evil which was conspicuously absent during ancient India was :
A. *Sati*-System B. *Devadasi*-System
C. Polygamy D. *Purdah*-System

29. Which, among the following, can be accepted as a novelty introduced by Mughal emperors to their buildings?
A. Domes B. Minarets
C. Arches D. Attached gardens

30. The first ruler of India who defeated Muhammud of Ghur was :
A. Mularaja II of Gujarat
B. Prithviraja Chauhan of Delhi
C. Jayachand of Kannauj
D. Parmaldeva of Bundelkhand

31. What important event happened in India in 1911?
A. Bengal was partitioned
B. Non-Cooperation movement was launched
C. India's capital was shifted from Calcutta to Delhi
D. Mahatma Gandhi presided over the Congress session

32. The first phase of the Congress Party (1885-1905) was characterized by its efforts to secure:
A. limited independence
B. complete freedom
C. Indianization of services
D. constitutional reforms

33. The Muslim League demanded a separate homeland for the Indian Muslims openly for the first time at its annual session held in Lahore in the year :

A. 1931 A.D. B. 1936 A.D.
C. 1940 A.D. D. 1941 A.D.

34. Under whose governorship did the East India Company secure the Diwani Rights in Bengal, Bihar and Odisha from Emperor Shah Alam?

A. Lord Cornwallis B. Lord William Bentinck
C. Lord Clive D. Lord Wellesley

35. The Simon Commission was generally boycotted by the Indian political parties. What was the reason for this general non-cooperation?

A. the Commission aimed at dividing the people
B. it was an 'all white' Commission
C. it came after the Jallianwala Bagh carnage
D. it was an eye wash

36. Aligarh Muslim University was founded by :

A. Dr. Saifuddin Kitchlu
B. Mohammad Ali Jinnah
C. Sir Syed Ahmed Khan
D. Maulana Mohammad Ali

37. Ibn Batutah was an African traveller visiting India during the time of :

A. Alivardi Khan B. Ala-ud-din Khalji
C. Iltutmish D. Mohammad-bin-Tughlaq

38. The battle of Wandiawash was fought in :

A. 1726 B. 1760
C. 1818 D. 1857

39. The abolition of *Sati* by government regulation was at the time of :

A. Warren Hastings B. Lord Wellesley
C. Lord Bentinck D. Lord Ahmerst

40. Pick out the wrong combination :

A. Dilwara Temple : Mt. Abu
B. Pashupati Temple : Kathmandu
C. Padmanabh Temple : Bangalore
D. Minakshi Temple : Madurai

41. Match the following:

(*a*) Chanhudaro (*b*) Kalibangan
(*c*) Lothal (*d*) Surkotada

1. Alleged discovery of the skeleton of horse.
2. Bead making.
3. Traces of a dock and ship on seal.
4. Evidence of ploughing the fields.

The Correct code is :

	(*a*)	(*b*)	(*c*)	(*d*)
A.	2	4	3	1
B.	2	1	3	4
C.	1	2	3	4
D.	2	1	4	3

42. Match the Harappan settlements with the banks of rivers on which they were located :

(*a*) Harappa 1. Ravi
(*b*) Mohenjodaro 2. Indus
(*c*) Ropar 3. Sutlej
(*d*) Kalibangan 4. Ghaggar
(*e*) Lothal 5. Bhogava

Codes :

	(*a*)	(*b*)	(*c*)	(*d*)	(*e*)
A.	1	2	3	4	5
B.	1	2	3	5	4
C.	2	1	3	5	4
D.	2	1	4	3	5

43. The Goddess 'Kannagi' whose many temples were erected during the 'Sangam Age' was the goddess of:

A. Chastity B. Love
C. Prowess D. Wisdom

44. The Jain goal of life is to attain deliverance from the fetters of mudane existence, the way to which lies through three jewels. Which one of the following was not included among the 'three jewels' of Jainism?

A. Right faith B. Right action
C. Right knowledge D. Right conduct

45. The most striking feature of the Ashokan pillar is polish. Name the Ashokan pillar which is considered to be the most graceful of all Ashokan pillars.

A. Sarnath
B. Rampurva
C. Laurya-Nandangarh
D. Rummindei

46. Which are the correct statements?

1. The land grants, started in Satavahana period, paved the way for feudal developments in India.
2. Silk and spices were the Chief Indian export articles of Indo-Roman trade.
3. The Guptas issued the largest number of gold coins in ancient India.
4. The first memorial of a 'SATI' dated 510 A.D. is found at Eran in Madhya Pradesh.

A. 1 and 2 B. 1, 3, and 4
C. 1 and 4 D. 1, 2, 3 and 4

47. Who among the following patronised the 'Gandhara' (Indo-Greek style) School of Art?

A. Ashoka, the Great
B. Harsha Vardhana
C. Kanishka
D. Chandragupta Vikramaditya

48. The Sultanate of Delhi had five ruling dynasties. The dynasty having longest and shortest period were :

A. Ilbari and Khalji
B. Tughlaq and Khalji
C. Tughlaq and Sayyid
D. Ilbari and Lodis

49. Which one of the following events took place at the last during reign of Muhammad-bin-Tughlaq?
A. Introduction of token currency
B. Increase of land-revenue in Doab
C. Transfer of Capital from Delhi to Devagiri.
D. Conquest of Khurasan and Iraq

50. The most learned medieval Muslim ruler who was well versed in various branches of learning including astronomy, mathematics and medicine was :
A. Jalaluddin Khilji
B. Sikander Lodi
C. Ghiyasuddin Tughlaq
D. Muhammad-bin-Tughlaq

51. The 'Sufis' had 12 silsilas. They propounded the idea of Union with God through:
A. Love B. Rituals
C. Fasts D. Prayers

52. Match the following:

(*a*) Peshwa	1. Foreign affairs
(*b*) Panditrao	2. Audit and accounts
(*c*) Amatya	3. Providing grants to scholars
(*d*) Sumant	4. General supervision
	5. Military affairs

Select the correct code :

	(*a*)	(*b*)	(*c*)	(*d*)
A.	2	3	4	5
B.	4	1	2	3
C.	4	3	2	1
D.	3	1	4	2

53. The Regulating Act of 1773 can be regarded as the first measure to :
A. assert the right of British Parliament to legislate for India
B. separate the legislature from the executive
C. separate the judiciary from the executive
D. centralise law-making

54. What was the exact constitutional status of the Indian Republic on 26th January, 1950?
A. A Democratic Republic
B. A Sovereign, Democratic Republic
C. A Sovereign, Secular, Democratic Republic
D. A Sovereign, Socialist, Secular, Democratic Republic

55. When the British obtained the grant of Diwani of Bengal, Bihar and Odisha they acquired the right to :
A. maintain law and order in these territories
B. administer civil justice and collect revenue in these territories
C. collect revenue and establish revenue administration in these territories
D. militarily defend these territories

56. Which of the following were responsible for the growth of nationalism in India during the British rule?
1. Economic exploitation of India.
2. Impact of western education.
3. Role of the Press.
Select the correct answer using the codes given below :
Codes:
A. 1, 2 and 3 B. 1 and 2
C. 2 and 3 D. 1 and 3

57. Which one of the following nationalist leaders has been described as being radical in politics but conservative on social issues?
A. G.K. Gokhale B. B.G. Tilak
C. Lala Lajpat Rai D. Madan Mohan Malviya

58. Provincial Autonomy in British India was envisaged by the :
A. Act of 1909 B. Act of 1919
C. Act of 1935 D. Act of 1947

59. Dyarchy means :
A. double government
B. a government in which the centre is very powerful
C. a government based on division of power between centre and provinces
D. None of the above

60. The Indian National Congress observed 'Independence Day' for the first time on 26th January in :
A. 1920 B. 1925
C. 1930 D. 1947

61. .... is situated near the banks of Sabarmati River
A. Bhavnagar B. Aurangabad
C. Ahmedabad D. Rajkot

62. Sericulture is:
A. science of the various kinds of serum
B. artificial rearing of fish
C. art of silkworm breeding
D. study of various cultures of a community

63. The most abundant constituents of earth's crust are:
A. Igneous rocks
B. Sedimentary rocks
C. Metamorphic rocks
D. Granite

64. Indian Standard Time is based on:
A. 80°E longitude B. 82½°E longitude
C. 110°E longitude D. 25°E longitude

65. Tides in the oceans are caused by :
A. Gravitational pull of the moon on the earth's surface including sea water
B. Gravitational pull of the sun on the earth's surface only and not on the sea water
C. Gravitational pull of the moon and the sun on the earth's surface including the sea water
D. None of these

66. Nagarjunasagar Project is situated on the river:
A. Tungabhadra B. Cauvery
C. Krishna D. Godavari

67. The difference between the Indian Standard Time and the Greenwich Mean Time is:
A. –3½ hours B. +3½ hours
C. –5½ hours D. +5½ hours

68. Which of the following dams is not on Narmada river?
A. Indira-Sagar Project
B. Maheshwar Hydel Power Project
C. Jobat Project
D. Koyna Power Project

69. Which of the following statements is **not true** about the availability of water on the earth, the crisis for which is going to increase in the years to come?
A. About 97.5 per cent of the total volume of water available on the earth is salty
B. 80 per cent of the water available to us for use comes in bursts as monsoons
C. About 2.5 per cent of the total water available on the earth is polluted water and cannot be used for human activities
D. Possibility is that some big glaciers will melt in the coming ten-fifteen years and sea level will rise by 3-4 metres all over the earth

70. Which of the following is **not** a cash crop?
A. Jute B. Paddy
C. Cashewnut D. Sugarcane

71. Through which States does Cauvery River flow?
A. Gujarat, M.P., Tamil Nadu
B. Karnataka, Kerala, Tamil Nadu
C. Karnataka, Kerala, Andhra Pradesh
D. M.P., Maharashtra, Tamil Nadu

72. Indian Standard Time is the local time of 82½°E which passes through :
A. Guntur B. Delhi
C. Allahabad D. Kolkata

73. The 17th parallel defines the boundary between:
A. North and South Korea
B. USA and Canada
C. North and South Vietnam
D. China and Russia

74. During the period of south-west monsoon, Tamil Nadu remains dry because:
A. the winds do not reach this area
B. there are no mountains in this area
C. it lies in the rain shadow area
D. the temperature is too high to let the winds cool down

75. Which of the following device measures depth of a sea?
A. Fathometer B. Anemometer
C. Altimeter D. Barometer

76. The biggest reserves of thorium are in :
A. India B. China
C. The Soviet Union D. U.S.A.

77. The Girnar Hills are situated in which of the following states?
A. Gujarat B. Karnataka
C. Madhya Pradesh D. Maharashtra

78. During December 22nd the sun is vertically over:
A. Tropic of Cancer
B. Tropic of Capricorn
C. The Equator
D. None of the above

79. Photosphere is described as the :
A. Lower layer of atmosphere
B. Visible surface of the sun from which radiation emanates
C. Wavelength of solar spectrum
D. None of the above

80. Broadly, there are three layers of the earth of the crust, the mantle and the core. The crust forms what percentage of the volume of the earth?
A. 0.5% B. 2.5%
C. 7.5% D. 12.5%

81. The grassland of Argentina is known as :
A. Pampas B. Campos
C. Savanna D. None of the above

82. Different seasons are formed because :
A. Sun is moving around the earth
B. of revolution of the earth around the Sun on its orbit
C. of rotation of the earth around its axis
D. All of the above

83. Eskers and Drumlins are features formed by:
A. underground water
B. running water
C. the action of wind
D. glacial action

84. Match List-I and List-II and select the correct answer using the codes given below the Lists :

List-I (Rivers)	**List-II (Towns)**
(*a*) Ghaghara	1. Lucknow
(*b*) Brahmaputra	2. Hoshangabad
(*c*) Narmada	3. Ahmedabad
(*d*) Sabarmati	4. Guwahati
	5. Ayodhya

	(a)	(b)	(c)	(d)
A.	4	5	1	2
B.	5	4	2	3
C.	5	4	3	1
D.	3	5	2	1

85. Which of the statements as regards the consequences of the movement of the earth is not correct?
A. Revolution of the earth is the cause of the change of seasons.
B. Rotation of the earth is the cause of days and nights.
C. Rotation of the earth causes variation in the duration of days and nights.
D. Rotation of the earth effects the movement of winds and ocean currents.

86. The world is divided into :
A. 12 time zones
B. 20 time zones
C. 24 time zones
D. 36 time zones

87. The 'Kiel' canal links the :
A. Pacific and Atlantic Oceans
B. Mediterranean Sea and Red Sea
C. Mediterranean Sea and Black Sea
D. North Sea and Baltic Sea

88. Match the following :

List-I	List-II
(a) Himadri	1. Outer Himalayas
(b) Shivalik	2. Inner Himalayas
(c) Himanchal	3. Middle Himalayas
(d) Sahyadri	4. Western Ghats

Codes:

	(a)	(b)	(c)	(d)
A.	1	2	3	4
B.	4	2	3	1
C.	2	1	3	4
D.	1	2	3	4

89. The term 'Regur' refers to:
A. Laterite soils
B. Black Cotton soils
C. Red Soils
D. Deltaic Alluvial Soils

90. Location of sugar industry in India is shifting from north to south because of:
A. cheap labour
B. expanding regional market
C. cheap and abundant supply of power
D. high yield and high sugar content in sugarcane

91. Consider the following statements :
1. Ozone is found mostly in the Stratosphere.
2. Ozone layer lies 55-75 km above the surface of the earth.
3. Ozone absorbs ultraviolet radiation from the Sun.
4. Ozone layer has no significance for life on the earth.

Which of the above statements are correct?
A. 1 and 3 B. 2 and 4
C. 2 and 3 D. 1 and 4

92. Which of the following is not a chemical coagulant used in water treatment?
A. Polyaluminium Chloride (PAC)
B. Nitrogen dioxide
C. Aluminium Sulfate (Alum)
D. Aluminium Chloride

93. Darjeeling and Dharamsala would be the right places to visit if one wanted to get a clear view respectively of :
A. Kanchanjunga and Dhauladhar ranges
B. Nandadevi and Dhauladhar ranges
C. Kanchanjunga and Nandadevi ranges
D. Nandadevi and Nanga Parvat

94. Atmosphere exists because:
A. The Gravitational force of the Earth
B. Revolution of the Earth
C. Rotation of the Earth
D. Weight of the gases of atmosphere

95. Victoria lake is located in the continent:
A. Africa
B. Asia
C. North America
D. South America

96. The famous Lagoon Lake of India is :
A. Dal Lake
B. Chilka Lake
C. Pulicat Lake
D. Mansarover

97. Where are most of the earth's active volcanoes concentrated?
A. Indian Ocean
B. Pacific Ocean
C. Aral Sea
D. Atlantic Ocean

98. Through which of the following states does the river Chambal flow?
A. U.P., M.P., Rajasthan
B. M.P., Gujarat, U.P.
C. Rajasthan, M.P., Bihar
D. Gujarat, M.P., U.P.

99. Which country is called the sugar bowl of the world?
A. Cuba B. India
C. Argentina D. USA

100. The area covered by forest in India is about:
A. 46% B. 33%
C. 23% D. 21.71%

101. A closed economy is the one which :
A. does not permit emigration or immigration
B. permits emigration but no immigration
C. engages in no foreign trade
D. engages in no foreign and domestic trade or transit

102. In a developed economy the major share of employment originates in the :
A. primary sector B. tertiary sector
C. secondary sector D. any of the above

103. The Economic and Social Commission for Asia and Pacific (ESCAP) is located at :
A. Bangkok B. Kuala Lumpur
C. Manila D. Singapore

104. Commercial vehicles are not produced by which of the following companies in India?
A. TELCO B. Ashok Leyland
C. DCM Daewoo D. Birla Yamaha

105. In India, the Public Sector is most dominant in:
A. transport
B. steel production
C. commercial banking
D. organised term-lending financial institutions

106. The main argument advanced in favour of small scale and cottage industries in India is that:
A. cost of production is low
B. they require small capital investment
C. they advance the goal of equitable distribution of wealth
D. they generate a large volume of employment

107. The most serious economic problems of India are:
A. Poverty and unemployment
B. Stagnation, not poverty
C. Unemployment, not poverty
D. Underdevelopment, not poverty

108. Which of the following is not one of the three central problems of an economy?
A. What to produce
B. How to produce
C. When to produce
D. For whom to produce

109. If saving exceeds investment, the national income will:
A. fall B. rise
C. fluctuate D. remain constant

110. In which of the following industries in India are the maximum number of workers employed?
A. Sugar B. Jute
C. Textiles D. Iron and Steel

111. Terrace Cultivation is practiced mostly:
A. in urban areas
B. on slopes of mountains
C. on tops of hills
D. in undulating tracts

112. Which of the following is a Selective Credit Control method?
A. Bank Rate
B. RBI directives
C. Cash Reserve Ratio
D. Open market operations

113. Which of the following taxes is not shared by the Central Government with the States?
A. Union excise duties
B. Customs duty
C. Income tax
D. Estate duty

114. ICICI is the name of a:
A. Financial Institution
B. Chemical Industry
C. Cotton Industry
D. Chamber of Commerce and Industry

115. Structural Unemployment arises due to
A. Deflationary conditions
B. Heavy industry bias
C. Shortage of raw material
D. Inadequate productive capacity

116. What is the full form of NPA in Context of Banking system?
A. Non-Performing Assets
B. National Productivity Authority
C. National Productivity Association
D. Non-Paying Assets

117. The largest public sector bank in India is:
A. Central Bank of India
B. Punjab National Bank
C. State Bank of India
D. Indian Overseas Bank

118. Which of the following statements best explains the term contraband goods?
A. Goods produced only for exports
B. Goods produced in joint sector only
C. Goods for the trading of which licence is not required
D. Goods that are forbidden, from export, import or even possession, by law

119. Price in the market is fixed by:
A. Stock exchange rates
B. The demand and supply ruling in the market at a particular time
C. The Finance Minister
D. None of the above

120. Devaluation of currency helps to promote:
A. National Income
B. Savings
C. Imports at lower cost
D. Exports

121. Balanced economic growth can be achieved only if:
A. All the sectors of economy grow at the same rate
B. Population growth is arrested
C. All the inter dependent sectors grow in harmony
D. Basic and heavy industries are assigned highest priority

122. P.V. Sindhu is associated with which of the following sport?
A. Badminton
B. Weightlifting
C. Swimming
D. Tennis

123. 'MODVAT' stands for:
A. Ad Valorem tax on output
B. Deduction of cost of inputs from the value of output
C. Reduction in import duties
D. Imposition of tax on professions

124. Who among the following is the first to receive 'Dada Saheb Phalke' award?
A. Shivaji Ganeson
B. Devika Rani
C. Dr. Raj Kumar
D. None of the above

125. The term 'devaluation' means:
A. Reducing the value of a currency in terms of another currency
B. Increasing the value of a currency
C. Revising the value of a currency
D. None of the above

126. Per capita net availability of pulses has shown a tendency of:
A. Increase over time
B. Decrease over time
C. Constant over time
D. First increase then decrease

127. National Income is the same as:
A. Net national product at market price
B. Net domestic product at market price
C. Net national product at factor cost
D. Net domestic product at factor cost

128. Which one of the following is not an example of indirect tax?
A. Goods and Services Tax
B. Excise duty
C. Customs duty
D. Expenditure tax

129. The major aim of devaluation is to:
A. encourage imports
B. encourage exports
C. encourage both exports and imports
D. discourage both exports and imports

130. Structural unemployment arises due to:
A. deflationary conditions
B. heavy industry bias
C. shortage of raw materials
D. inadequate productive capacity

131. When was the Family Planning Programme officially started in India?
A. 1950 B. 1952
C. 1956 D. 1962

132. When was the Reserve Bank of India nationalised?
A. 1947 B. 1949
C. 1950 D. 1951

133. Which of the following is *not* a feature of the Indian economy?
A. High rate of population growth
B. Disguised unemployment
C. Lowest rate of adult literacy
D. High rate of exports

134. The 'Relative Deprivation' approach for measuring poverty has been adopted by:
A. developing countries
B. developed countries
C. under-developed countries
D. None of the above

135. One of the main factors that led to rapid expansion of Indian exports is:
A. Imposition of import duties
B. Liberalisation of the economy
C. Recession in other countries
D. Diversification of exports

136. Sustainable economic development means an increase in the rate of growth of real:
A. total and per capita product
B. total and per capita product and level of literacy rate
C. total and per capita product and life expectancy at birth
D. total and per capita product, taking into account the cost of degradation of the quality of environment in this process

137. Functional unemployment occurs when:
A. unemployed have no qualification for job
B. people frequently change their job
C. people were thrown out from job due to recession
D. None of these

138. Which among the following does **not** have a 'free trade zone'?
A. Kandla B. Mumbai
C. Visakhapatnam D. Thiruvanantpuram

139. Sun Belt of USA is important for which one of the following industries?
A. Cotton textile
B. Petrochemicals
C. Hi-tech electronics
D. Food Processing

140. Commercial banking system in India is
A. unit banking B. branch banking
C. mixed banking D. None of the above

141. Who gives recognition to political parties in India?
A. Parliament
B. President
C. Supreme Court
D. Election Commission

142. The Quorum of the Legislative Council is :
A. one-fourth of its total membership
B. one-third of its membership
C. one-tenth of its membership
D. 25

143. The Indian Constitution is:
A. federal
B. unitary
C. a happy mixture of the federal and unitary
D. federal in normal times and unitary in times of emergency

144. Universal adult franchise implies a right to vote to all:
A. adult residents of the State
B. adult male citizens of the State
C. residents of the State
D. adult citizens of the State

145. When a resolution prefering a charge against the President has been passed by a specified majority in the House, it is sent to the other House for investigation. If, as a result of such an investigation, a resolution is passed through a specified majority by the other House, declaring that the charge has been sustained, the President shall leave his office. The specified special majority must not be less than :
A. two-third of the members present and voting
B. one-third of the members present and voting
C. three-fourth of the members present and voting and two-third of the total membership
D. two-third of the total membership

146. Which one of the following judicial powers of the President of India has been *wrongly* listed?
A. he appoints the Chief Justice and other judges of the Supreme Court
B. he can remove the judges of the Supreme Court on grounds of misconduct
C. he can consult the Supreme Court on any question of law or fact which is of public importance
D. he can grant pardon, reprieves and respites to persons punished under Union Law

147. The Vice-president of India can be removed from his office before the expiry of his term if :
A. the Rajya Sabha passes a resolution by a majority of its members and the Lok Sabha agrees with the resolution
B. if the Supreme Court of India recommends his removal
C. the President so desires
D. None of the above

148. The Chief Justice of a High Court in India is appointed by the :
A. Governor of the State
B. Prime Minister of India
C. Chief Justice of the Supreme Court
D. President of India

149. Which of the following statements is constitutionally not true about the passing of the Union Budgets and Finance Bill in India?
1. Under the law, Finance Bill should be adopted by both the Houses of the Parliament within 45 days of its introduction.
2. If the Finance Bill is not adopted within specified period, the government loses its authority to levy the taxes proposed in the budgets.
3. In the absence of full budget, a vote-on-account gives the power to the government to spend.
4. Government cannot raise revenues without a proper approval of the Finance Bill

A. Only 2 B. Only 3
C. Only 4 D. Only 1, 2 and 3

150. Normally, on whose advice the President's Rule is imposed in a State?
A. Chief Minister
B. Legislative Assembly
C. Governor
D. Chief Justice of High Court

151. Which Article of the Indian Constitution deals with Amendment procedure?
A. Article 368 B. Article 358
C. Article 367 D. All of these

152. Government is the agency through which the will of:
A. the state is expressed
B. the people is expressed
C. the head of the state is expressed
D. the majority is expressed

153. In a unitary system of government :
A. The centre is all powerful
B. The centre is weaker than the states
C. The centre and states stand at par
D. The states and centre are supreme in their respective spheres

154. In Cabinet System of Government the real executive authority rests with :
A. The Council of Ministers
B. The Prime Minister
C. The Constitution
D. The Parliament

155. The Head of the State under a parliamentary government:
A. is an elected representative
B. is a hereditary person
C. is a nominated person
D. may be any one of the above

156. In the event of a ministerial proposal being defeated on the floor of the legislature, under the parliamentary system :
A. the government waits for a general no-confidence motion
B. the minister concerned is taken to task by the Prime Minister
C. the minister is forced to resign
D. the whole Council of Ministers resign

157. The "due process of law" is an essential characteristic of the judicial system of:
A. UK B. France
C. USA D. India

158. Under the Constitution it is :
A. obligatory for the President to accept the advice of the Council of Ministers but is not obliged to follow it
B. obligatory for the President to accept the advice of the Council of Ministers
C. not obligatory for the President to seek or accept the advice of the Council of Ministers
D. obligatory for the President to seek the advice of the Council of Ministers if his own party is in power

159. Which one of the following statements is correct?
A. the Presiding Officer of Rajya Sabha is elected every year
B. the Presiding Officer of Rajya Sabha is elected for a term of two years at a time
C. the Presiding Officer of Rajya Sabha is elected for a term of six years
D. the Vice-President of India is the ex-officio Presiding Officer of Rajya Sabha

160. The introduction of "no confidence" motion in the Lok Sabha requires the support of at least:
A. 50 members B. 70 members
C. 60 members D. 80 members

161. The High Court comes under :
A. State List
B. Union List
C. Concurrent List
D. None of the above

162. Which one of the following has been wrongly listed as a Fundamental Duty of the Indian citizens?
A. to develop scientific temper, humanism and spirit of inquiry and reform
B. to work for raising the prestige of the country in the international sphere
C. to protect and improve the natural environment
D. to strive towards excellence in all spheres of individual and collective activity

163. Which one of the following is not a Fundamental Duty as outlined in Article 51A of the Constitution?
A. to abide by the Constitution and respect its ideals
B. to defend the country and render national service when called upon to do so
C. to work for the moral upliftment of the weaker sections of society
D. to preserve the rich heritage

164. The main characteristics of the Directive Principles of State Policy given in the Indian Constitution are :
A. not enforceable by any court
B. fundamental in the governance of the country
C. 'Like instruments, instructions, political manifesto and a code of moral precepts which have to guide governors of the country'
D. no law can be passed, which is opposed to these principles

165. Of the following which are true?
A. In a State, the Legislative Council is dominant with regard to non-financial bills and the Legislative Assembly with regard to financial (money) bills

B. Vidhan Parishad can virtually block legislation even if the same is passed by the Vidhan Sabha

C. In case of a tie between the two Houses, the Governor is duty-bound to call a joint session of the two Houses to have the issue settled on a majority verdict

D. If a Bill is twice approved by the Vidhan Sabha, it becomes law even if rejected by the Vidhan Parishad

166. Which one of the following types of emergency can be declared by the President?

A. Emergency due to threat of war and external aggresion

B. Emergency due to break-down of constitutional machinery in a State

C. Financial emergency on account of threat to the financial credit of India

D. all the three emergencies

167. The chairman of which of the following parliamentary committees is invariably from the members of ruling party?

A. Committee on public undertakings

B. Public accounts committee

C. Estimates committee

D. Committee on delegated legislation

168. Which of the following is not a formally prescribed device available to the members of parliament?

A. Question hour

B. Zero hour

C. Half-an-hour discussion

D. Short duration discussion

169. Which of the following is not a tool of executive control over public administration?

A. Power of appointment and removal

B. Line agencies

C. Appeal to public opinion

D. Civil services code

170. If the Speaker of the State Legislative Assembly decides to resign, he should submit his resignation to the:

A. Judges of the High Court

B. Deputy Speaker

C. Chief Minister

D. Finance Minister

171. The President of India can nominate to the Rajya Sabha:

A. 6 members B. 9 members

C. 15 members D. 12 members

172. India is a Federal State because of:

A. dual judiciary

B. dual citizenship prevalent here

C. share of power between the Centre and the States

D. rigid Constitution

173. Residuary Subjects are those subjects which are:

A. contained in the State list

B. contained in the Union list

C. contained in the Concurrent list

D. not covered by any of the three lists

174. Which of the following writs can be issued, by the Supreme Court, to enforce Fundamental Rights?

A. Writ of Habeas Corpus

B. Writ of Mandamus

C. Writ of Quo Warranto

D. All of these

175. When the offices of both the President and the Vice-President of India are vacant, who will discharge their functions?

A. Prime Minister

B. Home Minister

C. Chief Justice of India

D. The Speaker

176. The Supreme Court tenders advice to the President of India on a matter of law or fact:

A. on its own

B. only when such advice is sought

C. only if the matter relates to some basic issue

D. only if the issue poses a threat to the unity and integrity of the country

177. Six months shall **not** intervene between two sessions of the Indian Parliament because :

A. it is the customary practice

B. it is the British convention followed in India

C. it is an obligation under the Constitution of India

D. None of the above

178. The States of the Indian Union can be recognised or their boundaries altered by:

A. the Union Parliament by a simple majority in the ordinary process of legislation

B. two-thirds majority of both the Houses of Parliament

C. two-thirds majority of both the Houses of Parliament and the consent of the legislatures of concerned States

D. an executive order of the Union government with the consent of the concerned State governments

179. The Basic Feature theory of the Constitution of India was propounded by the Supreme Court in the case of:
A. Minerva Mills Vs. Union of India
B. Golaknath Vs. State of Punjab
C. Maneka Gandhi Vs. Union of India
D. Keshavananda Vs. State of Kerala

180. Which one of the following writs is issued by a court in case of illegal detention of a person?
A. Habeas corpus
B. Mandamus
C. Certiorari
D. Quo-warranto

181. Name the instrument with the help of which a sailor in a submarine can see the objects on the surface of the sea.
A. Telescope B. Periscope
C. Gycroscope D. Stereoscope

182. 'HEMOPHILLIA' is the disease of ....
A. liver B. blood
C. brain D. bones

183. Vitamin A is abundantly found in ....
A. Brinjal B. Tomato
C. Carrot D. Cabbage

184. .... is not soluble in water.
A. Vitamin A B. Vitamin B
C. Vitamin C D. None of these

185. The blood vessels with the smallest diameter are called ....
A. capillaries B. arterioles
C. venules D. lymphatics

186. Out of the following .... has the greatest elasticity.
A. steel B. rubber
C. aluminium D. annealed copper

187. Cooking gas is a mixture of which of the following two gases?
A. Carbon Dioxide and Oxygen
B. Butane and Propane
C. Carbon Monoxide and Carbon Dioxide
D. Methane and Ethylene

188. The substance most commonly used as a food preservative is:
A. sodium carbonate B. tartaric acid
C. acetic acid D. benzoic acid

189. Normally, the substances that fight against diseases in human systems are known as:
A. dioxyribonucleic acids
B. carbohydrates
C. enzymes
D. antibodies

190. The SI unit of temperature is ....
A. Kelvin
B. Celsius
C. Fahrenheit
D. None of the above

191. Where is the 'Indira Gandhi Rashtriya Manav Sangrahalaya' located?
A. Gwalior B. Bhopal
C. Sanchi D. Jabalpur

192. In which year was the Tansen Award founded?
A. 1979 B. 1980
C. 1981 D. 1982

193. The maximum rain in Madhya Pradesh occurs at:
A. Pachmarhi B. Bhind
C. Gwalior D. Betul

194. Which of the following cities is Headquarters of west Central Railway Zone?
A. Gwalior B. Jabalpur
C. Rewa D. Ratlam

195. Pandav Caves, a famous Tourist spot is situated in:
A. Raisen B. Pachmarhi
C. Sagar D. None of these

196. In which city is the tourism spot Ashrafi Palace situated?
A. Chanderi B. Mandu
C. Gwalior D. Orcha

197. Which of the following states has the largest number of people belonging to Scheduled Tribe (According to Census 2011)?
A. Bihar B. West Bengal
C. Madhya Pradesh D. Punjab

198. Which of the projects is a joint venture of Uttar Pradesh, Madhya Pradesh and Bihar?
A. Ban Sagar B. Laxmibai
C. Barona D. Tava

199. In which year was the Bharat Bhawan established in Bhopal?
A. 1981 B. 1982
C. 1983 D. 1984

200. Marble is found in which district?
A. Jhabua B. Hoshangabad
C. Betul D. Jabalpur

201. What is the number of Rajya Sabha seats in Madhya Pradesh?
A. 10 B. 11
C. 12 D. 13

202. Who was the first woman Chief Minister of Madhya Pradesh?
A. Meera Kumar B. Sushma Swaraj
C. Uma Bharti D. Sarla Grewal

203. The 'Baiga tribe' is majorly found in:
A. Shivpuri, Jhabua, Dhar
B. Shahdol, Sidhi, Dhar
C. Mandala, Shahdol, Balaghat
D. Sidhi, Jhabua, Balaghat

204. Where is the Railway Coach factory in Madhya Pradesh?
A. Beena B. Morena
C. Bhopal D. Hoshangabad

205. Which religion is the predominant religion of the state Madhya Pradesh?
A. Muslim B. Hinduism
C. Sikhism D. Buddhism

206. Which is the first district of Madhya Pradesh to produce energy from biomass?
A. Betul B. Morena
C. Gwalior D. Mandsaur

207. In which city is the Thakur Ranmat Singh stadium situated?
A. Itarsi B. Rewa
C. Satna D. Bhopal

208. When was the 'Lok Vaniki' programme launched by the Government of Madhya Pradesh?
A. 1998 B. 1999
C. 1997 D. 1992

209. Kapildhara waterfall is situated on which river?
A. Narmada B. Son
C. Tapti D. Shipra

210. Gas released during Bhopal Gas Tragedy was:
A. Methyl Isothicoynate
B. Ethyl Isothicoynate
C. Methyl Isocyanate
D. Ethyl Isocyanate

211. .... Airport is the busiest airport in Madhya Pradesh.
A. Devi Ahilyabai Holkar
B. Raja Bhoj
C. Jabalpur
D. Gwalior

212. Madhya Pradesh has a Special Economic Zone in ....
A. Jabalpur B. Bhopal
C. Bhojpur D. Ujjain

213. The name of airport in Bhopal is ....
A. Devi Ahilyabai Holkar Airport
B. Dumna Airport
C. Panna Airport
D. Raja Bhoj International Airport

214. .... has the largest reserves of diamond in India.
A. Maharashtra B. Uttar Pradesh
C. Madhya Pradesh D. Rajasthan

215. Bhoja was an Indian King from the .... dynasty.
A. Paramara B. Mughul
C. Nanda D. Maurya

216. Which one of these Chief Ministers has not served a second term?
A. Bhagwantrao Mandloi
B. Sunderlal Patwa
C. Arjun Singh
D. Uma Bharti

217. .... is the state flower of Madhya Pradesh.
A. White Lily B. Rose
C. Lotus D. Jasmine

218. .... Baansagar project is located on river reserves of India.
A. Sone B. Bargi
C. Narmada D. Betwa

219. ...., a town in Dhar district of Madhya Pradesh is also known as Detroit of India.
A. Manawar B. Badnawar
C. Pithampur D. Mandu

220. .... is called "Heart of India".
A. Maharashtra B. Chattisgarh
C. Rajasthan D. Madhya Pradesh

221. One of the 12 Jyotirlingas in India is present in .... in Madhya Pradesh.
A. Rewa B. Ujjain
C. Sagar D. Indore

222. Indian Institute of Forest Management is located in ....
A. Indore B. Jabalpur
C. Bhopal D. Gwalior

223. Sharad Joshi Samman is given by Government of Madhya Pradesh for achievement in the field of ....
A. Sports B. Writing
C. Music D. Dance

224. .... award is presented by the Government of Madhya Pradesh in the field of Hindustani classical music.
A. Lata Mangeshkar B. Iqbal
C. Kabir D. Tansen

225. Ujjain is located at the eastern bank of .... river.
A. Son B. Narmada
C. Tapti D. Shipra

226. .... is the state tree of Madhya Pradesh.
A. Teak B. Sal
C. Banyan D. Bamboo

227. Malwa Utsav is held in .... in Madhya Pradesh.
A. Ujjain B. Bhopal
C. Gwalior D. Jabalpur

228. Tomb of Tansen is located in ....
A. Gwalior B. Indore
C. Ujjain D. Morena

229. The Central Institute of Agricultural Engineering is situated in ....
A. Indore B. Bhopal
C. Jabalpur D. Rewa

230. The famous Bagh Caves are situated in .... district of Madhya Pradesh.
A. Satna B. Dhar
C. Bhopal D. Gwalior

231. Born in Indore and a long time member of the Rajya Sabha, he was the CM of Maharashtra and then re-signed. His name is:
A. Madhav Rao Scindia
B. Kalyan Kumar
C. Pramod Mahajan
D. Prithviraj Chauhan

232. The war that brought erstwhile states like Indore, Nagpur and Rewa under the British was the:
A. III Battle of Panipat
B. Battle of Chausa
C. III Anglo Maratha war
D. II Battle of Khanwa

233. The three regions that were merged as Madhya Pradesh were ....
A. The Central Provinces, Berar and Central India
B. The Kaimur, Satpura and Vindhyan Plateau
C. The Malwa, Satpura and the Vindhya Plateau
D. The Madhya Bharath, Vindhya Pradesh and Bhopal

234. The two most important minerals of Madhya Pradesh are ....
A. Copper and Iron ore B. Iron Ore and Coal
C. Zinc and Manganese D. Gold and Diamond

235. Golden triangle of Madhya Pradesh are the regions of ....
A. Dhar, Singurali and Chhindwara
B. Singurali, Vidisha and Rewa
C. Gwalior, Jhansi and Khajuraho
D. Vidisha, Gwalior and Ujjain

236. .... in Madhya Pradesh is famous for its tigers.
A. Chitrakoot B. Jabalpur
C. Datia D. Bandhavgarh

237. What is common among the following?
Badhai, Saira, Jawara, Kalsa.
A. All are names of crops grown in Madhya Pradesh.
B. All are types of dance forms in Madhya Pradesh.
C. All are food types that is common in Madhya Pradesh.
D. All are different festivals celebrated in Madhya Pradesh.

238. The Sanctuary that is located in Bhind is the ....
A. Bhind Sanctuary
B. Kanha Sanctuary
C. Chambal Gharial Sanctuary
D. Shivpuri Sanctuary

239. The Dindori district is a part of ....
A. Satpura Sanctuary
B. Kanha National Park
C. Bori Sanctuary
D. Sanjay Dubri Sanctuary

240. Most of Madhya Pradesh has Sal and Teak trees. Which among the following are the closest features exhibited by these trees?
A. They have broad leaves
B. They are very tall trees
C. They have cone shaped leaves
D. They have breathing roots

241. Naurendhi sanctuary covers the districts of ....
A. Sagar, Damoh, Narasinghpur and Raisen
B. Ratlam, Dhar and Siddhi
C. Only Sagar
D. Raisen and Ratlam

242. Which of the following was known as the summer capital of Scindia rulers of Gwalior?
A. Ranikhet B. Shivpuri
C. Jabalpur D. Chitrakoot

243. Sardarpur Sanctuary is managed for protection of ....
A. Kharmor B. Chausingha
C. Nilgai D. Gharial

244. Bina Refinery is located in the ....
A. Chanderi B. Sagar
C. Satna D. Ujjain

245. River Banas is a tributary of the ....
A. Chambal B. Narmada
C. Tapti D. Betwa

246. When you visit the Ajaigarh fort, the river that you can see is the ....
A. Tapti and Narmada B. Yamuna
C. Ken D. Khuddar

247. Kwari river flows through the district of ....
A. Morena B. Gwalior
C. Rewa D. Indore

248. Sunar is a tributary of ....
A. Narmada B. Chambal
C. Son D. Tapti

249. In which of the following districts is manganese found in abundance?
A. Balaghat and Chhindwara
B. Anuppur and Bhind
C. Sehore and Vidisha
D. Harda and Gwalior

250. Welspun Solar Project is located in ....
A. Vidisha B. Siddhi
C. Neemuch D. Dhar

251. Western part of the Narmada Valley and the southern part of the Vindhya is a region that is called:
A. Nimar B. Vihdhmar
C. Japar D. Narmad

252. Common tribes in Madhya Pradesh for whom tattooing is an integral part of the lifestyle are:
A. Gonds B. Baigas
C. Kikars D. Bhils

253. The state that ranks number one in population of Special Tribes is:
A. Rajasthan B. Chhattisgarh
C. Madhya Pradesh D. Uttarakhand

254. The tribes who have got their names from the older part of the peninsular India are:
A. Gonds B. Bhils
C. Kakaris D. Angas

255. The standard meridian of India passes through:
A. Bhopal B. Durg
C. Ujjain D. Singrauli

256. The game reserve of Maharaja of Rewa has now been converted into ....:
A. Mahadev Sanctuary
B. Bandipur Sanctuary
C. Bandhavgarh Sanctuary
D. Panna Reserve

257. The oldest forest preserve in India is found in ....
A. Bori Wildlife Sanctuary
B. Kanha National Park
C. Van Vihar Park
D. Bandhvagarh National Park

258. Acchnakamar is a sanctuary. This is located in the district ....
A. Rewa B. Annuppur
C. Ratlam D. Morena

259. The Gandhi Sagar Sanctuary is located at ....
A. Mandsaur B. Son
C. Rewa D. Jabalpur

260. The Sanctuary that has many rock shelters is:
A. Ken Gharial B. Shivpuri
C. Narsinghgarh D. Kanha

261. Nauradhi is a sanctuary that is located in ....
A. Sagar B. Morena
C. Rewa D. Banjar

262. Sanctuary that is located in Morena is ....
A. Son Sanctuary
B. Kuno Sanctuary
C. Ghatigaon Sanctuary
D. Bandhavgarh Sanctuary

263. Chambal Originates from ....
A. Sagar District B. Rewa District
C. Janapav Hills D. Mikkai Ranges

264. Bina and Dhasaan are tributaries of ....
A. Chambal B. Tapti
C. Narmada D. Betwa

265. Kshipra is a river that merges into ....
A. Chambal B. Narmada
C. Son D. Swarna

266. The major city that Kshipra passes through is ....
A. Ujjain B. Morena
C. Gwalior D. Sagar

267. Largest road bridge of Madhya Pradesh is located across .... river.
A. Narmada B. Tapti
C. Chambal D. Tawa

268. Which river is called the "Ganga of Madhya Pradesh"?
A. Narmada B. Chambal
C. Betwa D. Tapti

269. Mandhar is a waterfall that is formed by the confluence of ....
A. Narmada and Tapti
B. Narmada and Tawa
C. Chambal and Narmada
D. Chambal and Tapti

270. The district of Guna is divided by .... river:
A. Tawa B. Tamsa
C. Sindh D. Jamni

271. Highest percentage of land holdings in Madhya Pradesh lies in
A. less than 1 hectare B. 1-2 hectares
C. more than 2 hectares D. None of these

272. Highest percentage of land occupied in Madhya Pradesh by
A. cereals B. pulses
C. oilseeds D. vegetables

273. *Sujat, Kalawal* and *Malavraj* are varieties of which crops produced in Madhya Pradesh?
A. Jowar B. Wheat
C. Bajra D. Rice

274. *Laloo* is a variety of
A. small grain rice B. medium grain rice
C. long grain rice D. Both B and C

275. Balaghat district in Madhya Pradesh lies in agro-climatic regions of
A. Wheat zone B. Rice zone
C. Wheat-Rice zone D. Wheat-Jowar zone

276. Khandwa and Rajgarh are main producers of
A. Lime B. Orange
C. Banana D. Papaya

277. Turmeric in Madhya Pradesh is mainly produced in
A. Khandwa, Badwani B. Guna, Mandsaur
C. Ujjain, Shajapur D. Rajgarh, Chhindwara

278. The Madhya Pradesh state Agro-Industries Development Corporation Ltd. is headquartered at
A. Jabalpur B. Bhopal
C. Satna D. Indore

279. Madhya Pradesh Seed Certification Agency was established in
A. 1963 B. 1972
C. 1980 D. 1985

280. Madhya Pradesh State Livestock and Poultry Development Corporation was established in
A. 1871 B. 1975
C. 1978 D. 1982

281. When was the Adivasi Lok Kala Academy established?
A. 1957 B. 1980
C. 1965 D. 1985

282. 'Devani Gayan' is a song of which festival?
A. Holi B. Dusshera
C. Harvest season D. Diwali

283. Which dance drama is devoted to Lord Megnad?
A. Manch B. Gammat
C. Khamb Swang D. Chahur

284. Which among the following is the major sources of irrigation in Madhya Pradesh?
A. Canals B. Wells and Tubewells
C. Ponds D. Other sources

285. Which among the following districts of Madhya Pradesh is not benefitted from Wainganga canal?
A. Balaghat B. Morena
C. Gwalior D. Both B and C

286. Halali canal in Madhya Pradesh emerges from river
A. Chambal B. Barna
C. Halali D. Wainganga

287. Gandhi Sagar Dam is located on the river
A. Wainganga B. Chambal
C. Betwa D. Barna

288. Samrat Ashok Sagar is constructed across the river
A. Halali B. Chambal
C. Narmada D. Barna

289. Which among the following is not a part of Narmada Valley Project?
A. Tawa Reservoir
B. Maan Dam
C. Rani Avanti Bai Lodhi Sagar Project
D. Omkareshwar Dam

290. The folk dance form called 'Matki' is prevalent in which of the following regions?
A. Bundelkhand B. Malwa
C. Vindhyachal D. Baghelkhand

291. The Madhya Pradesh State Industrial Corporation was founded on
A. April, 1965 B. September, 1965
C. October, 1965 D. December, 1965

292. The railway sleepers in Madhya Pradesh are manufactured at
A. Bhopal B. Budhani
C. Indore D. Dindori

293. Maheshwar is famous for
A. Silk Saree Industry B. Ahilya Ghat
C. Ahilya Museum D. All of the above

294. The note printing press in Madhya Pradesh is located at
A. Hoshangabad B. Nepanagar
C. Dewas D. Ujjain

295. Leather complex in Madhya Pradesh is located at
A. Dewas B. Ujjain
C. Chhindwara D. Shajapur

296. Which chemical fertilizer is mostly used in Madhya Pradesh?
A. Nitrogen B. Potash
C. Phosphate D. Sulphur

297. The biggest undertaking of Madhya Pradesh Government is
A. Madhya Pradesh Finance Corporation
B. Madhya Pradesh Electricity Corporation
C. Madhya Pradesh Transportation Corporation
D. Madhya Pradesh Small Industries Corporation

298. The air cargo complex, Indo-German tool room and dry sea-port in Madhya Pradesh are located at ....
A. Mandideep B. Pithampur
C. Ujjain D. Korba

299. Under the Madhya Pradesh Ladli Laxmi Yojana, the beneficiary is paid the total amount on attaining the age of:
A. 18 B. 23
C. 21 D. 16

300. A new oil processing unit in Madhya Pradesh is proposed at
A. Malanpur B. Pithampur
C. Aagasaud D. Mandideep

301. Software Technology Park is located at
A. Ratlam B. Gwalior
C. Indore D. All of these

302. The Cement Corporation of India is in which district of Madhya Pradesh?
A. Jabalpur B. Durg
C. Katni D. Raisen

303. The first gem purifying centre in Madhya Pradesh is established at
A. Jabalpur B. Sidhi
C. Shivni D. Indore

304. The largest cotton textile producing district of Madhya Pradesh is
A. Indore B. Jabalpur
C. Raigarh D. Shivpuri

305. What was the capital of the Muslim Sultanate of Malwa?
A. Bhopal B. Gwalior
C. Mandu D. Hoshangabad

306. Which among the following thermal power stations is located in Umaria district of Madhya Pradesh?
A. Satpura B. Sanjay Gandhi
C. Chandani D. Vindhyachal

307. Which thermal station is a joint venture of Madhya Pradesh and Rajasthan?
A. Birsinghpur-II B. Pench
C. Malwa D. Satpura

308. Nepanagar is getting electricity from
A. Chandani Thermal B. Vindhyachal
C. Amarkantak D. Birsinghpur

309. Gandhi Sagar Dam is located on the river
A. Wainganga B. Chambal
C. Betwa D. Berna

310. Jawaharsagar hydropower project is on river
A. Pench B. Baansagar
C. Chambal D. Sone

311. Where is Madhya Pradesh Tribal Museum located?
A. Indore B. Jhabua
C. Bhopal D. Kargone

312. In Madhya Pradesh electricity was first produced in
A. Sohagpur B. Gwalior
C. Umaria D. Jabalpur

313. The energy capital of Madhya Pradesh is
A. Shivni B. Korba
C. Rajgarh D. Singrauli

314. The first solar village (district) of Madhya Pradesh is
A. Itarasi B. Sehore
C. Indore D. Panchmarhi

315. For how many days is the Gangaur festival celebrated?
A. 5 B. 9
C. 10 D. 15

316. Gandhi Sagar Power Station is located in
A. Mandsaur district B. Ujjain
C. Jhabua D. Umaria

317. When was the first bio gas plant established in Bhopal?
A. 1980 B. 1983
C. 1984 D. 1985

318. Indira Sagar Vidyut Kendra is located at
A. Punasa B. Khandwa
C. Omkareshwar D. Maheshwar

319. Parsili is situated in the district of:
A. Indore B. Jabalpur
C. Sidhi D. Ujjain

320. MP Urja Vikas Nigam was established in—
A. 1982 B. 1984
C. 1972 D. 1965

ANSWERS

1 B	**2** C	**3** D	**4** C	**5** B	**6** C	**7** A	**8** C	**9** C	**10** D
11 C	**12** A	**13** C	**14** A	**15** A	**16** D	**17** A	**18** B	**19** A	**20** D
21 A	**22** C	**23** B	**24** C	**25** D	**26** C	**27** B	**28** D	**29** D	**30** B
31 C	**32** D	**33** C	**34** C	**35** B	**36** C	**37** D	**38** B	**39** C	**40** C
41 A	**42** A	**43** A	**44** B	**45** C	**46** D	**47** C	**48** B	**49** B	**50** D
51 A	**52** C	**53** A	**54** B	**55** B	**56** A	**57** B	**58** C	**59** A	**60** C
61 C	**62** C	**63** B	**64** B	**65** C	**66** C	**67** D	**68** D	**69** D	**70** B
71 B	**72** C	**73** C	**74** C	**75** A	**76** A	**77** A	**78** B	**79** B	**80** A
81 A	**82** B	**83** D	**84** B	**85** C	**86** C	**87** D	**88** C	**89** B	**90** D

91	92	93	94	95	96	97	98	99	100
A	B	A	A	A	B	B	A	A	D
101	102	103	104	105	106	107	108	109	110
C	B	A	D	D	D	A	C	D	C
111	112	113	114	115	116	117	118	119	120
B	B	B	A	D	A	C	D	B	D
121	122	123	124	125	126	127	128	129	130
C	A	A	B	A	D	C	D	B	D
131	132	133	134	135	136	137	138	139	140
B	B	D	A	B	D	B	D	D	C
141	142	143	144	145	146	147	148	149	150
D	C	D	D	D	B	A	D	C	C
151	152	153	154	155	156	157	158	159	160
A	B	A	A	A	D	C	B	D	A
161	162	163	164	165	166	167	168	169	170
B	B	C	B	D	D	C	B	B	B
171	172	173	174	175	176	177	178	179	180
D	C	D	D	C	B	C	A	D	A
181	182	183	184	185	186	187	188	189	190
B	B	C	A	A	A	B	D	D	A
191	192	193	194	195	196	197	198	199	200
B	B	A	B	B	B	C	A	B	D
201	202	203	204	205	206	207	208	209	210
B	C	C	C	B	A	B	B	A	C
211	212	213	214	215	216	217	218	219	220
A	A	D	C	A	D	A	A	C	D
221	222	223	224	225	226	227	228	229	230
B	C	B	D	D	C	A	A	B	B
231	232	233	234	235	236	237	238	239	240
D	C	D	B	C	D	B	C	B	A
241	242	243	244	245	246	247	248	249	250
A	B	A	B	A	C	A	A	A	C
251	252	253	254	255	256	257	258	259	260
A	B	C	A	D	C	A	B	A	C
261	262	263	264	265	266	267	268	269	270
A	B	C	D	A	A	D	C	A	C
271	272	273	274	275	276	277	278	279	280
A	A	B	C	B	C	A	B	C	D
281	282	283	284	285	286	287	288	289	290
B	D	C	B	D	C	B	A	D	B
291	292	293	294	295	296	297	298	299	300
B	A	D	C	A	A	B	B	C	C
301	302	303	304	305	306	307	308	309	310
A	C	A	A	C	B	D	A	B	C
311	312	313	314	315	316	317	318	319	320
C	B	D	A	B	A	C	A	C	A

REASONING ABILITY

Directions : *In each of the following series determine the order of the letters. Then from the given options select the one which will complete the given series.*

1. BMK, DLM, FKO, HJQ, ?
A. JIR B. JIT
C. JHS D. JIS

2. A, CD, FGH, ?
A. IJKL B. KLMN
C. JKLM D. LMNO

3. BXJ, ETL, HPN, KLP, ?
A. PHR B. NIR
C. NHR D. MHR

4. PUF, QVG, RWH, ?
A. SXI B. SYZ
C. SXJ D. SVI

5. DEF, HIJ, MNO, ?
A. RTV B. STU
C. PTU D. SRU

Directions : *Which of the following groups of letters will complete the given series?*

6. ab---b-bbaa-
A. babba B. abaab
C. abbab D. baaab

7. aa-ab--aaa-a
A. baaa B. abab
C. aaab D. aabb

8. -baa-aab-a-a
A. baab B. abab
C. aaba D. aabb

9. -a cca-ccca-acccc-aaa
A. ccaa B. acca
C. caac D. caaa

10. c-bbb--abbbb-abbb-
A. abccb B. bacbb
C. aabcb D. abacb

Directions : *In the following questions, select the number(s) from the given options for completing the given series.*

11. 3, 9, 27, 81, 243, ?
A. 486 B. 729
C. 972 D. 359

12. 1, 6, 12, 19, 27, ?
A. 38 B. 35
C. 36 D. 54

13. 2, 6, 14, 30, 62, ?
A. 126 B. 128
C. 120 D. 130

14. 8, 48, 16, 96, 32, ?
A. 192 B. 150
C. 64 D. 288

15. 2, 8, 14, 24, 34, 48, ?
A. 66 B. 62
C. 58 D. 64

Directions : *In the given series find the number which is wrong.*

16. 5, 25, 120, 625, 3125, 15625
A. 15625 B. 625
C. 120 D. 5

17. 4, 8, 11, 22, 18, 36, 24, 50
A. 8 B. 22
C. 36 D. 24

18. 2, 4, 12, 24, 72, 142, 432
A. 432 B. 12
C. 142 D. 72

19. 2, 3, 4, 4, 6, 8, 9, 12, 16
A. 3 B. 9
C. 6 D. 12

20. 97, 91, 86, 83, 79, 77, 76, 76
A. 86 B. 76
C. 91 D. 83

Directions : *In the questions given below establish the relationship between the two words. Then from the given options select one which has the same relationship as of the given two words.*

21. ADULT : BABY : : FLOWER : ?
A. Seed B. Bud
C. Fruit D. Butterfly

22. WRITER : READER : : PRODUCER : ?
A. Creator B. Contractor
C. Creature D. Consumer

23. ENTRANCE : EXIT : : LOYALTY : ?
A. Treachery B. Patriotism
C. Fidelity D. Reward

24. MOTHER : MATERNAL : : FATHER : ?
A. Eternal B. Detrimental
C. Paternal D. Formidable

Directions : *In the questions given below one term is missing. Based on the relationship of the two given words find the missing term from the given options.*

25. GFC : CFG : : RPJ : ?

A. JRP B. JPR
C. PJR D. RJP

26. BCF : DEG : : MNQ : ?

A. OPR B. PQS
C. OPP D. QRT

27. NATION : ANITNO : : HUNGRY : ?

A. HNUGRY B. UNHGYR
C. YRNGUH D. UHGNYR

28. SSTU : MMNO : : AABC : ?

A. GGHH B. IJKK
C. XXYZ D. NOOP

Directions : *Three of the following four in each question are alike in a certain way and so form a group. Select the group of letters that does not belong to that group.*

29. A. ACE B. LOR
C. GIK D. VXZ

30. A. TSR B. LKJ
C. PQO D. HGF

31. A. EF LM B. KJ SR
C. XW HG D. ED YX

32. A. JOPK B. BOPC
C. QOPR D. TOPS

33. A. DfH B. MoQ
C. UwY D. InO

34. A. JKkL B. OPpQ
C. DEEf D. VWwX

35. A. BdfH B. FHJL
C. RTvX D. uVwX

36. A. DFHEG B. TWXUV
C. OQSPR D. JLNKM

37. A. FEUV B. DCXW
C. BAZY D. HGTS

38. A. UTSR B. XYZW
C. ONML D. IHGF

Directions : *In the following questions select the right option which indicates the correct code for the word or letter given in the question.*

39. If CHAIR is coded as FKDLU then RAID is coded as:

A. ULGD B. ULKG
C. ULDG D. UDLG

40. If CONDEMN is coded as CNODMEN, then TEACHER is coded as :

A. TEACHER B. TAEECHR
C. TCAEEHR D. TAECEHR

41. In a code language COME is written as XLNV and ABLE as ZYOV. How will MOLLY be written in that code?

A. NLOBO B. NLBOO
C. LNOOB D. NLOOB

42. In a certain code PROFESSION is written as EFORPNOISS. In the same code DICTIONARY will be written as :

A. YRANOITCID
B. ITCIDYRANO
C. ITCIDYRNAO
D. ITCDIYARNO

43. JUNE is coded as NXPF, how will STAY be coded in the same manner?

A. WWCZ B. WVCZ
C. WWDB D. VWZC

Directions : *In the following questions study the coded patterns and then select the right option from the given alternatives.*

44. In a certain language, (a) 'go ju mi' stands for 'plenty of money'; (b) pao ju go nei vu' for 'money creates lots of problems'; (c) 'kol vu nei' for 'problems create tension'; and (d) 'sol tun ju haw' for 'still money is needed'. Which of the following words stand for 'money'?

A. nei B. ju
C. haw D. go

45. In a certain language, (a) 'FOR' stands for 'old is gold'; (b) 'ROT' stands for 'gold is pure'; (c) 'ROM' stands for 'gold is costly'. How will 'pure old gold is costly' be written?

A. TFROM B. FOTRM
C. FTORM D. TOMRF

46. In a certain code '415' means 'milk is hot'; '18' means 'hot soup'; and '895' means 'soup is tasty'. What number will indicate the word 'tasty'?

A. 9 B. 8
C. 5 D. 4

47. In a certain code '643' means 'she is beautiful', '593' means 'he is handsome', and '567' means 'handsome meets beautiful'. What number will indicate the word 'meets'?

A. 5 B. 3
C. 7 D. 6

48. In a certain code language, (a) 'dugo hui mul zo' stands for 'work is very hard'; (b) 'hui dugo ba ki' for 'Bingo is very smart'; (c) 'nano mul dugo' for 'cake is hard', and (d) 'mul ki qu' for 'smart and hard'. Which of the following words stand for 'Bingo'?

A. jalu B. dugo
C. ki D. ba

49. Among five friends, A is heavier than B; C is lighter than D; B is lighter than D but heavier than E. Who among them is the heaviest?

A. B B. C
C. A D. Can't say

50. Pune is bigger than Jhansi, Sitapur is bigger than Chittor. Raigarh is not as big as Jhansi, but is bigger than Sitapur. Chittor is not as big as Sitapur. Which is the smallest?

A. Jhansi B. Pune
C. Chittor D. Sitapur

51. Ajay works more than Ram. Alok works as much as Raju. Pankaj works less than Alok. Ram works more than Alok. Who works the most of all?

A. Ajay B. Ram
C. Alok D. Raju

52. Vipul is taller than Hans. Hans is taller than Anand. Alok is taller than Ashok. Ashok is taller than Hans. Who among them is the tallest?

A. Vipul B. Alok
C. Ashok D. Cannot be determined

53. Pramod is taller than Gopal. Gopal is shorter than Madhu. To find out who among them is the tallest, which of the following further informations is necessary?

A. Madhu is taller than Gopal.
B. Madhu is shorter than Pramod's brother
C. Pramod is taller than Madhu.
D. Pramod is taller than Madhu's brother.

54. Among five friends P, Q, R, S and T, who is the youngest? To arrive at the answer which of the following information given in the statements (*a*) and (*b*) is sufficient?

(*a*) R is younger than P and T.
(*b*) S is younger than Q.

A. Only (*a*) alone is sufficient
B. Either (*a*) or (*b*) is sufficient
C. Both (*a*) and (*b*) together are needed
D. Both (*a*) and (*b*) together are not sufficient

55. Sushma is richer than Rashmi whereas Anand is richer than Priya. Arun is as rich as Rashmi. Shoba is richer than Sushma.

Which of the following statements is correct according to the above propositions?

A. Rashmi is poorer than Priya.
B. Priya is richer than Arun
C. Arun is poorer than Sushma.
D. Anand is richer than Rashmi

56. A is elder to B while C and D are elder to E who lies between A and B. If C be elder to B, which one of the following statements is necessarily true?

A. E is elder to B B. A is elder to C
C. C is elder to D D. D is elder to C

57. Vikram is taller than Rajan but shorter than Annie. Jamal is taller than Annie. Sita is taller than Vikram. Rajan is shorter than Sita. Who is the shortest of all in the group?

A. Sita B. Rajan
C. Vikram D. Cannot be determined

58. Suresh is as much older than Kamal as he is younger than Prabodh. Navin is as old as Kamal. Which of the following statements is wrong?

A. Suresh is older than Navin
B. Kamal is younger than Suresh
C. Prabodh is not the oldest
D. Navin is younger than Prabodh

Directions: *In the following questions, understand the arrangement pattern and then select the right answer from the given options :*

59. Five boys are sitting in a row. Raghu is not adjacent to Shyam or Amit. Ajay is not adjacent to Shyam. Raghu is adjacent to Mayank. If Mayank is at the middle in the row, then Ajay is adjacent to whom out of the following?

A. Amit B. Raghu
C. Mayank D. Shyam

60. Mini is to the right of Rajni but to the left of Ananta. Saya is to the right of Mini but to the left of Jaya. Who is on the extreme left if all the girls are facing North?

A. Jaya B. Mini
C. Rajni D. Saya

61. Kittu is in-between Mohan and Sohan. Raju is to the left of Sohan and Shyam is to the right of Mohan. If all of the friends are sitting facing South, then who is on their extreme right?

A. Mohan B. Sohan
C. Kittu D. Shyam

62. A, B, C, D and E are running one behind the other. C is not near E and A is not near D. B is next to A and E is not near D. Who is in the middle?

A. B B. E
C. A D. Cannot be said

63. O, P, Q, R, S and T are standing on a bench according to their height. P is taller than O but shorter than S. Only S is taller than T. R is shorter than P but taller than Q. Who is the shortest?

A. O B. Q

C. P D. Cannot be said

Directions : *In the following questions, select the right answer from the given options to depict the correct direction/distance.*

64. Kittu walks towards East and then towards South. After walking some distance he turns towards West and then turns to his left. In which direction is he walking now?

A. North B. South

C. East D. West

65. A person is driving towards West. What sequence of directions should he follow so that he is driving towards South?

A. left, right, right B. right, right, left

C. left, left, left D. right, right, right

66. Richa drives 8 km to the South, turns left and drives 5 km. Again, she turns left and drives 8 km. How far is she from her starting point?

A. 3 km B. 5 km

C. 8 km D. 13 km

67. Dingi runs 40 km towards North then turns right and runs 50 km. He turns right and runs 30 km, and once again turns right and runs 50 km. How far is he from his starting point?

A. 90 km B. 50 km

C. 10 km D. 5 km

68. Debu walks towards East then towards North and turning 45° right walks for a while and lastly turns towards left. In which direction is he walking now?

A. North B. East

C. South-East D. North-West

Directions : *In each of the following questions keenly study the relationship mentioned between the persons, and then from the given options select the right relationship as the answer.*

69. 'A' is the father of 'B' and 'C'. 'B' is the son of 'A' but 'C' is not the son of 'A'. What is 'C's' relation with 'A'?

A. Daughter B. Son

C. Niece D. Nephew

70. A lady said, "The person standing there is my grandfather's only son's daughter". How is the lady related to the standing person?

A. Sister B. Mother

C. Aunt D. Cousin

71. Ravi is the brother of Amit's son's son. What is Amit's relation to Ravi?

A. Cousin B. Father

C. Grandfather D. Son

72. Mayank said, "My mother is the sister of Rajat's brother." What is Rajat's relation with Mayank?

A. Cousin B. Maternal uncle

C. Uncle D. Brother-in-law

73. Introducing Lily, Raghav said, "Her father is my mother's only son". How is Lily related to Raghav?

A. Aunt B. Daughter

C. Mother D. Sister

74. If the day before yesterday was Thursday, when will Sunday be?

A. Tomorrow B. Day after tomorrow

C. Today D. Two days after today

75. There are twenty people working in an office. The first group of five works between 8:00 A.M. and 2:00 PM. The second group of ten works between 10:00 AM to 4:00 PM. And the third group of five works between 12 noon to 6:00 PM. There are three computers in the office which all the employees frequently use. During which of the following hours the computers are likely to be used most?

A. 1:00 PM - 3:00 PM

B. 12 noon - 2:00 PM

C. 2:00 PM - 4:00 PM

D. 10:00 AM - 12 noon

76. If the seventh day of a month is three (3) days earlier than Friday, what day will it be on the nineteenth day of the month?

A. Sunday B. Monday

C. Wednesday D. Friday

77. Radha remembers that her father's birthday is after 16th but before 21st of March, while her brother Mangesh remembers that his father's birthday is before 22nd but after 19th of March. On which date is the birthday of their father?

A. 19th B. 20th

C. 21st D. Cannot be determined

78. A man is three (3) years older than his wife and four (4) times as old as his son. If the son attains an age of fifteen (15) years after three (3) years, what is the present age of the mother?

A. 45 years B. 51 years

C. 48 years D. 60 years

79. A clock is so placed that at 12 noon its minute hand points towards north-east. In which direction does its hour hand point at 1:30 P.M.?

A. East B. West

C. North D. South

80. If in the above question clock is turned through an angle of 135° in an anticlockwise direction, in which direction will its minute hand point at 8.45 P.M.?
A. East B. West
C. North D. South

81. A couple married in 1980 had two children, one in 1982 and the other in 1984. Their combined ages will equal the years of the marriage in?
A. 1986 B. 1985
C. 1987 D. 1988

82. Manoj left home for the bus stop 15 minutes earlier than the usual time. It takes 10 minutes to reach the stop. He reached the stop at 8.40 A.M. What time does he usually leave home for the bus stop?
A. 8.30 A.M. B. 8.55 A.M.
C. 8.45 P.M. D. None of these

83. Mamuni went to the movies nine days ago. She goes to the movies only on Thursday. What day of the week is today?
A. Sunday B. Tuesday
C. Thursday D. Saturday

84. If Thursday was the day after the day before yesterday five days ago, what is the least number of days ago when Sunday was three days before the day after tomorrow?
A. Two days ago B. Three days ago
C. Four days ago D. Five days ago

85. 1.12.91 is the first Sunday. Which is the fourth Tuesday of December 91?
A. 31.12.91 B. 24.12.91
C. 17.12.91 D. 26.12.91

86. If the third day of a month is Monday, which of the following will be the fifth day from 21st of that month?
A. Tuesday B. Monday
C. Wednesday D. Thursday

87. Keshav runs a factory in three shifts of eight hours each with 210 employees. In each shift minimum of 80 employees are required to run the factory effectively. No employee can be allowed to work for more than 16 hours a day. At least how many employees will be required to work for 16 hours every day?
A. 30 B. 60
C. Data inadequate D. None of these

88. If 15 horses eat 15 bags of gram in 15 days, in how many days will one horse eat one bag of grain?
A. 15 days B. 1/15 days
C. 1 day D. 30 days

89. A century leap year is divisible by :
A. 4 B. 16
C. 40 D. 400

90. If the fifth day of a month is Friday, which of the following will be the Seventh day from 10th of that month?
A. Tuesday B. Monday
C. Wednesday D. Thursday

91. Day after tomorrow is my birthday. On the same day next week falls 'Holi'. Today is Monday. What will be the day after 'Holi'?
A. Wednesday B. Thursday
C. Friday D. Saturday

92. A clock shows the time as 3:30 P.M. If the minute hand gains 2 minutes every hour, how many minutes will the clock gain by 4 a.m.?
A. 23 Minutes B. 24 Minutes
C. 25 Minutes D. 26 Minutes

93. Two brothers were expected to return home on the same day. Rajat returned 3 days earlier but Rohit returned 4 days later. If Rajat returned on Thursday, what was the expected day when both the brothers were to return home and when did Rohit Return?
A. Wednesday, Sunday
B. Thursday, Monday
C. Sunday, Thursday
D. Monday, Friday

94. In a row of trees, one tree is fifth from either end of the row. How many trees are in the row?
A. 11 B. 8
C. 10 D. 9

95. Jaya ranks 5th in a class of 53. What is her rank from the bottom in the class?
A. 49th B. 48th
C. 47th D. 50th

96. Mohan ranks twenty-first in a class of sixty-five students. What will be his (Mohan's) rank if the lowest candidate is assigned rank 1?
A. 44th B. 45th
C. 46th D. Data inadequate

97. If Rahul finds that he is 12th from the right in a line of boys and 4th from the left, how many boys should be added to the line such that there are 28 boys in the line?
A. 12 B. 14
C. 20 D. 13

98. In a row of boys, Rajan is tenth from the right and Suraj is tenth from the left. When Rajan and Suraj interchange their positions, Suraj will be twenty-seventh from the left. Which of the following will be Rajan's position from the right?
A. Tenth B. Twenty-sixth
C. Twenty-ninth D. None of these

99. Mahesh and Suresh are ranked 11th and 12th respectively from the top in a class of 41 students. What will be their respective ranks from the bottom?
A. 32nd and 33rd B. 29th and 30th
C. 30th and 31st D. 31st and 30th

100. Uma ranked 8th from the top and 37th from bottom in a class. How many students are there in the class?
A. 47 B. 46
C. 45 D. None of these

101. In a queue, Sadiq is 14th from the front and Joseph is 17th from the end, while Jane is in between Sadiq and Joseph. If Sadiq be ahead of Joseph and there be 48 persons in the queue, how many persons are there between Sadiq and Jane?
A. 5 B. 6
C. 7 D. 8

102. Rohan ranked eleventh from the top and twenty-seventh from the bottom among the students who passed the annual examination in a class. If the number of students who failed in the examination was 12, how many students appeared for the examination?
A. 48
B. 49
C. 50
D. Cannot be determined

103. Some boys are sitting in a row. P is sitting fourteenth from the left and Q is seventh from the right. If there are four boys between P and Q, how many boys are there in the row?
A. 19 B. 21
C. 25 D. 23

104. How many 6's are there in the following series of numbers which are preceded by 7 but not immediately followed by 9?
6 7 9 5 6 9 7 6 8 7 6 7 8 6 9 4 6 7 7 6 9 5 7 6 3
A. One B. Two
C. Three D. Four

105. In a chess tournament each of six players will play every other player exactly once. How many matches will be played during the tournament?
A. 12 B. 15
C. 30 D. 36

106. How many 4's are there in the following series which are preceded by 7, but are not preceded by 8?
3 4 5 7 4 3 7 4 8 5 4 3 7 4 9 8 4 7 2 7 4 1 3 6
A. 1 B. 2
C. 3 D. 4

107. How many even numbers are there in the following series of numbers, each of which is immediately preceded by an odd number, but not immediately followed by an even number?
5 3 4 8 9 7 1 6 5 3 2 9 8 4 3 5
A. Nil B. 1
C. 2 D. 3

108. If all the numbers from 1 to 51 which are exactly divisible by 3 are arranged in descending order, which of the following numbers will come at the seventh and tenth places from the top?
A. 33 & 27 B. 33 & 21
C. 21 & 30 D. 33 & 24

109. If "+" means "–"; "–" means "×"; "×"means "÷" and "÷" means "+", then
$15 \times 5 \div 10 + 5 - 3 = ?$
A. 9.5 B. 0
C. – 2 D. 24

110. If "+" means "–"; "–" means "×"; "×"means "÷" and "÷" means "+", then
$15 \times 3 \div 15 + 5 - 2 = ?$
A. 0 B. 10
C. 20 D. 6

111. If "+" means "÷"; "×" means "–"; "÷"means "+" and "–" means "×", then
$16 \div 8 \times 6 - 2 + 12 = ?$
A. 22 B. 24
C. 23 D. 20

112. If "+" means "×"; "–" means "÷"; "÷"means "+" and "×" means "–", then what will be the value of 20 ÷ 40 – 4 × 5 + 6 = ?
A. 60 B. 1.67
C. 150 D. 0

113. If "+" means "×"; "–" means "÷"; "×"means "–" and "÷" means "+", then
$5 + 8 - 4 \times 2 \div 9 = ?$
A. 15 B. 13
C. 17 D. 11

Directions: *In each question given below which one number can be placed at the sign of interrogation?*

114.

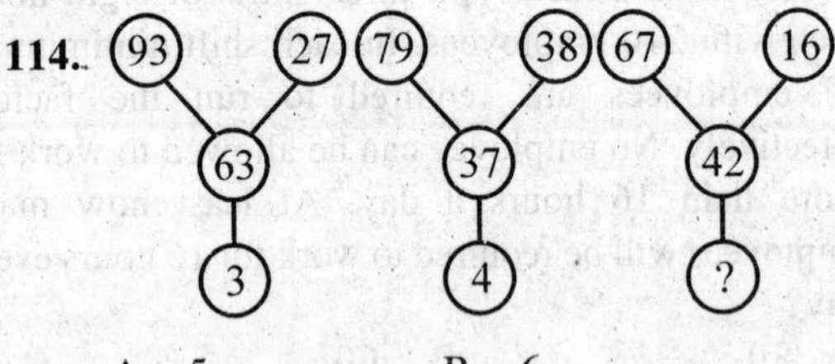

A. 5 B. 6
C. 8 D. 9

115.

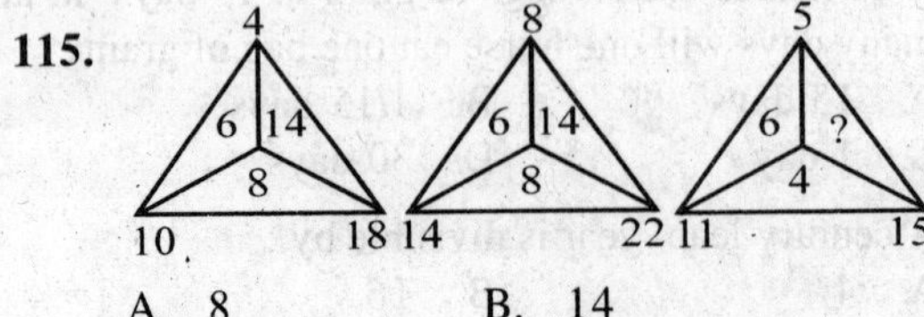

A. 8 B. 14
C. 10 D. 6

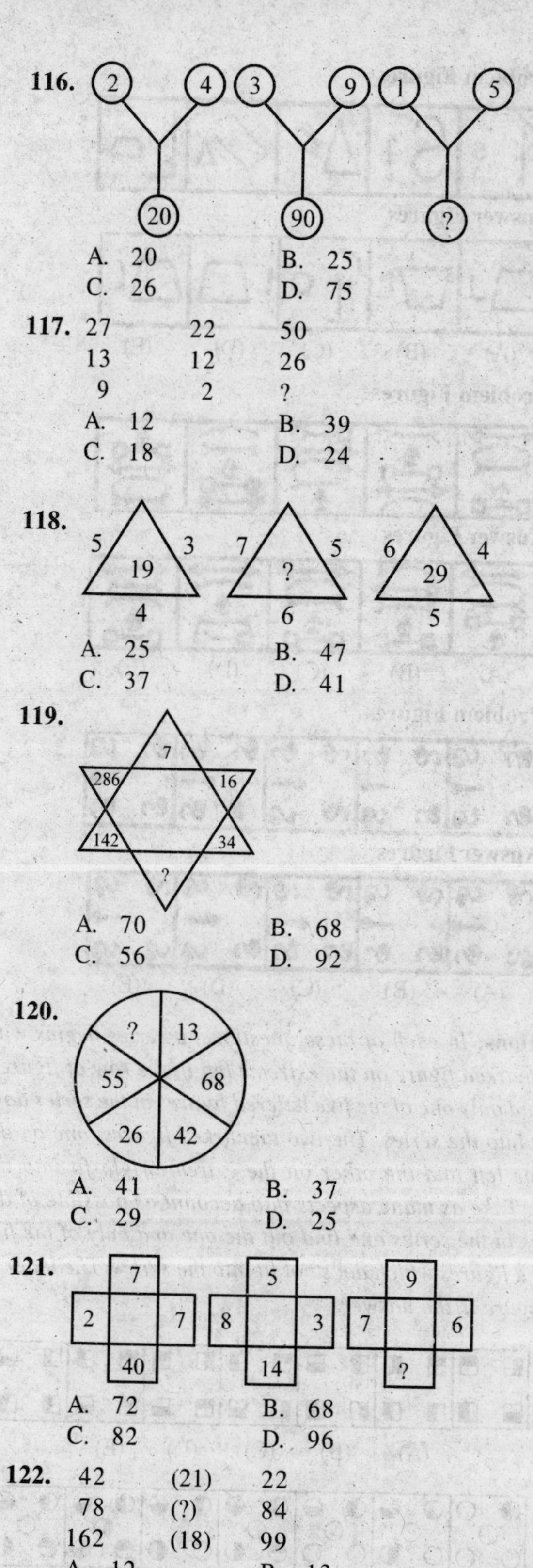

116. (2) (4) → (20); (3) (9) → (90); (1) (5) → (?)

A. 20 B. 25
C. 26 D. 75

117.

27	22	50
13	12	26
9	2	?

A. 12 B. 39
C. 18 D. 24

118. Triangle 1: 5, 3, 4, centre 19; Triangle 2: 7, 5, 6, centre ?; Triangle 3: 6, 4, 5, centre 29

A. 25 B. 47
C. 37 D. 41

119. Star: 7, 16, 34, ?, 142, 286

A. 70 B. 68
C. 56 D. 92

120. Circle: ?, 13, 68, 42, 26, 55

A. 41 B. 37
C. 29 D. 25

121. Figure 1: 7, 2, 7, 40; Figure 2: 5, 8, 3, 14; Figure 3: 9, 7, 6, ?

A. 72 B. 68
C. 82 D. 96

122.

42	(21)	22
78	(?)	84
162	(18)	99

A. 12 B. 13
C. 60 D. 72

123. Triangle 1: 16, 7, 10, centre 107; Triangle 2: 25, 20, 4, centre 209; Triangle 3: 19, 2, 17, centre ?

A. 68 B. 93
C. 175 D. 217

Directions : *The following questions are based on alphabet series in natural or reverse order and the combinations that can be made by changing the position of alphabet in given words.*

124. Which alphabet comes immediately before the sixth alphabet from the left extreme in alphabetical series?
A. U B. E
C. F D. V

125. Which letter is midway between G and S?
A. L B. N
C. M D. No letter

126. Which letter should be ninth letter to the left of ninth letter from the right if the first half of the alphabet is reversed?
A. I B. D
C. F D. E

127. If the alphabet is in reverse order, which letter will be eighth letter to the left of the seventh letter counting from the right end?
A. O B. P
C. N D. Q

128. What will be the fifth letter to the right of the thirteenth letter from the right?
A. R B. S
C. I D. O

Directions: *In each of the following questions which one of the five answer figures given below should come after the problem figures if the sequence are continued?*

129. Problem Figures

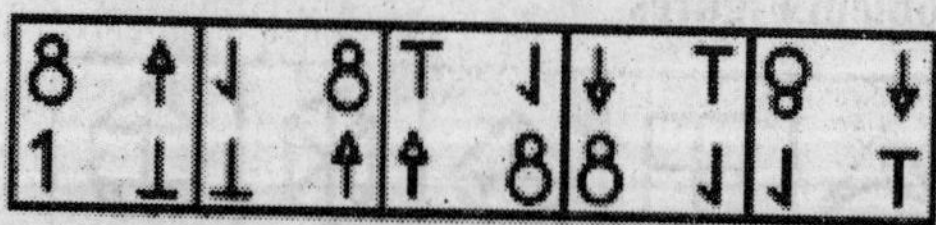

Answer Figures

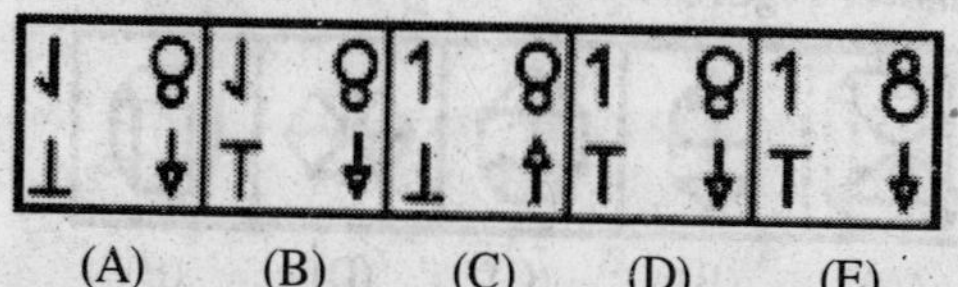

(A) (B) (C) (D) (E)

130. Problem Figures

Answer Figures

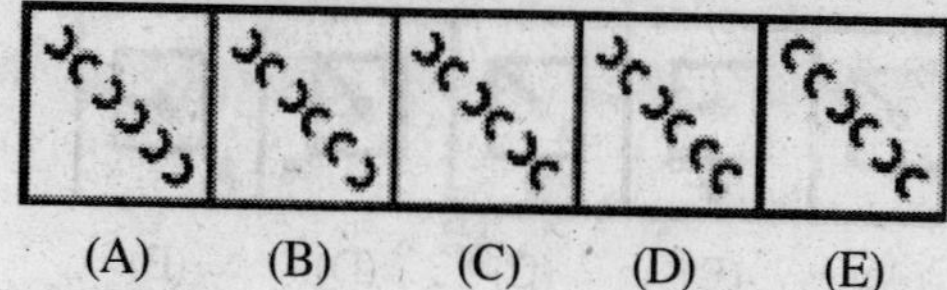

(A) (B) (C) (D) (E)

131. Problem Figures

Answer Figures

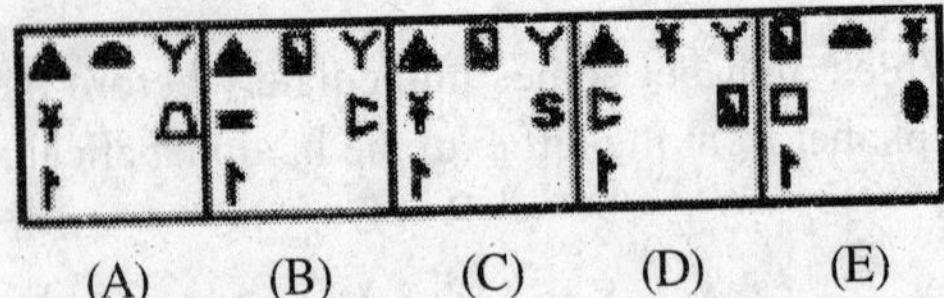

(A) (B) (C) (D) (E)

132. Problem Figures

Answer Figures

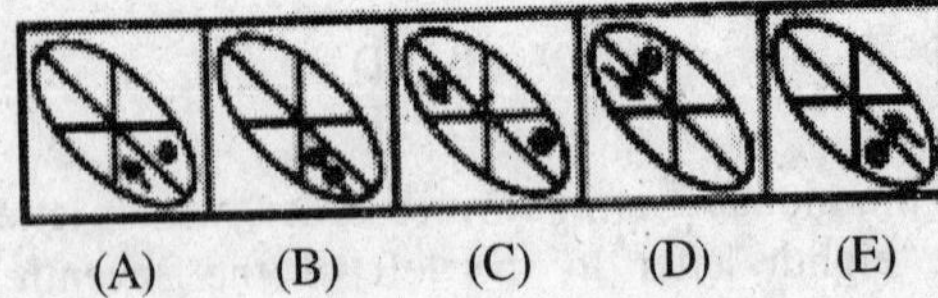

(A) (B) (C) (D) (E)

133. Problem Figures

Answer Figures

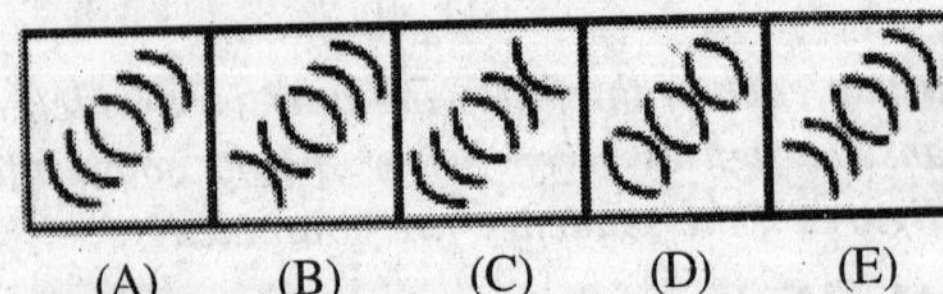

(A) (B) (C) (D) (E)

134. Problem Figures

Answer Figures

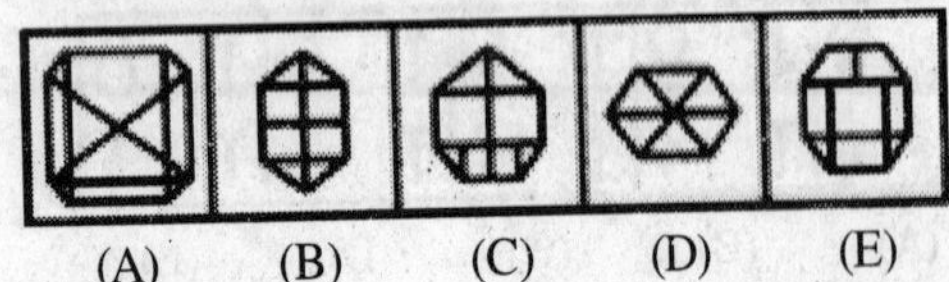

(A) (B) (C) (D) (E)

135. Problem Figures

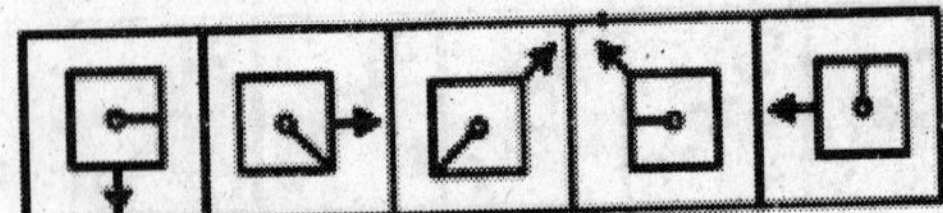

Answer Figures

(A) (B) (C) (D) (E)

136. Problem Figures

Answer Figures

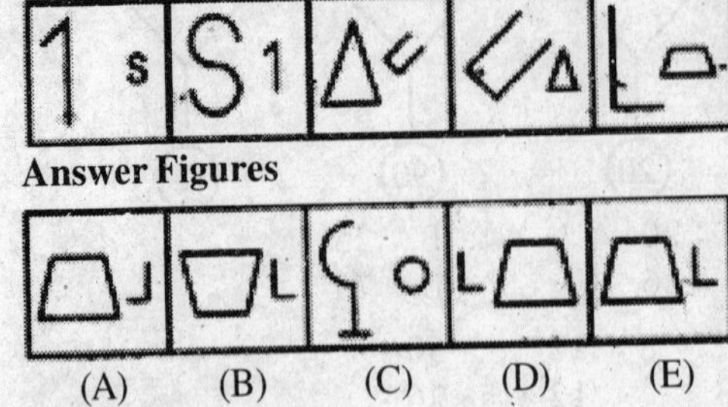

(A) (B) (C) (D) (E)

137. Problem Figures

Answer Figures

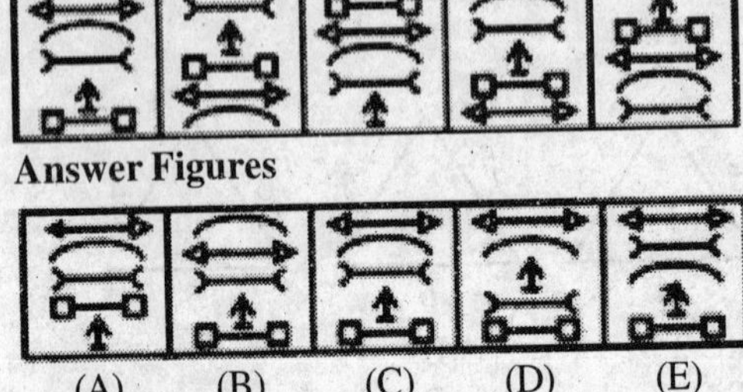

(A) (B) (C) (D) (E)

138. Problem Figures

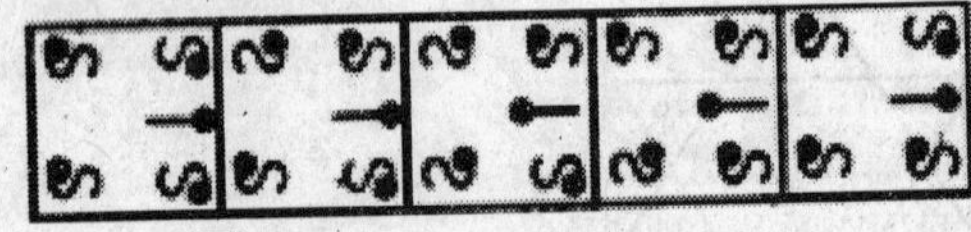

Answer Figures

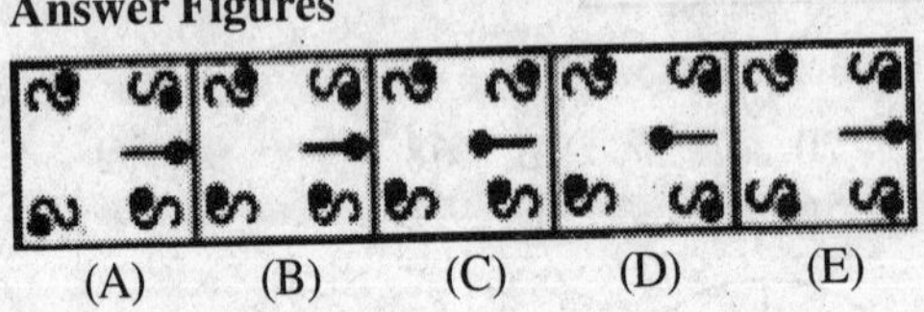

(A) (B) (C) (D) (E)

Directions: *In each of these questions, a series begins with an unmarked figure on the extreme left in the row of figures. One and only one of the five lettered figures in the series does not fit into the series. The two unmarked figures, one on the extreme left and the other on the extreme right fit into the series. Take as many aspects into account as possible of the figures in the series and find out the one and only of the five marked figures which does not fit into the series. The letter of that figure is the answer.*

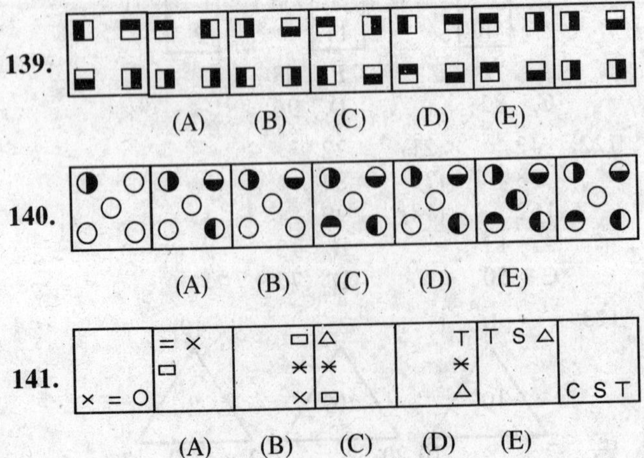

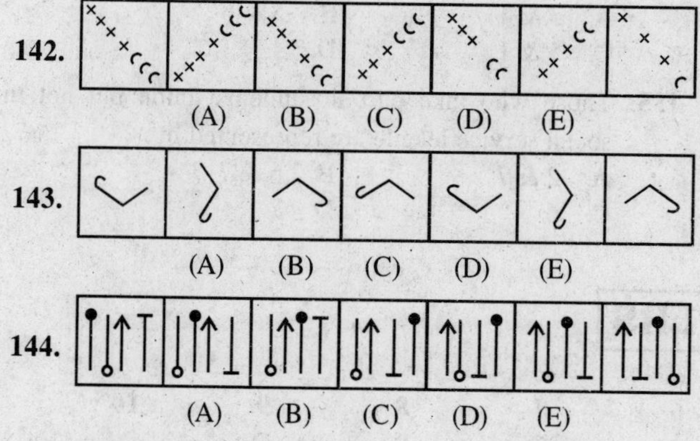

145. What is the number which is common to only two geometrical figures?

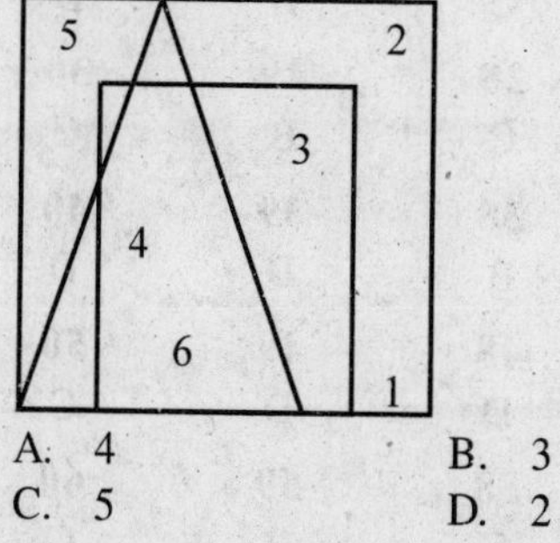

A. 4 B. 3
C. 5 D. 2

Directions: *In the following diagram, rectangle represents Hindi Announcers, circle represents English Announcers, square represents French Announcers, and triangle represents German Announcers.*

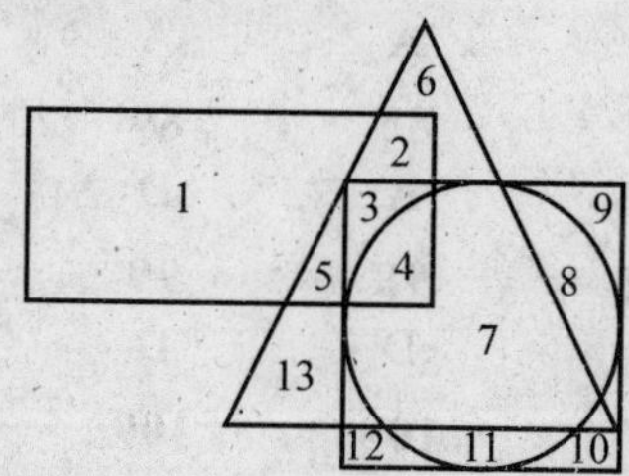

146. Which area represents those announcers who can present programmes in Hindi, French and German only?
A. 1 B. 2
C. 3 D. 4

147. Which area represents those announcers who can present programmes in French and English only?
A. 7 B. 9
C. 11 D. 13

Directions: *Study the diagram to answer these questions.*

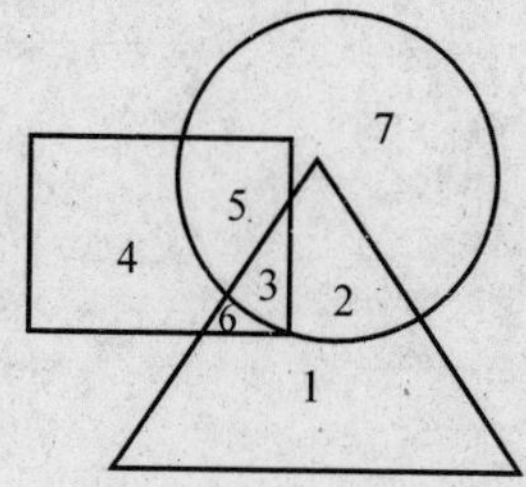

148. Which number is in all the geometrical figures?
A. 5 B. 6
C. 2 D. 3

149. Number 6 is in :
A. Rectangle and triangle
B. Circle and triangle
C. Rectangle and circle
D. Rectangle only

Directions: *In the following diagram*

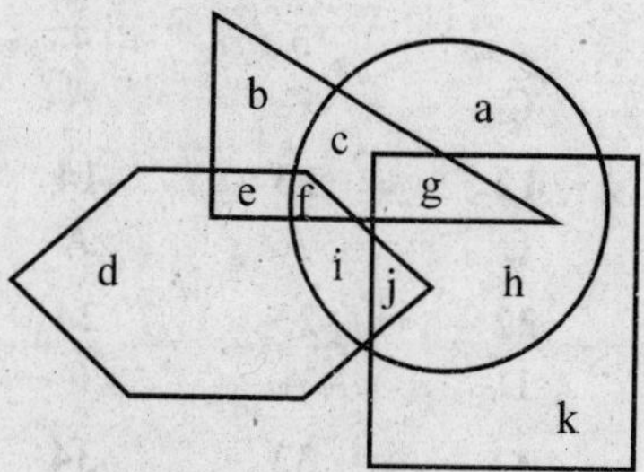

The Circle represents players
The Triangle represents outdoor games
The Hexagon represents indoor games and
The Square represents national level players
Study the diagram and answer the questions given below :

150. The letter in the section representing the players who play indoor games at national level is :
A. f B. i
C. j D. g

151. The letter representing the section of outdoor as well as indoor game players who do not play at the national level is :
A. c B. f
C. e D. i

152. The section representing national level players who do not play either outdoor or indoor games but still come under the category of players is :
A. k B. g
C. c D. h

153. Persons who play outdoor games but do not come under the category of players are represented in the section marked :
A. b B. c
C. a D. d

Directions: *Study the diagram given below.*

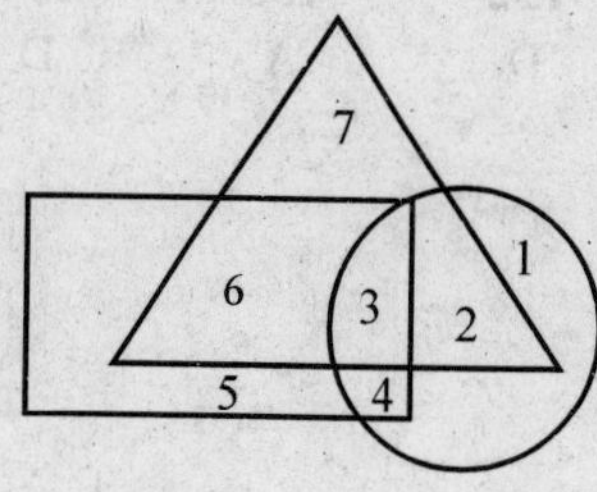

A college provides three different activities, students union represented by triangle, literary society represented by rectangle and social service league represented by circle.

154. Those who take part in both literary society and social service league but not in students union are represented by :

A. 3 & 4
B. 5 & 6
C. 5 & 1
D. 4

155. Those who take part in students union but not in social service league are represented by:

A. 2 & 7
B. 6 & 7
C. 6
D. 7

ANSWERS

1	2	3	4	5	6	7	8	9	10
D	C	C	A	B	D	C	B	D	A
11	**12**	**13**	**14**	**15**	**16**	**17**	**18**	**19**	**20**
B	C	A	A	B	C	D	C	B	D
21	**22**	**23**	**24**	**25**	**26**	**27**	**28**	**29**	**30**
B	D	A	C	B	A	D	C	B	C
31	**32**	**33**	**34**	**35**	**36**	**37**	**38**	**39**	**40**
A	D	D	C	D	B	A	B	D	D
41	**42**	**43**	**44**	**45**	**46**	**47**	**48**	**49**	**50**
D	B	A	B	A	A	C	D	D	C
51	**52**	**53**	**54**	**55**	**56**	**57**	**58**	**59**	**60**
A	D	C	D	C	A	B	C	B	C
61	**62**	**63**	**64**	**65**	**66**	**67**	**68**	**69**	**70**
D	A	D	B	D	B	C	D	A	A
71	**72**	**73**	**74**	**75**	**76**	**77**	**78**	**79**	**80**
C	B	B	A	B	A	B	A	A	D
81	**82**	**83**	**84**	**85**	**86**	**87**	**88**	**89**	**90**
A	D	D	A	B	C	D	A	D	C
91	**92**	**93**	**94**	**95**	**96**	**97**	**98**	**99**	**100**
B	C	C	D	A	B	D	D	D	D
101	**102**	**103**	**104**	**105**	**106**	**107**	**108**	**109**	**110**
C	B	C	C	B	D	C	D	C	B
111	**112**	**113**	**114**	**115**	**116**	**117**	**118**	**119**	**120**
C	D	C	D	C	C	A	D	A	C
121	**122**	**123**	**124**	**125**	**126**	**127**	**128**	**129**	**130**
B	B	A	B	C	D	A	B	D	C
131	**132**	**133**	**134**	**135**	**136**	**137**	**138**	**139**	**140**
D	A	C	E	C	E	C	B	A	E
141	**142**	**143**	**144**	**145**	**146**	**147**	**148**	**149**	**150**
A	C	C	E	B	C	C	D	A	C
151	**152**	**153**	**154**	**155**					
B	D	A	D	B					

NUMERICAL ABILITY

1. There are four numbers A, B, C and D. Average of the first three *i.e.*, A, B and C is 15 and that of B, C and D is 16. If the last number, *i.e.*, D is 19, then the first number is—
   A. 15 B. 16
   C. 17 D. 18

2. Of the three numbers, the first is twice the second and thrice the third. If the average of three is 22, the three numbers are—
   A. 12, 18, 36 B. 18, 12, 36
   C. 36, 12, 18 D. 36, 18, 12

3. If a person is standing on the sixth number in the queue from both the ends, the total persons in the queue are—
   A. 9 B. 11
   C. 12 D. 13

4. A number '*x*' when multiplied by 5 and added to three times its own gives 64, the number is—
   A. 8 B. 12
   C. 14 D. 18

5. A number which when multiplied by 11 is as much above 180 as it was originally below it. The number is—
   A. 25 B. 30
   C. 40 D. 45

6. The sum of a number and its reciprocal is thrice the difference of the number and its reciprocal. Find the number.
   A. $\sqrt{2}$ B. $\sqrt{3}$
   C. $\sqrt{5}$ D. $\sqrt{7}$

7. A boy was asked to find $\frac{7}{9}$ of a fraction. He made a mistake of dividing the fraction by $\frac{7}{9}$ and so got an answer which exceeded the correct answer by $\frac{8}{21}$. Find the correct answer.
   A. $\frac{2}{3}$ B. $\frac{5}{7}$
   C. $\frac{7}{12}$ D. $\frac{7}{15}$

8. There are 408 boys and 312 girls in a school, which are to be divided into equal sections of either boys or girls alone. Find the maximum number of boys or girls that can be placed in a section. Also find the total number of sections thus formed.
   A. 10, 20 B. 24, 30
   C. 24, 40 D. 30, 30

9. The sum of all possible two-digit number formed from three different one-digit natural numbers, when divided by the sum of the original three numbers is equal to—
   A. 11 B. 18
   C. 22 D. 36

10. There are four prime numbers written in ascending order. The product of the first three is 385 and that of the last three is 1001. The last number is—
    A. 19 B. 17
    C. 13 D. 11

11. If the number 357 ★ 25 ★ is divisible by both 3 and 5, then the missing digits in the unit's place and thousandth place respectively are—
    A. 0, 4 B. 5, 4
    C. 5, 6 D. 0, 6

12. The difference between two numbers is 1365. When the larger number is divided by the smaller one, the quotient is 6 and the remainder is 15. The smaller number is:
    A. 360 B. 295
    C. 270 D. 240

13. When a number is divided by 31, the remainder is 29. When the same number is divided by 16, what will be the remainder?
    A. 15 B. 13
    C. 11 D. Data inadequate

14. In dividing a number by 585, a student applied the method of short division. He divided the number successively by 5, 9 and 13 (factor of 585) and got the remainders 4, 8 and 12. If he had divided the number by 585, the remainder would have been:
    A. 584 B. 292
    C. 144 D. 24

15. When a number divided by 6 leaves a remainder 3. When the square of the same number is divided by 6, the remainder is:
    A. 3 B. 2
    C. 1 D. zero

16. The L.C.M. and H.C.F. of two numbers are 4284 and 32 respectively. If one of the numbers is 204, the other is

A. 672 B. 576
C. 676 D. 572

17. Two numbers are in the ratio of 8 : 15. If their H.C.F. is 4, the numbers are

A. 32 and 60 B. 16 and 30
C. 80 and 150 D. 64 and 120

18. The greatest number that will divide 366, 513 and 324 leaving the same remainder in each case is

A. 21 B. 18
C. 27 D. 42

19. The L.C.M. of two numbers is 45 times their H.C.F. If the sum of the L.C.M. and the H.C.F. of these two numbers is 1150 and one of the numbers is 125, then the other number is

A. 256 B. 225
C. 250 D. 255

20. The H.C.F. and the L.C.M. of two numbers are 50 and 250 respectively. On dividing one of these numbers by 2, 50 is obtained as quotient. The numbers are

A. 100, 125 B. 80, 100
C. 125, 100 D. 200, 250

21. Three bells ring respectively at an interval of 15 seconds, 20 seconds and 24 seconds. If they ring continuously for 12 minutes then how many times, during this period, will they ring together?

A. 2 times B. 6 times
C. 5 times D. 3 times

22. If the sum of two numbers is 55 and the H.C.F. and L.C.M. of these numbers are 5 and 120 respectively. Find the sum of their reciprocals.

A. $\frac{120}{11}$ B. $\frac{11}{120}$

C. $\frac{601}{55}$ D. $\frac{55}{601}$

23. The LCM of two numbers is 48. The numbers are in the ratio of 2 : 3. The sum of the numbers is

A. 64 B. 40
C. 32 D. 28

24. Find the greatest number that will divide 43, 91 and 183 so as to leave the same remainder in each case.

A. 13 B. 9
C. 7 D. 4

25. The greatest possible length which can be used to measure exactly the length 7m, 3m 85cm, 12m 95 cm is

A. 42 cm B. 35 cm
C. 25 cm D. 15 cm

26. A, B and C start at the same time in the same direction to run around a circular park. A completes a round in 252 seconds, B in 308 seconds and C in 198 seconds, all starting at the same point. After what time will they meet again at the starting point?

A. 46 minutes 12 seconds
B. 45 minutes
C. 42 minutes 36 seconds
D. 26 minutes 18 seconds

27. Which of the following has most numbers of divisors?

A. 182 B. 176
C. 101 D. 99

28. Which is of the following is a co-primes?

A. (23, 92) B. (21, 35)
C. (18, 25) D. (16, 62)

29. Let N be the greatest number that will divide 1305, 4665 and 6905, leaving the same remainder in each case. Then find the sum of the digits in N.

A. 8 B. 6
C. 5 D. 4

30. The greatest number which one dividing 1657 and 2037 leaves remainder 6 and 5 respectively, is:

A. 305 B. 235
C. 127 D. 123

31. One-third of a certain journey was covered at the rate of 25 km per hour, one-fourth at the rate of 30 km per hour and the rest at the 50 km per hour. What is the average speed per hour for whole journey?

A. $33\frac{1}{3}$ kmph B. $44\frac{1}{4}$ kmph

C. $22\frac{1}{2}$ kmph D. 33 kmph

32. A batsman has a certain average of runs for 16 innings. In the 17th innings, he makes a score of 85 runs thereby increasing his average by 3. What is the average after the 17th inning?

A. 33 runs B. 34 runs
C. 37 runs D. 36 runs

33. The average of 6 observations is 12. A new seventh observation is included and the new average is decreased by 1. The seventh observation is

A. 1 B. 3
C. 5 D. 6

34. The average age of 30 students in a class is 12 years. The average age of a group of 5 of the students is 10 years and that of another group of 5 of them is 14 years. The average age of the remaining students is

A. 8 years B. 10 years
C. 12 years D. 14 years

35. Out of the three given numbers, the first number is twice the second and thrice the third. If the average of three numbers is 121, what is the difference between the first and third number?

A. 144 B. 77
C. 99 D. 132

36. If the average marks of three batches of 55, 60 and 45 students is 50, 55 and 60, then average marks of all the students is:

A. 55 B. 54
C. 54.68 D. 55.68

37. The average of 8 numbers is 20. The average of first two numbers is $15\frac{1}{2}$ and that of the next three is $21\frac{1}{3}$. If the sixth number is less than the seventh and eighth numbers by 4 and 7 respectively, then the eighth number is:

A. 27 B. 25
C. 22 D. 18

38. A pupil's marks were wrongly entered as 83 instead of 63. Due to that the average marks for the class got increased by half. What is the number of pupils in the class?

A. 73 B. 40
C. 40 · D. 10

39. A cricketer whose bowling average is 12.4 runs per wicket takes 5 wickets for 26 runs and thereby decreases his average by 0.4. The number of wickets taken by him till the last match was:

A. 85 B. 80
C. 72 D. 64

40. The average weight of a class of 24 students is 35 kg. If the weight of the teacher is included, the average rises by 400 g. What is the weight of the teacher?

A. 55 kg B. 53 kg
C. 50 kg D. 45 kg

41. Nine men went to a hotel. Eight of them spent ₹ 3 for each over their meals and the ninth spent ₹ 2 more than the average expenditure of all the nine. What is the total money spent by them?

A. ₹ 29.25 B. ₹ 29.50
C. ₹ 29 D. ₹ 30

42. The average age of 24 students in a class is 10. If the teacher's age is included, the average increases by one. The age of the teacher is

A. 25 B. 30
C. 35 D. 40

43. The average of 5 consecutive even numbers A, B, C, D and E is 34. What is the product of B and D?

A. 1152 B. 1368
C. 1224 D. 1088

44. The average of 50 numbers is 30. If two numbers, 35 and 40 are discarded, then the average of the remaining numbers is nearly:

A. 29.68 B. 29.27
C. 28.78 D. 28.32

45. The average monthly salary of 20 employees of an organisation is ₹ 1500. If the manager's salary is added, then the average salary increases by ₹ 100. Find the manager's monthly salary?

A. ₹ 4800 B. ₹ 3600
C. ₹ 2400 D. ₹ 2000

46. The ratio of ages of A and B is 3 : 11. After 3 years the ratio becomes 1 : 3. What are the ages of A and B?

A. 9 years, 33 years
B. 10 years, 40 years
C. 9 years, 27 years
D. None of these

47. Two years ago, the ratio of Ram's and Mohan's age was 3 : 2 and at present 7 : 5. What are their present ages?

A. 14 years, 10 years
B. 15 years, 10 years
C. 13 years, 9 years
D. None of these

48. The ages of Samir and Saurabh are in the ratio of 8 : 15 respectively. After 9 years the ratio of their ages will be 11 : 18. What is the difference between their ages in years?

A. 20 years B. 21 years
C. 22 years D. 24 years

49. The present age of father is 34 years more than that of his son. 12 years ago, father's age was 18 times the age of his son. The present age of son in years is:

A. 12 B. 14
C. 16 D. 18

50. A mother is 25 years older than her daughter. Five years ago, the age of the mother was 6 times the age of the daughter. What is the present age of mother?

A. 25 years B. 29 years
C. 32 years D. 35 years

51. The difference between the present ages of P and Q is 4 years. The ratio of their ages after 5 years will be 9 : 8. The present age of P is:

A. 24 years B. 30 years
C. 32 years D. None of these

52. Ten years ago, the age of Divya was half of the age of Namrata. If the ratio of present ages of both is 3 : 4, the sum of their present ages is:

A. 35 years B. 30 years
C. 25 years D. 18 years

53. The ratio between the present ages of A and B is 5 : 3 respectively. The ratio between A's age 4 years ago and B's age 4 years hence is 1 : 1. The ratio between A's age 4 years hence and B's age 4 years ago is:

A. 4 : 1 B. 3 : 1
C. 2 : 1 D. 1 : 3

54. Ram got married 8 years ago. His present age is $\frac{6}{5}$ times his age at the time of marriage. Ram's sister was 10 years younger to him at the time of his marriage. What is the present age of Ram's sister?

A. 40 years B. 38 years
C. 36 years D. 32 years

55. A father said to his son, "I was as old as you are at present at the time of your birth." If the father's age is 38 years now. Five years ago the age of son was:

A. 38 years B. 33 years
C. 19 years D. 14 years

56. A fort has provision for 50 days. After 15 days a reinforcement of 150 men arrives and the provision now lasts 25 days. How many men were there in the fort?

A. 300 B. 225
C. 275 D. 200

57. In a fort there is provisions for 40 days for 275 persons. If after 16 days 125 persons leave the fort for how many more days the provisions will last?

A. 35 days B. 44 days
C. 45 days D. 53 days

58. 60 men could complete a work in 250 days. They worked together for 200 days. After that the work had to be stopped for 10 days due to bad weather. How many more men should be engaged to complete the work in time?

A. 20 B. 18
C. 15 D. 10

59. A contractor undertook to complete a project in 90 days and employed 60 men on it. After 60 days, he found that $\frac{3}{4}$ of the work has already been completed. How many men can he discharge so that the project may completed exactly on time?

A. 15 B. 20
C. 30 D. 40

60. A flagstaff 17.5 m high casts a shadow of length 40.25 m. The height of the building, which casts a shadow of length 28.75m under similar condition will be:

A. 21.25 m B. 17.5 m
C. 12.5 m D. 10 m

61. If 5 men or 9 women can do a piece of work in 19 days, then 3 men and 6 women will do the same work in how many days?

A. 21 B. 18
C. 15 D. 12

62. A certain number of men can finish a piece of work in 100 days. If there were 10 men less, it will take 10 days more for the work to be finished. How many men were there originally?

A. 110 B. 100
C. 82 D. 75

63. Some persons can do a piece of work in 12 days. Two times the number of such persons will do half of that work in:

A. 12 days B. 3 days
C. 6 days D. 4 days

64. 2 men and 7 boys can do a piece of work in 14 days; 3 men and 8 boys can do the same in 11 days. Then 8 men and 6 boys can do three times of this work in

A. 30 days B. 4 days
C. 21 days D. 18 days

65. If 3 men or 6 boys, working 7 hours a day can do a piece of work in 10 days; how many days will it take to complete a piece of work twice as large with 6 men and 2 boys working together for 8 hours a day?

A. 9 B. $8\frac{1}{2}$
C. $7\frac{1}{2}$ D. $6\frac{1}{2}$

66. If 15 men can do a certain amount of work in 20 days working 8 hours a day, in how many days will 10 men do three times the work working 6 hours a day?

A. 120 days
B. 70 days
C. 100 days
D. None of these

67. 40 men consume 60 kgs of rice in 15 days, then in how many days will 30 men consume 12 kgs of rice?

A. 9 days B. $6\frac{1}{4}$ days
C. 4 days D. $3\frac{1}{4}$ days

68. 56 men can complete a piece of work in 24 days. In how many days can 42 men complete the same piece of work?

A. 48 B. 32
C. 20 D. 16

69. Running at the same constant rate, 6 identical machines can produce a total of 270 bottles per minute. At this rate, how many bottles could 10 such machines produce in 4 minutes?

A. 1400 B. 1600
C. 1800 D. 2000

70. 400 persons, working 9 hours a day complete $\frac{1}{4}th$ of the work in 10 days. The number of additional persons, working 8 hours a day, required to complete the remaining work in 20 days, is:
A. 275 B. 250
C. 675 D. 200

71. Starting from a point at a speed of 4 km/hr a man reaches at a certain place and returns back to the point from where he had started journey on bicycle at the speed of 16 km/hr. His average speed during the entire journey will be :
A. 6.4 km/h B. 8.4 km/h
C. 5.4 km/h D. 10 km/h

72. A motorist covers a certain distance at a average speed of 48 km/h in 45 minutes. What speed in km/h he must maintain to cover the same distance in 30 minutes?
A. 66 km/h B. 79 km/h
C. 80 km/h D. 72 km/h

73. A policeman saw a thief at a distance of 200 m. The policeman and the thief started running at the same time. If the policeman runs at a speed of $4\frac{1}{6}$ m per second and the thief at a speed of $3\frac{1}{3}$m per second, after what time the policeman will catch the thief?
A. 12 min B. 10 min
C. 9 min D. 4 min

74. A monkey wants to climb up a glazed pole. He climbs 12 metres in 1 minute and then he slips back 3 metres in the next minute. If the pole is 63 metre high, how long does he take to climb at the top of the pole?
A. $11\frac{1}{4}$ min B. $12\frac{1}{2}$ min
C. $12\frac{3}{4}$ min D. $14\frac{3}{4}$ min

75. The distance between two stations A and B is 300 km. A train leaves the station A with a speed of 40 km/hr. At the same time another train departs from the station B with a speed of 50 km/hr. How much time will these two trains take to cross each other?
A. 3 hrs 40 min B. 3 hrs 20 min
C. 2 hrs 20 min D. 3 hrs 45 min

76. Nilesh goes to school from his village at the speed of 4 km/hr and returns from school to village at the speed of 2 km/hr. If he takes 6 hours in all, then what is the distance between the village and the school?
A. 8 km B. 6 km
C. 5 km D. 4 km

77. By increasing the speed of the bus by 10 km/hr the time of journey for 72 km is reduced by 36 minutes. What was the original speed of the bus?
A. 30 km/hr B. 35 km/hr
C. 40 km/hr D. 45 km/hr

78. A train covers a distance in 50 minutes, if it runs at a speed of 48 km/hr on an average. The speed at which the train must run to reduce the time of journey to 40 minutes will be:
A. 70 km/hr B. 60 km/hr
C. 55 km/hr D. 50 km/hr

79. A certain distance is covered by a vehicle at a certain speed. If half of this distance is covered by another vehicle in double the time, the ratio of the speeds of the two vehicles is:
A. 4 : 1 B. 1 : 4
C. 2 : 1 D. 1 : 2

80. A is faster than B. A and B each walk 24 km. The sum of their speeds is 7 km/hr and sum of times taken by them is 14 hours. What is the speed of A?
A. 7 km/hr B. 5 km/hr
C. 4 km/hr D. 3 km/hr

81. A and B working together complete a work in 35 days. If A takes 60 days to complete it, how long would B alone take to complete it?
A. 64 days B. 72 days
C. 81 days D. 84 days

82. A few children working together can do a piece of work in 18 days. If the number of children employed on the work is made double, how long would they take to complete half of the work?
A. $4\frac{1}{2}$ days B. $2\frac{1}{3}$ days
C. $8\frac{3}{4}$ days D. $6\frac{1}{2}$ days

83. 10 men or 18 boys can do a piece of work in 15 days. In how many days would 25 men and 15 boys complete the same work working together?
A. $5\frac{1}{2}$ days B. $4\frac{1}{2}$ days
C. $6\frac{2}{3}$ days D. $2\frac{1}{3}$ days

84. A cistern is filled by a tap in $3\frac{1}{2}$ hours. Due to a leak in the bottom of the cistern, it takes half an hour longer to fill the cistern. If the cistern is full, how long will it take the leak to empty it?
A. 28 hours B. 29 hours
C. $31\frac{1}{3}$ hours D. 38 hours

85. A is twice as good a workman as B and thrice as good a workman as C. If C alone can do a piece of work in 24 days, how long would the three persons take to finish the work working together?

A. $3\frac{3}{11}$ days B. $4\frac{4}{7}$ days
C. $4\frac{4}{11}$ days D. $3\frac{4}{11}$ days

86. If 3 men and 5 women can do a piece of work in 8 days and 2 men and 7 boys can do the same work in 12 days. Find the number of boys, the work done by whom can equate the work done by 10 women.

A. 19 boys B. 21 boys
C. 23 boys D. 15 boys

87. 8 men alone can complete a piece of work in 12 days. 4 women alone can complete the same piece of work in 48 days and 10 children alone can complete the piece of work in 24 days. In how many days can 10 men, 4 women and 10 children together complete the piece of work?

A. 6 B. 8
C. 10 D. 15

88. A works twice as fast as B. If B can complete a piece of work independently in 12 days. Find in how many days A and B together can complete the work?

A. 8 days B. 6 days
C. 4 days D. 18 days

89. A contractor undertook to complete a project in 90 days and employed 60 men on it. After 60 days, he found that $\frac{3}{4}$ of the work has already been completed. How many men can he discharge so that the project may be completed exactly on time?

A. 15 B. 20
C. 30 D. 40

90. A can do a piece of work in 25 days and B can do it in 20 days. They work together for 5 days and then A goes away. In how many days will B finish the remaining work?

A. 33 days B. 20 days
C. 11 days D. 10 days

91. A boat goes 6 km upstream and back to the starting point in 2 hours. If the current of the stream runs at the rate of 4 km/hr, find the speed of the boat in still water.

A. 6 km/hr B. 8 km/hr
C. 10 km/hr D. 12 km/hr

92. A boat covers 24 km upstream and 36 km downstream in 6 hours, while it covers 36 km upstream and 24 km downstream in 6½ hours. Find the speed of the current.

A. 2 km/hr B. 4 km/hr
C. 6 km/hr D. 8 km/hr

93. A man can row 5 km/hr in still water and the speed of the stream is 1.5 km/hr. He takes an hour when he travels upstream to a place and back again to the starting point. How far is the place from the starting point?

A. 2.275 km B. 3.5 km
C. 1.5 km D. None of these

94. The speed of a boat in still water is 6 km/hr and the speed of the stream is 1.5 km/hr. A man rows to a place at a distance of 22.5 km and comes back to the starting point. Find the total time taken by him.

A. 8 hours B. 10 hours
C. 12 hours D. 4 hours

95. A boat covers 20 km downstream and 6 km upstream in 3 hours, while it covers 30 km downstream and 12 km upstream in 5 hours. What is the speed of boat in still water?

A. 6 km/hr B. 8 km/hr
C. 10 km/hr D. 12 km/hr.

96. Samir can travel 12 miles downstream in a certain river in 6 hours less than it takes him to travel the same distance upstream. But when he could double his rowing rate for his 24-mile round trip, the downstream 12 miles would then take only one hour less than the upstream 12 miles. Find the speed of the current in miles/hour.

A. $2\frac{2}{3}$ B. $2\frac{1}{3}$
C. $1\frac{2}{3}$ D. $1\frac{1}{3}$

97. A boat takes 6 hours to travel from place M to N downstream and back from N to M upstream. If the speed of the boat in still water is 4 km/hr; what is the distance between two places?

A. 6 kms B. 8 kms
C. 12 kms D. Data inadequate

98. A man can row upstream at 8 km/hr and downstream at 13 km/hr. The speed of the stream is:

A. 2.5 km/hr B. 4.2 km/hr
C. 5 km/hr D. 10.5 km/hr

99. A man's speed with the current is 15 km/hr and the speed of the current is 2.5 km/hr. The man's speed against the current is:

A. 12.5 km/hr B. 10 km/hr
C. 9 km/hr D. 8.5 km/hr

100. A motorboat, whose speed is 15 km/hr in still water goes 30 km downstream and comes back in a total of 4 hours 30 minutes. What is the speed of the stream (in km/hr)?

A. 10 B. 6
C. 5 D. 4

101. A shopkeeper buys 26 kgs of milk @ ₹ 16 per kg. He also buys from another source an inferior quality of milk @ ₹ 10 per kg. How much quantity of the latter should he buy to mix it with the former so that he can sell the mixture @ ₹ 14 per kg without making any loss?

A. 13 kgs B. 12 kgs
C. 14 kgs D. 16 kgs

102. Two vessels A and B contain mixture of milk and water in the ratio 4 : 1 and 9 : 11 respectively. They are mixed in the ratio of 3 : 2. Find the ratio of milk : water in the resulting mixture.

A. 34 : 16 B. 33 : 17
C. 16 : 34 D. 17 : 33

103. A shopkeeper has 50 kgs of rice. He sells a part of it at 20% profit and the rest at 40% profit. If he gains 25% on the whole, find the quantity of each part.

A. 12.5 kgs and 37.5 kgs
B. 37.5 kgs and 12.5 kgs
C. 23.5 kgs and 21.5 kgs
D. 21.5 kgs and 23.5 kgs

104. A man bought a certain quantity of sugar for ₹ 8000. He sells one-fourth of it at 20% loss. At what per cent profit should he sell the remainder stock so as to make an overall profit of 20%?

A. 20% B. 30%
C. 35% D. 40%

105. ₹ 675 was divided among 75 boys and girls. Each boy gets ₹ 20 whereas a girl gets ₹ 5. Find the number of boys and girls.

A. 20, 55 B. 15, 60
C. 25, 50 D. 30, 45

106. A vessel contains mixture of liquids A and B in the ratio 3 : 2. When 20 litres of the mixture is taken out and replaced by 20 litres of liquid B, the ratio changes to 1 : 4. How many litres of liquid A was there initially present in the vessel?

A. 12 litres B. 18 litres
C. 24 litres D. 22 litres

107. A container is full of milk. One-third of milk is taken out of it and replaced by same quantity of water. Then again one-third of the mixture is taken out of it and replaced by the same quantity of water. The process is repeated 4 times. If 16 litres of milk is left in the container at the end of 4th operation, find the capacity of the container.

A. 76 litres B. 81 litres
C. 82 litres D. 85 litres

108. The cost of type-I rice is ₹ 15 per kg and type-II is ₹ 20 per kg. If both type I and type II are mixed in the ratio of 2 : 3, then find the price per kg of the mixed variety.

A. ₹ 19.50 B. ₹ 19
C. ₹ 18.50 D. ₹ 18

109. In what ratio must a grocer mix two varieties of tea worth ₹ 60 a kg and ₹ 65 a kg so that by selling the mixture at ₹ 68.20 a kg he may gain 10%?

A. 4 : 5 B. 3 : 5
C. 3 : 4 D. 3 : 2

110. A vessel contains 80 litres of milk. 16 litres of milk was taken out of the vessel and replaced by water. Then 16 litres of mixture was withdrawn and again replaced by water. The operation was repeated for third time. How much milk is now left in the vessel?

A. 96.40 litres B. 50.36 litres
C. 40.96 litres D. 32.76 litres

111. A student who secures 20% marks in an examination fails by 30 marks. Another student who secures 32% gets 42 marks more than those required to pass. The percentage of marks required to pass is:

A. 20 B. 25
C. 28 D. 30

112. In a college election, a candidate secured 62% of the votes and is elected by a majority of 144 votes. The total number of votes polled is:

A. 600 B. 800
C. 925 D. 1200

113. In an organisation, 40% of the employees are matriculates, 50% of the remaining are graduates and the remaining 180 are postgraduates. How many employees are graduates?

A. 360 B. 240
C. 300 D. 180

114. The population of a village is 4500. $\frac{5}{9}$th of them are males and rest females. If 40% of the males are married, then the percentage of married female is :

A. 35 B. 40
C. 50 D. 60

115. A's income is 10% more than B's. How much per cent is B's income is less than A's?

A. 10% B. 7%
C. $9\frac{1}{11}\%$ D. $6\frac{1}{2}\%$

116. If the price of a television set is increased by 25%, then by what percentage should the new price be reduced to bring the price back to original level?

A. 15% B. 20%
C. 25% D. 30%

117. In an election one of the two candidates gets 40% votes and loses by 100 votes. Total number of votes is :

A. 500 B. 400
C. 600 D. 1000

118. The gross income of a person is ₹ 20000. 10% of his income is exempted from income tax and his net income is ₹ 19100. The rate of income tax is :

A. 3% B. 2%
C. 4% D. 5%

119. The owner of a cell phone shop charges his customer 32% more than the cost price. If a customer paid ₹ 6600 for the cell phone, then what was the cost price of the cell phone?

A. ₹ 5000 B. ₹ 5500
C. ₹ 5800 D. ₹ 6100

120. If the cost of pins reduced by ₹ 4 per dozen, 12 more pins can be purchased for ₹ 48. The cost of pins per dozen after reduction is:

A. ₹ 8 B. ₹ 12
C. ₹ 16 D. ₹ 20

121. In an examination 80% of the students passed in Mathematics and 70% passed in English, while 10% students failed in both the subjects. If 360 students passed in both the subjects, find the total number of students who appeared in the examination.

A. 400 B. 600
C. 630 D. 640

122. Electric tax is increased by 20% and its consumption is decreased by 20%. The change in the expenditure is:

A. 4% decrease B. 4% increase
C. 5% decrease D. 5% increase

123. The selling price of certain commodity was reduced by 25%. As a result of it, the sales increased by 30%. What was the effect of it on cash collected by daily sales?

A. 2.5% decrease B. 2.5% increase
C. 5% decrease D. 5% increase

124. The wheat sold by a grocer contained 10% low quality wheat. What quantity of good quality wheat should be added to 150 kgs of wheat so that the percentage of low quality wheat becomes 5%?

A. 50 kgs B. 85 kgs
C. 135 kgs D. 150 kgs

125. Nilam spends 15% of her monthly income on household expenses. She spends 17% of the monthly income in travelling and 6% on medical expenses and saves the rest ₹ 15,500. What is her monthly income?

A. ₹ 20,000 B. ₹ 25,000
C. ₹ 30,000 D. ₹ 35,000

126. Ashok bought 25 kg of rice at the rate of ₹ 6 per kg and 35 kg of rice at the rate of ₹ 7 per kg. He mixed the two and sold the mixture at the rate of ₹ 6.75 per kg. What was his gain or loss in the transaction?

A. ₹ 16 gain B. ₹ 16 loss
C. ₹ 10 gain D. None of these

127. Profit after selling a commodity for ₹ 425 is same as loss after selling it for ₹ 355. The cost of the commodity is :

A. ₹ 285 B. ₹ 390
C. ₹ 295 D. ₹ 400

128. Ram bought 4 dozen apples at ₹ 12 per dozen and 2 dozen at ₹ 16 per dozen. He sold all of them to earn 20%. At what price per dozen did he sell the apples?

A. ₹ 14.40 B. ₹ 16.00
C. ₹ 16.80 D. ₹ 16.20

129. At what price must Kantilal sell a mixture of 80 kg sugar at ₹ 6.75 per kg with 120 kg at ₹ 8 per kg to gain 20%?

A. ₹ 7.50 per kg
B. ₹ 8.20 per kg
C. ₹ 8.35 per kg
D. ₹ 9 per kg

130. A person bought an article and sold it at a loss of 10%. If he had bought it for 20% less and sold it for ₹ 55 more, he would have had a profit of 40%. The C.P. of the article is :

A. ₹ 200 B. ₹ 225
C. ₹ 250 D. None of these

131. A dealer sold a machine to a shopkeeper at 20% profit. The shopkeeper sold the machine to a customer so as to get 25% profit for himself. The difference between the selling price of the dealer and that of the shopkeeper was found to be ₹ 129. What is the initial price of the machine?

A. ₹ 410 B. ₹ 420
C. ₹ 430 D. ₹ 440

132. A man bought a horse and cart. If he sold the horse at 10% loss and the cart at 20% gain he would not loss anything. If he sold the horse at 5% loss and the cart at 5% gain he would lose ₹ 10 in the bargain. What did he pay for each?

A. ₹ 400, ₹ 200
B. ₹ 300, ₹ 300
C. ₹ 250, ₹ 350
D. ₹ 350, ₹ 250

133. The marked price of a radio is 20% more than its cost price. If a discount of 10% is given on the marked price, the gain percentage is:

A. 8 B. 10
C. 12 D. 15

134. A dishonest dealer sells his goods at the cost price and still earns a profit of 60% by underweight. What weight does he use for a kg?

A. 625 gms B. 750 gms
C. 800 gms D. 850 gms

135. A man sells two horses for ₹ 990 each. On one he gains 10% and the other he loses 10%. What is his total percentage of gain or loss in the transaction?

A. 1% gain B. 1% loss
C. 2% gain D. 2% loss

136. A lent a sum of ₹ 1250 to B at a certain rate of interest for 3 years and a sum of ₹ 1500 to C at the same rate of interest for 2 years. If he was paid total ₹ 258.75 as interest in both cases, find the rate of interest at which money was lent by him.

A. $4\frac{1}{6}\%$ B. $6\frac{1}{4}\%$
C. $2\frac{1}{7}\%$ D. $3\frac{5}{6}\%$

137. A invested ₹ 5000 at a certain rate of simple interest and ₹ 4000 for the same period at 1% higher rate of interest. If the interest in both cases is same, the former rate of interest is :

A. 3% B. 4%
C. 6% D. 5%

138. If a certain sum of money at simple interest amounts to ₹ 1900 in 3 years and to ₹ 2050 in 5 years, the rate per cent per annum is :

A. 4½% B. 3½%
C. 2½% D. 5¼%

139. A certain sum of money lent out on simple interest amounts to ₹ 1760 in 2 years and to ₹ 2000 in 5 years. Find the sum.

A. ₹ 1650 B. ₹ 1500
C. ₹ 1580 D. ₹ 1600

140. Out of the sum of ₹ 1550, a part was lent out at 5% p.a. simple interest and the remaining at 8% p.a. simple interest. If the total interest in both cases after 3 years is ₹ 300, the sum of money lent out at 8% p.a. simple interest was:

A. ₹ 760 B. ₹ 775
C. ₹ 750 D. ₹ 780

141. If simple interest on a certain sum of money for 4 years at 5% p.a. is same as the simple interest on ₹ 840 for 10 years at the rate of 4% p.a., the sum of money is:

A. ₹ 1780 B. ₹ 1660
C. ₹ 1680 D. ₹ 1620

142. What equal instalment of annual payment will discharge a debt which is due as ₹ 848 at the end of 4 years at 4% per annum simple interest?

A. ₹ 200 B. ₹ 212
C. ₹ 225 D. ₹ 250

143. Madhavi lent ₹ 5000 to Kamla for 5 years and ₹ 3000 to Vimla for 4 years. Find the rate of interest, if Madhavi gets an interest of ₹ 600 in the end.

A. 1.62% B. 2.5%
C. 3% D. 4%

144. A sum of money doubles itself in 7 years at simple interest. In how many years it will become four fold?

A. 10 years B. 14 years
C. 21 years D. 35 years

145. An amount doubles itself at the end of 8 years with a certain rate of simple interest. What will be the total simple interest on ₹ 8000 at that rate at the end of 4 years?

A. ₹ 2000 B. ₹ 4000
C. ₹ 6000 D. None of these

146. The compound interest on a certain sum of money invested for 3 years at 5% per annum is ₹ 1891.50. What will be the simple interest on the same sum at the same rate for 2 years?

A. ₹ 1700 B. ₹ 1200
C. ₹ 1500 D. ₹ 2100

147. A sum of money lent out at a certain rate of simple interest amounts to ₹ 6600 in 2 years and to ₹ 6900 in 3 years. What will be the compound interest on the same sum of money if lent out at the same rate for 2 years?

A. ₹ 605 B. ₹ 715
C. ₹ 615 D. ₹ 595

148. A man deposits ₹ 1200 in a bank on the 1st day of each year. If the bank pays 5% per annum compound interest on deposited sum of money, what will be the amount to his credit on the 10th day of the second year?

A. ₹ 2560 B. ₹ 2460
C. ₹ 2370 D. ₹ 2860

149. If the difference between compound and simple interest on a certain sum of money for 3 years at 5% per annum is ₹ 244, the sum is :

A. ₹ 40000 B. ₹ 25000
C. ₹ 30000 D. ₹ 32000

150. A man purchased a sewing machine for ₹ 5000. If due to sustained use value of this sewing machine depreciates by 6% annually, find its value after 3 years.

A. ₹ 3775.67 B. ₹ 4152.92
C. ₹ 4250.25 D. ₹ 4356.25

151. Find the sum on which the difference between compound and simple interest for 3 years at 10% per annum will be ₹ 868.

A. ₹ 29500 B. ₹ 27625
C. ₹ 28500 D. ₹ 28000

152. Samir invested ₹ 15000 at the rate of interest 10% p.a. for 1 year. If the interest compound six months. What amount will Samir get at the end of the year?

A. ₹ 16,500 B. ₹ 16525.50
C. ₹ 16537.50 D. ₹ 18,150

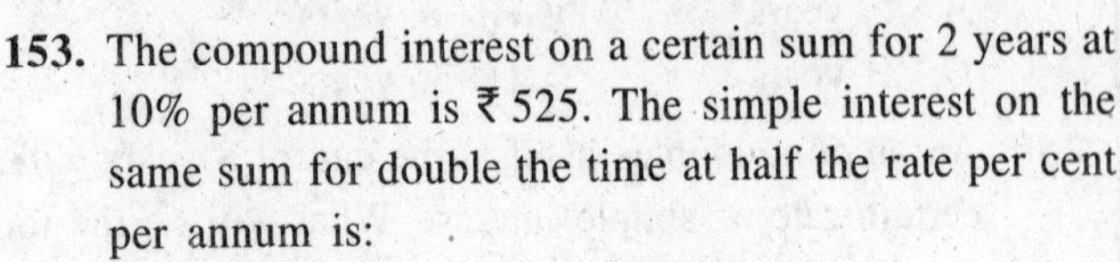

153. The compound interest on a certain sum for 2 years at 10% per annum is ₹ 525. The simple interest on the same sum for double the time at half the rate per cent per annum is:

A. ₹ 800 B. ₹ 600
C. ₹ 500 D. ₹ 400

154. The least number of complete years in which a sum of money put at 20% compound interest will be more than doubled is:

A. 6 B. 5
C. 4 D. 3

155. On a sum of money, the simple interest for 2 years is ₹ 660, while the compound interest is ₹ 696.30, the rate of interest being the same in both cases. Find the rate of interest.

A. 12% B. 11%
C. 10% D. 9%

156. If side of a square is reduced by 50%, its area will be reduced by

A. 50% B. 75%
C. 80% D. 60%

157. If each side of a square is doubled, its area will become

A. double B. four times
C. three times D. eight times

158. Three sides of a triangle are in the ratio of 17 : 15 : 8. If the perimeter of this triangle is 40 m, find its area

A. 50 sq. m. B. 49 sq. m.
C. 60 sq. m. D. 69 sq. m.

159. If the length of a rectangle is increased by 20% and width is decreased by 15%, then its area

A. decreases by 4% B. increases by 2%
C. decreases by 2% D. increases by 3%

160. If the length of a rectangle is increased by 20%, then by how much per cent its breadth must be decreased so as to keep its area unaltered?

A. 25% B. $8\frac{1}{3}\%$
C. $16\frac{2}{3}\%$ D. 20%

161. The ratio of length and breadth of a rectangular plot is 71 : 61 respectively. The area of the plot is 17324 m^2. What is perimeter of the plot?

A. 264 m B. 284 m
C. 528 m D. 614 m

162. If the length and breadth of a rectangular field are increased, the area increases by 50%. If the increase in length was 20%, by what percentage was the breadth increased?

A. 20% B. 25%
C. 30% D. 40%

163. The length and breadth of a varandah is 40 m and 15 m respectively. How many stone slabs of size 6 decimetre × 5 decimetre each are needed in flooring it:

A. 1000 B. 2000
C. 3000 D. 4000

164. The circumference of a circular plot is 396 m. What is the area of the circular plot?

A. 9,446 m^2 B. 9,856 m^2
C. 12,474 m^2 D. 18,634 m^2

165. If the sides of an equilateral triangle are increased by 20%, 30% and 50% respectively to form a new triangle, the increase in the perimeter of the equilateral triangle is:

A. 25% B. $33\frac{1}{3}\%$
C. 50% D. 100%

166. If a solid sphere of 3 cm radius is melted and recast into a right circular cone whose base radius is same as that of the sphere, the height of the cone will be

A. 8 cm B. 12 cm
C. 6 cm D. 5 cm

167. Diameter of a roller is 2.4 m and it is 1.68 m long. If it takes 1000 complete revolutions once over to level a field, the area of the field is

A. 12672 sq. m B. 12671 sq. m
C. 12762 sq. m D. 11768 sq. m

168. If each edge of a cube is increased by 10%, then by how much per cent will the surface area of this cube be increased?

A. 21% B. 18%
C. 15% D. 20%

169. Height and base radius of a solid cylinder are 14 m and 4 m respectively. It is melted and recast into a solid cone of the same base radius as that of the cylinder, what will be the height of the cone?

A. 21 m B. 42 m
C. 48 m D. 54 m

170. A room is in the form of a cube of side 10 m. How many bales of cotton can be kept in it if each bale covers 5 cu m space?

A. 100 B. 175

C. 200 D. 225

171. Three cubes having side 2 cm, 3 cm and 4 cm respectively are melted together to form a new cube. The side of the new cube will be

A. 3.526 cm B. 4.628 cm

C. 4.626 cm D. 4.528 cm

172. If base diameter of a cylinder is increased by 50%, then by how much per cent its height must be decreased so as to keep its volume unaltered?

A. 45.56% B. 55.56%

C. 50.16% D. 62.33%

173. The surface area of a cube is 600 sq. m. Its diagonal is

A. $10\sqrt{3}$ cm B. $5\sqrt{3}$ cm

C. $4\sqrt{2}$ cm D. $10\sqrt{2}$ cm

174. The base diameter of a conical tomb is 28 m and its slant height is 50 m. Find the cost of white washing its curved surface at the rate of 80 paise per sq. m?

A. ₹ 1860 B. ₹ 1760

C. ₹ 1950 D. ₹ 1875

175. The volume of a cuboid is 1120 cu cm and its height is 5 cm while the length and the breadth of the cuboid are in the ratio 8 : 7. The length of this cylinder exceeds the breadth by

A. 4 cm B. 2 cm

C. 7 cm D. 5 cm

Directions: *In the following number series, one of the numbers does not fit into the series. Find the wrong number.*

176. 2, 5, 10, 18, 26, 37, 50

A. 2 B. 5

C. 37 D. 18

177. 3 , 18, 38, 78, 123, 178, 243

A. 123 B. 178

C. 3 D. 38

178. 380, 188, 92, 48, 20, 8, 2

A. 188 B. 92

C. 48 D. 20

179. 5, 11, 23, 47, 96, 191, 383

A. 11 B. 23

C. 47 D. 96

180. 89, 78, 86, 80, 85, 82, 83

A. 78 B. 86

C. 80 D. 85

181. 58, 57, 54, 50, 42, 33, 32

A. 57 B. 54

C. 50 D. 32

182. 2, 20, 27, 44, 64

A. 27 B. 8

C. 20 D. 44

Directions: *Complete the following series.*

183. 1 4 9 16 25 36 49 ....

A. 54 B. 56

C. 64 D. 81

184. 11 13 17 19 23 29 31 37 41 ....

A. 43 B. 47

C. 53 D. 51

185. 3 7 6 5 9 3 12 1 15 ....

A. 18 B. 13

C. –1 D. 3

186. 85432 ÷ 2106 + 59.5614 = ?

A. 100 B. 60

C. 80 D. 140

187. $\sqrt{67621}$ = ?

A. 320 B. 260

C. 200 D. 280

188. 9.7 % of 5011 + 55.03 % of 4991

A. 5500 B. 7200

C. 6000 D. 4200

189. 730 × 199 = ?

A. 350000 B. 335000

C. 300000 D. 34600

190. .0144 × 0.36 = ?

A. 0.5 B. 0.005

C. 0.05 D. 0.005

191. 31% of 1508 + 26% of 2018

A. 1500 B. 2000

C. 1000 D. 1200

192. 3015 + 13594 + 3738 = ?

A. 40000 B. 36000

C. 42000 D. 46000

193. 6012 × 119 = ?

A. 560000 B. 448000

C. 900000 D. 720000

194. 2712.1563 ÷ 1805.4018 + 3.4982 = ?

A. 9 B. 8

C. 4 D. 5

195. 4182. 365 ÷ 20.886 = ?

A. 300 B. 200

C. 150 D. 250

ANSWERS

1	2	3	4	5	6	7	8	9	10
B	D	B	A	B	A	C	B	C	C
11	**12**	**13**	**14**	**15**	**16**	**17**	**18**	**19**	**20**
C	C	D	A	A	A	A	A	B	A
21	**22**	**23**	**24**	**25**	**26**	**27**	**28**	**29**	**30**
B	B	B	D	B	A	B	C	D	C
31	**32**	**33**	**34**	**35**	**36**	**37**	**38**	**39**	**40**
A	C	C	C	D	C	B	B	A	D
41	**42**	**43**	**44**	**45**	**46**	**47**	**48**	**49**	**50**
A	C	A	A	B	A	A	B	B	D
51	**52**	**53**	**54**	**55**	**56**	**57**	**58**	**59**	**60**
D	A	B	B	D	B	B	C	B	C
61	**62**	**63**	**64**	**65**	**66**	**67**	**68**	**69**	**70**
C	A	B	C	C	A	C	B	C	C
71	**72**	**73**	**74**	**75**	**76**	**77**	**78**	**79**	**80**
A	D	D	C	B	A	A	B	A	C
81	**82**	**83**	**84**	**85**	**86**	**87**	**88**	**89**	**90**
D	A	B	A	C	B	A	C	B	C
91	**92**	**93**	**94**	**95**	**96**	**97**	**98**	**99**	**100**
B	A	A	A	B	B	D	A	B	C
101	**102**	**103**	**104**	**105**	**106**	**107**	**108**	**109**	**110**
A	B	B	B	A	B	B	D	D	C
111	**112**	**113**	**114**	**115**	**116**	**117**	**118**	**119**	**120**
B	A	D	C	C	B	A	D	A	B
121	**122**	**123**	**124**	**125**	**126**	**127**	**128**	**129**	**130**
B	A	A	D	B	C	B	B	D	C
131	**132**	**133**	**134**	**135**	**136**	**137**	**138**	**139**	**140**
C	A	A	A	B	D	B	A	D	C
141	**142**	**143**	**144**	**145**	**146**	**147**	**148**	**149**	**150**
C	A	A	C	B	B	C	B	D	B
151	**152**	**153**	**154**	**155**	**156**	**157**	**158**	**159**	**160**
D	C	C	C	B	B	B	C	B	C
161	**162**	**163**	**164**	**165**	**166**	**167**	**168**	**169**	**170**
C	B	B	C	B	B	A	A	B	C
171	**172**	**173**	**174**	**175**	**176**	**177**	**178**	**179**	**180**
C	B	A	B	B	D	C	C	D	A
181	**182**	**183**	**184**	**185**	**186**	**187**	**188**	**189**	**190**
C	C	C	A	C	A	B	D	A	B
191	**192**	**193**	**194**	**195**					
C	A	D	D	B					